READINGS IN GENDER AND CULTURE IN AMERICA

READINGS IN GENDER AND CULTURE IN AMERICA

Edited by

Nancy P. McKee

Washington State University

Linda Stone

Washington State University

Prentice
Hall

UPPER SADDLE RIVER, NEW JERSEY 07458

Library of Congress Cataloging-in-Publication Data

Readings in gender and culture in America/edited by Nancy P. McKee, Linda Stone.
   p. cm.
  Includes bibliographical references.
  ISBN 0-13-040485-3
   1. Sex role—United States—History. 2. United States—Social conditions. I. McKee,
Nancy Patricia. II. Stone, Linda.

HQ1075.5.U6 R42 2001
305.3'0973—dc21   2001054897

AVP, Publisher: Nancy Roberts
Editorial assistant: Lee Peterson
Marketing manager: Chris Barker
Editorial/production supervision: Kari Callaghan Mazzola
Prepress and manufacturing buyer: Ben Smith
Electronic page makeup: Kari Callaghan Mazzola and John P. Mazzola
Interior design: John P. Mazzola
Cover director: Jayne Conte
Cover design: Bruce Kenselaar
Cover art: Stacy Heller/Stock Illustration Source, Inc.

This book was set in 10/12 Meridien by Big Sky Composition
and was printed and bound by RR Donnelley & Sons Company.
The cover was printed by Phoenix Color Corp.

 © 2002 by Pearson Education, Inc.
Upper Saddle River, New Jersey 07458

Printed in the United States of America
10 9 8 7 6 5 4 3 2 1

ISBN 0-13-040485-3

Pearson Education LTD., London
Pearson Education Australia PTY, Limited, Sydney
Pearson Education Singapore, Pte. Ltd
Pearson Education North Asia Ltd, Hong Kong
Pearson Education Canada, Ltd., Toronto
Pearson Educación de Mexico, S.A. de C.V.
Pearson Education—Japan, Tokyo
Pearson Education Malaysia, Pte. Ltd
Pearson Education, Upper Saddle River, New Jersey

To the students, both men and women, whom we have taught,
and to those whom we have yet to teach,
who find in the study of gender a pathway to a more humane world.

CONTENTS

PREFACE

In 1999 Prentice Hall published the first edition of our book *Gender and Culture in America*, which we have used in an undergraduate course of the same name. The text presents an overall historical and ethnographic account of the events that shaped gender in the United States, not only for the heterosexual and white majority but also for persons of other sexual and ethnic identities. We found, however, that our students craved something more immediate. They wanted to explore some of the experiences of particular groups and persons from a more individual vantage point. Ethnographic perspectives and historical trends, they felt, were useful in presenting the overall picture, but they wanted to know what it felt like to be a Chinese American girl in the United States, or how university students thirty-five years ago experienced their education and planned for the future. In short, they wanted to be engaged with issues of American gender and culture in a more personal way. As if in response to student concerns, Larry Armstrong, our field editor and sales representative from Prentice Hall, suggested to us that we put together a reader to accompany our text.

Readings in Gender and Culture in America follows the same general organization as *Gender and Culture in America*. As with that book, anthropology is the primary informing discipline. Thus we take a comparative view of cultural and subcultural variation. The collection also takes a historical perspective, with the aim of illuminating the present by an understanding of the past. In this we follow the maxim of Alfred L. Kroeber, one of the founding fathers of American anthropology, who said, "Anthropology is history, or it is nothing." The contents are eclectic. Though the majority of the selections in this volume are articles drawn from scholarly books and journals, we have also included data from a recent study commissioned by a feminist advocacy group, excerpts from a classic ethnography, and several life history accounts, at least one of them best described as literature. Like most anthropologists, we take all accounts of human life and culture as grist for our mill.

The collection moves from a theoretical overview of issues of American gender and culture to an exploration of topics concerning gender within the dominant U.S. population throughout American history. We then move to the role of gender among Americans of alternative sexual preference and identity, and then to gender issues among significant ethnic minority groups. The last topic explored before the conclusion is the role played by gender in charting a path through college and career.

Though this reader is intended to accompany our book *Gender and Culture in America* and act as a supplement to it, the reader does not depend upon *Gender and Culture in America* and can easily be used independently. Each chapter opens with an overview of the contents of the articles included in it. Each article is then preceded by an introduction and followed by several discussion questions. These questions may be used as stimuli for face-to-face or electronic exploration of the material, or they may be used for written work. Many of the articles are also accompanied by a key terms list, in which unfamiliar words, names, or other terms (listed in the order in which they first appear in the article) are defined. The key terms list accompanying Gloria Anzaldúa's article, "La Conciencia de la Mestiza," contains complete translations of all the Spanish words, phrases, and sentences included in that article.

We would like to acknowledge the assistance of the following people: Larry Armstrong, our Prentice Hall field editor and sales representative, who first suggested this collection to us; Lee Peterson, assistant to our editor, Nancy Roberts, who was always at the end of the telephone line to provide advice and answers; Edward C. Joyce, who suggested (and provided) one of the selections in this volume that we would otherwise have overlooked; Hannah McKee-Kennedy, who supplied valuable help in securing copyright permissions and preparation of the manuscript; Diana Ames, who also assisted in manuscript preparation; and Berta Herrera Trejo, who weeded out errors in our translation of Gloria Anzaldúa's Spanish. We would also like to thank the following reviewers, who made helpful suggestions: Dorothy K. Billings, Wichita State University; Miriam Chaiken, Indiana University of Pennsylvania; and Caroline Brettell, Southern Methodist University.

Nancy P. McKee
Linda Stone

READINGS IN GENDER AND CULTURE IN AMERICA

INTRODUCTION TO ISSUES OF GENDER AND CULTURE IN AMERICA

CHAPTER 1

Gender in the United States today is a multifaceted and often contentious topic. How does this society characterize and evaluate men and women? Is this society "patriarchal," or governed by male authority? What is the variation in gender construction by region, class, or ethnic group? The opening articles in this book lay out a number of concepts and theoretical approaches to gender that can help us to better understand cultural constructions of gender in the United States. The first article, by Michelle Zimbalist Rosaldo, was published in 1974 as an opening essay to her well-known edited volume, *Woman, Culture, and Society* (Rosaldo and Lamphere 1974). This was a path-breaking book that helped launch the anthropology of women.

At the time, many women anthropologists were concerned with gender inequality in their own society and with the male bias they saw in anthropological scholarship. While many ethnographies described various cultural groups from a distinctly male point of view, *Woman, Culture, and Society* brought women to the fore. It also sought explanations for what many of the book contributors understood to be a cross-cultural universal—the subordination of women to men. The book emphatically discounted biological explanations for female subordination (affirming that biology is *not* destiny) and pointed the way to seeing gender as cultural construction.

In her essay Rosaldo suggested that a dichotomy between the public and the domestic or private spheres of life universally underlies women's subordination. On account of their reproduction and nurturing of children, women everywhere are largely confined to the domestic sphere, whereas men are active in public life. Rosaldo then claims that the domestic or private sphere of women is everywhere culturally devalued compared to the public sphere of men.

Rosaldo also uses the theories of two other anthropologists, both of whom published important articles in her book, and both of whose theories center on women's reproduction and motherhood as fundamental to their subordination. The first is Nancy Chodorow (1974), who developed a theory of the development of feminine and masculine personalities. Women are largely responsible for child

1

rearing, but this has different consequences for the personality development of their male and female children. As little girls grow up they stay connected with their mother, modeling their behavior on her and identifying, as women, with her. Little boys, on the other hand, must break away from the mother and cease to identify with her in order to achieve manhood. Chodorow relates this difference in child development to a greater male independence, assertiveness, and other aspects of a masculine personality, and to attributes of dependence, weaker ego boundaries, and greater sense of connection with others in a feminine personality. In addition, males must renounce and devalue the world of women to achieve manhood, which fosters the cultural devaluation of women.

The second theorist covered in Rosaldo's article is Sherry Ortner (1974), who held that women are universally subordinate to men because they are associated with "nature" whereas men are associated with nature's more highly valued opposition, "culture." Woman is seen as closer to nature than man on account of her body and its procreative functions. Men, by contrast, "transcend" nature and participate in the "higher" realms of artistic, symbolic, and technological expressions of culture.

There have been a number of developments in gender studies since Rosaldo's time. For one thing, many scholars disputed that women are universally subordinated to men. Some of them pointed to cases of gender equality, or near equality, particularly in hunter-gatherer groups such as the !Kung of the Kalahari desert in Africa. Another trend has been to include men and relations between men and women in studies of gender. There is also more interest today in intersections among gender, race and class, or seeing gender in relation to other dimensions of inequality, both in terms of cultural ideology and in terms of discriminatory practices. Finally, the universality of dichotomies such as public/private and nature/culture was questioned. Charges were made that these kinds of dichotomies were prevalent in Western societies, but violated the thought or worldview of other cultural traditions. Or, the dichotomies were criticized as being too simple, not easily fitting many real situations. In a review of the strengths and weaknesses of Rosaldo's public/private dichotomy, Louise Lamphere (who was co-editor of *Woman, Culture, and Society*) wrote the following:

> [M]any of us have tired of the domestic–public dichotomy. We feel it is constraining, a 'trap,' while some new approaches try to get away from dichotomous thinking. These approaches do one of several things. Often they take history seriously, examining women's situation as it has evolved, often in a colonial context. Furthermore they treat women as active agents ... as people who have interests, often divergent from men, and who act on them. [And these newer approaches] do not treat all women as part of a single universal category of 'woman.' Rather women are usually analyzed in terms of their social location. Age, class, race, ethnicity and kinship are all likely to divide women, so newer analyses examine women's strategies and identities as they are differently shaped. (Lamphere 1993, 72)

For all this, the public/private dichotomy has been usefully applied to gender in many situations, particularly in the United States and in other Western countries. Rosaldo (1980) herself came to suggest that the concept grew out of our Western Victorian heritage and that, while it may not always apply cross-culturally, it is still a relevant dichotomy in the Western world. We will see later in this book how the concept has been and still is applied in the United States.

The next piece in this chapter is more recent and focuses directly on gender in North America. This selection is a chapter from Holly Devor's book, *Gender Blending: Confronting the Limits of Duality*, published in 1989. This book grew out of Devor's research on what she calls "gender blending" women, or women who exhibit a mixture of masculine and feminine gender characteristics and are often mistaken for men. In the chapter reproduced here, Devor discusses several concepts, such as the self in relation to gender identity, child socialization, shared conceptual frameworks of gender (which she refers to as cognitive schema), gender roles, and patriarchy. From her discussion one gets a good sense of how these and other basic concepts from the social sciences are applied to mainstream, or dominant, gender constructions in the United States. Devor refers to ways in which masculine attributes and associations are more highly valued in these constructions, confirming for mainstream American society what Rosaldo held to be a cross-cultural universal.

References

Chodorow, Nancy. 1974. "Family Structure and Feminine Personality." Pp. 43–66 in *Woman, Culture, and Society*, ed. Michelle Zimbalist Rosaldo and Louise Lamphere. Stanford, CA: Stanford University Press.

Devor, Holly. 1989. *Gender Blending: Confronting the Limits of Duality*. Bloomington, IN: Indiana University Press.

Lamphere, Louise. 1993. "The Domestic Sphere of Women and the Public Sphere of Men: The Strengths and Limitations of an Anthropological Dichotomy." Pp. 67–77 in *Gender in Cross Cultural Perspective*, ed. Caroline B. Brettell and Carolyn F. Sargent. Englewood Cliffs, NJ: Prentice Hall.

Ortner, Sherry B. 1974. "Is Female to Male as Nature Is to Culture?" Pp. 67–87 in *Woman, Culture, and Society*, ed. Michelle Zimbalist Rosaldo and Louise Lamphere. Stanford, CA: Stanford University Press.

Rosaldo, Michelle Zimbalist. 1980. "The Uses and Abuses of Anthropology." *Signs* 5 (3): 389–417.

Rosaldo, Michelle Zimbalist, and Louise Lamphere, eds. 1974. *Woman, Culture, and Society*. Stanford, CA: Stanford University Press.

Woman, Culture, and Society: A Theoretical Overview

Michelle Zimbalist Rosaldo

In this now classic article, Michelle Rosaldo asserts that women's subordination to men is universal. She notes that there is variation in female subordination, that some societies are more gender egalitarian than others, and that there is considerable cross-cultural variation in gender roles. Nevertheless, she maintains that there is "a universal asymmetry in cultural valuations of the sexes." The activities and roles of men are everywhere more highly valued than those of women, and men everywhere have some authority over women, though women may exercise considerable power. Rosaldo suggests that underlying the universal subordination of women is an opposition between the public and the private (or domestic) spheres of life. All cultures value the public and extradomestic over the private and domestic; and in all cultures it is women who are associated with the domestic sphere whereas men are associated with the public sphere. Thus men have active roles and responsibilities in the extradomestic world of politics, the military, official positions within public institutions and so forth, whereas women's activities and roles are largely confined to the domestic household and the rearing of children. For Rosaldo, this "structural opposition" between public and private spheres does not determine or cause universal female subordination but rather underlies it, so that through this opposition we can better understand the universality of female subordination and ways that it might be alleviated.

Rosaldo then goes on to discuss the ways in which the public/domestic opposition underlies women's subordination to men along a number of dimensions. Here her discussion gains strength and her cross-cultural examples are compelling. Using her domestic/public opposition she covers the following issues: (1) the development of a distinctively female personality; (2) the ways that men are culturally granted authority over women; (3) how the status of men is culturally viewed as achieved, whereas that of women is seen as ascribed; (4) the closer identification of women than men with "nature"; (5) the ways that women are cross-culturally seen as anomalous, dangerous, and often as ritually "polluting"; and (6) the different roles that women and men tend to play in economic production. It is in this reading that we see Rosaldo's use of the important theories and concepts developed by Nancy Chodorow and Sherry Ortner that we discussed earlier.

Rosaldo's central thesis raises two problems. First, assuming that the domestic sphere is everywhere culturally less valued than the public sphere, why is this so? Rosaldo does not adequately address this question. It is tempting to wonder: Is it because it is associated with women? But of course this just returns us to the original question (Why are women culturally less valued than men?) and leads us in circles. A second question that Rosaldo does answer is: Why are women associated with the domestic sphere? Rosaldo's answer is that this is because women bear and nurse children. But this answer raises problems in terms of how Rosaldo views biology in relation to gender. Like most feminist writers of her time, Rosaldo downplayed the significance of biological factors. Though she grants that biological factors may play some role in gender, biology, she insists, "becomes significant only as it is interpreted by human actors." Biological factors on their own are not capable of explaining moral evaluations, or why men are granted more social value

than women. Biological factors are not significant, yet Rosaldo also asserts that it is biol-
ogy that "dictates women will be mothers," hence she falls back on the biologically dictated
fact of motherhood to place women in the domestic sphere.

Despite these muddles in her model, Rosaldo's public/private opposition is a powerful
tool by which to look at gender in many situations in some societies, and it is particularly
applicable to gender relations in American society.

As anthropologists looking at the roles and activities of women, we are confronted, from the outset, with an apparent contradiction. On the one hand, we learn from the work of Mead and others of the extraordinary diversity of sex roles in our own and other cultures. And on the other, we are heirs to a sociological tradition that treats women as essentially uninteresting and irrelevant, and accepts as necessary, natural, and hardly problematic the fact that, in every human culture, women are in some way subordinate to men.

The purpose of this paper is to develop a perspective that at once incorporates earlier observations while at the same time suggesting systematic dimensions within which the social relations of the sexes can be investigated and understood. After a brief discussion of variation, I attempt to document aspects of what I take to be a universal asymmetry in cultural evaluations of the sexes. Women may be important, powerful, and influential, but it seems that, relative to men of their age and social status, women everywhere lack generally recognized and culturally valued authority. The secondary evaluation of women can be approached from a number of perspectives. Here, rather than put forth a single causal explanation, I propose a structural model

that relates recurrent aspects of psychology and cultural and social organization to an opposition between the "domestic" orientation of women and the extra-domestic or "public" ties that, in most societies, are primarily available to men. This approach, developed further in some of the other papers in this volume, enables us to make sense of a number of very general characteristics of human sex roles and to identify certain strategies and motivations, as well as sources of value and power, that are available to women in different human groups. As such, it provides an introduction to the various "sources of power" for women that are treated in detail later in this book.

Asymmetries in Cultural Evaluations of the Sexes

The fact that what Westerners take to be the "natural" endowments of men and women are hardly necessary, natural, or universal (as an ethnocentric perspective might lead one to expect) was first emphasized in the work of Margaret Mead. In her words, "If those temperamental attitudes which we have traditionally regarded as feminine—such as passivity, responsiveness, and a willingness to cherish children—can so easily be set up as the masculine pattern in one tribe, and, in another, be outlawed for the majority of women as for the majority of men, we no longer have any basis for regarding aspects of such behavior as sex linked" (1935: 279–280). And to some extent Mead was right. There are, in fact, groups like the New Guinea Arapesh, in which neither sex shows much aggression or assertiveness, and there are societies like our own, in which children of both sexes are more egoistic than boys in other parts of the world (Chodorow, 1971). The same sort of variability attaches to almost every kind of behavior one can think of: there are societies in which women trade or garden, and those in which men do; societies where women are queens and those in which they must always defer to a man; in parts of New Guinea, men are (like Victorian women) at once prudish and flirtatious, fearful of sex yet preoccupied with love magic and cosmetics that will lead the maidens—who take the initiative in courtship—to be interested in them.

But there are also limits to variation. Every known society recognizes and elaborates some differences between the sexes, and although there are groups in which men wear skirts and women wear pants or trousers, it is everywhere the case that there are characteristic tasks, manners, and responsibilities primarily associated with women or with men. Cross-cultural studies of child rearing (Barry, Bacon, and Child, 1957) reveal certain temperamental differences between the sexes, and studies of adults indicate that it is women, and not men, who have the primary responsibility for raising children; this fact seems to make it unlikely that women will be a society's hunters, warriors, or the like (Brown, 1970b). Differences in physical constitution, and especially in endurance and strength, may also lead to characteristic differences in male and female activities.

But what is perhaps most striking and surprising is the fact that male, as opposed to female, activities are always recognized as predominantly important, and cultural systems give authority and value to the roles and activities of men. Contrary to some popular assumptions, there is little reason to believe that there are, or once were, societies of primitive matriarchs, societies in which women predominated in the same way that men predominate in the societies we actually know (see Bamberger [in Rosaldo and Lamphere, 1974]). An asymmetry in the cultural evaluations of male and female, in the importance assigned to women and men, appears to be universal. Mead recognized this in observing that "whatever the arrangements in regard to descent or ownership of property, and even if these formal outward arrangements are reflected in the temperamental relations between the sexes, the prestige values always attach to the activities of men" (1935: 302).

Nor is this difficult to document. We find in some parts of New Guinea, for example, that women grow sweet potatoes and men grow yams, and yams are the prestige food, the food one distributes at feasts. Or again, in the Philippine society I studied, men hunted in groups while women gardened (for the most part) individually; and although a woman's rice became the food supply of her immediate family, its dietary staple, meat was always shared by the community and was the most highly valued food. The same pattern obtains in other hunting societies, where women may help on the hunt but the catch is the men's to distribute, and meat, unlike the nutritious grubs and nuts a woman gathers,[1] is socially valued and shared. Among aboriginal groups in Australia, only the meat, which men distribute, is felt to be a proper "food" (Kaberry, 1939).

Cultural expressions of sexual asymmetry may be associated with economics, but they are often found in other domains of activity as well. Among the Arapesh, studied by Mead (1935, 1971), the roles of men and women were seen as cooperative and complementary, but a wife was felt to be a "daughter" to her husband, and at the time of the dominant male ritual (when men played on secret flutes) she was required to act like an ignorant child. Among the nearby Tchambuli (Mead, 1935), the women were traders, controlling the family economics; yet there the men were artists and ritual specialists, and although the women had little respect for masculine secrets, they still found it necessary to adhere to, and engage in, a ritual order that marked them as inferior—in morality and knowledge—to men. Again, in certain African societies like the Yoruba (Lloyd, 1965), women may control a good part of the food supply, accumulate cash, and trade in distant and important markets; yet when approaching their husbands, wives must feign ignorance and obedience, kneeling to serve the men as they sit. Even the Iroquois, who, according to Murdock, "of all the people of the earth approach most closely to that hypothetical form of society known as the matriarchate" (1934: 302), were not ruled by women; there, powerful women might instate and depose their rulers, but Iroquois chiefs were men.

Still another form of cultural subordination is revealed in the linguistic practices of women of the Merina tribe in Madagascar (Keenan, 1974). There it is felt that in order to be cultured, sophisticated, and respectable, one must learn how to speak indirectly. Rather than being assertive, men are masters of an allusive, formal style in public speech. Women, on the contrary, are said not to know the subtleties of polite language. They are, in effect, cultural idiots, who are expected to blurt out what they mean. And so again, in the public ideology women are inferior. Yet they too have their methods of influence; in public meetings, men cluster together, whispering polite and evasive words of discreet opinion, while women, who are political outsiders, manage to influence public decisions by simply shouting out what they think.

For a final example, consider the Jewish ghetto communities of Eastern Europe (Zborowski and Herzog, 1955). In these communities, women had an extraordinary amount of influence. They were strong and self-confident mothers whose sons were their loyal supporters; as community gossips, they shaped most political events; in the household, a woman kept control of the pocketbook and effectively dictated family spending; and finally, in wealthier families, women and not men were the workers, running the family business, usually a small local store. Yet, in spite of all this, wives would defer to their husbands, and their greatest joy in life was to have a male child. A woman's work was rewarded by having the son become a scholar, a man whose actual activities might have little influence on the everyday life of the community but who stood, nonetheless, as its source of pride and moral value, its cultural ideal.

Taken individually, no one of these examples is surprising, yet a single thread runs through them all. Everywhere, from those societies we might want to call most egalitarian to those in which sexual stratification is most marked, men are the locus of cultural value. Some area of activity is always seen as exclusively or predominantly male, and overwhelmingly and morally important. This observation has its corollary in the fact that everywhere men have some *authority* over women, that they have a culturally legitimated right to her subordination and compliance. At the same time, of course, women themselves are far from helpless, and whether or not their influence is acknowledged, they exert important pressures on the social life of the group. In other words, in various circumstances male authority might be mitigated, and, perhaps rendered almost trivial, by the fact that women (through gossiping or yelling, playing sons against brothers, running the business, or refusing to cook) may have a good deal of informal influence and *power*.[2] While acknowledging male authority, women may direct it to their own interests, and in terms of actual choices and decisions, of who influences whom and how, the power exercised by women may have considerable and systematic effect.

This distinction between power and culturally legitimated authority, between the ability to gain compliance and the recognition that it is right, is crucial to our study of women. Social scientists have by and large taken male authority for granted; they have also tended to accept a male view that sees the exercise of power by women as manipulative, disruptive, illegitimate, or unimportant. But it is necessary to remember that while authority legitimates the use of power, it does not exhaust it, and actual methods of giving rewards, controlling information, exerting pressure, and shaping events may be available to women as well as to men. This point is elaborated in later essays. Here it is necessary simply to note that in acknowledging the universal fact of male authority, we are not denying women importance.

The kinds of power available to women, and the reasons they have been traditionally ignored, will be clarified by examining those features of women's position that present special problems for study. We begin by asking what to make of the fact of male authority. Why is sexual asymmetry a universal fact of human societies? What is its importance and how is it related to other aspects of men's and women's lives? Once these complex relations are understood, we can ask how and in what situations male systems of authority are reduced or mitigated in importance, what sources of power are available to women, and what sorts of social arrangements give what sorts of value to women's lives.

Most available accounts of the asymmetrical relations of the sexes have attempted to explain them in terms of a universal and necessary cause. These explanations range from the rather implausible assertion that at some moment in human history men "took" power away from women (Engels, 1891)[3] to more suggestive accounts relating sexual asymmetry to male envy of female reproductive powers (Bettelheim, 1954) or to aspects of the human biological endowment (Bardwick, 1971). Different hormonal cycles, infant activity levels, sexual capacities, or emotional orientations have all been proposed as possible sources of the cultural subordination of women to men.

But it seems reasonable to ask what the available facts, or the promise of future information (deriving from, say, advances in biological studies, or archaeological research), can tell us. Will they explain the constant factor in the secret flute cults of the Arapesh, the Merina woman's lack of subtlety, or the bowing and scraping of the Yoruba wife? Although there is no doubt that biology is important, and that human society is constrained and directed in its development by facts of a physical kind, I find it difficult to see how these could possibly lead to moral evaluations. Biological research may illuminate the range in human inclinations and possibilities, but it cannot account for the interpretation of these facts in a cultural order. It can tell us about the average endowments of groups or of particular individuals, but it cannot explain the fact that cultures everywhere have given Man, as a category opposed to Woman, social value and moral worth.

I look, rather, to human social and cultural organization. Paraphrasing Parsons (1964: 58), I would suggest that anything so general as the universal asymmetry of sex roles is likely to be the result of a constellation of different factors, factors that are deeply involved in the foundation of human societies. Biology may be one of these, but biology becomes significant only as it is interpreted by human actors and associated with characteristic modes of action (De Beauvoir, 1968: 29–33). Because biology dictates that women will be mothers, it seems that an analysis of the balance of forces in human social systems, and of the organization of human families in particular, will give the most promising results. In the discussion that follows, I will suggest that characteristic asymmetries in the experience of men and women—asymmetries ranging from their emotional orientations to the fact that men have public authority—an be understood in terms, not of biology directly, but of a near-universal fact of human experience. The fact that, in most traditional societies, a good part of a woman's adult life is spent giving birth to and raising children leads to a differentiation of domestic and public spheres of activity that can, I think, be shown to shape a number of relevant aspects of human social structure and psychology.[4]

Domestic and Public Orientations

In what follows, it will be seen that an opposition between "domestic" and "public" provides the basis of a structural framework necessary to identify and explore the place of male and female in psychological, cultural, social, and economic aspects of human life.[5] "Domestic," as used here, refers to those minimal institutions and modes of activity that are organized immediately around one or more mothers and their children; "public" refers to activities, institutions, and forms of association that link, rank, organize, or subsume particular mother-child groups. Though this opposition will be more or less salient in different social and ideological systems, it does provide a universal framework for conceptualizing the activities of the sexes. The opposition does not *determine* cultural stereotypes or asymmetries in the evaluations of the sexes, but rather underlies them, to support a very general (and, for women, often demeaning) identification

of women with domestic life and of men with public life. These identifications, themselves neither necessary nor desirable, can all be tied to the role of women in child rearing; by examining their multiple ramifications, one can begin to understand the nature of female subordination and the ways it may be overcome.

Although the fact that women give birth to and nurse children would seem to have no necessary entailments, it appears to provide a focus for the simplest distinction in the adult division of labor in any human group. Women become absorbed primarily in domestic activities because of their role as mothers. Their economic and political activities are constrained by the responsibilities of child care, and the focus of their emotions and attentions is particularistic and directed toward children and the home. So, for instance, Durkheim was able to speculate that "long ago, woman retired from warfare and public affairs, and consecrated her entire life to her family" (1964: 60). And Simmel points out that woman "because of her peculiar functions was relegated to activities within the limits of her home, confined to devote herself to a single individual and prevented from transcending the group-relations established by marriage [and] family" (1955: 180).

Historical or functional accounts aside, it is striking that, in these two cases as in numerous others, the domestic orientation of woman is felt to be the critical factor in understanding her social position. This orientation is contrasted to the extra-domestic, political, and military spheres of activity and interest primarily associated with men. Put quite simply, men have no single commitment as enduring, time-consuming, and emotionally compelling—as close to seeming necessary and natural—as the relation of a woman to her infant child; and so men are free to form those broader associations that we call "society," universalistic[6] systems of order, meaning, and commitment that link particular mother-child groups. Although I would be the last to call this a necessary arrangement or to deny that it is far too simple as an account of any particular empirical case, I suggest that the opposition between domestic and public orientations (an opposition that must, in part, derive from the nurturant capacities of women) provides the necessary framework for an examination of male and female roles in any society. Obvious as it may seem, its ramifications are enormous to isolate those interrelated factors that make woman universally the "second sex."

Personality

Chodorow's paper [in Rosaldo and Lamphere (1974)] develops a theory relating adult sex-role behavior to the fact that women raise children, and shows how early involvement with a female figure has characteristic consequences for the development of both boys and girls. A few of her observations seem particularly relevant to the perspective developed here. First, insofar as a young girl has a mother to love and to follow, she also has the option of becoming a "little mother," and consequently of being absorbed into womanhood without effort. Female manners and activities are acquired in a way that seems easy and natural. The young girl's family provides her with an adequate and intelligible picture of most of the possibilities and important relationships that will define her throughout life. This continuity, characteristic of a young girl's development through puberty, is in radical contrast to the experience of boys, who must *learn* to be men. Adult male activities, whether hunting, politics, or farming, are rarely visible or available to young children, and fathers are often away from the home. At some point the boy must break away from his mother and establish his maleness as a thing apart. Therefore, when his sister is learning "to be a mother," he is apt to be

restless and assertive and to seek out horizontal ties with male peers.

Three aspects of Chodorow's sophisticated argument seem particularly important. First, girls are most likely to form ties with female kin who are their seniors; they are integrated vertically, through ties with particular people, into the adult world of work.[7] This contrasts with young boys, who, having few responsibilities in late childhood, may create horizontal and often competitive peer groups, which cross-cut domestic units and establish "public" and overarching ties. In this respect, childhood activities and organization are apt to mirror the world of adults.

Second, Chodorow highlights the sense in which a young girl's early development may proceed without conflict or challenge in a group that never questions her membership, where her age rather than her abilities or achievement is likely to define her status. This is both a liability and a privilege. Growing up as a subordinate must be difficult, and if one's mother has accepted a derogatory self-image, identification with the mother can hardly be unproblematic. Such women, confusing themselves with their mothers, often have a weak ego or an uncertain sense of self. At the same time, they may enjoy a sense of ease, love, and acceptance in the process of becoming an adult. Male peer groups, by contrast, are difficult to enter; status, power, and sense of worth are often difficult to achieve. The boy's peer group, like adult male associations, is defined in part through its opposition to the family; and to establish himself, to "be a man," the boy is often required to dissociate himself, ritually or in fact, from the home. In this sense, then, a woman's status comes "naturally" (and even in societies that practice female initiation these ceremonies appear to be more a celebration of natural, biological developments than a "proof" of femininity or a challenge to past ties), whereas "becoming a man" is a feat.

Finally, growing up in a family, the young girl probably has more experience of others as individuals than as occupants of formal institutionalized roles; so she learns how to pursue her own interests, by appeals to other people, by being nurturant, responsive, and kind. She develops a "feminine" psychology. Boys, in contrast, are apt to know manhood as an abstract set of rights and duties, to learn that status brings formal authority, and to act in terms of formal roles. Their success or failure is judged in terms of male hierarchies, whereas most women, as wives, mothers, or sisters, gain respect, power, and status through their personal relations with men.

The fact that children virtually everywhere grow up with their mothers may well account for characteristic differences in male and female psychologies, and may also provide a partial psychological motive for men who, in Mead's terms (1949: 168), "need" to achieve an independent sense of worth and identity in order to become full adults.

Authority

A second consequence of the domestic, or familiar, orientation has to do with the ways in which women are perceived by the rest of society. Women are felt to be close to their children; they have access to a kind of certainty, a sense of diffuse belonging, not available to men. Men who are physically and socially distant from their children may well have political and economic claims on them; but their claims tend to be based more on their abstract authority than on personal commitment. In their absence or failure to perform as providers and symbols of status, they may lose their place in the home. This can be seen in our own society, in a father who awkwardly fondles his baby or in the woman-focused families of Blacks (Liebow, 1967; Stack [in Rosaldo and Lamphere, 1974]) and other poor urban groups. In parts of Indonesia, men spend most of their time in long-distance trading, and are treated as outsiders, or guests, in the home (Tanner [in Rosaldo and Lamphere, 1974]).

But distance itself can, and often does, provide interactional support for male claims to authority. In many parts of the world there is a radical break between the life of men—as reflected in their politics, separate sleeping quarters, and rituals—and the life of the domestic group. To the extent that men live apart from women, they of course cannot control them, and women may be able to form informal groups of their own. Yet men are free to build up rituals of authority that define them as superior, special, and apart. In New Guinea, for example, men often have collective sleeping quarters, a practice associated with secret rituals and a lore that teaches young men that their health, strength, and beauty are damaged and diminished through their ties to the home. In parts of the Arab world (Fernea, 1965) women interact mostly with women, and men with men; wives meet their husbands briefly when serving dinner and occasionally for a few hours in bed. Interaction is highly structured and limited, subject to the mood of the man. Among the camel-herding Tuareg (Murphy, 1964) of the central Sahara, social roles are often ambiguous and overlapping, because of a preference for endogamy and bilateral reckoning of kin. Furthermore, women enjoy a good deal more freedom and social recognition than they do in most other Islamic societies. For men, it seems likely that the difficult, cooperative work situations of daily life tend to break down social distance; slaves and nobles, women and men, must cooperate in tending the herds. In order to distance themselves from a web of complex social relationships, and to protect their integrity and sense of personal esteem, Tuareg men have adopted the practice of wearing a veil across the nose and mouth. The veil is drawn most tightly when a man confronts a superior. But significantly, high-status men wear their veils more strictly than do slaves or vassals; women have no veils; and to assure his distance, no man is supposed to permit his lover to see his mouth. (In parts of American society, it would seem that men wear their veil of a newspaper in the subways and at breakfast with their wives.)

Such rituals enforce the distance between men and their families; for the individual, they provide a barrier to becoming embedded in an intimate, demanding world. Distance permits men to manipulate their social environment, to stand apart from intimate interaction, and, accordingly, to control it as they wish. Because men can be separate, they can be "sacred"; and by avoiding certain sorts of intimacy and unmediated involvement, they can develop an image and mantle of integrity and worth.

Women, by contrast, would have considerable difficulty in maintaining distance from the people they interact with. They must care for children, feed and clean them, and perform the messy chores. Their social interaction is more difficult for them to structure, being intimate and subject to variation in their own and their children's moods. Women's lives are marked by neither privacy nor distance. They are embedded in, and subject to, the demands of immediate interaction. Women, more than men, must respond to the personal needs of those around them: their public image is more difficult for them to manipulate or control; and where that image is concerned, familiarity may breed contempt. The rituals of authority are not available to woman; only when she is old and free of the responsibility of children, when she is dissociated from child rearing and also from sexuality, can a woman build up the respect that comes with authority.

Achieved and Ascribed Status

My earlier observations indicated that women's early experience in growing up has continuity. Whatever pain is in fact associated with female socialization, most cultures assume that it is relatively easy for a young girl to become a woman; people in most societies seem to take that process for granted. A man's experience lacks this continuity; he may be wrenched from the domestic sphere in which he spent his earliest years, by means of a series of rituals or initiations that teach him to distrust or despise the world of his mother, to seek his manhood outside the home. A woman becomes a woman by following in her mother's footsteps, whereas there must be a break in a man's experience. For a boy to become an adult, he must prove himself—his masculinity—among his peers. And although all boys may succeed in reaching manhood, cultures treat this development as something that each individual has achieved.

Unlike the two or three generations of a woman's domestic group, the male peer group often has no natural criteria that uniquely determine membership, order relationships, or establish chains of command. Instead, order within male groups, and in the social world in general, is felt to be a cultural product, and men elaborate systems of norms, ideals, and standards of evaluation that permit them to order relationships among themselves. If "becoming a man" is, developmentally, an "achievement," social groups elaborate the criteria for that achievement and create the hierarchies and institutions we associate with an articulated social order. Insofar as achievement in this sense is a prerequisite of manhood, then men create and control a social order in which they compete as individuals. Womanhood, by contrast, is more of a given for the female, and in most societies we find relatively few ways of expressing the differences among women. In Simmel's words, "the most general of her qualities, the fact that she was a woman and as such served the functions proper to her sex, caused her to be classified with all other women under one general concept"

(1955: 180). Womanhood is an ascribed status; a woman is seen as "naturally" what she is.

One consequence of this can be seen in those traditional descriptions of social structure that report what are, for the most part, activities of men. Men are, in a real sense, identified with and through those groups of kin or peers that cut across domestic units; ranked in hierarchies of achievement, they are differentiated in their roles. These systems of ranking, grouping, and differentiation comprise the explicit social order that social scientists typically describe. Women, for their part, lead relatively comparable lives, both within a culture and from one culture to the next.[8] Their activities, in comparison with those of men, are relatively uninvolved with the articulation and expression of social differences. Therefore, we find, in most societies, relatively few institutionalized roles for women, and relatively few contexts in which women can legitimately make claims. Women's contributions to extra-domestic relations are rarely made explicit; women are given a social role and definition by virtue either of their age or of their relationship to men. Women, then, are conceived almost exclusively as sisters, wives, and mothers. Whereas men achieve rank as a result of explicit achievement, differences among women are generally seen as the product of idiosyncratic characteristics, such as temperament, personality, and appearances.[9]

Because cultures provide no fine social classification for kinds of women and their interests, women are seen and come to see themselves as idiosyncratic and irrational. Bateson, for example, reports that "structural phrasings" of motives and relations are pronounced among men in Iatmul (New Guinea) culture, whereas "among the women emotional phrasings of reasons for behaviour are very much more frequent than among the men" (1958: 253). We are also told that Iatmul men are given

to histrionic displays of status, whereas women behave in a casual, happy-go-lucky mode. Again, Landes says of the Ojibwa that "only the male half of the population and its activities fall under the traditional regulations, while the female half is left to spontaneous and confused behavior"; successful women may rival men in their achievements, but "they do not pursue these in systematic male fashion" (1971: v). Women's lives appear to be unstructured and "spontaneous" (see also Paul [in Rosaldo and Lamphere, 1974]) in comparison with those of men.

Such perceptions are not, of course, unique to foreign cultures, but seem to be quite general. In the West, thinkers from Durkheim to Parsons have said that women are more "affective" or "expressive," less "intellectual" or "instrumental" than men. The claim has been made that this difference is a functional necessity of the family as a social group (Zelditch, 1955, 1964). Yet increasing evidence belies this assumption and suggests that the "expressive" character of women is as much a cultural interpretation, or cliché, as an accurate reflection of the ways in which women act and think.

If, following Durkheim, we are willing to suppose that the structure and nature of social relationships themselves influence cultural perceptions and modes of thinking, we can now illuminate this long-standing claim of social science. It reflects, not a natural or necessary endowment, but a very general cultural theme. Since women must work within a social system that obscures their goals and interests, they are apt to develop ways of seeing, feeling, and acting that seem to be "intuitive" and unsystematic—with a sensitivity to other people that permits them to survive. They may, then, be "expressive." But it is also important to realize that cultural stereotypes order the observer's own perceptions. It is because men enter the world of articulated social relations that they appear to us as intellectual, rational, or instrumental; and the fact that women are excluded from that world makes them seem to think and behave in another mode.

Nature and Culture

There is yet another implication of this discussion. Insofar as men are defined in terms of their achievement in socially elaborated institutions, they are participants, *par excellence*, in the man-made systems of human experience. On a moral level, theirs is the world of "culture." Women, on the other hand, lead lives that appear to be irrelevant to the formal articulation of social order. Their status is derived from their stage in a life cycle, from their biological functions, and, in particular, from their sexual or biological ties to particular men. What is more, women are more involved than men in the "grubby" and dangerous stuff of social existence, giving birth and mourning death, feeding, cooking, disposing of feces, and the like. Accordingly, in cultural systems we find a recurrent opposition: between man, who in the last analysis stands for "culture," and woman, who (defined through symbols that stress her biological and sexual functions) stands for "nature," and often for disorder.[10]

This point is elaborated in Ortner's paper [in Rosaldo and Lamphere, 1974]. But it may be worth while to review some of its implications here. What is perhaps most striking is the fact that cultural notions of the female often gravitate around natural or biological characteristics: fertility, maternity, sex, and menstrual blood. And women, as wives, mothers, witches, midwives, nuns, or whores, are defined almost exclusively in terms of their sexual functions. A witch, in European tradition, is a woman who sleeps with the devil; and a nun is a woman who marries her god. Again, purity and pollution are ideas that apply primarily to women, who must either deny their physical bodies or circumscribe their dangerous sexuality.

Women as Anomalies

The fact that men, in contrast to women, can be said to be associated with culture reflects another aspect of cultural definitions of the female. Recent studies of symbolic culture have suggested that whatever violates a society's sense of order will be seen as threatening, nasty, disorderly, or wrong. Douglas (1966) has called this sort of thing "anomalous." The idea of "order" depends, logically, on "disorder" as its opposite, yet society tries to set such things aside.

Now I would suggest that women in many societies will be seen as something "anomalous." Insofar as men, in their institutionalized relations of kinship, politics, and so on, define the public order, women are their opposite. Where men are classified in terms of ranked, institutional positions, women are simply women and their activities, interests, and differences receive only idiosyncratic note. Where male activities are justified and rationalized by a fine societal classification, by a system of norms acknowledging their different pursuits, women are classified together and their particular goals are ignored. From the point of view of the larger social system, they are seen as deviants or manipulators; because systems of social classification rarely make room for their interests, they are not publicly understood.

But women defy the ideals of the male order. They may be defined as virgins, yet be necessary to the group's regeneration. They may be excluded from authority, yet exercise all sorts of informal power. Their status may be derived from their male relations, yet they outlive their husbands and fathers. And insofar as the presence of women does introduce such contradictions, women will be seen as anomalous and defined as dangerous, dirty, and polluting, as something to be set apart.

A few examples may clarify this position. In many patrilineal ideologies (see Denich [in Rosaldo and Lamphere, 1974]), women are seen as unnecessary or superfluous, yet at the same time vitally important to men: they are needed as wives, as sisters to be exchanged for wives, and as procreators who produce workers and heirs for the groups. Because they are important, they are powerful, yet theirs is a power opposed to formal norms. A woman may, for example, be the mediator between her own kin group and that of the man she has married; her manipulations and choice of male allies may be of crucial importance to her kin. In such situations, cultures may elaborate the idea of her pollution; a woman's activities are circumscribed by calling them dangerous, by making them something to fear. Douglas (1966), for example, says of the Lele of the Kasai in southern Africa that men, who are dependent on women's political manipulations, are afraid to eat food cooked by menstruating women and rigorously abstain from sex, from contact with polluting women, before any important event. An extreme and now classic case is reported by Meggit (1964) in New Guinea. The Mae Enga of the Western Highlands say that they "marry their enemies"; women are pawns in a tenuous political alliance. Yet the in-marrying woman is always, of course, an outsider, and her influence is always feared. So, young Mae Enga boys are taught at an early age to fear the association of women; they learn that sexual indulgence deforms them and that menstrual blood can bring on disease. Pollution ideas are so extreme that marriage itself is seen as extremely dangerous; and to avoid the pollution of childbirth, a man may wait as much as three months before he dares to look at his newborn child.

Elsewhere, of course, women in conventional roles are not threatening. A woman who is a wife and a mother is benign. Danger is perceived only when a woman fails to bear children, or when her husband or children have died. In some societies danger or blame attaches to a woman who lives to mourn the death of her male kin. That many societies give far more cultural elaboration to the role of "widow" than to that of "widower" suggests that such conflicts do arise.[11] Men may take an active part in the rituals of mourning, but it is the women, not the men, who cry longer or louder, or in some other way are forced to show more suffering at death. In Madagascar, for example, women dance with the bones of dead people (Bloch, 1971); in the Mediterranean, women who have lost a close relative are likely to wear black for the rest of their lives. In parts of New Guinea, joints of a young girl's finger are severed when there is a death in the family; high-caste Indian women used to throw themselves on the funeral pyres of their husbands; and in other parts of the world, widows are strangled, commit suicide, or the like.

The sense that the widow is anomalous—that she, rather than the ghost of the dead person or some other close kin, must bear the weight of a loss—seems to be most elaborate in those groups in which a woman is defined exclusively in and through her male relations. Harper (1969) illustrated this in a paper on high-caste Brahmins in southern India. Among members of this group, marriage is seen as a necessary but terrible fact of a woman's maturity. Girls are indulged as little children because their parents pity their imminent fate; before puberty they are married into a group containing none of their kinswomen; they are subordinated to a hostile mother-in-law, and to ensure their purity and exclusive attachment to a single man, they are denied a role in production activities and confined to the house. It is said that a woman should pray to die before her husband. If he dies first, she as an outsider is apt to be suspected as the mystical source of his demise. When these poor women, who have been excluded from any social role of their own, are widowed, they in fact become social anomalies, without meaning or place. Others see them as pariahs, as evildoers and poisoners; they are despised and feared. It is significant that low-caste groups in the same area have no such beliefs about widows; there women have a role in social life and production, and widows remarry at will.

Finally, women may be "anomalies" because societies that define women as lacking legitimate authority have no way of acknowledging the reality of female power. This difference between rule and reality is reflected in our own society when we speak of powerful women as "bitches"; elsewhere in the world, the powerful woman is often considered a witch. Nadel, in his study of the Nupe of Nigeria (1952), described a situation where, in spite of a male-oriented political and religious system, women had become long-distance traders, thus acquiring a substantial income of their own. What is more, these women had access to contraceptives and illicit sex in faraway markets, defying a dominant norm that made reproduction a husband's prerogative and right. The Nupe, then, came to see societies of female traders as societies of witches. In so doing, they acknowledged the women's real power while labeling it illegitimate and wrong.

Production

A final reflex of the opposition between domestic and public spheres of activity is seen in the relations of production, in the place of men and women in economic life. Here it is particularly difficult to generalize, because female economic activities are truly varied, ranging from the American woman's housework to the African woman's long-distance trade. Yet the economic organization of women does seem to be relatively less public than that of men; women tend to work individually, or in small, loosely organized groups. And the products of female labor

tend to be directed to the family and the home. Even when the products of women's labor are distributed in the larger community, it is often in support of male prestige.

Several papers [in Rosaldo and Lamphere, 1974] show the consequences of different modes of female labor as well as the different ways in which a woman's reproductive capacities themselves are integrated into the economic life of a society (see Sanday, Sacks, and O'Laughlin). But whatever the variation, it is clear that the relatively domestic and particularistic orientation of women obtains in the vast majority of social groups. In most hunting bands, for instance, both men and women may hunt and gather, but only gathering is felt to be woman's work. Gathering requires little formal planning or organization; groups of women search the brush together, each doing the same kind of work and each acquiring foodstuffs, which may be shared informally with neighbors but are used primarily to meet individual family needs. Among the Ilongots, the Philippine group I studied, rice is a woman's product and possession; adult women usually have their own gardens and individual granaries in which rice is stored for household use. Hunting, on the other hand, is a responsibility of men as members of the community, and game is distributed through the community as a whole, since it is difficult to store. Even when men hunt individually, and dry and sell their catch, they exchange game for prestige goods, which are used for bride-price payments, gifts, and redress in the case of feuds. Finally, Bateson comments that in Iatmul (New Guinea) society both men and women fish for food, but when women fish "there is none of the excitement which the men introduce into their fishing expeditions. Each woman goes off by herself to do her day's work" (1958: 143).

Although one may find exceptions, then, it is generally the case that woman's economic orientation, like her emotional and social orientation, is relatively more individual and particularistic than that of men. This leads me to restate Engels's suggestive claim (see Sacks [in Rosaldo and Lamphere, 1974]) that women were once involved in "social production" and, with the development of technology and capital, have been relegated to the domestic sphere. Rather, it seems that a domestic/public asymmetry is general in economic forms of human organization as in other forms. Advanced and capitalistic societies, although they are extreme in this regard, are not unique.

Sources of Power and Value

The preceding discussion has suggested that characteristic aspects of male and female roles in social, cultural, and economic systems can all be related to a universal, structural opposition between domestic and public domains of activity. In many ways this claim is far too simple. It is easy—in American society, for example—to identify the domestic sphere of the suburban housewife, and oppose it to the public, social world of industry, finance, and prestige. However, domestic groups themselves are highly varied—ranging from Mbuti leantos, which are hardly dissociated from the life of the community, to the famous Iroquois longhouse (Brown, 1970a), which holds several families and is itself a kind of social sphere. In fact, as Lamphere shows in a later paper, variations in domestic group structure are importantly related to variations in the types of female power.

Yet the complexities of particular cases do not undermine our global generalization, which points, not to absolute, but to relative orientations of women and men. Furthermore, by using the structural model as a framework, we can identify the implications for female power, value, and status in various cross-cultural articulations of domestic and public roles. Although the model has no necessary implications for the future,

it permits us to identify two sorts of structural arrangements that elevate women's status: women may enter a public world, or men may enter the home.[12] By seeing how women have manipulated, elaborated, or undermined their domestic affiliations, we begin to appreciate women's roles as actors in various social systems, and also to identify the kinds of changes that women might effect in our own.

The model leads me to suggest, first, that women's status will be lowest in those societies where there is a firm differentiation between domestic and public spheres of activity and where women are isolated from one another and placed under a single man's authority, in the home. Their position is raised when they can challenge those claims to authority, either by taking on men's roles or by establishing social ties, by creating a sense of rank, order, and value in a world in which women prevail. One possibility for women, then, is to enter the men's world or to create a public world of their own. But perhaps the most egalitarian societies are those in which public and domestic spheres are only weakly differentiated, where neither sex claims much authority and the focus of social life itself is the home.

To begin (and without specifying particular criteria for reckoning women's status), it is clear that women who are cut off from ties with peers, who are circumscribed in their movements and activities, have an unenviable fate. A good example comes from Campbell's excellent description of the sheepherding Greek Sarakatsani (1964). Men spend their days in the hills, tending animals, while women are strictly confined to the home. An adolescent girl is taught early to limit her movements, to walk modestly, and never to run. Her sex is the stuff of the devil; her body is so feared that she rarely washes her torso; and if she so much as looks eye to eye with a man she is thought to invite assault. Upon marriage, she enters a hostile and distant household, where men and women alike resent any signs that she and her husband are close. For her, the sole joy in life is the son who grows up to support her, guaranteeing comfort when she is old. Yet her son's future status itself depends on her actions, and she must guard her own purity and preserve her husband's good name. She cannot so much as complain of her husband's abuses lest she defame him. Effectively she is his servant, and as Campbell suggests (1964), he is her god (see Denich [in Rosaldo and Lamphere, 1974]).[13]

Other social arrangements, however, accord women more power and value. In some, a woman's opinions and her ability to bring a high bride-price or make ties with particular men are important factors in forging political alliances between groups. In others, her economic contribution and in particular, her control of foodstuffs permit her to influence men. Where domestic and public spheres are firmly differentiated, women can manipulate men and influence their decisions by strategies as diverse as refusing to cook for their husbands (see Paulme, 1963), winning their sons' loyalties, setting spouse against kinsmen, or instigating what the rest of society may recognize as a "tragedy" in the home (see Wolf, 1972; Collier, 1973 [and in Rosaldo and Lamphere, 1974]). Finally, there are societies like our own, in which domestic and public spheres are distinguished, but in which privileged women, by taking on men's roles (becoming doctors, lawyers, or even members of the army), achieve considerable status and power. This seems to be the case with the classic queens and female chieftains of Africa (Lebeuf, 1963; Hoffer [in Rosaldo and Lamphere, 1974]). Among the Lovedu (Krige and Krige, 1943), for instance, a woman may win power, status, and autonomy by taking over her husband's estate or by accumulating capital and marrying wives (the Lovedu have queens who, in the ritual aspects of marriage, perform in the role of a man).

Women in men's roles, however, tend to constitute an elite segment of female humanity; few women in history have achieved a dominant position in the working world, and even fewer have competed with male politicians and become political leaders or queens. More commonly, in those societies where domestic and public spheres are firmly differentiated, women may win power and value by stressing their differences from men. By accepting and elaborating upon the symbols and expectations associated with their cultural definition, they may goad men into compliance, or establish a society unto themselves. Thus, for instance, the traditional American woman can gain power covertly, by playing up to her husband's vanity (privately directing his public life). Or in everything from charities to baking contests, she may forge a public world of her own. Elsewhere, women may form trading societies, church clubs, or even political organizations, through which they force thoughtless men into line. Among the Iroquois (Brown, 1970a), women's power was rooted in a predominantly female organization of domestic life and agricultural labor; men spent long periods away from home hunting or warring, and women worked together, controlled the distribution of foodstuffs, decided on marriages, and generally dominated community concerns. Again, in the prestigious female political and religious societies of West Africa (Lebeuf, 1963; Leis, Hoffer [in Rosaldo and Lamphere, 1974]), women have created fully articulated social hierarchies of their own.

The ideas of purity and pollution, so often used to circumscribe female activities, may also be used as a basis for assertions of female solidarity, power, or value. In the simplest case, we might note that a woman who is feared often has power; many a New Guinea man will observe his wife's wishes for fear that an angry woman will serve him food while she is menstruating, or step over him, letting blood drip, while he sleeps. Again, roles like that of the witch or mid- wife (see Paul [in Rosaldo and Lamphere, 1974]) seem to be used by women who, by stressing aspects of their special or anom- alous position, take on powers uniquely their own. What is more, pollution beliefs can provide grounds for solidarity among women. Women may, for example, gather in menstrual huts, to relax or to gossip, cre- ating a world free from control by men. Or again, as Lewis (1971) has indicated, anom- alous and powerless women in many parts of the world may be particularly vulnera- ble to possession by spirits; on the basis of such possession, women form cult groups that rival the religious organizations of men. Finally, women as both secular and religious prostitutes, as women who never marry yet have intercourse with a wide range of men, may again be making positive use of their "anomalous" sexuality. Because it is both feared and desired, it gives them a real source of power, and in certain situations the brothel and temple may be spheres where women prevail.

If assertions of sexuality can give power to women, so too can its denial. Victorian women won status by denying their own sexuality and treating male sexual drives as a sin. Purity beliefs seem to be particularly attractive to women, who very often elabo- rate the norms concerned with purity, the rules for strict dress and demeanor, modesty, cleanliness, and prudishness, which they use as a device for contrasting their world and the men's world—establishing grounds for order and status among themselves. So, for example, in a Spanish village I studied, women were vicious in their condemnation of the seductive female; they elaborated a system of strict norms for the period of mourning, and the pure and respectable woman spent most of her life in drab black clothing. Groups of these women gathered during the day at the fountain in the center of the village, defining that center as their

own. As is the case elsewhere in the Mediterranean, they saw themselves as purer, more moral and stable, than men, and men, in the fields or the bar or the cities, were rarely in sight. At the fountain, women gossiped and exchanged valuable information. Their dazzlingly white sheets and severe sexless garments testified to their purity; and while men dirtied themselves in work, compromise, and public competi- tion, women had a moral sphere all their own. Perhaps the extreme case of a women's society founded on the idiom of purity, on a lack of involvement with men, is the convent. Brides of Christ need not be tainted by mortal men's foibles. Instead, they establish a pure and moral society, a world wholly their own.

These examples suggest that the very symbolic and social conceptions that appear to set women apart and to circumscribe their activities may be used by women as a basis for female solidarity and worth. When men live apart from women, they in fact cannot control them, and unwittingly they may provide them with the symbols and so- cial resources on which to build a society of their own. Such women's groups, ranging from convents and brothels to informal neighborhood friendships in China (see Wolf, 1972 [and in Rosaldo and Lamphere, 1974]) or African political organizations and cults (Leis, Hoffer [in Rosaldo and Lam- phere, 1974]), are available to women in men's absence, and they add social and moral value to an otherwise domestic role.

Extra-domestic ties with other women are, then, an important source of power and value for women in societies that create a firm division between public and domestic, or male and female, roles. As suggested ear- lier, however, there is another possibility. Societies that do not elaborate the opposi- tion of male and female and place positive value on the conjugal relationship and the involvement of both men and women in the home seem to be most egalitarian in terms of sex roles. When a man is involved in domestic labor, in child care and cooking, he cannot establish an aura of authority and distance. And when public decisions are made in the household, women may have a legitimate public role.

Because none of the other papers [in Rosaldo and Lamphere, 1974] consider this alternative, it might be valuable to treat one example at length. Among the Ilongots, the Philippine society I studied, a man's hunting is more highly valued than the gardening done by women, but the two modes of production are conceived as complementary and the division of labor is not strict. Rituals for hunting and gardening draw on the same complex repertoire of magical objects; in the house when food is being distributed, women cook and allot rice portions, while men cook, cut, and distribute bits of meat. During the day, when women are gardening, men spend long hours with their children, and husband and wife may keep an infant between them while they sleep. A marriage forms a core, an enduring and cooperative social unit; the only Ilongot expression for "family" means "married couple" or "those who have intercourse together."

In fact, there is little in everyday Ilongot life to suggest an asymmetrical relation of the sexes. There are no men's houses or public plazas, no locus for an independent, ranked, and organized hierarchical world of men.[14] Most political confrontations take place in the large one-room households; although men may predominate in such contexts, women are rarely forbidden to speak. The one activity that marks men as special is headhunting. Like male cults and secret rituals elsewhere in the world, this is associated with the attainment of manhood; it is the one activity in which men are definitely set apart. Yet it is particularly interesting to note that headhunting is not felt to be obligatory, nor is it desirable for a man to take a head more than once. The overly anxious killer is thought to be aggressive,

and headhunting does not provide a basis on which men readily rank one another or compete among themselves.

In other words, it appears that involvement of men in the domestic sphere and, correspondingly, participation of women in most public events, have a number of related consequences. In an area of the world in which men have traditionally won authority through their competitive success in warfare, Ilongot headhunters seem nonetheless to play down a male ethic of authority and achievement, of systems of ranking among men. Because boys' earliest experiences are shaped by the intimacy of fathers as well as mothers, they are relatively unconcerned with a need to "achieve," or to denigrate women; men involved in domestic tasks demand no submission from their wives. In social and political life, Ilongots evince little stratification, and although sexual asymmetry is certainly present, it is minimized by the fact that women have the right, and the confidence, to speak their minds. Finally, in the home we find relatively egalitarian relations between the sexes, cooperation rather than competition, and a true closeness of husband and wife.

The same point, I think, can be made for other societies considered in the anthropological literature to be "egalitarian." In these, as in Ilongot society, men control prestigious rituals and symbols, but the aura of male authority is minimized through men's involvement in the home. So, for example, the Mbuti pygmies of Africa (Turnbull, 1961) live in groups where domestic units are separated from one another by mere lean-tos and men and women cooperate in both domestic and economic pursuits. Mbuti men do have a secret flute cult, but it is not used to dominate women or to create rankings among themselves. Another example is the Arapesh, as well as those other New Guinea groups (e.g., Wogeo, described in Hogbin, 1970) that, in a culture area characterized by elaborate and institutionalized expressions of sexual antagonism, seem to have stressed the complementarity of women and men. In these, as opposed to other groups in the area, the "secret" of male flute cults is enforced only weakly. And among the Arapesh, men and women together are said to "give birth to" and "grow" their children; they participate jointly in domestic life. Here again the mutual and complementary involvement of men and women in domestic activities promotes a sense of equality. An egalitarian ethos seems possible to the extent that men take on a domestic role.

Conclusion

I have tried to relate universal asymmetries in the actual activities and cultural evaluations of men and women to a universal, structural opposition between domestic and public spheres. I have also suggested that women seem to be oppressed or lacking in value and status to the extent that they are confined to domestic activities, cut off from other women and from the social world of men. Women gain power and a sense of value when they are able to transcend domestic limits, either by entering the men's world or by creating a society unto themselves. Finally, I suggested that the most egalitarian societies are not those in which male and female are opposed or are even competitors, but those in which men value and participate in the domestic life of the home. Correspondingly, they are societies in which women can readily participate in important public events.

It is interesting to note that American society participates to some extent, especially on the level of ideology (though not, of course, in economic or other forms of organization), in the last complementary ideal. Americans talk about sexual equality, and American rituals from churchgoing to holiday dinners are intended to involve the nuclear family as a whole. Schneider, in an innovative study (1968), has suggested that the idea of "sexual intercourse," of conjugal solidarity, is a central metaphor in American kinship; husband and wife form a core unit, an ordering principle for reckoning relationships, and also a cultural ideal. In a similar way, I indicated that "those who have intercourse together" means "family" for the Ilongots. There too, the union of man and woman is seen as crucial, and again it is associated with an egalitarian sexual ideology.

Unlike the Ilongot, however, American society is in fact organized in a way that creates and exploits a radical distance between private and public, domestic and social, female and male. It speaks, on one level, of the conjugal family, while on another it defines women as domestic (an invisible army of unemployed) and sends its men into the public, working world. This conflict between ideal and reality creates illusions and disappointments for both men and women.

In concluding, I would like to suggest that this conflict is at the core of the contemporary rethinking of sex roles: we are told that men and women should be equals and even companions, but we are also told to value men for their work. So far, women concerned to realize their equality have concentrated on the second half of this paradox, and have sought grounds for female solidarity and opportunities for women in the men's working world. We have conceived of our liberation on the model of women's societies and African queens. Yet as long as the domestic sphere remains female, women's societies, however powerful, will never be the political equivalents of men's; and, as in the past, sovereignty can be a metaphor for only a female elite. If the public world is to open its doors to more than the elite among women, the nature of work itself will have to be altered, and the asymmetry between work and the home reduced. For this, we must, like the Ilongots, bring men into the sphere of domestic concerns and responsibilities.

Certainly it is difficult to imagine modeling our society after that of the Ilongot cultivators and hunters. Yet we need today to combine political goals with utopian visions, and to this end the Ilongot example can help. It provides us with an image of a world in which the domestic/public opposition is minimized and dissociated from sexual ascriptions. And it suggests that men who in the past have committed their lives to public achievement will recognize women as true equals only when men themselves help to raise new generations by taking on the responsibilities of the home.

NOTES

Author's Note: Neither this paper nor this book would have been conceived had I not had the opportunity in 1971, at Stanford University, to teach a course on women with Ellen Lewin, Julia D. Howell, Jane Collier, Janet Shepherd Fjellman, and Kim Kramer. Many of their ideas appear in the collective paper "Power Strategies and Sex Roles" (Lewin et al., 1971) and are echoed in the discussion that follows. Since that time, discussions with Jane Atkinson, Amy Burce, Nancy Chodorow, Jane Collier, Peggy Comstock, Mary Felstiner, Carol Nagy Jacklin, Louise Lamphere, Bridget O'Laughlin, Sherry Ortner, and Ellen Rogat have influenced the development of the ideas presented here. I am indebted to all of them, as well as to Renato Rosaldo, Arthur Wolf, Karl Heider, and Harumi Befu for their comments on this manuscript.

1. The fact that female gathering rather than male hunting may provide the bulk of a group's nutritional requirements has been suggested by Lee (1968) and others. Linton (1973) uses this, as well as the facts of human newborn development, to criticize the "man the hunter" view of human evolution.
2. The classic distinction between power, authority, and influence was developed by Weber (1947). M. G. Smith proposes the following definition: "Authority is, in the abstract, the right to make a particular decision and to command obedience. . . . Power . . . is the ability to act effectively on persons or things, to make or secure favourable decisions which are not of right allocated to the individuals or their roles" (1960: 18–19). Whether power is exercised through influence or force, it is inherently competitive, whereas authority entails a hierarchical chain of command and control. Although the idea of authority implies positive actions and duties, the exercise of power has no positive sanctions, only rules that specify "the conditions of illegality of its operation" (p. 20). Later essays will show that, although women may have neither the right nor the duty to make decisions, they often have a systematic influence on decisions that are made. And although social norms may not acknowledge the positive use of power by women, they often specify the limits or illegality of such power, treating the powerful or influential woman as disruptive, anomalous, and so on. A more technical discussion of power, authority, and influence is given by Lamphere [in Rosaldo and Lamphere, 1974].
3. See also Bachofen (1967) and Davis (1972). Although many societies have myths that seem to confirm this interpretation (myths in which, for example, men "steal" an important cultural artifact from the women, see Bamberger [in Rosaldo and Lamphere, 1974]), I would prefer to see these as cultural reflections of the often tenuous and conflict-ridden nature of male claims to authority, rather than as historical accounts (see Murphy, 1959).
4. The importance of the woman's role as mother is not a new idea, but it was first suggested to me by Nancy Chodorow as the critical fact in understanding woman's status. See her paper "Being and Doing" (1971).
5. It should be stressed that, whereas a number of the empirical observations put forth here might seem to support those theorists who have claimed that men, as opposed to women, have a biological propensity for forming social "groups" (e.g., Tiger, 1969), my point is that what universals can be found in the social organization and position of

men and women can be traced to social rather than biological considerations. The universal association of women with young children and its various social, cultural, and psychological implications are seen as likely but not necessary (or desirable) outcomes, and they are more readily derived from organizational factors than from biology.

6. The use of "universalistic" and "particularistic" here resembles, but is different from, the meanings proposed in Parsons and Shils (1951: 82). Parsons used these terms to differentiate societies in which status is achieved and allocated on the basis of individual attributes, defined and evaluated in generalized terms, from those in which positions of status are determined by kin relations and the like. I speak of the women's world as "relatively particularistic" in all societies because it is governed by informal and personal knowledge of individuals, in contrast to the male world, which is relatively more concerned with formal norms of relationship and publicly recognized characteristics of roles.

7. The Mae Enga (Meggit, 1964, 1965), who believe that flesh grows "vertically" on the bones of women and "horizontally" on the bones of men, and that this accounts for the fact that girls mature more quickly and easily than men do, seem to have formulated a symbolic statement of the sociological generalization suggested here.

8. The wives of herders, agriculturalists, and businessmen lead lives that are conceptualized in remarkably similar terms. Women, who are characterized everywhere as "the other," are often seen by missionaries and colonialists as the easiest people to interact with, convert, or educate; the hispanization of the New World, for example, seems to have depended in large part upon the colonialists' use of native women as lovers and domestics, and therefore as mediators between two worlds (Mary Felstiner, 1973). The fact that sisters can be married off to foreigners (whether in the New Guinea Highlands or the crowned courts of Europe), that women can be "exchanged" (Lévi-Strauss, 1949), corresponds to the fact that cultural conceptions of women's roles are universally very similar; much of what women do in any one society may be seen to have immediately available equivalents in any other.

9. This generalization has its exceptions; in West Africa (Little, 1951) and in parts of Melanesia (Deacon, 1934), for example, women establish a fine societal classification of ranks among themselves. In general, however, women are not differentiated except in terms of age, relationship to men, or idiosyncratic (and institutionally irrelevant) characteristics. The contrast between categories used for men and women seems to parallel a contrast identified by Cancian (n.d.) between folk statements of what "good" and "bad" men do. "Good" norms are organized in terms of social institutions and provide criteria for ranking achievement in well-articulated social spheres; "bad" norms, by contrast, are only loosely organized, and refer to such considerations as temperament, appearance, sociability—idiosyncratic characteristics that do not lend themselves to organized and public systems of rank.

10. The tendency to associate women rather than men with Nature, and in particular with sexuality, in contemporary Western thought is documented in Ellman's witty observations concerning the popular "association . . . between female reproductive organs and the female mind" (1968: 12). Ellman shows how, in literary discussion, there is a stereotyped and "repeated association of women . . . with nature and of men with art" (p. 61). De Beauvoir (1953) saw the same thing, as in the nineteenth century did Bachofen (1967), whose claim that modern civilization was preceded by matriarchy is based, in large part, on the notion that nature, and especially fertility (rather than logical prowess), was once highly valued in human societies.

11. The belief that extremes in mourning practices reflect the tenuous or anomalous position of the mourner (whose position in relation to a social group is refined solely in and through his or her ties to the deceased) is confirmed by an apparent exception. Fortune (1932) reported extremes in mourning practices among the Dobuans, where widows and widowers alike must spend a year in virtual isolation mourning the lost spouse. Dobuan residence arrangements require that couples spend alternate years in the husband's or wife's matrilineal village. This means that neither spouse has an opportunity to establish regular ties with his or her affines, and neither can be anything but an outsider to the affinal group. When one dies, the sole basis for social ties between spouse and affines

is lost and the spouse stands in an "anomalous" relationship—of familiarity without institutional meaning—to the deceased. He or she is then forced to spend a full year grieving at the outskirts of the spouse's village, before their ties can be severed. At the end of mourning, the spouse is barred forever from reentering the village of the deceased.

12. For conceptual purposes, these possibilities are distinguished, although actual societies may be characterized by combinations of the two.

13. In accord with our emphasis on how women see their lives, it is important to add that a Sarakatsani woman's status is at a low point in late adolescence and the first years of marriage. When her sons marry, they take over their father's position as head of household, and her powers and privileges are heightened, while those of her husband wane.

14. Recent mission influence has established an institution outside the household, the Church. It has also introduced the explicit Christian idea of the subordination of the wife to her husband. Ilongot women more than men seem open to conversion, but it is significant that leadership roles in the Church (the first formal, institutionalized, important, and explicit leadership roles within Ilongot society) have all been assumed by men.

REFERENCES

Bachofen, J. J. 1967. Myth, Religion and Mother Right. Selected Writings. Ralph Mannheim, trans. Bollingen Series, 84. Princeton, NJ.

Bardwick, Judith M. 1971. Psychology of Women: A Study of Bio-Cultural Conflicts. New York.

Barry, Herbert, M. K. Bacon, and I. L. Child. 1957. "A Cross-Cultural Survey of Some Sex Differences in Socialization," *Journal of Abnormal and Social Psychology* 55: 327–332.

Bateson, Gregory. 1958. Naven. Stanford, CA.

Bettelheim, Bruno. 1954. Symbolic Wounds: Puberty Rites and the Envious Male. New York.

Bloch, Maurice. 1971. Placing the Dead. London.

Brown, Judith K. 1970a. "Economic Organization and the Position of Women Among the Iroquois," *Ethnohistory* 17 (3–4): 151–167.

——— 1970b. "A Note on the Division of Labor by Sex," *American Anthropologist*, 72: 1073–1078.

Campbell, J. K. 1964. Honor, Family and Patronage. Oxford.

Cancian, Francesca. n.d. What Are Norms? Chicago. Forthcoming.

Chodorow, Nancy. 1971. "Being and Doing," in Vivian Gornick and B. K. Moran, eds., Women in Sexist Society. New York.

Collier, Jane F. 1973. Law and Social Change in Zinacantan. Stanford, CA.

Davis, Elizabeth Gould. 1972. The First Sex. Baltimore, MD.

Deacon, A. Bernard. 1934. Malekula: A Vanishing People. London.

De Beauvoir, Simone. 1953. The Second Sex. New York. Originally published in French in 1949.

Douglas, Mary. 1966. Purity and Danger. New York.

Durkheim, Emile. 1964. The Division of Labor in Society, trans. George Simpson. New York. Originally published in French in 1911.

Ellman, Mary. 1968. Thinking About Women. New York.

Engels, Friedrich. 1891. The Origin of the Family, Private Property and the State, 4th ed. Moscow.

Felstiner, Mary. 1973. Personal communication.

Fernea, Elizabeth. 1965. Guests of the Sheik: An Ethnography of an Iraqi Village. Garden City, N.Y.

Fortune, Rio. 1932. Sorcerers of Dobu. London.

Harper, E. B. 1969. "Fear and the Status of Women," *Southwestern Journal of Anthropology* 25: 81–91.

Hogbin, Ian. 1970. The Island of Menstruating Men. Scranton, PA.

Kaberry, Phyllis. 1939. Aboriginal Women, Sacred and Profane. London.

Keenan, Elinor. 1974. "Norm-Makers, Norm-Breakers: Uses of Speech by Men and Women in a Malagasy Community," in R. Bauman and J. Sherzer, eds., Explorations in the Ethnography of Speaking. Cambridge, Eng. (In press.)

Krige, E. Jenson, and J. D. Krige. 1943. The Realm of a Rain Queen. London.

Landes, Ruth. 1971. The Ojibwa Woman. New York.

Lebeuf, Annie. 1963. "The Role of Women in the Political Organization of African Societies," in Denise Paulme, ed., Women of Tropical Africa. Berkeley, Calif. Originally published in French in 1960.

Lee, Richard B. 1968. "What Hunters Do for a Living, or How to Make Out on Scarce Resources," in Richard B. Lee and Irven DeVore, eds., Man the Hunter, pp. 30–48. Chicago.

Lévi-Strauss, Claude. 1949. Les structures élémentaires de la parenté. Paris.

Lewin, Ellen, J. Collier, M. Rosaldo, and J. Fjellman. 1971. "Power Strategies and Sex Roles." Paper presented at the 70th Annual Meeting of the American Anthropological Association. New York.

Lewis, I. M. 1971. Ecstatic Religion. London.

Liebow, Elliot. 1967. Tally's Corner. Boston.

Linton, Sally. 1973. "Woman the Gatherer: Male Bias in Anthropology," in Sue-Ellen Jacobs, Women in Perspective: A Guide for Cross-Cultural Studies. Urbana, IL.

Little, Kenneth. 1951. The Mende of Sierra Leone—A West African People in Transition. London.

Lloyd, P. C. 1965. "The Yoruba of Nigeria," in James L. Gibbs, ed., Peoples of Africa, pp. 547–582. New York.

Mead, Margaret. 1935. Sex and Temperament in Three Primitive Societies. London.

———— 1949. Male and Female. New York.

———— 1971. The Mountain Arapesh. New York. Originally published in 1938.

Meggit, M. J. 1964. "Male-Female Relationships in the Highlands of Australian New Guinea," American Anthropologist, 66 (4, part II): 204–224.

———— 1965. "The Mae Enga of the Western Highlands," in Lawrence P. and M. J. Meggit, eds., Gods, Ghosts and Men in Melanesia. Oxford.

Murdock, George P. 1934. Our Primitive Contemporaries. New York.

Murphy, Robert. 1959. "Social Structure and Sex Antagonism," Southwestern Journal of Anthropology, 15.

———— 1964. "Social Distance and the Weil," American Anthropologist, 66: 1257–1274.

Nadel, S. F. 1952. "Witchcraft in Four Societies: An Essay in Comparison," American Anthropologist, 54.

Parsons, Talcott. 1964. Social Structure and Personality. New York.

Parsons, Talcott, and Edward Shils, eds. 1951. Toward a General Theory of Social Action. Cambridge, MA.

Paulme, Denise. 1963. "Introduction," in Denise Paulme, ed., Women of Tropical Africa. Berkeley, Calif. Originally published in French in 1960.

Schneider, David. 1968. American Kinship: A Cultural Account. Englewood Cliffs, NJ.

Shapiro, Judith. 1970. "Yamomamo Women: How the Other Half Lives." Paper presented at the 69th Annual Meeting of the American Anthropological Association, San Diego.

Simmel, Georg. 1955. Conflict and the Web of Group Affiliations, trans. Kurt Wolff and Reinhard Bendix. New York. Originally published in German in 1922–1923.

Smith, Michael G. 1960. Government in Zazau. London.

Tiger, Lionel. 1969. Men in Groups. New York.

Turnbull, Colin. 1961. The Forest People. New York.

Weber, Max. 1947. The Theory of Social and Economic Organization, trans. and ed. Talcott Parsons. New York.

Wolf, Margery. 1972. Women and the Family in Rural Taiwan. Stanford, Calif.

Zborowski, Mary, and Elizabeth Herzog. 1955. Life Is with People. New York.

Zelditch, Morris. 1955. "Role Differentiation in the Nuclear Family," in Parsons and R. Bales, eds., Family, Socialization and Interaction Process, pp. 307–352. New York.

———— 1964. "Cross-Cultural Analysis of Family Structure," in H. T. Christensen, ed., Handbook of Marriage and the Family, pp. 462–500. Chicago.

KEY TERMS

ethnocentric   The tendency to interpret and evaluate other cultures by the standards or values of one's own.

Victorian   A nineteenth-century era noted for sexual repression and a sharp split between the public (male) and domestic (female) spheres of life. The term derives from the rule of England's Queen Victoria (ruled 1837–1901).

DISCUSSION QUESTIONS

1. Rosaldo makes a sharp distinction between the domestic/female and the public/male spheres of life. To what extent do you think this distinction is relevant to everyday life in your own society? Do you see any ways in which this distinction has blurred or lessened in importance since Rosaldo wrote in 1974?
2. How does Rosaldo think we might alleviate the subordination of women? Do you think her recommendations are useful? To what extent do you think they are feasible?
3. How does Rosaldo view the United States in terms of gender equality? In general, does she rank it as better or worse than other societies? Why? Do you agree with her assessment?

BECOMING MEMBERS OF SOCIETY

LEARNING THE SOCIAL MEANINGS OF GENDER

HOLLY DEVOR

This piece synthesizes a great deal of research on mainstream gender relationships in North America. Devor focuses her discussion on how children learn gender identity, and on how fundamental gender identity is to the child's development of a sense of self. Borrowing from sociologist George Herbert Mead, she distinguishes between the personal self, or "I" and the social self, or "me," showing how societal expectations of gender become integrated with one's personal and social self.

Another concept Devor uses is "cognitive schema," which refers to socially shared cognitive frameworks for organizing knowledge and experience. Throughout the world, gender figures prominently in the cognitive schema that children learn in order to interpret the world around them. Devor then outlines the dominant gender schema of North American society, characterizing it as "biologically deterministic." This is a very interesting observation. Essentially Devor is saying that biology does not really determine or shape gender, but rather it is a North American cultural perception that it largely does so. She lays out the American gender schema as one in which "social factors" can influence gender roles, but only to a limited extent; Americans see gender roles as largely set by basic biological sexual difference.

Devor goes on to characterize this cultural schema of gender as "patriarchal," by which she means it grants dominance and privilege to males. Again we see in this work the use of biology in an American cultural framework through which gender is constructed. Devor writes that mainstream North American ideology gives a higher evaluation to male attributes and characteristics (egoistic dominance, competitiveness) than to female ones (passivity, dependence, cooperativeness) and sees male aggression and dominance as a natural outgrowth of innate male predispositions. Women in this cultural view are "naturally" maternally oriented, which leaves them dependent on men for support and protection.

Next she reviews an important body of literature on gender in relation to body postures and speech patterns in American society, showing how male patterns of posture and speech exude dominance and aggression whereas those of females express passivity and submission. Learning these body postures and speech patterns is again a part of our socialization to gender identity.

The Gendered Self

The task of learning to be properly gendered members of society only begins with the establishment of gender identity. Gender identities act as cognitive filtering devices guiding people to attend to and learn gender role behaviors appropriate to their statuses. Learning to behave in accordance with one's gender identity is a lifelong process. As we move through our lives, society demands different gender performances from us and rewards, tolerates, or punishes us differently for conformity to, or digression from, social norms. As children, and later adults, learn the rules of membership in society, they come to see themselves in terms they have learned from the people around them.

Children begin to settle into a gender identity between the age of eighteen months and two years.[1] By the age of two, children usually understand that they are members of a gender grouping and can correctly identify other members of their gender.[2] By age three they have a fairly firm and consistent concept of gender. Generally, it is not until children are five to seven years old that they become convinced that they are permanent members of their gender groupings.[3]

Researchers test the establishment, depth, and tenacity of gender identity through the use of language and the concepts mediated by language. The language systems used in populations studied by most researchers in this field conceptualize gender as binary and permanent. All persons are either male or female. All males are first boys and then men; all females are first girls and then women. People are believed to be unable to change genders without sex change surgery, and those who do change sex are considered to be both disturbed and exceedingly rare.

This is by no means the only way that gender is conceived in all cultures. Many aboriginal cultures have more than two gender categories and accept the idea that, under certain circumstances, gender may be changed without changes being made to

Source: Holly Devor, "Becoming Members of Society: Learning the Social Meanings of Gender." Pp. 43–62 in *Gender Blending: Confronting the Limits of Duality*, ed. Holly Devor. Bloomington: Indiana University Press, 1989. Reprinted with the permission of Indiana University Press.

biological sex characteristics. Many North and South American native peoples had a legitimate social category for persons who wished to live according to the gender role of another sex. Such people were sometimes revered, sometimes ignored, and occasionally scorned. Each culture had its own word to describe such persons, most commonly translated into English as "berdache." Similar institutions and linguistic concepts have also been recorded in early Siberian, Madagascan, and Polynesian societies, as well as in medieval Europe.[4]

Very young children learn their culture's social definitions of gender and gender identity at the same time that they learn what gender behaviors are appropriate for them. But they only gradually come to understand the meaning of gender in the same way as the adults of their society do. Very young children may learn the words which describe their gender and be able to apply them to themselves appropriately, but their comprehension of their meaning is often different from that used by adults. Five year olds, for example, may be able to accurately recognize their own gender and the genders of the people around them, but they will often make such ascriptions on the basis of role information, such as hair style, rather than physical attributes, such as genitals, even when physical cues are clearly known to them. One result of this level of understanding of gender is that children in this age group often believe that people may change their gender with a change in clothing, hair style, or activity.[5]

The characteristics most salient to young minds are the more culturally specific qualities which grow out of gender role prescriptions. In one study, young school age children, who were given dolls and asked to identify their gender, overwhelmingly identified the gender of the dolls on the basis of attributes such as hair length or clothing style, in spite of the fact that the dolls were anatomically correct. Only 17

percent of the children identified the dolls on the basis of their primary or secondary sex characteristics.[6] Children, five to seven years old, understand gender as a function of role rather than as a function of anatomy. Their understanding is that gender (role) is supposed to be stable but that it is possible to alter it at will. This demonstrates that although the standard social definition of gender is based on genitalia, this is not the way that young children first learn to distinguish gender. The process of learning to think about gender in an adult fashion is one prerequisite to becoming a full member of society. Thus, as children grow older, they learn to think of themselves and others in terms more like those used by adults.

Children's developing concepts of themselves as individuals are necessarily bound up in their need to understand the expectations of the society of which they are a part. As they develop concepts of themselves as individuals, they do so while observing themselves as reflected in the eyes of others. Children start to understand themselves as individuals separate from others during the years that they first acquire gender identities and gender roles. As they do so, they begin to understand that others see them and respond to them as particular people. In this way they develop concepts of themselves as individuals, as an "I" (a proactive subject) simultaneously with self-images of themselves as individuals, as a "me" (a member of society, a subjective object). Children learn that they are both as they see themselves and as others see them.[7]

To some extent, children initially acquire the values of the society around them almost indiscriminately. To the degree that children absorb the generalized standards of society into their personal concept of what is correct behavior, they can be said to hold within themselves the attitude of the "generalized other."[8] This "generalized other" functions as a sort of monitoring or measuring device with which individuals may judge their own actions against those of their generalized conceptions of how members of society are expected to act. In this way members of society have available to them a guide, or an internalized observer, to turn the more private "I" into the object of public scrutiny, the "me." In this way, people can monitor their own behavioral impulses and censor actions which might earn them social disapproval or scorn. The tension created by the constant interplay of the personal "I" and the social "me" is the creature known as the "self."

But not all others are of equal significance in our lives, and therefore not all others are of equal impact on the development of the self. Any person is available to become part of one's "generalized other," but certain individuals, by virtue of the sheer volume of time spent in interaction with someone, or by virtue of the nature of particular interactions, become more significant in the shaping of people's values. These "significant others" become prominent in the formation of one's self-image and one's ideals and goals. As such they carry disproportionate weight in one's personal "generalized other."[9] Thus, children's individualistic impulses are shaped into a socially acceptable form both by particular individuals and by a more generalized pressure to conformity exerted by innumerable faceless members of society. Gender identity is one of the most central portions of that developing sense of self.

Gender as a Cognitive Schema

The important molders of children's concepts of social standards reside within the immediate family group, but very early in life children become exposed to the standards of others in a larger social context. Often the various people in children's lives give them conflicting or confusing messages as to the nature of social standards. Children are only able to make sense of such

variety according to their cognitive abilities and within the context of the experiences they have already had and the lessons they have already learned.

Certain ways of understanding social exchanges become more firmly established through repeated experience with them. These cognitive frameworks become more useful to children as they learn that they are the ways that many other people around them share. Different societies, or social groupings within societies, teach children and adults their own ways of recognizing and organizing knowledge. When members of societies share common ways of understanding the people, objects, and events of their lives, they use similar conceptual structures to organize their experience into cognitive bits which make sense to them, and which may be effectively communicated to others. Any conceptual structure that organizes social experience so that this sort of understanding and shared meaning can exist is called a cognitive schema.

Cognitive schemata are therefore basic to social organization and communication. They make it possible for persons to come to common understandings of shared experiences. Without socially accepted cognitive schemata, individuals who experienced the same events could place such diverse interpretations on their simultaneous experiences that it would be difficult to believe that they had all been at the same place at the same time.[10]

Most societies use sex and gender as a major cognitive schema for understanding the world around them.[11] People, objects, and abstract ideas are commonly classified as inherently female or male. The attributes, qualities, or objects actually associated with each class vary widely from society to society, but most do use gender as a most basic groundwork. Gender, then, becomes a nearly universally accepted early cognitive tool used by most children to help them understand the world. This means that children learn that gender is a legitimate way to classify the contents of the world and that others will readily understand them if they communicate through such a framework. Children also learn from those around them what to allocate to the categories of male and female, what elements of all things are considered to fall under the influence of the feminine principle, and which are classified as within the masculine sphere.

In North American society, the gender schema most widely in use is biologically deterministic. While there is some widespread belief and understanding that social factors have an influence on questions of gender, the dominant view remains that biological demands set the limits on the possible effects of social factors. In the script of the dominant gender schema, and in the parlance of the everyday world, the relationship between the main concepts is roughly as follows:[12] It is presumed that there are normally two, and only sexes, that all persons are either one sex or the other, and that no person may change sexes without extensive surgical intervention. Sex is believed to so strongly determine gender that these two classifications are commonly conflated to the extent that the terms are used interchangeably, and many people fail to see any conceptual difference between the two. Thus it is also believed that there are two, and only two, genders, and that individuals can effectively change genders only by also changing their sex. Gender roles are that part of the sex/gender bundle that may culturally vary within the constraints of biological imperatives. Gender roles, usually seen to be somewhat determined by social factors, are therefore thought to be less precisely tied to sex and gender than sex and gender are to each other.

Thus, sex is seen as wholly determining gender and largely determining gender role. The practices of gender roles are thought to be biologically constrained by the demands of one's biological sex/gender and socially defined by one's particular rearing within their gender.

The specifics of the definitions of appropriate gender roles for members of each sex/gender class in North American societies vary mainly by age, race, regionality, socioeconomic class, ethnicity, and by membership in sexually defined minority groups. Nonetheless, each sub-group generally subscribes to the main premises of the dominant gender schema and forms its particular definitions of appropriate gender roles from within those limitations.

In strongly sex-typed societies, or individuals, a gender schema tends to be a predominant mode of thought. In any given situation, there are always a number of cognitive frameworks one might use to understand the dynamics of that situation. Other major frameworks which might be used to understand situations involving human beings might revolve around race, social class, age, or physical size, but sex-typed individuals, and societies, tend to regard gender as one of the most significant factors in understanding themselves and the situations they find themselves in.

During the period in children's lives when they are first learning their gender identity and gender role, they also learn the definitions and usages of a gender schema. Children learn that they are girls or boys and that everyone else is either a girl or a boy. They learn that girls and boys are different by virtue of the different ways that they act and look, and that certain objects and ideas are associated with maleness and femaleness. As children assimilate the concepts and classifications of the gender schema of their social group, they learn to define themselves and those around them by its terms of reference. A process begins in young minds whereby it becomes not only legitimate but also expedient to sift all experience through the mesh of a gender schema.[13]

Children who are raised within a society which revolves around a gender schema learn to embrace those aspects of the schema which apply to the gender group that they have been assigned to. Because an element of our gender schema is that there are two distinct, non-overlapping gender groups, children also learn to reject those elements of their schema which do not apply to themselves. But it is important that members of society do not so thoroughly reject the gender lessons of the other gender that they become unable to recognize its members and respond appropriately to their cues. As gender schemata are highly complex and can be used to understand almost any experience, children are engaged in this process with increasing sophistication as their cognitive abilities improve with age.

The Male Standard

In North America, the dominant gender schema is patriarchal, and its assumptions underlie psychological, social, economic, and political definitions of gender. Psychological examinations of personality, for instance, routinely start by dividing subjects into classifications of male and female. The results obtained from such research thus have built into them the parameters of gender. In ways such as this, the division of persons by gender is both legitimized and reinforced. The same kind of emphasis carries through into social, political, and economic research as well as into research involving animals. Gender is thus forced to become a relevant variable in almost every situation studied.

Research has been undertaken to investigate what people do when they are denied information which readily allows them to use their gender schema as an organizer of information. In one study, adults were exposed to infants whose sex was not disclosed to them. It was found that when adults assumed a sex for a child in the study they most often assumed the child to be male.[14]

The attribution of a gender, and the more frequent assumption of maleness, suggest schematic information processing according to a patriarchal gender schema which claims that (1) all persons must be either male or female, and that (2) maleness is primary and generally inclusive of lesser categories.

Adults themselves are so thoroughly imbued with the dominant gender schema that it is virtually impossible to gather any group of them who would be so totally devoid of gender cues as to make suitable confederates for similar studies. Kessler and McKenna, in the mid 1970s, however, did devise a study using line drawings of adults exhibiting mixtures of common gender cues in order to examine how adults recognize and ascribe gender in other adults. By combining nine sex or gender cues (long hair, short hair, wide hips, narrow hips, breasts, flat chest, body hair, penis, and vulva) with two non-gender cues ("unisex" pants and shirt), they were able to produce ninety-six different combinations of characteristics which they overlaid on simple drawings having the same arms, hands, legs, feet, shoulders, waistlines, and faces. The ninety-six different drawings were each shown to equal numbers of male and female adults who were asked to identify the figure they were shown as male or female, to rate the confidence that they had in their appraisal, and to suggest how the figure might be changed to render it a member of the other sex or gender. The results of this study strongly suggested that people see maleness almost whenever there is *any* indication of it. A single strong visual indicator of maleness tended to take precedence in the attribution process over almost any number of indications of femaleness.[15]

Common wisdom and, to a large degree, medical opinion tell us that gender is determined on the basis of genitalia. Thirty-two of the figures used in the Kessler and McKenna study had their genitalia covered by a non–gender specific pair of pants while displaying various combinations of the other possible characteristics. Male and female cues were evenly distributed among the thirty-two drawings of figures wearing pants, but more than two-thirds (69 percent) of the 320 people who viewed these figures saw them as male. Surprisingly, a majority of the figures (57 percent) wearing pants and showing bare breasts were among those seen as male.[16] Thus, more than half of the people who viewed the figures displaying bare breasts were able to ignore, or rationalize away, a major female secondary sex characteristic and somehow still label the figure in the drawing as male.

The tendency to see maleness was even more pronounced among the remaining 640 persons who viewed drawings of figures with exposed genitals. Kessler and McKenna found that although in theory genitalia determine the sex of an individual, in fact, only male genitals serve this function. In this study, it was overwhelmingly the presence or absence of the male genital cue which determined the sex attributed to the drawings. (No figure had both male and female genitals portrayed.) The drawings which exhibited a penis were almost unanimously (96 percent) identified as male regardless of the presence of any number of female cues such as breast or wide hips.[17] The female genital cue did not have this same power.

The presence of a vulva in a drawing was, by contrast, sufficient to elicit a female identification in only a little less than two-thirds (64 percent) of the representations. In the remaining more than one-third (36 percent) of the drawings where a vulva was in evidence, the people who viewed the drawings were able to disregard that information in favor of male cues which were also present. There were only two combinations of cues that produced a rate of female identification equal to the rate of male identification achieved with the presence of the penis in combination with *any* other cues (male or female). These were the drawings which showed a figure with vulva and wide hips, wearing a "unisex" shirt and long hair; or a figure with vulva, no body hair, breasts, and long hair. In other words, for a figure to be seen virtually every single time as male required only the presence of a penis; for a figure to be identified as female equally as often required the presence of a vulva *plus* one of two specific combinations of three additional cues.[18] Thus, the power of the presence of a penis to elicit a male identification was a full 50 percent stronger than the ability of the presence of a vulva to cue a female identification.

This study demonstrates that even in situations of conflicting, confusing, or absent gender cues, people were willing, able, and likely to attribute gender. It also shows that when there is a doubt as to the gender of an individual, people have a pronounced tendency to see maleness. This study also suggests that maleness is readily seen whenever there are indicators of it, whereas femaleness is seen only when there are compelling female cues and an absence of male cues. This way of seeing corresponds closely to patriarchal gender schema notions of maleness as a positive force and femaleness as a negative force; of maleness as a presence and femaleness as an absence; of maleness as primary and femaleness as derivative. Thus, in North American society, the dominant gender schema rests on and supports patriarchy. It assumes that maleness and its attributes are the definitive standard against which all gender questions shall be judged. This means that femaleness, as well as all that becomes associated with it, is defined by the dominant patriarchal gender schema as inherently flawed and lacking.

Gender Role Behaviors and Attitudes

The clusters of social definitions used to identify persons by gender are collectively known as femininity and masculinity. Masculine characteristics are used to identify persons as males, while feminine ones are used as signifiers for femaleness. People use femininity or masculinity to claim and communicate their membership in their assigned, or chosen, sex or gender. Others recognize our sex or gender more on the basis of these characteristics than on the basis of sex characteristics, which are usually largely covered by clothing in daily life.

These two clusters of attributes are most commonly seen as mirror images of one another with masculinity usually characterized by dominance and aggression, and femininity by passivity and submission. A more even-handed description of the social qualities subsumed by femininity and masculinity might be to label masculinity as generally concerned with egoistic dominance and femininity as striving for cooperation or communion.[19] Characterizing femininity and masculinity in such a way does not portray the two clusters of characteristics as being in a hierarchical relationship to one another but rather as being two different approaches to the same question, that question being centrally concerned with the goals, means, and use of power. Such an alternative conception of gender roles captures the hierarchical and competitive masculine thirst for power, which can, but need not, lead to aggression, and the feminine quest for harmony and communal well-being, which can, but need not, result in passivity and dependence.

Many activities and modes of expression are recognized by most members of society as feminine. Any of these can be, and often are, displayed by persons of either gender. In some cases, cross-gender behaviors are ignored by observers, and therefore do not compromise the integrity of a person's gender display. In other cases, they are labeled as inappropriate gender role behaviors. Although these behaviors are closely linked to sexual status in the minds and experiences of most people, research shows that dominant persons of either gender tend to

use influence tactics and verbal styles usually associated with men and masculinity, while subordinate persons, of either gender, tend to use those considered to be the province of women.[20] Thus it seems likely that many aspects of masculinity and femininity are the result, rather than the cause, of status inequalities.

Popular conceptions of femininity and masculinity instead revolve around hierarchical appraisals of the "natural" roles of males and females. Members of both genders are believed to share many of the same human characteristics, although in different relative proportions; both males and females are popularly thought to be able to do many of the same things, but most activities are divided into suitable and unsuitable categories for each gender class. Persons who perform the activities considered appropriate for another gender will be expected to perform them poorly; if they succeed adequately, or even well, at their endeavors, they may be rewarded with ridicule or scorn for blurring the gender dividing line.

The patriarchal gender schema currently in use in mainstream North American society reserves highly valued attributes for males and actively supports the high evaluation of any characteristics which might inadvertently become associated with maleness. The ideology which the schema grows out of postulates that the cultural superiority of males is a natural outgrowth of the innate predisposition of males toward aggression and dominance, which is assumed to flow inevitably from evolutionary and biological sources. Female attributes are likewise postulated to find their source in innate predispositions acquired in the evolution of the species. Feminine characteristics are thought to be intrinsic to the female facility for childbirth and breastfeeding. Hence, it is popularly believed that the social position of females is biologically mandated to be intertwined with the care of children and a "natural" dependency on men for the maintenance of mother-child units. Thus the goals of femininity and, by implication, of all biological females are presumed to revolve around heterosexuality and maternity.[21]

Femininity, according to this traditional formulation, "would result in warm and continued relationships with men, a sense of maternity, interest in caring for children, and the capacity to work productively and continuously in female occupations."[22] This recipe translates into a vast number of proscriptions and prescriptions. Warm and continued relations with men and an interest in maternity require that females be heterosexually oriented. A heterosexual orientation requires women to dress, move, speak, and act in ways that men will find attractive. As patriarchy has reserved active expressions of power as a masculine attribute, femininity must be expressed through modes of dress, movement, speech, and action which communicate weakness, dependency, ineffectualness, availability for sexual or emotional service, and sensitivity to the needs of others.

Some, but not all, of these modes of interrelation also serve the demands of maternity and many female job ghettos. In many cases, though, femininity is not particularly useful in maternity or employment. Both mothers and workers often need to be strong, independent, and effectual in order to do their jobs well. Thus femininity, as a role, is best suited to satisfying a masculine vision of heterosexual attractiveness.

Body postures and demeanors which communicate subordinate status and vulnerability to trespass through a message of "no threat" make people appear to be feminine. They demonstrate subordination through a minimizing of spatial use: people appear feminine when they keep their arms closer to their bodies, their legs closer together, and their torsos and heads less vertical than do masculine-looking individuals. People also look feminine when they point

their toes inward and use their hands in small or childlike gestures. Other people also tend to stand closer to people they see as feminine, often invading their personal space, while people who make frequent appeasement gestures, such as smiling, also give the appearance of femininity. Perhaps as an outgrowth of a subordinate status and the need to avoid conflict with more socially powerful people, women tend to excel over men at the ability to correctly interpret, and effectively display, nonverbal communication cues.[23]

Speech characterized by inflections, intonations, and phrases that convey nonaggression and subordinate status also make a speaker appear more feminine. Subordinate speakers who use more polite expressions and ask more questions in conversation seem more feminine. Speech characterized by sounds of higher frequencies are often interpreted by listeners as feminine, childlike, and ineffectual.[24] Feminine styles of dress likewise display subordinate status through greater restriction of the free movement of the body, greater exposure of the bare skin, and an emphasis on sexual characteristics. The more gender distinct the dress, the more this is the case.

Masculinity, like femininity, can be demonstrated through a wide variety of cues. Pleck has argued that it is commonly expressed in North American society through the attainment of some level of proficiency at some, or all, of the following four main attitudes of masculinity. Persons who display success and high status in their social group, who exhibit "a manly air of toughness, confidence, and self-reliance" and "the aura of aggression, violence, and daring," and who conscientiously avoid anything associated with femininity are seen as exuding masculinity.[25] These requirements reflect the patriarchal ideology that masculinity results from an excess of testosterone, the assumption being that androgens supply a natural impetus toward aggression, which in turn impels males toward achievement and success. This vision of masculinity also reflects the ideological stance that ideal maleness (masculinity) must remain untainted by female (feminine) pollutants.

Masculinity, then, requires of its actors that they organize themselves and their society in a hierarchical manner so as to be able to explicitly quantify the achievement of success. The achievement of high status in one's social group requires competitive and aggressive behavior from those who wish to obtain it. Competition which is motivated by a goal of individual achievement, or egoistic dominance, also requires of its participants a degree of emotional insensitivity to feelings of hurt and loss in defeated others, and a measure of emotional insularity to protect oneself from becoming vulnerable to manipulation by others. Such values lead those who subscribe to them to view feminine persons as "born losers" and to strive to eliminate any similarities to feminine people from their own personalities. In patriarchally organized societies, masculine values become the ideological structure of the society as a whole. Masculinity thus becomes "innately" valuable and femininity serves a countrapuntal function to delineate and magnify the hierarchical dominance of masculinity.

Body postures, speech patterns, and styles of dress which demonstrate and support the assumption of dominance and authority convey an impression of masculinity. Typical masculine body postures tend to be expansive and aggressive. People who hold their arms and hands in positions away from their bodies, and who stand, sit, or lie with their legs apart—thus maximizing the amount of space that they physically occupy—appear most physically masculine. Persons who communicate an air of authority or a readiness for aggression by standing erect and moving forcefully also tend to appear more masculine. Movements that are abrupt and

stiff, communicating force and threat rather than flexibility and cooperation, make an actor look masculine. Masculinity can also be conveyed by stern or serious facial expressions that suggest minimal receptivity to the influence of others, a characteristic which is an important element in the attainment and maintenance of egoistic dominance.[26]

Speech and dress which likewise demonstrate or claim superior status are also seen as characteristically masculine behavior patterns. Masculine speech patterns display a tendency toward expansiveness similar to that found in masculine body postures. People who attempt to control the direction of conversations seem more masculine.[27] Those who tend to speak more loudly, use less polite and more assertive forms, and tend to interrupt the conversations of others more often also communicate masculinity to others. Styles of dress which emphasize the size of upper body musculature, allow freedom of movement, and encourage an illusion of physical power and a look of easy physicality all suggest masculinity. Such appearances of strength and readiness to action serve to create or enhance an aura of aggressiveness and intimidation central to an appearance of masculinity. Expansive postures and gestures combine with these qualities to insinuate that a position of secure dominance is a masculine one.

Gender role characteristics reflect the ideological contentions underlying the dominant gender schema in North American society. That schema leads us to believe that female and male behaviors are the result of socially directed hormonal instructions which specify that females will want to have children and will therefore find themselves relatively helpless and dependent on males for support and protection. The schema claims that males are innately aggressive and competitive and therefore will dominate over females. The social hegemony of this ideology ensures that we are all raised to practice gender roles which will confirm this vision of the nature of the sexes. Fortunately, our training to gender roles is neither complete nor uniform. As a result, it is possible to point to multitudinous exceptions to, and variations on, these themes. Biological evidence is equivocal about the source of gender roles,[28] psychological androgyny is a widely accepted concept.[29] It seems most likely that gender roles are the result of systematic power imbalances based on gender discrimination.[30]

Gendered Values

Feminine people experience, and therefore understand, the world from a very different status position than do masculine persons. Their differing access to power and privilege engender in them different value systems, priorities, and goals. Many theorists have suggested that the early childhood experiences of boys and girls begin the process of shaping them into their assigned gender roles by creating deep psychological needs in individuals which predispose them toward the social roles into which they will be encouraged to grow.

Nancy Chodorow hypothesized that the primary emotional bonds of all children are the ones they first had with their mothers. She suggested that the closeness of these first bonds acts as a largely unconscious model for people in the relationships they form in later life. She maintained that the desire to recreate mother-child bonds is a motive force behind attitudes of both masculinity and femininity. Chodorow argued that femininity revolves around the need to replicate the primary symbiotic bonds experienced by young girl children with their mothers. She also suggested that masculinity stems, in part, from the need to reproduce the one-on-one emotional closeness lost to young male children as they are forced to reject their bonds to their mothers

and cleave to social definitions of masculinity. Chodorow's argument essentially states that our emotional lives are driven by needs to feel symbiotically attached to other persons in the way that we all once felt, however briefly, with our mothers. But because of the different gender role training that males and females receive from the moment of birth onward, both the symbiotic stage and the separation-individuation processes are experienced differently by the two sexes. Therefore our attempts to recreate our infantile states, and our adult relational needs, reflect these differences.

The men that boys become strive, on one level, to duplicate the emotional closeness and security of their earlier mother-child bonds within the privacy of their emotionally intimate relationships. On another level, masculine people suffer from a need to assert their masculinity through independence from women, and freedom from dependency in any guise.[31] The role of masculinity, therefore, requires of those who wish to enjoy its privileges, that they regard vulnerability to other people as a dangerous weakness at the same time as they crave emotional intimacy. These conflicting needs make emotionally intimate relationships very problematic. It is difficult, if not impossible, for people to conduct satisfying intimate relationships when they are suspicious of emotional intimacy. The recreation of the closeness of a mother-child bond is therefore stymied by the successful practice of masculinity, because masculinity is, in essence, about separation and emotionally distant relationships.

Feminine persons, who tend to grow out of more secure and enduring attachments to their mothers, also wish to simulate the experience of union in their intimate relationships. Heterosexual women, however, are often frustrated in their attempts to find intimacy with the men in their lives, because of the conflicting masculine needs to receive unconditional love and to assert independence from the source of that love. Women therefore tend to turn to other women and, more commonly, to their own children for a reconstruction of the love they received as children. But the recreation of a mother-child bond through motherhood is not an entirely satisfactory solution. Those women who become mothers do not have the opportunity to feel themselves playing the desired role of child in the mother-child dyad. For this feeling, they must have the cooperation of another adult. Hence women's often frustrated desire for intimacy with men can be supplemented, but not fully replaced, by emotional intimacy with children.

Chodorow argues that in societies where women do virtually all early child care, and in which there exists a dichotomized, male-dominated, and hierarchical gender schema, femininity has two major components: maternal and heterosexual. The heterosexual component of femininity serves as a means for women to achieve both maternity and some satisfaction of their needs for emotional intimacy. Femininity, as characterized by Chodorow, is motivated by a need for union with others, a need which is socially channeled toward childbearing and heterosexuality.

The socially dominant needs of masculinity also require that femininity be defined heterosexually so that the masculine psychological goal of surrogate mothering for grown males may be accomplished.[32] Child rearing is an integral part of femininity which, although it may serve other important masculine goals of egoistic dominance,[33] is often only a tolerated impediment to the emotional goals of masculinity. Masculinity then might be characterized as a cluster of psychological needs which vibrate with the conflict between a largely unconscious need for emotional submersion and a continuously socially reinforced gender role need for independence.

Not all females equally accept the feminine role. Some females reject the heterosexual component of the female role without abandoning an interest in the recreation of the mother-child bond. Many women turn directly to other women, rather than to children, for an approximation of the sort of love that they recall from their childhoods. Many women desire, and do have, children without forming heterosexual bonds to men. Many women form loving bonds with other women and children in non-heterosexual family groups. Concerning these other ways of satisfying the need for intimacy and union, Adrienne Rich has asked:

> If women are the earliest sources of emotional caring and nurture for both female and male children, it would seem logical from a feminist perspective at least, to pose the following questions: whether the search for love and tenderness in both sexes does not originally lead toward women; *why in fact would women ever redirect that search*; why species survival, the means of impregnation and emotional/erotic relationships should ever become so rigidly identified with each other; and why such violent strictures should be found necessary to enforce women's total emotional, erotic loyalty and subservience to men. (Emphasis in the original)[34]

The answers to these questions might be found in an analysis which focuses on the masculine needs of motherly attention and egoistic independence within a morality which allows the assertion of masculine needs to dominate over a more cooperative balancing of masculine and feminine goals.

Catharine MacKinnon analyzed heterosexuality as a defining characteristic of femininity, and hence the social meaning of femaleness. She argued that social recognition of femaleness is defined entirely within sexual terms. More specifically, she proposed that to be seen as female one must be heterosexual, and that to claim femaleness and not be heterosexually within the power of males is to be in defiance of the social meaning of femaleness.[35] Femininity, from this perspective, can be seen as a structure designed for the purpose of satisfying the egoistic needs of males for dominance, and heterosexuality can be seen as a component of femininity which ensures that females are accessible to those who need and demand patriarchal power. It is through the institution of heterosexuality that females remain in intimate and continued contact with the people who require them to function in support of masculinity. The institution of heterosexuality ensures that females never stray far from a masculine reminder of patriarchal definitions of femininity.

Masculinity is less rigidly defined in terms of heterosexuality. Although masculinity requires access to the sexuality of women, it does not pivot around that sexuality in the same way as the feminine role does. Masculinity has other dimensions which can be sufficient to independently delineate one as male. Outwardly directed states are more important to masculinity than are emotional or home-centered interests. Economic achievement, bureaucratic power, physical strength, aggression, and emotional toughness are major indicators of masculinity;[36] heterosexuality is a minor indicator. Insufficient or nonexistent heterosexuality will cast a doubt on a person's masculinity,[37] but if other more outwardly directed qualities are strongly in evidence, the negative effect of a defective heterosexuality may be diminished or erased.

Thus, although adult femininity and masculinity share common elements, the function of those elements is quite different. Both masculinity and femininity are in part defined through their heterosexual and child-caring roles, but those roles carry very different values in their applications to the lives of men and women. The feminine role, to a great degree, derives from the need of the masculine role for support functions. Masculinity requires emotional nurturing from a quasi-maternal source; femininity is dedicated to satisfying that requirement. Masculinity further requires independence from that quasi-maternal source of emotional stability, and to this end the dominant patriarchal gender schema attributes greater masculinity to outwardly reaching, emotionally cool, achievement activities; and greater femininity to the child rearing which femininity offers as an alternative source of emotional intimacy to those who find themselves emotionally abandoned by their masculine partners.

These different motivations and statuses result in different moral standards for feminine and masculine persons, different styles of interaction based on differing standards of right and wrong, differing value systems, and differing assumptions about the motivations and goals of others. More masculine people, who tend to relate to the world on the basis of an assumption of the separation of individuals and place a high moral value on the results of separation, find intimacy threatening. More feminine people, who tend to value and strive for interactive styles and situations which are based in a desire for attachment and communion, place the highest value on caring for the needs and feelings of others. As a result of these differences, women tend to approach moral questions and problems within a context of conflicting responsibilities, while men tend to approach these same situations as questions of conflicting rights.[38]

Masculinity fosters an ethic wherein separate and independent individuals assert their rights within a set of laws which provide guidelines for resolving whose competing interests will take precedence when conflicts arise. It is understood as inevitable and fair, in such a system of justice, that there will exist a hierarchy of rights and individuals. Where separation is the theme, order is the method.

Femininity demands an approach to questions of morality from another perspective. Feminine morality is predicated on the desire for the greatest communal good for the greatest number of people. Feminine justice is based in an ethic of caring for others and directs conflicts to be resolved through a minimizing of power differences. Where attachment is the theme, empathy is the method.

An aggressive assertion of power sustains a masculine ethic of domination through rights, while a contextual and supportive balancing of power through empathy and nurturance underlies the feminine ethic of cooperation. In North American patriarchal society, aggressive masculine striving for egoistic dominance backed by a patriarchal social, political, and economic reality ensures the negative social valuation of femininity, the marginal status of femaleness, and the subordination of the ethic of cooperation.

Gender Role Strain

When people come together in social exchanges, they bring with them the sum of their experiences to that point, the cognitive schemata they used to make sense of those experiences, and the results of the application of the latter to the former. Each individual in social interaction acts, and perceives the actions of others, from the perspective of their own gender role values, training, and experience. All persons in society are constantly engaged in an ad hoc process of negotiation aimed at interpreting experience and developing shared meanings. Each of these interactions is built upon an exchange of social cues which individuals use to construct their understandings of the meanings of actions, words, and events. Such dyadic and small group negotiations of meaning take place within a larger shared contextual framework made up of the cognitive schemata and norms of a society. All interpretations of interactions

between members of a society are normally understood within that larger context at the same time as cognitive schemata are applied idiosyncratically and subjectively to everyday events.

Social actors simultaneously receiving information from others are also attempting to project information about themselves which both reflects their self-images and conforms to their understandings of the requirements of their social setting.[39] This process is open-ended, to some degree, as people are often willing to reformulate earlier conclusions as new information suggests a more "sensible" interpretation of prior events.[40] Nonetheless, all members of society are social actors attempting to manage the impressions that they make on others, so that they might be perceived in the most advantageous light possible.

Individuals are able to understand social experiences only within the restrictions imposed on them by their own frames of reference, or from within the boundaries of their own cognitive schemata.[41] To simplify and organize experience so as to make it more manageable, people call upon a loosely organized commonsense "stock of knowledge at hand,"[42] which they presume that "anyone like us necessarily knows."[43] Such a stock of knowledge constitutes a set of cognitive schemata that offer them guidelines around which they may structure their perceptions. Together, people involved in face-to-face interactions strive to develop a shared understanding of the meaning of their experiences through an ongoing interactive process, which is actually a subtle bargaining process about whose version of reality will become accepted as the working definition in an interaction.[44]

When two individuals meet they must establish certain facts about themselves as a basis for the smooth progress of their interaction. As all individuals in society are presumed to belong to gender groups which are governed by certain etiquettes and proprieties, adult members of society generally consider that a social failure has occurred if a person's gender is not displayed obviously, immediately, and consistently.

A subtle but powerful process of interaction revolves around the cueing and countercueing of gender display. Members of society signal to one another, through their simple everyday talk and actions, the complex message which is an unmistakable gender.[45] Social actors exchange this information through both direct and indirect means of communication. Persons put forward presentations which they would like to have accepted by their audiences as the "true" state of affairs. Observers respond in ways which indicate either acceptance or the need for further negotiations to establish a mutually acceptable definition of their situation. In the case of gender attributions, these cues and responses are largely nonverbal, but vast in number. And because, as Goffman maintained, "any scene . . . can be defined as an occasion for the depiction of gender difference, and in any scene a resource can be found for effecting this display,"[46] there may be no plausible excuse for adults to fail to properly display their gender.

Children, on the other hand, who are young enough to be conceivably still learning the proper application of their society's gender schema, are usually benignly tolerated if they fail to display gender behaviors appropriate to their assigned genders. But this tolerance is not evenly distributed between the two gender classes. Masculinity would seem to be more highly valued in children than is femininity. Boys are strongly encouraged toward masculinity, while masculine behavior in female children is tolerated as quite harmless, perhaps even salubrious. Feminine behavior in male children, on the other hand, is only poorly tolerated and often seen as a cause for alarm,[47] while femininity is valued but not required in prepubescent girls.

Girl children who exhibit masculine behaviors are colloquially known as "tomboys," boy children who display femininity are called "sissies." Both parents and peers show strong disapproval of femininity in boys, the label "sissy" carrying with it significant social stigma. On the other hand, "tomboy" is used in a tongue-in-cheek pejorative way when applied to prepubescent girls. There almost seems to be a guarded respect for girls who enjoy some of the privileges and skills which are usually reserved for the socially dominant gender. Masculine girls call forth an amused, bittersweet admiration for their striving to socially "better" themselves. By contrast, feminine boys evoke, in most people, a disdain for their seeming disregard for the superior opportunities and privileges available to them. Masculinity in children then, as in adults,[48] is more highly valued than femininity, regardless of the gender of the children exhibiting it.

Children learn the greater value of masculine behaviors and the lesser value of feminine ones by observing the actions of the adults around them. Although children do receive a great deal of social training as to the "correct" ways for boys and girls to act, they also receive the message of the dominant gender schema that maleness is the standard against which all things associated with gender are measured. Thus, children learn that to be masculine is better than to be feminine: to be male and masculine is to be best; to be female and masculine is to be second best; to be female and feminine is to be a "good girl," but second class; and to be male and feminine is to be a traitor. Masculine males take full advantage of their superior social options, and so gain the greatest social approval and rewards. Masculine females can improve their social status by acquiring some of the characteristic behavior patterns of men, thereby cueing others to grant them some of the respect and privileges usually reserved for men. Feminine females behave in accordance with their prescribed social roles. They therefore earn social approval for their conformity, but the role they perform affords them fewer rights and privileges than masculinity does. Feminine males forfeit many of the special advantages usually associated with maleness, because they not only fail to cue for them, but also compromise the appearance of innate, biologically based, male rights to socially dominant roles. They therefore elicit disrespect and distrust from most members of society, because they not only turn their backs on their own opportunities for social power, but they also threaten the credibility of other men's claims of "natural" superiority. Thus, it is not cross-gender role behavior that is censured so much as it is gender behavior which lowers an individual's or a gender class's social value.

Cognitive developmental theorists have suggested that people desire to learn and conform to what is appropriate for their gender grouping. This process of identification and modeling is complicated by the diversity in gender schema definitions. There may exist severe, or subtle, disjunctions between the gender schemata projected by various "significant others," or between "significant others" and a person's "generalized other." As the actual prescriptions and proscriptions of gender schemata are constantly in flux and undergoing challenge from competing social and cultural ideological sources, individual representatives of society subscribe to different individual versions of a gender schema which in itself contains confusions and contradictions. The media, peers, schools, workplaces, and families may deliver sharply competing messages about desirable gender role behaviors. When social agents transmit their gender schemata, they are rarely clear and uncontradictory.

Further complications arise despite the best intentions and abilities of people to subscribe to a gender schema as they understand it. People also carry within themselves certain individual dispositions and talents. It is not uncommon that gender role requirements as outlined in a gender schema conflict with the personalities, talents, and dispositions of growing and changing people. Such conflicts can result in gender role strain, wherein individuals find it difficult to negotiate their assigned gender role as they understand it.[49] In such situations the disjuncture between a person's "I" and "me" can become uncomfortably large, and a sense of oneself as a coherent "self" might become endangered. Such conflict might result in an internalized power struggle between one's "I" and one's "generalized other." In other words, when people do not see themselves as they believe others see them, and as they themselves believe they ought to be, personality disintegration is possible.

Persons experiencing such conflict have several avenues open to them. They might adjust their behavior, so that others can see them more as they see themselves. They might choose to alter their definitions of themselves so that they see themselves as others see them. Or they may shift their locus of social standards to reside with a different social group whose criteria coincide more exactly with their personal self-images. This last option can allow people suffering from an I/me conflict to align the way that other people see them with the way that they see themselves by changing their "significant others" to persons whose values match their own.

The first option has certain inherent limitations. When persons perceive that their private definitions of themselves vary significantly from their public image, they may attempt to display their private selves more openly in an attempt to bring others to see them as they "really" are. But one must be cautious not to display attributes which might bring social censure; therefore individuals who perceive themselves to be experiencing a conflict between their public and private selves may be able to use this option only in limited ways if their private self-image is not in conformity with social norms.

Another way to negotiate a more perfect conjunction of "I" and "me" is to adjust one's personal self-image to match more closely the way one is seen by others. This approach has the advantage of running the least risk of offending public sensibilities. It is safer in that social expectations are being met rather than questioned, but it carries with it the greatest challenge to the self because it necessitates alteration of the "I," the most deeply rooted and intensely personal part of the self.

The method for partially relieving gender role strain which least threatens the self, and most effectively avoids conflict and social disapproval, revolves around the constituency of the "generalized other." People may choose to allow the standards of certain individuals or ideologies to take prominence within their cognitive schemata. A gender schema need not be one's preeminent cognitive schema, nor must it be constructed according to the demands of the dominant ideologies of society. Individuals or groups of individuals may choose either to give other cognitive schemata dominance within their own cognitive frameworks, or to minimize their use of gender schemata whenever possible in their own lives and social interactions. Gender role strain might therefore be relieved by a willful effort to shift one's cognitive schema priorities.

Such a shift could be reinforced and bolstered by a similar effort to shift one's "significant others" and "generalized others" to include persons of similar persuasions. Gender role strain may then be lessened to the degree that individuals are able to restrict their social contacts to persons of similar minds. Such a strategy would be limited in its effectiveness to the same degree that any social deviation might be. Major social

deviations are rarely tolerated easily, and individual or group deviation from gender schema prescriptions can be perceived as extremely threatening to a social order which is, to a large degree, predicated on the use of gender as a major cognitive schema. Those who threaten the social order can be, and often are, severely punished for their transgressions.

Each option must be understood within a larger social context. Gender schemata exist in society as widely accepted ways of making sense out of everyday experience; everyone may not agree on exactly how a schema is to be defined but, in general, gender schemata are universally used cognitive techniques and, as such, are a most basic part of social sense. If individuals were to contradict, in behavior, speech, attitude, or in any other way, the basic tenets of the gender schema of their society, they would be challenging a widely accepted social definition of sense. One result of such a situation might be that such individuals would simply be misunderstood. If such misunderstanding were viewed benignly, there might be no further implications. Were this behavior aschematic enough, it might be considered dangerous, criminal, or even insane. The ramifications in such situations could be severe.

Persons who find themselves unable to conform satisfactorily to their assigned gender role may become socially stigmatized for such failure. Normally, in North American society, when people join together in social situations, they expect from one another a certain level of social collusion so that all participants in an interaction will be able to share a common meaning and understand the intentions and actions of one another. The most generally applicable way to establish a common language of communication is to agree to collectively subscribe to elements of the dominant social language. This dominant social language is composed not only of words but also of a shared understanding of the meanings of nonverbal communications and by a set of values and attitudes.[50] Persons who do not, willingly or unwillingly, share in these common creations of meaning become people who carry with them a stigma. Persons who carry a stigma come to be seen by others as "not quite human," and they can thus become partially or fully disqualified from social acceptance.[51]

People who are aware that they have a disjuncture in their gendered selves between their "I," their "me," and their "generalized other" must manage themselves in such a way so as to minimize any possible stigma which might result from others becoming aware of their situation. Such people may attempt to disguise or compensate for the offending parts of their gender behavior which they feel unable or unwilling to modify. Individuals who take such an approach carry with them at all times the awareness that they are secretly in transgression of social laws. At any time they may become exposed not only as persons with stigma but also as persons engaged in deceit.

Inappropriate gender role behaviors are treated differently depending on the ways in which they are inappropriate. Minor transgressions of prescribed gender roles normally elicit social ridicule or chastisement. More major transgression can earn one the status of mentally ill. Sufficient variation from the norm can cause one to forfeit the gender attribution which they would normally expect on the basis of their sex and gender identity. Most extremely, chronic transgressions of gender role norms can lead to insecurity in, or even loss of, one's gender/sex identity. Hence, the power of gender role norms lies in the threat of possible loss of basic identity as a result of insufficient conformity to their demands. This power is possible only because of the strength of the dominant gender schema to define the core person in terms of these behaviors.

Thus, stigmatized persons, who believe themselves to be stigmatized for reasons beyond their control, have few options open to them. They may allow their nonconforming "I's" to be fully visible to public scrutiny and become subject to the full force of social affront at social nonconformity. They may attempt to hide whatever offending behavior that they are able to and run the risk of exposure and the subsequent further discredit associated with falsehood, as well as suffer the anxiety of leading a life mired in duplicity. Or they may allow their stigma to become public while safeguarding themselves by limiting their social contact to persons who will be sympathetic to their situation. In any case, full social acceptance and peace of mind are not easily available to persons who do not conform to the requirements of the "generalized others" among whom they live.

NOTES

1. Much research has been devoted to determining when gender identity becomes solidified in the sense that a child knows itself to be unequivocally either male or female. John Money and his colleagues have proposed eighteen months of age because it is difficult or impossible to change a child's gender identity once it has been established around the age of eighteen months. Money and Ehrhardt, p. 243.
2. Mary Driver Leinbach and Beverly I. Fagot, "Acquisition of Gender Labels: A Test for Toddlers," *Sex Roles* 15 (1986), pp. 655–666.
3. Maccoby, pp. 225–229; Kohlberg and Ullian, p. 211.
4. See Susan Baker, "Biological Influences on Human Sex and Gender," in *Women: Sex and Sexuality*, ed. Catherine R. Stimpson and Ethel S. Person (Chicago: University of Chicago Press, 1980), p. 186; Evelyn Blackwood, "Sexuality and Gender in Certain Native

American Tribes: The Case of Cross-Gender Females," *Signs* 10 (1984), pp. 27–42; Vern L. Bullough, "Transvestites in the Middle Ages," *American Journal of Sociology* 79 (1974, 1381–1389; J. Cl. DuBois, "Transsexualisme et Anthropologie Culturelle," *Gynecologie Practique* 6 (1969), pp. 431–440; Donald C. Forgey, "The Institution of Berdache among the North American Plains Indians," *Journal of Sex Research* 11 (Feb. 1975), pp. 1–15; Walter L. Williams, *The Spirit and the Flesh: Sexual Diversity in American Indian Culture* (Boston: Beacon, 1986).

5. Maccoby, p. 255.
6. Ibid., p. 227.
7. George Herbert Mead, "Self," in *The Social Psychology of George Herbert Mead*, ed. Anselm Strauss (Chicago: Phoenix Books, 1962, 1934), pp. 212–260.
8. G. H. Mead.
9. Hans Gerth and C. Wright Mills, *Character and Social Structure: The Psychology of Social Institutions* (New York: Harcourt, Brace and World, 1953), p. 96.
10. Consider, for example, the different interpretations of symptoms of physical illness given by Western medical practitioners and shamanistic peoples: invasion by bacteria or viruses, versus invasion by evil spirits.
11. Weisner.
12. See Introduction for definitions of the terms "sex," "gender," "gender role."
13. Bern, "Gender Schema Theory: A Cognitive Account" and "Gender Schematic Theory and Its Implications."
14. Seavey, Katz, and Zalk.
15. Kessler and McKenna, pp. 145–146.
16. Ibid., pp. 149–150.
17. Ibid., p. 151.
18. Ibid., pp. 151–153.
19. Egoistic dominance is a striving for superior rewards for oneself or a competitive striving to reduce the rewards for one's competitors even if such action will not increase one's own rewards. Persons who are motivated by desires for egoistic dominance not only wish the best for themselves but also wish to diminish the advantages of others whom they may perceive as competing with them. See Maccoby, p. 217.
20. Judith Howard, Philip Blumstein, and Pepper Schwartz, "Sex, Power, and Influence Tactics in Intimate Relationships," *Journal of Personality and Social Psychology* 51 (1986), pp. 102–109; Peter Kollock, Philip Blumstein, and Pepper Schwartz, "Sex and Power in Interaction: Conversational Privileges and Duties," *American Sociological Review* 50 (1985), pp. 34–46.
21. Chodorow, p. 134.
22. Jon K. Meyer and John E. Hoopes, "The Gender Dysphoria Syndromes: A Position Statement on So-Called 'Transsexualism'," *Plastic and Reconstructive Surgery* 54 (Oct. 1974), pp. 444–451.
23. Erving Goffman, *Gender Advertisements*; (New York: Harper Colophon Books, 1976) Judith A. Hall, *Non-Verbal Sex Differences: Communication Accuracy and Expressive Style* (Baltimore: Johns Hopkins University Press, 1984); Nancy M. Henley, *Body Politics: Power, Sex and Non-Verbal Communication* (Englewood Cliffs, New Jersey: Prentice Hall, 1979); Marianne Wex, *"Let's Take Back Our Space": "Female" and "Male" Body Language as a Result of Patriarchal Structures* (Berlin: Frauenliteraturverlag Hermine Fees, 1979).
24. Karen L. Adams, "Sexism and the English Language: The Linguistic Implications of Being a Woman," in *Women: A Feminist Perspective*, 3rd edition, ed. Jo Freeman (Palo Alto, Calif.: Mayfield, 1984), pp. 478–491; Hall, pp. 37, 130–137.
25. Pleck, p. 139.
26. Goffman, *Gender Advertisements*; Hall; Henley; Wex.
27. Adams; Hall, pp. 37, 130–137.
28. See Chapter 1.
29. See Chapter 2.
30. Howard, Blumstein, and Schwartz; Kollock, Blumstein, and Schwartz.
31. Chodorow.

32. Ibid., p. 139.
33. Ibid., p. 207.
34. Adrienne Rich, "Compulsory Heterosexuality and Lesbian Existence," *Signs* 5 (1980), pp. 631–660, esp. p. 637.
35. Catharine A. MacKinnon, "Feminism, Marxism, Method, and the State: Toward Feminist Jurisprudence," *Signs* 8 (1983), pp. 635–678; and "Feminism, Marxism, Method, and the State: An Agenda for Theory," *Signs* 7 (1982), pp. 515–544.
36. Pleck, p. 140.
37. Ibid., p. 4.
38. Gilligan.
39. Erving Goffman, *The Presentation of the Self in Everyday Life* (New York: Doubleday, 1959), p. 35.
40. Aaron Cicourel, *Cognitive Sociology: Language and Meaning in Social Interaction* (New York: The Free Press, 1974), pp. 52–58.
41. Erving Goffman, *Frame Analysis: An Essay on the Organization of Experience* (Cambridge, Mass: Harvard University Press, 1974), pp. 22, 39.
42. Kenneth Leiter, *A Primer of Ethnomethodology* (New York: Oxford University Press, 1980), p. 5.
43. Harold Garfinkel, *Studies in Ethnomethodology* (Englewood Cliffs, New Jersey: Prentice Hall, 1967), p. 54.
44. Goffman, *Presentation*, p. 9.
45. Garfinkel, p. 181; Goffman, *Gender Advertisements*, p. 8.
46. Goffman, *Gender Advertisements*, p. 9.
47. Saul Feinman, "Approval of Cross-Sex-Role Behavior," *Psychological Reports* 35 (1974), pp. 643–648; Norma Costrich et al., "When Stereotypes Hurt: Three Studies of Penalties of Sex-Role Reversals," *Journal of Experimental Social Psychology* 11 (1975), pp. 520–530.
48. Jones, Chernovetz, and Hansson, pp. 310–311.
49. Pleck, p. 9.
50. Goffman, *Presentation*.
51. Erving Goffman, *Stigma: Note on the Management of Spoiled Identity* (Englewood Cliffs, New Jersey: Prentice Hall, 1963), p. 5.

References

Adams, Karen L. "Sexism and the English Language: The Linguistic Implications of Being a Woman." *Women: A Feminist Perspective.* 3rd ed. Edited by Jo Freeman. Palo Alto, Calif.: Mayfield, 1984.

Baker, Susan W. "Biological Influences on Human Sex and Gender." *Women: Sex and Sexuality.* Edited by Catherine R. Stimpson and Ethel S. Person. Chicago: University of Chicago Press, 1980.

Bern, Sandra L. "Gender Schema Theory: A Cognitive Account of Sex Typing." *Psychological Review* 88 (1981), 354–364.

———. "Gender Schematic Theory and Its Implications for Child Development: Raising Gender-aschematic Children in a Gender-schematic Society." *Signs* 8 (1983), 598–616.

Blackwood, Evelyn. "Sexuality and Gender in Certain Native American Tribes: The Case of Cross-Gender Females." *Signs* 10 (1984), 27–42.

Bullough, Vern. "Transvestites in the Middle Ages." *American Journal of Sociology* 79 (1974), 1381–1389.

Chodorow, Nancy. *The Reproduction of Mothering: Psychoanalysis and the Reproduction of Mothering.* Berkeley: University of California Press, 1978.

Cicourel, Aaron. *Cognitive Sociology: Language and Meaning in Social Interaction.* New York: The Free Press, 1974.

Costrich, Norma, Joan Feinstein, Louise Kidder, Jeanne Marecek, and Linda Pascale. "When Stereotypes Hurt: Three Studies of Penalties of Sex-Role Reversals." *Journal of Experimental Social Psychology* 11 (1975), 520–530.

Dubois, J. Cl. "Transsexualisme et Anthropologie Culturelle." *Gynecologie Practique* 6 (1969), 431–440.

Feinman, Saul. "Approval of Cross Sex-Role Behavior." *Psychological Reports* 35 (1974), 643–648.

Forgey, Donald. "The Institution of Berdache among the North American Plains Indians." *Journal of Sex Research* 11 (Feb. 1975), 1–15.

Garfinkel, Harold. *Studies in Ethnomethodology*. Englewood Cliffs, New Jersey: Prentice Hall, 1967.

Gerth, Hans, and C. Wright Mills. *Character and Social Structure: The Psychology of Social Institutions*. New York: Harcourt, Brace and World, 1953.

Gilligan, Carol. *In a Different Voice: Psychological Theory and Women's Development*. Cambridge, Mass.: Harvard University Press, 1982.

Goffman, Erving. *The Presentation of Self in Everyday Life*. New York: Doubleday, 1959.

———. *Stigma: Note on the Management of Spoiled Identity*. Englewood Cliffs, New Jersey: Prentice Hall, 1963.

———. *Frame Analysis: An Essay on the Organization of Experience*. Cambridge, Mass.: Harvard University Press, 1974.

———. *Gender Advertisements*. New York: Harper Colophon Books, 1976.

Hall, Judith A. *Non-Verbal Sex Differences: Communication Accuracy and Expressive Style*. Baltimore: Johns Hopkins University Press, 1984.

Henley, Nancy M. *Body Politics: Power, Sex and Non-Verbal Communication*. Englewood Cliffs, New Jersey: Prentice Hall, 1979.

Howard, Judith, Philip Blumstein, and Pepper Schwartz. "Sex, Power, and Influence Tactics in Intimate Relationships." *Journal of Personality and Social Psychology* 51 (1986), 102–109.

Jones, Warren, Mary E. O'C. Chernovetz, and Robert O. Hansson. "The Enigma of Androgyny: Differential Implications for Males and Females?" *Journal of Consulting and Clinical Psychology* 46 (1978), 298–313.

Kessler, Suzanne, Wendy McKenna. *Gender: An Ethnomethodological Approach*. New York: John Wiley and Sons, 1978.

Kollock, Peter, Philip Blumstein, Pepper Schwartz. "Sex and Power in Interaction: Conversational Privileges and Duties." *American Sociological Review* 50 (1985), 34–46.

Leinbach, Mary Driver, and Beverly I. Fagot. "Acquisition of Gender Labels: A Test for Toddlers." *Sex Roles* 15 (1986), 655–666.

Leiter, Kenneth. *A Primer of Ethnomethodology*. New York: Oxford University Press, 1980.

Maccoby, Eleanor. *Social Development: Psychological Growth and the Parent-Child Relationship*. New York: Harcourt, Brace, Jovanovich, 1980.

MacKinnon, Catharine A. "Feminism, Marxism, Method, and the State: Toward Feminist Jurisprudence." *Signs* 8 (1983), 635–678.

———. "Feminism, Marxism, Method and the State: An Agenda for Theory." *Signs* 7 (1982), 515–544.

Mead, George Herbert. "Self." *The Social Psychology of George Herbert Mead*. Edited by Anselm Strauss. Chicago: University of Chicago Press, 1962 (1934).

Meyer, Jon K., and John E. Hoopes. "The Gender Dysphoria Syndromes: A Position Statement on So-Called 'Transsexualism'." *Plastic and Reconstructive Surgery* 54 (Oct. 1974), 444–451.

Money, John, and Anke A. Ehrhardt. *Man and Woman, Boy and Girl: The Differentiation and Dimorphism of Gender Identity from Conception to Maturity*. Baltimore: Johns Hopkins University Press, 1972.

Pleck, Joseph H. *The Myth of Masculinity*. Cambridge, Mass.: M. I. T. Press, 1981.

Rich, Adrienne. "Compulsory Heterosexuality and Lesbian Existence." *Signs* 5 (1980), 631–660.

Seavey, Carol, Phyllis Katz, and Sue R. Zalk. "Baby X: The Effects of Gender Labels on Adult Responses to Infants." *Sex Roles* 2 (1975), 103–109.

Weisner, Thomas S. "Some Cross-Cultural Perspectives on Becoming Female." *Becoming Female: Perspectives on Development*. Edited by Claire B. Kopp and Martha Kirkpatrick. New York: Plenum Press, 1979.

Wex, Marianne. *"Let's Take Back Our Space": "Female" and "Male" Body Language as a Result of Patriarchal Structures.* Berlin: Frauenliteraturverlag Hermine Fees, 1979.

Williams, Walter L. *The Spirit and the Flesh: Sexual Diversity in American Indian Culture.* Boston: Beacon, 1986.

KEY TERMS

cognitive schema   Plural: schemata. The conceptual structures that organize social experience into shared meanings.

patriarchal   Having to do with a social system characterized by male dominance.

deconstruct   To analyze by exposing the constituent cultural assumptions.

symbiotic   Characterized by mutual beneficial relationship.

salubrious   Healthful.

DISCUSSION QUESTIONS

1. Both Rosaldo and Devor write about biology in relation to gender. What are the similarities and contrasts in the way that biology figures into their views of gender?

2. What does Devor mean by her claim that in American culture, sex is believed to be the primary determiner of gender? In making this claim, what exactly does she mean by the terms "sex" and "gender"? And what does she mean by "gender role"?

3. Holly Devor writes about mainstream, or dominant, American culture, noting that there are variations by class, ethnic group, etc., in terms of gender constructions. Among what groups in the United States do you see variation from her model? How is this variation expressed?

CHAPTER 2

Cultural History, 1600–1900

Constructions of gender in American society (and the current debates on gender issues) grow out of this country's past, its cultural history. And despite important social and economic changes affecting the lives of women and men in recent years, that past is in many ways still with us, still shaping our perceptions of what it means to be a man or a woman. The readings in this chapter give us glimpses into the lives of women and men over a broad sweep of three centuries, from 1600–1900, from Puritan times to the dawn of the twentieth century. Most of these articles emphasize the nineteenth century, with a focus on the white middle class. These readings thus show gender constructions which, though dominant in American society, were often less significant or absent among other classes and ethnic groups (see Chapters 4–6).

The first article takes us to Puritan New England in the late 1600s and early 1700s. Puritans believed that men and women were spiritually equal, but there was no question that, socially speaking, women were subordinate to men. The authority of husbands over wives was sanctioned by religion and reinforced by a broader community authority. As with so many aspects of Puritan life, sexual activity was subject to strict regulation and public scrutiny. From a modern point of view Puritans may have had "strict" standards, but in fact, as this first article shows, they were remarkably open about sex. Sexual intercourse was considered perfectly natural and ideally pleasurable for both women and men. The problem was not sex, but sex outside marriage.

It is this subject—adultery—that Laurel Thatcher Ulrich takes up in her article "The Serpent Beguiled Me." Using court records of adultery cases, Ulrich reveals the words of the accused, the witnesses, the neighbors, and friends. She takes us into a world where women seem sexually naive yet themselves complicit in sexual transgressions, where a woman's chastity is significant not as an attribute of her person but as her husband's property. And in Ulrich's work we see how closely Puritan gender and sexuality are governed by a hierarchical social structure and close-knit community life.

By the 1800s, life for the American middle classes had changed dramatically. The population had expanded and commercial centers developed. Later, after the Civil War, industrialization transformed the economy and brought a sharp split between the workplace and the home. The next two articles by Carroll Smith-Rosenberg and Nancy F. Cott focus on middle-class women of this nineteenth century, Victorian period. In contrast to the home-based production of previous centuries where husbands and wives cooperatively ran a farming enterprise, in the nineteenth century, middle-class men went off to work while a woman's place was in the home. In this era there developed what came to be know as the "Cult of True Womanhood," which defined the ideal woman as pious, submissive, virtuous, nurturing, and caring for others (Welter 1966). As a wife, the True Woman was oriented toward domesticity, creating a "haven in a heartless world" for her husband who struggled in the outside competitive male world of work and politics. Thus developed the split between male/public and female/domestic spheres, discussed in Michelle Rosaldo's article in this book's introductory chapter. Though no longer widely considered a cross-cultural universal, as Rosaldo initially supposed, this separating of male and female spheres was and in some ways continues to be a fundamental feature of gender constructions in the United States, as we will see in later chapters of the book.

Earlier Americans had seen women as physically and mentally weaker than men, but it was not until the nineteenth century that women and men came to be seen as utterly different, with these differences rooted in their contrasting reproductive biologies. That of men was relatively simple and required little energy, leaving men unencumbered to chart their individual course in the public world outside the home. Women, by contrast, were ruled by their complicated reproductive organs, forever endangered by extra-domestic activities and interests. Smith-Rosenberg's article treats this aspect of Victorian womanhood, showing how medical theory of the time saw female puberty and menopause, and through these events, women themselves.

Yet, as we see in Cott's article, late-eighteenth- and early-nineteenth-century middle-class New England women were not entirely confined to the home, however much that may have been an ideal backed by medical prescriptions. There was indeed one arena of life—Protestant religion—in which many women were not only active outside the home but assertive, confident, and striving to come to terms with their spiritual selves. By the early nineteenth century women's relatively greater participation in Protestant Christian activities and institutions was so conspicuous that historians now refer to this period as the "feminization of Protestantism." Women not only excelled over men in church attendance but also in their participation in prayer groups, missionary activity, church-related charitable work, and conversion to evangelical religious movements. In many ways women's religious activism made them resemble men in the public world of work and politics, but with one important exception: In their public roles men of the period were often competitive, whereas women active in Protestant activities or movements formed close, affective bonds with other women.

The final article in this chapter looks at men of the nineteenth century, emphasizing themes that continue into the mid-twentieth century. Here Michael S. Kimmel delineates an American "cult of masculinity" that centers on the image of the Cowboy. The Cowboy is a strong, lone figure, emotionally detached, and often aggressive as his physical strength and manhood are constantly challenged in the wilderness he seeks to tame.

Focusing on nineteenth- and twentieth-century political leaders, Kimmel shows how American political life both reflected and helped produce the "cult of masculinity." An interesting point in Kimmel's work is that American masculinity is something that must continually be proven, and is therefore perpetually insecure. In his later book, *Manhood in America* (1996), Kimmel discusses more fully how American manhood became tied to individual socio-economic success—a perpetually insecure proposition in the competitive capitalist economy that emerged in nineteenth-century America.

In this brief historical review of pre-twentieth-century gender constructions in middle-class America, we note a number of themes. One is the way that ideas about who we are as men and women are often reflected in ideas about and treatments of the body. In this chapter, that connection is clearest in Smith-Rosenberg's article on medical interpretations of female puberty and menopause. A second theme is the close connections between gender and religion, seen here in the discussion of Puritan gender and in women's later roles in Protestant activism. Interestingly, Puritan Christianity seems to reinforce patriarchy and privilege male religious roles whereas later Protestantism opens new avenues for women. A third theme is American individualism, a cultural value that figures into Kimmel's views of American masculinity. With the notable exception of women's participation in Protestant activism, expressions of individualism were considered unwomanly among the American middle classes before the 1900s. All of these themes—gender in relation to the body, religion, and individualism—continue for the middle classes into the twentieth century, as covered in the book's next chapter.

REFERENCES

Kimmel, Michael S. 1996. *Manhood in America: A Cultural History.* New York: The Free Press.
Welter, Barbara. 1966. "The Cult of True Womanhood, 1820–1860." *American Quarterly* 18: 151–174.

The Serpent Beguiled Me

Laurel Thatcher Ulrich

How "puritanical" were the Puritans? What were men and women's sexual behaviors and attitudes toward sex in the seventeenth and eighteenth centuries really like? Laurel Thatcher Ulrich's article throws light on these questions through analysis of official adultery accusations and court records of Puritan New England. Her study opens with what to modern eyes is a bizarre case of adultery between Mary Rolfe and Henry Greenland in New England in 1693. The roles of the many participants, their remarks and actions make little sense to us until Ulrich places them in the context of Puritan culture and, especially, gender constructions. Ulrich interprets this and other cases of adultery in terms of Puritan social structure, religious traditions, and ambivalence toward sexuality. She elucidates the Puritan concept of female chastity as male property, the important role of older women as guardians of female sexual morality, and the fine line between expectations of female hospitality and sexual accessibility. In the end, Puritans, according to Ulrich, saw women much as they saw the biblical Eve, not really sinful but rather easily beguiled, weak and vulnerable by nature.

It might have been a Restoration comedy.[1] In the spring of 1663 John Rolfe, a Newbury fisherman, went off to Nantucket, leaving behind a comely and "merily disposed" young wife named Mary. Being "a verie loving husband," Rolfe arranged for Mary to "live Cherfully as he thought and want for nothing" in his absence. Betty Webster, a single woman in the neighborhood, agreed to stay with Mary. Betty's stepfather, Goodman John Emery, promised to be a father to both. But Rolfe's careful arrangements proved a snare. No sooner had he sailed out of Newbury harbor than two strangers from old England sailed in. Henry Greenland and John Cordin, physicians and gentlemen, came to lodge at the Emery house.

Mary confided to Betty Webster that "Mr Cording was as pretty a Carriadg man as Ever shee saw in hir life." But Greenland proved more interesting still. He was uninhibited by the pious manners of the Newbury folk. At supper, before Goodman Emery could half finish prayer, "Mr Grenland put on his hatt and spread his napkin and stored the sampe and said Com Landlord light supper short grace." Mary was both enticed and troubled by his attentions. When he pulled her toward him by her apron strings, she resisted at first, only giving way, as she said, "to save my apron." One minute she rebuked him for acting "an uncivell part." The next she was laughing and eating samp with him out of one dish and with one spoon.

Late one night Betty was in bed with Mary, who was nursing her baby, when Henry Greenland knocked on the window. Frightened, the women made no answer. "Bettye, Bettye," Greenland called. "Will you let me stand here and starve with the cold?" Betty answered that they were already in bed, that they would not let him in, that

---

they were afraid of him. When he continued to plead, protesting that he "would doe them noe hirt, but desired to smoke a pipe of tobacco," Betty let him in. Still in bed, Mary told her to rake up the fire to give Mr. Greenland some light. While the maid bent over the hearth, Greenland pulled off his clothes and climbed into bed with Mary, who fainted.

"Sir," cried Betty, "what have you done? You have put the woman into a fitt."

"The Devell has such fitts," said Greenland, scrambling out of bed. "It is nothing but a mad fitt."

"What offence have I given that you should speke such words?" Mary exclaimed. Seeing that his conquest was conscious, Greenland jumped back into bed. "Lord help me," she cried.

At that moment Henry Lessenby, a neighbor's servant, just happened to walk by. He had earlier observed Greenland's attentions to Goody Rolfe. Hearing the cry, he ran to the Rolfe door and knocked loudly. "Lye still," whispered Greenland, "for now there are two witnesses, we shall be tried for our lives." But Lessenby was not to be discouraged by silence. He climbed through the window, stumbled into the room in the dark, and felt his way to the bedside. In the dim light from the fireplace he discerned a gentleman's clothes on a box by the bed. Reaching for the pillow, he felt a beard. Just as he suspected, it was Greenland.

Lessenby might have raised a commotion, but he chose instead to act the part of the stage servant who, loving a secret, is drawn through vanity or cupidity into the intrigues of his betters. As he later reported it, "The woman and I went adore [outdoors] to Consider what was best to be done so we thought becas he was a stranger and a great man it was not best to make an up Rore but to let him go way in a private maner."

Here the plot calls for deeper entanglements, for pacts between the gentleman and the maid, half-kept promises whispered

on the doorstep in the dark, and finally the return of the cuckolded husband. But this little drama was not enacted on the London stage but in a Massachusetts village. In this case the young wife was rescued by an old wife, the husband was avenged, and the denouement was played in the county court. Goody Rolfe had a pious mother and an observant sister. At meeting on Sunday, Sarah Bishop saw that Mary had been crying and alerted their mother.

Goody Bishop visited the Rolfe house the next morning. As she approached, she met a boy rushing out with a glass—to get liquor for Dr. Greenland, he said. For two hours she sat in the house, watching and observing and waiting for Greenland to leave. Finally she had a chance to question Mary, who seemed to fear telling her mother all that had happened. Mary admitted that the gentleman had "with many Arguments inticed her to the act of uncleanness," but she insisted that "God had hitherto helped her resist him."

"Will you venture to lay under these temptations & concealed wickedness?" exclaimed the mother. "You may Provoak God to Leave you & then you will come under Great Blame."

"I know not what to doe," Mary sighed. "Hee is in Creditt in the Towne, some take him to be godly & say hee hath grace in his face, he have an honest loke, he have such a carrige that he deceive many: It is saide the Governer sent him a letter Counting it a mercy such an Instrument was in the Country, and what shall such a pore young woman as I doe in such a case, my husband being not at home?"

Goody Bishop was troubled. "These things are not to bee kept private," she insisted. "Goodman Emery beeing grand Jury-man must present them." But when confronted, Goodman Emery proved unwilling to act the part of moral guardian. (Had he seen too much "merriness" on Mary's part?) He promised to keep closer watch on Greenland, to lock up the hard drink, and to see that the Doctor stayed home when half drunk, but he felt matters were best kept quiet for the moment. He could see no harm done.

Goody Bishop was not to be soothed by promises. On her way home she encountered *Goody* Emery and explained to her all that had happened. The wife proved more sympathetic than the husband. Together the two women returned to the Rolfe house, pressed Mary and Betty further, and concluded that Greenland's actions had been "more gross" than they had first believed.

"I dare not keep such things as these private upon my owne head," said Mary's mother as the two women parted.

"Doe wisely," answered her friend.

That night, having asked for God's direction, Goody Bishop revealed all that she knew to a "wise man" in the town, asking for his advice. He directed her to the magistrates. Henry Greenland was tried by jury at his own request, perhaps counting on his good reputation in the town, but was convicted of attempted adultery and fined the whopping sum of £30. The citizens of Newbury supported the pious mother against the dazzling stranger. John Rolfe returned from Nantucket avenged.

To understand this village morality play, we must determine the historical meaning of the characters. That they do not represent the classical stage triangle—husband, wife, and lover—is in itself significant. What can we make of a plot which casts a mother as moral guardian, a dashing Englishman as assailant, and a pretty young bride as victim?

One obvious interpretation would make Puritanism the real protagonist.[2] Surely Goody Bishop represents the community surveillance characteristic of the rule of the saints. As Mary Rolfe's mother, she upheld a morality thundered from the pulpit and enforced by the court. As for Henry Greenland, the libertine Englishman, he was a Thomas Morton (or Tom Jones) caught in a society he did not understand, incriminated as much by his attitude as by his acts. How many of his reported boasts—that it didn't matter that he had a wife in England, that Mary need not worry about consequences, that he could afford two wives— were in jest? He insisted that he meant no harm, but in Newbury his carefree words condemned him. In this view, Mary Rolfe hardly matters. The real conflict was between two cultures—Puritan Massachusetts and Merry England.

Yet a close examination of the case suggests that the most serious division was not between the town and the stranger but within the community itself—and perhaps in the mind of Mary Rolfe. Dragged into court by outraged neighbors, John Emery angrily reported that before the fateful night someone had put "fig dust" (tobacco shavings) and pebbles in Greenland's bed. Had Mary Rolfe surreptitiously invited the pretty gentleman to rap on her window and ask for a light? Had Betty Webster or someone else in Emery's family been playing tricks on them both?[3]

Since the 1930s, discussion of sexual behavior in New England has focused on the relationship between religion and repression. Despite the efforts of Edmund S. Morgan to dispel the stereotype of the "sad and sour" saints, historians continue to ask, "How 'Puritan' were the Puritans?"[4] Michael Zuckerman insists they were hostile to the flesh.[5] Philip Greven says that some of them were.[6] For our purposes, the question is badly put. To understand the historical drama in Newbury, one must give less attention to ideology than to gender, taking the characters pretty much at their surface value. Goody Bishop was an old woman. Mary Rolfe was a young woman. Henry Greenland was an aggressive male. The really crucial issues are exposed in the action itself, with all its confusion and apparent inconsistency. Mary Rolfe was obviously attracted to Greenland. She was also afraid of him. She openly flirted with him. At the same time, she was troubled by her own feelings and by the potential consequences of her behavior.

Her dilemma was created by the coexistence in one rural village of a hierarchal social order (by no means limited to New England), a conservative religious tradition (not exclusively Puritan), and sex-linked patterns of sociability (rooted in English folkways). All three elements determined her behavior. Accustomed to deference—to her mother, to her husband, to the selectman next door—she was easily dazzled by the genteel appearance and apparent good name of Greenland. What right had she to question his behavior? Though taught to fear God, she had not yet acquired the kind of confidence in her own sense of right which propelled her mother to challenge both a popular gentleman and a respected neighbor by bringing the case to court. Finally, in her easy compliance with Greenland's initial advances, Mary Rolfe was responding to a lifetime of instruction in femininity. Massachusetts girls, like ordinary Englishwomen everywhere, knew how to light pipes for strangers.

Keith Thomas has argued that the double standard in sexual relations is but one manifestation of a hierarchal system which included not just the subordination of one class to another but the subordination of female to male. Thus, from medieval times "the absolute property of the women's chastity was vested not in the woman herself, but in her parents or her husband."[7] In these terms, Henry Greenland's pursuit of Mary Rolfe was not just an attempted seduction, it was a trespass upon the "property rights of John Rolfe, who in fact successfully sued Greenland for damages soon after his return from sea. (There was no question, of course, of *Mistress* Greenland suing anyone, even though she too arrived in New England not long after the case came to court.[8])

Throughout the Christian world the property concept of chastity was challenged by a religious concept which upheld the value of marital purity and premarital fidelity for both sexes. Potentially at least, this opened the way for a more egalitarian legal system, though in Massachusetts reliance on the Mosaic law created some strange contradictions. Following Leviticus 20, the Laws and Liberties of 1648 established the death penalty for adultery, yet defined the crime according to the marital status of the woman, effectively reinforcing the old notion of a man's property rights in his wife.[9] A married man who engaged in sexual relations with an unmarried partner risked only a fine or a whipping for fornication. A married woman who did the same risked death. The inequity could work the other way, of course. A single man who engaged in sexual relations with a married partner risked death; a single woman who did the same risked only a fine or a whipping—and pregnancy!

In practice, adultery was such a heinous crime in the Bay Colony that convictions were rare.[10] Married folk of either sex were usually punished more or less equally for the lesser crimes of "attempted adultery," "uncleanness," or "lascivious carriage." In prosecuting fornicators, Massachusetts courts moved even closer to a single standard. A woman's accusation, especially if witnessed by the midwives at the time of delivery, was sufficient to convict a man, all his protests notwithstanding.[11]

The legal record is quite clear—in sexual matters, as in most other areas of life, New England women were subject to men, though entitled to protection. The more difficult question is determining how all of this translated into gender roles, which of course were enacted not in court but in the intimate arena of ordinary life.

Sharing rooms, beds, benches, trenchers, and even spoons, ordinary New Englanders had little opportunity to develop the elaborate sense of personal space so essential to "polite" interaction. Chairs were rare. Bedrooms hardly existed. Although in some families the parents' bedstead was curtained for warmth or privacy, it almost always occupied "public" space.[12] In many dwellings, as in Mary Rolfe's, the front door opened on a bed.

Sexual experience had not yet acquired the ceremonial sanctity of a separate setting. Even if the notion had suggested itself, there was little possibility of segregating sex in the larger sense from the daily round of life. Procreation was everywhere, in the barnyard as well as in the house. Since sleeping quarters were crowded and darkness provided the only privacy, many children must have gained their first awareness of copulation from half-muffled sounds and shapes in the night. For a wife there might be advantages to all this crowding. When Abigail Willey of Oyster River wanted to prevent her husband from "coming to her," she planted her two youngest children in the middle of the bed, rather than pushing them to one side as usual. The night John Bickford slept with her mother, seven-year-old Judith Willey told a New Hampshire court, the bed "crakled" so she could not sleep.[13] Goody Willey's extramarital affair was deviant, but the context in which it occurred was not.

There were proprieties, of course. A respectable woman did not undress before her male servants, nor did she lie under the covers with a man not her husband, but she might sleep in the same room with either.[14] She did not sing and drink with strangers in the tavern, though out of common hospitality she would certainly smoke at her own hearth or doorstep with any of her husband's friends.[15] She did not sit on her neighbor's lap or kiss him in the barn, but with good conscience she could share his horse.[16] Lynn folks were shocked when Goody Leonard stood laughing at the millpond where a group of servants were skinny-dipping, forcing the "more modest"

of the men to put on their shirts in the water, letting them drop "by degrees" as they came out.[17] But relatives at Ipswich as well as friends at the Isles of Shoals were just as surprised at the jealousy of William Row, who became angry if any man "saluted" his wife with a kiss, a custom which was apparently as acceptable in New England as in old.[18] Even the sermon literature stressed the affability of the good wife, a quality expressed in the very word "consort." From childhood, daughters were taught to please, to smile and fetch and carry, to stand on the table and sing.[19] If for some women affability translated into accessibility, the distance was shorter than we might think.

Such evidence is easily misinterpreted, however. Twentieth-century readers, enjoying the "earthiness" of seventeenth-century court records, may mistake verbal openness for an easy and matter-of-fact attitude to the flesh. The opposite was often nearer the truth. In premodern societies sexual tensions are close to the surface and frequently vented in bawdy stories or in epithets hurled across a fence in anger. To impugn a person's sexual integrity was a particularly potent form of slander in early New England, suggesting that the values enshrined in formal law were widely acknowledged but tenuously held.

How else can one explain the "presentation" in York County Court of Goody Mendum of Kittery, whose crime consisted of calling Mistress Alice Shapleigh "a pedlers Trull"? In a less close-knit society a wild accusation flung at the wife of a town official would hardly deserve the dignity of attention. In seventeenth-century Kittery it called for a forced retraction, not only in court but in church.[20] Because this was a society which still depended primarily upon external rather than internal controls, many New Englanders responded not so much to guilt as to shame. The opinion of one's neighbor was everything. As Goody Bishop expressed it, a body might as well take an axe and knock one of her cows on the head as to take away her daughter's good name.[21]

Whore. Jade. Bawd. Strumpet. Trull. Such words came quickly to the tongues of village gossips. They meant everything and nothing. Certainly there were loose women in most country towns, women like the widow Sarah Stickney of Newbury, who had more than one illegitimate child and little reputation to lose. When Samuel Lowell rode by in a cart, she called, "A you roge, yonder is yor Child under the tree, goe take it up and see it," an action that did not prevent her from successfully suing for child support from John Atkinson, a married father of nine. When Goody Atkinson railed at Sarah and called her "an impudent baud," she spat in her face.[22] In their wider application, however, the epithets turned not on specific behavior but on an underlying ambiguity surrounding sexuality. This is partly explained in religious terms. For Calvinists, the old proverb "There but for the Grace of God go I" had a literal meaning.[23] Because the potential for evil was innate, lust might break out anywhere. But for many New Englanders, religion was but a thin overlay on a traditional fatalism, an inability to see oneself as in any sense a shaper of events. Such an attitude affected both sexes, of course, but in the traditional world fatalism and femininity were powerfully linked.[24]

The serpent beguiled me, and I did eat. New England ministers did not berate women for the sin of Eve. In fact, in referring to the transgression in Eden they almost always spoke of the "sin of Adam," perhaps unconsciously assuming male pre-eminence even in evil but at least sometimes intentionally countering the ancient misogyny.[25] Eve's sin was in one sense hardly a sin at all. Her transgression was an inevitable consequence of her nature—weak, unstable, susceptible to suggestion. She was "beguiled."[26]

There was no question of one sex being more or less sinful than another. Outside of family and community government, males were carnal, sensual, and devilish. Puritan writers were amazed at the sexual restraint of Indian men, who never raped their captives. They could only attribute this amazing preservation of New England women to divine intervention.[27] No, both sexes were culpable. But they were different. Men required restraint, especially when drunk. Women needed protection, not because they were innocent but because they were not. They were physically and sexually vulnerable, easily aroused, quick to succumb to flattery. Widows were considered especially susceptible to temptation. Their humble—and frequent—confessions in court and church reinforced folk wisdom: "He who wooeth a widow must go stiff before."[28]

As might be expected, the vocabulary describing the sexual misbehavior of women was richer and more direct than that for men. Even the epithets *cuckold* and *pimp* turn on female rather than on male promiscuity. The opposite of *whore* was *rogue*, a term which mixed sexual and more general meanings.[29] For a woman, sexual reputation was everything; for a man, it was part of a larger pattern of responsibility. A *whore* bestowed her favors indiscriminately, denying any man exclusive right to her body. A *rogue* tricked or forced a woman into submission with no regard for consequences. The words mirror traditional gender relationships. A woman gave; a man took. Because the female role was in its nature more ambiguous, less clearly active without quite being passive, a woman could lose her reputation simply in being attacked. "Whore! baud!" Patrick Morrin shouted at Mary Water when she ran from the house after an attempted assault.[30]

So Mary Rolfe smiled when Henry Greenland pulled on her apron strings. She ate out of his dish and laughed at his jokes, and perhaps enjoyed the game of conquest and resistance. When the plot grew more serious, she found herself confused. To call for help would be an admission of complicity. Who would believe her story against a man in credit in the town, especially when everyone knew she was young, pretty, and "often merrily disposed"? Her only recourse was to petition the court and confess herself "a poor young woman and in an aflicted Condition." The same vulnerability which led to her trouble might save her from it.

If the role of Mary Rolfe was clear, so was that of Goody Bishop. She had earned her position through experience. In New England, ultimate authority to police sexual behavior was given to men—to justices, juries, ministers, and elders. In reality, primary responsibility for controlling female sexuality was in the hands of women. The formal role of midwives in fornication cases grew out of a larger and more pervasive system of informal justice. just as Goody Bishop instinctively turned to Goody Emery in determining her course in response to Henry Greenland, so older women throughout New England acted as advisers, counselors, and ultimately as judges, though sometimes their visible role was intentionally muted.

In September of 1664 Elizabeth Perkins, Sr., and Agnes Ewens of Topsfield sent word to the Essex County Court that "they did not desire to testify but would depose if called." They explained that

> what had brought them forth was the busy prattling of some other, probably the one whom they had taken along with them to advise a young woman, whose simple and foolish carriages and words, having heard of, they desired to advise better. . . . They desired to be excused from testifying because what was told them was a private confession which they had never to that day divulged, and the woman had never offended since that time but had lived gravely and soberly.[31]

In this case the two women assumed a kind of "professional immunity" from the inquisitions of the county officials. Their consciousness of their own importance is striking, but the role they had played was not unusual.

A hierarchal social structure which made female chastity the property of men, a religious tradition which demanded morality from both sexes, and patterns of feminine behavior rooted in traditional fatalism and in the rhythms of village life—against this backdrop men and women in northern New England played out an old drama of conquest and seduction.

Gorgeana, Province of Maine, 1650. For more than a year Jane Bond had been troubled with "fat Robert," who came to her house on at least four occasions when her husband was away "to the East." The first time he "strived with her but hardly knew hur boddy fully." Six months later he came again. When he tried to crawl through the window, she opened the door and let him in. "Robert Collins leave my company and medell not with me," she told him. "If not I will make you a shame to all New England." But though she tried, she "could not save hir selfe." Whether this had anything to do with alcohol is not clear, but when he came the third time at twilight and sat on her doorstep, she would not open the door. "I would have given you some drinke," he said. She answered, "I know not what is in it." About midnight on a May evening as she was making a cake to leave with her children, who would be alone the next day, Collins again came to the door, this time pushing the door almost off the hinges. He asked her to move her youngest child out of the bed and lie with him. She refused. He forced her.

"Put your finger but a littell in the fier you will not be able to Induer it," she told him, "but I must suffer eternally." Then she added, "You burn in your lust."

The next day Jane went to her neighbor Mary Tappe. Her heart was heavy, she was troubled to be so much alone, she said, and she was afraid to live so. Someone had been at her house the night before.

"It might be cattle," the neighbor answered.

"Noe, Jane said, "it was not cattell." Who then had been there? Jane simply repeated over and over again, "Alase I am but one, I dare not reveale it."

"Why did you not cry out?" Mary asked.

"Alase," she answered. "I may Cry tell my hart ake."[32]

Salem, Essex County, 1672. Elizabeth Goodell was careful to tell the justice of the peace that the language and actions of her brother-in-law John Smith "were such as most tend to the way of his calling in dealing with Cattel and not so like unlawful dalliances tending to uncleanness." No attempted rape—just continual and persistent annoyance. The record is never more specific, but the unbrotherly kisses, the meaningful looks, and the well-placed pats are easy to picture. These "assaults" and "affronts" had been going on for years, ever since her son Zachary was a little boy. Smith approached Elizabeth at her sister's house when he was there digging a well, at Giles Corey's house while Goody Corey was bringing in the linen from the bushes, and once at her own house on the Lord's day while her husband was at meeting. He became so insistent as they rode together to his wife's lying-in that she was forced to jump from the horse. Working in a swamp near her dwelling, he called for fire. When she refused to stay and smoke with him, he chased her up a hill.

Why didn't she complain? A male neighbor testified that he had come into the room after one alleged assault. If there was really a problem, she should have said something then. All he could see was "laughing and smoking."

Female neighbors said that Elizabeth was afraid. She told them that Smith was "an ugly rogue" and she was frightened that if she told, he would kill her or her children or "hurt her creatures." Even if he

were tried and convicted, she explained, "what a sad life should I have with my Husbands relations."[33]

Kittery, York County, 1710. When John White, the tinker, came to Mary Jenkins' house asking to borrow a canoe, she was glad to see him. Her husband, Rowland, was frequently at sea and she was afraid of Indians, who had taken captives in her own neighborhood. She told White that if he would stay the night, she would go with him to Mr. Kelley's house in town to get the canoe. He stayed. She sent to a neighbor's house for a pipe and tobacco, and the two of them sat up most of the night talking and smoking, "on two chairs," she said. Near morning he threw her on the bed and said he would "have his will of her," keeping his face so close to hers she could not scream. "I was in Souch a fit," she told the court, "that I do not know all hee dead or how Long hee Stayed."

About daylight Mary's mother knocked on the door. White answered. "Your Daughter would not Lett me come away," he explained. "She was afraid of the Indians."

Goody Muggeridge worried. Mary had given birth to an illegitimate child before she married Jenkins as his third wife. She urged her daughter not to tell her husband of White's visit. Knowing he "did not allow of any man to Be att their house affter it was Night," she was afraid he would "Go Neare to Kill her." Mary decided upon half-truth. When Jenkins returned, she told him that "The Tinker Lay att there house the Night before," but that Goody Pope also lay there, that White had refused the women's offer to give up the bed, that he had slept on chairs, and that he was "an honest and civil man." At a neighbor's house next day Jenkins casually engaged Sarah Pope in conversation and found she had not slept with his wife. When Goody Muggeridge came to the house later, she found her daughter sitting under a tree. She refused to go inside, saying "she wished her selfe Dead her husband had soe Kikt her and hurt her."[34]

Despite differences in circumstances, in place, and in time, the three stories illustrate common themes. In each case a woman advertently or inadvertently encouraged her aggressor. In each case she found herself unable to complain. Her fears were complex. There was the danger of beating but also the larger threat of disrupting the hierarchy of relations in which she found herself. Behind that was a deep sense of complicity in the crime.

The stories are grim in the telling, but they do not end here. When Jane Bond broke her silence, she found she was not alone. The record does not explain exactly how Robert Collins came to trial. In the formal record male witnesses predominate, as was frequently the case, but the triggering event seems to have been that first tentative confession to Mary Tappe. When questioned, six-year-old Henry Bond revealed that "fat Robert" was the man who had been with his mother. Once word was out, Henry Norton, who lived in the house next door, remembered hearing a strange sound in the night. Robert Knight thought that he had heard one too. Goody Knight was sure she had seen someone go by the house early in the morning; she thought it was Robert Collins. Pleading "not guilty," Collins was tried by jury, acquitted of the "forcement," which might have brought death, but sentenced to the extremely harsh punishment of "forty stripes but one," the maximum corporal punishment ever administered in New England. In addition he was fined £10, half to go "to the cuntrey," half to Nicholas Bond.[35]

The role of neighborhood women is even more prominent in the case of Elizabeth Goodell. Bit by bit, she too began to talk—to her sister, to her husband, and to trusted friends. Their advice was mixed. Some suggested a private hearing, some a formal complaint. Elizabeth went "down to towne to acquaint Major Hathorne with it but was discouraged by others and being foolish & not acquainted with the law, did forbear." While she hesitated, the scandal quickly and inexorably "spread abroad." Within a few weeks the magistrates were summoning her. Thus, without filing a formal complaint and perhaps without quite consciously meaning to do so, she had brought John Smith to court. She told the magistrates she was sorry about the gossip. She repented of speaking "foolishly vainly or slitely of such matters" and acknowledged it "a dishonor to the Sect of women," but she could not "wrong the truth." She hoped her brother-in-law would not "suffer more than he hath deserved." The court sentenced him to be whipped on the next lecture day.[36]

The outcome of the third case was quite different. Although Mary Jenkins finally convinced her husband that John White had forced her, she could not convince the court. Her first mistake seems to have been in violating the trust of the female community by lying about the presence of Sarah Pope on the fateful night. When the story became known, Mary Rice and Sarah Keene went to Mary and pressed her for details. They later reported the entire conversation to the magistrates. In examination Goody Keene had been as relentless as any state prosecutor. She focused upon the "fit" which Mary had described in her complaint. "Were you sencable when the Tinker was in the vary act?" she asked.

"No," Mary replied. But she insisted that "By what he said and the Circumstances affter ward" she knew that he had raped her.

Keene admonished her for attempting to take away a man's life without better proof than her thoughts. "Did hee Ly with you after you where in your fitte?"

Mary said, "No."

"Then . . . he Never Lay with you atole," Keene answered. "For you said hee did not

Ly with you before your fitte Nor after your fitte and in your fitte you whare not Sencebel hee laid with you." Mary Jenkins and John White were *both* sentenced to fifteen stripes at the post.[37]

In each case the role which the neighbor women performed was traditional. In New England, however, this role had been reinforced and strengthened by the involvement of the county courts. This is why the position of young women like Mary Rolfe cannot be understood without examining the position of older women like Mary Bishop. Older women derived their authority both from their established position in the community and from gender. They not only understood enticement, they also knew its consequence—as no magistrate could. Proved in life, they were capable of recognizing and of judging sin. Experience—not innocence—was the supreme female virtue in rural New England.

This chapter began by considering history as drama. It is perhaps appropriate that it should end by examining fiction as history. The eighteenth century has often been considered a pivotal point in the transformation from external to internal controls of sexual behavior. By the end of the seventeenth century in New England the authority of the county courts to enforce morality had already begun to slip. Fines replaced whippings, and convictions failed to keep pace with the growth in deviant behavior. Although churches continued to demand confession for fornication from members, their jurisdiction was narrow. At mid-century, family government was also under strain as parents lost the ability to control the timing of marriage for their children. The last years of the eighteenth century and the first years of the nineteenth saw the creation of a system of repression based upon internalized guilt.[38]

At the heart of the so-called "Victorian morality" which replaced the old "Puritan repression" was an altered concept of female sexuality. Man continued carnal, sensual, and devilish, but Woman assumed an active role as purifier of society. Female chastity became the touchstone of public virtue, purity the radiant light of the home. One of the most potent emblems of this transformation, as many historians have recognized, was Samuel Richardson's novel *Pamela*. Richardson took an old theme, the seduction of a maidservant by her master, and created an epic of middle-class morality. By resisting the increasingly frantic advances of Mr. B, the lovely Pamela won his admiration as well as his love.

Critics continue to argue over the meaning of the story. Was Pamela really as innocent and as artless as she appeared, or was she simply a shrewd bargainer who knew how to play her virtue as the ultimate trump, refusing to become a mistress until she had become a bride? Esther Burr (the daughter of Jonathan Edwards) didn't like the novel. She couldn't understand how a virtuous woman could marry her oppressor, a man who had not only kidnapped her but attempted to rape her as well.[39] Most modern readers probably share Burr's perception. In the eighteenth century, however, *Pamela* was wildly popular, especially among readers of an emerging middle class. It represented problems and solutions which they could understand and share. Keith Thomas may be right in suggesting that one consequence of the elevation of female chastity was the "total desexualization of women," and in arguing that Richardson exemplified this phenomenon in his creation of an idealized heroine who was "delicate, insipid, fainting at the first sexual advance, and utterly devoid of feeling toward her admirer until the marriage knot was tied."[40]

Such an analysis reads backward toward *Pamela* from the nineteenth century. The novel takes on a different significance, however, if we read forward from the seventeenth-century folk world which we have described. Significantly, the three main characters in the long Lincolnshire section of Richardson's novel, like the three main characters in the Rolfe-Greenland story, are a young woman, an old woman, and an aggressive male.

The climactic struggle of the novel is between Pamela and her "rough-natur'd Governess," Mrs. Jewkes, the old housekeeper who has been paid to watch over Pamela after she has been kidnapped and eventually to deliver her up to the lecherous master. As Robert Erickson has shown, Richardson drew upon the rich lore of English midwifery and witchcraft in creating the character Of Mrs. Jewkes, playing upon the role of the old wife as a woman who mediated at the mysteries of creation and of death, and who, in traditional society as well as in literature, was capable of expanding "into a figure of great autonomous power."[41] In that final fateful scene in Lincolnshire, Mrs. Jewkes and Mr. B both stand over a prostrate Pamela, whose virtuous fainting has ironically vanquished them both.

When this scene is set against the real-life dramas from northern New England, its meaning becomes startlingly clear. Pamela's triumph was not in retaining her virtue but in seizing responsibility for her own behavior. Facing the tempter, she was not beguiled. If chastity was property in Richardson's novel, it belonged to the heroine, not to her father or to any other man. Using her own assets, Pamela won the title of wife. But victory over the sensual advances of Mr. B was achieved only by overcoming the governance of Mrs. Jewkes, who had failed in her role as protector. It is as though Richardson were saying that the lore of the old wife was insufficient to protect a young woman in the changing world of the eighteenth century. Bereft of parents and of guardians, she must acquire a new world of values, breaking out of the ancient community of women into the sequestered paradise of an idealized marriage.

ABBREVIATIONS TO ACCOMPANY NOTES

ECR *Records and Files of the Quarterly Courts of Essex County, Massachusetts*, I–IX (Salem: Essex Institute, 1911–1975).

MPCR *Province and Court Records of Maine*, I–VI (Portland: Maine Historical Society, 1928–1975).

NEQ *New England Quarterly.*

NH Court Manuscript Court Records, New Hampshire State Archives, Concord, N.H.

NLD Sybil Noyes, Charles Thornton Libby, and Walter Goodwin Davis, *A Genealogical Dictionary of Maine and New Hampshire* (Portland, Me.: Southworth-Anthoensen Press, 1928).

NOTES

1. The Greenland-Rolfe case described was reconstructed from depositions in *ECR*, III, 47–55, 65–67, 70, 75, 88–91. All dialogue is in the original. Greenland eventually removed to Kittery, where he was continually in trouble and where his wife was accused of witchcraft. *NLD*, 288; NH Court, I, 1, 267.
2. Lawrence Stone, *The Family, Sex, and Marriage in England 1500–1800* (London: Harper & Row, 1977), p. 523; Keith Thomas, "The Double Standard," *Journal of the History of Ideas* XX (1959), 203.

3. *ECR, III,* 66.

4. Edmund S. Morgan, "The Puritans and Sex," *NEQ,* XV (1942), 591–607.

5. Michael Zuckerman, "Pilgrims in the Wilderness: Community, Modernity, and the Maypole at Merry Mount," *NEQ,* L (1977), 265–267.

6. Philip J. Greven, Jr., *The Protestant Temperament* (New York: Alfred A. Knopf, 1977), pp. 24–140.

7. Thomas, "Double Standard," p. 213 and passim.

8. *ECR,* III, 88, 48.

9. *The Laws and Liberties of Massachusetts,* 1648 (Cambridge, Mass.: Harvard U. Press, 1929), pp. 6, 23; George Lee Haskins, *Law and Authority in Early Massachusetts* (New York: Macmillan, 1960), pp. 149–150.

10. Haskins, *Law and Authority,* p. 149; Morgan, "Puritans and Sex," p. 602.

11. William H. Whitmore, ed., *The Colonial Laws of Massachusetts . . . 1660* (Boston, 1880), p. 257. Stone, *Family, Sex, and Marriage,* p. 623, believes New England courts gave up trying to punish a sin. The continuing conviction of married fornicators argues against this. Between 1653 and 1727 the York courts tried 274 cases of fornication, 61 percent involving couples who had already married, eliminating the economic motive for prosecution. The midwives' testimony was crucial in cases of single women; e.g., *MPCR,* VI, 121–127.

12. In describing the effort of colonial New Englanders to achieve sexual privacy, David Flaherty clearly demonstrates its lack. *Privacy in Colonial New England* (Charlottesville: U. Press of Virginia, 1972), pp. 76–84.

13. *NH Court,* VII, 225, 227.

14. *ECR,* V, 351–354; *MPCR,* 1, 85.

15. *ECR,* II, 35.

16. *ECR,* II, 420.

17. *ECR* V, 351–354.

18. *ECR,* V, 228–229; G. E. and K. R. Fussell, *The English Countrywoman* (New York: Benjamin Blom, 1971), p. 27; *Stone, Family, Sex, and Marriage,* p. 520.

19. E.g., Nicholas Noyes, "A Consolatory Poem," in Cotton Mather, *Meat Out of the Eater* (Boston, 1703), p. 186; Cotton Mather, *Virtue in Its Verdure* (Boston, 1725), p. 23, and *Life Swiftly Passing* (Boston, 1716), p. 3; Benjamin Colman, *A Devout Contemplation* (Boston, 1714), p. i.

20. *MPCR,* I, 176.

21. *ECR,* III, 90.

22. *ECR,* VIII, 99, 259–263, 288–289, 296, 308, 433.

23. Morgan, "Puritans and Sex," p. 594 and passim; Eli Faber, "Puritan Criminals: The Economic, Social, and Intellectual Background to Crime in Seventeenth-Century Massachusetts," *Perspectives in American History,* XI (1977–1978), p. 85.

24. Sherry Ortner, "Is Female to Male as Nature Is to Culture?" in *Woman, Culture, and Society,* ed. Michelle Zimbalist Rosaldo and Louise Lamphere (Stanford, Calif.: Stanford U. Press, 1974), pp. 67–87.

25. E.g., Cotton Mather, *Ornaments for the Daughters of Zion* (Boston, 1692), p. 50. I have never found a reference to original sin as "Eve's Sin." As in the primer, "In Adam's fall we die all."

26. Natalie Davis, *Society and Culture in Early Modern France* (Stanford, Calif.: Stanford U. Press, 1975), pp. 124–125.

27. William Hubbard, *A Narrative of the Troubles with the Indians* (Boston, 1677), pp. 61, 77; [Elizabeth Hanson], *God's Mercy Surmounting Man's Cruelty* (Philadelphia, 1728), pp. 35–36; Cotton Mather, *Good Fetch'd Out of Evil* (Boston, 1700), pp. 33–34.

28. *The Works of Aristotle* (Philadelphia, 1798), pp. 16–19; Stone, *Family, Sex, and Marriage,* p. 281; Nancy F. Cott, "Eighteenth-Century Family and Social Life Revealed in Massachusetts Divorce Records," *Journal of Social History,* X (1976), 33–35; Charles Carlton, "The Widow's Tale: Male Myths and Female Reality in Sixteenth and Seventeenth Century England," *Albion,* X (1978), 118–129.

29. E.g., *MPCR*, II, 43, 92; IV, 48–50; VI, 98.

30. *ECR*, V, 21–22.

31. *ECR*, III, 194. It is hardly surprising that in *formal* court actions, male witnesses would predominate (Cott, pp. 26–27), especially in eighteenth-century divorce cases, which went to the Council rather than to county courts.

32. *MPCR*, I, 140–143.

33. *ECR*, V, 52–55.

34. *MPCR*, III, 378–380.

35. *MPCR*, I, 142–143.

36. *ECR*, V, 54–55.

37. *MPCR*, III, 379.

38. Daniel Scott Smith and Michael S. Hindus, "Premarital Pregnancy in America 1640–1971," *Journal of Interdisciplinary History*, V (Spring 1975), pp. 537–570.

39. Laurie Crumpacker and Carol Karlsen, paper delivered at the Fourth Berkshire Conference on the History of Women, Mt. Holyoke, August 1978. For additional evidence that *Pamela* was read in New England, see *Gentleman's Progress: The Itinerarium of Dr. Alexander Hamilton*, 1744, ed. Carl Bridenbaugh (Chapel Hill, N.C.: U. of North Carolina Press for Institute of Early American History and Culture, 1948), p. 112; and Clifford K. Shipton, *New England Life in the Eighteenth Century* (Cambridge, Mass.: Harvard U. Press, 1963), p. 185.

40. Thomas, "Double Standard," pp. 214–215.

41. Robert A. Erickson, "Mother Jewkes, Pamela, and the Midwives," *ELH*, XLIII (1976), pp. 500–516.

Key Terms

Restoration   The period between the resumption of the British throne by Charles II in 1660 and the revolution of 1688.

Goodman   A term of reference and address for the male head of household among the New England Puritans. A goodman's wife was addressed and referred to with the term "Goody," followed by the husband's last name.

sampe   Also "samp." A porridge made from hominy.

selectman   A member of a group of town officials chosen to oversee community affairs in New England.

trull   A prostitute.

Discussion Questions

1. One striking difference between adultery cases among the Puritans and adultery in contemporary society is that the Puritans saw these marital transgressions as rightfully a matter of *public* knowledge and concern. Why was this so? What was it about Puritan society that made people's sexual conduct a legitimate part of everyone's business?

2. Today in the United States, adultery is largely seen as a private concern of the parties involved. Or is it? What about adultery cases among political leaders and politicians? Compare what you understand of adultery in Ulrich's article with, for example, the impeachment case of President Bill Clinton.

3. Compare the cultural construction of womanhood among the New England Puritans (as described by Ulrich) and the nineteenth-century American middle class (as described by Smith-Rosenberg and, for New England, Cott). The differences are readily apparent, but what are some similarities?

Puberty to Menopause

THE CYCLE OF FEMININITY IN NINETEENTH-CENTURY AMERICA

Carroll Smith-Rosenberg

Nineteenth-century America saw the florescence of a very particular image of woman among the middle classes. Ideally chaste but dangerously sexual, women's lives were believed most strongly governed by their reproductive organs. In this article, Carroll Smith-Rosenberg comments on Victorian womanhood from the perspective of nineteenth-century medicine. Using medical texts and advice from physicians, she focuses on the two "crises" in woman's reproductive cycle, puberty and menopause. During both these crises, physicians urged considerable restraint on the activities and undertakings of women and warned of severe physical and mental consequences should they do otherwise. Smith-Rosenberg shows how medical theory of these feminine biological events allowed society to control female sexuality within the framework of reproduction and encouraged women to confine themselves within the domestic sphere.

Adolescence and the coming of old age are pivotal processes in human experience. On one level, they are socially defined crises, points of entrance into new social roles and responsibilities. More primitively, they are physiological processes that each individual and each culture must incorporate into basic patterns of social structure and ideology. They are marked by hormonal and emotional flux, maladjustment and depression—in the case of old age, by disease and fears of disease. The coming and fading of sexual maturity, moreover, force cultures and individuals to deal with the question of human sexuality. The menstrual blood and wet dreams of puberty, the hot flashes of menopause are physical signposts that even the most sexually repressed and denying culture must acknowledge and rationalize in terms consistent with its social values generally (as must each individual within that culture, in terms appropriate to his or her particular psychic needs). Few values are more central to this process than those relating to women and women's role.

This essay proposes to examine Victorian American attitudes toward puberty and menopause in women. It will do so from one specific perspective—the perspective of the medical profession as expressed in both its professional and its popular writings. Since puberty and menopause are both physiological processes and possible triggers of disease, every nineteenth-century gynecology textbook and the most popular medical guides devoted sections to them, as, of course, did the professional journals. In non-medical Victorian literature, on the other hand, these subjects remained veiled.[1]

Puberty, menstruation, and menopause could be specifically medical problems as well. The depressions and irritability of adolescence, the breast and uterine cancer of the aging woman were conditions physicians had to face—and if not cure, at least explain, and in explaining hope to mitigate. The physician's hypothetical explanation of these disorders thus served to express and rationalize the often intractable realities of puberty and menopause—and, at the same time, helped the physician act out his own role as healer. Inevitably, as well, the physician's would-be scientific views reflected and helped shape social definitions of the appropriate bounds of woman's role and identity. In exploring these medical arguments, then, I want to stress not their internal consistency and even less their scientific significance, but, rather, the ways in which they represent a particular nineteenth-century attempt to resolve the perplexing interplay of socially defined sex roles and the ambivalence surrounding puberty and menopause.

Woman, Victorian society dictated, was to be chaste, delicate, and loving. Yet her Victorian contemporaries assumed that behind this modest exterior lay a complex network of reproductive organs that controlled her physiology, determined her emotions, and dictated her social role. She was seen, that is, as being both higher and lower, both innocent and animal, pure yet quintessentially sexual. The central metaphor in these formulations, central both emotionally and in content, pictures the female as driven by the tidal currents of her cyclical reproductive system, a cycle bounded by the pivotal crises of puberty and menopause and reinforced each month by her recurrent menstrual flow.[2]

The extent to which the reproductive organs held sway over woman's body had no parallel in the male. Male sexual impulses, nineteenth-century physicians and laymen alike maintained, were subject to a man's will; they were impulses that particular men could at particular times choose to indulge or to repress.[3] Not so with woman's sexuality. Woman's sexual and generative organs were hidden within her body, subject not to her will but to a biological clock of which women were only dimly aware and which they were clearly unable to control. Each month, for over thirty years, these organs caused cyclical periods of pain, weakness, embarrassment, irritability, and, in some cases, even insanity. "Woman's reproductive organs are pre-eminent," one mid-century physician explained in typical phrases. "They exercise a controlling influence upon her entire system, and entail upon her many painful and dangerous diseases. They are the source of her peculiarities, the centre of her sympathies, and the seat of her diseases. Everything that is peculiar to her, springs from her sexual organization."[4]

Such views had been familiar since classical antiquity. Between 1840 and 1890, however, physicians, reflecting a growing physiological sophistication generally, and, more specifically, increasingly circumstantial knowledge of the female reproductive system, were able to present a far more elaborate explanation of woman's peculiar femininity—and hence a rationale for her role as wife and mother.[5] Woman became a prisoner not only of her reproductive functions but quite explicitly of two tiny and hitherto ignored parts of that system—the ovaries. "Ovulation fixes woman's place in the animal economy, one doctor explained in 1880. "With the act of menstruation is wound up the whole essential character of her system." "A woman's system is affected," health reformer J. H. Kellogg commented as late as 1895, "we may almost say dominated, by the influence of these two little glands. . . . Either an excess or a deficiency of the proper influence of these organs over the other parts of the system may be productive of disease."[6]

The ovaries began their dictatorship of woman's life at puberty. They released her, often exhausted and debilitated, at menopause. Puberty and menopause were thus seen as peculiarly sensitive physiological turning points in a woman's life—stages at which new physical and emotional equilibria had to be established.[7] Both men and women, of course, experienced such crises of developmental readjustment. For women, however, such periods of crisis and resolution occurred more frequently, and seemed both more dangerous and more sexual. Puberty was, for example, more precipitate and difficult for women—and was followed immediately by the monthly crisis of menstruation, by pregnancy, childbirth, lactation, and finally menopause. As late as 1900, a physician could picture the dangers in these melodramatic terms:

> Many a young life is battered and forever crippled in the breakers of puberty; if it crosses these unharmed and is not dashed to pieces on the rock of childbirth, it may still ground on the ever-recurring shadows of menstruation, and lastly, upon the final bar of the menopause ere protection is found in the unruffled waters of the harbor beyond the reach of sexual storms.[8]

Another physician, perhaps influenced by the moral and religious strivings pictured in *Pilgrim's Progress*, entitled his guide to woman's health *Woman and Her Thirty Year Pilgrimage*.[9]

Puberty and menopause were, moreover, inseparably linked in nineteenth-century medical thought. The way in which a woman negotiated the physiological dangers of puberty was believed to determine her health not only during her child-bearing years but at menopause as well. A painful, unhealthy, or depressed puberty sowed the seeds for disease and trauma at menopause. Indeed, so intertwined

were these events that physicians used the age of puberty to predict the age when menopause would occur. Puberty and menopause were, as one nineteenth-century physician revealingly expressed it, "the two termini of a woman's sexual activity."[10] One woman physician even went so far as to liken the menopausal woman to a preadolescent; menopause, she wrote, was "the transition of the (sexual) system from an active ovarian state to the quiet condition of a non-ovulating girl."[11]

Such medical and biological arguments helped, of course, to rationalize woman's traditional role. But they served other social purposes as well. They expressed, that is, the age-old empirical understanding that puberty and menopause were indeed periods of stress—crises of both emotional and social identification and physical health. And they served as well to provide the physician—armed with still-primitive gynecological skills and an equally primitive body of physiological knowledge with a system with which to explain such biological and emotional realities. The nineteenth century was a time when pregnancies and obstetrical trauma were far more common than today. It was crucial to the physician's professional role, and thus to the psychic comfort of his female patients as well, that he be provided with explanations with which to counsel and to comfort.

At puberty a girl became a woman. Physicians remarked that the change was often startlingly dramatic. Many doctors indulged in romantic eulogies to the young woman's physical and anatomical attributes. They admired her newly rounded limbs, her "swelling breasts," her broadened hips, the transparent nature of her skin, which reflected every blush. Her unfolding beauty was charming indeed. "How sensitive—how tremulous is now her nervous system!" one such physician remarked. "It is as if," another doctor wrote, "a new being, almost, is created."[12]

Yet this beauty, like the opening blossom to which the pubescent girl was so frequently compared, was at the same time weak, dependent, and fragile. Puberty, the nineteenth century never doubted, brought strength, vigor, and muscular development to boys; to women it brought increased bodily weakness, a newfound and biologically rooted timidity and modesty, and the "illness" of menstruation. With puberty, English clinician Michael Ryan explained to his medical audience, "all parts of [a man's] . . . body became developed . . . the principles of life superabound in his constitution, and he vigorously performs all the noble pursuits assigned him by nature. Woman, on the contrary, delicate and tender, always preserves some of the infantile constitution."[13]

Yet the creation of this fragile and ethereal creature was frequently traumatic; female adolescence was often a stormy period. (The emotional difficulties of adolescence were hardly a discovery of the late nineteenth century; they were well known to physicians throughout the century.) Girls would suddenly become moody, depressed, petulant, capricious, even sexually promiscuous. Adolescence, explained a late-nineteenth-century advice book for mothers, is naturally a time of restlessness and of nerve irritability. Her mind is confused with vague dissatisfaction with all about her, and vaguer desires which she vainly endeavors to define even to herself. . . . Her feelings are especially sensitive and easily hurt." It was a "period of storm and stress," of "brooding, depression and morbid introspection."[14]

Victorian physicians drew upon their "ovarian" model of female behavior both to explain such erratic behavior and to contain it within traditional social bounds. The onset of puberty, they explained, marked perhaps the greatest crisis in a woman's life—a crisis during which a new physiological and emotional equilibrium was being created, an equilibrium that would control a woman's life for the next thirty years. If a

girl, especially at the very outset of puberty, violated the laws of her body, a dire chain of pain and disease, of dysmenorrhea, miscarriage, even sterility would surely follow. As one physician explained in his domestic medical text,

> It is now that every hidden germ of disease is ready to spring up; and there is scarcely a disorder to which the young and growing female is subjected, which is not at this time occasionally to be seen, and very often in a fatal form. . . . Coughs become consumptive and scrofula exerts its utmost influence in the constitution and deforms the figure of the body. . . . The dimensions of that bony outlet of the female frame is also altered and diminished on which so much of safety and comparative ease depends in childbirth. This, indeed, is the cause of almost every distressing and fatal labor that occurs and it is at this period of life . . . that such an unspeakable misfortune may be prevented.

If a woman was to fulfill her ordained role as mother of numerous and healthy offspring, her own mother must carefully oversee her puberty—and be aware of even the slightest evidence of ill-health.[15]

Woman's body, doctors contended, contained only a limited amount of energy—energy needed for the full development of her uterus and ovaries. At the commencement of puberty, then, a girl should curtail all activity. One doctor advised the young woman to take to her bed from the first signs of a discharge until menstruation was firmly established, months or perhaps years later. Not all doctors took so extreme a position, but most did warn that a girl should not engage in any absorbing project at this time. Indeed physicians routinely used this energy theory to sanction attacks upon any behavior they considered unfeminine; education, factory work, religious or charitable activities, virtually any interests outside the home during puberty were deplored, as was any kind of sexual forwardness such as flirtations, dances, and party-going.[16]

There was only one right way for a young woman to behave at puberty. From the onset of menstruation until marriage, she must concentrate on the healthy development of her reproductive organs and the regulation of her menses. Physicians prescribed an elaborate regimen to maintain sexual and general health, a regimen that remained remarkably consistent throughout the nineteenth century. Young women were told to avoid the display of any strong emotions, especially anger, at puberty. They should spend much of their time in the fresh air, enjoy moderate exercise, avoid down beds, corsets, or liquor and other stimulating beverages. Ample rest and a simple diet of unstimulating food were equally necessary. The life-style most frequently advocated for the young woman consisted of a routine of domestic tasks, such as bed-making, cooking, cleaning, and child-tending. These would appropriately serve, physicians argued, to provide the best regimen for the full and proper development of her maternal organs.[17]

Medical theories of puberty thus served a number of functions. Such concepts functioned as a way in which physicians—and society generally—could recognize the development and centrality of woman's sexual nature—while at the same time controlling and limiting that sexuality within a reproductive framework. The theories conceded the existence of sexuality and emotionality as normal aspects of adolescence, but served to warn women that they must control these emotions and limit their activities to the home; otherwise, disease, insanity, and even death would surely follow.

Still more subtly, these hypothetical physiological arguments suggest, by implication, a good deal about the social and psychic realities of female adolescence—and their latent function for the physicians who intoned them. Let me be a bit more specific. Nineteenth-century medical discussions of puberty suggested that mother-daughter

relations may often have broken down at puberty, thus leaving the young girl isolated from an important emotional support system during a critical and stormy period. Physicians wrote repeatedly of girls left in culpable ignorance by their prudish mothers, terrified at what they could only construe as vaginal hemorrhaging. Many such girls, physicians reported, tried fearfully to stop the flow, immersing their bodies in icy water or wrapping wet clothes around their abdomens. Others, seized with shame and terror, ran away from home, exposed themselves to inclement weather, or wandered the streets at night not wanting to return home. One woman reported that it had taken her "a life time" to forgive her mother for the fear and loneliness she had felt when she was first menstruating.[18] Indeed, so common in medical writings are versions of this traumatic first menstruation that it becomes a kind of primal feminine scene, one encompassing in a single exemplary situation a universe of veiled emotion—emotions that nineteenth-century doctors recognized and attempted to mitigate by castigating those mothers who failed to support their daughters at so critical a period.[19]

Though warnings about rest, diet, and the need for maternal supervision that mark the medical discussions of puberty may seem quaint, perhaps repressive, they tell us a good deal about the female experience of puberty; they tell us that adolescence was traumatic, that it implied an often painful restructuring of intra-familial and social identities—in short, the hypothetical pathology of the critical period and its possibly irreversible damage expressed a consciousness of the real crisis a young girl faced at this time. The emotionally charged picture of first menstruation, its isolation, fears, and dangers, served, that is, to express and rationalize a rather complex insight into the several dimensions of puberty.

Insecurity and a sense of isolation and unworthiness are, of course, not peculiar to adolescent girls in Victorian America. These feelings reflect a multitude of anxieties: fear that menstrual blood might indeed be the result of injury due to masturbation; a fear—probably unconscious and perhaps dating to infancy, of a growing social autonomy and sexual maturity, the reactivation of a fundamental struggle between mother and daughter for both love and independence—a struggle that psychiatrists now suggest predates any Oedipal conflict. Puberty and menstruation do, after all, force every woman to ask and attempt to answer that fundamental question: What is the nature and meaning of my femaleness?

Part of this stress surrounding female puberty was due to the ambivalent and unresolved attitudes that surrounded menstruation itself. The history of attitudes toward menstruation is age-old, varied, yet surprisingly consistent; it was a period of danger, of shame, of punishment. Judeo-Christian folklore attributed menstruation to God's curse on the daughters of a sinning Eve. Because of Eve's transgression, woman needed more forgiveness and regeneration than man, one physician argued, and thus "this special secretion was given them." "Many girls," another reported, "consider [menstruation] as a humiliating badge of their inferiority to the stronger sex." Not surprisingly, many women believed that menstrual blood was peculiarly contaminated; if retained within the body it would corrupt the blood generally and lead to disease.[20]

Physicians, or many of them, tried to counter these feelings of shame and resentment. The tactic normally chosen, of course, was to wash the menstrual blood white in the rhetorical spirituality of marriage and motherhood. "Menstruation is allied to Maternity," one doctor wrote, "leading us to regard this function with reverence." "How strange," another wrote reassuringly, "that woman should regard with shame and distaste this function to which she owed health and life itself."[21] Yet, not surprisingly, such words of paternalistic reassurance were often mixed with expressions of distaste and doubt. One of America's leading gynecologists, for instance, prefaced a medical school lecture on the female reproductive system by "begging" his students "to accompany me in this disagreeable task," while another physician commented in passing that menstrual blood had a rank smell which any man could detect. Others argued that it was not in fact blood but some strange and unclassifiable discharge.[22]

There are other indications in the medical literature that many physicians were ambivalent toward the menstruating woman. Doctors, for instance, frequently began discussions of puberty and menstruation by elaborately recounting ancient myths that granted menstrual blood distinctive and magical powers. Forcefully denying the truth of these myths, the doctors then argued that, quite the contrary, menstruation made women weak, diseased, and dependent.[23] The recurrence of this particular formulation suggests that it may well have proved psychically functional to those male physicians who so tirelessly intoned it; certain physicians may well have felt ambivalent about menstruation or female genitalia—and, by implication, about their own masculinity. Their elaborate and stylized exposition and then destruction of such myths might thus have served the dual psychological purpose of permitting physicians first to displace their own fears of menstruating women onto classical writers or primitive peoples—an effective distancing technique—and then consciously to ridicule and deny the validity of such displaced fears. Their coupling this denial of feminine powers with the theory that menstruating women were indeed weak and fragile supports this hypothesis.

The other patterns found in nineteenth-century medical discussions of menstruation tend to reinforce such a psychological interpretation. A significant number of physicians drew a suggestive nexus between women's sexual appetite and menstruation—seeing menstruation as either the monthly apex of women's sexual desires or as a system to aid women in controlling such impulses. George Rowe wrote in 1844: "In God's infinite wisdom . . . might not this monthly discharge be ordained for the purpose of controlling woman's violent sexual passions . . . by unloading the uterine vessels . . . so as to prevent the promiscuous intercourse which would prove destructive to the purest . . . interests of civil life. . . ."[24]

The insatiate and promiscuous woman is one of man's most primitive and fearful fantasies, a fantasy that in individual men was clearly productive of anxiety such as that evident in Rowe's pious praise of menstruation. Closely paralleling the image of the sexually powerful woman is that of the maniacal and destructive woman. Menstruation, nineteenth-century physicians warned, could drive some women temporarily insane; menstruating women might go berserk, destroying furniture, attacking family and strangers alike, and even killing their infants. Those "unfortunate women," subject to such excessive menstrual influence, Edward Tilt wrote, should, for their own good and that of society, be incarcerated for the length of their menstruating years.[25]

Like puberty, menopause was seen as a physiological crisis, its course shaped by a woman's preceding sexual experiences, its resolution determining her future health.[26] If a woman had followed a sound regimen throughout life and had no predisposition to malignant disease, menopause could bring with it a golden age of health and freedom from the periodic inconvenience, pain, and depression of menstruation. The menopausal period could thus become the "Indian summer" of a woman's life—a period of increased vigor, optimism, and even of physical beauty.[27]

Far more frequently, however, menopause marked the beginning of a period of depression, of heightened disease incidence, and of early death. "There is a predisposition to many diseases, and these are often of a melancholy character," one physician noted in the 1830s. The host of diseases that might develop as a result of the cessation of menstruation included, as one doctor lamented, "almost all the ills the flesh is heir to."[28] They ranged from the classic flushes of menopause, through dyspepsia, diarrhea, severe vaginitis, vaginal inflammation, prolapsed uterus, rheumatic pains, paralysis, apoplexy, and erysipelas to uterine hemorrhaging, tumors, uterine and breast cancer, tuberculosis, scrofula, and diabetes.[29] Emotional or psychological symptoms characterized menopause as well. Irritability, depression, hysteria, melancholy, episodes of severe emotional withdrawal and insanity, seemed particularly common.[30] Clearly, nineteenth-century physicians used menopause as an all-purpose explanation for the heightened disease incidence of the older female; all of her ills were directly or indirectly diseases of the uterus and ovaries.

Physicians postulated a number of mechanisms to explain this pattern of ill health. The diseases of menopause, one theory argued, were rooted in a "plethora," which resulted after the cessation of the menses from the retention of the monthly menstrual blood. It was to such a plethora, or suffusion of the body with fluids, that physicians attributed the hot flashes, circulatory diseases, palpitations, and vaginal hemorrhaging of menopause. "The stoppage of any customary evacuations, however small, is sufficient to disorder the whole frame and often to destroy life itself," William Buchan explained in his extraordinarily influential *Domestic Medicine*.[31] By mid-century, physicians evolved additional explanations of such diseases in older women. Each month, some contended, the menstrual blood had carried off the seeds of illness and in this way repressed a host of contagious and constitutional ailments that then flourished with the repression of menstruation. Still others argued that the diseases of menopause, especially cancer of the uterus and breast, were rooted in systemic exhaustion consequent upon the unceasing cycle of menstruation, pregnancy, and lactation.[32]

But the most significant cause of a woman's menopausal disease, virtually every doctor believed, lay in her violation of the physiological and social laws dictated by her ovarian system. Education, attempts at birth control or abortion, undue sexual indulgence, a too-fashionable life-style, failure to devote herself fully to the needs of husband and children—even the advocacy of woman's suffrage—all might guarantee a disease-ridden menopause.[33]

One of the common causes of hemorrhaging, ovarian tumor, or insanity at menopause was not, however, a life filled with hygienic misdeeds, but, rather, a momentary lack of judgment in old age—that is, engaging in sexual intercourse during or after menopause. "My experience teaches me that a marked increase of sexual impulse at the change of life is a morbid impulse," Edward Tilt wrote in his widely read study of menopause. "Whenever sexual impulse is first felt at the change of life, some morbid ovario-uterine condition will be found to explain it. . . . It, therefore, is most imprudent for women to marry at this epoch without having obtained the sanction of a medical man." Female sexuality and reproduction thus formed a comforting nexus, the destruction of which clearly threatened certain Victorian physicians.[34]

Doctors warned that women must treat menopause as the beginning of old age. Women should alter their style of life and retire from the world into the bosom of their family. "We insist," wrote Walter Taylor in 1872, "that every woman who hopes for a healthy old age ought to commence her prudent cares as early as the 40th year

or sooner. . . . She should cease to endeavor to appear young when she is no longer so, and withdraw from the excitements and fatigues of the gay world even in the midst of her legitimate successes, to enter upon that more tranquil era of her existence now at hand. . . . Most American mothers," he added with unintentional irony, "can find at hand enough to do for their own families . . . to absorb all their energies."[35] The regimen almost universally prescribed for menopausal women closely paralleled that recommended for their pubescent daughters and granddaughters, a regimen of quiet, avoidance of mental activities, the shunning of new activities and a commitment to domesticity.[36]

Such ideas seem obviously formal and defensive. Male physicians displayed a revealing disquietude and even hostility when discussing their menopausal patients. In the medical literature, the menopausal woman often appeared as ludicrous or physically repulsive. Edward Tilt, for instance, claimed that she characteristically had a "dull stupid look," was "pale or sallow," and tended to grow a beard on her chin and upper lip. Doctors scoffed at women who, long sterile or just married at menopause, believed themselves pregnant. These women, doctors commented heartily, suffered from a little flatulence, somewhat more hysteria, and, most of all, obesity. Such a woman's fantasied fetus, another doctor joked, was just her belly's double chin. More critical were doctors' comments about women who deliberately attempted to appear young after they had reached menopause. Menopausal depression—other physicians remarked—grew out of pique at no longer being considered young and attractive.[37]

Indeed, such hostility and even contempt marked male medical discussions of menopausal women that one woman physician, in a valedictory address to the 1864 class at Woman's Medical College in Philadelphia, cited such animosity as an important reason for women's becoming physicians. Referring specifically to male physicians' treatment of menopausal women, she exhorted: "You will also vindicate the right, scarcely yet conceded to women, to grow *old* without reproach...."[38]

But how did women view this stage of life? From what I can detect thus far from diaries, letters, and the medical literature, I would answer that women viewed menopause with utter ambivalence. Doctors routinely noted that women faced menopause with dread and depression. "Suffering at the later period of life is accepted by many women as unavoidable and proper," one doctor remarked. Another physician commented upon a woman's "fear[s] as her age warns her that she is approaching that mysterious change. Every morbid impulse of her life is discussed with her friends.... She anxiously dwells on every little disorder, so charged is her mind with vague fears...." "Indeed," wrote a third some seventy years earlier, "so replete is this time with horrors to some that we may very justly suspect apprehension to be the cause of some of the distressing symptoms...."[39]

There is much, however, to indicate that many women looked forward to menopause as a release from the bondage of menstruation and pregnancy. Doctors, as already mentioned, did report that despite a general pattern of disease and depression, the health of some women improved dramatically with menopause. Indeed, menopause was seen as a specific for long-term depression, lassitude, and hysteria. Other doctors remarked how fresh and lovely some menopausal women looked—with a lightness to their step and a countenance free from anxiety.

The comments of a conservative and socially prominent Philadelphia Quaker matron, Elizabeth Drinker, may throw some light on this sense of freedom. Drinker recorded in her diary a conversation she had with her daughter Sally, who was about

to give birth. Each of Sally's births had been protracted and painful; her youngest sister had, just the day before, almost died in childbirth, surviving only to be permanently crippled. Sally was filled with foreboding at the beginning of this labor. "My poor dear Sally was taken unwell last night, ..." Drinker wrote in October 1799.

> She in pain at times, forerunning pains of a lingering labour, a little low spirited, poor dear Child. This day is 38 years since I was in agonies bringing her into this world of troubles; she told me with tears that this was her birth day. I endeavour'd to talk her into better spirits, told her that the time of her birth was over by some hours, she was now in her 39th year, and that this might possibly be the last trial of this sort, if she could suckle her baby for two years to come, as she had several times done heretofore.[40]

Elizabeth and Sally Drinker were not the only women who viewed menopause as a release from "a world of troubles." Menopause was indeed an ultimate birth-control technique, and many women welcomed it for that reason. Their feelings were well captured by a woman physician when she described the obstetrical history and feelings of a representative patient at the coming of menopause. As a young woman and newly in love, the patient had believed marriage the summit of human happiness. Within a year, however, she became pregnant "and such pains as accompanied this [birth] she had never before believed that woman could endure." Many pregnancies followed this first, "until ten, twelve or even fifteen children have been born, with an accumulation of troubles to correspond.... Then her remarks assume a different tone.... She wrings her hands ... and weeps as she begs her young friends to pause and consider before they leave home at so early an age; for marriage and maternity are not a romance...." It is against a background of such experience that the nineteenth-century woman approached menopause. "She is no longer exposed to the direful risks and pain of child bearing," a male physician remarked some fifty years earlier. "She thanks God for that and takes comfort in the thought."[41]

Perhaps the most forceful mid-nineteenth-century expression of a positive view of menopause was articulated by social reformer and suffrage advocate Eliza Farnham. "My acquaintance with women of the nobler sort," Farnham wrote, "has convinced me that many a woman has experienced, at times, a secret joy in her advancing age." Indeed, Farnham continued, menopause could become woman's golden age; when she was freed from the physical and emotional demands of childbirth and child-rearing, her spiritual nature could develop to its fullest. She found the postmenopausal years the period of woman's "super-exaltation" and condemned those men who had taught women to dread menopause as "an absolutely uncompensated loss of power." "That day is long since past for enlightened women," she continued and will be soon for their less understanding sisters. . . . For women developed enough to have opinions and take any ground, teach each other very rapidly. Their presence in the field of masculine errors is like sunlight to the mists of early dawn."[42]

Borrowing Eliza Farnham's imagery, let us examine the forms shrouded by the mists of these Victorian metaphors. On the very simplest level these ideas served as an absolute biological justification for woman's restricted role. They served as well to express and explain traditional empirical observations and folk wisdom concerning the real biological, emotional, and social significance—and stress—of puberty, menstruation, and menopause. They created, moreover, an ideal metaphor in which the Victorian physician could express a characteristic and revealingly inconsistent ambiguity toward woman's sexual and social nature. Within this system, woman was seen at the same time as a higher, more sensitive, more spiritual creature—and as a prisoner of tidal currents of an animal and uncontrollable nature (and in this way denied the two cardinal Victorian virtues of control and rationality). At the same time this formula also permitted Victorians to recognize the sometimes ominous force of female sexuality and to render such sexuality safe by subordinating it to the limited ends of child-bearing and nursing.

It is tempting, indeed, to elaborate a psychological interpretation of these nineteenth-century gynecological metaphors and formulations concerning puberty and menopause. They are suggestively consistent, for example, with a theory developed some years later by Karen Horney. Horney argued that male fear of a woman is a basic human emotion that predates the Oedipal dread of castration. In developing this hypothesis, Horney suggested that those men fearful of woman's sexuality attempt to defend against their anxiety in two ways. First, they denigrate women, especially those aspects of woman's body most closely associated with her genitals. Second, they overcompensate for their fears and hostility by romanticizing women, especially those parts of a woman's body and behavior not immediately associated with genital sexuality.[43]

The conventional formulas of nineteenth-century medical writers are remarkably compatible with Horney's hypothetical male "dread of women." Woman's "disagreeable," diseased—and hidden—sexual organs contrasted unfavorably in the medical literature, that is, with her "blushing" cheeks, her parted lips, her graceful bearing, her luminous eyes. In addition to defending against primal fears, as suggested by Horney, these particular rhetorical formulas may have also served as a means through which "respectable" males could cope with sexuality in the specifically repressive moral and religious climate of mid-nineteenth-century England and the United States.[44]

But such interpretations raise serious methodological problems for the historian. I have attempted in some ways to paint a group psychological portrait of individuals at a distance of one hundred years, individuals of whom we know little more than their formal writings. These writings are suggestive, but to assert more would clearly be gratuitous. Whole segments of past societies cannot be placed upon a couch that, at best, accommodates a single individual. And contemporary psychoanalytic theory can hardly be said to have provided final statements in regard to the development of human personality. Specifically, for example, though Horney's hypothesis may indeed be plausible, it is a theory unproved and unprovable.

NOTES

1. This is not to say that the question of adolescence and aging in women did not appear in nineteenth-century fiction; quite the contrary. Fictional discussions, however, lack the explicit physiological and sexual detail that characterized medical accounts. There were indeed so many popular nineteenth-century medical guides for women that they may be said to constitute a specific genre; all discussed such issues with varying degrees of explicitness. This article is based on a study of popular women's medical guides and of medical literature written for a professional medical audience: gynecological textbooks, monographs, and journal articles.

2. For an expanded study of this metaphor and its implications for woman's social role see Carroll Smith-Rosenberg and Charles Rosenberg, "The Female Animal: Medical and Biological Views of Women in Nineteenth-Century America," *Journal of American History* 60 (September 1973), in press.

3. Charles West, *Lectures on the Diseases of Women*, 2 vols. (London: John Churchill, 1861), vol. 1, no. 1; A. J. C. Skene, *Education and Culture as Related to the Health and Diseases of Women* (Detroit: George S. Davis, 1889), p. 22.

4. John Wiltbank, *Introductory Lecture for the Session, 1853–1854* (Philadelphia: Edward Grattan, 1854), p. 7.

5. This changing ideology reflected, of course, more than a simple improvement in medical knowledge. It reflected both a rapid growth in the prestige of science as a reference area in the mid- and late nineteenth century, as well as the growing conflict that centered on women's role. As the traditional role of wife and mother seemed increasingly under attack, the medical and biological defenses of that role increased proportionately. For a general discussion of the role of scientific language and metaphor and the growing emotional relevance of science in dealing with such social problems see Charles E. Rosenberg, "Science and American Social Thought," in *Science and Society in the United States*, eds. David D. Van Tassel and Michael G. Hall (Homewood, Ill.: The Dorsey Press, 1966), pp. 135–162.

6. William Pepper, "The Change of Life in Women," *Clinical News* I (1880): 505; J. H. Kellogg, *Ladies' Guide in Health and Disease* (Battle Creek, Mich.: Modern Medicine Publishing Co., 1895), p. 371. See as well Edward H. Dixon, *Woman and Her Diseases* (New York: author, 1846), p. 71; Charles Meigs, *Females and Their Diseases* (Philadelphia: D. G. Brinton, 1879), p. 332. A number of women physicians disagreed. Disease in women originated not in diseased ovaries, they argued, but in the unhealthy and restrained way women lived—without exercise, fresh air, or serious employment to occupy their minds. For a classic example of this "feminist" argument see Alice Stockham, *Tokology*, rev. ed. (Chicago: Sanitary Publishing Co., 1887), p. 257. With this particular exception, however, I found a remarkable uniformity in medical opinions on the specific issues discussed in this essay both in terms of chronology, that is, between the late eighteenth century and the late nineteenth, and between representatives of the medical establishment and so-called quack doctors.

7. Edward Tilt, *The Change of Life in Health and Disease*, 4th ed. (New York: Bermingham & Co., 1882), p. 14; P. Henry Chavasse, *Physical Life of Man and Woman* (Cincinnati: National Publishing Co., 1871), p. 155; Caleb Ticknor, *Philosophy of Living* (New York: Harper & Bros., 1836), pp. 304–305.

8. Alexander Hamilton, *A Treatise on the Management of Female Complaints* (New York: Samuel Campbell, 1792), pp. 98–99; Gunning Bedford, *Lecture Introductory to a Course on Obstetrics and Disease of Women and Children* (New York: Jennings, 1847), p. 8; Meigs, *Females and Their Diseases*, p. 334; George J. Englemann, "The American Girl To-day: The Influence of Modern Education on Functional Development," *Transactions of the American Gynecological Society* 25 (1900): 9–10.

9. [W. W. Bliss], *Woman and Her Thirty Year Pilgrimage* (New York: William M. Littell, 1869).

10. This was a pattern that remained constant throughout the century. See for example: Joseph Brevitt, *The Female Medical Repository* (Baltimore: Hunter & Robinson, 1810), p. 39; John Burns, *Principles of Midwifery*, 2 vols. (Philadelphia: Edward Parker), p. 138; J. Smedley, "The Importance of Making a Physical Exploration during the Climacteric Period," *Hahnemannean Monthly* 8 (1886): 487; William Capp, *The Daughter* (Philadelphia: F. A. Davis, 1891), p. 65; Kellogg, *Ladies' Guide*, p. 371.

11. A. M. Longshore-Potts, *Discourses to Women on Medical Subjects* (San Diego, Calif.: author, 1890), pp. 32, 94.

12. Dixon, *Woman and Her Diseases*, p. 21; William P. Dewees, *A Treatise on the Diseases of Females* (Philadelphia: H. C. Carey & J. Lea, 1826), p. 56. Again, this pattern can be found in medical literature throughout the nineteenth century. See for example: William Buchan, *Domestic Medicine Adapted to the Climate and Diseases of America*, 2nd ed. (Philadelphia: R. Folwell, 1801), pp. 356–357; Samuel Bard, *A Compendium of the Theory and Practice of Midwifery* (New York: Collins & Co., 1819), p. 39; Albert Hayes, *Physiology of Woman* (Boston: Peabody Medical Institute, 1869), pp. 86–87; Longshore-Potts, *Discourses to Women*, p. 67.

13. Michael Ryan, *Philosophy of Marriage*, 4th ed. (London: J. Bailliere, 1843), p. 143; Frederick Hollic, *The Marriage Guide, or Natural History of Generation* (New York: T. W. Strong, c. 1860), p. 111; Dewees, *Treatise*, pp. 20–21; William Alcott, *The Young Woman's Book of Health* (Boston: Tappan, Whittemore & Mason, 1850), pp. 120–121.

14. [Dr. Porter], *Book of Men, Women and Babies* (New York: De Witt & Davenport, 1855), p. 90; Hayes, *Physiology of Women*, p. 86; Meyer Solis-Cohen, *Girl, Wife and Mother* (Philadelphia: The John C. Winton Co., c. 1911), p. 27; Capp, *The Daughter*, p. 55.

15. Edward Clarke, *Sex in Education* (Boston: James R. Osgood & Co., 1873), p. 47; J. H. Kellogg, *Plain Facts about Sexual Life* (Battle Creek, Mich.: Office of the Health Reformer, 1877), pp. 52–53; Buchan, *Domestic Medicine*, p. 357; Meigs, *Females and Their Diseases*, p. 165; Hayes, *Physiology of Women*, p. 79.

16. For two classic expositions of this argument see: Clarke, *Sex in Education*, and Azel Ames, Jr., *Sex in Industry* (Boston: James R. Osgood, 1875). See as well: T. A. Emmet, *The Principles and Practice of Gynecology* (Philadelphia: Henry C. Lea, 1879), p. 21; Rebecca Crumpler, *A Book of Medical Discourses, In Two Parts* (Boston: Cashman, Keating & Co., 1883), p. 121; and Smith-Rosenberg and Rosenberg, "The Female Animal."

17. Hamilton, *Treatise*, p. 100; John See, *A Guide to Mother and Nurses* (New York: author, 1833), pp. 13–14; Tulio Suzzara Verdi, *Maternity, A Popular Treatise for Young Wives and Mothers* (New York: J. B. Ford and Co., 1870), p. 347; Mrs. E. R. Shepherd, *For Girls: A Special Physiology*, 20th ed. (Chicago: Sanitary Publishing Co., 1888), pp. 132–137; Stockham, *Tokology*, p. 254.

18. Shepherd, *For Girls*, pp. 8–9; Dixon, *Woman and Her Diseases*, p. 75; M. K. Hard, *Woman's Medical Guide* (Mt. Vernon, Ohio: W. H. Cochran, 1848), p. 6; Augustus K. Gardner, *Conjugal Sins* (New York: G. J. Moulton, 1874), p. 22; Henry B. Hemenway, *Healthful Womanhood and Childhood* (Evanston, Ill.: V. T. Hemenway & Co., 1894), p. 16.

19. See *Guide to Mothers*, p. 12; Lydia Maria Child, *The Family Nurse* (Boston: Charles J. Hendee, 1837), p. 43; Calvin Cutter, *The Female Guide* (West Brookfield, Mass.: Charles A. Mirick, 1844), p. 49; Potter, *How Should Girls Be Educated?* p. 5; Capp, *Daughter*, vol. 2, 3.

20. Clarke, *Sex in Education*, p. 27; Elizabeth Evans, *The Abuse of Maternity* (Philadelphia: J. B. Lippincott and Co., 1875), p. 26. There was a lengthy medical debate over the nature of menstrual blood, in which these popular beliefs were discussed. See note 23.

21. Henry C. Wright, *Marriage and Parentage* (Boston: Bela Marsh, 1854), p. 32; Stockham, *Tokology*, p. 252.

22. Meigs, *Females and Their Diseases*, p. 53; Charles E. Warren, *Causes and Treatment of Sterility in Both Sexes* (Boston: International Medical Exchange, 1890), pp. 58–59. Until quite late in the nineteenth century some physicians doubted whether menstrual blood was in fact blood, or if it was not a special discharge which drew off germs and waste from the circulatory system and thus each month cleansed a woman's system. See for example: Samuel Pancoast, *The Ladies' Medical Guide*, 6th ed. (Philadelphia: John E. Potter, c. 1859), pp. 154–155; Longshore-Potts, *Discourses to Women*, p. 69; Shepherd, *For Girls*, pp. 137–138, for this argument. For refutations see A. M. Mauriceau, *The Married Woman's Medical Companion* (New York: author, 1855), pp. 30–31, and T. R. Trall, *Sexual Physiology* (New York: Miller, Wood & Co., 1866), p. 58.

23. An excellent example of this formula is found in Hayes, *Physiology of Woman*, pp. 84–85. In this passage Hayes significantly refers to menstruation as "an internal wound, the real cause of all this tragedy." For a male physician to refer to menstruation as a "tragedy" seems a bit disproportionate unless Hayes is referring unconsciously to some other primitively perceived tragedy, as for instance castration or death. For an interesting discussion of male fear of menstruation and female genitalia see Karen Horney, "Denial of the Vagina," in *Feminine Psychology*, and with an introduction by Harold Kelman (New York: Norton, 1967). The common medical argument and folk belief that menstruation spoiled the milk of a nursing mother and indeed that such milk could cause convulsions or death in the infant may also be related to a general fear of menstrual blood.

24. George Robert Rowe, *On Some of the Most Important Disorders of Women* (London: John Churchill, 1844), pp. 27–28; William Carpenter, *Principles of Human Physiology*, 4th American ed. (Philadelphia: Lea and Blanchard, 1850), p. 698; Hollick, *Marriage Guide*, p. 95.

25. Tilt, *Change of Life*, p. 13; Horatio R. Storer and Franklin Fiske Heard, *Criminal Abortion* (Boston: Little, Brown and Company, 1868), p. 90 n.; Verdi, *Maternity*, p. 345.

26. Dixon, *Woman and Her Diseases*, p. 101; Tilt, *Change of Life*, pp. 10–12; Bard, *Compendium*, pp. 78–79.

27. Tilt, *Change of Life*, pp. 12–16; Dewees, *Treatise*, p. 94; Hayes, *Physiology of Women*, p. 95.

28. Joseph Ralph, *A Domestic Guide to Medicine* (New York: author, 1835), p. 130; L. H. Mettler, "Menopause," *Medical Register* 2 (1887): 323.

29. Tilt, *Change of Life*, contains the classic list of menopausal diseases—118 in all, pp. 106–246. See, as well, B. F. Baer, "The Significance of Menorrhagia Recurring about or after the Menopause," *American Journal of Obstetrics* 17 (1884): 461–462; Lawson Tait, "Climacteric Diabetes in Women," *The Practitioner* 36 (June 1886): 401–408; William Pepper, "The Change of Life in Women," pp. 505–506; Dewees, *Treatise*, pp. 94–103; Denman, *Introduction to Midwifery*, pp. 192–193; Sara E. Greenfield, "The Dangers of Menopause," *Woman's Medical Journal* (Toledo) 12 (1902): 183–185.

30. See, for example, C. J. Aldrich, "The Role Played by Intestinal Fermentation in the Production of the Neurosis of Menopause," *Physician and Surgeon* (Detroit) 19 (1897): 438–444; Philander Harris, "The Dangers of Certain Impressions Regarding the Menopause," *Transactions of the Medical Society of New Jersey* (1898), pp. 317–325; Dewees, *Treatise*, p. 103.

31. Buchan, *Domestic Medicine*, p. 360. This was the most popular physiological explanation of menopausal problems. See as well: West, *Diseases of Women*, p. 44; Hays, *Physiology of Women*, p. 96; Tilt, *Change of Life*, pp. 54, 85.

32. Denman, *Midwifery*, pp. 189–191; Dixon, *Woman and Her Diseases*, p. 103; Shepherd, *For Girls*, pp. 138–139; Mettler, "Menopause," p. 323; Longshore-Potts, *Discourses to Women*, pp. 94–95; "Change of Life in Women," pp. 505–506.

33. Dewees, *Treatise*, pp. 92, 95; Rowe, *On Some Common Disorders*, p. 36; George Woodruff Johnston, "Certain Facts Regarding Fertility, Utero-Gestation, Parturition and the Puerperium in the So-Called 'Lower' or 'Laboring' Classes," *American Journal of Obstetrics and Diseases of Women and Children* 21 (May 1888): 19.

34. Tilt also reported giving menopausal women anaphrodisiacs to control their sexual impulses. *Change of Life*, pp. 79, 93–94; Kellogg, *Plain Facts*, p. 80.

35. Taylor, *A Physician's Counsels to Women*, pp. 93–94.

36. See *Guide to Mothers and Nurses*, p. 18; Brevitt, *Woman's Medical Repository*, pp. 52–53; Longshore-Potts, *Discourses to Women*, p. 95.

37. Tilt, *Change of Life*, pp. 16, 39, 94–95; Taylor, *Physician's Counsels to Women*, pp. 85, 90–92; Bard, *Compendium*, p. 80; Burns, *Principles of Midwifery*, p. 162.

38. Ann Preston, *Valedictory Address to the Graduating Class, Female Medical College of Pennsylvania at the Twelfth Annual Commencement, March 16, 1864* (Philadelphia: William S. Young, Printer, 1864), p. 9.

39. Dewees, *Treatise*, p. 92; Aldrich, "Neuroses of Menopause," pp. 153–154; Baer, "Menorrhagia . . . Menopause," p. 451; Hal C. Wyman, "The Menopause-Gangliasthenia: A Clinical Lecture in the Michigan College of Medicine," *Michigan Medical News* 5 (1882): 313; Mauriceau, *Married Woman's Private Medical Companion*, p. 7.

40. This quote as well as many other lengthy excerpts from Elizabeth Drinker's diary are reprinted in Cecil K. Drinker, *Not So Long Ago: A Chronicle of Medicine and Doctors in Colonial Philadelphia* (New York: Oxford University Press, 1937), pp. 59–60.

41. Meigs, *Females and Their Diseases*, p. 55; Longshore-Potts, *Discourses to Women*, pp. 98–102.

42. Eliza W. Farnham, *Woman and Her Era*, 2 vols. (New York: A. J. Davis & Co., 1864), pp. 56–57.

43. Horney, *Feminine Psychology*. See especially her essays on "Fear of Woman," "Denial of the Vagina," and "Female Masochism."

44. For a discussion of such issues see Charles E. Rosenberg, "Sexuality, Class and Role in Nineteenth-Century America," *American Quarterly* (May 1973): in press.

DISCUSSION QUESTIONS

1. In general, how have social attitudes toward menstruation and menopause changed in the United States since the nineteenth century? What remnants of nineteenth-century values and attitudes toward menstruation and menopause do you detect in twenty-first-century attitudes? One interesting place to look for both remnants and changes is in popular culture, especially television. You might even ask, "What's so 'sanitary' about products marketed as 'sanitary protection'?" Why choose that euphemism?

2. Some people argue that in spite of new medical views of menstruation and menopause, American society still sees women as more largely governed by their reproductive biology than are men. What examples of this idea do you see expressed in popular magazines, television commercials, or other sources in American popular culture?

RELIGION [AND THE BONDS OF WOMANHOOD]

NANCY F. COTT

The previous article highlighted middle-class Victorian images of women that fostered their restriction to domesticity and defined them as weak and passive by nature. But that was not the whole picture. As Nancy F. Cott shows in the following article, religion was one area of life in which many late-eighteenth- and early-nineteenth-century New England women could be and were positively assertive. Cott discusses the gender ideology of both men and women of the time in New England that was used to

account for and promote women's religious expressions. She also shows how this religious participation, while fostering ideals of female submissiveness, became an avenue of feminine self-definition and assertion, giving women a sense of personal choice and individual commitment. In nineteenth-century Protestantism, New England women found both self-consciousness and community with other women. Cott also explores the extent to which women's participation in their various maternal associations and moral reform societies was a prelude to later demands for equal rights or was merely reinforcing women's subordination and confinement to particular spheres of life. This participation may be seen to have reflected in various ways both of these dimensions of women's history.

Woman was "fitted by nature" for Christian benevolence, announced a Presbyterian minister in Newburyport, Massachusetts, in 1837—"religion seems almost to have been entrusted by its author to her particular custody." As he saw it, Christianity had performed a unique service for women by bringing them social advantages as well as spiritual hope, and women had incurred a corresponding obligation.[1] The numbers and activity of women in New England churches suggest that they found benefits indeed in their religious devotion—but did their perception of the benefits, and the minister's, exactly coincide?

The Puritans who settled Massachusetts Bay worshipped a patriarchal God, but as early as the mid-seventeenth century women outnumbered men in the New England churches. While the church hierarchy remained strictly male the majority of women in their congregations increased, and ministers felt compelled to explain it.[2] "As there were three Marys to one John, standing under the Cross of our Dying Lord," Cotton Mather wrote in 1692, "so still there are far more Godly Women in the World, than there are Godly Men; and our Church Communions give us a Little Demonstration of

it." Mather offered two explanations for the persistent pattern. Because of Eve's sins God had decreed that woman's lot would include subjection to man, and pain in childbirth; but he had mercifully converted these curses into blessings. The trials that women had to endure made them "tender," made them seek consolation, and thus turned them toward God and piety. Mather also thought that women had more opportunity and time to devote to "soul-service" than men had because they were ordinarily at home and had little "Worldly Business." Two decades later, when the Reverend Benjamin Colman praised women for showing "more of the Life & Power of Religion" than men, he discerned similar causes: women's "natural Tenderness of Spirit & Your Retiredness from the Cares & Snares of the World; so more especially in Your Multiplied Sorrows the curse pronounc'd upon our first Mother Eve, turn'd into the greatest blessing to Your Souls." Writers later in the eighteenth century dropped the references to Mother Eve and focused instead on the religious inclination "naturally" present in female temperament. In the British work *A Father's Legacy to his Daughters*, which was widely reprinted in New England after 1775, Dr. John Gregory maintained that women were more "susceptible" to religion because of their "superior delicacy," "modesty," "natural softness and sensibility of . . . dispositions," and "natural warmth of . . . imagination." (Men, he assumed naturally had harder hearts and stronger passions, and were more dissolute and resistant to religious appeal because of the greater freedom they enjoyed.) Gregory also thought that women needed the consolations of religion, since they suffered great difficulties in life yet could "not plunge into business, or dissipate [them]selves in pleasure and riot" (as men might) for diversion. An influential British Evangelical named Thomas Gisborne made a similar appraisal of women's religious inclinations at the turn of the century, giving more weight, however, to women's distress and fear in childbirth as motivations of their piety.[3]

By the early nineteenth century New England ministers took for granted that women were the majority among Christians. They had assimilated the eighteenth-century argument that "women are happily formed for religion" by means of their "natural endowments" of sensibility, delicacy, imagination, and sympathy.[4] It testified how far New England Protestantism had become a matter of "the heart" rather than "the head" between the seventeenth and the nineteenth century—just as it had become a religion chiefly of women rather than men—that such characteristics manifested a "religious" temperament.[5] Recalling Christ's blessing of the meek and merciful, the Reverend Joseph Buckminster asked a Boston women's organization in 1810 if it was "surprising, that the most fond and faithful votaries of such a religion should be found among a sex, destined by their very constitution, to the exercise of the passive, the quiet, the secret, the gentle and humble virtues?" Men, the "self-styled lords of Creation," pursued wealth, politics or pleasure, but "the dependent, solitary female" sought God. Because of their softheartedness women were attuned to Christianity, Buckminster thought, and they appreciated Christianity because it valued domestic life. He summed up dramatically, "I believe that if Christianity should be compelled to flee from the mansions of the great, the academies of the philosophers, the halls of legislators, or the throng of busy men, we should find her last and purest retreat with woman at the fireside; her last altar would be the female heart; her last audience would be the children gathered around the knees of a mother; her last sacrifice, the secret prayer, escaping in silence from her lips, and heard perhaps only at the throne of God."[6] Christianity was essentially female, his pronouns revealed.

Buckminster and his colleagues developed a power rationale for women's special obligations to Christianity. They reasoned that women's devotion to the religion only fair recompense for the gospel's service in elevating them to their "proper" rank. Only Christianity, they claimed, made "men willing to treat females as equals, and in some respects, as superiors"; only Christianity "exalt[ed] woman to an equal rank with man in all the felicities of the soul, in all the advantages of religious attainment all the prospects and hopes of immortality"; only Christianity redeemed human nature from the base passions taught reverence for domestic relations.[7] Drawing comparisons from history and from other cultures (readily at hand because of the foreign-mission movement), ministers affirmed that New England women owed their social rank to the progress of Christian civilization. This was an omnipresent theme.[8]

Contrasts between the condition of women in New England and in the countries to which missionaries traveled made it plausible that the Christian gospel had "civilized" men's attitudes to women. To appeal to a female charitable society for funds in 1829, the male trustees of the New Hampshire mission society asserted that "heathen" women were "ignorant—degraded—oppressed—enslaved. They are never treated by the other sex as companions and equals. They are in a great measure outcasts from society. They are made to minister to the *pleasures* of man; they are made to do the *work* of men; but, admitted to the enjoyment of equal rights, and raised to the respectability and happiness of free and honourable social intercourse, they are not." New Hampshire women by contrast were respected and free, and had access to knowledge.[9] Rebeccah Lee, wife of the pastor in Marlborough, Connecticut, urged this point of view on the members of several female societies there. "To the Christian religion we owe the rank we hold in society, and we should feel our obligations," she declared.

> It is that, which prevents our being treated like beasts of burden—which secures us the honourable privilege of human companionship in social life, and raises us in the domestic relations to the elevated stations of wives and mothers. Only seriously reflect upon the state of our sex, in those regions of the globe unvisited and unblessed with the light of Christianity; we see them degraded to a level with the brutes, and shut out from the society of lordly *man*; as if they were made by their Creator, not as the companions, but as the slaves and drudges of domineering masters. . . . Let each one then ask herself, how much do I owe?[10]

The "feminization" of Protestantism in the early nineteenth century was conspicuous.[11] Women flocked into churches and church-related organizations, repopulating religious institutions. Female converts in the New England Great Awakening between 1798 and 1826 (before the Methodist impact) outnumbered males by three to two.[12] Women's prayer groups, charitable institutions, missionary and education societies, Sabbath School organizations, and moral reform and maternal associations all multiplied phenomenally after 1800, and all of these had religious motives. Women

thus exercised as fully as men the American penchant for voluntary association noted by Tocqueville in the 1830s, but women's associations before 1835 were *all* allied with the church, whereas men's also expressed a variety of secular, civic, political, and vocational concerns.[13]

This flowering of women's associational activities was part of the revival movement of the early nineteenth century in which Protestants tried to counteract religious indifference, rationalism, and Catholicism and to create an enduring and moral social order. Ministers were joined by lay persons, often (not always) of wealthy and conservative background, in giving the Awakening its momentum. They interpreted the aftermath of the French Revolution in the 1790s as proof of the dangers of a "godless" society, and feared that the American republic, with its growing urban populations, its Catholic immigrants, its Western inhabitants far from New England culture and clergy, might fall victim to similar "godless" influence. They saw religious education not only as a means to inculcate true faith but as a route to salvation on this earth, since it could teach the restraints demanded for an orderly society. The lay activities of the revival intended education, religious conversion, and the reformation of individual character whether they took the form of distributing bibles and tracts among the urban poor and Western frontier residents, raising money to train ministers or missionaries to evangelize the unchurched, setting up Sabbath schools for children to begin the business of Christian training early, or other myriad forms.[14]

Ministers' religious and denominational aims, conservatives' manipulation of religious benevolence for social control, humanitarians' perceptions of the needs of the poor, and women's orientation toward religious and gender-group expression all contributed to the proliferation of Christian women's societies. Since the prayer meetings called during religious revivals were often sex-segregated, they could serve as prototypes of religious organizations exclusively for women. The British Evangelical movement also supplied explicit models of charitable and humanitarian efforts by women.[15] These several motives and predispositions help to explain the extraordinarily swift rise and geographical dispersion of women's religious benevolent associations. Under the combined forces of local ministers, agents of national benevolent organizations, and individual women who took to heart their obligations, female religious and charitable societies were established in all the larger cities of New England shortly after the turn of the century—in Middlebury and Montpelier, Concord and Portsmouth, Portland and Eastport, Providence and Newport, Hartford and New Haven, Boston, Salem, and Newburyport. Small towns in Vermont such as Jericho Center, Danville, Cornwall, Thetford, and Castleton had female religious and missionary societies before 1816. Scores of religious charitable societies were formed among New Hampshire women in rural towns between 1804 and 1814. With the encouragement of agents of the New Hampshire Bible Society, women founded local affiliates in 138 towns between 1820 and 1828. Women belonged to dozens of female charitable societies and "education" societies (which raised funds to educate ministers) in Connecticut towns by 1815; and societies for prayer, for propagation of the gospel, for missionary and charitable purposes were even more numerous in Massachusetts. The Boston Female Society for Missionary Purposes corresponded with 109 similar societies in 1817–1818.[16]

Why did women support religion so faithfully? Perhaps Cotton Mather's and Benjamin Colman's reasoning deserves some credence. The specter of death in childbirth repeatedly forced women to think on the state of their souls. And women's domestic occupations may have

diverted them from piety less than the "snares" of the world did men; besides, ministers and pious women made every effort to conflate domestic values with religious values. Domestic occupations offered women little likelihood of finding a set of values and symbols to rival the ones proposed by evangelical Christianity. For women at home in New England society, Christian belief had a self-perpetuating force that was not likely to be disrupted by experience that would provide alternative and equally satisfying explanations.[17] Yet women whose occupations took them outside the home, and single women generally, were prominent in the female religious community. Early factory workers participated in revivals, as Catherine Sedgwick, a Unitarian opposed to evangelical fervor, reported to her brother in 1833: "We have had the religious agitators among us lately—They have produced some effect on the factory girls & such light & combustible materials."[18] Perhaps the eighteenth-century reasoning about women's temperament suiting them for Christian faith had a deeper truth. Characteristics expected in women and in Christians—those of the "tender heart"—increasingly coincided during the eighteenth century, because women supported Christianity more consistently than men, and became ministers' major constituency.[19] By the early nineteenth century, the clergy claimed that women supported (or should support) Christianity because it was in the interest of their sex to do so; that reassured the faithful, whether or not it accurately described their motives.

It is less than satisfying, however, to attribute New England women's religiosity to their mortal risks in childbirth or to a socialization process that inculcated domestic piety and "Christian" temperament in them. Skeptics at the time suggested other reasons. Harriet Martineau, a witty and politically astute British visitor who criticized hypocrisies in American women's expected roles, noticed that "in New England, a vast deal of [women's] time is spent in attending preachings, and other religious meetings: and in paying visits, for religious purposes, to the poor and sorrowful." She even found it plausible "that they could not exist without religion," but considered that an unhealthy circumstance. Women were "driven back upon religion as a resource against vacuity," in her view.[20]

(Although Martineau seems to have meant vacuity of *mind* rather than *time*, some evidence suggests that women without pressing demands on their time were indeed the *most* devoted to religion. Single women or childless wives not responsible for the whole of their own support were the most likely to record their religious musings unfailingly. Abigail Brackett Lyman began a journal of that sort in her teens when she made a public profession of faith, and continued, as she reflected several years later, "to inscribe nothing in my journal but devotional exercises from the period above-mentioned till some time after my marriage when cares increasing & being obliged to entertain considerable company I found it impossible to continue this laudable practice." Another ardent convert remarked plaintively, while she was still single, "Most of my associates were settled in life but I saw that those who had been zealous and devoted before their marriage had mostly declined in piety when pressed with the domestic cares of a family. I said to myself Why is it so? It cannot be because there is anything in that state subversive of piety for it is of Divine appointments."[21]

Martineau's insight was still more piercing. She said women "pursue[d] religion as an occupation" because they were constrained from exercising their full range of moral, intellectual, and physical powers in other ways. With an extension of her allusion religious activities can be seen as a means used by New England women to define self and find community, two functions that worldly occupations more likely performed for men. Traditionally, of course, religion had enlightened individuals of both sexes about their identity and placed them in a like-minded community; but women's particular needs and the configuration of religious institutions at this time enhanced those social functions. In an era when Protestantism was a "crusade," when ministers presented evangelical Christianity as embattled and yet triumphant, religious affiliation announced one's identity and purpose. "I made religion the principal business of my life," Nancy Thompson summarized the effect of her conversion at nineteen. Abigail Lyman exhorted herself in 1800 (before the Second Great Awakening had progressed widely) "to Live up to the Professions of Religion I had made—to dare to be singular in this day when iniquity abounds."[22]

Religion stretched before the convert a lifetime of purposeful struggle holding out heartening rewards. It provided a way to order one's life and priorities. The evangelical theology of the early nineteenth century made that process of ordering amenable to personal choice. "The salvation of our precious souls is not to be effected independent of our exertions," Lyman wrote in her journal, "—we are free agents and as such should work out our salvation with fear and trembling. . . . We may believe and rely on the faith of Revelation—and form our actions and tempers by its pure and perfect precepts—or we may resist the truth—appose [sic] its influence & harden our hearts in sin—either the one or the other all are constantly doing." Yet an individual made the religious choice in submission to God's will rather than through personal initiative. The morphology of religious conversion echoed women's expected self-resignation and submissiveness while it offered enormously satisfying assurance to converts. Nancy Meriam, a devout young woman of Oxford, Massachusetts, recorded in her religious notes of 1815, "There is sweetness in committing ourselves to God which the world knows nothing of. The idea that I am intirely [sic] in the hands of God fills my mind with a secret pleasure which I cannot describe."[23]

Yet religious identity also allowed women to assert themselves, both in private and in public ways. It enabled them to rely on an authority beyond the world of men and provided a crucial support to those who stepped beyond accepted bounds—reformers, for example. Women dissenters from Ann Hutchinson to Sarah Grimke displayed the subversive potential of religious belief. Religious faith also allowed women a sort of holy selfishness, or self-absorption, the result of the self-examination intrinsic to the Calvinist tradition. In contrast to the self-abnegation required of women in their domestic vocation, religious commitment required attention to one's own thoughts, actions, and prospects. By recording their religious meditations women expressed their literacy and rising self-consciousness in a sanctioned mode. Vigilance for their souls and their conformity to God's requirements compelled them to scrutinize their lives. And the more distinctly Christianity appeared a preserve of *female* values, the more legitimate (and likely) it became for religious women to scrutinize their gender-role. If the popular sales of the published memoirs of female missionaries are any guide, that model of religious commitment, which proposed a submission of self that was simultaneously a pronounced form of self-assertion, had wide appeal. Time and again women who made note of little reading except the Bible read the memoirs of Mrs. Newell, missionary to Burma (1814), and responded perhaps as a young matron of Woodmont, Connecticut, did: "O that I could feel as she did . . ., it appears to me as though I had ought to feel willing to contribute freely to spread the gospel among the heathen."[24]

No other avenue of self-expression besides religion at once offered women social approbation, the encouragement of male leaders (ministers), and, most important, the community of their peers. Conversion and church membership in the era of the Second Great Awakening implied joining a community of Christians. As historians have noted, the individual convert in the revival entered "a community of belief in which he [or she] was encouraged to make a decision that would be a positive organizing principle for his [or her] own life." During these decades the sacramental dimension of the church faded in the light of a new conception, "a voluntary association of explicitly convinced Christians for the purpose of mutual edification in the worship of God and the propagandization of the Christian faith as the group defined it." Because the vigor of religion had sunk during the late eighteenth century, the "awakened" Christian community defined itself to an unusual extent by its adversary and evangelical relation to the outside world, as well as by its intramural purposes. "He that is not with us said the Saviour is against us," Abigail reiterated.[25]

Being a Christian in this period meant becoming a member of a voluntary community not only in a psychological but in a literal sense, for piety implied group evangelical activity. Associative activity flowed naturally from church membership. The motive to advance personal piety and the cause of Christianity, together with the desire to act cooperatively, and (often) the local minister's support, influenced women to form associations even before they had specific aims. The process of organization of the Female Religious and Cent Society in Jericho Center, Vermont, seems to have been typical. In 1805 a number of women joined together because they wished to "do good" and aid the cause of religion, but they did not know what path to take. They began meeting for prayer. (This was the simplest form religious association took, and probably the most widespread, but also the most difficult to find record of.[26]) With their minister's assistance they formed a society and began to raise money for the missionary movement. The articles of their society proclaimed in 1806 that they would meet fortnightly "for social prayer and praise and religious instruction and edification." They also pledged mutual support and group intimacy, resolving that "all persons attending the meeting shall conduct themselves with seriousness and solemnity dureing [sic] the Exercises nor shall an Illiberal remark be made respecting the performance of any of the members, neither shall they report abroad any of the transactions of the society to the prejudice of any of its members." The society prospered. In 1816, when it joined with a Young Ladies' Society that had been formed in 1812 under another minister's guidance, and founded the Female Cent Society of Jericho, the new group had seventy members.[27]

Women's diaries reveal the efforts, and the high esteem, given to religious associations. As a young matron in Greenfield, Massachusetts, in 1815 Sarah Ripley Stearns joined a group of "youthful females" who hoped to improve themselves in piety. The same year she helped found a female charitable society, with the goal of aiding destitute children to attend school and church. She noted when the "band of associated females" met at her house, and remarked that their "Benevolent Institution" was one of her chief sources of enjoyment. In 1816 she endeavored to found a maternal association, a "Juvenile Institution," and a "heathen school society." She carried on these activities during the years in which she bore three children, despite her laments that household cares left her little time for diary writing, pious reading, or church attendance.[28]

Sarah Connell Ayer of Maine involved herself even more thoroughly. Although her youth had been frivolous, the deaths of four infants during her first five years of marriage turned her increasingly to religion and its community of consolation. (The deaths of children, in these years, may have given women more powerful motivation toward religiosity then ever did fears of their own mortality in childbirth.) By the time Sarah Ayer was twenty-four she saw nothing more pleasant "than to spend an evening in conversation with a few pious friends." In early 1816 she belonged to a female missionary society, prayer meeting, and donation society in Portland, and was devoted to her orthodox Congregationalist minister. After giving birth to two children who survived, she joined the Maternal Association and found its meetings "profitable." In 1822 her husband's appointment as surveyor of the port induced the family to move to Eastport. There Mrs. Ayer found the Congregationalist minister too Unitarian for her taste, and missed her Portland friends greatly. "We loved to meet together, to talk of Heaven as our final home, Christ as our Saviour; we shared each others joys and sorrows, and found the one heightened and the other alleviated by sympathy. Ah! how prone am I to murmur when things go contrary to my own inclinations," she wrote in her diary. Soon, however, she reestablished comparable activities in Eastport. At first she discovered a compatible community among the Baptists, and then worked with a small group of orthodox Congregationalists—seventeen women and three men—to set up a church to her preference. By the late 1820s she participated in a maternal association, a female prayer society, a benevolent society, and Sabbath School class.[29]

The ease with which women moved among evangelical societies, and participated in several at once, suggests that associating under the ideological aegis of evangelical Christianity mattered more to them than the specific goals of any one group. The founding members of the Female Religious Biographical and Reading Society (or "Berean Circle") associated in 1826 because they were "convinced of the importance and utility of the benevolent associations of the present day, and wish[ed] to unite our efforts in the same worthy objects, and also desir[ed] to improve and impress our own minds by obtaining religious instruction."[30] The occurrence of such associations in virtually every Protestant church implied that professing faith had come to include participating in group activity. Whether local ministers, state organizations, or pious individuals launched them, such associations created peer groups which became part of their members' definition of Christian piety.

The chosen Christian community also entered into a woman's self-definition. Rachel Willard Stearns, who set herself off from her Congregational family by converting to Methodism, exemplified that effect in a pronounced way. She appreciated the Methodist small-group meetings, she said, because "if we have been gay or trifling, or anger or revenge have had a place in our hearts, we do not wish to go, if we stay away, then the others will think there is something wrong. . . . I am thankful that I have placed myself under the watch-care and discipline of a church, where when I do wrong they will tell me of it. . . ."[31] Stearns's Methodism brought her to an especially intense religious self-concept; but religion performed an analogous social function for women in traditional denominations.

Within their Christian peer groups women examined their own behavior, weighed the balance between self and sacrifice in their lives, and sought appropriate models. In October 1828 the Berean Circle discussed the question, "Can an individual who is more strongly activated by selfish motives than by a view to the glory of God be a Christian?" They recorded their conclusions: "If their *habitual prevailing* motives are selfish they cannot; for the most important point in conversion is the change from selfishness to benevolence. We are not required to be so disinterested as to leave

our own *chief* happiness out of view. This subject led to much interesting conversation." Several years later the group was engaged in similar topics, pursuing such questions as "Is an ungoverned temper, proof of an unsanctified heart?" Women's remarks in diaries suggest unanimously the deep satisfaction derived from occasions for discussion. One recorded that her meeting provided "much pleasure," another that it was "instructive and entertaining," a third that "I returned much refreshed in spirit."[32]

A shift in ministers' views also encouraged women's religious activities. The seventeenth-century clergy had tended to stress Eve's legacy, and hence to focus on woman being the "first in transgression." During the eighteenth century, ministers turned their attention from Eve to other promising models of female character in the Bible, in order to justify the idea that women could bear the standard of the religious community.[33] From the 1790s to the 1820s ministers of several denominations endorsed the view that women were of conscientious and prudent character, especially suited to religion. Drawing often on the text of Proverbs 31, they showed the model Christian woman to be a modest and faithful wife, an industrious and benevolent community member, and an efficient housekeeper who did not neglect the refinements of life. Fervently they described how pious women could influence others in the community and in their own families. From Baptists to Unitarians, clergymen agreed that family religion communicated from parents to children was the natural, divinely approved, most effective means of reproducing true Christian character.[34] By the pastors' own admission, mothers had more impact on children in this regard than fathers did. The reasoning of a Wolfborough, New Hampshire, Sabbath School convention reiterated the pervasive idea that mothers (and by extension, all women) propagated religion best. They resolved in 1834: "Whereas the influence of females on little children ordinarily determines their future character and eternal destiny, and as it has been most effectually exerted in bringing them to Christ, therefore, *Resolved*, that it is the sacred duty of all females to use every effort to promote the cause of Sabbath Schools."[35]

No other public institution spoke to women and cultivated their loyalty so assiduously as the churches did. Quickened by religious anxiety and self-interest, the clergy gave their formulations of women's roles unusual force. They pinned on women's domestic occupation and influence their own best hopes. Their portrayal of women's roles grew in persuasive power because it overlapped with republican commonplaces about the need for virtuous citizens for a successful republic. It gained intensity because it intersected with new interest in early childhood learning. Ministers declared repeatedly that women's pious influence was not only appropriate to them but crucial for society. "We look to you, ladies," said Joseph Buckminster, "to raise the standard of character in our own sex; we look to you, to guard and fortify those barriers, which still exist in society, against the encroachments of impudence and licentiousness. We look to you for the continuance of domestick purity, for the revival of domestick religion, for the increase of our charities, and the support of what remains of religion in our private habits and publick institutions."[36]

Ministers addressed women as a sex and, at the same time, as an interest group in the polity that had special civil and social responsibilities and special powers to defend its interests. "I address you as a class," said a Boston pastor to the mothers of the Mount Vernon Maternal Association, "because Your duties and responsibilities are peculiar."[37] Ministers viewed women's sex-role as a social role, in other words. It meant no lessening of women's consciousness of the responsibilities borne to them by gender

that the interests and obligations proposed to them were the ministers own interests, and that the latter looked ahead to a rising generation of sons (the *men* who would lead society). Under ministers' guidance women could conclude that their sex shared not simply a biological but a social purpose. They were entrusted with the morals and faith of the next generation. According to prevailing conceptions of republican virtue, this was a task having political impact.[38]

Maternal and moral reform societies—the two wings (as it were) of the women's religious-voluntary movement—illustrated vividly how women took to heart the social role proposed by ministers. Both kinds of societies institutionalized the idea that women's pious influence, especially as exerted over their own children, could reform the world.

Maternal associations have left few traces because they were organized locally only (with no state or national superstructure) and had no official organ of communication.[39] They were grass-roots responses to the contemporary cultural and religious elevation of the mother's role. Their members felt obliged to prepare themselves to guide their children properly, in order to raise a generation of Christians and thus accomplish a moral reformation. The appearance of such associations suggests how the perception of motherhood as a social role as well as a personal role led women to seek supportive peer groups. The women who formed the Dorchester Maternal Association in Massachusetts in 1816 did so because they were "aware of our highly responsible situation as Mothers & as professing Christians" and wished to "commend our dear offspring" to God. They considered it each member's duty to pray and to read appropriate works, to pray with her children, and "to suggest to her sister members such hints as her own experience may furnish or circumstances seem to render necessary."[40] In

Portland, Maine, mothers created in 1815 a widely copied format for a maternal association, providing for election of officers, monthly meetings for reading and discussion, and attendance at every third meeting of the members' daughters between age three and sixteen, and sons between three and fourteen.[41]

The spate of evangelically-oriented child-rearing books during the 1830s seems to have encouraged mothers to give institutional form to their developing consciousness, and maternal associations multiplied, John S. C. Abbott's *The Mother at Home* became a much-used part of the library of the Maternal Association of Jericho Center, Vermont, a group formed in 1833 by mothers "deeply impressed with the importance of bringing up children in the nurture and admonition of the Lord," who associate[d] for the purpose of devising and adopting such measures, as may seem best calculated to assist us in the performance of this duty." Women who created maternal associations seemed burdened with the weight of responsibility in motherhood as well as impressed by its power. Mary Hurlbut, at twenty-eight the mother of four children, described the formation of her association in New London, Connecticut, in 1833: "11 mothers who feeling the greatness of their responsibilities & the need of Almighty aid, meet together unitedly to plead for their Children & for grace & strength to help—O that the Lord would bless this little band of sisters." Mothers in Hamilton, Massachusetts, began a maternal association in 1833 because "the immense influence we were exerting upon our beloved children, & that that influence would be felt through eternity, pressed upon our consciences." Every two weeks they met to discuss such topics as how "to train up our children for the service of the church" and "the best methods of instilling into our children habits of *Self-Denial*." The aim and the ambiance of the meetings are evoked in a member's intentions "that in order to make their meetings profitable to ourselves, there should be perfect and unreserved freedom & that the ladies should feel so much confidence in each other as to express their feelings and opinions without reserve—that our object in associating ourselves was mutual benefit & instruction & this could not be effected unless the sentiments of each other were elicited."[42]

Women who joined maternal associations thus asserted their formative power over their children's lives, took up evangelical goals, and complemented the private job of child rearing by approaching their common occupation cooperatively with their peers. Women joined moral reform societies to accomplish different immediate aims, but with similar reasoning. Moral reform societies intended to eliminate the sin of "licentiousness," which appeared in the permitted lust of men and the prostitution of women. The Boston Female Society for Missionary Purposes was probably the earliest to adopt such goals, in 1817. The Boston Female Moral Reform Society and others similarly titled were formed for that purpose in the 1830s. These groups had four main tactics. Two were direct: to reform and resurrect "fallen" women, and to publicize and ostracize men who visited prostitutes. Two were long-term, preventive, moral education measures: to kindle self-respect in women and to bring up both sexes in the next generation to uphold chastity and marital fidelity. Twenty-nine local societies enlisted as auxiliaries when the Boston society became the "New England" Female Moral Reform Society in 1838, and scores more in New England towns affiliated with the New York organization.[43]

Like maternal associations, moral reform societies focused women's energies on the family arena in order to solve social problems. The Boston society's rhetoric breathed fire: "Our mothers, our sisters, our daughters are sacrificed by the thousands every year on the altar of sin, and who are the agents in this work of destruction? Why, our fathers, our brothers, and our sons." But the moral reformers' aim took them outside the family. It also gave them a unique sexual perspective on sin. Since they believed that men practiced licentiousness, and women suffered it, they were sensitive to prevailing sexual injustice. They opposed the double standard of sexual morality as much as they opposed licentiousness, resolving "to make the impure man lose his character as effectually as the impure woman," urging the virtuous to "esteem the licentious man as little as they do the licentious woman," and further insisting that "this work must begin with the ladies. They are the injured and they must rise and assert their rights."[44]

Although it portrayed women as sacrificial victims to male lust, the language of moral reform evoked women's power; power to avenge, power to control and reform. The visiting committee of the Boston Female Moral Reform Society described the city's prostitutes as "abandoned girls, who having been ruined themselves by the treachery and depravity of man, have sworn to glut their vengeance by dragging to their own depths in guilt and infamy such young men as might otherwise have been the flower and stamina of our country."[45] In moral reform activities women took up (literally with a vengeance) the power that ministers had for decades told them they possessed. Ministers taught that women had beneficial influence on men's habits; hence the moral reformers thought it possible to eliminate male lust, and devised a program to end licentiousness by ostracizing "impure" men. Ministers emphasized that women's power centered in their influence over their children; hence the moral reformers vowed to stop prostitution by rearing self-controlled children. Ministers told women that they had a special obligation to uphold Christianity and oppose sin, and also that women were especially suited to help one another; hence

moral reformers believed that their collective opposition to sexual exploitation was valiant Christian service.

In taking up these sexually designated powers and duties moral reformers moved toward asserting women's "rights." They disavowed false delicacy, and urged women to acquaint themselves with human anatomy and physiology in order to understand their sexual nature and instruct their children scientifically.[46] Their ideology encouraged women's self-esteem, denied female inferiority outright, and disapproved women's subservience to men's whims and wishes. In an address to the society in Worcester, Massachusetts, Mary Ann Brown counseled every young woman to "consider [her]self *inferior by nature to no man*," and to marry no one but a principled man who would "receive her as *an equal and be willing that she shall stand upon the broad platform of human rights, free and untrammeled, and accountable only to her God.*"[47] As far as was possible moral reform societies put into action and ideology the predisposition of evangelical associations to organize women and provoke their gender-group consciousness.

From the simplest prayer group, through "cent" and "mite" societies, education and missionary support groups to maternal and moral reform societies, women's religious voluntary associations had a dual potential: to encourage women's independence and self-definition within a supportive community, or to accommodate them to a limited, clerically defined role. Like women's religious involvement generally, therefore, they had an ambiguous effect on women's autonomy and status. Religious voluntary associations provided women with a community of peers outside the family, without contravening the importance of the family. For those who had to move around the country—more often for their fathers' or husbands' reasons than their own—the personal and national implications of these cooperative endeavors transferred easily. Women softened the shock of displacement and maintained a continuing sense of belonging to a female Christian community by finding or re-creating associations like the ones they had left, as Sarah Connell Ayer did. Such evangelical activity grouped women with one another, obviously, and put women's interests and capabilities in a category different from men's. It reaffirmed members' shared womanhood while giving each one perspective on her own life. She could compare her experience with her peers, with the poor widows or female orphans or the "heathen" whom they hoped to benefit, or even with the ministers and young men whom the women's "mites" would educate. Since it illustrated different kinds and degrees of female subordination—and disclosed the *social* as well as the "natural" construction of women's roles— that comparison might lead some women to consider changes in their own position. Furthermore, in their associations women wrote and debated and amended constitutions, elected officers, raised and allotted funds, voted on issues, solicited and organized new members; in other words, they familiarized themselves with the processes of representative government in an all-female environment, while they were prevented from it in the male political system.

Did women who contributed their "mites" to missionary funds mark out new social boundaries for themselves, or become pawns of manipulative ministers and conservative laymen? Were women who united for religious self-improvement conforming more than graciously to their prescribed roles? Did anxious mothers in maternal associations forge new social power or resign themselves to the domestic fireside? Lucy Stone, who became an early and ardent supporter of the women's rights movement, and refused to have the word *obey* in her marriage contract or give up her

own name for her husband's, quickly rebelled against the self-sacrifice implicit in women's evangelical societies. While she was sewing for an education society it occurred to her "how absurd it was for her to be working to help educate a student who could earn more money toward his own education in a week, by teaching, than she could earn in a month; and she left the shirt unfinished and hoped that no one would ever complete it."[48] Most women, however, did not move on from evangelical societies to advocate equal education, equal pay, and political rights for women.[49] Church-related voluntary associations commanded a much larger membership through the nineteenth century than did the women's rights movement proper. Powerful restraints inhered in the very concerns that brought women into evangelical association: religious conviction and family role. Because they brought women together on the basis of religious and familial definitions, voluntary societies could hinder the prospect of further change, especially if they diverted women from and compensated them for their isolation and subordination, and, offered assurances of usefulness and sisterly companionship.

Women's religious associationism cannot be neatly classified either as a protofeminist or, on the contrary, as a crypto-conservative or merely compensatory phenomenon. It preserved conventional appearances but gave them a new direction. Evangelical activity fostered women's emergence as social actors whose roles were based on female responsibilities rather than on human rights. While evoking women's group-consciousness and sense of sex-identified social purpose—both of which were requisite before any woman would perceive her sex-oppression—evangelical associationism directly served to elucidate the doctrine of woman's sphere, a "different but equal" doctrine.

Ministers' addresses to women turned in the same direction. Positive appeals to women to contribute to society with benevolent works, pious influence, and child nurture dominated ministers' attitudes from 1790 to 1820, but in the next decades their sermons more often sprang from negative tenets, such as Gardiner Spring's of 1825 that "there are spheres for which a female is not fitted, and from which the God of nature has proscribed her."[50] Of course even their calls for women's social participation had implied this kind of constraint, for ministers defined women primarily as members of families and then, secondarily, as individuals in society. Women's contribution through domesticity was not a possible or preferred option but the only permissible role. Even ministers' promises of women's social power contained implicit threats about their limitations.

Between 1790 and 1820, however, ministers had seemed more interested in the promise. Their only explicit prohibitions pertained to clerical prerogatives. The Reverend Walter Harris, a Congregationalist of New Hampshire, explained in 1814 that women could considerably assist and advance the preaching of the Gospel, but "God has made known, that it is his will that females should not be public teachers of religion, nor take an active part in the government of his church on earth." As Methodist evangelists adopted the unorthodox tactic of encouraging women to pray aloud in public, ministers of opposing denominations strengthened their Prohibition against women's preaching. George Keely, a Baptist, protested in 1819, "that woman appears to me lost to modesty and prudence, who has boldness enough to teach or exhort where men are present. If she were a relative of mine, I should request her to change her name and remove to a distance where her connections were not known."[51]

These strictures forboded a hardening of boundaries in ministers' appraisal of the social role of women. Without abandoning their earlier estimate of woman's influence ministers clarified its limitations. Rather than the book of Proverbs, they chose texts from Titus and Paul, requiring women to be "keepers at home," and "silent in the churches." The Reverend Joseph Richardson of Hingham, Massachusetts, interpreted the text of Titus for the women there in 1832, advising them, "the world concedes to you the honor of exerting an influence, all but divine; but an influence you lose the power to exert, the moment you depart from the sphere and delicacy of your proper character."[52]

Ministers used the concept of "woman's sphere" to esteem female importance while containing it. In their sermons of the 1830s the theme of order in family and society took precedence, vividly emphasizing the necessity for women to be subordinate to and dependent on their husbands.[53] Clergymen focused on woman's place their own alarm at changing social patterns. The widespread tendency toward erosion of accustomed authority and deference made the fulfillment of women's promised social importance problematic. Ministers warned that women who betrayed their subordinate place in the family would destroy themselves. Inverting their reasoning about Christianity's special benefit to women, they threatened that women would suffer more than men if the Christian social order dissolved. Should "the wife who possesses a mind of superior cultivation and power to her husbands . . . be in subjection to his authority?" asked Richardson, and answered, "yes, because this is conformable to the general order God has established. Many private citizens may possess minds of powers and gifts superior to those of riders and magistrates, to whose authority it is their duty to submit. Subordination to principles and laws of order is absolutely essential to the existence of the social state. Break up the order of the social state and woman must become the most abject and helpless of all slaves."[54]

Evangelical religion thus imparted a twofold message and possibility to women in these years, especially since its clerical guides needed both to elevate women as religion's supporters and yet (in order to sustain social stability, as they saw it) to reaffirm women's subordination to men. In most ministers' interpretation evangelical Christianity confined women to pious self-expression, sex-specific duties, and subjection to men. But by promoting women in activities deemed appropriate for their sex and "sphere" evangelical religion nourished the formation of a female community that served them as both a resource and a resort outside the family. And it endowed women with vital identity and purpose that could be confirmed among their peers.

NOTES

1. Jonathan Stearns, *Female Influence, and the True Christian Mode of its Exercise: A Discourse delivered in the 1st Presbyterian Church in Newburyport, July 30, 1837* (Newburyport: John G. Tilton, 1837), p. 11. He had to qualify his assertion with "almost," I assume, in order to encourage male church-goers and also to account for the exclusion of women from the ministry.
2. Women's majority did not increase in a linear fashion from the seventeenth to the nineteenth centuries because during the Great Awakening of the 1740s proportionally more men converted than during nonrevival years. On the sex ratio among church members during the seventeenth century see Edmund S. Morgan, "New England Puritanism: Another Approach," *WMQ* 3d ser., 18 (1961):236–242; Darrett Rutman, "God's Bridge Falling Down—'Another Approach' to New England Puritanism Assayed," *WMQ* 3d ser., 19 (1962):408–421; on the early eighteenth century see Cedric Cowing, "Sex and Preaching in the "Great Awakening," *AQ* 20 (1968):625–634; J. Bumsted, "Religion, Finance and Democracy in Massachusetts: The Town of Norton as a Case Study," *JAH* 57 (1971):817–831; James Walsh, "The Great Awakening in the First Congregational Church of Woodbury, Connecticut, *WMQ* 3d ser., 28 (1971):543–552; Gerald F. Moran, "Conditions of Religious Conversion in the First Society of Norwich, Connecticut, 1718–1744," *JSH* 5 (1972):331–343; Philip J. Greven, Jr., "Youth, Maturity, and Religious Conversion: A Note on the Ages of Converts in Andover, Massachusetts, 1711–1749," *Essex Institute Historical Collections* (April 1972):119–134; on the early nineteenth century see Nancy F. Cott, "Young Women in the Second Great Awakening," *FS* 3 (1975):15–29; Donald Mathews, "The Second Great Awakening as an Organizing Process," *AQ* 21 (1969), esp. p. 42; Whitney R. Cross, *The Burned-Over District* (New York: Harper Torchbooks, 1965), esp. pp. 84–89; and Barbara Welter, "The Feminization of Religion in Nineteenth-Century America," in Mary Hartman and Lois Banner, eds., *Clio's Consciousness Raised* (New York: Harper Torchbooks, 1973).
3. Cotton Mather, "Ornaments for the Daughters of Zion" (Cambridge, Mass., 1692), pp. 44–45; Benjamin Colman, *The Duty and Honour of Aged Women* (Boston, 1711) pp. ii–iii; Dr. John Gregory, *A Father's Legacy to his Daughters* (London: John Sharpe, 1822), pp. 11–12; Thomas Gisborne, *An Enquiry into the Duties of the Female Sex* (London, reprinted Philadelphia: James Humphreys, 1798), pp. 182–183. I cite these English works because of the evidence that they were read in New England; on this, see Nancy F. Cott, "In the Bonds of Womanhood: Perspectives on Female Experience and Consciousness in New England, 1780–1830" (Ph.D. diss., Brandeis University, 1974), pp. 225–227.
4. Quotation from Daniel Chaplin. *A Discourse Delivered before the Charitable Female Society in Groton [Massachusetts], October 19, 1814* (Andover, Mass., 1814), p. 9.
   When I speak of "New England ministers' views" in what follows, my opinions primarily derive from my reading of 65 sermons concerning or addressed to women between 1792 and 1837, of which 54 were written between 1800 and 1820, and 57 were delivered to meetings of female associations in New England towns and cities. The denomination best

represented were the Trinitarian Congregationalists, Presbyterians, Episcopalians, Baptists, and others together gave the rest. Denominational differences did not perceptibly vary ministers' assessments of women's roles, however. But note that I am not dealing here with the Methodist contribution or the influence of Charles G. Finney's revivalism, which occurred chiefly after 1835 in New England. I have presented the ministers' views in greater detail in "In the Bonds of Womanhood," chap. 3. A complete listing of the sermons appears at the end of this book.

5. Jonathan Edwards was, of course, a central figure in this transformation. See Chapter 5, "Sisterhood," esp. note 15.

6. Joseph Buckminster, "A Sermon Preached before the Members of the Boston Female Asylum, September 1810," hand-copied and bound with other printed sermons to the BFA, pp. 7–9, BPL.

7. Chaplin, *A Discourse*, p. 12; Pitt Clarke, *A Discourse Delivered before the Norton Female Christian Association, on . . . June 13, 1818* (Taunton, Mass., 1818), p. 11; Samuel Worcester, *Female Love to Christ* (Salem, Mass., 1809), pp. 12–13.

8. E.g., see Daniel Clark, *The Wise Builder, a Sermon Delivered to the Females of the 1st Parish in Amherst, Mass.* (Boston, 1820), pp. 17–18, 23–24; John Bullard, *A Discourse, delivered at Pepperell, September 19, 1815, before the Charitable Female Society* (Amherst, N.H., 1815), pp. 9–10, Benjamin Wadsworth, *Female Charity an Acceptable Offering . . .* (Andover, Mass., 1817), pp. 27–28; David T. Kimball, *The Obligation and Disposition of Females to Promote Christianity . . .* (Newburyport, 1819), p. 4.

9. *16th Annual Report on the concerns of the Female Cent Institution, New Hampshire* (Concord, N.H., 1829), pp. 3–4 (quotation), 4–6.

10. Mrs. Rebeccah Lee, *An Address, Delivered in Marlborough, Connecticut, September 7, 1831* (Hartford, 1831), p. 4. She also noted, "There is not a town or village in our country, perhaps, where females are not actively engaged in this good cause, and from us much is expected in the present day."

11. The term is Barbara Welter's, in "The Feminization of Religion."

12. See Ebenezer Porter, *Letters on Revivals of Religion* (Andover, Mass.: The Revival Association, 1832); p. 5; and Cott, "Young Women in the Second Great Awakening." Beginning in 1830 Methodist evangelism under Charles G. Finney encouraged women's religious activity, particularly their public praying, more vigorously than other denominations. On the contribution of Methodist practice to Congregational and Presbyterian revival measures in the northeast before Finney, see Richard Carwardine, "The Second Great Awakening in the Urban Centers: An Examination of Methodism and the 'New Measures,'" *JAH* 59 (1972):327–341.

Studies of many individual communities will be necessary before the precise impact of the revivals on the sex ratio among church members can be ascertained. Recent historical research on the Second Great Awakening suggests that the proportion of men among the converts was greater during revival years than ordinary years, but only large enough to reduce the female majority somewhat, not to undermine it. See Mary P. Ryan, "A Woman's Awakening: Revivalist Religion in Utica, New York, 1800–1835," paper delivered at the Third Berkshire Conference on the History of Women, Bryn Mawr, Pa., June 10, 1976, and Paul E. Johnson, "A Shopkeeper's Millennium: Society and Revivals in Rochester, N.Y., 1815–1837" (Ph.D. diss., University of California at Los Angeles, 1975).

13. See Alexis de Tocqueville, *Democracy in America*, ed. Phillips Bradley (New York: Vintage Books, 1945), 1:198–205, 2:114–118, 123–128. Cf. Richard D. Brown, "The Emergence of Voluntary Associations in Massachusetts, 1760–1830," *Journal of Voluntary Action Research* 2 (1973), esp. 68–70.

14. See Clifford S. Griffin, "Religious Benevolence as Social Control, 1815–1860," *MVHR* 44 (1957), esp. 440–442; Charles I. Foster, *An Errand of Mercy: The Evangelical United Front, 1790–1837* (Chapel Hill, N.C.: University of North Carolina Press, 1960). A recent critique by Lois Banner, "Religious Benevolence as Social Control: A Critique of an Interpretation," *JAH* 60 (1973): 23–41, stresses the organizational dynamics of the Protestant denominations and the sincere educational and humanitarian aims of proponents.

15. Merle Curti, "American Philanthropy and the National Character," *AQ* 10 (1958):425. The first female charitable institution in the United States, the Society for the Relief of Poor Widows and Small Children, was founded in 1796 in New York by a newly arrived Scotswoman, Isabella M. Graham, on the model of a London institution for poor relief.

16. The formation of the national benevolent societies, such as the American Bible Society, the American Sabbath School Association, etc., did not occur until 1815 and after. Documentation of the existence of women's associations occurs in the titles of ministers' sermons, in printed constitutions and reports and manuscript records of the societies themselves, in women's diaries and letters, and in local histories. In addition to titles listed in the back of Cott's *The Bonds of Womanhood*, see documents from the Jericho Center Female Religious Society, Cent Society, and Maternal Association, and constitution and rules of the Maternal Association in Dorchester, Mass., Dec. 25, 1816, CL; documents of the Charitable Female Society in the 2d parish in Bradford, 1815–1821, of the West Bradford Female Temperance Society, 1829–1834, of the Female Religious, Biographical, Reading Society (Berean Circle), 1826–1832, of the Belleville Female Benevolent Society, or Dorcas Society, 1839–1840, and of the Hamilton Maternal Association, 1834–1835, EI; *Report on the Concerns of the New Hampshire Cent Institution* (Concord, 1814, 1815, 1816); *The Rules, Regulations, &c of the Portsmouth Female Asylum* (Portsmouth, 1815); Edward Aiken, *The First Hundred Years of the New Hampshire Bible Society* (Concord, 1912), p. 66; Mrs. L. H. Daggett, ed., *Historical Sketches of Women's Missionary Societies in America and England* (Boston, n.d.), p. 50; *Annual Reports of the Education Society of Connecticut and the Female Education Society of New Haven* (New Haven, 1816–1826); *An Account of the Rise, Progress, and Present State of the Boston Female Asylum* (Boston, 1803); *Constitution of the Salem Female Charitable Society, Instituted July 1st, 1801* (printed circular, 1801); *Reminiscences of the Boston Female Asylum* (printed, Boston, 1844); *Account of the Plan and Regulations of the Female Charitable Society of Newburyport* (Newburyport, 1803); *A Brief Account of the Origin and Progress of the Boston Female Society for Missionary Purposes, with extracts from the reports of the society in May 1817 and 1818* (Boston, 1818); *Report of the Boston Female Society for Missionary Purposes* (Boston, 1825); *Constitution of the Female Samaritan Society instituted in Boston, Nov. 19, 1817 and revised 1825* (Boston, 1833); *Constitution of the Female Society of Boston and the Vicinity for Promoting Christianity among the Jews, instituted June 5, 1816* (Boston, n.d.); *Constitution of the Fragment Society, Boston, founded 1817* (Boston, 1825); *Constitution of the Female Philanthropick Society, instituted Dec. 1822* (Boston, 1823); *Boston Fatherless and Widows Society, founded 1817, Annual Report* (Boston, 1836); *Second Annual Report, Third Annual Report, of the Boston Female Moral Reform Society* (Boston, 1837, 1838); *Constitution of the Maternal Association of Newburyport* (printed, 1815); *Constitution of the Maternal Association of the 2d Parish in West-Newbury, adopted Sept. 1834* (printed, n.d.); *Constitution of the Maternal Association* (Dedham, Mass., n.d.); *Constitution of the Maternal Association of the New Congregational Church in Boston, Mass., organized Oct. 6, 1842* (Boston, 1843); *Diary of Sarah Connell Ayer* (Portland, Me., 1910), pp. 213–215, 226, 228, 237, 285–307; diary of Mary Hurlbut, Feb. 10, 1833, CHS. See also Keith Melder, "'Ladies Bountiful': Organized Women's Benevolence in Early Nineteenth-Century America," *New York History* 48 (1967):231–265; Mary B. Treudley, "The Benevolent Fair: A Study of Charitable Organizations Among Women in the First Third of the Nineteenth Century," *Social Service Review* 14 (1940):506–522.

17. This line of argument was suggested to me by Gordon Schochet's reasoning about patriarchalism in the seventeenth century in "Patriarchalism, Politics, and Mass Attitudes in Stuart England," *Historical Journal* 12 (1969), esp. 421–425.

18. Catherine Sedgwick to Robert Sedgwick, Sept. 15, 1833, Sedgwick Collection, MHS. See also the diary of Mary Hall, a Lowell operative, NHHS; and Almond H. Davis, ed., *The Female Preacher, or Memoir of Salome Lincoln* (Providence, R.I., 1843).

19. Lonna Malmsheimer suggests that the numerical predominance of women in New England churches forced adjustments in ministers' views of their character during the eighteenth century, in "New England Funeral Sermons and Changing Attitudes toward Women, 1672–1792" (Ph.D. diss., University of Minnesota, 1973).

20. Harriet Martineau, *Society in America* (New York: Saunders and Otley, 1837), 2:255–257, 229, 363. Martineau strenuously objected to women working to raise money to educate young clerics (as they did in "education" societies); see pp. 363, 415–420.

21. Journal of Abigail Brackett Lyman, Jan. 1, 1800, in Helen Roelker Kessler, "The Worlds of Abigail Brackett Lyman" (M. A. thesis, Tufts Univ., 1976), appendix A; "A Short Sketch of the life of Nancy Thomson [*sic*]," autobiographical fragment in the diary of Nancy Thompson (Hunt), c. 1813, *CHS*. See also the journal of Mary Treadwell Hooker, 1795–1812, *CSL*.

22. "Short Sketch," diary of Nancy Thompson, c. 1808; journal of Abigail Brackett Lyman, Jan. 30, 1800; see also diary of Lucinda Read, March 30, 1816, *MHS*.

23. Journal of Abigail Brackett Lyman, Oct. 3, 1802; Nancy Meriam, "Religious Notes, 1811–1815," April 9, 1815, *WHS*; also see Cott, "Young Women in the Second Great Awakening, on this theme. William McLoughlin summarizes the idea of "compliance with the terms of salvation" thus: "The process of conversion . . . became a shared act, a complementary relationship. Man striving and yearning; God benevolent and eager to save; the sinner stretching out his hands to receive the gift of grace held out by a loving God. This belief in man's free will or his partial power to effect his own salvation had in earlier Calvinist days been condemned as the heresy of Arminianism. For this reason most nineteenth-century ministers preferred to call themselves Evangelicals." *The American Evangelicals 1800–1900* (New York: Harper Torchbooks, 1968), p. 10.

24. Diary of Mrs. S. Smith, March 29, 1825, *CSL*. See also the diary of Mary Treadwell Hooker; diary of Sarah Ripley Stearns, May 1, 1814, and March 19, 1815, Stearns Collection, *SL*; correspondence between Almira Eaton and Weltha Brown, 1812–1822, Hooker Collection, *SL*.

25. Richard D. Birdsall, "The Second Great Awakening and the New England Social Order," *Church History* 39 (1970):357; Sidney E. Mead, "The Rise of the Evangelical Conception of the Ministry in America, 1607–1850," in H. Richard Niebuhr and Daniel L. Williams, eds., *The Ministry in Historical Perspective* (New York: Harper and Bros., 1956), p. 224; journal of Abigail Brackett Lyman, Oct. 3, 1802. Historians of religion consistently maintain that during the last two decades of the eighteenth century American churches "reached a lower ebb of vitality . . . than at any other time in the country's religious history," in the words of Sydney E. Ahlstrom, *A Religious History of the American People* (New Haven: Yale University Press. 1972), p. 365. Douglas Sweet protests the consensus in "Church Vitality and the American Revolution," *Church History* 45 (1976):341–357. The Second Great Awakening, beginning in the late 1790s, decisively changed the religious climate. Estimates for New England, which generally was the region of highest church affiliation, are unavailable, but Winthrop S. Hudson estimates that church members in the United States as a whole increased from 1 out of 15 in the population in 1800, to 1 out of 8, in 1835, raising the churches' "constituency" from 40 percent to 75 percent of the population; *Religion in America: An Historical Account* (2d ed., New York: Scribners, 1973), pp. 129–130.

26. Mary Orne Tucker mentions her attendance at such a meeting in her diary, April 12, 1802, *EI*; see also *The Writings of Nancy Maria Hyde of Norwich, Conn.* (Norwich, 1816), pp. 182–183, 189–190, 192–193, 201–202, 203–205.

27. Documents of the Jericho Center, Vermont, Female Religious Society, Cent Society, and Maternal Associations. By 1824 the Cent Society had 120 subscribers.

28. Sarah Ripley Stearns diary, 1814–1817, esp. Dec. 24, 1815, March 2, March 31, July 14, Oct. 13, 1816, June 1817.

29. *Diary of Sarah Connell Ayer 1805–1835*, pp. 209, 211, 213, 214, 215, 225, 226, 228, 231–233, 236–237, 239–240, 254, 278, 282–305. There is a gap in the diary between 1811 and 1815, the years in which Ayer bore and buried her first four children.

30. Record book of the Female Religious, Biographical, Reading Society (the Berean Circle), 1826–1832, *EI*. The society was probably located near Newburyport, though its exact location is not clear.

31. Diary of Rachel Willard Stearns, July 19, 1835, Stearns Collection, *SL*.

32. Record book of the Berean Circle, Oct. 15, 1828, Jan. 17, 1832; Mary Orne Tucker diary, April 12, 1802; *The Writings of Nancy Maria Hyde*, pp. 189–190; diary of Nancy Meriam, May 12, 1819, *WHS*.

33. See Malmsheimer, "New England Funeral Sermons."

34. See, for example, Amos Chase, *On Female Excellence* (Litchfield, Conn., 1792); John C. Ogden, *The Female Guide* (Concord, N.H., 1793); George Strebeck, *A Sermon on the Character of the Virtuous Woman* (New York, 1800); William Lyman, *A Virtuous Woman the Bond of Domestic Union and the Source of Domestic Happiness* (New London, Conn., 1802); Nathan Strong, *The Character of a Virtuous and Good Woman* (Hartford, 1809); Ethan Smith, *Daughters of Zion Excelling* (Concord, N.H., 1814); Daniel Clark, *The Wise Builder* (Boston, 1820); and Cott, "In the Bonds of Womanhood," pp. 105–115.

35. Quoted by Henry C. Wright in his journal, 6:135, June 18, 1834, *HCL*.

36. Buckminster, "A Sermon Preached . . . 1810," pp. 24–25.

37. Pastor's address appended to *Constitution of the Maternal Association of the New Congregational Church* (Boston, 1843), p. 5.

38. E.g., Wad Cotton told the women of Boylston, Massachusetts, that bringing domestic missionaries to unchurched Western residents would be "the means not only of the salvation of their souls, but also of the political salvation of our country." *Causes and Effects of Female Regard to Christ* (Worcester, 1816), p. 13.

39. The monthly *Mother's Magazine*, begun by Mrs. A. G. Whittelsey in 1833 in Utica, N.Y., served informally as an organ of communication, advising on programs and topics for maternal associations.

    Mary P. Ryan's data from Utica indicates that the members of maternal societies there (c. 1825–1835) were predominantly middle-class (wives of mechanics, shopkeepers, etc.) in contrast to the higher status of members of missionary societies formed there slightly earlier (c. 1805–1815), who were predominantly wives of large proprietors, merchants, etc. See "A Woman's Awakening: Revivalist Religion in Utica, New York, 1800–1835."

40. Constitution and rules of the Maternal Association in Dorchester, Massachusetts, Dec. 25, 1816, *CL*.

41. The constitutions of the maternal associations of Newburyport, Dedham, 2d Parish of West-Newbury, and New Congregational Church of Boston copied that format; see note 16.

42. Constitution of the Jericho Center Maternal Association, *CL*; diary of Mary Hurlbut, Feb. 10, 1833 *CHS* (a penciled note added later on this page of the diary states that the maternal association continued to meet for 42 years); "Record Book of the Maternal Association, Hamilton, Massachusetts, 1834–1835, copied by A. W. Dodge for her friend Mrs. Judith N. Hill, 1835," *EI*. A member of the Hamilton association said that every one of her nine children had experienced religious conversion early; she explained that "she began when they were very young to discipline them. She thought children were subject to it at a much earlier age than we had generally any idea—she believed that it could be done at the expiration of one month after their birth—She also subjected them to habits of *self-denial* and *self-control* at an early age. And she made it a constant practice to pray with her children." I have no further evidence to corroborate *so* early an imposition of self-denial. But the document strongly suggests a link between mothers' new, evangelically-oriented concentration on child-rearing and the self-repressive "Victorian personality."

43. The Boston Society for Missionary Purposes, originally a foreign mission group, became interested in a "city mission" to prostitutes in 1817–1818 (see *A Brief Account*, and 1825 *Report*, cited in note 16); *Second Annual Report, Third Annual Report of the Boston Female Moral Reform Society*; on the New York Female Moral Reform Society, see Carroll Smith-Rosenberg, "Beauty, The Beast, and the Militant Woman," *AQ* 23 (1971), esp. 575–576, regarding the New England affiliates.

44. *Second Annual Report; Advocate of Moral Reform*, New York (Sept. 1835), 1:72.

45. *Third Annual Report*, p. 16; cf. the report of the missionary of the Boston Female Society for Missionary Purposes, *A Brief Account*, p. 8.

46. See *Third Annual Report*, p. 18, which notes approvingly Mary Gove's classes on physiology for women, held in Boston; and *Advocate of Moral Reform* for frequent rejections of false delicacy.

47. Mary Ann B. Brown, *An Address on Moral Reform, Delivered before the Worcester Female Moral Reform Society, Oct. 22, 1839* (n.p., n.d.), p. 14.

48. Quoted from Alice Stone Blackwell, *Lucy Stone* (Boston: Little Brown, 1930), p. 20, in Eleanor Flexner, *Century of Struggle* (New York: Atheneum, 1970), p. 34. Lucy Stone's marriage protest, signed by herself and her husband, is reprinted in Aileen S. Kraditor, ed., *Up from the Pedestal* (Chicago: Quadrangle Books, 1970), pp. 149–150.

49. Keith Melder's article "'Ladies Bountiful',," while generally helpful, portrays the women's benevolent associations as predecessors of the women's rights movement without discerning their more complex and ambiguous overall impact.

50. Gardiner Spring, *The Excellence and Influence of the Female Character; Preached at the Request of the N.Y. Female Missionary Society* (2d ed., New York, 1825), p. 3. Spring was a conservative Presbyterian.

51. Walter Harris, *A Discourse to the Members of the Female Cent Society in Bedford, New Hampshire, July 18, 1814* (Concord, 1814), p. 10; George Keely, *The Nature and Order of a Gospel Church . . .* (Haverhill, Mass., 1819), p. 24. On Methodist practices, see note 12.

52. Joseph Richardson, *A Sermon on the Duty and Dignity of Woman Delivered April 22, 1832* (Hingham, Mass., 1833), p. 15. Cf. Samuel P. Williams (a Presbyterian), in *Plea for the Orphan* (Newburyport, 1822), p. 3: "Christianity, alone, has marked with precision, the official boundaries between the two great divisions of mankind; clearly defined the duties of their several relations, and wisely assigned the stations which they may occupy with appropriate dignity."

53. For an extended view of women as dependent, see "Claims of Christianity on Females," *Universalist and Ladies' Repository* 2 (1834):309, 325, 340, 356, 388, 396. The magazine was conducted by Universalist ministers.

54. Richardson, *A Sermon*, p. 13.

KEY TERM

New England Great Awakening   A Protestant religious revival that swept through New England (as well as other parts of the United States) in the late eighteenth and early nineteenth centuries. In the Great Awakening, preachers delivered "hellfire and brimstone" sermons, inviting converts to break with traditional sects and find personal salvation ("rebirth") through their own spiritual effort and joining with new, less established Protestant sects.

DISCUSSION QUESTIONS

1. Nancy F. Cott covers the nineteenth century "feminization of Protestantism," showing how the Protestant faith provided a special arena of self-expression for New England women. To what extent is this still going on today in the United States? Are women today more active than men in Protestant organizations, and, if so, why?

2. What were some of the issues that concerned activist Protestant women in nineteenth-century New England? What kinds of issues concern today's activist Protestant women? How are the two sets of issues similar? How are they different?

3. Does it seem to you that activist Christian women in the United States today come from a segment of society that may be considered the equivalent of the segment from which nineteenth-century female Christian activists were drawn? Describe these segments, pointing out any differences you see. What about geography? Has the focus shifted away from New England?

THE CULT OF MASCULINITY

AMERICAN SOCIAL CHARACTER AND THE LEGACY OF THE COWBOY

MICHAEL S. KIMMEL

The nineteenth century saw the emergence of a "Cult of True Womanhood," as discussed in the introduction to this chapter. In this next piece, historian Michael S. Kimmel finds an American "cult of masculinity" that he traces over the same period and further, into the twentieth century. To Kimmel, American masculinity has been a "compulsive masculinity, a masculinity that must always prove itself and that is always in doubt," and, as such, a masculinity characterized by violence, aggression, competitiveness, and insecurity. Kimmel sees this compulsive masculinity as epitomized by the American Cowboy, a cultural hero who in many ways has embodied U.S. national identity through the course of its history. Kimmel's article traces the development of the cult of masculinity by focusing on political leaders from Andrew Jackson through Ronald Reagan. He shows how styles of leadership, political rhetoric, and domestic and foreign policy have resonated with the Cowboy ethic in U.S. politics.

In this historical treatment of masculinity, Kimmel draws attention to the use of Cowboy symbols as political ploys, but he also shows the very real socioeconomic consequences of Cowboy ethics in the political sphere. At the end of the article Kimmel discusses how the cult of masculinity in American political life started to break down at the close of the twentieth century. Not all readers may agree with Kimmel's interpretation of U.S. history, but his work stands as a stunning and thought-provoking example of how political posturing, policymaking, national identity, war, and peace are inseparable from cultural constructions of gender.

> *Doctor, I can't stand anymore being frightened like this over nothing. Bless me with manhood! Make me brave! Make me strong!*
>
> —Philip Roth, *Portnoy's Complaint*[1]

Is there a distinctive "American social character,"[2] a unique combination of attitudes, aspirations, and activities that sets the American apart from other nationalities? Is the American a type that can be instantly recognized and categorized? Traditionally, analysts of the American personality have given three sorts of answers in their attempts to define the American social character. One sort of assessment often reads like horoscopes, so vague and blandly noncommittal that anyone could believe them to be true. The adjectives that define this distinctively American character type would also be instantly recognized, I'm afraid, as the "essential" defining features of the Afghani, the Burmese, the Senegalese, the

Australian, or even the German personality. For example, one respected social scientist lists fifteen "value orientations" of the American personality, among them: achievement and success, humanitarianism, efficiency and practicality, belief in progress, valuing of material comfort, and a belief in freedom, equality, scientific rationality, nationalism, individualism, and conformity.[3] Political scientist Harold Laski listed an orientation to the future, dynamism, worship of bigness, sense of destiny, fluidity of classes, pioneer spirit, individualism, anti-statism, versatility, empiricism, hard work, and a sense of property among his components of the American "spirit."[4] Max Lerner's sprawling classic, *America as a Civilization* (1957), reads like a catalog of contradictory adjectives intended to capture the extremes of American life. Americans, he claims, are mobile and restless, resilient, and temperamental, "over-organized in some areas and under-organized in others," composed of "vendible" and "authoritarian" personalities. Not only are they "extremely moral" but also habitually "moral breaking"; what's more, they also subscribe to an ethic in which the "reigning moral deity . . . is fun."[5]

If this analytic imprecision is confusing, it is no less so than a second mode of understanding the American social character. In this version of American exceptionalism, the American personality is cast as an indescribably and existentially unique formation. In this depiction, bland platitudes are replaced by soaring superlatives, frequently referring to a mythic, historical, even sacred destiny awaiting fulfillment. "We Americans are the peculiar, chosen people," wrote Herman Melville in 1850, "the Israel of our time." Over a century later, the English observer D.W. Brogan caricatured American exceptionalism when he remarked in *The American Character* that Americans assume that "all modern historical events are either American or unimportant."[6]

A third school of thought is more ambivalent. Some authors are not sure exactly what an American is; they are sure only that he or she is not a European. What makes the American unique is his or her difference from the European. The seemingly unlimited frontier and the absence of a feudal heritage allowed the full flowering of what had only been a tendency in Europe. "America is Europe with all the walls down," noted one astute observer. To Richard Hofstadter, one of the United States' most celebrated historians, U.S. anti-intellectualism is a sharp contrast to the European kind. Europeans theorize and plan, he argued, while Americans act on the basis of their primitive instincts and imagination to advance a new world order based on individual abilities and accomplishments.[7] As Alexis de Tocqueville, that perceptive French aristocrat, observed in the 1830s, the "spirit of the Americans is averse to general ideas; it does not seek theoretical discoveries."[8] If the European thinks, the American acts; the European is careful, precise, elegant, while the American counterpart is reckless, rough, and daring. (Think, for example, of the contrast between James Bond and Dirty Harry.) Geographic limits bind the European to civil law, but the peculiar American relationship to nature—the twin myths of the limitless frontier and of inexhaustible resources—allows us to continue to see the New World as the state of nature, ruled by natural law, unrestrained by the historic obligation to civilization. (This relationship to nature has been said to justify both intervention in world affairs and U.S. isolation.)[9]

Different as these three types of analysis may be, they all use several similar adjectives, which may describe some essential elements of an American social character, a cultural personality that explains present-day U.S. foreign policy.

Interestingly enough, these common characteristics—violence, aggression, extreme competitiveness, a gnawing insecurity—are also the defining features of compulsive masculinity, a masculinity that must always prove itself and that is always in doubt.

And American violence and aggression, these observers tell us, are distinctly American. For example, the American acts aggressively, not like a bully, seeking a confrontation, but rather in response to provocation. American school children are invariably taught that the United States has "never lost a war and never been the aggressor," which is a remarkable achievement, since the United States has only been invaded twice (in 1812 and 1941) since 1800 but has invaded scores of countries itself. American aggression is peculiar, wrote anthropologist Margaret Mead, because it is "seen as a response rather than as primary behavior." In *And Keep Your Powder Dry* (1944, revised in 1968), Mead explained that ours is an "aggressiveness which can never be shown except when the other fellow starts it . . . which is so unsure of itself that it had to be proved."[10]

Americans, Mead continued, "fight best when other people start pushing us around." As an editorial in the *Chicago Tribune* put it in 1883, "Having been kicked, it is time to kick back, and kick back hard, and keep on kicking back until they are kicked into something like reciprocity." American aggression is usually, in this mythic representation, retaliatory, a response to an apparent injury. And the retaliation is swift, effective, and inevitably disproportionately severe. Once provoked, the United States tends to get carried away by a boundless fury. Not one, but two atomic bombs were thought necessary and suitable retaliation against an already weakened enemy.

At the individual behavioral level, is it any wonder that the United States leads all modern industrial democracies in rapes, aggravated assaults, homicides, and robberies, and ranks among the highest in group violence and assassination? The National Commission on the Causes and Prevention of Violence suggested that "proving masculinity may require frequent rehearsals of toughness, the exploitation of women, and quick, aggressive responses." Such an analysis raises a most important issue, specifically that American aggression and violence conform to this compulsive masculinity, a socially constructed gender identity that is manifest both in individual behavior and in foreign and domestic policies. It is the central argument of this article that the aggregate compulsive masculinity in the United States makes it a dangerous country in the modern world.

In the rest of this article I will trace the development of the cult of masculinity among U.S. political leaders through the course of U.S. history, indicating several of the forces that gave rise to it. Then I shall discuss the cult of masculinity in recent years and suggest a few reasons why this construct, both as a model for individual leaders and as a national posture, is beginning to break down, even at the moment it appears to be so vigorously reasserted. But first, let's look briefly at the constituent elements of masculinity, and observe how it so easily becomes a cult of excessive masculinity.

U.S. History as a Test of Manhood

The psychologist Robert Brannon has identified four components of the dominant traditional male sex role in the rules that define how a man is supposed to behave.[11] The first rule, "no sissy stuff," suggests that a stigma is attached to any behavior that appears even vaguely feminine. The second rule, "be a big wheel," says that success and status are vital elements of masculinity, and that men crave admiration. A man must also "be a sturdy oak," exuding a manly air of toughness, confidence, and self-reliance, so that others may come to rely on him. A final rule admonishes men to "give 'em hell," to evince an aura of aggression, violence, and daring. While this version of masculinity was originally intended to delineate the pressures on individual men to adopt a traditional kind of behavior, even a cursory glance at U.S. history, and the administrations of its political leaders, reveals a marked national preoccupation with masculinity. For the United States has been the archetypal male society, both because traditional masculinity permeates every facet of its political life, and because American men are never certain of our masculinity, never secure in our identity, always restless, eternally anxious, unrelentingly competitive. It's as if only Americans can be "real men."

Nowhere is the dynamic of American masculinity more manifest than in our singular contribution to the world's storehouse of cultural heroes: the cowboy. It was the United States that gave the world the cowboy legend, and Americans continue to see him as the embodiment of the American spirit. Even if the rest of the world finds him somewhat poignantly anachronistic, the United States has been trying to live up to the cowboy ideal ever since he appeared on the mythical historical stage.

Ideally, the cowboy is fierce and brave, willing to venture into unknown territory and tame it for its less-than-masculine inhabitants. As soon as the environment is subdued though, he must move on, unconstrained by the demands of civilized life, unhampered by clinging women and whining children. The cowboy is a man of impeccable ethics, whose faith in natural law and natural right is eclipsed only by the astonishing fury with which he demands adherence to them. He moves in a world of men, in which daring, bravery, and skill are constantly tested. He lives by his physical strength and rational calculation; his compassion is social and generalized, but he forms no lasting emotional bonds with any single person. The cowboy therefore lives alone—on the range, in the woods, settling the west. Like the United States' view of itself as the lone voice of reason in a hostile

sea, the cowboy's mission was to reassert natural law against those forces that would destroy it (monarchy and aristocracy in the nineteenth century and communism in the twentieth, each of which is considered a foreign ideology, imported from Europe).

The American-as-cowboy theme resonates through the history of the United States. The pioneers and explorers of the early nineteenth century—Daniel Boone, Davey Crockett, Kit Carson—remain some of the nation's most potent cultural heroes, blazing the trail westward. The virgin land of the American west "gave America its identity," writes one commentator; the frontier was the place where manhood was tested, where, locked in a life or death struggle against the natural elements and against other men, a man discovered if he truly was a real man.[12]

If we see the cowboy as the embodiment of the American identity, Americans expect no less from their contemporary leaders, from the men they elect as the personification of American aspirations. Almost every presidential administration has been marked by a concern for masculinity; at times this is muted by a relative security, while at other times a convulsively bellicose masculinity becomes the defining feature of the administration. No American president better has expressed this compulsive masculine style than Andrew Jackson—a "man of violent character and middling capacities" according to Tocqueville—who carved out a distinctly American identity against both the effete "European" banks of the eastern establishment and the frighteningly "primitive" native American population.

Jackson's Indian policies illustrate well the tragic consequences of compulsive masculinity as a political style, particularly in combination with the needs of an expanding capitalist economy. By dispossessing the Indians of their land through a strategy of "internal colonialism" and genocide, Americans began to fulfill their destiny as possessors, a destiny that resounded through the nineteenth and twentieth centuries in countless imperialist adventures and reverberates today in Central America, the Middle East, and Southeast Asia. In *Fathers and Children* (1975), a brilliant psychoanalytically informed cultural history of Jacksonian America, political scientist Michael Rogin suggests that while the black man represented a "sexual Oedipal threat to the white man," the Indian represented a pre-Oedipal aggressive threat to the mother-child relationship." Such aggression (whether real or imagined) was sufficient provocation for Jackson and his new-born country, whose response was to reassert the authority of the Great White Father against his "red children." Thus Jackson said to three Florida Indian chiefs that they had listened to bad counsel, which

> compelled your Father the President to send his white children to chastise and subdue you, and thereby give peace to his children both red and white. . . . I give to you a plain, straight talk, and do not speak with a forked tongue. It is necessary that you be brought together, either within the bounds of your old Nation, or at some point, where your Father the President may be enabled to extend to you his fatherly care and assistance.[13]

The Indians were to be "resettled," forcibly removed from their traditional homelands, and placed on reservations (not unlike the relocation camps for Japanese Americans during the Second World War and the "strategic hamlets" of the Vietnam War), where they would be protected from the excesses of less enlightened whites. "Like a kind father," explained Jackson's military aide, "the President says to you, there are lands enough for both his white and his red children. His white children are strong, and might exterminate his red, but he will not permit them. He will preserve his red children."[14]

The consequences of this forced resettlement onto reservations, a profound infantilization of the subject population, had far-reaching consequences for native American identity. For the white Americans, the consequences were different. "By killing Indians whites grounded their growing up in a securely achieved manhood, and securely possessed their land."[15] Masculinity became linked to the subjugation of other people and the secure appropriation of their land.

Post-Bellum Flexing

Masculinity in the United States is certain only in its uncertainty; its stability and sense of well-being depend on a frantic drive to control its environment. And no sooner did this identity establish itself in the mid-nineteenth century than the walls of the male establishment began to crack. The bloody Civil War, an orgy of fratricide, left a significant legacy to the American self-image. For one thing, wartime industrialization contributed to a dramatic reshaping of the nature of work in American society. The independent artisan, the autonomous small farmer, the small shopkeeper was everywhere disappearing—before the Civil War, 88 percent of American men were farmers or self-employed businessmen—replaced by an industrial working class that was tuned to the demands of the assembly line, and that held less and less control over its labors or its fruits. The organization of the Knights of Labor and the Populist Movement tried to stop this massive proletarianization, but in the end, like their European counterparts, American workers lost their struggle to retain the integrity of their work. Rapid industrialization also exacerbated the separation of work and home and extended the period of childhood socialization, contributing to what many observers labeled a "feminization" of American life.[16] Women, as mothers, public school teachers, and Sunday school teachers were thought to be softening the American character and replacing heroic male virtues of valor and honor with a generous compassion and emotional expressiveness. As William James put it, "There is no more contemptible type of human character than that of the nervous sentimentalist and dreamer, who spends his life in a weltering sea of sensibility and emotion, but who never does a concrete manly deed."[17] Finally, the frontier itself began to close, forcing America back onto itself. "For nearly three centuries," wrote Frederick Jackson Turner in 1896, "the dominant fact in American life has been expansion. And now the frontier is gone, and with its going has closed the first period of American history."

To counteract the effects of the closing of the frontier and the loss of patriarchal control over home and workplace, the twenty years preceding the entry of the United States into the First World War witnessed a striking resurgence of concern about masculinity. Writers extolled martial virtues and the heroic individual squaring off against faceless bureaucrats, and celebrated the charisma of the warrior, the willingness to die for what is natural and real. "The greatest danger that a long period of profound peace offers to a nation is that of creating effeminate tendencies in young men," noted one author in 1898. Psychologist Theodore Roszack observes that the years leading up to 1914 read "like one long drunken stag party where boys from every walk of life and ideological persuasion goad one another on to ever more bizarre professions of toughness, daring, and counterphobic mania— until at last the boasting turns suicidal and these would-be supermen plunge the whole Western society into the blood bath of world war.[18] Imperialist adventures took on qualities of national purification; military madness offered moral regeneration through the creation of an overseas empire. "Every argument that can be made for the Filipinos could be made for the Apaches," argued Theodore Roosevelt against those who cautioned restraint in the Philippines. Here, then, was the new frontier.

To sabotage the feminization of American culture meant, of course, a recharged opposition to women's suffrage, a certain subterfuge of American male values. "The American Republic stands before the world as the supreme expression of masculine force," proclaimed the Illinois Association Opposed to Women's Suffrage in 1910. The nation had grown soft and lazy, and America would soon lose its dominance in world affairs if its young boys did not metamorphose into vigorous, virile men. A spate of books of advice appeared for young men to guide their development, sabotage women's influence, and urge the adoption of traditional masculinity. Senator Albert Beveridge of Indiana's *Young Man and the World* (1906) counseled boys to "avoid books, in fact avoid all artificial learning, for the forefathers put America on the right path by learning from completely natural experience."[19]

It is interesting that, to counter these arguments about feminization, many early feminists and suffragists argued that the cult of masculinity was the true threat to the American way of life. Alice Duer Miller's amusing but effective rejoinder to those who would exclude women from public affairs has a contemporary ring, but was written in 1915. In "Why We Oppose Votes for Men"[20] she writes

1. Because Man's place is in the army.
2. Because no really manly man wants to settle any question otherwise than by fighting about it.
3. Because if men should adopt peaceable methods women will no longer look up to them.
4. Because men will lose their charm if they step out of their natural sphere and interest themselves in other matters than feats of arms, uniforms and drums.
5. Because men are too emotional to vote. Their conduct at baseball games and political conventions shows this, while their innate tendency to appeal to force renders them particularly unfit for the task of government.

Perhaps the most revealing event in the drive to counter the forces of feminization and maintain traditional manhood was the founding of the Boy Scouts of America in 1910. The Boy Scouts celebrated a masculinity tested against, and proved, in the world of nature and other men, far from the restraints of home, hearth, school, and church. The Boy Scouts stressed chivalry, courage, honor, activity, and thoughtfulness; Theodore Roosevelt claimed that "all daring and courage, all iron endurance of misfortune make for a finer and nobler type of manhood." "Spectatoritis," wrote E.T. Seton in *The Boy Scouts of America* (1910) had turned "robust, manly, self-reliant boyhood into a lot of flat-chested cigarette smokers with shaky nerves and doubtful vitality."[21] The Boy Scouts provided an institutional sphere for the validation of masculinity that had been previously generated by the flow of daily social life and affirmed in one's work. As one official Boy Scout manual put it in 1914,

> The Wilderness is gone, the Buckskin Man is gone, the painted Indian has hit the trail over the Great Divide, the hardships and privations of pioneer life which did so much to develop sterling manhood are now but a legend in history, and we must depend upon the Boy Scout movement to produce the MEN of the future.[22]

As no one else before him, President Theodore Roosevelt epitomized these masculine virtues, and he was heralded as the most manly of American presidents. His triumph over his frail body (he was dangerously asthmatic as a child) and his transformation into a robust, vigorous physical presence served as a template for the revitalized American social character in the twentieth century. Roosevelt's foreign policy was militaristic and expansionist; the Roosevelt corollary to the Monroe Doctrine extended the frontier once again, in the guise of "manifest destiny" to include the entire western hemisphere. "The nation that has trained itself to a cancer of unwarlike and isolated ease is bound, in the end, to go down before other nations who have not lost the manly and adventurous virtues," he argued. Or again: "There is no place in the world for nations who have become enervated by soft and easy life, or who have lost their fiber of vigorous hardiness and masculinity." A newspaper editor from Kansas praised Roosevelt's masculinity—his "hard muscled frame" and his "crackling voice"— as a model for Americans.[23]

Rough Riding Off to World War

Teddy Roosevelt and his band of Rough Riders may have symbolized a hyper-masculine style in America, but he was surely not alone. All across Europe, turn-of-the-century leaders symbolically flexed their muscles and prepared themselves for the ultimate test of their virility. Insecure masculinity is not uniquely American, but rather emerges in the nineteenth century as the bourgeoisie ascends to national political dominance. According to the French historian and critic Michel Foucault, it is the bourgeois preoccupation with order and control and with an interminable ordering and disciplining of the natural and social environment that defines the era of bourgeois hegemony. In this regard, the United States is not unique, but presents perhaps the least adulterated case of the pathological insecurity of the bourgeois man about his own masculinity. The reassertion of manhood was the dominant theme of the political rhetoric of the entire era. U.S. general Homer Lea put it that "manhood marks the height of physical vigor among mankind, so the militant successes of a nation mark the zenith of its physical greatness."[24] Patrick Pearse, the Irish revolutionary poet, believed that bloodshed "is a cleansing and sanctifying thing and the nation which regards it as a final horror has lost its manhood."[25] Or, perhaps most strikingly, Spanish political philosopher Juan Donoso-Cortes, who claimed that "when a nation shows a civilized horror of war, it receives directly the punishment of its mistake. God changes its sex, despoils it of its common mark of virility, changes it into a feminine nation, and sends conquerers to ravish it of its honor."[26]

Every American generation since 1840 had fought in a war, and the generation of 1914 carried the additional burden of a masculinity-in-question, challenged by cultural softness, leisure, feminization, and a decade of peace. There was a lot on the line for America as a virile nation and enormous pressures on individual soldiers to prove themselves in battle, to emerge as a man among men. When poet Joyce Kilmer was killed in battle, one magazine offered this eulogy: "Kilmer was young, only 32, and the scholarly type of man. One did not think of him as a warrior. And yet from the time we entered the war he could think of but one thing—that he must, with his own hands, strike a blow at the Hun. He was a man."[27] And such tests of manliness were not limited to the U.S. infantry; businessmen and entrepreneurs also embraced the cowboy myth and yearned to outwit the competition and emerge as men among men. Recent biographies of robber barons such as John D. Rockefeller, Andrew Carnegie, Andrew Mellon, Henry Ford, and Leland Stanford reveal a startlingly common preoccupation with masculinity, in which their supremacy was proved daily on the corporate battlefield.[28]

If Teddy Roosevelt had been America's idealized version of a "real man" when the nation entered the First World War, by the war's end the country had discovered a new style of man and a new masculinity. Woodrow Wilson was, in many ways, Roosevelt's antithesis. Roosevelt harked back to Andrew Jackson, but Wilson was reminiscent of idealistic visionaries like Abraham Lincoln and Thomas Jefferson. Whereas Roosevelt was a man of action, vigorous and impulsive, Wilson was thoughtful and contemplative, rational, paternal, and intellectual. Roosevelt was the heroic patriarch, always "Old Rough and Ready"; Wilson was the meditative fatherly executive, who always listened to others' problems.

Yet both conformed to the four elements of the male role: they were "sturdy oaks" and "big wheels," they were not "sissies" and they "gave 'em hell." Each combined those elements in a somewhat different way, and both were vigorous reformers and among the most important supporters of American progressivism in the years after the war. Both believed that their domestic and foreign policies were expressions of their masculinity and that reformism at home and militarism abroad were the most consistent strategies for the continued assertion of American masculinity. One author recently argued that many of the most prominent progressives were impelled to political reform as a compensation for feelings of inadequate masculinity. Even if the "cowboy-president" now shared center stage in the American psyche with the "professor-president," compulsive masculinity was never written out of America's cultural drama.

The Japanese attack on Pearl Harbor in 1941 again inspired a new generation of American men to test their masculinity on the fields of battle. As always, Americans went into war armed with a moral imperative, believing that they alone carried the moral burden of the fate of the earth. This mythic legacy is so powerful that almost fifty years after Pearl Harbor youngsters in the United States continue to play American GI against German and Japanese.

Post-War Cowboys

Since the end of the Second World War, the cult of masculinity in American politics has remained a dominant theme. The Cold

War and the "race for space" introduced an intractable national competitiveness, so that a contest over whether the Soviet Union or the United States is the "better" society is indelibly etched into the national consciousness. Interestingly enough, space exploration, diplomatic negotiations, and even international hockey games have taken their place alongside the battlefield as the testing ground of an insecure and compulsive masculinity. And lucky for us that they have, too, for the nuclear stakes are too high for men who need to prove their manhood at every turn. Nonetheless, the exaggerated competitiveness, the terror of appearing soft and weak, has marked the administration of each post-war president. John F. Kennedy, who proclaimed his administration as "The New Frontier," was possessed, according to biographer Joe McCarthy, by a "keyed up, almost compulsive competitiveness."[29] And Richard Nixon was chronically terrified of appearing to be "soft" on communism or on anything else. Bruce Mazlish, author of the psychoanalytic study *In Search of Nixon*, wrote that Nixon was "afraid of being acted upon, of being inactive, of being soft, of being thought impotent, of being dependent on anyone else."[30]

Frequently, a president's machismo is expressed in opposition to Congress, whose incapacity for resolute action stems, the presidents suggest, from their immediate dependence on their constituents and their ultimate less-than-total manhood. Thus Barry Goldwater promised that Nixon's impressive resolve would overcome the "weak-kneed, jelly-backed attitude" of some members of the Congress on the Vietnam war, and in 1972 Gerald Ford argued that the Congressional vote on the Super-Sonic Transport, a questionably efficient and unquestionably overpriced airplane would determine whether each Congressman was "a man or a mouse."

In many ways, the post-war era, and especially the 1980s, resembles the turn of the century, in which similar economic and social changes have structured individual men's struggles and America's national struggle, to appear heroic and masculine. The closing of the frontier is today evidenced by the rising tide of struggles for national liberation and the promise of decolonization in the Third World. The dramatic transformation of the nature of work in the past two decades finds even the assembly line worker threatened by Third World workers on the one hand and by computers and robots in an increasingly service economy on the other. And it is widely believed that American culture has entered a new era of feminization, opposition to military adventures in Central America, a deepening concern for the devastation of the environment, the impressive gains registered by the women's movement and the gay movement in challenging traditional sexual scripts, and a growing trend toward a surface androgyny. (This movement toward androgyny was more marked in the 1960s when long hair, love beads, sandals, and bell-bottoms adorned a counter-culture of men dedicated to abandoning traditional masculinity; today it is more evident in the growing trend of "cross dressing.") And, as at the turn of the century, there is a flood of advice about behavior for both men and women.

Among America's political leaders, the cult of masculinity has found no better expression in recent years than in Lyndon Johnson and Ronald Reagan. (As a liberal Democrat and conservative Republican respectively, Johnson and Reagan demonstrate that compulsive masculinity knows no one political party.) Johnson was so deeply insecure about it that his political rhetoric resonated with metaphors of aggressive masculinity; affairs of state appeared to be conducted as much with his genitals as with political genius. There was a lot at stake for Johnson, as David Halberstam noted in his monumental study, *The Best and the Brightest*:

> He has always been haunted by the idea that he would be judged as being insufficiently manly for the job, that he would lack courage at a crucial moment. More than a little insecure himself, he wanted very much to be seen as a man; it was a conscious thing. . . . [H]e wanted the respect of men who were tough, real men, and they would turn out to be the hawks. He had unconsciously divided people around him between men and boys. Men were activists, doers, who conquered business empires, who acted instead of talked, who made it in the world of other men and had the respect of other men. Boys were the talkers and the writers and the intellectuals, who sat around thinking and criticizing and doubting instead of doing.[31]

Johnson's terror of an insufficient masculinity, especially that he would be seen as less of a man than John Kennedy, impelled him to escalate the war in Vietnam. When opposed, by enemies real or imagined, Johnson attacked their manhood. When informed that one member of his administration was becoming a dove on Vietnam, Johnson retorted, "Hell, he has to squat to piss." And as he celebrated the bombings of North Vietnam, Johnson declared proudly, "I didn't just screw Ho Chi Minh. I cut his pecker off."[32]

And just as Teddy Roosevelt rode the rising tide of recharged vitality from San Juan Hill to the White House, so did Ronald Reagan, riding in from his western ranch, hitch his political fortunes to the cult of compulsive masculinity. Reagan capitalized on Carter's "failure of will" in the botched invasion of Iran, and his alleged softness on domestic issues such as civil rights and environmental issues. Reagan sits tall in the saddle, riding roughly over the environment, Central America, Grenada, toward the gunfight at the nuclear arsenal, the ultimate test of the modern cowboy's mettle.

The quickest gun in the west is now the fastest finger to the button of nuclear annihilation. President Reagan is the country's most obvious cowboy-president.[33]

And he may also be one of our last. The limitations of the cult of masculinity in American politics are slowly being revealed. A growing "gender gap," a difference in the political attitudes and preferences between men and women, threatens the unfettered continuation of macho politics. During the invasion of Grenada, the *New York Times* reported, the gap between male and female support for Reagan reached 20 percent, the most significant difference on record in U.S. political history. The conservative political agenda, long linked to the expression of manhood through mercilessly tough foreign policies and equally compassionless domestic strategies, has also shown signs of shifting away from cowboy euphoria. The cowboy swagger of the former Secretary of the Interior James Watt as he attempted to sell or lease some of the country's most valuable land was too much even for the laissez-faire, free-drilling right wing. Even conservatives have counseled against the invasion of Central America, and Reagan was urged to withdraw from Lebanon. Across Europe, demonstrations against America's apocalyptic posturing with nuclear weapons have cast further doubts on the suitability of the cowboy as a policy maker for the 1980s.

The disappearance of the cowboy as the model of American masculinity will be a gain, not a loss. His disappearance as an individual hero, a template for individual role-modeling, may help free U.S. men from the constraints of a compulsively competitive masculinity and create new options for men as nurturing fathers, expressive husbands and lovers, and generous, sympathetic friends. Similarly, the decline of the cowboy ethic in American political life may finally permit the United States to cease proving its masculinity through every policy and every act of state. By giving up the insecure quest for macho heroism, the United States might become at last a compassionate democracy, concerned with human dignity and justice, which would allow it to become finally a truly heroic nation.

NOTES

An earlier version of this article was published as "Der Mãinnlichkeitskult: Amerikanischer Sozialcharakter und das Vermãchtnis des Cowboys" in Andreas Guha and Sven Papke, eds., *Amerika: Der Riskante Partner* (Bonn: Athenãum, 1984). I am grateful to Bob and Joann Brannon, Michael Kaufman, Marty Oppenheimer, and Joseph Pleck for critical comments and support through various drafts.

1. Philip Roth, *Portnoy's Complaint* (New York: Random, 1969).
2. Although I continue to use the word "American" in several places throughout this essay, I have tried to limit its use to those places in which I join the discourse on the "American personality" or the "American character." But even there, I do not use the term to refer to all the Americas, but rather to the United States in particular. In those places where I am not engaged in the discourse about the American personality, I have tried to use the more accurate (if more cumbersome) specific term "United States" or "U.S."
3. Robin M. Williams, *American Society* (New York: Alfred Knopf, 1951).
4. Harold Laski, *The American Democracy* (New York: Viking, 1948).
5. Max Lerner, *America as a Civilization* (New York: Alfred Knopf 1957), 62, 550, 655, 675.
6. D.W. Brogan, *The American Character* (New York: Vintage, 1954), 176.
7. Richard Hofstadter, *The Paranoid Style in American Politics* (New York: Basic Books, 1965).
8. Alexis de Tocqueville, *Democracy in America*, 2 vols. (New York: Doubleday, 1974), vol. 1, 326.
9. Lerner, *op. cit.*, 920.
10. Margaret Mead, *And Keep Your Powder Dry* (New York: William Morrow, 1965), 151, 157.
11. Deborah David and Robert Brannon, "The Male Sex Role," in David and Brannon, eds., *The Forty-Nine Percent Majority* (Reading: Addison-Wesley, 1976), 12.
12. It is curious that the United States does not evince a concept of "Motherland" in the same way as other advanced capitalist nations do. Perhaps the westward expansion was cast in such terms, as "taming" and "subduing," that the protection afforded an archetypal mother was replaced by the violent subjugation of a wild territory, an errant child. Michael Kaufman suggested to me that part of the answer lies in the patriarchal, yet not traditionally paternal, nature of the U.S. state (as opposed to individual politicians), again, perhaps, a father of fury and not a father of compassion.
13. Michael Rogin, *Fathers and Children* (New York: Vintage, 1975), 79, 199.
14. *Ibid.*
15. *Ibid*, 125.
16. Ann Douglas, *The Feminization of American Culture* (New York: Alfred Knopf, 1977).
17. Cited by Robert Bellah *et al.*, *Habits of the Heart* (Berkeley: University of California Press, 1985), 120.
18. Theodore Roszak, "The Hard and the Soft: The Force of feminism in Modern Times," in T. and B. Roszak, eds., *Masculine/Feminine* (New York: Harper & Row, 1969), 92.
19. Albert Beveridge, *The Young Man and the World* (New York: Appleton, 1906).
20. Reprinted in David and Brannon, *op. cit.*, 215.
21. Ernest T. Seton, *The Boy Scouts of America* (New York: Doubleday, 1910), xi, quoted in Jeffrey Hantover, "The Boy Scouts and the Validation of Masculinity," in E.H. Pleck and J.H. Pleck, *The American Man* (Englewood Cliffs: Prentice-Hall, 1980), 294.
22. D.C. Beard, *Boy Scouts of America* (1914), 109, cited by Jeffrey Hantover, *op. cit.*, 293.
23. Quoted by Joe Dubbert. "Progressivism and the Masculinity Crisis," in Pleck and Pleck, *op. cit.*, 313.
24. T. Roszak, *op. cit.*, 92.
25. *Ibid.*
26. *Ibid.*

27. "Quoted in Peter Filene, "In Time of War," in Pleck and Pleck, *op. cit.*, 324.

28. *Cf.* Philip Slater, *Wealth Addiction* (New York: E.P. Dutton, 1980).

29. Joe McCarthy, *The Remarkable Kennedys* (New York: Dial, 1960), 30, quoted in Mark Fasteau, "Vietnam and the Cult of Toughness in Foreign Policy," in Pleck and Pleck, *op. cit.*, 385.

30. Bruce Mazlish, *In Search of Nixon* (New York: Basic, 1972), 116.

31. David Halberstam, *The Best and the Brightest* (New York: Random House, 1972), 531, quoted by M. Fasteau, *op. cit.*, 394–395.

32. *Ibid.*, 396.

33. President Reagan may be a "cowboy president" in his foreign policy posturing, especially vis-à-vis the mythic Communist monolith that stretches from Central America to Africa to the Soviet Union. But his domestic policies—while no less compulsively masculine and compassionless—are cast in a "Father Knows Best" kind of paternalism that, I believe, softens their impact and lends an air of kindliness to rather systematically unkind domestic policies. This "successful" blend of patriarchy and paternalism—a father of fury *and* a father of compassion—might be the key to Reagan's popularity.

KEY TERMS

vendible   Saleable; capable of being sold.

Andrew Jackson   Seventh president of the United States (1829–1837).

Knights of Labor   A late-nineteenth-century organization that addressed concerns of laborers in this period of massive unemployment, economic depression, and suppressive government actions against workers' strikes.

Populist movement   An 1890s political movement in the United States that represented farmers and laborers. The movement addressed the concerns of the common people and advocated a more equitable distribution of the country's wealth.

Theodore (Teddy) Roosevelt   Twenty-sixth president of the United States (1901–1909).

Rough Riders   Those men who joined a voluntary cavalry regiment under Theodore Roosevelt in the Spanish-American War.

Woodrow Wilson   Twenty-eighth president of the United States (1913–1921).

Progressivism   The political doctrine of early-twentieth-century American reformers, who advocated increased democracy, the regulation of big business, restraints on corrupt political bosses, and general measures to help the poor. An outgrowth of the Populist movement, progressivism greatly influenced the political platforms of both President Theodore Roosevelt (Republican) and later President Woodrow Wilson (Democrat).

DISCUSSION QUESTIONS

1. Kimmel's analysis of the Cowboy legacy in American political leaders stops with Ronald Reagan. He claims that the "cult of masculinity" in American political life started to break down at the close of the twentieth century and predicts that Reagan may be our last "cowboy-president." What has happened since Reagan? Discuss the policies and rhetoric of the administrations of George Bush, Bill Clinton, and George W. Bush in terms of contemporary constructions of gender in U.S. culture. How are constructions of gender being expressed or used in American political life at present?

2. Another interesting way to come at the legacy of Cowboy politics is to consider how women fit into that world. Can women be political Cowboys? Can you think of any women who have tried? How successful have they been? How have Americans generally responded to them? What about First Ladies? Can you think of any First Ladies who have been cowboys? With what success? What roles have most First Ladies taken? How have they articulated their roles, and how have they meshed with their husbands' roles?

THE TWENTIETH CENTURY

CHAPTER 3

Over the twentieth century, middle-class America saw a dramatic change: a breaking down of the boundary between male/public and female/private spheres. Women moved into the public sphere, pursuing individualistic interests like those of men. More and more women entered occupations that previously were virtually all-male fields, such as medicine, politics, and religious ministries. Today nearly half of the U.S. work force consists of women, and women are nearly on a par with men in terms of education. Still, women on average have lower-paying jobs than men and occupy less prestigious occupations. Pay inequity, unequal opportunities for career advancement, and sexual harassment in the workplace have been at the forefront of gender issues in the late twentieth century.

Probably the greatest factor behind women's entry into the public sphere was their increasing participation in higher education. Ironically, women's education beyond high school was initially spearheaded by those who wanted to see them become better wives and mothers, not career women. In the late nineteenth and early twentieth century, women's colleges opened with a view to enhancing women's domestic roles, and women's higher education was largely restricted to fields like literature, art, and home economics. But once higher education for women was set in motion, many women used it to carve out new roles for themselves and in the process came to question their society's gender assumptions.

It was a long time, however (not until the 1960s), before sizable numbers of middle-class women agitated for gender equality, or saw women as comparable to men in terms of ability and potential in the public sphere. The earlier nineteenth-century view that stressed the biologically-based *differences* between men and women went largely unchallenged for the first half of the century. For example, women secured the right to vote in 1920, but women suffragists argued that, with voting power, women would bring feminine virtue, caring, and humanitarian concerns into politics. They were not saying that women should be able to vote because they are essentially no different from men. Much later, in the

1960s "women's liberation movement," middle-class feminists downplayed male–female difference and argued that women are as capable as men in any field, or in any endeavor. Biological differences were seen as irrelevant, or as an excuse for excluding women from particular occupations or life choices. These women fought for autonomy and self-expression, which they saw as previous prerogatives of men. They wanted to be seen not just as wives and mothers but as persons in their own right.

This 1960s movement was related to an important economic shift in middle-class America at mid-century. The so-called "American dream"—a suburban home with a husband as breadwinner supporting a nonworking wife and dependent children—was affordable for the middle class only for a few decades after World War II. After that, a middle-class lifestyle (especially to keep the house payments up and to properly educate the children) required that wives as well as husbands go out to work. It was under these conditions that "women's liberation" was born. This movement came to demand gender equality in all facets of life, challenging the significance of male–female biological difference. At the same time, some women felt boredom and a sense of isolation in their role of suburban housewife/mother.

The entrance of women into the public sphere brought tremendous conflicts in its wake, and we are still coping with these conflicts today. Many of the problems center on middle-class American "motherhood" as discussed in the first article in this chapter by John R. Gillis. His article is thoroughly historical and covers a rather vast amount of time. But what it all leads up to is the present problem of mothers working outside the home. For many people this is unacceptable, the doom of the American family, the cause of problems with youth and rising rates of divorce, an affront to cherished "family values." But motherhood, according to Gillis, is now in a crisis because of the way that motherhood has come to be defined, not because of an inherent incompatibility between mothers working outside the home and the successful rearing of children. He draws attention to the cultural evolution of American mothering into something intensive, life-long, and doable only by one person, the biological mother. *Motherhood*, he says, was not always and is not elsewhere so closely tied to *maternity* as it is in contemporary middle-class America.

This cultural construction of motherhood carries implications beyond the immediate setting of women's child rearing and work outside the home. As we will see in Chapter 7 of this book, many young women college students expect to have careers, but are already preparing themselves for part-time, interrupted, or home-based work to accommodate future children. This trend will perpetuate the predominance of women in the lower-paying, less prestigious occupations. Perhaps unconsciously, many college women are making choices now that reflect the construction of motherhood described by Gillis.

Another issue challenging young women in the United States today returns us to a topic raised in the last chapter, namely, the ways in which gender constructs are reflected in ideas and ideals about the body. Middle-class American ideals for women's bodies have shifted about considerably over the past two hundred years. A more rounded, voluptuous figure was sought in the late eighteenth and early nineteenth century. Then in the 1920s, the thinner look of the "flapper" became popular, along with bobbed hair and shortened skirts. In the 1950s a plumper body with large breasts and full hips was favored. Now, of course, rather extreme thinness is the ideal. For the American middle-class, the ideal male body is now big and muscular, a far cry from the thin and lighter shape of the nineteenth-century ideal.

What does all of this mean? Some observers have suggested that an obsession with the body, a feeling that it is forever imperfect, an "enemy" we must constantly fight against, is distinctive of American middle-class culture. If so, it may be a very old idea, traceable to a Puritan heritage that saw the body as weak and vulnerable, the route of Satan into the soul. Quite possibly, something of this idea remains in contemporary life. But an obsessive concern with the shape and appearance of one's body, especially among women, is truly a twentieth-century phenomena. In the article "Fat Talk: Body Image among Adolescent Girls," we see how girls' discourse on being "fat" reveals how they feel about themselves and how they seek social acceptance. This piece also shows the extent to which the self is identified with the body for adolescent girls, and the anxiety this produces.

Both male and female bodies have been subject to what Leonore Tiefer calls "medicalization," or the way that corporeal functions and "dysfunctions" are interpreted as medical issues, subject to medical intervention. We saw some "medicalization" of female puberty and menopause in the last chapter. Gillis's article also refers to the "medicalization" of childbirth in America, where pregnant women near labor are hospitalized and treated passively as patients in need of medical authority and treatment.

In the last article in this chapter, Tiefer discusses the "medicalization" of male impotence. She describes how male impotence has increasingly come to be seen not as a sociocultural or even psychological problem, but rather as a simple, almost mechanical defect in some men, easily treated with mechanical or medical interventions. But behind the "problem" itself, Tiefer notes some interesting cultural assumptions about the penis and its relationship to American constructions of masculinity.

MOTHERS GIVING BIRTH TO MOTHERHOOD

JOHN R. GILLIS

"Motherhood," like gender itself, is culturally constructed, or so argues John R. Gillis in the article opening this chapter on gender and culture in twentieth-century America. Gillis's article places twentieth-century American motherhood in the perspective of a larger history of motherhood in middle-class America, showing us that current conceptions are actually quite recent and differ markedly from those of the past. This helps us to see U.S. cultural views of motherhood as contingent on both time and place, rather than absolute or simply "natural." Gillis demonstrates that in the American past, nurturing of children was more widely shared among a variety of people, the role of "mother" was largely encompassed by the more important role of "wife," and that children were more fully incorporated into a social group and cared for collectively rather than seen as the responsibility of primarily one person. American ideas about children and childrearing have also changed dramatically.

Gillis highlights his points with discussion of the changing practices of birth and early childhood rituals through three centuries. His historical perspective throws new light on contemporary motherhood and its attendant stresses in U.S. culture. A key point is that, in the past, a woman's nurturing of her children was more integrated with her other roles. In the twentieth century, more and more women in the United States began working full-time outside the home, whereas over the same period, "motherhood" was increasingly constructed as a singular and all-consuming role for women. "Never," he writes, "have mothers been so burdened by motherhood." Current discussions about the conflicts between women's careers and their reproduction will benefit from this historical review of motherhood in mainstream America.

There have always been mothers but motherhood was invented.

—Ann Dally, *Inventing Motherhood*[1]

Because we assume that the physical act of giving birth naturally produces the desire and ability to nurture, we are stunned when we learn of birth mothers abusing or murdering their children, even though almost two of every three infants who die violently are killed by their own parents. When Susan V. Smith of South Carolina drowned both her sons in 1994, many of her neighbors found themselves searching for the answer to the question: "How could a mother do that to her children?"[2] We simply cannot believe that in giving birth a woman does not also give birth to herself as a mother. Yet many cultures make a distinction between maternity and motherhood, and even in Western

Source: From *A World of Their Own Making* by John Gillis. Copyright © 1996 by Basic Books, Inc. Reprinted by permission of Basic Books, a member of Perseus Books, L.L.C.

society the connection between giving birth and giving nurture is surprisingly recent. It was not until 1875 that English-speaking people began talking about "true motherhood" as if maternity and motherhood were one and the same. Only in our own century have these terms become so completely identified that we have felt compelled to invent a new vocabulary—surrogate mothers, adoptive mothers, foster mothers—to describe those who do not combine maternity and motherhood in the prescribed manner.

The meanings of motherhood and fatherhood are never stable or transparent but forever contested and changing. Whatever may be universal about the biology of conception, pregnancy, and birth, maternity has no predetermined relationship to motherhood, and paternity no fixed relationship to fatherhood; both vary enormously across cultures and over time.[3] The many meanings of motherhood and fatherhood are not only reflected in the various images, symbols, and rituals associated with birth but are shaped by them. Faced with the ultimate mystery of human reproduction, we turn to rituals to provide us with a sense of meaningfulness. Birth has always been marked culturally, but whereas its rites once served to create and sustain a distinction between maternity and motherhood, today they underline the identity between these concepts. When a woman gives birth in the late twentieth century, she does so not once but four times: to the child, to herself as mother, to the man as father, and to the group that in our culture we are most likely to call family.[4]

Our equation of maternity with motherhood is not only relatively recent but historically unprecedented by the standards of the Western world. In earlier centuries, giving birth and giving nurture were often incompatible for demographic and economic reasons as well as cultural ones. Because of the high levels of both fertility and mortality that prevailed in Europe and North America until the nineteenth century, there was simply no way that all women who gave birth could also mother all their children. Maternal mortality never fell below 7 percent until this century. Until about a century ago, infant mortality rates, calculated as the percentage of infants who die before they reach their first birthday, ranged from 15 to 25 percent; only about half of all those born lived to the age of twenty-one. To replace these losses, women's fertility rates remained very high. Children came so quickly that it was often impossible for a woman to nurture all who were born to her, and she was likely to die before all her children left home.[5] The lifelong, intensive involvement with the individual child that has become the standard of motherhood in our own times was simply impossible for many women before the twentieth century. As a consequence, maternity and motherhood were understood as quite separable, not unlike the current understanding of fatherhood, in which the term "to father" means merely to generate and implies none of the nurturing capacities that currently attach to the words "to mother."[6]

Children in earlier periods did not lack for mothering, however. There existed a wide range of alternative sources of nurture. Wet-nursing had always been practiced and seems to have increased in the seventeenth and eighteenth centuries.[7] Placing out infants to women who would suckle them for an extended period was common not only among upper-class women, many of whom considered breast-feeding distasteful and unfashionable, but among working women who had neither the time nor the energy for the task. . . .[8] It was not until the nineteenth century that wet-nursing went into a precipitous decline, which began when infants were no longer being sent out to nurse and nurses were required to live in under close maternal supervision. Eventually, the very idea of the nonmaternal breast became incompatible with good motherhood, and by 1900 the wet-nurse had become a thing of the past, associated with so-called primitive cultures but having no place in civilized society. Mothers either suckled their own infants or bottle-fed, a method made safe by the milk pasteurization techniques developed late in the nineteenth century.

The convergence of maternity and motherhood proceeded fastest among the middle classes, but even at that social level it was still common in the nineteenth century for older children to be informally adopted by relatives.[9] This practice remained quite widespread among the working classes well into the early decades of this century.[10] In neighborhoods where kin lived nearby, children often took meals and slept apart from their biological parents; in families with many offspring, older siblings were frequently sent to live with more distant relatives—to "claim kin," as it was called in England—a form of intrafamily relief.[11] This was merely an extension of the ancient practice of circulating children for their own good, which in earlier times had been more likely to involve movement among unrelated households. In sixteenth-century England, 60 percent of those between the ages of fifteen and twenty-four were living apart from their parents, mainly as servants.[12] From the early nineteenth century onward, however, the movement of the children of the poor into the households of the better-off began to slow down. Girls continued to be sent away into domestic service, but working-class boys stayed closer to home. Still, it was not until the interwar period of the twentieth century that parents could expect most if not all of their children to be their responsibility until they saw them married, and even then the newlyweds were likely to return to one of the parental homes until they could find a place of their own.

As John Boswell has shown, Christian culture in earlier times never held parents wholly responsible for bringing up all their children. Giving up a child to the church through the medieval institution of oblation was regarded as an act of both piety and good sense. Protestants eliminated this practice but established foundling hospitals and orphanages, which served a similar purpose. They too saw nothing immoral or unnatural about giving up one's children to the "kindness of strangers." In the eighteenth century, one-quarter of all the children born in Toulouse, France, were turned over to the care of others.[13]

In this country as well, the foundling home and the orphanage remained vital institutions until the early twentieth century, housing large numbers of children—mainly for short rather than permanent placement, however. It was only after the Second World War that these institutions were closed down and Western societies turned to adoptive families and foster homes as the exclusive means of caring for displaced children. This change followed the general shift in thinking of parenting as an individual rather than a collective responsibility, one best carried out by one set of parents rather than several. Even now we assume that foster or adoptive mothers are second-best to what we call "real" or "natural" mothers. There has always been a certain suspicion of stepmothers, but the fine lines we draw between different kinds of mothers, always maintaining biological motherhood as the norm, is a distinctly recent phenomenon. Stepmotherhood and grandmotherhood were not sharply defined categories until the nineteenth century, when, as Ann Dally points out, motherhood itself finally emerged "as a concept rather than a mere statement of fact."[14] Until that time, anyone who mothered was called "Mother," regardless of biology. The term was applied to the mistresses of brothels and to the keepers of journeymen's hostels. In colonial New

England, all older women, whether they had children or not, were called mothers.[15] In Europe it was common to call midwives "good mothers."[16] Mothering knew no age, race, or gender boundaries. Older sisters who brought up their siblings were referred to as "little mothers"; slave women who nursed white children were called "mammies"; and nurturing qualities were attributed to men as well as to women throughout the medieval and early modern periods.[17] Until the nineteenth century, the term "to father" still retained nurturing as well as generative connotations.[18] Only in this century has maternity come to bear all the weight of the symbolic as well as practical meanings that were once attached to all who mothered rather than to the one particular person who gave birth.

. . .

. . . [U]ntil the twelfth century Christianity had no central mother figure. In her earliest representations, Mary was associated more with virginity than maternity, and the mother of Jesus was envisioned by the church more as the queen of heaven than as a mother as such. Only when Mary began to be represented as a mother in the late Middle Ages did she attract the devotion previously attached to pagan goddesses. For the first time it became possible to envision maternal as well as virgin saints. "In the Virgin," writes Clarissa Atkinson, "Christians discovered and made manifest in art and worship the powers of a sacred female common to many of the world's religions."[19]

In Mary, mother of Christ, late medieval Christians found a symbolic mother to live by. Her cult reached its apogee during the fourteenth and fifteenth centuries, when, as we have already seen, the Holy Family also became central to Catholic devotions, offering safe storage for the ideals of an emerging family system in which the nuclear unit was conceived for the first time as

a moral core. It was at this time that Jesus acquired a father as well as a mother; for the next three centuries, the father figure was to compete with the mother figure for the right to symbolize nurturance. This was particularly true in Protestant lands, where the Reformation of the sixteenth century brought the Holy Family down to earth, finding new sources of symbolic reassurance within its own communities of godly households. A similar shift was apparent in Catholic countries, where the Holy Family also ceased to have a sacramental value and became a model for real families. The cult of Mary would continue to be a source of comfort to Catholics right up to the present day, but everywhere there was an increased emphasis on the heads of households providing the sense of protection and security that had once been sought elsewhere, at the roadside shrine or in monastic institutions.

. . .

From the sixteenth through the early nineteenth centuries, motherhood was still subordinated to wifehood. As Clarissa Atkinson has described it, Protestantism placed a greater premium on "woman's role as a wife, consort, helpmeet, and lover—like Eve before the Fall, a central figure but secondary and complementary to her husband."[20] In the household economy of the commercial phase of capitalism, women were often partners, though normally junior partners, in farming and proto-industrial enterprises. Even as employment outside the household became closed to them, they were increasingly active in production both for household use and for the expanding market economy. Our notion of "housework," a term invented only in 1841 to describe domestic tasks, is incapable of encompassing all the skills acquired and practiced by women prior to the mid-nineteenth century.[21] The demands on a wife's time and energy were such that many found it difficult, if not impossible, to mother full-time. Until very late, the goodwife took precedence over the good mother.

Premodern rituals of pregnancy and birth reflected the tensions between wifehood and motherhood and reconciled the two by representing maternity as an episode in a woman's life rather than the beginning of an all-consuming career. Contrary to what we have been led to believe, birthing rites in earlier periods were not necessarily more elaborate than those of the modern era. Today women are the subject of intense and highly ritualized attention from conception onward, culminating with hospitalized birth, which Robbie Davis-Floyd has described as an "event more elaborate than any heretofore known in the 'primitive' world.[22] Through this modern rite of female passage a modern woman is left with few doubts about her primary identity. She may be a wife, consort, helpmeet, and lover, but she is above all a mother.

All societies mark birth and give it a meaning consistent with their material conditions and cultures. The birthing rites of the seventeenth and eighteenth centuries acknowledged maternity but reconciled it to women's other roles. They did so by representing pregnancy and maternity as something that happened to a woman, as an episode in her life in which she was more the object of natural and supernatural forces than a subject in control of her own body. As Jacques Gelis reminds us: "To the country mind, in times gone by, men had to wait for nature to accomplish her work within the time she herself had set. It could be neither hindered nor precipitated. In a word, nature must go at her own pace, and the child 'come' in its own time.[23] When Protestants substituted the will of God for the whim of nature, they did not grant any additional agency to mothers. Indeed, their completely theocentric universe deprived

women of access to the charms and potions that had provided comfort to Catholics. In America as well, the Protestant woman "could only throw herself on the mercy of God, and the midwife dared do nothing that might appear magical."[24] As a result, the prospect of birth became more rather than less terrifying.

Like all rites of passage, birth during this period consisted of three stages—separation, transition, and reincorporation.[25] But unlike our contemporary version of the birthing ritual, which heavily emphasizes the social separation of the pregnant woman, the premodern birth process placed the most symbolic weight on the final phase, the incorporative rites of baptism of the child and the churching of the woman. These are best described as communal rites of progression rather than as individual rites of passage, for their purpose was not to underline the separateness of mother and child but to restore the household and communal relationships disrupted by the arrival of the little stranger.[26]

Traditional rites made little of the preparation for birth and a great deal of its consequences. Prior to the nineteenth century, births were hardly anticipated, for it was thought unlucky to preempt either nature or divine will by preparing for birth in too overt a manner. There was no sure way of confirming pregnancy until the woman felt the movement of the fetus, the so-called quickening, though much effort was put into divining conception by various magical means. According to the contemporary understanding of fertilization, male seed was endowed with the greatest generative powers. The position of intercourse was said to determine the sex of the child, and men believed they could tell at ejaculation whether or not conception had occurred. But there were myriad other ways to divine pregnancy, none of which required medical attention.[27]

Prenatal medical care was in fact quite rare, though there was a great deal of lore about how a woman should conduct herself either to ensure a healthy birth or, if the baby was unwanted, to end the pregnancy. Her thoughts and actions were assumed to affect the child in her womb, though it was also believed that others, especially the father, could also influence it.[28] As for what we would call the fetus, it was thought of as a fully formed child from the seventh month onward, with a will of its own, just biding its time before entering the world. Although the child was thought to be influenced by its mother's behavior, it was assumed to have as much, if not more, control over the woman's body as did the woman herself, lending further credence to the notion that pregnancy was something that happened to her rather than a condition she was entirely responsible for.[29]

There is evidence that husbands monitored the health of their wives very closely, keeping diary records, as did the Reverend Ralph Josselin.[30] But for the most part, pregnancy went unmarked. There were no changes in behavior or dress, no efforts to collect baby clothes or pick out a name; such acts were thought to be presumptuous, even unlucky.[31] Indeed, there was as much to fear as to celebrate since, as mentioned earlier, the maternal death rate never fell below 7 percent and often went higher.[32] There was no way to avoid morning sickness or labor pains, which doctors, midwives and mothers alike still thought of as either naturally or divinely ordained, brought upon women by Eve's misconduct and therefore something they should accept rather than resist. From the fourteenth century onward, maternal suffering replaced virginal status as a way of demonstrating female holiness. "The definition of a good mother as a suffering mother was firmly lodged in the ideologies of sanctity and of motherhood," notes Atkinson.[33] And this was as true of Protestantism as of Catholicism, though Catholic women still had the sufferings of Mary to give them psychological comfort.

. . .

Most women continued their normal routines right up to the moment of labor. In the ordinary language of the seventeenth and eighteenth centuries, pregnancy and birth were described not as a condition but as an activity—"breeding"—not all that different from a housewife's other enterprises.[34] While many women sought a little rest and indulgence during their pregnancies, eighteenth-century medical advice books encouraged them to remain active in everyday tasks, for they were thought to be plethoric, requiring leaner diets and more rather than less exercise.[35] In any case, pregnant woman hardly stood out in a population in which virtually all married women were bearing children until illness or death prevented it. As Jacques Gelis has noted, "This simultaneous and permanent presence of pregnancy was an essential element of the 'human landscape' in past centuries. The community was perpetually pregnant with itself."[36]

Few women did much in anticipation of birth itself. A few who could afford to leave their busy households seem to have returned to their mothers; in England aristocratic women "went to Town," London being the favorite place to deliver.[37] But most households could not afford to dispense with their female members even for a short period. Thus, most women were at or near home when birth pains began, and often as surprised by the onset of labor as were their husbands and neighbors. The beginning of labor was interpreted as the child's efforts to get out of the womb. The flurry of activity that it precipitated may strike us as chaotic, even careless, but it was consistent with the traditional understanding of the body as subject to natural and supernatural forces beyond human control.

The first step once birth was imminent was to call for the midwife and to separate and isolate the birthing mother.[38] A "lying-in chamber" was designated and closed off, the doors shut and the windows draped, so that none of the normal sounds, smells, or activities of the household could penetrate.[39] Sometimes birth would take place in the warmest place, normally the kitchen. If a bedroom was chosen, it was completely rearranged so as to deconstruct its familiar features, including the bed itself. Few women gave birth in their own beds, for the birthing position of the time was either standing or squatting, and it was normal to substitute a special cot or birthing chair.[40] Suddenly and deliberately removed from her role as wife and helpmeet, the expectant mother was as isolated as if she had been removed to a birthing hut in the African rain forest.[41]

The midwife was joined by a half-dozen "gossips," neighborhood matrons who were there to witness the birth and assist as best they could. They busied themselves preparing special food and drink, usually a caudle of either hot wine or spiced porridge, sharing birth stories, and praying for a safe delivery. Birth was considered a women's affair, and only when the life was threatened was the male doctor called in.[42] Every effort was made to prevent husbands from seeing or hearing what was often a painful and sometimes a lethal process. They awaited news in the company of male friends, drinking the "groaning malt," drowning the anxiety that birth invariably evoked—the fear of losing not only a mother and child but also their indispensable helpmeet and companion.[43]

The father's absence from the birthing room might suggest the lack of a concept of paternity, but in reality the opposite was the case. Men were said to feel a pregnancy, to share morning sickness and suffer the so-called husband's toothache, even experiencing labor pains.[44] The rituals of couvade, common to virtually all societies, constituted a parallel rite of progression in which paternity was formally acknowledged by the father and the community. In addition, the law recognized paternity by assigning rights in the child to the father rather than to the mother.[45]

Once the ritual separation had been accomplished, the waiting began. Little effort was made to hasten nature's pace or to substitute human for the divine will. Midwives sometimes liked to hurry events for their own convenience, but medical opinion prior to the nineteenth century was against inducing labor. In fact, midwives were no more sensitive or tolerant of the mother's wishes than were male doctors.[46] The common language of the time—"with child," "brought to bed," "lying-in"—reinforced the notion of the mother as an object of forces beyond her control.[47] Birth was the moment of greatest danger to her, to the child, and to everyone attending her. It had once been a moment when every available magical means would be brought to bear, but by the eighteenth century these were largely unavailable to women of the middle and upper classes. In Protestant America it was said that "no midwives can do what angels do," a reference to the fatalism that attended birth during this period.[48]

Once the child was delivered, it was the task of the midwife to cut the umbilical cord, separating the child symbolically as well as physically from the mother. Instead of being brought immediately to the breast, the child was often taken to the hearth symbolically identifying it with the house rather than with the mother.[49] It was then swaddled and shown to the father, his friends, and the other neighbors gathered at the house at the news of the event. The neglect of the mother in the immediate postpartum period was not as cruel as it may seem. She was regarded as out of danger and needing rest, but, of equal significance, she was not supposed to show too much affection toward the child. The mother love that is so much celebrated in our day was regarded with great suspicion during the eighteenth century.[50] Any display of emotion suggested that the woman was still under the control of the natural and supernatural forces associated with birth. Both she and the child needed protection from these; both needed a time and a space to gain, or regain, the full measure of their humanity before reincorporation into family and community.[51]

The birthing ritual did not end with the biological event but continued for some days and even weeks until all its most important phase, the rites of incorporation, were complete. For the child this meant a second birth through the rite of baptism. Ralph Josselin wrote at the birth of his first child in 1642, "God wash it from it[s] corruption and sanctify it and make it his owne."[52] Cleansing was one of the traditional functions of baptism, but even before the child was brought to the font it had ordinarily undergone several folk rites of purification, separating it symbolically from the womb and forces of nature that had brought it into the world. Great attention was given to shaping the child's head, as if it had to be remade in a human image.[53] Swaddling served similar symbolic purposes, for it "was these clothes which made the child human, just as the wider ceremony of childbirth of which swaddling was a part made the delivery an act of culture, not merely of nature.[54]

In the traditional narrative of birth, the wife "presented" the child to the husband, who in turn re-presented the child to the world with great flare and ceremony. Among the eighteenth-century gentry, birth, especially of a first-born son, was celebrated with bonfires, feasting, and distribution of largesse. Among the middle classes, patriarchal rites were more restrained but

followed a similar pattern of celebrating with family and friends.[55]

. . .

Mothers, still confined to the lying-in chamber by the strict conventions of the day, were rarely present at the church when their children were baptized.[56] They played little part in the immediate postpartum festivities, which were presided over by the paterfamilias. If the infant was to be wet-nursed, the mother might get only a brief glimpse before it was taken away, not to be seen again for months, sometimes even years. In the meantime, she had entered into her period of "lying in," a ritualized period of up to a month when she was in a transition state, betwixt and between, neither fully a wife nor fully a mother. The physical act of giving birth was not at that time deemed sufficient to endow her with the wholeness and sanctity we now see as naturally conferred by maternity. Maternity was an event, not a cultural category capable of endowing a woman with motherhood as we would understand it. Indeed, seeing birth as something that happened to her allowed a woman to return to her household roles relatively unchanged by the biological experience.

Restoring a new mother to the fullness of womanhood required a period of several weeks, called "her month"; this final stage of the traditional ritual of progression would return her to her role as wife and coworker. For the first week the new mother was supposed to remain immobilized in bed, drinking the special caudle and eating a restricted diet. She would receive a carefully orchestrated series of visitors—women relations first, later female friends—sharing caudle with them.[57] The husband was the first male to enter the lying-in chamber, but it was thought dangerous to have sex during "her month," and even the mother's breast, which has such erotic meaning in modern culture, was then regarded with distaste, even fear.[58] Gradually the lying-in chamber would be opened up and restored to its original order, and the new mother would venture into the other rooms of the house. She would not leave the house, however, until the end of the month, which was normally marked by the religious rite of "churching," the religious ceremony of purification and thanksgiving to which was attached so much significance during this period.[59]

. . .

Even as the literate classes turned increasingly to private thanksgiving, public churching remained extremely popular throughout the eighteenth and nineteenth centuries, kept alive by women who valued it for its power to reconnect them with their households and communities.[60] During "her month," the domestic order was turned upside down, and husbands took on many of the wifely duties. New mothers were even spared their usual sexual duties until they were churched, a rite of incorporation that, as David Cressy writes, "established a ritual closure to this state of affairs, allowing the resumption of sexual relations between husband and wife and the restoration of normal domestic order.[61] According to John Brand's eighteenth-century description, "on the day when such a Woman was Churched, every Family, favoured with a call, were bound to set Meat and Drink before her.[62] In America this event was called the "groaning-party." While the womenfolk rejoiced indoors, the men drank and fired off guns in recognition that a moment of danger had passed and their symbolic universe was once again in proper order.[63]

It is not surprising that churching remained popular among women of all classes throughout the eighteenth century. The upper classes differed from the lower only in their preference that it be a private ceremony, performed at home.[64] For all women,

however, it signaled a return to their primary identity as wife and helpmeet, and as part of the community of women. Today we think of birth (and especially first birth) as a new beginning that initiates motherhood and starts a family, thereby bringing a woman into the fullness of her femininity. Earlier generations, who did not equate maternity with motherhood or insist that nurturance was the sole responsibility of the individual mother, endowed birth with an entirely different meaning, making of it less a rite of individual passage and more a rite of progression for the entire community.

Rituals like these did not simply reflect behavior, they shaped it. The traditional rites of churching and baptism incorporated mothers and children into the community in a way that underlined, not a woman's own individual motherhood, but her connection to all mothers, and her children's connection to all children. The rites encouraged women to see their offspring as separate from themselves and to see mothering as one task among many, one that could be shared with others, including men. This is not to say that they did not care deeply about their children. It was precisely because parents were so concerned with the well-being of their offspring under conditions of high mortality and economic uncertainty that they were willing to entrust them to the kindness of strangers for both the short and the long term.[65] Taking care of children was central to a house mistress's duties, but in the era of the patriarchal household the role of wife subsumed that of mother. Until the nineteenth century, children looked beyond their own natural families for mothering and fathering. In turn, mothers and fathers looked to children who were not their own to fulfill their duty and desire to be good parents.

As long as a distinction was maintained between maternity and motherhood, mother figures, both idealized and demonized, were by no means confined to the domestic sphere. In the Middle Ages, maternal icons had populated the cosmos. By the seventeenth century, they had been brought down to earth but were still associated with godly households. It was not until the nineteenth century that "true motherhood" came to be associated with all women by virtue of giving birth. For the first time, motherhood was fully sacralized. "Human mothers had been honored before, but not in such an inflated manner. Flesh-and-blood mothers had never been held up to the standards of the Virgin Mary. Even the Virgin Mary had not been held to her own standards." In earlier centuries, the mother of Jesus had been allowed a certain freedom from the domestic role, but now she too was "completely redomesticated into a Victorian mother."[66] In Catholic countries, her cult grew in strength, providing women with a powerful representation of domesticated motherhood. But in Protestant lands, it was mothers themselves who would be fashioned into icons of true motherhood. By the end of the nineteenth century, they were objects of worship in both North America and Europe.

The symbolic treatment of pregnancy and birth was already showing some changes in the early nineteenth century. Middle-class women were beginning to treat their pregnancies differently: they were less likely to discuss what they called their "condition" with their husbands, and more likely to seek out male doctors for prenatal attention. Beginning their withdrawal from the world much earlier, most would no longer leave home during the period they now referred to as their "confinement."[67] These changes were anticipated in the new language of maternity that had appeared among the educated classes of Europe and North America at the end of the eighteenth century.

. . .

Lady Sarah Napier could write in 1818 that "no one can say 'breeding' or 'with child' or 'lying-in' without being thought indelicate. . . . 'In the family way' and 'confinement' have taken their place."[68] In the new United States, the term "pregnancy" was eclipsed by a whole series of euphemisms—"in the family way," "expecting," and "in a delicate condition."[69]

The term "expecting" conveyed a notion of anticipation that had been absent earlier. Birth ceased to be an event, something that happened to a woman, and became a condition women were expected to internalize and represent to the larger world. The ritual of birth itself was changing, with more attention paid to the first phase of separation and less to the last phase of incorporation, which became truncated, even nonexistent, among, middle-class women. Pregnant women were now advised to refrain from travel and exercise, and while working-class women had no choice but to continue their everyday activities, those who could afford to remove themselves from contact with the world did so. A pregnant woman was no longer welcome in public places, and she was discouraged from participating in many social occasions. She was not subject to these new prohibitions because, as in the past, she was considered too much under the influence of nature and dangerous to herself and others, but rather because, as Ludmilla Jordanova has observed, women were now seen as "the carriers and givers of life, and as a result, a pregnant woman was both the quintessence of life and an erotic object."[70] As such, she needed the protection afforded by domestic seclusion.

A rite that had taken only a few days now stretched over months. By the time the child arrived, middle-class women were fully prepared and had made all the necessary arrangements. Whereas upper-class women had previously traveled to their mothers, mothers now came to them.[71] The lying-in chamber was a thing of the past, for the birthing room, now normally the bedroom, was to be kept as nearly as possible in a normal state, with doors and windows open. There was no rearrangement of furniture, but rather an effort was made to maintain a homelike atmosphere. The conjugal bed replaced the birthing stool, emphasizing the compatibility between the roles of wife and mother and minimizing the strange and dangerous aspects of the female body in labor.[72]

The Victorian middle classes were the first to insist on home birth. "Thus confinement for childbirth was withdrawal to the supreme source of a woman's identity and purpose, the home," write Richard and Dorothy Wertz. "There, in her domain, a woman relearned who she was and, in maternity, performed her essential duty. Thereafter she might return, richly renewed, to society."[73] The symbols of home and motherhood were mutually reinforcing. No longer did a middle-class woman have need of an extended period of lying-in culminating with churching. Birth itself was capable of sanctifying a woman; it was a redeeming experience, a defining moment in the life of all women, a performance in which the mother was now the central actor. "Labour is a drama, painful to the individual, and exerting a painful interest in those around her," wrote W. Tyler Smith in the 1848 *London Lancet*.[74]

. . .

It is all the more significant therefore that women were choosing to have men present at births rather than the "gossips" who had been the traditional witnesses. By the 1840s and 1850s, not only were most middle-class home births attended by male doctors, but for the first time husbands were present in the birthing room.[75] Elaborate precautions were taken to preserve women's modesty, and doctors were trained to deliver by touch rather than by sight.[76] While most birth mothers were never entirely comfortable having male

doctors present, and the doctors seem to have been wary of the presence of husbands, middle-class women and the medical profession appear to have worked out an arrangement that met the requirements of all concerned. As historians have suggested, the women's willingness to have men in attendance had less to do with medical concerns than with the cultural imperative to have a "guaranteed performance. . . . They may have wanted a representative male to see their pain and suffering in order that their femininity might be established and their pain verified before men."[77]

. . . Guilt seems to have replaced fear as the primary paternal emotion in the nineteenth century. Previously afraid to be present during the mysterious moment of birth, middle-class men now felt a powerful need to support their wives at their moment of greatest pain and danger.[78] Unlike working-class fathers, who continued to experience their wives' travails in the traditional form of couvade well into this century, middle-class men could no longer imagine their bodies as functioning like those of women. Among them, the term "to father" had already taken on its modern meaning: to inseminate. They were increasingly detached during the nine months of gestation and played virtually no role at all in the preparations for birth. The old rites of passage to fatherhood, the groaning malt and the ritual presentation of the child to its *pater*, had all but fallen away by the nineteenth century. Perhaps the middle-class man eagerly accepted the invitation to enter the birthing room for the first time because the only remaining symbolic connection to his child was through the mother.

Women were the central actors in the transformed rites of birth. Previously, maternity was something that happened to a woman, her maximum moment of vulnerability and suffering. Now the test of true womanhood was not only how well a woman bore physical suffering but how she responded emotionally to her newborn. This shift coincided precisely with the redefinition of women as the more delicate, more feeling sex, and with the reevaluation of mother love, which ceased to be seen as so dangerous it required a lying-in period to recover from and became instead central to "true motherhood," born of the sacred moment of birth.[79] Melesina Trench described the birth of her first child in 1787 in terms that were to become standard in the next century: "When I looked in my boy's face, when I heard him breathe, when I felt the full pressure of his little fingers, I understood the full force of Voltaire's declaration: Le chef d'oeuvre d'amour est le coeur d'une mere. . . . My husband's delight of his son nearly equalled mine."[80] In Mrs. Gaskell's Victorian novel *Ruth* (1853), the initial interaction between mother and child is rendered in precisely the same terms: "That baby touch called forth her love; the doors of her heart were thrown wide open for the little infant to go in and take possession."[81]

Until the moment of giving birth, a woman's femininity had been only potential; afterward, she was a true woman. Gone was the ritual separation of mother and child, the head shaping and the swaddling. The new mother was no longer considered a danger to herself and others, to be immobilized and quarantined until she underwent rites of purification. The breast, simultaneously naturalized and eroticized, became identified with both nurturance and pleasure; for middle-class Victorian women, breast-feeding became a symbol of true motherhood.[82] Doctors recommended it because it made women "more soft and beautiful," more rather than less attractive to their husbands.[83] In Dickens's novel of the same name, David Copperfield dreams that "a baby smile upon her breast might change my child-wife [Dora] into a woman."[84] In the traditional birth ritual, the postpartum period had served to symbolically disconnect mother and child, returning the

woman to her multiple roles as wife and helpmeet. Now this time was used to symbolize fusion, as if, as Judith Lewis has put it, "the experience of motherhood presumably began only after the child's birth—precisely when it was thought to have ended a century earlier.[85]

Having ceased to be a moment of supernatural and physical danger, birth was represented as magical, transformative of the identities not just of the mother but also of the father and child. And what had once been a moment of communal reaffirmation now served primarily as a celebration of female kin connections. Attending their daughters' confinements became for older women a source of renewal of their own sense of motherhood. Queen Victoria set the example, insisting that her daughters wear her maternity gown and give birth in the same bed where they themselves had been born.[86] Few women were able to symbolize their connections in quite so dramatic a manner, but in time a whole set of all-female cerebrations, including the baby and bridal shower, would arise.[87]

The old rites had emphasized incorporation; the new underlined separation. With birth symbolically disassociated from death and danger, the traditional practices of baptism and churching seemed neither necessary nor proper. Infant mortality rates remained relatively high, but among the middle classes the sickly child was no longer hastened away to be given the magical protection of baptism but was immediately placed under a doctor's care. Baptism could wait until the child and mother were physically ready. In the eighteenth and early nineteenth centuries, this ceremony was likely to take place at home, but after 1850 church christenings regained their popularity among the middle classes; they did not regain, however, their communal aspect or the magic that was still a part of working-class baptisms.[88] It was now the mother and child who provided the focus for these family ceremonials; they have remained the center of attention ever since, virtually displacing the father from his previous role in the baptism ceremony.

Churching went the way of the traditional baptism. Educated women recited prayers of thanksgiving in the privacy of their homes, leaving the public ceremony to the working classes.[89] The doctor now determined when a woman was ready to end her confinement. The new rite of passage, focused on separation, dispensed with all the old symbols of incorporation.[90] Maternity by itself had become sufficient to establish not only true motherhood but also fatherhood. In the absence of the old rites of paternity, fathers came to rely on birth to give meaning to their fatherhood, and they were drawn to the bedside by the powerful symbols present there. In the rescripted drama of birth, the husband became a father when he beheld mother and child together, joined by the powerful icon of the breast. For Amos Alcott, a new American father, this sight was an almost religious experience that made "it seem that I was, indeed, a Father."[91]

By the end of the nineteenth century, middle-class women were congratulating themselves on having mastered the natural and super-natural forces that still made birth such a mysterious and deadly process to many working-class women. "We can take care of our bodies, study them, worry about them, treat them, in short, much as one does a favorite horse, and then demand that they serve us absolutely," one American woman wrote in *Good Housekeeping* in 1915.[92] But this sense of control over nature had been achieved largely through science and in collaboration with the male medical establishment. By 1900 middle-class women were ready to take the step of demanding painless birth, an option that had been available since the 1840s but that they had been unwilling to adopt because

suffering remained so closely identified with true motherhood. But now a generation of "New Women," many of them feminists eager to enter the wider world, were ready to dispense with what they regarded as an outmoded superstition. By the 1920s a variety of anesthetics, including "twilight sleep," had become popular in middle-class circles.[93] The physicality of birth was thereby separated from suffering as women asserted the superiority of mind over body.

Ironically, women's heightened desire to control their own bodies increased their dependency on the male medical profession and led directly to the hospitalization of birth, which began after the First World War and had become almost universal by the 1950s. In the nineteenth century, only the destitute went to hospitals to give birth. They were dangerous places until the 1880s, and the stigma attached to them was reflected in the fact that in 1900 only 5 percent of American births took place there. By 1939, however, one-half of all births took place in hospitals and three-quarters of all urban births were hospitalized. The middle classes led the way in placing themselves under medical care; the working classes followed when they could afford it![94]

Beginning in the 1920s, middle-class women were coming to hold the medical view of their bodies as machines, prone to breakdown and failure. This was the rationale for hospitalization, inspiring *Century Illustrated Magazine* to give its own version of the contemporary colloquy between a woman and her doctor:

> "But is the hospital necessary at all?" demanded a young woman of her obstetrician friend. "Why not bring the baby at home?"
>
> "What would you do if your automobile broke down on a country road?" the doctor countered with another question.
>
> "Try and fix it," said the modern chauffeuse.
>
> "And if you couldn't?"
>
> "Have it hauled to the nearest garage."

"Exactly. Where the trained mechanics and their necessary tools are," agreed the doctor. "It's the same with the hospital."[95]

Doctors had begun to see all birth as potentially pathogenic and to establish what they believed to be scientifically valid procedures to ensure the health and safety of both mother and child; middle-class women, increasingly taught to think scientifically about their own bodies and those of their children, readily accepted this rationale. Intensified prenatal care placed them in the category of patients, inducing them "to regard themselves as objects."[96] Saved from suffering but denied the central role in the drama of birth that their mothers and grandmothers had claimed, these otherwise liberated women found themselves subjected to procedures that initially had been designed to promote hygiene but that rapidly became rigidly routinized, denying the very humanity of mother and child that hospital birth was supposed to protect and enhance.[97]

Hospitalization's emphasis on separation began at the moment of admission. The woman was immobilized in a wheelchair and whisked away from her escort to be "prepped"—gowned, her pubic hair shaved, given an enema, bedded, sedated, and monitored, usually in splendid isolation. She was now on hospital time; should labor come too slowly, it was likely to be induced. (In the twentieth century, noticeably few births occur on weekends, normally a doctor's free time.)[98] Once labor began, the routines become even more invasive. The birth mother's sense of vulnerability was enhanced by the so-called lithotomy position, "her buttocks at the table's edge, her legs widespread in the air, her vagina totally exposed."[99] Other technological procedures, none of which had been proven to enhance the birthing process, were then deployed and, indeed, continue to be used to this day. In the

United States episiotomy has become an almost universal practice, used in 90 percent of all births. Almost one-quarter of all American births are now performed by cesarean section, which places a woman's mind and body at an even further remove. Mirrors are provided so that the woman can observe the whole process, placing her in the position of witnessing herself, the ultimate reminder that in the modern scientific construction of birth it is the doctor, not the mother, who delivers the child.[100]

In the hospital, birth ceased to be a family event. The father's role was reduced to that of the nervous bystander, pacing the halls during labor, glimpsing the newborn through the glass of the nursery, his visits strictly limited. But the mother's access to the baby was also drastically restricted. it was handed by the doctor to the nurses, who washed and bundled it, a kind of secular baptism signifying the child's incorporation, not into the family or community, but into a technological world claiming full credit for its birth.[101] From the 1920s onward, mothers' access to their infants was governed by notions of "scientific motherhood," which emphasized scheduled feeding and sleeping and gave little support to breast-feeding or to the mothers themselves. It has been noted that, "while child experts became more sensitive to baby . . . they were increasingly insensitive to mother."[102]

Women's efforts to transcend nature through science began as part of a progressive effort to gain equal access to the men's world of work, education, and political power. By the 1940s, however, some women were questioning "twilight sleep" and anesthetized birth, along with other tenets of scientific motherhood like scheduled feeding. Margaret Mead demanded of her doctor, Benjamin Spock, that he assist her in achieving the fullest possible consciousness during the birth of her children.

She also insisted on breast-feeding on demand, another radical departure from the technologic model of child-rearing.[103] Educated women had been the first to internalize an image of themselves as machines, but by the 1950s they were beginning to complain of the factorylike conditions of the delivery wards. "The practice of obstetrics is the most modern and medieval, the kindest and the cruelest," wrote one mother of three. "Women are herded like sheep through the obstetrical assembly line, are drugged and strapped on tables while their babies are forceps-delivered. Obstetricians today are businessmen who run baby factories. Modern painkillers and methods are used for the convenience of the doctor, not to spare the mother."[104]

By this time a small number of middle-class women on both sides of the Atlantic had become followers of Grantley Dick Read's "natural childbirth" movement. They eschewed drugs out of a fear of possible damage to their infants' brains and began to listen to Spock's notions about a more flexible, commonsensical approach to child-rearing. Accepting that their own feelings and those of their children might be a better guide than the doctors and child care experts, they began to challenge the doctrines of scientific motherhood through their own experiences of mothering.

Although this new attitude upset the medical profession, the natural childbirth and child-rearing movements were no threat to postwar conventions of marriage and family. In fact, the followers of the Read, Lamaze, and Bradley methods were all concerned about restoring birth to its place as a family ritual, enhancing the "togetherness" that was so highly prized in the postwar era. All were staunch defenders of the conventional nuclear family, with its gendered division of labor. No unwed fathers were admitted to Read's natural childbirth classes, and the training provided to properly married couples reinforced the

highly gendered notion of childbirth and child care that assigned to fathers the role of secondary parent.[105] Fathers' supportive role still ended at the admissions desk, for the entry of fathers into the delivery room was resisted until the 1970s. But even when this barrier fell, fathers were subjected to a gendered set of rules and procedures that reduced them largely to the role of bystander and often left them feeling frustrated and alienated by the experience. Natural childbirth managed to restore women to a central role in the drama of birth but failed to provide symbols of the father's connection to the newborn. Birth continued to be defined as a female rite of individual passage, underlining the gendered nature of parenthood and reinforcing the connection between maternity and motherhood, while emphasizing the distinction between paternity and fatherhood.

Aware that hospital procedures, even when administered with the greatest consideration, are inevitably alienating and discomforting, many people had begun by the 1980s to advocate a return to birthing at home or, as the next best thing, in homelike birthing centers. This movement, together with the parallel return to midwife-assisted births, continues to grow in both Europe and the United States but has yet to displace medicalized childbirth procedures as the modern rite of passage for most women. In the United States, more than 85 percent of all births continue to occur in hospital settings, with only 1 percent taking place at home; in Europe the percentages of home births are higher but the symbolic construction of motherhood has not changed very much. Scientific motherhood continues to hold sway. Robbie Davis-Floyd has estimated that 70 percent of all American births conform to what she calls the technocratic model, with standard procedures of modern medicine constituting the rite of passage preferred by most women.[106] Even when they choose birthing centers, women insist on medically trained assistance, so that, whether under the bright lights of the delivery room or in the softer ambience of the birthing center, mothers still struggle to achieve the illusive sense of true motherhood under the sign of science.

Despite all the changes in location, little has altered over the two hundred years since birth ceased to be something that happens to a woman and became the ultimate source of adult female identity. Never have the rituals surrounding birth been so extended or elaborate; never has birth played so central a role in our imaginings of what family should be; never has so much time and effort been devoted to its anticipation and to its memory. But it remains a rite of individual passage, separating the new mother and underlining her singular relationship to the child. In earlier centuries, mothers certainly experienced postpartum depression, but there is evidence that the current absence of incorporative rituals leads to an overwhelming sense of isolation, a feeling of being "lost and alone."[107] Men are once again part of the birthing scene, but largely as witnesses, with their still and video cameras at the ready. It is still women who give modern family life's most demanding performance. It is something they most eagerly anticipate and look back on with a great deal of satisfaction. While they are going through their rite of passage, however, many find themselves overwhelmed, even to the point of becoming destructive to themselves and to their children.

Women give birth not only to children but to their husband's fatherhood, their own motherhood, and the family itself.[108] Weddings create couples, but it is birth that makes a family. We say that a young couple expecting their first child are "starting a family." We celebrate not only wedding anniversaries but children's birthdays; indeed, the latter have become the most important rites of progression for modern families,

moments to synchronize calendars and symbolize unity. Childless couples are considered less than complete, and we talk about a family whose children have grown up as if it is no longer really a family.[109] While fathers as well as mothers experience this change, it is women who are most affected by "empty nest syndrome," a sense of loss only a little less painful to them than the onset of menopause, which until recently was equated with the loss of purpose in a woman's life.[110]

In the past, when maternity was separable from motherhood, it was possible to imagine motherless families and familyless mothers. Then, it was the absence of a patriarch that endangered the household, while today a family without a mother is the one most likely to be placed under the jurisdiction of the state. Prior to the nineteenth century, custody of children, even of infants, was invariably assigned the responsibility for children.[111] We have no trouble imagining fatherless families, but a motherless family is unthinkable. In the twentieth century, law, psychology, and the social sciences have combined to declare the mother-child bond primary. Mothers are assigned all the credit when children turn out well, and all the blame when they turn out badly, for never has motherhood loomed so large in Western culture's sense of its own well-being.

Mother's voice, mother's smile, and mother's love first became central symbols in the Victorian period. But we can also detect the beginnings of modern mother-blaming in the same period, suggesting that idealization and demonization are two sides of the same coin. It was then that mothers first became the objects of intense nostalgia, particularly among sons who were forced to leave family behind in their quest for success in an uncertain, fragmented world that made the wholeness and certainty mothers stood for so unattainable and therefore so attractive. Daughters were also drawn to their mothers, but in a somewhat different way. They were more likely to remain within her orbit and to experience her as a real person rather than an idealized icon. Today, as more daughters enter careers, they too have found it harder to recognize the real woman behind the powerful image of motherhood. Daughters seem to find it as difficult to separate fantasy and reality when it comes to motherhood. As they have entered the world of work and politics, they have had increasing difficulty in seeing the human dimension of mothers, including their own.[112]

Fantasies about mothers have spread in proportion to the increasing complexity and difficulty of modern mothering. In the nineteenth century, when servants and kinfolk were more likely to be involved in the upbringing of children, the praise and blame were more likely be divided among several mother figures. The British upper classes have been notoriously fond of their nannies, but just as apt to project negative feelings onto them.[113] Today, when mothers are more likely to raise their own children, they are also more likely to be the objects of both idealization and demonization. The higher the standard that mothers set for themselves, the more likely they are to be blamed, and to blame themselves. As Ann Dally has put it: "In our times, there has been less idealization of women and wives, but idealization of the mother has reached unprecedented proportions. The result is that we now face a crisis of motherhood."[114]

In a world largely emptied of a sense of place, mothers have become fixed points in our mental landscapes. They must always be there for us, even in their physical absence. By 1900 it had become difficult to imagine any mother substitutes. Hymns composed for the new Mother's Day, invented just before the First World War, extolled mothers' singularity and centrality: "We find no second mother/We find no second home."[115] Today Europeans and Americans still return to mother's for Sunday

dinner and at Christmas. It is her memory that is most honored and her grave that is most visited. Mother's Day is still a far more important occasion than Father's Day, which was invented in North America in 1908.[116] The spread of Mother's Day in the twentieth century testifies to the greater symbolic power of motherhood, which has been appropriated by all kinds of commercial, religious, and political movements. But the desire to honor the idea of motherhood has too often been accompanied by a neglect of the plight of actual mothers. Regimes like Nazi Germany, which placed huge burdens on women, were the most zealous in their promotion of Mother's Day. And in our own country, in the current debates about welfare, the same idealization goes hand in hand with neglect of the dire conditions facing many real mothers.[117]

There is really no role in modern society quite like motherhood. Wifehood and husbandhood are disposable through divorce, and fathers can practice a kind of serial fatherhood in which they are allowed to try again when they fail with their first set of children.[118] But mothers are forever the mothers to the children they bear in a culture that privileges blood tie as its primary symbol of permanence and connection.[119] Motherhood is considered a full-time, lifelong career, and child-rearing, which was once understood as a set of learned tasks, is seen as an instinct that comes as naturally to women as the sex drive does to men.[120] While it could be argued that the physical burdens of child-rearing have diminished, the psychological and cultural work of motherhood has increased enormously. No longer a set of well-defined tasks that can be shared with others, modern mothering demands, as John Bowlby, the leading advocate of mother-child bonding, formulated it in 1951, "constant attention day and night, seven days a week and 365 in the year."[121]

For much of this century, the ideology of true motherhood demanded that women stay at home to meet the supposedly insatiable needs of their children; even now, as women cope with the equally greedy claims of the workplace, their time and presence are more in demand than those of men, even when both parents are earning the same salaries. Studies have shown that women have much greater difficulty mentally separating work and home than men. Even the physical separation of home and work does not automatically create cognitive distance for women in the same way that it does for men. Mothers who are thousands of miles from home remain responsible for its day-to-day operations. Studies show that they are more likely to check in by calling home and that they worry more than men.[122] Mothers are always mentally at home in ways that fathers are not. They do not have access to the rituals that allow men to create mental distance, for much more fuss is still made over men's home leavings and comings than women's. By and large, the symbols and images of both home and workplace underscore men's claims to the role of principal breadwinner, disguising and even erasing working women's contributions. Thus, even as the conditions of men's and women's work change, the cultural constructions remain the same, sustaining the image in the absence of reality.

Today motherhood is given far more ritual attention than fatherhood. It is something of a paradox that birth should have become such an elaborate rite of passage in an era of declining fertility and at a time when only about one-quarter of the average woman's life is involved with active childbearing and child-rearing. In the days when a married woman's life span was entirely taken up with mothering, there was no need to underline that basic function. Today our culture demands that motherhood be honored even at the expense of mothers themselves. All our private and public celebrations of motherhood—birthdays, anniversaries, Mother's Day—reflect our need to find through symbol and ritual a sense of nurture and protection that mothers by themselves can never fully provide. In earlier periods, society was able to turn to holy mothers and exemplary members of the community to reassure itself of the enduring qualities of good motherhood. Today we look to mothers themselves, who are placed in the unenviable position of having to live up to an ideal that only a superwoman could fulfill.

Unable to accept their own humanity and the shortcomings this inevitably entails, many women feel a disconnection between the idealized motherhood they are expected to live up to and the realities of everyday mothering. Modern culture has thus added yet another task to mother's work: representing herself to herself and to others as something she can never completely be. Never before has this cultural imperative taken up so much space and time in women's lives. Never have mothers been so burdened by motherhood.

NOTES

1. Ann Dally, *Inventing Motherhood: The Consequences of an Ideal* (London: Burnett Books, 1982), p. 17.
2. "Disillusioned Town Reviles Woman Accused of Killings," *New York Times*, November 5, 1994; see also Susan Chira, "Murdered Children: In Most Cases, a Parent Did It," ibid.
3. Dana Raphael, "Matrescence, Becoming a Mother: An 'Old/New' Rite of Passage," in *Being Female: Reproduction, Power, and Change*, ed. Dana Raphael (The Hague: Mouton, 1975), pp. 65–71.
4. Robbie E. Davis-Floyd, *Birth as an American Rite of Passage* (Berkeley: University of California Press, 1992), pp. 13, 38.

5. Even among the relatively healthy American populations, rates of orphanage were very high; see Richard Wertz and Dorothy Wertz, *Lying-in: A History of Childbirth in America* (New York: Free Press, 1977), p. 3; Peter Laslett, *Family Life and Illicit Love in Earlier Generations* (Cambridge: Cambridge University Press, 1977), Chapter 4.

6. Shari Thurer, *Myths of Motherhood: How Culture Reinvents the Good Mother* (Boston: Houghton Mifflin, 1994), p. 213.

7. Ibid., p. 177; Elisabeth Badinter, *Mother Love: Myth and Reality: Motherhood in Modern History* (New York: Macmillan, 1981), p. 48; Valerie Fildes, *Wet-nursing: A History from Antiquity to the Present* (Oxford: Basil Blackwell, 1988), Chapters 6–8.

8. Fildes, *Wetnursing*, Chapter 8.

9. Leonore Davidoff and Catherine Hall, *Family Fortunes: Men and Women of the English Middle Class, 1780–1850* (Chicago: University of Chicago Press, 1987), pp. 222–223.

10. Ellen Ross, *Love and Toil: Motherhood in Outcast London, 1870–1918* (New York: Oxford University Press, 1993), pp. 133–137.

11. Carl Chinn, *They Worked All Their Lives: Women of the Urban Poor in England, 1880–1939* (New York: St. Martin's Press, 1988), Chapters 2–4; Michael Anderson, *Family Structure in Nineteenth-Century Lancashire* (Cambridge: Cambridge University Press, 1971), pt. 3.

12. Illana Krausman Ben-Amos, *Adolescence and Youth in Early Modern England* (New Haven, Conn.: Yale University Press, 1994), p. 2.

13. John Boswell, *The Kindness of Strangers: The Abandonment of Children in Western Europe, Late Antiquity to the Renaissance* (New York: Pantheon, 1988), p. 11.

14. Dally, *Inventing Motherhood*, p. 17.

15. Laura Thatcher Ulrich, *Good Wives: Image and Reality in the Lives of Women in Northern New England, 1650–1750* (New York: Vintage, 1980), p. 158.

16. Jacques Gelis, *History of Childbirth: Fertility, Pregnancy, and Birth in Early Modern Europe* (Cambridge: Polity, 1991), p. 105.

17. On the phenomenon of "little mothers," see Elizabeth Roberts, *A Woman's Place: An Oral History of Working-Class Women, 1890–1940* (Oxford: Basil Blackwell, 1984), pp. 24–25, 173; Chinn, *They Worked All Their Lives*, pp. 26–36; on the familial relationship of whites and blacks on American slave plantations, see Mechal Sobel, *The World They Made Together: Black and White Values in Eighteenth-Century Virginia* (Princeton, N.J.: Princeton University Press, 1987), Chapter 10; on the nurturing qualities attributed to men, see Davidoff and Hall, *Family Fortunes*, pp. 329–335.

18. For a fuller discussion, see Chapter 9.

19. Clarissa Atkinson, *The Oldest Vocation: Christian Motherhood in the Middle Ages* (Ithaca, N.Y.: Cornell University Press, 1991), pp. 115, 143.

20. Atkinson, *The Oldest Vocation*, p. 220.

21. Thurer, *Myths of Motherhood*, p. 90.

22. Davis-Floyd, *Birth as an American Rite of Passage*, pp. 1–2.

23. Gelis, *History of Childbirth*, p. 65.

24. Wertz and Wertz, *Lying-in*, p. 23.

25. On rites of passage generally, see Arnold van Gennep, *Rites of Passage* (Chicago: University of Chicago Press, 1960).

26. On rites of progression, see David Cheal, "Relationships in Time: Ritual, Social Structure, and the Life Course," *Studies in Symbolic Interaction* 9 (1988): 98.

27. Audrey Eccles, *Obstetrics and Gynecology in Tudor and Stuart England* (Kent, Ohio: Kent State University Press, 1982), pp. 24–26, 60; Angus McClaren, *Reproductive Rituals: The Perception of Fertility in England from the Sixteenth to the Nineteenth Century* (London: Methuen, 1984), Chapters 1–2.

28. McLaren, *Reproductive Rituals*, pp. 13–30; Gelis, *History of Childbirth*, pp. 47–56, and Chapter 6.

29. Gelis, *History of Childbirth*, p. 58.

30. Alan Macfarlane, *The Family Life of the Reverend Ralph Josselin* (New York: W. W. Norton, 1970), pp. 81–91.

31. Gelis, *History of Childbirth*, pp. 67ff.; American death records in the eighteenth century include many infants who died without names; Sandra Brant and Elissa Cullman, *Small Folk: A Celebration of Childhood in America* (New York: E. P. Dutton, 1980), p. 43.

32. Thurer, *Myths of Motherhood*, p. 171.

33. Atkinson, *The Oldest Vocation*, p. 193.

34. Ralph Josselin used this language; and it continued among the upper classes until the late eighteenth century; Macfarlane, *The Family Life of the Reverend Ralph Josselin*, pp. 84–85; see also Judith S. Lewis, *In the Family Way: Childbearing in the English Aristocracy, 1760–1860* (New Brunswick, N.J.: Rutgers University Press, 1986), p. 72; Madeleine Riley, *Brought to Bed* (South Brunswick, N.J.: A. S. Barnes, 1968), p. 4.

35. Eccles, *Obstetrics and Gynecology in Tudor and Stuart England*, pp. 45–47, 60–65; Ann Oakley, *The Captured Womb: A History of the Medical Care of Pregnant Women* (Oxford: Basil Blackwell, 1984), pp. 22–24.

36. Gelis, *History of Childbirth*, p. 45.

37. On aristocratic women, see Lewis, *In the Family Way*, pp. 52–54, 156–158.

38. Van Gennep, *Rites of Passage*, p. 41.

39. Eccles, *Obstetrics and Gynecology in Tudor and Stuart England*, pp. 94–95; Adrian Wilson, "Participant or Patient? Seventeenth-Century Childbirth from the Mother's Point of View," in *Patients and Practitioners: Lay Principles of Medicine in Pre-Industrial Societies*, ed. Roy Porter (Cambridge: Cambridge University Press, 1985), p. 135; Wertz and Wertz, *Lying-in*, Chapter 1.

40. Lewis, *In the Family Way*, p. 151; Wilson, "Participant or Patient?" p. 135; Edward Shorter, *The Making of the Modern Family* (New York: Basic Books, 1975), p. 145; Eccles, *Obstetrics and Gynecology in Tudor and Stuart England*, p. 92; Gelis, *History of Childbirth*, pp. 97–98, 130–132.

41. Wilson, "Participant or Patient?" pp. 132–135; Shorter, *The Making of the Modern Family*, pp. 48–56; Ralph Houlbrooke, *English Family Life, 1576–1716: An Anthology from Diaries* (Oxford: Basil Blackwell, 1989), pp. 129–130; Wertz and Wertz, *Lying-in*, pp. 12–14.

42. Shorter, *The Making of the Modern Family*, pp. 293–294.

43. Wilson, "Participant or Patient?" pp. 133–136.

44. Gelis, *History of Childbirth*, pp. 38, 155; Lisa Cody, "The Politics of Body Contact: The Discipline of Reproduction in Britain, 1688–1834" (Ph.D. dissertation, University of California at Berkeley, 1993), conclusion.

45. Nigel Lowe, "The Legal Status of Father: Past and Present," in *The Father Figure*, eds. L. McKee and M. O'Brien (London: Tavistock, 1982), pp. 26–28; Riley, *Brought to Bed*, pp. 68, 105–113.

46. Wertz and Wertz, *Lying-in*, pp. 20–23; Wilson, "Participant or Patient?" pp. 129–130; Shorter, *The Making of the Modern Family*, pp. 38–39; Gelis, *History of Childbirth*, pp. 134–135.

47. Riley, *Brought to Bed*, pp. 3–4; Lewis, *In the Family Way*, p. 72.

48. Quoted in Wertz and Wertz, *Lying-in*, p. 21.

49. Gelis, *History of Childbirth*, p. 163.

50. Ruth Bloch, "American Feminine Ideals in Transition: The Rise of the Moral Mother, 1785–1815," *Feminist Studies* 4, no. 2 (1978): 101–126; Badinter, *Mother Love*, pt. 1.

51. Gelis, *History of Childbirth*, p. 183.

52. Alan Macfarlane, *The Family Life of Ralph Josselin* (New York: W. W. Norton, 1970), p. 88.

53. Eccles, *Obstetrics and Gynecology in Tudor and Stuart England*, p. 83; Joseph Illick, "Child-rearing in Seventeenth-Century England and America," in *The History of Childhood*, ed. Lloyd deMause (New York: Psychohistory Press, 1974), p. 307; *Notes and Queries*, 5th series (September 14, 1878): 205, and (September 28, 1878): 255–256.

54. Wilson, "Participant or Patient?" p. 137.

55. Macfarlane, *The Family Life of Ralph Josselin*, pp. 88–89; Houlbrooke, *English Family Life*, p. 131; on folk rites, see John Brand, *Observations on Popular Antiquities* (London: Chatto and Windus, 1877), pp. 340–341.

56. Wilson, "Participant or Patient?" p. 138.

57. Eccles, *Obstetrics and Gynecology in Tudor and Stuart England*, pp. 95–97; Wilson, "Participant or Patient?" pp. 137–138; Lewis, *In the Family Way*, pp. 194–199; van Gennep, *Rites of Passage*, p. 48; Gelis, *History of Childbirth*, pp. 188–194.

58. Linda Pollock, *Forgotten Children: Parent-Child Relations from 1500 to 1900* (Cambridge: Cambridge University Press, 1983), p. 215; Eccles, *Obstetrics and Gynecology in Tudor and Stuart England*, pp. 14, 98.

59. Wilson, "Participant or Patient?" p. 138; Lewis, *In the Family Way*, pp. 195–197.

60. Peter Rushton, "Purification or Social Contract? Ideologies of Reproduction and the Churching of Women after Childbirth," in *The Public and Private*, eds. Eva Gamarnikow, et al. (London: Heinemann, 1983), pp. 124–131.

61. David Cressy, "Thanksgiving and the Churching of Women in Post-Reformation England," *Past and Present* 141 (November 1993); 115.

62. Brand, *Observations on Popular Antiquities*, p. 228.

63. Wertz and Wertz, *Lying-in*, pp. 5–10.

64. Lewis, *In the Family Way*, pp. 201–202; Adrian Wilson, "The Ceremony of Childbirth and Its Interpretation," in *Women as Mothers in Pre-Industrial England*, ed. Valerie Fildes (London: Routledge, 1990), p. 92.

65. Pollock, *Forgotten Children*, pp. 111–113; Boswell, *Same-Sex Unions*, pp. 428–434.

66. Thurer, *Myths of Motherhood*, p. 186.

67. Wertz and Wertz, *Lying-in*, pp. 79–80.

68. Quoted in ibid.

69. Wertz and Wertz, *Lying-in*, p. 79.

70. Ludmilla Jordanova, "Naturalizing the Family: Literature and the Bio-medical Sciences in the Late Eighteenth Century," in her *Languages of Nature: Critical Essays on Science and Literature* (London: Free Association Press, 1986), p. 105.

71. Lewis, *In the Family Way*, pp. 53–54.

72. Ibid.; Pollock, "Forgotten Children," p. 36; John Conquest, "Letters to a Mother, on the Management of Herself and Her Children in Health and Disease" (London: Longman, 1848), pp. 39–46; Shorter, "The Making of the Modern Family," p. 145.

73. Wertz and Wertz, *Lying-in*, p. 80.

74. Quoted in Mary Poovey, "Scenes of an Indelicate Character: The Medical Treatment of Victorian Women," in Catherine Gallagher and Thomas Laqueur, *The Making of the Modern Body* (Berkeley: University of California Press, 1987), p. 157.

75. J. Jill Suitor, "Husbands' Participation in Childbirth: A Nineteenth-Century Phenomena," *Journal of Family History* 6 (1981): 278–293; Shorter, *The Making of the Modern Family*, p. 294; Lewis, *In the Family Way*, pp. 177–183; J. H. Walsh, *A Manual of Domestic Economy Suited to Families Spending from 100 to 1000 a Year* (London, 1857), p. 558.

76. Wertz and Wertz, *Lying-in*, pp. 85–87.

77. Ibid., p. 65.

78. John H. Miller, "'Temple and Sewer': Childbirth, Prudery and Victoria Regina," *The Victorian Family*, ed. A. S. Wohl (London: Croom Helm, 1978), pp. 34–36; Riley, *Brought to Bed*, pp. 122–123.

79. Lewis, *In the Family Way*, pp. 58–59, 71–72; Miller, pp. 35–39; Jan Lewis, "Mother's Love: The Construction of an Emotion in Nineteenth-Century America" (paper delivered at the Pittsburgh Symposium, July 1988).

80. Quoted in Pollock, *Forgotten Children*, p. 206.

81. Quoted in Miller, "Temple and Sewer," p. 35; for other literary representations, see Riley, *Brought to Bed*, pp. 28–29.

82. Jordanova, "Natural Facts," pp. 50ff.; Thurer, *Myths of Motherhood*, pp. 199–200.

83. Conquest, *Letters to a Mother*, p. 93; Fildes, *Women as Mothers*, p. 401.

84. Quoted in Riley, *Brought to Bed*, p. 5.

85. Lewis, *In a Family Way*, pp. 73–84.

86. Miller, "Temple and Sewer," pp. 37–38.

87. David Cheal, *The Gift Economy* (London: Routledge, 1988), pp. 99–100.

88. James Obelkevich, *Religion and Rural Society: South Lindsey, 1825–1875* (Oxford: Clarendon Press, 1976), pp. 127–130.

89. Rushton, "Purification or Social Contract?" pp. 118–123; David Clark, *Between Pulpit and Pew: Folk Religion in a North Yorkshire Fishing Village* (Cambridge: Cambridge University Press, 1982), pp. 114–123.

90. Suitor, "Husbands' Participation in Childbirth," pp. 284–287; Miller, "Temple and Sewer," p. 36.

91. Quoted in Pollock, *Forgotten Children*, p. 205; see also Riley, *Brought to Bed*, pp. 115–124.

92. Quoted in Wertz and Wertz, *Lying-in*, p. 106.

93. Ibid., Chapter 4.

94. Ibid., pp. 133–135.

95. Quoted in Davis-Floyd, *Birth as an American Rite of Passage*, p. 51.

96. Wertz and Wertz, *Lying-in*, p. 168.

97. Ibid., p. 173.

98. Gelis, *History of Childbirth*, p. 272.

99. Davis-Floyd, *Birth as an American Rite of Passage*, p. 123.

100. On the meaning of mirrors, see ibid., pp. 132–135.

101. Ibid., pp. 68–69.

102. Thurer, *Myths of Motherhood*, p. 255.

103. Wertz and Wertz, *Lying-in*, pp. 180–182.

104. Letter to the editor, *Ladies' Home Journal* (May 1958), quoted in ibid., p. 172.

105. Wertz and Wertz, *Lying-in*, p. 185.

106. Davis-Floyd, *Birth as an American Rite of Passage*, p. 282.

107. For a summary of these studies, see ibid., pp. 41–43.

108. Ibid., p. 38.

109. Joan Busfield and Michael Paddon, *Thinking about Children: Sociology and Fertility in Post-War Britain* (Cambridge: Cambridge University Press, 1977), pp. 134–156.

110. Carroll Smith-Rosenberg, "Puberty to Menopause: The Cycle of Femininity in Nineteenth-Century America," in Smith-Rosenberg, *Disorderly Conduct: Visions of Gender in Victorian America* (New York: Oxford University Press, 1985), pp. 182–196; Gail Sheehy, *The Silent Passage: Menopause* (New York: Random House, 1992).

111. Lowe, "The Legal Status of Father," pp. 28–42.

112. Orvar Löfgren and Jonas Frykman, *Culture Builders: A Historical Anthropology of Middle-Class Life* (New Brunswick, N.J.: Rutgers University Press, 1987), pp. 118–125; Nancy Friday, *My Mother/My Self: A Daughter's Search for Identity* (New York: Delacourte, 1977).

113. Jonathan Gathorne-Hardy, *The Rise and Fall of the British Nanny* (London: Hodder and Stoughton, 1972).

114. Dally, *Inventing Motherhood*, p. 17.

115. John Gillis, *For Better, For Worse: British Marriages, 1600 to the Present* (New York: Oxford University Press, 1985), p. 253; on the importance of symbols of the mother as a nurturer, see Joan Brumberg, *Fasting Girls: The Emergence of Anorexia Nervosa as a Modern Disease* (Cambridge, Mass.: Harvard University Press, 1988), Chapter 5.

116. Leigh Schmidt, "The Humbug of Modern Ritual: The Invention of Father's Day" (paper delivered at the Davis Center of Princeton University, November 1994).

117. Karen Hausen, "Mothers, Sons, and the Sale of Symbols and Goods: The 'German Mother's Day' 1923–1933," in *Interest and Emotion: Essays on the Study of Family and Kinship*, eds. Hans Medick and David Sabean (Cambridge: Cambridge University Press, 1984), pp. 371–414.

118. Frank F. Furstenberg, Jr., "Good Dads—Bad Dads: Two Faces of Fatherhood," in *The Changing American Family and Public Policy*, ed. Andrew Cherlin (Washington, D.C.: Urban Institute Press, 1988), pp. 193–216.

119. Barbara Katz Rothman, *Recreating Motherhood: Ideology and Technology in a Patriarchal Society* (New York: W. W. Norton, 1989), p. 32.

120. Ornella Moscucci, *The Science of Women: Gynecology and Gender in England, 1800–1929* (Cambridge: Cambridge University Press, 1990), pp. 15–40.

121. Quoted in Dally, *Inventing Motherhood*, p. 101.

122. Christema Nippert-Eng is currently researching this question in a contemporary American context.

KEY TERM

churching   The religious ritual by which a new mother emerges from a period of seclusion and undergoes a church ceremony of purification. Originally a Catholic ritual, churching was also adopted by some Protestant sects. The practice was common in Europe and America through the eighteenth century, after which it became increasingly uncommon. It still occasionally occurs today.

DISCUSSION QUESTIONS

1. What does Gillis mean by his title "Mothers Giving Birth to Motherhood"? Is it only, or even largely, mothers who are "giving birth" to a cultural construction of motherhood?
2. Gillis reports that the "natural childbirth" movement may have challenged the medical model of childbirth, but it actually promoted conventional ideas of marriage and the family in the United States. On what basis does he argue this?
3. Gillis lays out the stresses and strains of contemporary motherhood, but does not in this selection suggest solutions to these problems. What are some possible solutions implied by his discussion? Do you see any other ways that motherhood could become less burdensome in the future?

FAT TALK

BODY IMAGE AMONG ADOLESCENT GIRLS

MIMI NICHTER AND NANCY VUCKOVIC

Nearly every middle-class American girl or woman, of whatever ethnic background, is or has been obsessively concerned with her body. In "Fat Talk" the authors focus on adolescent girls and discuss data from their Teen Lifestyle Project. For this study the authors interviewed adolescent girls from the eighth through twelfth grades in two urban southwestern schools in the United States. They also discussed body issues with these girls in small gatherings ("focus groups"). Nichter and Vuckovic found that the most common expression they heard from these girls was "I'm so fat" and their article discusses just what this means to the girls themselves. From this study, then, we hear what the girls themselves have to say about body ideals, weight control, dieting, boys, the influence of the media, and the influence of their mothers. The study shows that "I'm so fat" is a nearly ritualized expression with multiple meanings and social goals. In some contexts girls utter this phrase to monitor what other girls think of them; in other cases it is a cry for social

support, and in yet other cases it is a strategy to affirm or enhance one's social position. In all cases it appears intended to evoke the response "No, you're not." Through this discourse on fat and the body, young girls are forming and negotiating their own sense of self and their position within a peer group. Interestingly, the study also found that these adolescent girls seek to pursue "the perfect body," which they define as a female who is 5 feet 7 inches and weighs 110 pounds. In addition, a primary motivation behind this pursuit is the belief that the perfect body will bring attention from boys and therefore a perfect life. As we will see in a later chapter of this book, a similar concern with male attention continues to strongly influence the lives of college women.

Routinized forms of indirect speech are an important component of social exchange in many cultures. In a region of South India where one author worked, a common greeting was "Are your meals finished?" If the person responded "yes," the next question would be "What did you have?" (Nichter 1978). As her stay in the field area continued, it became clear that the greeting was not really about food at all. The meal was only a reference point; what was being indexed were events in an individual's home, life, or emotional feeling state. If a large meal with several dishes was described, it would indicate that something special had happened in the speaker's house that day; a small meal would indicate that it was an ordinary day. Discourse utilizing the idiom of food indirectly provided a great deal of information about one's family situation. It also gave permission for a playful interchange of small talk. Although the people involved were quite poor and there was little variety in their diets, responses to the question were varied, involving humor, exaggeration, and deception. Each response was an invitation for further talk.

In the United States, where food is abundant and diverse, weight is a reference point

for conventionalized statements about the way people feel about themselves and events in their lives. Such statements may not reflect actual behavior, but rather index important personal and cultural concerns. The issue of weight also promotes ritual exchanges which serve multiple purposes in conversation.

One statement often heard in the United States, particularly among white, middle-class adolescent females, is "I'm so fat." During ethnographic interviews with adolescent girls about body image and dieting, we were struck with the commonality of the statement, particularly as it emerged in focus group discussions. In this chapter, cultural meanings of talk about weight, which we term *fat talk*, are discussed. Of particular note is the role fat talk plays in the negotiation of self and peer group interaction among adolescent females.

The present chapter represents a departure from many of the existing studies on adolescent weight control behavior. While literature on eating-disordered females has relied on case studies (e.g., Millman 1980; Orbach 1987). Research on weight control among normal adolescent females has largely been behaviorally based, focusing

Source: Mimi Nichter and Nancy Vuckovic, "Fat Talk: Body Image among Adolescent Girls." Pp. 109–131 in *Many Mirrors: Body Image and Social Relations,* ed. Nicole Sault. New Brunswick, NJ: Rutgers University Press, 1994. Reprinted by permission of the authors.

on such issues as present dieting status, methods adopted to lose weight, and extent of bodily dissatisfaction (Casper and Offer 1990; Desmond et al. 1986; Greenfield et al. 1987; Rosen and Gross 1987). Despite reports of a "dieting epidemic" among adolescent females (Berg 1992), researchers have not given voice to those afflicted. Specifically, the meaning of weight control to adolescent females has not been explored from the perspective of their lived experience. Instead, girls have been asked to self-report their behavior into researcher-specified variables. An ethnographic approach allowed the researchers to explore the meaning of weight-related behaviors among this cohort rather than imposing meaning through survey questions. This chapter attempts to broaden the scope of weight-related studies by examining how adolescents' preoccupation with weight manifests itself in discourse.

Sample

This chapter reports on data collected by the Teen Lifestyle Project, a longitudinal project on body image, dieting, and smoking among adolescent females.[1] Ethnographic interviews were conducted with informants once during each school year. The pilot study population consisted of 60 girls in the eighth, tenth, and twelfth grades at two urban schools in the southwestern United States. The longitudinal study began In the fall of 1989 with a cohort of 300 girls in the eighth and ninth grades at four urban middle and high schools. Over the three years the cohort was followed, 47 girls left the study because they moved out of town, were unreachable, or declined participation because of increasing time commitments at school. The total number of girls who remained in the study at the end of the third year was 253. Attrition of the subjects, approximately 15 percent, was lower than anticipated.

Informants came from a range of lower- to upper-middle-class families. Seventy-three percent of the girls were Caucasian, 16 percent Hispanic, with the remaining 11 percent of the girls of Asian and African-American ethnicity. The majority of these girls were within normal height and weight ranges. The mean height and weight for the eighth grade cohort was 120 pounds, five feet, three inches, while the mean for the ninth grade cohort was 125 pounds, five feet, four inches.

Research Method

The project utilized anthropological research methods. Ethnographic interviews were generally conducted one on one, with a student spending approximately one hour talking with an interviewer. The format of the discussion was a structured, open-ended interview. In addition to individual interviews, some girls ($N = 74$) took part in focus-group interviews formed by the girls themselves and consisting of one or two interviewers and three to five informants.[2] The format of these interviews was likewise structured but open-ended. While individual interviews focused on perceived body image, dieting, and smoking behavior, focus-group interviews elicited generalized attitudes about these issues as well as about perceived group behaviors. Focus-group interviews proved an extremely important methodology for obtaining occurrences of interactional speech between informants (Labov 1972), including how weight control issues emerged in discourse among friends.

We first became aware of the prevalence of talk about feeling fat in response to a general question raised in focus-group interviews: "Do you think that a lot of girls your age are concerned about their weight?" Girls generally responded with head nods and laughs, which led us to ask, "How do you know that?" Girls then described how their friends complained about being fat and began to act out common conversations using the expression "I'm so fat." In order to investigate the commonality of fat talk more closely, we asked each informant during an individual interview, "Do you hear many girls saying 'I'm so fat'? What do you think it means when they say that?" The vast majority of girls acknowledged that they heard this expression used frequently.

In addition to ethnographic interviews, one survey, developed by project researchers, was administered each year to quantify subjects' report of dieting and smoking behaviors. The same instrument, with minor modifications, was administered during each year of the longitudinal phase.

Fat Talk: An Overview

The following excerpt from a focus-group discussion typifies the kind of exchange which occurs among adolescent females. The conversation took place between two fourteen-year-old girls in response to a question about the reasons for weight control.

JESSICA: I'm so fat.

TONI: Shut up, Jessica. You're not fat—you know how it makes you really mad when Brenda says she's fat?

JESSICA: Yeah.

TONI: It makes me really mad when you say that cuz it's not true.

JESSICA: Yeah, it is.

TONI: Don't say that you're fat. Don't you think we'd have said something to Brenda by now, if she, all the time said, "I'm so fat. I'm so fat." Don't you think we'd have said something by now. "Brenda, Brenda, I don't think you're overweight, I think you're chunky or whatever."

JESSICA: You wouldn't say that!

TONI: Well, we're best friends, Jessica, and I mean, she would rely on me to tell her something that was like, you know how people, like something's wrong with someone. You don't want to tell them but you do because you want to, you want . . . them . . . to help them, you know.

Females, and to a lesser degree males, engage in ritualized talk about their weight (Hope 1980). According to our informants, the previous dialogue—the "I'm so fat" discourse—is frequently repeated during the course of a day. By the time a white middle-class female reaches adolescence, she has probably become a competent user of the discourse, whether or not she actually practices weight control.

Fat talk is multivocal. At times, the statement "I'm so fat" can be used as an idiom of distress (Nichter 1981; Swartz 1987), allowing a person to allude to widely diffuse feelings. Fat talk constitutes a final common pathway (Carr 1978) describing a wide range of feelings about uncontrol. The speaker does not have to be specific. Sometimes, when feeling bad, rather than saying "I'm so sad," a person may say "I'm so fat" to index that she is depressed. One informant remarked that among her family and friends, the saying "I'm having a fat day" indicated that things in general were not going well.

When examining the "I'm so fat" interchange, we find disparity between the message's inherent properties or meanings and its effects (Austin 1962). The statement "I'm so fat" is not just an observation about one's weight. It is a call for support from one's peers, for affirmation that one is in fact *not* fat. It can also act as an apology or excuse for behavior, or as an invitation to listeners to reaffirm group solidarity. The hearer uses contextual cues provided by the speaker and the situation to interpret the message so that it is understood in the manner in which it was intended by the speaker (Grice 1975). When "I'm so fat" is said in the girls' locker room, the impetus for the statement may come from the vulnerability of exposing one's body to the sight of others. Understanding this cultural cue, it is then appropriate for the listener to respond in a way that mitigates the speaker's discomfort. When the statement comes before eating, it provides an apology or excuse by the speaker for the indulgence at hand (in effect, a secular "grace" before eating).

A Call for Positive Strokes

During adolescence, there is an increased concern with emotional self-understanding and negotiation of status among one's peers. Not uncommonly, discussion among friends—"girl talk"—centers around the identification and negotiation of group norms (Eckert 1990). These discussions provide an opportunity for girls to influence or change group norms through disclosure of personal opinions or experience. At the same time, girl talk serves as a mechanism of social control by encouraging girls to measure themselves against the standards set by the group.

Another main goal of conversation during this developmental period becomes understanding the self in relation to others, with vulnerability in self-disclosure as one mechanism for achieving this goal (Gottman and Mettetal 1986). Saying "I'm so fat" performs the function of disclosing vulnerability and may give other girls the impression that one is "withholding nothing." Through the sharing of thoughts and feelings, friends increase each other's self-esteem, provide feedback, and help support one another (Sullivan 1953). Research on female adolescent development reports that girls are socialized to rely heavily on external acceptance and feedback to inform their identity (Steiner-Adair 1990).

Not uncommonly, a speaker says "I'm so fat" to a friend to evoke a positive response such as "Oh, no you're not." This response tells the initiator that her fears of fat are ungrounded, as the following comment illustrates: "People say 'Oh, I'm fat,' you know, and you're supposed to tell them 'Oh no, you're not.' It's just like something that people say." Our fourteen-year-old informants were well aware that this was an appropriate response:

INTERVIEWER: What usually happens when someone says [I'm so fat]?

JAMIE: About six or seven girls go "No you're not!" Probably it's just because, you know, you like to hear that people don't think you're fat. And it's mostly like in gym, cuz when you change into your gym clothes those are so bunchy anyway they make you look fat. And, uh, but I'd say, I'd say not very many of them mean that, mean it when they say it. They just want to hear "Oh no you're not."

It was generally agreed upon by our informants that girls who say "I'm so fat" are not significantly overweight and are not usually the girls who attempt to change their weight for sustained periods of time. Rather, for many girls, the motivation in saying "I'm so fat" is to gauge what other people think about them. As one informant noted, it makes you feel good about yourself when people say "No, you're not fat": "They're always like 'I'm so fat,' like that. Then I'm like, 'No, you're not.' 'Yes, I am.' Some people I know that say that are really skinny and they just wanna be, they just want people to say that they're skinny so that they'll feel better about themselves. I go 'No you're not,' but they keep on saying that so they can hear you saying that they're not fat." In response to one girl's discussion of feeling fat, an interviewer asked: "Do you tell your friends that you feel fat?" She replied: "Yeah, and they sit there going 'No you're not,' but I don't know really if they're telling me the truth. I really would like to know. Even if I say 'Tell me the honest to God truth,' they'll probably say 'No, you're not.' And they're probably saying 'Yes, you are,' but I don't really know that but I would like to."

Some of our informants noted that girls who were significantly overweight would not say "I'm so fat" as that would call attention to their problem. It is also inappropriate for another to call attention to their fatness. Similarly, in a discussion of survey results collected from junior high school students, Ogaitis et al. (1988) note that given the option of "talking with a friend about eating concerns," only a few of those students who actually were over- or underweight expressed interest in doing so. Girls who felt they were overweight (but were normal weight) were more likely to want to talk about such concerns than girls who actually were overweight.

There seem to be tacit cultural sanctions at play which prevent females from commenting on another's overweight or recent weight gain. Although we find discourse about weight loss and thinness, we do not find corresponding discussion among women about another's weight gain or overweight. The presence and conspicuous absence of certain phrases in everyday conversation provide examples of how these sanctions operate. A statement such as "Gee you look great. Have you lost weight?" is generally welcomed as a compliment. Yet few women would approach another female—even a close friend—with the comment "You look like you've gained some weight."

Absolving Oneself of Guilt

Another time "I'm so fat" is said is at the beginning of a meal, particularly before eating calorie-laden food or enjoying a buffet-style meal where an individual is faced with making public food choices. Stating that *you know* you are already fat is an admission that you know you shouldn't be eating, that you know you should be on a diet. It is a public presentation of responsibility and concern for one's appearance (Hope 1980). The admission of a little guilt forestalls further scrutiny (Barthes 1973) and frees the speaker to do as she pleases. This statement also puts her in control of the situation. She has announced that she knows the true state of her body and has therefore precluded anyone else from telling her.

Marker of Group Affiliation

"I'm so fat" is sometimes used as a marker of group affiliation. As one girl noted, "Sometimes I think girls just say it to fit in with the group. One person will start saying it [I'm so fat] and everyone will say 'God, I am too!'" Several researchers have noted the importance of crowd or group affiliation across adolescence (Brown et al. 1986; Dunphy 1972). Group identification is a central developmental task of early adolescence, with a more autonomous sense of identity achieved in late adolescence.

Group fat talk offers the opportunity for all group members to obtain affirmation that they look good. It becomes a way for group members to share positive strokes as well as to build group solidarity. For example, one girl noted, "I don't know, like somebody will make a comment in the like girls' locker room or something and everybody like adds 'Oh my god, look at these legs of mine' or something, you know. 'You think you're fat! Look at me!' It's fun though. I mean, it's not really fun, but . . . You get input on what everybody else thinks."

One informant explained that even though she didn't really think she was too fat, she felt she had to say it when she was with her friends. In fact, she was fed up with fat talk and diet talk but knew that if she did not acknowledge that she shared those feelings, she would separate herself from the group by implying that she was perfect. In other words, saying that she didn't diet would be an admission that she didn't need to work on herself—that she was satisfied. To be satisfied with one's appearance displaces the goal of working toward the perfect future. As she explained, "I was talking to my friends, and they wanted to lose weight even though they weren't really fat. They just wanted to be the perfect weight."

With a high degree of agreement, our informants described the perfect girl as between one hundred and one hundred ten pounds with a height of five feet, seven inches.[3] Ethnographic interviews revealed that among many of our teen informants, the right weight was perceived as a ticket to the perfect life. Words such as *perfect* have the power to evoke an entire framed scenario (Fillmore 1977; Quinn 1982). Thus, the girl with the perfect body who can "eat and eat and eat and not gain anything" is described as being "perfect in every way." By extension, the girl with the perfect body has a perfect life: she gets the boy of every girl's dreams. One informant stated: "Most girls buy *Seventeen* magazine and see all the models and they're really, really skinny, and they see all these girls in real life that look like that. They have the cutest guy in the school and they seem to have life so perfect." The perfect girl provokes jealousy, sometimes to the point that girls feel their own efforts are futile: "You just see all these older girls, like when you go to the mall, and there's like, it's like, 'why was I born?' because they're so perfect."

Despite the desire to be perfect, a female who is extremely attractive may find herself shunned by her female peers. Some informants noted that when they saw a beautiful girl at school, in the mall, or even on television, they would label her a bitch. Since the perfect girl's flaw is not visible, it is assumed to exist in her personality. One girl remarked: "If a girl is really pretty, then I want to see her flaw. All of it—all of it. I want to know every single part of her flaw (laughs)." Not uncommonly, girls would decide that they hated this girl, despite the fact that they didn't know her. Some girls remarked, "I want to hurt her" or "I feel like killing her." Spiteful comments afford the speaker a feeling of superiority at a time when she may be experiencing the opposite emotion.

While the previous statements describe interactions among strangers, some slender adolescents in our study spoke of similar though less malicious experiences involving acquaintances. These girls described how their friends practically "accused" them of being thin, "as if it were my fault or something." One ninth grader thought that girls reacted to her in this way due to jealousy. Other girls felt that comments about their thinness implied that they had an eating disorder.

> VANESSA: Brandy and I were talking one day about when you say, "Oh, you're so skinny." How do you think that makes someone feel? Good or bad?
>
> ERIN: I think it would make me feel totally happy.
>
> VANESSA: It makes me feel bad. "Oh, you're so skinny." What is that supposed to mean, you know? Do I have a problem? I don't know, it just makes me feel uncomfortable.

The ambiguity of the message "you're so thin" caused some girls to complain that they didn't like to hear it. Even when it was meant as a compliment, it was difficult to accept as that, for to do so would be to indicate satisfaction with one's self. Denial becomes the appropriate counter to the compliment.

From a clinical standpoint, if so many girls are talking about being fat, what is the potential impact on girls who are at risk for eating disorders? Girls who are anorexic and bulimic also participate in this discourse but may mean it literally. When friends respond "No you're not" to their complaints of being fat, these responses may not be believed. For distressed girls, the impact of fat talk may not be transient. Indeed, this discourse pattern may serve to normalize and legitimize a position that is potentially dangerous.

Misuse of Fat Talk

While one needs to be involved with the "I'm so fat" discourse in order to maintain group affiliation, a majority of informants emphasized that it is important not to overuse it. To continually complain about body dissatisfaction is to provoke the anger of your friends. Several informants described girlfriends whose constant body complaints led them to respond that they indeed were too fat. They noted, "When she says 'I'm so fat' we just say 'yeah, you are' to shut her up." Another informant described her strategy for dealing with what she perceived to be an annoying situation: "I think they just say it so they can hear other girls say 'Oh no you're not, you're skinny.' It kind of makes me mad. My friend in eighth grade said that every day, so when she'd say it I'd just say 'Oh.' She'd get mad and say, 'Well aren't you going to say something?' She stopped doing it. She just wanted attention. Now I just look at people when they say it." Other girls noted:

> Even the thin people, they'll walk around saying "I'm so fat." I just want to hit them on the head. Maybe their idea of gaining weight is like one or two pounds and they like weigh one hundred. I just want to say 'Shut up, you don't even know what being fat is."

> It annoys me. Because a lot of them are like totally skinny. They're like perfect. And they're like, "Oh, look at my butt. It's like cheese." And that's really annoying because they know they're not fat. They just want to get the attention. They want to hear they're not fat. Like from other people. So that annoys me really.

Teens: A Homogenous Group?

We have been discussing adolescent girls as if they belong to a singular, homogenous group, but from observational and interview data we learned that girls tend to cluster into particular social groups. Group membership is particularly salient during adolescence due to its perceived ability to facilitate friendships and social interaction as well as provide emotional support (Brown 1990). We wanted to assess to what extent social-group affiliation influenced girls' desire to be thin and their use of fat

talk. Specifically, did those girls who considered themselves "stoners" or "mods" adopt similar discourse patterns to girls who were "preps"?[4] Through their dress, stoner and mod girls seemed to adopt counter-culture values. Did these girls also reject mainstream notions of preferred body size, resulting in less fat talk?

Through ethnographic interviews with girls from a variety of social groups, we found that among white middle-class adolescents, desire for thinness crosscut social groups. One self-identified stoner informant was asked whether she thought there was pressure among girls in her group to be thin. She noted:

> STACY: There's pressure to be thin in all groups. I think with stoners it's not as bad, but it's still there.

> INTERVIEWER: Stoners seem to be against other things—like adopting dress that preps are wearing. So why do you think the importance of being thin still holds?

> STACY: Everyone loves to be thin (laughs). Every girl wants to be thin. Well, the guys are still after thin girls.

Another girl, who considered herself a mod, commented: "The mod chicks and the punker girls that I know, they all, I think it's the same with every girl. Cuz all my friends, no matter how skinny they are think they are fat. And no matter what they are, they think they're fat, even if they're not. I think everyone wants to be attractive."

Who Are They Doing It For?

Why is fat talk such a salient discourse strategy among adolescent females? In this section we ask for whom they are doing it and suggest that fat talk and dissatisfaction with weight are a result of several factors, including social comparison with other girls, a desire to be popular with boys, and media and family influences.

Teenage girls exist in a highly interactional environment in which comparison to other girls is commonplace. Early adolescent thinking has been characterized as excessively concerned with physical appearance, bodily changes, and personal behavior. Cognitive developmentalists such as Elkind (1967) have described how an adolescent believes that *others* are even more preoccupied with his or her appearance and behavior than he or she is. Elkind notes: "The adolescent takes the other person's point of view to an extreme degree. He is so concerned with the point of view of others and how they regard him that he often loses sight of his own point of view" (1967:153). From Elkind's perspective the adolescent, especially in early adolescence, is always on stage, viewing himself or herself as the main actor, with peers as an imaginary audience. This concept of adolescent egocentrism may help explain the importance of peers during adolescence. Research findings reported by Pesce and Harding (1986) reveal that such perceptions are more common among girls than boys.

Researchers have noted that in contrast to males, for whom identity development is the outcome of increasing experience of separation and autonomy, the female personality develops through attachment and relation to others (Chodorow 1978; Gilligan 1982). While feminists have argued that gender differences are socially constructed, research has found that girls are more social in their orientation than boys (Berndt 1982; Blyth et al. 1982; Fischer and Naurus 1981). In a series of time studies (Richards and Larson 1989), girls were found to be more social than boys before adolescence and became even more social with adolescence. Girls spend more time talking than boys, more time grooming in front of friends (Duckett et al. 1989), and more time doing homework in the company of friends (Leone and Richards 1989).

Intimacy, emotional closeness, and trust are more characteristic of girls' rather than boys' relationships at all ages (Youniss 1980). Through interactions with friends, social skills such as the ability to empathize with and understand the point of view of others are learned and practiced (Rubin 1980). This social orientation is also reflected in girls' greater concern for physical appearance. Girls are taught from an early age that attractiveness is an intrinsic part of pleasing and serving others and, in turn, of securing love (Brownmiller 1984, Striegel-Moore et al. 1986). Exploring the impact of cultural standards on adolescent girls and boys, Wooley and Wooley (1984) found that girls are more influenced by and therefore more vulnerable to mandated cultural standards of the ideal body.

Clearly, social comparison with regard to body size is important for females. Striegel-Moore et al. found that college-age informants engaged in frequent comparisons between their own bodies and those of other women, "as if they needed to check where they stood" (1986:945). One adolescent informant in our study stated, "People just compare themselves to popular people who are really skinny. You just look at other girls and wish you were like them."

To assess how important girls considered thinness with regard to friendship with other girls, we asked informants to agree or disagree with the statement "A girl has to be thin to be popular with other girls." Survey responses among eighth and ninth graders indicate that for the large majority of girls (85 percent, $N = 241$), thinness is not considered a prerequisite for friendships with other girls. In a focus-group interview, however, two girls described how being thin was an important factor for membership in the highly desirable "popular group":

> I think that for people that are socially active, that go to a lot of parties and see a lot of other people from other schools, you know, it is important. I don't think

that a lot of, like really overweight people feel comfortable at a party, you know, because of first impressions. People *do* look at your weight. They do notice that. I guess if you're more socially active, you'd feel more comfortable being, being at a decent weight.

Boys' Influence on Girls' Discourse

In interviews, we asked girls why they thought talk about being fat emerged so commonly in discussions with their friends. One obvious reason adolescent girls believe it is important to be thin is to attract boys. To assess the perceived importance of thinness in relation to boys, we asked our eighth- and ninth-grade informants to respond on the survey to the following statement: "A girl has to be thin to be popular with boys." Almost half of our informants (44 percent) believed that boys preferred girls who were thin and that a girl would have difficulty being popular with boys unless she were thin. The remaining 56 percent disagreed that thinness was a requirement for popularity with boys.

Some informants overtly complained about how fat they were in front of boys to obtain a contradictory response from them. One girl explained this behavior: "Sometimes you need a guy to tell you, like, it sounds better when a guy tells you you're skinny than when a girl does, you know what I mean? Cuz you're not trying to look skinny for girls. You're doing it for yourself and for guys."

The desire to be thin to please boys sometimes resulted in changes in food consumption patterns in the presence of boys. While such patterns have been documented among adult women, our findings show that these patterns are socialized early in adolescence. Eighth-grade girls in our study described how they would eat "just a few fries or a bite from a salad" if they were with boys, so as not to appear "piggish." They explained that boys didn't like to see girls eat a lot of food, that it

was somehow unfeminine for girls to do so. Boys, on the other hand, were described as "inhaling" food whenever possible (Nichter and Nichter 1991).

Influence of the Media

Another powerful influence on girls' perception of self is the media and the role models presented therein (Nichter and Nichter 1991). Television programs present slender women as the dominant image of popularity, success, and happiness (Aldebaran 1975; Collins 1988; Garner et al. 1980; Horvath 1979, 1981). Other sources of this image are the approximately four hundred to six hundred advertisements we are exposed to daily. Downs and Harrison (1985) estimate that one in every eleven commercials includes a direct message about beauty. These messages are almost exclusively directed toward women. Similar messages are disseminated to adolescent girls in the guise of self-improvement features found in "teenzines." Both articles and advertisements in these publications convey the message that "the road to happiness is attracting males . . . by way of physical beautification" (Evans et al. 1991:110). We asked girls if they thought the media affected their self-image. One girl responded with regard to magazines: "On the front cover they always say 'How to lose weight, how to look skinnier.' I think that's good because they give you tips on how you can manage your weight and lose it. But it's also bad because then it's like 'Am I fat?' And then I start saying, 'Hmm, maybe I can lose weight.'"

Mothers and Daughters

In addition to pressures from sources outside the home, ethnographic data indicate that girls are significantly influenced by familial dieting behavior, particularly that of the mother. Over 30 percent of the girls questioned in the Teen Lifestyle Project survey reported that they had been told by their mothers that they needed to lose weight, although less than 5 percent of those girls were clinically overweight. It is likely that a mother's advice reflects her own concern about weight control. While 59 percent of our informants described their mothers' weight as "just about right," 68 percent reported that their mothers were commonly dieting. Some girls noted that when their mothers began a diet, they would also have to diet. An eighth-grade girl explained, "Well, me and my mom are like, both built the same way, so if she gets fat that means I have to go on a diet." With regard to fat talk, some girls reported that they said "I'm so fat" to their mothers and that their mothers also used the phrase.

Weight Watching: Myth or Reality?

Through ethnographic research, we have found that discourse and action about dieting are as multivocal as those about feeling fat. Saying you are on a diet indexes an intention of gaining control over your environment. Among our adolescent informants, the need for control or the ability to control is often short-lived. We have found that the same girls who "talk fat" often do not engage in sustained weight-reducing action:

> Well, I mean, everybody thinks they're fat. Well not everybody, but, you know, most people, I guess, well, I mean, I don't know. If you see people your age that look skinny but weigh more than you, you know, it feels good, right? But sometimes I'll think I'm fat or something. After usually I get weighed. You know, but, I never really do anything about it. I just say "I'm going on a diet," you know?

Despite some girls' statements that diets are more a matter of intention than action, national survey results continue to show high rates of dieting behavior among adolescent girls. As part of the Teen Lifestyle

Project annual survey, girls were asked, "Are you trying to change your weight now?" Responses indicate that on the day of the survey, 44 percent of the girls were trying to lose weight while 51 percent were *not* trying. The remaining 5 percent were trying to gain weight.

While our survey results seemed to substantiate the commonality of dieting among adolescents and the similarity of our sample to a much larger national sample ('Body-Weight Perceptions' 1991), we emphasize that survey data taken alone can be misleading. Three important questions need to be clarified: What do teenagers mean when they say they are dieting? What behaviors and practices are associated with dieting? What is the duration of a teenager's diet? These kinds of questions are generally not included in self-report surveys (Nichter et al. 1993).

In interviews, we asked girls to define what it meant to go on a diet. Responses ranged from "eating right" (i.e., eating "good" food as opposed to "junk" foods) to "just eating salads" or "cutting down on what you eat" to "Jane Fonda every day." As one eighth grader noted: "Dieting—well it's like eating the right foods or like not eating anything—like between those two." As these responses indicate, concepts of dieting are varied and loosely defined.

An important finding which emerged from interviews was that diets among teenagers were extremely short-lived. Some girls said a diet just lasted a few hours—from breakfast until lunch, when temptation in the cafeteria or boredom would compel them to have something to eat:

> INTERVIEWER: Do you ever diet with your friends?
>
> SANDY: Yeah, but it didn't work. I was dieting with my friend Sheila, and like, I'd say I wouldn't eat but then like a few hours later I'd eat like a candy bar or something.

To others, dieting meant eating a candy bar with a diet Coke and then skipping meals.

Still others talked about dieting as a social ritual, an almost amusing pastime to engage in with friends: "Well, we both thought we were fat, so we thought we would go on a diet together. And we kept saying, 'Oh, we'll do it tomorrow,' and the next day, 'Oh, we'll do it tomorrow.' And it kept going on and finally we did but then we just ate whatever we wanted." Others drew on the resources available to them from mothers and older sisters:

MELANIE: We like, we like would be over at her house and we went, we went through *all* the diet books and um all of the magazine articles and everything, and we like planned out what we would eat a day. What we would eat every day, and how many calories they had and what, what exercises we'd do. And everything. That didn't last for too long (laughs). That lasted about a week.

INTERVIEWER: Is that because you got bored with it or just . . .

MELANIE: We just, Amy started. Amy went off it at lunch, and so I'd be like, "ok, well she's off then I will," and I ate this huge old dinner.

A few girls who had more serious weight problems spoke of counting calories or joining weight loss programs with the support of their parents.

Some girls said they never actually went on a diet but controlled their weight by watching what they ate each day (Nichter et al. 1993). As one girl explained, "If you consider it a diet, then you're in trouble because then you'll *have* to lose weight. If you don't lose weight, then, you know, you realize you've failed." For this informant and for many others who shared her thinking, to define or label how she was going to eat was to establish expectations and be faced with potential failure. Furthermore, if she didn't say she was dieting, a little cheating would be no big thing.

Survey questions on dieting behavior among teenagers which ask girls to self-report their behavior into researcher-specified categories may lead to misreporting. To date, data on adolescent dieting behavior have been obtained from cross-sectional surveys in which behaviors are assessed generally without attention to issues of intensity and duration. Among adolescents, labels may misrepresent habitual behavior. Being a dieter may represent a range of behaviors, and thus cross-sectional surveys may mask the variety of behaviors which can occur under the same label.[5]

Questionnaires not grounded in preliminary ethnographic research may impose categories not culturally appropriate for a teenage population. Taking into account the variety of meanings and durational differences noted among respondents, what do survey data reveal? When adolescent girls say they are dieting, do they mean they start a diet in the morning that lasts until noon? Do they overreport dieting because they feel they *should* be on a diet? Do they underreport because they don't call their restrictive eating a diet for fear of failure?

Attention to the details of language may facilitate the creation of survey questions. For example, after identifying the category of "watching what one ate" as distinct from "dieting to lose weight," we included several survey questions to quantify this phenomenon and the behaviors associated with it. Results revealed that a significant number of girls classified themselves as "watchers" as opposed to "dieters" (Nichter et al. 1993). Further study of the relationship between data and ethnographic records is important to the validation of both methodologies. Sociolinguistic and semantic theories may provide useful tools in studying the meanings that can be derived from either method of culture study.

What is important to consider with regard to survey data is not merely the number of girls purporting to be dieting, but what is indexed by talk of dieting. As we have demonstrated, for many girls, talking about body dissatisfaction and the need to lose weight is a strategy for improving one's social position. It provides a plan of action toward a more perfect life. From one girl's perspective, "If I was thin, I'd be totally happy."

Discussion

Our society encourages engagement in body work—directed effort to improve the body in an attempt to achieve perfection. Improving one's body no longer means simply losing weight. Adolescent girls discussed their desire to develop a toned physique with a hint of muscle definition. The imperative to maintain a thin, toned body is not merely a matter of aesthetics. Bound into the image are expectations and hopes for acceptance and a deeply embodied cultural model which reflects a "taken-for-granted social world" in which events and relations take place in a simplified, prototypic manner (D'Andrade 1987; Holland and Skinner 1987; Quinn and Holland 1987). Within this world, thin females are popular, desirable, and successful. Conversely, overweight females are ostracized and expected to have less satisfying personal lives than their thinner counterparts (Dion et al. 1972: Seid 1988). Previous research (Vuckovic-Moore 1990) has revealed that a cultural model exists which equates weight control with morality. Within this model, "good" behavior leads to thinness, while "bad" behavior results in overweight.

It is apparent that adolescent girls and women are "worshipping at the shrine of slimness" (Brumberg 1988:257). The discourse we are hearing among teenage girls shows evidence of ritual talk about weight and a rhetoric indicative of a cultural mandate for weight control. Under such a mandate, even if a girl is not actually working on herself, she must at least talk about it. Talking about weight control in itself constitutes action as it serves to create and project an image of self. By engaging in fat talk, females present themselves to others as responsible beings concerned about their appearance. As noted by Rodin et al. (1985), our culture promotes an extremely thin female beauty ideal and thus creates a normative discontent with weight. The woman who experiences herself as dissatisfied with her weight resembles rather than deviates from her peers.

Our examination has stressed the need to look not only at reports of weight-related behavior (as previous research has done), but at the speech which accompanies or replaces such behavior. Discourse about weight may be particularly prevalent during adolescence, when concern about appearance is high, but appetite, social settings, and parental presence may preclude other actions. The litany of weight-related discourse and its importance in peer-group social activity indicate that adolescent girls are greatly concerned about body size. Irrespective of what action girls are taking to achieve their body goals, they are attempting to reproduce the cultural ideal through their discourse.

NOTES

1. Research for this chapter was conducted within a larger study of adolescent behavior, Food Intake, Smoking, and Diet among Adolescent Girls, funded by the National Institute of Child Health and Human Development, grant number HD24737.
2. Focus-group interviewing is a methodology that involves talking to several people at a time about a particular topic. Through experience we learned that focus groups which disregarded social networks did not function effectively because girls were reluctant to express their opinions in front of others they did not consider their friends. To assure more open discussions, we asked girls to form a group of friends with whom they would

feel comfortable discussing issues about body image and dieting. During the focus-group interviews these topics were discussed generally and not specifically in regard to individual behaviors.

3. The ideal girl was also described as having a good figure, long blonde hair, and big blue eyes. To many girls the ideal girl is a living manifestation of the Barbie doll. According to Susan Brownmiller, the ideal girl exhibits the characteristics of fairy princess: "Who can imagine a fairy princess with hair that is anything but long and blonde, with eyes that are anything but blue. . . . The fairy princess remains one of the most powerful visual symbols of femininity the Western world has ever devised, and falling short of her role model, women are all feminine failures to some degree" (1984:67).

4. Preps are characterized as very involved in school activities and often come from wealthier families. Their style of dress, hair, and makeup follows the latest mainstream fashion dictates. Jocks are the more athletically oriented preps. Stoners are characterized as indifferent toward school and as smokers and users of drugs. Their wardrobe revolves around jeans and t-shirts advertising heavy metal rock bands. Mods are another fringe group, often students involved in the arts. Their style tends to be an amalgam of fashion from previous eras.

5. The fact that the same label can identify a variety of behaviors came to our attention when analyzing smoking behavior. Girls who smoked as few as two or three cigarettes a week sometimes referred to themselves as smokers, whereas some girls who smoked more frequently thought of themselves as nonsmokers.

REFERENCES

Alderbaran, V. 1975. "Uptight and Hungry: The Contradiction in Psychology of Fat." *Journal of Radical Therapy* 5:5–6.

Austin, J. 1962. *How to Do Things with Words*. Cambridge: Harvard University Press.

Barthes, R. 1973. *Mythologies*. Trans. A. Davis. London: Paladin.

Berg, F. 1992. "Harmful Weight Loss Practices Are Widespread among Adolescents." *Obesity and Health*, July/August, pp. 69–72.

Berndt, T. 1982. "The Features and Effects of Friendship in Early Adolescence." *Child Development* 53:1447–1460.

Blyth, D., J. Hill, and K. Thiel. 1982. "Early Adolescents' Significant Others: Grade and Gender Differences in Perceived Relationships with Familial and Non-Familial Adults and Young People." *Journal of Youth and Adolescence* 11:425–450.

"Body-Weight Perceptions and Selected Weight-Management Goals and Practices of High School Students–United States, 1990." 1991. *Mortality and Morbidity Weekly Report* 40:741–750.

Brown, B. B. 1990. "Peer Groups and Peer Cultures." In *At the Threshold: The Developing Adolescent*, ed. S. S. Feldman and Glen R. Elliot, pp. 171–196. Cambridge: Harvard University Press.

Brown, B. B., S. A. Eicher, and S. Petrie. 1986. "The Importance of Peer Group ('Crowd') Affiliation in Adolescence." *Journal of Adolescence* 9:73–96.

Brownmiller, S. 1984. *Femininity*. New York: Linden Press/Simon & Schuster.

Brumberg, J. J. 1988. *Fasting Girls*. Cambridge: Harvard University Press.

Carr, J. E. 1978. "Ethno-Behaviorism and the Culture-Bound Syndromes: The Case of Amok." *Culture, Medicine and Psychiatry* 2:269–293.

Casper, R., and D. Offer. 1990. "Weight and Dieting Concerns in Adolescents: Fashion or Symptom?" *Pediatrics*, September, pp. 384–390.

Chodorow, N. 1978. *The Reproduction of Mothering*. Berkeley: University of California Press.

Collins, M. E. 1988. "Education for Healthy Body Weight: Helping Adolescents Balance the Cultural Pressure for Thinness." *Journal of School Health* 58(6):227–231.

D'Andrade, R. G. 1987. "A Folk Model of the Mind." In *Cultural Models in Language and Thought*, ed. D. Holland and N. Quinn, pp. 112–148. New York: Cambridge University Press.

Desmond, S., J. Price, N. Gray, and J. O'Connell. 1986. "The Etiology of Adolescents' Perceptions of Their Weight." *Journal of Youth and Adolescence* 15(6):461–474.

Dion, K., E. Berscheid, and E. Walster. 1972. "What Is Beautiful Is Good." *Journal of Personality and Social Psychology* 24:285–290.

Downs, C., and S. Harrison. 1985. "Embarrassing Age Spots or Just Plain Ugly? Physical Attractiveness Stereotyping as an Instrument of Sexism on American Television Commercials." *Sex Roles* 13:9–19.

Duckett, E., M. Raffaelli, and M. Richards. 1989. "'Taking Care': Maintaining the Self and the Home in Early Adolescence." *Journal of Youth and Adolescence* 18(6):549–564.

Dunphy, D. C. 1972. "Peer Group Socialization." In *Socialization in Australia*, ed. F. J. Hunt. Sydney: Angus and Robertson.

Eckert, Penelope. 1990. "Cooperative Competition in Adolescent 'Girl Talk.'" *Discourse Processes* 13:91–122.

Elkind, D. 1967. "Egocentrism in Adolescents." *Child Development* 38:1025–1034.

Evans, E. D., J. Rutber, C. Sather, and C. Turner. 1991. "Content Analysis of Contemporary Teen Magazines for Adolescent Females." *Youth and Society* 23(1):99–120.

Fillmore, Charles. 1977. "Frame Semantics and the Nature of Language." In *Origin and Evolution of Language and Speech*, ed. S. Harnad, H. Stecklis, and J. Lancaster. New York: New York Academy of Science.

Fischer, J., and L. Naurus. 1981. "Sex Roles and Intimacy in Relationships." *Psychology of Women Quarterly* 5:164–169.

Garner, D., P. Garfinkel, D. Schwartz, and M. Thompson. 1980. "Cultural Expectations of Thinness in Women." *Psychological Reports* 47: 483–491.

Gilligan, Carol. 1982. *In a Different Voice: Psychological Theory and Women's Development*. Cambridge: Harvard University Press.

Gottman, J., and G. Mettetal. 1986. "Speculations about Social and Affective Development: Friendship and Acquaintanceship through Adolescence." In *Conversations of Friends*, ed. J. Gottman and J. Parker, pp. 192–240. Cambridge: Cambridge University Press.

Greenfield, D., D. M. Quinlan, P. Harding, E. Glass, and A. Bliss. 1987. "Eating Behavior in an Adolescent Population." *International Journal of Eating Disorders* 6:(1):99–111.

Grice, H. 1975. "Logic and Conversation." In *Syntax and Semantics 3: Speech Acts*, ed. P. Cole and J. Morgan, pp. 41–58. London: Academic Press.

Holland, Dorothy, and Deborah Skinner. 1987. "Prestige and Intimacy: The Cultural Models Behind Americans' Talk about Gender Types." In *Cultural Models in Language and Thought*, ed. D. Holland and N. Quinn, pp. 78–111. New York: Cambridge University Press.

Hope, C. 1980. "American Beauty Rituals." In *Rituals and Ceremonies in Popular Culture*, ed. R. B. Browne, pp. 226–237. Bowling Green, Ohio: Bowling Green University Press.

Horvath, T. 1979. "Correlates of Physical Beauty in Men and Women." *Social Behavior and Personality* 7:145–151.

Labov, W. 1972. *Language in the Inner City*. Philadelphia: University of Pennsylvania Press.

Leone, C. M., and M. H. Richards. 1989. "Classwork and Homework in Early Adolescence: The Ecology of Achievement." *Journal of Youth and Adolescence* 18(6):531–548.

Millman, Marcia. 1980. *Such a Pretty Face*. New York: W. W. Norton.

Nichter, Mark. 1981. "Idioms of Distress: Alternatives in the Expression of Psychosocial Distress: A Case Study from South India." *Culture, Medicine and Psychiatry* 5:379–408.

Nichter, Mark, and Mimi Nichter. 1991. "Hype and Weight." *Medical Anthropology* 13:249–284.

Nichter, Mimi. 1978. Anthropological fieldwork. South Kanara District, Karnataka, India.

Nichter, Mimi, Cheryl Ritenbaugh, Mark Nichter, Nancy Vuckovic, and Mikel Aickin. 1993. "Weight Control Behavior among Adolescent Females: Report of a Multimethod Study." Typescript.

Ogaitis, S., T. T. Chen, and G. P. Cernada. 1988. "Eating Attitudes, Dieting and Bulimia among Junior High School Students." *International Quarterly of Community Health Education* 9(1):51–61.

Orbach, Susie. 1987. "Anorexia and Adolescence." In *Fed Up and Hungry*, ed. Marilyn Lawrence, pp. 74–85. New York: Peter Bedrick Books.

Pesce, R., and C. Harding. 1986. "Imaginary Audience Behavior and Its Relationship to Operational Thought and Social Experience." *Journal of Early Adolescence* 6:83–94.

Quinn, Naomi. 1982. "'Commitment' in American Marriage: A Cultural Analysis." *American Ethnologist* 3:775–798.

Quinn, Naomi, and Dorothy Holland. 1987. "Culture and Cognition." In *Cognitive Models in Language and Thought*, ed. D. Holland and N. Quinn, pp. 3–40. New York: Cambridge University Press.

Richards, M. H., and R. Larson. 1989. "The Life Space and Socialization of the Self: Sex Differences in the Young Adolescent." *Journal of Youth and Adolescence* 18(6):617–626.

Rodin, J., L. Silberstein, and R. Striegel-Moore. 1985. "Women and Weight: A Normative Discontent." In *Psychology and Gender: Nebraska Symposium on Motivation, 1984*, ed. T. B. Sonderegger. Lincoln: University of Nebraska Press.

Rosen, J., and J. Gross. 1987. "The Prevalence of Weight Reducing and Weight Gaining in Adolescent Boys and Girls." *Health Psychology* 6:131–147.

Rubin, Z. 1980. *Children's Friendships*. Cambridge: Harvard University Press.

Seid, R. P. 1988. *Never Too Thin: Why Women Are at War with Their Bodies*. New York: Prentice-Hall.

Steiner-Adair, Catherine. 1990. "The Body Politic: Normal Female Adolescent Development and the Development of Eating Disorders." In *Making Connections: The Relational Worlds of Adolescent Girls at Emma Willard School*, ed. Carol Gilligan, Nona P. Lyons, and Trudy J. Hanmer, pp. 162–182. Cambridge: Harvard University Press.

Striegel-Moore, R., L. Silberstein, and J. Rodin. 1986. "Toward an Understanding of Risk Factors for Bulimia." *American Psychologist* 41:246–263.

Sullivan, H. 1953. *The Interpersonal Theory of Psychiatry*. New York: W. W. Norton.

Swartz, Leslie 1987. "Illness Negotiation: The Case of Eating Disorders." *Social Science and Medicine* 24(7):613–618.

Vuckovic-Moore, Nancy. 1990. "Things That Are Good and Things That Are Chocolate: A Cultural Model of Weight Control as Morality." M.A. thesis, University of Arizona.

Wooley, W., and S. Wooley. 1984. "Feeling Fat in a Thin Society: Women Tell How They Feel about Their Bodies." *Glamour Magazine*, February, pp. 198–252.

Youniss, J. 1980. *Parents and Peers in Social Development*. Chicago: University of Chicago Press.

Youth Risk Behavior Survey, Center for Disease Control. 1991. *Journal of the American Medical Association*, November 27, pp. 2811–2812.

DISCUSSION QUESTIONS

1. The article on "Fat Talk" discusses how weight concerns and the ideal of a perfect thin body figure into self-definition and group affiliation among adolescent girls in the United States. Is there now any comparable "body talk" among adolescent boys or, for that matter, adult men in U.S. culture? If so, do these boys and/or men belong to any particular groups? Whatever your answer, what does it tell us about constructions of masculinity? How do males' styles of body talk differ from females' styles?

2. If you look at five or six hundred years of paintings of women considered beautiful in their own time, you notice that fashion in body type has changed dramatically. Even if you look at photographs of famous actresses and other beauties in the United States of only fifty or sixty years ago, you will notice that the female body type that was fashionable then is different from what is popular now. Can you identify a trend? Why do you think this trend has developed? Do you think it has anything to do with medical information? Technology? Changes in social and economic trends? Do you think that the current fashion in female bodies is likely to remain the same long into the future? Why?

3. Nichols and Vuckovic mention the association of weight with morality. To some extent, slenderness is considered evidence of a "good," or moral life, and obesity is seen as evidence of a "bad," or immoral life. Similarly, a slim person is often seen as disciplined and energetic, while a fat person is viewed as self-indulgent and slothful. What examples have you seen of these stereotypes in American popular culture?

4. Why weight? That is, why has *weight* become the dimension of physical appearance that has consumed the interest of so many Americans in the past century?

In Pursuit of the Perfect Penis

THE MEDICALIZATION OF MALE SEXUALITY

Leonore Tiefer

So much has been written about the medical understandings (and misunderstandings) of female sexuality, especially in the nineteenth century, that it is easy to overlook a somewhat similar process of "medicalizing" male sexuality in the twentieth century. Leonore Tiefer looks at this issue, focusing on male impotence. Tiefer first discusses the importance of sexual performance to male gender identity, then reviews the recent history of explanations of and treatments for impotence, showing how these reflect cultural ideas about male sexuality and male relationships with their sexual partners. Increasingly, impotence has come to be seen as a medical matter with a simple mechanical solution. While this medicalization has a certain allure, Tiefer cautions that it may also obscure underlying social and psychological issues. The real problem of male impotence, Tiefer suggests, is the rigid cultural construction of masculinity in terms of male sexual performance with the ever-elusive "perfect penis."

Sexual virility—the ability to fulfill the conjugal duty, the ability to procreate, sexual power, potency—is everywhere a requirement of the male role and, thus, "impotence" is everywhere a matter of concern. Although the term has been used for centuries to refer specifically to partial or complete loss of erectile ability, the first definition dictionaries give for impotence never mentions sex but refers to a general loss of vigor, strength, or power. Sex therapists, concerned about these demeaning connotations, have written about the stigmatizing impact of the label "impotent":

> The word *impotent* is used to describe the man who does not get an erection, not just his penis. If a man is told by his doctor that

Source: Leonore Tiefer, "In Pursuit of the Perfect Penis: The Medicalization of Male Sexuality." Pp. 165–184 in *New Directions in Research on Men and Masculinity*, ed. Michael S. Kimmel. Copyright © 1987 Sage Publications, Inc. Reprinted by permission of Sage Publications, Inc.

he is impotent, the man turns to his partner and says he is impotent, they are saying a lot more than that the penis cannot become erect. (Kelley, 1981, p. 126)

Yet a recent survey of the psychological literature found that the frequency of articles with the term "impotence" in the title has risen dramatically since 1970, in contrast with the almost total disappearance of the term "frigidity," a term with comparable pejorative connotations and comparable frequency of use from 1940 to 1970 (Elliott, 1985).

In this article I would like to show how the persistence and increased use of the stigmatizing and stress-inducing label of impotence reflects a significant moment in the social construction of male sexuality. The factors that create this moment include the increasing importance of life-long sexual activity in personal life, the insatiability of mass media for appropriate sexual topics, the expansionist needs of specialty medicine and new medical technology, and the highly demanding male sexual script. I will show how these factors interact to produce a medicalization of male sexuality and sexual impotence that limits many men even as it offers new options and hope to others. Let me begin with a discussion of men's sexuality, and then discuss what medicine has recently had to offer it.

Male Sexuality

Sexual competence is part—some would say the *central* part—of contemporary masculinity, whether we are discussing the traditional man, the modern man, or even the "new" man:

What so stokes male sexuality that clinicians are impressed by the force of it? Not libido, but rather the curious phenomenon by which sexuality consolidates and confirms gender. . . . An impotent man always feels that his masculinity, and not just his sexuality, is threatened. In men,

gender appears to "lean" on sexuality . . . the need for sexual performance is so great. . . . In women, gender identity and self-worth can be consolidated by other means. (Person, 1980, pp. 619, 626)

Gagnon and Simon (1973) explained how, during adolescent masturbation, genital sexuality (i.e., erection and orgasm) acquires nonsexual motives such as the desire for power, achievement, and peer approval that have already become important during preadolescent gender role training. "The capacity for erection is an important sign element of masculinity and control" (Gagnon & Simon, 1973, p. 62) without which a man is not a man. Gross (1978) argues that by adulthood few men can accept other successful aspects of masculinity in lieu of adequate sexual performance.

. . .

Psychologically, then, male sexual performances may have as much or more to do with male gender role confirmation and homosocial status as with pleasure, intimacy, or tension release. This may explain why men express so many rules concerning proper sexual performance: Their agenda relates not merely to personal or couple satisfaction but to acting "like a man" in intercourse in order to qualify for the title elsewhere.

We can draw on the writings of several authorities to compile an outline of the ten sexual beliefs to which many men subscribe (Doyle, 1983; Zilbergeld, 1978; LoPiccolo, 1985): (1) Men's sexual apparatus and needs are simple and straightforward, unlike women's. (2) Most men are ready, willing, and eager for as much sex as they can get. (3) There is suspicion that other men's sexual experiences approximate ecstatic explosiveness more closely and more often than one's own. (4) It is the responsibility of the man to teach and lead his partner to experience pleasure and orgasm(s). (5) Sexual prowess is a serious, task-oriented business, no place for experimentation, unpredictability, or play. (6) Women prefer intercourse to other sexual activities, particularly "hard-driving" intercourse. (7) All really good and normal sex must end in intercourse. (8) Any physical contact other than a light touch is meant as an invitation to foreplay and intercourse. (9) It is the responsibility of the man to satisfy both his partner and himself. (10) Sexual prowess is never permanently earned; each time it must be reproven.

Many of these demands directly require—and all of them indirectly require—an erection. Nelson (1985) pointed out that male sexuality is dominated by a genital focus in several ways: Sexuality is isolated from the rest of life as a unique experience with particular technical performance requirements; the subjective meaning for the man arises from genital sensations first practiced and familiar in adolescent masturbation and directly transferred without thought to the interpersonal situation; and the psychological meaning primarily depends on the confirmation of virility that comes from proper erection and ejaculation.

It is no surprise, then, that any difficulty in getting the penis to do what it "ought" can become a source of profound humiliation and despair, both in terms of immediate self-esteem and the destruction of one's masculine reputation, which is assumed will follow.

> Few sexual problems are as devastating to a man as his inability to achieve or sustain an erection long enough for successful sexual intercourse. For many men the idea of not being able to "get it up" is a fate worse than death. (Doyle, 1983, p. 205)

> What's the worst thing that can happen? I asked myself. The worst thing that can happen is that I take one of these hip, beautiful, liberated women to bed and I can't get it up. I can't get it up! You hear me? She tells a few of her friends. Soon around every corner there's someone laughing at my failure. (Parent, 1977, p. 15)

Biomedical Approaches to Male Sexual Problems

Within the past decade, both professional and popular discussion about male sexuality has emphasized physical causes and treatments for sexual problems. There is greater awareness and acceptance within the medical profession of clinical and research work on sexuality, and sexually dissatisfied men are increasingly willing to discuss their problems with a physician (Bancroft, 1983). The professional literature on erection problems has focused on methods of differentiating between organic and nonorganic causes (LoPiccolo, 1985). Recent reviews survey endocrine, neurological, medication-related, urological, surgery-related, congenital, and vascular causes and contrast them with psychological and relationship causes (Krane, Siroky, & Goldstein, 1983).

Although the physiological contributions to adequate sexual functioning can be theoretically specified in some detail, as yet few diagnostic tests exist that enable specific identification of one type of pathophysiological contribution versus another. Moreover, as yet few medical treatments are available for medically caused erectile disorders aside from changing medications (particularly in the case of hypertension) or correcting an underlying disease process. The most widely used medical approach is an extreme one: surgical implantation of a device into the penis that will permit intromission. This is the penile prosthesis.

The history of these devices is relatively short (Melman, 1978). Following unsuccessful attempts with bone and cartilage, the earliest synthetic implant (1948) was of a plastic tube placed in the middle of the penis of a patient who had had his urethra removed for other reasons. Today, several different manufacturers produce slightly different versions of two general types of implant.

One type is the "inflatable" prosthesis. Inflatable silicone cylinders are placed in the *corpora cavernosa* of the penis, the cylindrical bodies of erectile tissue that normally fill with blood during erection. The cylinders are connected to a pump placed in the scrotum that is connected to a small, saline-filled reservoir placed in the abdomen. "When the patient desires a tumescent phallus, the bulb is squeezed five or six times and fluid is forced from the reservoir into the cylinder chambers. When a flaccid penis is wanted, a deflation valve is pressed and the fluid returns to the reservoir" (Melman, 1978, p. 278).

The other type of prosthesis is a pair of semirigid rods, now made of silicone, with either a bendable silver core or a hinge to allow concealment of the erection by bending it down or up against the body when the man is dressed.

Because these devices have been implanted primarily by private practitioners, the only way to estimate the number of implant operations is from manufacturers' sales figures. However, many devices are sold that are not used. A French urologist estimated that 5,000 parents were given penile implants in 1977 alone (Subrini, 1980). It seems reasonable to guess that by the mid-1980s hundreds of thousands of men had received implants.

· · ·

Postimplant follow-up studies have typically been conducted by surgeons interested in operative complications and global measures of patient satisfaction (Sotile, 1979). Past reports have encouraged the belief that the devices function mechanically, are adjusted to by the man and his partner without difficulty, and result in satisfactory sexual function and sensation. But recent papers are challenging these conclusions. One review of the postoperative follow-up literature was so critical of methodological weaknesses (brief follow-up periods, rare

interviews with patients' sexual partners, few objective data or even cross-validation of subjective questions about sexual functioning among others) that the authors could not summarize the results in any meaningful way (Collins & Kinder, 1984). Another recent summary criticized the implants' effectiveness:

> First, recent reports indicate that the percentage of surgical and mechanical complications from such prosthetic implants is much higher than might be considered acceptable. Second, despite claims to the contrary by some surgeons, it appears likely that whatever degree of naturally occurring erection a man is capable of will be disrupted, and perhaps eliminated by the surgical procedures and scarring involved in prosthetic implants. Finally, it has been my experience that, although patients are typically rather eager to have a prosthesis implanted and report being very happy with it at short-term surgical follow-up, longer term behavioral assessment indicates poor sexual adjustment in some cases. (LoPiccolo, 1985, p. 222)

Three recent urological papers report high rates of postoperative infection and mechanical failure of the inflatable prosthesis, both necessitating removal of the device (Apte, Gregory, & Purcell, 1984; Joseph, Bruskewitz, & Benson, 1984; Fallon, Rosenberg, & Culp, 1984) In the first paper, 43 percent of patients required at least one repeat surgery; in the second paper, the device malfunctioned in 47 percent of 88 cases operated on since 1977; in the third, 48 percent of 95 patients have had their prosthesis malfunction in one way or another since 1977.

· · ·

Public Information about Penile Prostheses

Public sexual information is dominated by health and medical science in both language and substance. Newspapers present "new" discoveries. Magazines have "experts" with advanced health degrees outline "new" norms and ways to achieve them. Television and radio talk-show guests, health-degreed "experts," promote their latest book or therapeutic approach as "resources" are flashed on the screen or mentioned by the host. Sexuality is presented as a life problem—like buying a house, having a good relationship, dealing with career choices—the "modern" approach is to be rational, orderly, careful, thorough, up-to-date, and in tune with the latest pronouncements of the experts.

The public accepts the assumption that scientific discoveries improve our ability to manage and control our lives and welcomes new biomedical developments in areas perceived to be dominated by the physical or by standards of health and illness. Sexual physiology has a tangibility that "love" and "lust" lack, increasing its propriety as a language for public discourse. When biomedicine, health, and physiology are considered the appropriate sexual discourse, scientists and health care providers are the appropriate authorities.

The media have presented information about penile prostheses in the same straightforward, rational, scientific, informative way as other "news" about sexuality. One article in *The New York Times* in 1979 presented the findings of a urological paper that had appeared in the *Journal of the American Medical Association* the day before. It gave the address of the prosthesis manufacturer as well as typical financial cost, length of hospital stay, and insurance coverage. A *JAMA* editorial, criticizing the study's inattention to the patients' sexual partners, was mentioned.

An article in *Vogue* exclusively discussed new medical/surgical approaches to impotence under a typically simple and optimistic title, "Curing Impotence: The Prognosis Is Good." The financial cost of the devices is mentioned as well as an in-development "electrostimulatory device to be inserted in the anus before intercourse and controlled by a ring or wristwatch-like switch so that patients can signal appropriate nerves to produce an erection" (Hixson, 1985, p. 406). The style is technical and mechanical and so simple and cheerful that it is hardly amazing to read in a sentence following the anal electrode description, "While psychological impotence problems probably also require psychological treatment, the doctors feel that successful electronic intercourse may provide the confidence needed by some men" (p. 406).

Literature for patients has been developed by the major prosthesis manufacturers and is available at patient education centers, in doctors' waiting rooms, and through self-help groups such as Impotents Anonymous. A typical booklet is seven pages of high-quality glossy paper, with photographs of healthy young couples in a garden, watching a beautiful sunset, sitting by the ocean (Mentor Corporation, 1984). Entitled *Overcoming Impotence*, the text reads

> Impotence is a widespread problem that affects many millions of men. It can occur at any age and at any point in a man's sexual life. The myth of impotence as an "old man's disease" has finally been shattered. Impotence is a problem of men but also affects couples and families. Now, as a result of recent medical advances, impotence need no longer cause frustration, embarrassment and tension. New solutions are now available for an age-old problem.

In the second section, on causes of impotence, the booklet reads as follows:

> The causes can be either physical or psychological. For many years, it was believed that 90 percent of impotent men had a psychological cause for their problem; but as a result of recent medical research, it is now known that at least half of the men suffering from impotence can actually trace its origin to a physical problem.

After a lengthy discussion of the methods used to distinguish between physical and psychological impotence, the booklet continues in its relentlessly upbeat way:

> For the majority of men who are physically impotent and for those who are psychologically impotent and do not respond to counselling, a penile implant offers the only complete, reliable solution. It offers new hope for a return to satisfactory sexual activity and for the disappearance of the anxieties and frustrations of impotence.

This, of course, seems to be merely a straightforward technological solution to a technical problem. No mention is made of individual differences in adjustment to the prosthesis, or even that adjustment will be necessary at all. The mechanical solution itself will solve the problem; the person becomes irrelevant.

Other patient information booklets are similar: informative about the device and reassuring about the outcome. In addition to lengthy and detailed discussion of specific physical causes of impotence, brief mention is made of psychogenic impotence.

> Another group of patients have some type of mental barrier [sic] or problem. This latter group may account for as high as 50 percent of the people with impotence, but only a small number of these people are candidates for a penile implant. (Medical Engineering Corp., 1983)

Is it any wonder that men who "fail" the physical tests and are diagnosed as having psychogenic impotence cannot understand why they should be deprived of the device?

Urologists have begun in recent years to specialize in the diagnosis and surgical treatment of impotence. A quarterly publication from a prosthesis manufacturer "for surgeons practicing prosthetic urology" devoted a front page recently to the subject "Impotence Clinics: Investments in the Future" (American Medical Systems, 1984). Newspaper advertisements have begun to appear from groups of urologists with such names as Potency Plus in California. Another California group

calling itself Potential advertises "Impotence . . . there could be a medical reason and a medical solution." An ad in a New York newspaper is headlined "Potent Solution to Sexual Problem."

Another source of publicity about the physical causes and treatments for erectile difficulties has come from The Impotence Institute of America, an organization founded by a man who describes how his own search ended happily with an implanted penile prosthesis. Although the subhead on the not-for-profit institute's stationery is "Bringing a 'total-care' concept to overcoming impotency," the ten men on the board of directors are all urologists.

In 1982 the institute created two consumer-oriented groups, Impotents Anonymous (IA) and I-Anon, based on the Alcoholics Anonymous models (both the institute's founder and his wife had formerly been members of Al-Anon). Recent correspondence from the institute indicates 70 chapters of IA operating and another 20 planned. A 1984 news article about IA, "Organization Helps Couples with Impotence as Problem," repeated the now familiar information that "until five years ago most physicians believed that up to 95 percent of all erectile impotence stemmed from psychological problems, [but that] medical experts now agree that about half of all impotence is caused by physical disorders" (*New York Times*, 1984). The IA brochure cites the same numbers.

Let us turn now to a critique of the biomedical approach to male sexuality, beginning with this question of organic and psychogenic etiology.

Critique of the Biomedical Approach

The frequent claim that psychogenic impotence has been oversold and organic causes are far more common than realized has captivated the media and legitimated increased medical involvement in sexuality.

An *International Journal of Andrology* editorial summarizes the shift:

> Medical fashions come and go and the treatment of erectile impotence is no exception. In the 20s and 30s, physicians and surgeons looked for physical causes and tried out methods of treatment, most of which now seem absurd. Since that time there has been a widely held view that 90–95 percent of cases of impotence are psychologically determined. Where this figure came from was never clear [some sources cite Havelock Ellis], but it has entered into medical folklore. In the past five years or so, the pendulum has been swinging back. Physical causes and methods of treatment are receiving increasing attention. (Bancroft, 1982, 353)

In the Center for Male Sexual Dysfunction in the Department of Urology, Beth Israel Medical Center, New York City, over 800 men have been seen since 1981 because of erectile problems. Very few who, on the basis of a simple history and physical, could be unambiguously declared "psychogenic" were immediately referred for sex therapy; the remainder underwent a complete medical and psychological workup. Over 90 percent of these patients believed that their problem was completely or preponderantly physical in origin; yet we have found that only about 45 percent of patients have exclusively or predominantly medically caused erectile problems, and 55 percent have exclusively or predominantly psychologically caused problems. This approximately 50/50 split is, in fact, what is being observed by the mass media. But it is based on a sample of men usually referred by their primary physicians (over 75 percent) because of their likely medical etiology and their need for a comprehensive workup.

. . .

Obviously, one cannot describe the actual rate of occurrence of any particular problem (e.g., "organic impotence") without describing the population from which the sample comes. The urology departments' findings that approximately half of the patients seen for erectile problems have a medical cause *cannot* be generalized to other groups (e.g., men in general practitioners' waiting rooms reading prosthesis manufacturers' literature, men watching a TV program about impotence) without further normative data collection. It is important to emphasize that even men with diabetes, a known cause of peripheral neural and vascular difficulties that could result in impotence, are as often potent as not (Schiavi, Fisher, Quadland, & Glover, 1984; Fairburn, McCulloch, & Wu, 1982), a result that cannot be predicted from the duration of the diabetes or the presence of other physical complications.

An even more serious criticism of the biomedical trend is the common tendency to contrapose organic and psychogenic causes of impotence as mutually exclusive phenomena.

> Conceptually, most of the research suffers from the flaw of attempting to categorize the patients into discrete, nonoverlapping categories of organic *or* psychogenic erectile failure. Yet, many cases, and perhaps the majority of cases, involve *both* organic and psychogenic erectile factors in the genesis of erectile failure. (LoPiccolo, 1985, p. 221)

. . .

It is not so much, I believe, that all cases involve a mixture of factors but that all cases involve psychological factors to some degree. The director of a New York sexuality clinic sums up her impressions similarly:

> We have found in our work . . . that where organic determinants are diagnosed, inevitably there will also be psychological factors involved, either as co-determinants of the erectile dysfunction or as reactive to it. . . . A man's emotional reactions to

his erectile failures may be such that it serves to maintain the erectile problem even when the initial physiological causes are resolved. (Schreiner-Engel, 1981, p. 116)

The consequences of this implication are particularly serious given that, as LoPiccolo (1985) notes, "many physicians currently will perform surgery to implant a penile prosthesis if any organic abnormality is found" (p. 221). The effect of psychological factors is to make the dysfunction look worse than the medical problem alone would warrant. Altering the man's devastated attitudes will improve the picture, whatever else is going on.

Perelman (1984) refers to "the omnipresent psychogenic component existing in any potency problem regardless of the degree of organicity" (p. 181) to describe his successful use of cognitive-behavioral psychotherapy to treat men diagnosed with organic impotence. He reminds us that physical sexual function has a psychosomatic complexity that is not only poorly understood but that may have the "ability to successfully compensate for its own deficits" (p. 181). Thus the search for the etiology that characterizes so much of the biomedical approach to male sexual problems seems to have less to do with the nature of sexuality than the nature of the medical enterprise.

The Allure of Medicalized Sexuality

Men are drawn to a technological solution such as the penile prosthesis for a variety of personal reasons that ultimately rest on the inflexible central place of sexual potency in the male sexual script. Those who assume that "normal" men must always be interested in sex and who believe that male sexuality is a simple system wherein interest leads easily and directly to erection (Zilbergeld, 1978) are baffled by any erectile difficulties. Their belief that their penis is an instrument

immune from everyday problems, anxieties and fears" (Doyle, 1983, p. 207) conditions them to deny the contribution of psychological or interpersonal factors to male sexual responsiveness. This denial, in turn, results from fundamental male gender role prescriptions for self-reliance and emotional control (Brannon, 1976).

Medicalized discourse offers an explanation of impotence that removes control, and therefore responsibility and blame, for sexual failure from the man and places it on his physiology. Talcort Parsons (1951) originally argued that an organic diagnosis confers a particular social role, the "sick role," which has three aspects: (1) The individual is not held responsible for his or her condition; (2) illnesses are legitimate bases for exemption from normal social responsibilities; and (3) the exemptions are contingent on the sick person recognizing that sickness is undesirable and seeking appropriate (medical) help. A medical explanation for erectile difficulties relieves men of blame and thus permits them to maintain some masculine self-esteem even in the presence of impotence.

> Understandably, for many years the pattern of the human male has been to blame sexual dysfunction on specific physical distresses. Every sexually inadequate male lunges toward any potential physical excuse for sexual malfunction. From point of ego support, would that it could be true. A cast for a leg or a sling for an arm provides socially acceptable evidence of physical dysfunction of these extremities. Unfortunately, the psychosocial causes of perpetual penile flaccidity cannot be explained or excused by devices for mechanical support. (Masters & Johnson, 1970, pp. 187–188)

Perhaps in 1970 "devices for mechanical support" of the penis were not in widespread access, but we now have available, ironically, precisely the type of medical vindication Masters and Johnson suggested would be the *most* effective deflection of the "blame" men feel for their inability to perform sexually.

Men's willingness to accept a self-protective, self-handicapping (i.e., illness label) attribution for "failure" has been demonstrated in studies of excuse-making (Snyder, Ford, & Hunt, 1985). Reduced personal responsibility is most sought in those situations in which performance is related to self-esteem (Snyder & Smith, 1982). It may be that the frequent use of physical excuses for failure in athletic performance provides a model for men to use in sexuality. Medical treatments not only offer tangible evidence of nonblameworthiness, but they allow men to avoid psychological treatments such as marital or sex therapy, which threaten embarrassing self-disclosure and admissions of weakness men find aversive (Peplau & Gordon, 1985).

The final allure of a technological solution such as the penile prosthesis is its promise of permanent freedom from worry. One of Masters and Johnson's (1970) major insights was their description of the self-conscious self-monitoring that men with erectile difficulties develop in sexual situations. "Performance anxiety" and "spectatoring," their two immediate causes of sexual impotence, generate a self-perpetuating cycle that undermines a man's confidence about the future even as he recovers from individual episodes. Technology seems to offer a simple and permanent solution to the problem of lost or threatened confidence, as doctors from *Vogue* to the *Journal of Urology* have already noted.

The Rising Importance of Sexuality in Personal Life

Even though we live in a time when the definition of masculinity is moving away from reliance on physical validation (Pleck, 1976), there seems no apparent reduction in the male sexual focus on physical performance.

Part of the explanation for this must rest with the increasing importance of sexuality in contemporary relationships. Recent sociocultural analyses have suggested that sexual satisfaction grows in importance to the individual and couple as other sources of personal fulfillment and connection with others wither.

> I would say that with the collapse of other social values (those of religion, patriotism, the family, and so on), sex has been forced to take the slack, to become our sole mode of transcendence and our only touchstone of authenticity. . . . In our present isolation we have few ways besides sex to feel connected with each other. (White, 1980, p. 282)

. . .

The increasing pressure on intimate relationships to provide psychological support and gratification comes at the same time that traditional (i.e., economic and family-raising) reasons for these relationships are declining. Both trends place more pressure on compatibility and companionship to maintain the relationship. Given that men have been raised "not to be emotionally sensitive to others or emotionally expressive or self-revealing" (Pleck, 1981, p. 140), much modern relationship success would seem to depend on sexual fulfillment. Although some contemporary research indicates that marriages and gay relationships can be rated successful despite the presence of sexual problems (Frank, Anderson, & Rubinstein, 1978; Bell & Weinberg, 1978), popular surveys suggest that the public believes sexual satisfaction is essential to relationship success.

The importance of sexuality also increases because of its use by consumption-oriented capitalism (Altman, 1982). The promise of increased sexual attractiveness is used to sell products to people of all ages. Commercial sexual meeting places and playgrounds are popular in both gay and heterosexual culture. A whole system of therapists, books, workshops, and magazines sells advice on improving sexual performance and enjoyment. Restraint and repression are inappropriate in a consumer culture in which the emphasis is on immediate gratification.

The expectation that sexuality will provide ever-increasing rewards and personal meaning has also been a theme of the contemporary women's movement, and women's changing attitudes have affected many men, particularly widowed and divorced men returning to the sexual "market." Within the past decade, sexual advice manuals have completely changed their tone regarding the roles of men and women in sexual relations (Weinberg, Swensson, & Hammersmith, 1983). Women are advised to take more responsibility for their own pleasure, to possess sexual knowledge and self-knowledge, and to expect that improved sexual functioning will pay off in other aspects of life. Removing responsibility from the man for being the sexual teacher and leader reduces the definition of sexual masculinity to having excellent technique and equipment to meet the "new woman" on her "new" level.

. . .

The Medicalization of Impotence: Part of the Problem or Part of the Solution?

The increased use of the term "impotence" that Elliott (1985) reported can now be seen as part of a process of medicalization of sexuality. Physicians view the medical system as a method for distributing technical expertise in the interest of improved health (Ehrenreich & Ehrenreich, 1978). Their economic interests, spurred by the profit orientation of medical technology manufacturers, lie in expanding the number and type of services they offer to more and more patients. Specialists, in particular, have dramatically increased their incomes and prestige during the postwar era by developing high-reimbursement relationships with hospitals and insurance companies (Starr, 1982). In the sexual sphere, all these goals are served by labelling impotence a biomedical disorder, common in men of all ages, best served by thorough evaluation and appropriate medical treatment when any evidence of organic disorder is identified.

There are many apparent advantages for men in the medicalization of male sexuality. As discussed earlier, men view physical explanations for their problems as less stigmatizing and are better able to maintain their sense of masculinity and self-esteem. Accepting medicine as a source of authority and help reassures men who feel under immense pressure from role expectations but are unable to consult with or confide in either other men or women because of pride, competitiveness, or defensiveness. That "inhibited sexual excitement . . . in males, partial or complete failure to attain or maintain erection until completion of the [sic] sexual act" is a genuine disorder (American Psychiatric Association, 1980, p. 279) legitimates an important aspect of life that physicians previously dismissed or made jokes about. And, as I have said, permanent mechanical solutions to sexual performance worries are seen as a gift from heaven in erasing, with one simple operation, a source of anxiety dating from adolescence about failing as a man.

The disadvantages to medicalizing male sexuality, however, are numerous and subtle. (My discussion here is informed by Riessman's 1983 analysis of the medicalization of many female roles and conditions.) First, dependence on medical remedies for impotence has led to the escalating use of treatments whose long-term effects are not known and, in many cases, seem to be harmful. Iatrogenic ("doctor-caused") consequences of new technology and pharmacology are not uncommon and seem most worrisome when medical treatments are offered to men with no demonstrable organic disease. Second, the use of medical language mystifies human experience, increasing dependence on professionals and experts. If sexuality becomes fundamentally a matter of vasocongestion and myotonia (as in Masters & Johnson's famous claim, 1966, p. 7), personal experience requires expert interpretation and explanation. Third, medicalization spreads the moral neutrality of medicine and science over sexuality, and people no longer ask whether men "should" have erections. If the presence of erections is healthy and their absence (in whole or part) is pathological, then healthy behavior is correct behavior and vice versa, again increasing dependence on health authorities to define norms and standards for conduct.

The primary disadvantage of medicalization is that it denies, obscures, and ignores the social causes of whatever problem is under study. Impotence becomes the problem of an individual man. This effect seems particularly pertinent in the case of male sexuality in which the social demands of the male sexual role are so related to the meaning of erectile function and dysfunction. Recall the list of men's beliefs about sexuality, the evaluative criteria of conduct and performance. Being a man depends on sexual adequacy, which depends on potency. A rigid, reliable erection is necessary for full compliance with the script. The medicalization of male sexuality helps a man conform to the script rather than analyzing where the script comes from or challenging it. Research and technology are directed only toward better and better solutions. Yet the demands of the script are so formidable, and the pressures from the sociocultural changes we have outlined so likely to increase, that no technical solution will ever work—certainly not for everyone.

Medicine attracts public resources out of proportion to its capacity for health enhancement, because it often categorizes problems fundamentally social in origin as biological or personal deficits, and in so doing smothers the impulse for social change which could offer the only serious resolution. (Stark & Flitcraft, in Riessman, 1983, p. 4)

Preventive Medicine: Changing the Male Sexual Script

Men will remain vulnerable to the expansion of the clinical domain so long as masculinity rests heavily on a particular type of physiological function. As more research uncovers subtle physiological correlates of genital functioning, more men will be "at risk" for impotence. Fluctuations of physical and emotional state will become cues for impending impotence in any man with, for example diabetes, hypertension, or a history of prescription medication usage.

One of the less well understood features of sex therapy is that it "treats" erectile dysfunction by changing the individual man's sexual script.

. . .

Our thesis is that the rules and concepts we learn [about male sexuality] are destructive and a very inadequate preparation for a satisfying and pleasurable sex life. . . . Having a better sex life is in large measure dependent upon your willingness to examine how the male sexual mythology has trapped you. (Zilbergeld, 1978, p. 9)

Sexuality can be transformed from a rigid standard for masculine adequacy to a way of being, a way of communicating, a hobby, a way of being in one's body—and *being* one's body—that does not impose control but rather affirms pleasure, movement, sensation, cooperation, playfulness, relating. Masculine confidence cannot be purchased, because there can never be perfect potency. Chasing its illusion may line a few pockets, but for most men it will only exchange one set of anxieties and limitations for another.

REFERENCES

Altman, D. (1982). *The homosexualization of America, The Americanization of the homosexual*. New York: St. Martin's Press.

American Psychiatric Association. (1980). *Diagnostic and statistical manual of mental disorders* (3rd ed.). Washington, D.C.: Author.

Apte, S. M., Gregory, J. G., & Purcell, M. H. (1984). The inflatable penile prosthesis, reoperation and patient satisfaction: A comparison of statistics obtained from patient record review with statistics obtained from intensive followup search. *Journal of Urology, 131*, 894–895.

Bancroft, J. (1982). Erectile impotence: Psyche or soma? *International Journal of Andrology, 5*, 353–355.

Bancroft, J. (1983). *Human sexuality and its problems*. Edinburgh: Churchill-Livingstone.

Bell, A. P., & Weinberg, M. S. (1978). *Homosexualities: A study of diversity among men and women*. New York: Simon & Schuster.

Brannon, R. (1976). The male sex role: Our culture's blueprint of manhood, and what it's done for us lately. In D. David & R. Brannon (Eds.), *The forty-nine percent majority: The male sex role*. Reading, MA: Addison-Wesley.

Collins, G. F., & Kinder, B. N. (1984). Adjustment following surgical implantation of a penile prosthesis: A critical overview. *Journal of Sex and Marital Therapy, 10*, 255–271.

Doyle, J. A. (1983). *The male experience*. Dubuque, IA: William C. Brown.

Ehrenreich, B., & Ehrenreich, J. (1978). Medicine and social control. In J. Ehrenreich (Ed.), *The cultural crisis of modern medicine*. New York: Monthly Review Press.

Elliott, M. L. (1985). The use of "impotence" and "frigidity": Why has "impotence" survived? *Journal of Sex and Marital Therapy, 11*, 51–56.

Fairburn, C. G., McCulloch, D. K., & Wu, F. C. (1982). The effects of diabetes on male sexual function. *Clinics in Endocrinology and Metabolism, 11*, 749–767.

Fallon, B., Rosenberg, S., & Culp, D. A. (1984). Long-term follow-up in patients with an inflatable penile prosthesis. *Journal of Urology, 132*, 270–271.

Finkle, A. L., & Finkle, C. E. (1984). Sexual impotency: Counseling of 388 private patients by urologists from 1954–1982. *Urology, 23*, 25–30.

Frank, E., Anderson, C., & Rubinstein, D. (1978). Frequency of sexual dysfunction in "normal" couples. *New England Journal of Medicine, 299*, 111–115.

Gagnon, J. H., & Simon, W. (1973). *Sexual conduct: The social sources of human sexuality*. Chicago: Aldine.

Gross, A. E. (1978). The male role and heterosexual behavior. *Journal of Social Issues, 34*, 87–107.

Hixson, J. R. (1985, April). Curing impotence: The prognosis is good. *Vogue*, p. 406.

Impotence clinics: Investments in the future. (1984). *Colleagues in Urology Newsletter*, Fourth Quarter, p. 1. Minnetonka, MN: American Medical Systems.

Joseph, D. B., Bruskewitz, R. C., & Benson, R. C. (1984). Long-term evaluation of the inflatable penile prosthesis. *Journal of Urology, 131*, 670–673.

Kelley, S. (1981). Some social and psychological aspects of organic sexual dysfunction in men. *Sexuality and Disability, 4*, 123–128.

Krane, R. J., Siroky, M. B., & Goldstein, I. (1983). *Male sexual dysfunction*. Boston: Little, Brown.

LoPiccolo, J. (1985). Diagnosis and treatment of male sexual dysfunction. *Journal of Sex and Marital Therapy, 11*, 215–232.

Masters, W. H., & Johnson, V. E. (1966). *Human sexual response*. Boston: Little, Brown.

Masters, W. H., & Johnson, V. E. (1970). *Human sexual inadequacy*. Boston: Little, Brown.

Medical Engineering Corporation. (1983). *Patient information booklet discussing the surgical correction of impotency*. Racine, WI: Author.

Melman, A. (1978). Development of contemporary surgical management for erectile impotence. *Sexuality and Disability, 1*, 272–281.

Nelson, J. (1985). Male sexuality and masculine spirituality. *Siecus Report, 13*, 1–4.

Organization helps couples with impotence as problem. (1984, June 24). *New York Times*, Section 1, Pt. 2, p. 42.

Paff, B. (1985). Sexual dysfunction in gay men requesting treatment. *Journal of Sex and Marital Therapy, 11*, 3–18.

Parsons, T. (1951). *The social system*. New York: Free Press.

Peplau, L. A., & Gordon, S. L. (1985). Women and men in love: Gender differences in close heterosexual relationships. In V. E. O'Leary, R. K. Unger, & B. S. Wallston (Eds.), *Women, gender and social psychology*, Hillsdale, NJ: Lawrence Erlbaum.

Perelman, M. (1984). Rehabilitative sex therapy for organic impotence. In R. T. Segraves & E. J. Haeberle (Eds.), *Emerging dimensions of sexology*. New York: Praeger.

Person, E. S. (1980). Sexuality as the mainstay of identity: Psychoanalytic perspectives. *Signs, 5,* 605–630.

Pleck, J. H. (1976). The male sex role: Definitions, problems and sources of change. *Journal of Social Issues, 32,* 155–164.

Riessman, C. K. (1983). Women and medicalization: A new perspective. *Social Policy 14,* 3–18.

Schiavi, R. C. Fisher, C., Quadland, M., & Glover, A. (1984). Erectile function in nonimpotent diabetics. In R. T. Segraves & E. J. Haeberle (Eds.), *Emerging dimensions of sexology*. New York: Praeger.

Schmidt, G. (1983). Introduction: Sexuality and relationships. In G. Arentewicz & G. Schmidt, *The treatment of sexual disorders*. New York: Basic Books.

Schover, L. R., & Von Eschenbach, A. C. (1985). Sex therapy and the penile prosthesis: A synthesis. *Journal of Sex and Marital Therapy, 11,* 57–66.

Schreiner-Engel, P. (1981). Therapy of psychogenic erectile disorders. *Sexuality and Disability, 4,* 115–122.

Schumacher, S., & Lloyd, C. W. (1981). Physiological and psychological factors in impotence. *Journal of Sex Research, 17,* 40–53.

Segraves, R. T., Schoenberg, H. W., Zarins, C., Camic, P., & Knopf, J. (1981). Characteristics of erectile dysfunction as a function of medical care system entry point. *Psychosomatic Medicine, 43,* 227–234.

Snyder, C. R., Ford, C. E., & Hunt, H. A. (1985, August). *Excuse-making: A look at sex differences*. Paper presented at American Psychological Association annual meeting, Los Angeles.

Snyder, C. R., & Smith, T. W. (1982). Symptoms as self-handicapping strategies: The virtues of old wine in a new bottle. In G. Weary & H. L. Mirels (Eds.), *Integration of Sex and Marital Therapy, 5,* 90–102.

Sotile, W. M. (1979). The penile prosthesis: A review. *Journal of Sex and Marital Therapy, 5,* 90–102.

Starr, P. (1982). *The transformation of American medicine*. New York: Basic Books.

Subrini, L. P. (1980). Treatment of impotence using penile implants: Surgical, sexual, and psychological follow-up. In R. Forleo & W. Pasini (Eds.), *Medical sexology*. Littleton, MA: PSG Publishing.

Surgical implants correct impotence. (1979, June 12). *New York Times*, Section C, p. 3.

Tolson, A. (1977). *The limits of masculinity*. New York: Harper & Row.

Weinberg, M. S., Swensson, R. G., & Hammersmith, S. K. (1983). Sexual autonomy and the status of women: Models of female sexuality in U.S. sex manuals from 1950 to 1980. *Social Problems, 30,* 312–324.

White, E. (1980). *States of desire*. New York: E. P. Dutton.

Wise, T. N., Rabins, P. V., & Gahnsley, J. (1984). The older patient with a sexual dysfunction. *Journal of Sex and Marital Therapy, 10,* 117–121.

Zilbergeld, B. (1978). *Male sexuality*. Boston: Little, Brown.

DISCUSSION QUESTIONS

1. Discuss the ten sexual tenets that Tiefer claims many American men believe. Do you agree that these beliefs are widespread among men? Do you think women generally hold these same beliefs? What are some ways in which U.S. society perpetuates these beliefs about male sexuality?

2. Comparing Tiefer's article with that by Michael Kimmel in the last chapter, what do you feel has and has not changed in middle-class American constructions of masculinity over the past century?

ALTERNATIVE SEXUAL PREFERENCES AND GENDER IDENTITIES

CHAPTER 4

There is no question that the majority of the American population would describe itself as heterosexual, or "straight." But there is also no question that the non-heterosexual minority is increasingly visible, increasingly vocal, and increasingly unwilling to be ignored or to have its interests and needs overlooked. The non-heterosexual population is made up of lesbians, transgendered and transsexual individuals, gay men, and bisexuals, and it is worthy of study for at least three reasons. First, and most significant, it is a large and varied group with its own interests, goals, and history. Second, this group is currently in an exciting period of charting its own course. Third, this loose collection of communities and subcultures is interesting because of the light it reflects on American culture as a whole. If the essence of meaning lies in contrast, then the meaning of gender issues, generally, cannot fail to be illuminated by the juxtaposition of the perspectives and experiences of majority and minority gender communities.

The four selections contained in this chapter address a number of different issues that concern sexual preference and gender identity. Readers will probably notice some that we have not mentioned. Make sure you keep them in mind for further thought and future discussion. Keep in mind the following questions that may be said to bind the articles together—though they may take distinctively different positions on them.

1. What is the meaning of terms like *sexual preference* and *gender identity*? To what extent do such terms imply or reflect the notions of individual choice and cultural facilitation or conditioning? To what extent may they be said to involve biological determination—to be simply a "fact of life"? You will rapidly come to notice that different authors in this chapter represent different positions on this issue. They do not attempt to provide scientific answers to the question of *why* individuals are homosexual, transgendered, transsexual, or heterosexual; their goals in these articles are different. Try to see if it is possible to account for the basis of these differing positions. Are they based on an author's gender, for example, or on his or her sexual affiliation? Do you think it is possible to make a general statement about the origins of the authors' perspectives?

2. There is a general assumption within the American heterosexual population that it is possible to make a sharp distinction between those who are "straight"

and those who are not, and that all humans can be classified as either homosexual or heterosexual. Though this American dichotomy forms the background for all of the articles, some of them present alternative ways of thinking about the way people make sexual choices and assess (or construct) their own gender identities. Consider the variation in perspective represented in the selections in this chapter, and when you have finished reading them, consider whether you (still) believe that all of us must be *either* homosexual *or* heterosexual, and whether those designations are fixed in an individual for all time.

3. The authors of the selections in this chapter come from the gay, lesbian, and transgendered/transsexual communities, and they discuss varying perspectives even within each one of these groups. As you read the four articles presented here, ask yourself two questions. First, what binds these apparently very different groups together? Perhaps, in fact, they are *not* bound together except in the minds of the heterosexual population. Or perhaps this affiliation is looser in the minds of some authors than it is in the minds of others. Second, what kinds of variation exist among the groups and authors represented? There is the obvious variation in sexual interest (gay, lesbian, transgendered, of course, but there are others, too). Some variations have obviously to do with personal experience, and some seem to be more easily classified as theoretical or philosophical differences (though some would say that such differences are ultimately the result of personal experience, too).

4. Despite the varying perspectives the four authors in this chapter present with respect to the issue of why individuals are (or become) gay, lesbian, straight, or trans, the articles, taken together, suggest that the issues of sexual preference and gender affiliation do not have a single cause. Nonetheless, the articles do demonstrate, some more explicitly than others, that whatever the ultimate origin of sexual choice and gender identity, these behaviors are mediated and shaped by the cultures in which they occur. And by "culture," it is important not only to consider whether an individual is living in Mali or Monaco or Massachusetts, but *when* that person is living, and what cultural and historical events are swirling around her or him.

5. In light of the importance of the cultural and historical context of gender-based issues, it is important to note that in all of the four articles presented here the events of the 1960s and 1970s played an important role. During the late sixties and early seventies many social movements developed, some of which, including the civil rights movement, the War on Poverty, feminism, and gay liberation, dramatically changed American culture. These processes and upheavals were the context in which gay, transgendered and transsexual people, and lesbians were able to make their voices heard to the culture as a whole and to come together to form alternative subcultures.

6. Finally, each one of the four articles demonstrates the significance of the *individual* attainment of alternative gender roles, especially the process of "coming out," or publicly identifying oneself as a lesbian or a gay man. Though each coming out story is different, their authors all share the relief and sense of community derived from public affirmation of their identities and affiliation with other persons with whom they have shared identity as well as shared experiences.

The four articles presented here raise more questions than they resolve. This is neither bad nor surprising at a time when science and society are only beginning to deal with gender issues, and when American culture as a whole is still struggling to understand its gendered self and to realize that there are questions to ask. But though they provide few answers, these articles do destroy forever any stereotypes of The Undifferentiated Homosexual. And they provide a window into the complexity, variation, and vitality of lesbian, trans, and gay populations and communities.

OUT-TAKES

RON CALDWELL

The title of this selection is a pun. Instead of a silly joke, however, it is a gently humorous way of getting the reader to unravel the implications that the word "out-takes" contains. Literally, the term "out-takes" refers to pieces of a commercial film or videotape that are edited out, and that do not appear in the final product in theatres or television. In a more specialized, less usual sense, "out-takes" has to do with "takes" (perceptions) of "coming out" (publicly stating one's identity as a gay or lesbian person). On one level this piece is a thoughtful but straightforward account of the author's process of coming out to members of his family; there is the public part of the narrative that would make it into the finished videotape of his life. On another level the piece discusses how the author felt about coming out; that is the part that might have ended up on the cutting room floor.

Then there is the question of the author's perspective on the phenomenon of "coming out" and "being out." Many straight people who think of themselves as tolerant say something like, "I have no objection to anyone's sexual preference, as long as they keep it to themselves. But I don't understand why lesbians and gay men have to make such a point of their sexual identity." As you read through "Out-takes," keep that perspective (which we might call the "pseudo-tolerant position") in mind. Try to determine why the process of coming out is such a central experience for many lesbians and gay men, and why being out is such an essential part of their lives. If you are gay or lesbian yourself, this exercise will not be difficult. If you are heterosexual, try to imagine what your life would be like if you were "in the closet" (that is, not "out"). How much of your life would you have to conceal, deny, and even lie about? Sexual relationships frequently involve very strong emotions, and often contribute to the building of deep love and affection. What would it be like never to be able to acknowledge those relationships in public or even to your family and heterosexual friends? Even such relatively uncomplicated gestures as a parting kiss at an airport or holding hands on a stroll down the street would be impossible to someone in the closet. For straight readers, do these considerations change your perspective at all?

At the very end of this piece, Caldwell says that "until the collective groan of straight life dies in me, I'll be outing myself—to myself and everybody else—all the time." Caldwell is not a gay bigot: He loves, likes, and respects many heterosexual people, and he refuses to consider his homosexuality the central fact of his existence. On the other hand, he is also adamant that since it is an important element of his life, he will explore and celebrate it in the same way that straight writers explore and celebrate the sexual aspects of their lives.

I

Are those who read psychoanalysis destined to live it? I came out to my sister by a combination of wish fulfillment and a Freudian slip, which I used to think was the thing that stuck out from underneath my mother's dress.

Stacy dated a large lunk of a boy named Todd when she was a junior in high school in 1983. He was the laconic type, a sphinx without a secret. I think he must have been either incredibly bored with us or incredibly frightened. Todd had dropped Stacy off after a movie. I assume they made out in the car for a little while, but not too long, since my father would most certainly have been peeking out the window of his darkened bedroom, waiting to pounce on the opportunity to accuse Todd of untoward behavior, or my sister of coming on to her boyfriend like a Jezebel.

I was home on a weekend visit from college. By the time Stacy came into the house, our parents and our little brother were asleep. I met her with a hug at the back door and we crept into her bedroom and talked until past midnight. She and Todd had gone to see *Psycho II* and she, having the most vivid imagination in our family, was still a little frightened. We had already opened up to each other in many ways; we'd even had long talks about sex. I was anxious that she should have more information so that she could enjoy herself but keep from getting pregnant, and hoped to mitigate whatever guilt she might feel. But that night we just talked about the movies, gossiped, and commiserated about life in our peculiar family.

We fell asleep on her bed. At some point, I rolled over in the darkness, put my arm around her, and said, "Tony, I love you with all my heart." She woke up in time to hear it, and didn't go back to sleep the rest of the night.

It was two months before Stacy was able to sit me down and ask what it meant, only telling me the story after she'd inquired whether I really was in love with Tony. She had no one in our tiny Bible Belt town of Atlanta, Texas, to talk with about it, but by then she had accustomed herself to the idea and was *fine* with it. But she didn't tell anyone else.

My family may appear at the outset as typically East Texas, but I was born in Houston, lived there until I was ten, and went back as soon as I was old enough to go to college. We had urban roots. My mother's family was partly Jewish; I was raised in the Episcopal church, in some ways, for me at least, a much more liberal and liberating background than that of some of my friends in Atlanta, who were Fundamentalists.

From an early age I was aware of gay people. My parents had a close friendship with a male couple in Houston, and my mother's uncle is gay. It was not a difference that was of particular concern or interest, and did not carry with it, within my immediate family, any particular fear. That my parents expected, up till I was a young adult, for me to live pretty much the way they had goes without saying, but their attitude toward my sister's, brother's, and my sexual orientations, choices, and commitments was always accepting.

I've always been odd, and plenty of boys in grammar school called me "faggot" and "fruit" and "sissy" before I understood what the words implied; I could hear the hatred or revulsion, but not the meaning. I didn't mind being in love with Bobby Sherman, but I knew I wasn't supposed to tell anybody. When I was five and my father twenty-seven, I developed limp wrists and he became apoplectic (we used to worry about those elusive neighbors we never knew).

Source: Ron Caldwell, "Out-Takes." Pp. 265–274 in *Boys Like Us*, ed. Patrick Merla. New York: Avon Books, 1996. Reprinted by permission of Ron Caldwell.

Although I had, on several occasions, brought my lover to my parents', they didn't figure out what our relationship was. Since they had moved after I graduated from high school, I didn't have my own bedroom; they would put us in one queen-size bed, something my parents would never do with my brother and sister and their significant others—not before marriage, at least. I don't know what they'd have thought had they found Tony and me humping in the den in the middle of the night.

When I was twenty-one and she forty, in 1984, I sat my mother down and told her everything, to keep her on my side—to preserve the banality of my homosexuality in her mind, the first step in really coopting her. I wrote about it shortly thereafter:

Explaining Things to Mom

No, I do not think that it is tragic
Or unbearably lonely, not
Fearful or sordid or unpleasant.
It isn't hardness or intrusion of
One into one crouched on knees,
Dug into mattresses, not all
Bitter, broken idols, weakness.

I hold her hand, we sit
On the sofa and I wonder
What "happy" has meant
To her and my father
For twenty-five years.
We don't have exactly
What they have, no . . .

Ours is a soft, gentle
Sameness: Let-us-touch-
At-every-point for a moment.
She must understand
The touch of a stubbled face
Burning across lips
At four o'clock in the morning.

Nowadays, if my mother calls after a guy has stayed the night, I'll roll over, pick up the phone, and tell her, with a giggle, what we've been doing—in general terms. (She's particularly amused by stories that feature handcuffs.) This does not seem to me to be strange, and she's not scandalized. There might have been a time when shock value was my motive, but I don't think that's the case anymore. She seems genuinely glad to know that I'm not keeping anything important from her. She is good and gracious and witty, and she seems to like my friends. She has never treated my misery at the hands of love with anything short of acceptance and compassion.

The official coming out to my father wasn't for another few years. I had finished my master's thesis, a book of verse, at Boston University. Dad had expressed a little curiosity about what I was writing, but I was for the most part reticent to share it with him. Part of this had to do with the rocky nature of our relationship, which had never been very good. From where I stood he was The Law, a disciplinarian at home and a policeman abroad; I was afraid of him and could not confide in him. When I was twenty, in a stupid argument over the telephone, I'd let drop that I was completely and utterly and hopelessly miserable and it was all his fault. With a cache of gay sonnets out in the world, though, I felt I had to tell him. So I did the safe thing: I wrote him a letter.

Dear Dad—

Here's a letter to serve as an introduction to my thesis, which I sent via Mom some days ago and asked that she have bound. I think the printing came out pretty well. Though I have worked on many of the pieces for a long time, it still feels incomplete. I'm glad to have gotten it out of the way. Now I hope that I'll have some incentive to send some of them out and try to get published. We'll see.

All that business is secondary to the reason I'm writing today, which has more to do with the content of some of the poems. You're not naïve; I'm sure that nothing of mine that you have read or will read shocks you in the least, though you might be surprised to see how much of my private life has burst onto the printed page.

That could be a little uncomfortable, since we've never spoken about many of the thoughts, feelings, and philosophies you'll find that I have often and, sometimes I hope, provocatively expressed on the pages of my thesis.

Working this business out—how much to reveal, when, to whom—has occupied me for a long time, not so much because of my own insecurities, as a total uncertainty about how my "audience" would react. That's something none of us can ever know, so it makes little sense to second-guess and worry. With this letter and my thesis in your hands (or at least in your house), you can see the culmination of that process: A very important part of my life—its past, present, and future—is my involvement with other men. It colors my ideas and actions; it is sometimes central, sometimes trivial and amusing, but it is always there. It is time, I think, to reconcile my public and private selves with who I am in our family.

If I were more optimistic (or maybe stupid or callous or crazy), I'd say that this shouldn't make any difference to you. We've lived with the reality of my homosexuality for a long time without expressing the fact. You and I want different things out of life, and play different roles. These things alone mean that there will be differences in the ways we understand and work within the world. That is not to say that there is any insurmountable misunderstanding, nor has anything negative come to light. Because of your perspective this may be a challenge, but you're not alone. I'm here to help make sense of it for you as best I can.

You should know that I take my sexuality for granted, as everyone should. It would be silly, painful, and wrong to deny it and pretend that I am or could be different from the way I am, just as it would make little or no sense to see being gay as the central issue in my life all the time. It is a political problem a lot of the time. Sometimes taking political stands is important—and I'm not afraid or embarrassed to speak out to ensure that I and others like me are accepted as worthwhile citizens, productive people, with all the rights anyone should have by virtue of being born into the world. And with no fewer responsibilities. I haven't the slightest desire to prove anything political to you. This is about your being my father and my being your child.

The other time when my being gay is most central to my life is when love is involved. Then there will be a discernible difference. In my still rather short life, I have only been in love with Tony, and our relationship has lasted—and faltered, sometimes—for over five years. When it has faltered, it has been because our personalities and inclinations have been stretched to the limit, not because of any inherent flaw in the way that we love. Love is generic, I think, and always boundless, no matter who the lovers are. And life for us is not bizarre—it's fairly calm and domestic. For men in love the major difference is that the rules for taking care of each other are not always apparent. Decency, respect, attention, and devotion are still the operative words, though. We just don't seem to have too many models for the way we conduct our lives.

Besides making the poems a little more palatable, I write to let you know that I believe that the responsibility for bringing all of this out into the open rests with both of us. I can't do it alone. I'm not particularly shy about being gay, but there have rarely been ideal moments to talk these things out. When we see each other, neither of us wants to upset the proverbial apple cart. I'm much less inhibited when I write than I am in person—I am more comfortable here on the page, without the tension and second-guessing. And I can express myself at my own pace.

I'm not afraid of your rejecting me—I know that would never occur to you. You have never wanted me to feel alienated. What I want most is for you to feel you know and understand me better. I hope you don't think that my being gay is bad, or even unusual. It just *is*. After some time and practice you may even champion the cause—inasmuch as it is a cause. Nothing has changed except my willingness to express this. I am the same man who was the Eagle Scout, trumpet player, acolyte, and opinionated little man you've watched grow. But perhaps I will be all the more real, complete. You've always expected a lot out of me. Well, there's a lot here—it just might not be what you expected.

If there is anything I can do to make this easier, any questions I can answer, please call or write, and don't feel like you should be inhibited, either. I'm not defensive—I want whatever respect I'm due, regardless of and including my sexuality.

I hope you'll be interested to some extent, and that we'll be able to talk about this openly and unashamedly. That may take some time. It's taken twenty-five years to write this letter. I'm certainly not rushing anything.

Thanks for your patience, attention, and understanding, Dad.

"Love has no position, / Love's a way of living, / One kind of relation / Possible between / Any things or persons," according to W. H. Auden, a poet whom [our parish priest] referred to last Christmas as "a notorious homosexual"—whatever that means. Take care.

Love,
Ron

My letter makes me squirm now. I should have been more casual and blunt—but I was so much older then. Nonetheless, it served its purpose. The night he read it, my father phoned right away. He told me about his own gay friends, a couple named Larry and Ben, whom he and my mother had been close to in the sixties; he said it didn't matter, that he'd thought for a long time I might be gay, and just wanted me to be happy. I still don't really confide in him, but there is an understanding between us. We have far to go but my being gay isn't at issue.

My father did, however, ask me, when I came out to him, to hold off telling my little brother until he got out of high school. Dad thought Bret might have trouble understanding, that it might throw him into a tailspin and affect his work. That seemed reasonable and prudent, and I agreed.

Bret and I were raised in the same house, but under very different circumstances. Because of the seven-year gap in our ages, we hardly knew each other before he went to college. My sister, brother, and I had the same senior English teacher in high school, Ms. Trumble. In my glory days, I had been her champion ready-writer. (Oh, for half the

chutzpah and a quarter of the feverish concentration I had then.) Those poor students who followed me, including Stacy and Bret, had to read and discuss my essays. I loved Ms. Trumble (and still do); she adored language and was a very witty woman who wore bold print blouses and A-line skirts. She was a divorced Roman Catholic, Mr. Trumble having run off with a younger woman.

Naturally enough, my sister and brother felt quite differently about her. But Bret was aware of how much she had liked me and, when he found out that some of my poems had appeared in a literary journal, he thought she'd like to see them. He took the journal from my parents' nightstand, slipped it into his knapsack, and drove off to school. English was first period; he had an in-class writing assignment. He gave the journal to Ms. Trumble, told her I had some poetry in it, and went to work. Later on in the class, Ms. Trumble thanked him and gave him back the journal. He returned to his seat, found my name in the Table of Contents, and flipped to this poem:

An Other

Below his eye a bright blue vein—
Sleeplessness or age or nothing
But a variable to distinguish him
From others in a small way. Watching,
The composite is not half bad.
Twirl his hair through my fingers,
Close my eyes and sense the mattress
Rising up from the floor to meet us,
The draft blowing through the crevices
To chill our pasty feet. Then he does
The predictable expedient daring
Thing with gallant trepidation,
As if he were asking first, expecting
Denial. We have stood and embraced.
We have lain quite naked in full view
In the early light. We have walked
Arm in arm, forsaking nothing. It
Seems fine. Oh, but darling,

You are not the one to carry me
Through the day, not the one I would
Give up a good game of conversation
For. Some unsympathetic teacher
Taught me to look out for my spot
In a world-historical couple,
Not to settle for less: to find
The company of one who, with me,
Would land us in the pages of Dante,
Fiery passion and misunderstanding
In this world, and in the other.

Until that moment Bret had no idea I was gay. With the current of realization growing in his mind arose the terror of having brought me out to Ms. Trumble. It took us quite a few phone calls to get him through it. In the ensuing years, Bret's been my greatest political ally. He might have been even more pleased if I'd turned out to be African American, but my difference, such as it is, has been a touchstone for his own development as a good and gracious activist. I'm a very luck man.

II

I'm not sure I know exactly what "out" means. The queerer I get, the less I notice the abstract, though stark, contrast between myself and everybody else, and the less concerned I am about it. My being odd to the straight world is no longer new to me; by extension, what presumably links me to the millions of other people with whom I share this label seems less and less clear.

Coming out comes up all the time—on a date, when the moment of silence becomes unpleasant, because either too little or too much is happening over the dinner table. It's a convenient topic of conversation. On the other hand, I have no earthly idea what it means to be completely out, out of the closet. For a very long time, it seemed to me I didn't really have to come out at all, that somehow my mere aspect conveyed to the world that I was gay. As

for letting most people in on the truth, sometimes all it takes is a certain intensity of focus in one's gaze, an indeterminate posture, a gesture. Sometimes, no matter how obvious I try to make it, the message doesn't get through. Sometimes one just has to make a little speech about it, or write a letter.

Maybe I am one of a generation that has not known the kind of oppression experienced by my—what shall I call them?—*forelovers*, those men who found themselves in the arms of other men and liking it. I have not been photographed in public often enough with another man in my arms.

I remember a meeting of the Rice University Gay and Lesbian Alliance held at the apartment of a graduate student or renegade faculty member, I'm not sure which, in 1982. Those were somber days. Something had begun to kill us, but we knew not what it was. One had to call a number to get directions about where the meetings took place. The members would consent to appear in the yearbook, but only wearing brown paper bags over their heads. I don't like paper hats. Brown doesn't become me.

I was very much in love with Tony, a tall, handsome, ultimately unfaithful tennis player my age who'd transferred from Sewanee under a cloud. He lived on the second floor of the dormitory and I could hardly remember having a life before I met him. Everyone at Rice knew we were lovers—they had all figured it out before it was clear to the two of us—but no one gave us any grief about it. Tony and I went to the Gay and Lesbian Alliance because we wanted to meet other couples and find out how to *be*.

The talk at the meeting was lugubrious. We all sat around in a circle and, instead of jerking off like we probably wanted to, each person related what it was like for him to come out of the closet. When it came my turn, I looked at the question, and at the men who had spoken before me, and thought that

I, too, must answer. But I couldn't. I was either so well adjusted to my sexuality that I'd never seen the need formally to announce it, or I was so naïve that I didn't know the extent to which I was in denial. Granted, I had not yet told my family. My last girlfriend had found out through direct revelation, when she asked why I was being so distant and I burst out with it. She quickly took up with an intelligent but boring doofus with very long arms, reckless driving habits, and an extremely weak chin, who was cold on the question of marriage. But even boys on my hall, who seemed to me the most typical of macho American chemical engineering students, knew and didn't quake when we stood naked together in the communal shower. Tony and I were the subjects of gossip—which, if anything, I cultivated. As far as I know, we were not held up as objects of ridicule.

Once my father came to Houston with his friend Dennis, to the house I shared with Tony and a pair of straight friends. Dad and Dennis had a few hours to kill before they made some sort of business contact or connection. Dennis was wild in a conventional way; when he was away from his second wife, he liked to party. (No doubt that was how he'd met her, when he was on vacation from his first.) All the way down, Dennis had been insisting that my father, a devoted husband, go with him to Caligula XXI. My father didn't want to be a pill, but he didn't want to go unchaperoned to a sex club and leave open the possibility that Dennis would carry stories that weren't true back to Atlanta. Dad asked if I'd come along. I certainly did not want to, but there was pressure and bravado and nervousness. I convinced my lover to join us. At least we would have our own story to tell, I reasoned.

The four of us piled into a supercab pickup truck and drove out, out into the wilderness of strip malls that is South Texas, way out on the wrong end of Westheimer, to a large, irregularly shaped building hung with banners and plastic flags like the ones strung over used-car lots. We parked and went inside. Caligula XXI stank of smoke and drink and vinyl and Naugahyde and dust. Quite a few men stood around or were sitting, being served watered-down drinks by oddly unprepossessing women who looked not at all happy to be there.

Before long, Dennis ordered us a round of drinks, then began to wave a twenty-dollar bill at a heavy woman who looked about six months pregnant, with dimples and dark, sallow skin. She began to dance to the song that was already playing, jiggling her breasts in front of Dennis, wiggling her not insubstantial ass in his face while he laughed like an eight-year-old with his first porno magazine. When that ended, Dennis decided to procure a dancer for me. About five-foot-two and weighing at most ninety pounds soaking wet, she had the body of a prepubescent girl, with preternaturally small breasts.

Tony sat beside me, a hard, tense smile plastered on his face. The dancer ground her ass in my direction without actually touching me; she jiggled her small breasts in my face, wiggling and gyrating in various not very attractive ways (a comparable man doing the same things wouldn't have been any more appealing). The song was long and loud; at some point, Tony got up and ran out. Although I wasn't yet ready to make any confessions to my father and Dennis, I did whisper to the dancer that I was gay and ask her to stop. "Just relax," she said, "I'm almost done." When she finished, Dennis, the picture of macho glee, tipped her and ordered another drink. I went to look for Tony, and found him in tears in the parking lot.

Years later, I discovered that this had been the point at which my parents first spoke to each other about the possibility that I might be gay. Tony's reaction had been enough to convince them that *he* was. I think the incident was a marker of sorts. Although my father was not sure I was gay, he never afterward asked me whom I was dating or when I was planning to get married. My mother didn't tell my father after I told her—partly because she wanted me to tell him when I was ready, and partly, I think, because she wanted it to remain our secret.

Mostly, my coming to terms with—and bringing other people along in accepting—my sexuality seems to have occurred as a series of vignettes:

Marvin, a clerk at Sakowitz in downtown Houston, says I can borrow three pairs of theatrical tights if I tell him what I think about when I masturbate. I need the tights for a scene from *The Taming of the Shrew* we're doing in England class. I say, "Well, I think about sex mostly." "Do you ever think about men?" "Sure. I mean, sometimes. Doesn't everybody?" "No, not really, everybody doesn't." He suggests that we go and do something about it. I demur. He might have handed me the key to my sexual identity, but he was married; from my point of view at the time, he was old; I didn't like him. (Not that I wouldn't give in eventually.) A month later, Scott, my roommate, on the platform bed ten feet away, asks me if I've ever thought about having sex with a man. I had; we did. Seminal moment. We would have a close and turbulent sexual friendship. He would ask me to dress up as a cowboy. Later, he would suggest that I do myself in with a pair of single-edged razor blades provided by him. (I found out early that shared oppression doesn't guarantee solidarity.) The rest I've already told you.

My life is, I think, on a relative scale of human existence, pretty happy. I have many close friends who care about me and engage me in interesting ways. They form the backbone of my emotional life. Since I discovered that I am gay, sometime around my freshman or sophomore year in college, I have been involved—romantically

sexually—with men. For five years, I shared my life with Tony. We lived and traveled and planned and slept together, and it ended rather badly, not unlike many complex marriages among bright and ambitious young straight people. I have dated lots of other guys, one for over a year; some of them have become close friends in their own right. Everyone I have gotten to know from the time I was nineteen or twenty has had full knowledge of my situation, and those who have been resistant have either been left behind or left me behind. Being gay is not something I worry about.

I can see no reason for my general attitude to change. The important things I wish for my life are things that I wish for the world: that it were kinder to those who have no one to hold them and listen to them; that people move from intolerance, not to tolerance but to full understanding; that rigid norms based on fear and inexperience be put away. It occurs to me that there is not only no harm in my being who I am, there may be good in it.

These days, I wear a ring in each ear. The word *gay* appears in my curriculum vitae quite a few times. I volunteer at Gay Men's Health Crisis. I don't have any trouble emoting. I write stories about men having sex with each other, poems about the love of men I have never been or am no longer involved with. I love to look at men's bodies, to feel them, to watch the way they react or respond to pleasure. My greatest role in the amateur theater of life: Queen Leer. Every time I fall in love with a man on the subway takes me farther and farther away from that elusive crystalline norm most people hold themselves up to or against, the way of life they defend so loudly that it sounds like they're protesting too much. Do I reserve some secret patch of ambiguity I can transgress against? Sure I do. But until the collective groan of straight life dies in me, I'll be outing myself—to myself and everybody else—all the time.

Key Terms

come out From "to come out of the closet"; to declare one's homosexuality publicly.

Freudian slip An unconscious verbal error that displays a hidden truth about oneself.

Boston University A large private university in Boston, Massachusetts.

cache A hidden supply; a stash.

callow Unsophisticated; inexperienced.

W. H. Auden Distinguished British-born poet (1907–1973).

chutzpah Yiddish: brashness, "guts."

Dante Dante Alighieri; Italian poet (1265–1321), author of *The Divine Comedy*, a tour of heaven, purgatory, and hell.

touchstone A test for determining authenticity.

Rice University A private university in Houston, Texas.

Sewanee The University of the South, a small private university located in the isolated town of Sewanee, Tennessee, and usually referred to as "Sewanee."

sallow Of a yellowish/grayish tinge; said primarily and unflatteringly of skin tone.

preternatural Exceeding natural or common limits.

Sakowitz Texas-based department store.

demur To object.

curriculum vitae Latin: the course of [one's] life; a resume; sometimes called a "vita."

emoting Expressing emotion.

Discussion Questions

1. Caldwell says that when he was young he was sometimes called "faggot," "fruit," and "sissy" by his classmates, and that though he did not understand the precise meaning of the terms, he could easily decode the "hatred" and "revulsion" that inspired them. Most readers will probably remember similar events if they attended American schools. What, specifically, do you think causes children to react this way to classmates they believe to be homosexual? What about the fear and revulsion that Caldwell felt? It is one thing to note that a fellow student is atypical, and quite another to revile him or her for it. It is uncommon for an elementary school student to be very good (or awful) at spelling, fascinated and knowledgeable (or totally ignorant) about insects, or unusually good (or terrible) at playing the violin. And yet these traits are in themselves rarely enough to cause the kind of torment that Caldwell recounts, and that many of us remember from our own youth, even if we were not the objects of humiliation. So in constructing an answer to the question "Why?" make sure you don't just rely on the easy answer that "kids don't like anyone who's different."

2. Somewhat later in the piece, Caldwell tells us that "It would be silly, painful, and wrong . . . to pretend that I am or could be different from the way I am. . . ." But many lesbians and gay men feel that they *must* pretend that they are straight. What kinds of situations, relationships, and other phenomena might tempt some lesbians and gay men *not* to come out? Caldwell's family was loving and receptive to his announcement of his homosexuality, but his father asked him to keep his secret from one family member for a little while longer, because it might "confuse" him. What do you think about that kind of a request?

3. While a student at Rice University in Houston, Caldwell and his lover, Tony, went to meetings of the Gay and Lesbian Alliance (which Caldwell found generally dreary), because, he said, he wanted "to meet other [gay] couples and find out how to *be*." What does he mean by that? Is this a problem for heterosexual couples? If not, how do they

find out how to "be"? Why should lesbian and gay couples need special lesbian and gay examples? Aren't couples just couples, regardless of the gender mix? Construct a response that addresses the range of issues raised by this question.

4. One of the most interesting things Caldwell says is that when he came out to his mother, he wanted to "preserve the banality of [his] homosexuality in her mind." Why would he want to frame his sexual identity as "banal"? What does "banal" mean? It could be argued that Caldwell wants to preserve the banality of his homosexuality for his readers, as well. What are some of the ways in which he does this (use specific citations)?

CAPITALISM AND GAY IDENTITY

JOHN D'EMILIO

This is a particularly interesting article, with a distinctive and multifaceted point of view that is not immediately apparent from the title. It is also a controversial point of view with which many readers, both homosexual and heterosexual, will disagree, and thus it offers readers a chance to explore the controversy.

It is important to understand that any complex cultural issue has a number of reasonable and productive approaches and analyses, as well as a number of foolish and unproductive treatments. People of intelligence and good will can and do disagree frequently over matters of fact and interpretation. Such disagreements should result in lively and interesting debate rather than accusations of folly and stupidity. The issue of homosexuality is one to which many Americans have strong emotional responses, so it is particularly useful for many of us to gain practice in thinking critically, rather than emotionally, about the topic.

It is also important to make sure we avoid stereotyping lesbians and gay men and oversimplifying the issues that are of concern to them. The only reliable prediction one can make about all gay men and lesbians is that they are primarily or exclusively sexually interested in their own gender. Beyond that, they exhibit the same range of variation in emotional, cultural, and intellectual focus as any other collection of people.

The overarching point of D'Emilio's article is his contention that what he calls "gay identity" has developed primarily as a result of several hundred years of capitalist economic and social evolution. In the course of this evolution, the economic necessity that had held the largely self-sufficient nuclear family together has to a great extent diminished, as subsistence, socialization, and child care are handled by institutions outside the household. Though some kind of a family is still necessary for the care of children, the traditional nuclear family is no longer an absolute economic necessity, a phenomenon that permits alternative living arrangements, including some based on persons bound to each other by same-gender sexual interest.

In order to understand D'Emilio's history of the development of gay identity, it is essential to understand what he means by the term gay *identity, a phenomenon that he contends has not always existed. Is D'Emilio arguing that people who are sexually interested in their own gender have come to exist only comparatively recently, and in developed, capitalist countries? Certainly not. All educated Westerners are aware of the sexual interest that existed between men in ancient Greece. This interest was expected and was enacted (at least ideally) according to a well-understood etiquette, primarily between married men and younger, not-yet-married men. But Athenian society did not consider Socrates (married to the bad-tempered Xanthippe) to be "gay," though it was well-known that he had sexual relationships with men, especially his students. That was simply what privileged men of his time and place did. Anthropologists are aware of many other cultures in which same-gender sexual activity is common and often expected and encouraged, especially between males. But neither the society as a whole nor the men, themselves, consider participation in same-gender sexual activity "gay." A "gay identity" refers to the consciousness of a distinctive constellation of values, interests, and practices shared with others who are sexually interested in their own gender. It is, according to D'Emilio, the result of historical factors that have allowed "some men and women to organize a personal life around their erotic attraction to their own sex."*

The most controversial claim made by D'Emilio is that the percentage of people who are gay or lesbian is not fixed. Rather, he says, the proportion is increasing, and will likely continue to do so. This assertion appears to run counter to the claims made by many students of sexual preference, including the pioneering student of American sexual behavior, Alfred C. Kinsey, that the proportion of same-gender sexual preference in the population is roughly constant through time and space. But does D'Emilio contradict the traditional position? Keep this issue in mind for responding to one of the discussion questions.

For gay men and lesbians, the 1970s were years of significant achievement. Gay liberation and women's liberation changed the sexual landscape of the nation. Hundreds of thousands of gay women and men came out and openly affirmed same-sex eroticism. We won repeal of sodomy laws in half the states, a partial lifting of the exclusion of lesbians and gay men from federal employment, civil rights protection in a few dozen cities, the inclusion of gay rights in the platform of the Democratic Party, and the elimination of homosexuality from the psychiatric profession's list of mental illnesses. The gay male subculture expanded and became increasingly visible in large cities, and lesbian feminists pioneered in building alternative institutions and an alternative culture that attempted to embody a liberatory vision of the future.

In the 1980s, however, with the resurgence of an active right wing, gay men and lesbians face the future warily. Our victories appear tenuous and fragile; the relative freedom of the past few years seems too recent to be permanent. In some parts of the lesbian and gay male community, a feeling

Source: John D'Emilio, "Capitalism and Gay Identity." Pp. 3–16 in *Making Trouble: Essays on Gay History, Politics, and the University*, ed. John D'Emilio. New York: Routledge, 1992.

of doom is growing: analogies with Mc-Carthy's America, when "sexual perverts" were a special target of the Right, and with Nazi Germany, where gays were shipped to concentration camps, surface with increasing frequency. Everywhere there is the sense that new strategies are in order if we want to preserve our gains and move ahead.

I believe that a new, more accurate theory of gay history must be part of this political enterprise. When the gay liberation movement began at the end of the 1960s, gay men and lesbians had no history that we could use to fashion our goals and strategy. In the ensuing years, in building a movement without knowledge of our history, we instead invented a mythology. This mythical history drew on personal experience, which we read backward in time. For instance, most lesbians and gay men in the 1960s first discovered their homosexual desires in isolation, unaware of others and without resources for naming and understanding what they felt. From this experience, we constructed a myth of silence, invisibility, and isolation as the essential characteristics of gay life in the past as well as the present. Moreover, because we faced so many oppressive laws, public policies, and cultural beliefs, we projected this onto an image of the abysmal past until gay liberation, lesbians, and gay men were always the victims of systematic, undifferentiated, terrible oppression.

These myths have limited our political perspective. They have contributed, for instance, to an overreliance on a strategy of coming out—if every gay man and lesbian in America came out, gay oppression would end—and have allowed us to ignore the institutionalized ways in which homophobia and heterosexism are reproduced. They have encouraged, at times, an incapacitating despair, especially at moments like the present: How can we unravel a gay oppression so pervasive and unchanging?

There is another historical myth that enjoys nearly universal acceptance in the gay movement, the myth of the "eternal homosexual." The argument runs something like this: gay men and lesbians always were and always will be. We are everywhere; not just now, but throughout history, in all societies and all periods. This myth served a positive political function in the first years of gay liberation. In the early 1970s, when we battled an ideology that either denied our existence or defined us as psychopathic individuals or freaks of nature, it was empowering to assert that "we are everywhere." But in recent years it has confined us as surely as the most homophobic medical theories, and locked our movement in place.

Here I wish to challenge this myth. I want to argue that gay men and lesbians have *not* always existed. Instead, they are a product of history, and have come into existence in a specific era. Their emergence is associated with the relations of capitalism; it has been the historical development of capitalism—more specifically, its free labor system—that has allowed large numbers of men and women in the late twentieth century to call themselves gay, to see themselves as part of a community of similar men and women, and to organize politically on the basis of that identity.[1] Finally, I want to suggest some political lessons we can draw from this view of history.

What, then, are the relationships between the free labor system of capitalism and homosexuality? First, let me review some features of capitalism. Under capitalism, workers are "free" laborers in two ways. We have the freedom to look for a job. We own our ability to work and have the freedom to sell our labor power for wages to anyone willing to buy it. We are also freed from the ownership of anything except our labor power. Most of us do not own the land or the tools that produce what we need, but rather have to work for a living in order to survive. So, if we are free to sell our labor power in the positive sense, we are also freed, in the negative sense, from any other alternative. This dialectic—the constant interplay between exploitation and some measure of autonomy—informs all of the history of those who have lived under capitalism.

As capital—money used to make more money—expands, so does this system of free labor. Capital expands in several ways. Usually it expands in the same place, transforming small firms into larger ones, but it also expands by taking over new areas of production: the weaving of cloth, for instance, or the baking of bread. Finally, capital expands geographically In the United States, capitalism initially took root in the Northeast, at a time when slavery was the dominant system in the South and when noncapitalist Native American societies occupied the western half of the continent. During the nineteenth century, capital spread from the Atlantic to the Pacific, and in the twentieth, U.S. capital has penetrated almost every part of the world.

The expansion of capital and the spread of wage labor have effected a profound transformation in the structure and functions of the nuclear family, the ideology of family life, and the meaning of heterosexual relations. It is these changes in the family that are most directly linked to the appearance of a collective gay life.

The white colonists in seventeenth-century New England established villages structured around a household economy, composed of family units that were basically self-sufficient, independent, and patriarchal. Men, women, and children farmed land owned by the male head of household. Although there was a division of labor between men and women, the family was truly an interdependent unit of production: the survival of each member depended on the cooperation of all. The home was a workplace where women processed raw farm produces into food for daily consumption; where they made clothing, soap, and

candies; and where husbands, wives, and children worked together to produce the goods they consumed.

By the nineteenth century, this system of household production was in decline. In the Northeast, as merchant capitalists invested the money accumulated through trade in the production of goods, wage labor became more common. Men and women were drawn out of the largely self-sufficient household economy of the colonial era into a capitalist system of free labor. For women in the nineteenth century, working for wages rarely lasted beyond marriage; for men, it became a permanent condition.

The family was thus no longer an independent unit of production. But although no longer independent, the family was still interdependent. Because capitalism had not expanded very far, because it had not yet taken over—or socialized—the production of consumer goods, women still performed necessary productive labor in the home. Many families no longer produced grain, but wives still baked into bread the flour they bought with their husband's wages; or, when they purchased yarn or cloth, they still made clothing for their families. By the mid-1800s, capitalism had destroyed the economic self-sufficiency of many families, but not the mutual dependence of the members.

This transition away from the household family-based economy to a fully developed capitalist free labor economy occurred very slowly, over almost two centuries. As late as 1920, 50 percent of the U.S. population lived in communities of fewer than 2,500 people. The vast majority of blacks in the early twentieth century lived outside the free labor economy, in a system of sharecropping and tenancy that rested on the family. Not only did independent farming as a way of life still exist for millions of Americans, but even in towns and small cities women continued to grow and process food, make clothing, and engage in other kinds of domestic production.

But for those people who felt the brunt of these changes, the family took on new significance as an affective unit, an institution that produced not goods but emotional satisfaction and happiness. By the 1920s among the white middle class, the ideology surrounding the family described it as the means through which men and women formed satisfying, mutually enhancing relationships and created an environment that nurtured children. The family became the setting for a "personal life," sharply distinguished and disconnected from the public world of work and production.[2]

The meaning of heterosexual relations also changed. In colonial New England the birth rate averaged over seven children per woman of childbearing age. Men and women needed the labor of children. Producing offspring was as necessary for survival as producing grain. Sex was harnessed to procreation. The Puritans did not celebrate *hetero*sexuality but rather marriage; they condemned *all* sexual expression outside the marriage bond and did not differentiate sharply between sodomy and heterosexual fornication.

By the 1970s, however, the birth rate had dropped to under two. With the exception of the post–World War II baby boom, the decline has been continuous for two centuries, paralleling the spread of capitalist relations of production. It occurred even when access to contraceptive devices and abortion was systematically curtailed. The decline has included every segment of the population—urban and rural families, blacks and whites, ethnics and WASPS, the middle class and the working class.

As wage labor spread and production became socialized, then, it became possible to release sexuality from the "imperative" to procreate. Ideologically, heterosexual expression came to be a means of establishing intimacy, promoting happiness, and experiencing pleasure. In divesting the household of its economic independence and fostering the separation of sexuality from procreation, capitalism has created conditions that allow some men and women to organize a personal life around their erotic/emotional attraction to their own sex. It has made possible the formation of urban communities of lesbians and gay men and, more recently, of a politics based on a sexual identity.

Evidence from colonial New England court records and church sermons indicates that male and female homosexual behavior existed in the seventeenth century. Homosexual *behavior*, however, is different from homosexual *identity*. There was, quite simply, no "social space" in the colonial system of production that allowed men and women to be gay. Survival was structured around participation in a nuclear family. There were certain homosexual acts—sodomy among men, "lewdness" among women—in which individuals engaged, but family was so pervasive that colonial society lacked even the category of homosexual or lesbian to describe a person. It is quite possible that some men and women experienced a stronger attraction to their own sex than to the opposite sex—in fact, some colonial court cases refer to men who persisted in their "unnatural" attractions—but one could not fashion out of that preference a way of life. Colonial Massachusetts even had laws prohibiting unmarried adults from living outside family units.[3]

By the second half of the nineteenth century, this situation was noticeably changing as the capitalist system of free labor took hold. Only when *individuals* began to make their living through wage labor, instead of as parts of an interdependent family unit, was it possible for homosexual desire to coalesce into a personal identity—an identity based on the ability to remain outside the heterosexual family and to construct a personal life based on attraction to one's own sex. By the end of the century, a class of men and women existed who recognized their erotic interest in their own sex, saw it as a trait that set them apart from the majority, and sought others like themselves. These early gay lives came from a wide social spectrum: civil servants and business executives, department store clerks and college professors, factory operatives, ministers, lawyers, cooks, domestics, hoboes, and the idle rich: men and women, black and white, immigrant and native born.

In this period, gay men and lesbians began to invent ways of meeting each other and sustaining a group life. Already, in the early twentieth century, large cities contained male homosexual bars. Gay men staked out cruising areas, such as Riverside Drive in New York City and Lafayette Park in Washington. In St. Louis and the nation's capitol, annual drag balls brought together large numbers of black gay men. Public bathhouses and YMCAs became gathering spots for male homosexuals. Lesbians formed literary societies and private social clubs. Some working-class women "passed" as men to obtain better-paying jobs and lived with other women— lesbian couples who appeared to the world as husband and wife. Among the faculties of women's colleges, in the settlement houses, and in the professional associations and clubs that women formed, one could find lifelong intimate relationships supported by a web of lesbian friends. By the 1920s and 1930s, large cities such as New York and Chicago contained lesbian bars. These patterns of living could evolve because capitalism allowed individuals to survive beyond the confines of the family.[4]

Simultaneously, ideological definitions of homosexual behavior changed. Doctors developed theories about homosexual*ity,* describing it as a condition, something that was inherent in a person, a part of his or her "nature." These theories did not represent scientific breakthroughs, elucidations of previously undiscovered areas of knowledge; rather, they were an ideological response to a new way of organizing one's personal life.

The popularization of the medical model, in turn, affected the consciousness of the women and men who experienced homosexual desire so that they came to define themselves through their erotic life.[5]

These new forms of gay identity and patterns of group life also reflected the differentiation of people according to gender, race, and class that is so pervasive in capitalist societies. Among whites, for instance, gay men have traditionally been more visible than lesbians. This partly stems from the division between the public male sphere and the private female sphere. Streets, parks, and bars, especially at night, were "male space." Yet the greater visibility of white gay men also reflected their larger numbers. The Kinsey studies of the 1940s and 1950s found significantly more men than women with predominantly homosexual histories, a situation caused, I would argue, by the fact that capitalism had drawn far more men than women into the labor force, and at higher wages. Men could more easily construct a personal life independent of attachments to the opposite sex, whereas women were more likely to remain economically dependent on men. Kinsey also found a strong positive correlation between years of schooling and lesbian activity. College-educated white women, far more able than their working-class sisters to support themselves, could survive more easily without intimate relationships with men.[6]

Among working-class immigrants in the early twentieth century, closely knit kin networks and an ethic of family solidarity placed constraints on individual autonomy that made gayness a difficult option to pursue. In contrast, for reasons not altogether clear, urban black communities appeared relatively tolerant of homosexuality. The popularity in the 1920s and 1930s of songs with lesbian and gay male themes—"B.D. Woman," "Prove It on Me," "Sissy Man," "Fairey Blues"—suggests an openness about homosexual expression at odds with the mores of whites. Among men in the rural West in the 1940s, Kinsey found extensive incidence of homosexual behavior, but, in contrast with the men in large cities, little consciousness of gay identity. Thus, even as capitalism exerted a homogenizing influence by gradually transforming more individuals into wage laborers and separating them from traditional communities, different groups of people were also affected in different ways.[7]

The decisions of particular men and women to act on their erotic/emotional preference for the same sex, along with the new consciousness that this preference made them different, led to the formation of an urban subculture of gay men and lesbians. Yet at least through the 1930s this subculture remained rudimentary, unstable, and difficult to find. How, then, did the complex, well-developed gay community emerge that existed by the time the gay liberation movement exploded? The answer is to be found during World War II, a time when the cumulative changes of several decades coalesced into a qualitatively new shape.

The war severely disrupted traditional patterns of gender relations and sexuality, and temporarily created a new erotic situation conducive to homosexual expression. It plucked millions of young men and women, whose sexual identities were just forming, out of their homes, out of towns and small cities, out of the heterosexual environment of the family, and dropped them into sex-segregated situations—as GIs, as WACs and WAVES, in same-sex rooming houses for women workers who relocated to seek employment. The war freed millions of men and women from the settings where heterosexuality was normally imposed. For men and women already gay, it provided an opportunity to meet people like themselves. Others could become gay because of the temporary freedom to explore sexuality that the war provided.[8]

Lisa Ben, for instance, came out during the war. She left the small California town where she was raised, came to Los Angeles to find work, and lived in a women's boarding house. There she met for the first time lesbians who took her to gay bars and introduced her to other gay women. Donald Vining was a young man with lots of homosexual desire and few gay experiences. He moved to New York City during the war and worked at a large YMCA. His diary reveals numerous erotic adventures with soldiers, sailors, marines, and civilians at the Y where he worked, as well as at the men's residence club where he lived, and in parks, bars, and movie theaters. Many GIs stayed in port cities like New York, at YMCAs like the one where Vining worked. In his oral histories of gay men in San Francisco, focusing on the 1940s, Allan Bérubé has found that the war years were critical in the formation of a gay male *community* in the city. Places as different as San Jose, Denver, and Kansas City had their first gay bars in the 1940s. Even severe repression could have positive side effects. Pat Bond, a lesbian from Davenport, Iowa, joined the WACs during the 1940s. Caught in a purge of hundreds of lesbians from the WACs in the Pacific, she did not return to Iowa. She stayed in San Francisco and became part of a community of lesbians. How many other women and men had comparable experiences? How many other cities saw a rapid growth of lesbian and gay male communities?[9]

The gay men and women of the 1940s were pioneers. Their decisions to act on their desires formed the underpinnings of an urban subculture of gay men and lesbians. Throughout the 1950s and 1960s, the gay subculture grew and stabilized so that people coming out then could more easily find other gay women and men than in the past. Newspapers and magazines published articles describing gay male life. Literally hundreds of novels with lesbian themes were published.[10] Psychoanalysts complained about the new ease with which their gay male patients found sexual partners. And the gay subculture was found not just in the largest cities. Lesbian and gay male bars existed in places like Worcester, Massachusetts, and Buffalo, New York; in Columbia, South Carolina, and Des Moines, Iowa. Gay life in the 1950s and 1960s became a nationwide phenomenon. By the time of the Stonewall Riots in New York City in 1969—the event that ignited the gay liberation movement—our situation was hardly one of silence, invisibility, and isolation. A massive, grass-roots liberation movement could form almost overnight precisely because communities of lesbians and gay men existed.

Although gay community was a precondition for a mass movement, the oppression of lesbians and gay men was the force that propelled the movement into existence. As the subculture expanded and grew more visible in the post–World War II era, oppression by the state intensified, becoming more systematic and inclusive. The Right scapegoated "sexual perverts" during the McCarthy era. Eisenhower imposed a total ban on the employment of gay women and men by the federal government and government contractors. Purges of lesbians and homosexuals from the military rose sharply. The FBI instituted widespread surveillance of gay meeting places and of lesbian and gay organizations, such as the Daughters of Bilitis and the Mattahine Society. The post office placed tracers on the correspondence of gay men and passed evidence of homosexual activity on to employers. Urban vice squads invaded private homes, made sweeps of lesbian and gay male bars, entrapped gay men in public places, and fomented local witch hunts. The danger involved in being gay rose even as the possibilities of being gay were enhanced. Gay liberation was a response to this contradiction.

Although lesbians and gay men won significant victories in the 1970s and opened up some safe social space in which to exist, we can hardly claim to have dealt a fatal blow to heterosexism and homophobia. One could even argue that the enforcement of gay oppression has merely changed locales, shifting somewhat from the state to the arena of extralegal violence in the form of increasingly open physical attacks on lesbians and gay men. And, as our movements have grown, they have generated a backlash that threatens to wipe out our gains. Significantly, this New Right opposition has taken shape as a "pro family" movement. How is it that capitalism, whose structure made possible the emergence of a gay identity and the creation of urban gay communities, appears unable to accept gay men and lesbians in its midst? Why do heterosexism and homophobia appear so resistant to assault?

The answers, I think, can be found in the contradictory relationship of capitalism to the family. On the one hand, as I argued earlier, capitalism has gradually undermined the material basis of the nuclear family by taking away the economic functions that cemented the ties between family members. As more adults have been drawn into the free labor system, and as capital has expanded its sphere until it produces as commodities most goods and services we need for our survival, the forces that propelled men and women into families and kept them there have weakened. On the other hand, the ideology of capitalist society has enshrined the family as the source of love, affection, and emotional security, the place where our need for stable, intimate human relationships is satisfied.

This elevation of the nuclear family to pre-eminence in the sphere of personal life is not accidental. Every society needs structures for reproduction and childbearing, but the possibilities are not limited to the nuclear family. Yet the privatized family fits well with capitalist relations of production. Capitalism has socialized production while maintaining that the products of socialized labor belong to the owners of private property. In many ways, child rearing has also been progressively socialized over the past two centuries, with schools, the media, peer groups, and employers taking over functions that once belonged to parents. Nevertheless, capitalist society maintains that reproduction and child rearing are private tasks, that children "belong" to parents, who exercise the rights of ownership. Ideologically, capitalism drives people into heterosexual families: each generation comes of age having internalized a heterosexist model of intimacy and personal relationships. Materially, capitalism weakens the bonds that once kept families together so that their members experience a growing instability in the place they have come to expect happiness and emotional security. Thus, while capitalism has knocked the material foundation away from family life, lesbians, gay men, and heterosexual feminists have become the scapegoats for the social instability of the system.

This analysis, if persuasive, has implications for us today. It can affect our perception of our identity, our formulation of political goals, and our decisions about strategy.

I have argued that lesbian and gay identity and communities are historically created, the result of a process of capitalist development that has spanned many generations. A corollary of this argument is that we are *not* a fixed social minority composed for all time of a certain percentage of the population. *There are more of us* than one hundred years ago, more of us than forty years ago. And there may very well be more gay men and lesbians in the picture. Claims made by gays and nongays that sexual orientation is fixed at an early age, that large numbers of visible gay men and lesbians in society, the media, and the schools will have no influence on the sexual identities of the young, are wrong. Capitalism has created the material conditions for homosexual desire to express itself as a central component of some individuals' lives;

now, our political movements are changing consciousness, creating the ideological conditions that make it easier for people to make that choice.

To be sure, this argument confirms the worst fears and most rabid rhetoric of our political opponents. But our response must be to challenge the underlying belief that homosexual relations are bad, a poor second choice. We must not slip into the opportunistic defense that society need not worry about tolerating us, since only homosexuals become homosexuals. At best, a minority group analysis and a civil rights strategy pertain to those of us who already are gay. It leaves today's youth—tomorrow's lesbians and gay men—to internalize heterosexist models that it can take a lifetime to expunge.

I have also argued that capitalism has led to the separation of sexuality from procreation. Human sexual desire need no longer be harnessed to reproductive imperatives, to procreation; its expression has increasingly entered the realm of choice. Lesbians and homosexuals most clearly embody the potential of this split, since our gay relationships stand entirely outside a procreative framework. The acceptance of our erotic choices ultimately depends on the degree to which society is willing to affirm sexual expression as a form of play, positive and life-enhancing. Our movement may have begun as the struggle of a "minority," but what we should now be trying to "liberate" is an aspect of the personal lives of all people—sexual expressions.[11]

Finally, I have suggested that the relationship between capitalism and the family is fundamentally contradictory. On the one hand, capitalism continually weakens the material foundation of family life, making it possible for individuals to live outside the family, and for a lesbian and gay male identity to develop. On the other hand, it needs to push men and women into families, at least long enough to reproduce the next generation of workers. The elevation of the family to ideological preeminence guarantees that capitalist society will reproduce not just children but also heterosexism and homophobia. In the most profound sense, capitalism is the problem.[12]

How do we avoid remaining the scapegoats, the political victims of the social instability that capitalism generates? How can we take this contradictory relationship and use it to move toward liberation?

Gay men and lesbians exist on social terrain beyond the boundaries of the heterosexual nuclear family. Our communities have formed in that social space. Our survival and liberation depend on our ability to defend and expand that terrain, not just for ourselves but for everyone. That means, in part, support for issues that broaden the opportunities for living outside traditional heterosexual family units: issues like the availability of abortion and the ratification of the Equal Rights Amendment, affirmative action for people of color and for women, publicly funded day care and other essential social services, decent welfare payments, full employment, the rights of young people—in other words, programs and issues that provide a material basis for personal autonomy.

The rights of young people are especially critical. The acceptance of children as dependents, as belonging to parents, is so deeply ingrained that we can scarcely imagine what it would mean to treat them as autonomous human beings, particularly in the realm of sexual expression and choice. Yet until that happens, gay liberation will remain out of our reach.

But personal autonomy is only half the story. The instability of families and the sense of impermanence and insecurity that people are now experiencing in their personal relationships are real social problems that need to be addressed. We need political

solutions for these difficulties of personal life. These solutions should not come in the form of a radical version of the profamily position, of some left-wing proposals to strengthen the family. Socialists do not generally respond to the exploitation and economic inequality of industrial capitalism by calling for a return to the family farm and handicraft production. We recognize that the vastly increased productivity that capitalism has made possible by socializing production is one of its progressive features. Similarly, we should not be trying to turn back the clock to some mythic age of the happy family.

We do need, however, structures and programs that will help to dissolve the boundaries that isolate the family, particularly those that privatize child rearing. We need community- or worker-controlled day care, housing where privacy and community coexist, neighborhood institutions—from medical clinics to performance centers—that enlarge the social unit where each of us has a secure place. As we create structures beyond the nuclear family that provide a sense of belonging, the family will wane in significance. Less and less will it seem to make or break our emotional security.

In this respect, gay men and lesbians are well situated to play a special role. Already excluded from families as most of us are, we have had to create, for our survival, networks of support that do not depend on the bonds of blood or the license of the state, but that are freely chosen and nurtured. The building of an "affectional community" must be as much a part of our political movement as are campaigns for civil rights. In this way we may prefigure the shape of personal relationships in a society grounded in equality and justice rather than exploitation and oppression, a society where autonomy and security do not preclude each other but coexist.

Notes

This essay is a revised version of a lecture given before several audiences in 1979 and 1980. I am grateful to the following groups for giving me a forum in which to talk and get feedback: the Baltimore Gay Alliance, the San Francisco Lesbian and Gay History Project, the organizers of Gay Awareness Week 1980 at San Jose State University and the University of California at Irvine, and the coordinators of the Student Affairs Lectures at the University of California at Irvine.

Lisa Duggan, Estelle Freedman, Jonathan Katz, Carole Vance, Paula Webster, Bert Hansen, Ann Snitow, Christine Stansell, and Sharon Thompson provided helpful criticisms of an earlier draft. I especially want to thank Allan Bérubé and Jonathan Katz for generously sharing with me their own research, and Amber Hollibaugh for many exciting hours of nonstop conversation about Marxism and sexuality.

1. I do not mean to suggest that no one has ever proposed that gay identity is a product of historical change. See, for instance, Mary McInstosh, "The Homosexual Role," *Social Problems* 16 (1968): 182–192; Jeffrey Weeks, *Coming Out: Homosexual Politics in Britain* (New York: Quarter Books, 1977). It is also implied in Michel Foucault, *The History of Sexuality*, vol. 1: *An Introduction*, tr. Robert Hurley (New York: Pantheon, 1978). However, this does represent a minority viewpoint, and the works cited above have not specified how it is that capitalism as a system of production has allowed for the emergence of a gay male and lesbian identity. As an example of the "eternal homosexual" thesis, see John Boswell, *Christianity, Social Tolerance, and Homosexuality* (Chicago: University of Chicago Press, 1980), where "gay people" remains an unchanging social category through fifteen centuries of Mediterranean and Western European history.

2. See Eli Zaretsky, *Capitalism, the Family, and Personal Life* (New York: Harper & Row, 1976); and Paula Fass, *The Damned and the Beautiful: American Youth in the 1920s* (New York: Oxford University Press, 1977).

3. Robert F. Oaks, "'Things Fearful to Name': Sodomy and Buggery in Seventeenth-Century Norman and Mary Hammond," *Sinister Wisdom* 24 (1980): 57–62; and Jonathan Katz, *Gay American History* (New York: Crowell, 1976), pp. 16–24, 568–571.

4. For the period from 1870 to 1940 see the documents in Katz, *Gay American History*, and idem., *Gay/Lesbian Almanac* (New York: Crowell, 1983). Other sources include Allan Bérubé, "Lesbians and Gay Men in Early San Francisco: Notes Toward a Social History of Lesbians and Gay Men in America," unpublished paper, 1979; Vern Bullough and Bonnie Bullough, "Lesbianism in the 1920s and 1930s: A Newfound Study," *Signs* 2 (Summer 1977): 895–904.

5. On the medical model see Weeks, *Coming Out*, pp. 23–32. The impact of the medical model on the consciousness of men and women can be seen in Louis Hyde, ed., *Rat and the Devil: The Journal Letters of F. O. Matthiessen and Russell Cheney* (Hamden, Conn.: Archon, 1978), p. 47; and in the story of Lucille Hart in Katz, *Gay American History*, pp. 258–279. Radclyffe Hall's classic novel about lesbianism, *The Well of Loneliness*, published in 1928, was perhaps one of the most important vehicles for the popularization of the medical model.

6. See Alfred Kinsey et al., *Sexual Behavior in the Human Male* (Philadelphia: W. B. Saunders, 1948), and *Sexual Behavior in the Human Female* (Philadelphia: W. B. Saunders, 1953).

7. On black music, see "AC/DC Blues: Gay Jazz Reissues," Stash Records, ST-106 (1977); and Chris Albertson, *Bessie* (New York: Stein and Day, 1974). On the persistence of kin networks in white ethnic communities see Judith Smith, "Our Own Kind: Family and Community Networks in Providence," in *A Heritage of Her Own*, ed. Nancy F. Cott and Elizabeth H. Pleck (New York: Simon & Schuster, 1979), pp. 393–411; on differences between rural and urban male homoeroticism see Kinsey et al., *Sexual Behavior in the Human Male*, pp. 455–457, 630–631.

8. The argument and the information in this and the following paragraphs come from my book *Sexual Politics, Sexual Communities: The Making of a Homosexual Minority in the United States, 1940–1970* (Chicago: University of Chicago Press, 1983). I have also developed it with reference to San Francisco in "Gay Politics, Gay Community: San Francisco's Experience," *Socialist Review* 55 (January–February 1981): 77–104.

9. Donald Vining, *A Gay Diary, 1933–1946* (New York: Pepys Press, 1979); "Pat Bond," in Nancy Adair and Casey Adair, *Word Is Out* (New York: New Glide Publications, 1978), pp. 55–65; and Allan Bérubé, "Marching to a Different Drummer: Coming Out during World War II," a slide/talk presented at the annual meeting of the American Historical Association, December 1981, Los Angeles. A shorter version of Bérubé's presentation can be found in *The Advocate*, October 15, 1981, pp. 20–24.

10. On lesbian novels see *The Ladder*, March 1958, p. 18; February 1960, pp. 14–15; April 1961, pp. 12–13; February 1962, pp. 6–11; January 1963, pp. 6–13; February 196, pp. 12–19; February 1965, pp. 19–23; March 1966, pp. 22–26; and April 1967, pp. 8–13. *The Ladder* was the magazine published by the Daughters of Bilitis.

11. This especially needs to be emphasized today. The 1980 annual conference of the National Organization for Women, for instance, passed a lesbian rights resolution that defined the issue as one of "discrimination based on affectional/sexual preference/orientation," and explicitly disassociated the issue from other questions of sexuality such as pornography, sadomasochism, public sex, and pederasty.

12. I do not meant to suggest that homophobia is "caused" by capitalism or is to be found only in capitalist societies. Severe sanctions against homoeroticism can be found in European feudal society and in contemporary socialist countries. But my focus in this essay has been the emergence of a gay identity under capitalism, and the mechanisms specific to capitalism that made this possible and that reproduce homophobia as well.

KEY TERMS

sodomy   A diffuse category of sexual practices considered "unnatural" by the dominant population. Sodomy usually refers to homosexual activity generally, but especially anal intercourse, whether homosexual or heterosexual, and to human-animal sexual activity.

resurgence   Reawakening; renewed development.

ensuing   Resulting; following.

homophobia   Fear or dislike of homosexual persons.

heterosexism   The notion that practices and institutions that favor heterosexual persons and interests are fundamentally just and "natural."

share-cropping   A practice by which the renter of agricultural land receives a share of the harvest from that land, while the rest of the crop goes to the owner of the land, as rent. Share-cropping has existed all over the world for thousands of years, and was common in the southeastern United States until after World War II.

tenancy   The condition of being a tenant, or renter, rather than an owner of the land one occupies or farms.

cruising   Strolling in search of sexual activity or contacts. Used particularly by and about gay men.

drag ball   A dance or other social event at which many of the participants are men dressed in "drag" (i.e., as women).

DISCUSSION QUESTIONS

1. D'Emilio argues that "the relationship between capitalism and the family is fundamentally contradictory." Explain in concrete detail what he means by that provocative statement. What specific evidence do you see in contemporary American society that would bolster D'Emilio's argument? Do you see any evidence that would tend to counter D'Emilio's position? What kinds of solutions does D'Emilio propose to the problems produced by the relationship between capitalism and the family? Do they seem sensible to you? Why or why not? What solutions would you propose?

2. There has been a lot of concern in the past few years about "family values" and a recent backlash against lesbians and gay men on the part of some Americans disturbed about what they see as a decline in family values. What do you think is generally meant by the term "family values"? Do you think it is reasonable to be concerned about a decline in them? Or do you think it is more reasonable to talk about a *change* in family values? What has caused this change/decline? How do gay men and lesbians fit in here? Or do they fit in at all?

3. Thirty years ago an unmarried friend said, with what seemed to be a combination of exasperation and wonder at people's folly, "Marriage doesn't work." And certainly if American marriage were being graded like a midterm, it would receive an F, since more than half of all American marriages end in divorce. D'Emilio talks about the weakening of the "forces that propelled men and women into marriage and kept them there." Is marriage dead? Dying? What kept marriages alive fifty or a hundred and fifty years ago that isn't keeping them alive today? Americans usually believe that they should (and can) marry for love, and that love can (and will) keep marriages alive. What about love? The friend with the low opinion of marriage came from a large, traditional family, in which his parents and siblings had been married for many years. He, himself, is gay. Anthropologists often point to the insights that "outsiders" bring to the understanding of alien cultures. Do you think that the perspective of a gay man or lesbian might produce a view of marriage different from and in some ways more insightful than that of a heterosexual person?

4. And now the promised question about the fluctuation of the gay and lesbian population. Construct an argument that supports both D'Emilio's statement that "There are more of us than one hundred years ago" and the contention of those who argue that the proportion of the population with a primary or exclusive sexual interest in their own gender is roughly fixed through time and space.

TRANSGENDER WARRIORS

LESLIE FEINBERG

This selection, drawn from the beginning and the middle of Leslie Feinberg's book, Transgender Warriors *discusses "trans" gender expression in two different ways: first, by recounting Feinberg's own childhood as a "masculine girl," and second, by considering how transgendered and transsexual persons fit into the women's movement. At this point it will be helpful to consider the two terms* transgender *and* transsexual, *to see how the terms are related and how they differ. These are not words with which a dictionary is much help (at least not yet). And though most readers may have a general notion that they refer to individuals who "change their sex," it is worth distinguishing the two.*

A transgender *(or* transgendered) *individual is one who identifies to some extent with the "opposite sex," that is, the sex to which he or she was not assigned at birth, but who continues to identify primarily with and as a member of the sex to which he or she was assigned at birth. Transgendered persons may dress like the opposite sex, manifest their behavioral characteristics, and express sexual interest in their own sex, and may even undergo some medical procedures to bring their appearances more in line with cultural expectations for the other sex. By the terms of this definition, as well as her own self definition, Leslie Feirberg is a transgender person.*

Transsexuals, on the other hand, are persons who identify primarily with and as members of the sex to which they were not assigned at birth. Often, especially in industrialized countries like the United States, transsexuals make the transition to their new gender via surgical alteration of the genitalia and sometimes other parts of the body (breasts, adam's apple), and through hormone therapy. When the transition is completed, transsexuals in the United States are legally considered members of their new gender. Though most media publicity in the United States has focused on male-to-female transsexuals, this country now has a roughly equal number of female-to-male transsexuals.

Feinberg frequently uses the term "trans" to refer to both transgender and transsexual persons. The primary reason is certainly to be inclusive of both groups. But Feinberg may also use the term because she recognizes that many people outside the "trans" community fail to understand the distinction between the two groups.

In her discussion of her early years, Feinberg speaks persuasively of her pain and uncertainty as a child, growing up as a "masculine girl." When she wore the hairstyle and clothes in which she was most comfortable, strangers would ask whether she was a boy or a girl, an almost unbelievable expression of cruelty. She saw comedians on television cross-dressing, and she had heard adult conversations about Christine Jorgensen, a male-to-female transsexual whose story made the news in the 1950s. Still, she felt that she was essentially alone in the world. This was true not only because in the working-class surroundings in which she grew up she had no support for her style of gender expression, but also because she knew no one who had the same feelings she did, and had no idea that a large trans and lesbian community existed anywhere.

As Feinberg grew up, she came to focus not only on gender expression as a personal characteristic, but on gender and its expression as products of the oppression that is characteristic of capitalist cultural systems. She rejects the notion that maleness and femaleness are the result of fixed, biologically based boundaries, and points to the variety of gender expression that exists in traditional, tribal societies. Though anthropologists might argue with Feinberg's somewhat romanticized view of tribal cultures, her point about the cross-cultural range of gender expression is well-taken. And though Feinberg does not dwell on the distinction between sex and gender, it is probably a good idea to consider it at this point. The two terms are used in a number of overlapping ways by different authors (and even by the same one), but their central core definitions can be distinguished. In general, sex has to do with biological traits. Gender, by contrast, is usually considered to be the result of cultural definition. Thus, though sex and gender often coincide, they are not identical.

Feinberg's final goal in this selection is a call to all persons who identify as or with women to fight gender oppression wherever it occurs, regardless of the biological origin of the person oppressed. There are, she says, a number of ways of being a woman, and all women need to fight all gender oppression.

When I was born in 1949, the doctor confidently declared, It's a girl. That might have been the last time anyone was so sure. I grew up a very masculine girl. It's a simple statement to write, but it was a terrifying reality to live.

I was raised in the 1950s—an era marked by rigidly enforced social conformity and fear of difference. Our family lived in the Bell Aircraft factory housing projects. The roads were not paved; the coal truck, ice man's van, and knife-sharpener's cart crunched along narrow strips of gravel.

I tried to mesh two parallel worlds as a child—the one I saw with my own eyes and the one I was taught. For example, I witnessed powerful adult women in our working-class projects handling every challenge of life, while coping with too many kids and not enough money. Although I hated seeing them so beaten down by poverty, I loved their laughter and their strength. But, on television I saw women depicted as foolish and not very bright. Every cultural message taught me that women were only capable of being wives, mothers, housekeepers—seen, not heard. So, was it true that women were the "weak" sex?

In school I leafed through my geography textbooks and saw people of many different hues from countries far, far from my home. Before we moved to Buffalo, my family had lived in a desert town in Arizona. There, people who were darker skinned and shared different customs from mine were a sizeable segment of the population. Yet in the small world of the projects, most of the kids in my grade school, and my teachers, were white. The entire city was segregated right down the middle—east and west. In school I listened as some teachers paid lip service to "tolerance" but I frequently heard adults mouth racist slurs, driven by hate.

I saw a lot of love. Love of parents, flag, country, and deity were mandatory. But I also observed other loves—between girls and boys, and boys and boys, and girls and girls. There was the love of kids and dogs in my neighborhood, soldier buddies in foxholes in movies, students and teachers at school. Passionate, platonic, sensual, dutiful, devoted, reluctant, loyal, shy, reverent. Yet I was taught there was only one official meaning of the word *love*—the kind between men and women that leads to marriage. No adult ever mentioned men loving men or women loving women in my presence. I never heard it discussed anywhere. There was no word at that time in my English language to express the sheer joy of loving someone of the same sex.

And I learned very early on that boys were expected to wear "men's" clothes, and girls were not. When a man put on women's garb, it was considered a crude joke. By the time my family got a television, I cringed as my folks guffawed when "Uncle Miltie" Berle donned a dress. It hit too close to home. I longed to wear the boy clothing I saw in the Sears catalog.

My own gender expression felt quite natural. I liked my hair short and I felt most relaxed in sneakers, jeans and a t-shirt. However, when I was most at home with how I looked, adults did a double-take or stopped short when they saw me. The question, "Is that a boy or a girl?" hounded me throughout my childhood. The answer didn't matter much. The very fact that strangers had to *ask* the question already marked me as a gender outlaw.

My choice of clothing was not the only alarm bell that rang my difference. If my more feminine younger sister had worn "boy's" clothes, she might have seemed stylish and cute. Dressing all little girls and all little boys in "sex-appropriate" clothing actually called attention to our gender differences. Those of us who didn't fit stuck out like sore thumbs.

Being different in the 1950s was no small matter. McCarthy's anti-communist witch hunts were in full frenzy. Like most children, I caught snippets of adult conversations. So I was terrified that communists were hiding under my bed and might grab my ankles at night. I heard that people who were labeled "reds" would discover their names and addresses listed in local newspapers, be fired from their jobs, and be forced to pack up their families and move away. What was their crime? I couldn't make out the adults' whispers. But the lesson seeped down: keep your mouth shut; don't rock the boat. I overheard angry, hammering accusations on radio and television against grownups who had to answer to a committee of men. I heard the words: commie, pinko, Jew. I was Jewish.

We were the only Jews in the projects. Our family harbored memories of the horrors that relatives and friends had faced in Czarist Russia before the 1917 revolution and in Eastern Europe during World War II. My family lived in fear of fascism, and the McCarthy era stank like Nazism. Every time a stranger stopped us on the street and asked my parents, "Is that a boy or a girl?" they shuddered. No wonder. My parents worried that I was a lightning rod that would attract a dangerous storm. Feeling helpless to fight the powers that be, they blamed the family's problems on me and my difference. I learned that my survival was my own responsibility. From kindergarten to high school, I walked through a hail of catcalls and taunts in school corridors. I pushed my way past clusters of teenagers on street corners who refused to let me pass. I endured the stares and glares of adults. It was so hard to be a masculine girl in the 1950s that I thought I would certainly be killed before I

could grow to adulthood. Every gender image—from my Dick and Jane textbooks in school to the sitcoms on television—convinced me that I must be a Martian.

In all the years of my childhood, I had only heard of one person who seemed similarly "different." I don't remember any adult telling me her name. I was too young to read the newspaper headlines. Adults clipped their vulgar jokes short when I, or any other child, entered the room. I wasn't allowed to stay up late enough to watch the television comedy hosts who tried to ridicule her out of humanity.

But I did know her name: Christine Jorgensen.

I was three years old when the news broke that Christine Jorgensen had traveled from the United States to Sweden for a sex change from male to female. A passport agent reportedly sold the story to the media. All hell broke loose. In the years that followed, just the mention of her name provoked vicious laughter. The cruelty must have filtered down to me, because I understood that the jokes rotated around whether Christine Jorgensen was a woman or a man. Everyone was supposed to easily fit into one category or another, and stay there. But I didn't fit, so Christine Jorgensen and I had a special bond. By the time I was eight or nine years old, I had asked a baby-sitter, "Is Christine Jorgensen a man or a woman?"

"She isn't anything," my baby-sitter giggled. "She's a freak." Then, I thought, I must be a freak too, because nobody seemed sure whether I was a boy or a girl. What was going to happen to me? Would I survive? Would Christine survive?

As it turned out, Christine Jorgensen didn't just endure, she triumphed. I knew she must be living with great internal turmoil, but she walked through the abuse with her head held high. Just as her dignity and courage set a proud example for the thousands of transsexual men and women who followed her path, she inspired me—and who knows how many other transgendered children.

Little did I know then that millions of children and adults across the United States and around the world also felt like the only person who was different. I had no other adult role model who crossed the boundaries of sex or gender. Christine Jorgensen's struggle beamed a message to me that I wasn't alone. She proved that even a period of right-wing reaction could not coerce each individual into conformity.

I survived growing up transgendered during the iron-fisted repression of the 1950s. But I came of age and consciousness during the revolutionary potential of the 1960s—from the Civil Rights movement to the Black Panther Party, from the Young Lords to the American Indian movement, from the anti-Vietnam War struggles to women's liberation. The lesbian and gay movement had not yet emerged. But as a teenager, I found the gay bars in Niagara Falls, Buffalo, and Toronto. Inside those smoke-filled taverns I discovered a community of drag queens, butches, and femmes. This was a world in which I *fit*; I was no longer alone.

It meant the world to me to find other people who faced many of the same problems I did. Continual violence stalked me on the streets, leaving me weary, so of course I wanted to be with friends and loved ones in the bars. But the clubs were not a safe sanctuary. I soon discovered that the police and other enemies preyed on us there. Until we organized to fight back, we were just a bigger group of people to bash.

But we did organize. We battled for the right to be hired, walk down the street, be served in a restaurant, buy a carton of milk at a store, play softball or bowl. Defending our rights to live and love and work won us respect and affection from our straight co-workers and friends. Our battles helped fuel the later explosion of the lesbian and gay liberation movement.

I remember the Thaw Out Picnic held each spring during the sixties by the lesbian and gay community in Erie, Pennsylvania. Hundreds and hundreds of women and men would fill a huge park to enjoy food, dancing, softball, and making out in the woods. During the first picnic I attended, a group of men screeched up in a car near the edge of the woods. Suddenly the din of festivity hushed as we saw the gang, armed with baseball bats and tire irons, marching down the hill toward us.

"C'mon," one of the silver-haired butches shouted, beckoning us to follow. She picked up her softball bat and headed right for those men. We all grabbed bats and beer bottles and followed her, moving slowly up the hill toward the men. First they jeered us. Then they glanced fearfully at each other, leaped back into their car and peeled rubber. One of them was still trying to get his legs inside and shut the car door as they roared off. We all stood quietly for a moment, feeling our collective power. Then the old butch who led our army waved her hand and the celebration resumed.

My greatest terror was always when the police raided the bars, because they had the law on their side. They *were* the law. It wasn't just the tie I was wearing or the suit coat that made me vulnerable to arrest. I broke the law every time I dressed in fly-front pants, or wore jockey shorts or t-shirts. The law dictated that I had to wear at least three pieces of "women's" clothing. My drag queen sisters had to wear three pieces of "men's" clothing. For all I know, that law may still be on the books in Buffalo today.

Of course, the laws were not simply about clothing. We were masculine women and feminine men. Our *gender expression* made us targets. These laws were used to harass us. Frequently we were not even formally charged after our arrests. All too often, the sentences were executed in the back seat of a police cruiser or on the cold cement floor of a precinct cell.

But the old butches told me there was one night of the year that the cops never arrested us—Halloween. At the time, I wondered why I was exempt from penalties for cross-dressing on that one night. And I grappled with other questions. Why was I subject to legal harassment and arrest at all? Why was I being punished for the way I walked or dressed, or who I loved? Who wrote the laws used to harass us, and why? Who gave the green light to the cops to enforce them? Who decided what was normal in the first place?

These were life-and-death questions for me. Finding the answers sooner would have changed my life dramatically. But the journey to find those answers *is* my life. And I would not trade the insights and joys of my lifetime for anyone else's.

This was how my journey began. It was 1969 and I was twenty years old. As I sat in a gay bar in Buffalo, a friend told me that drag queens had fought back against a police bar raid in New York City. The fight had erupted into a four-night-long uprising in Greenwich Village—the Stonewall Rebellion! I pounded the bar with my fist and cursed my fate. For once we had rebelled and made history and I had missed it!

I stared at my beer bottle and wondered: Have we always existed? Have we always been so hated? Have we always fought back?

. . .

I feel the combined weight of women's and trans oppression in my own life. I am forced to battle both, simultaneously. As a result, I personally experience the relationship between women's and trans liberation, because these demands overlap in my own life.

Everywhere I've traveled across the United States talking about fighting trans oppression—from a crowded potluck supper in Tuscaloosa, Alabama, to an overflow audience in a cavernous university auditorium near Northampton, Massachusetts—women of all ages turn out, enthusiastically ready to discuss how the trans movement impacts on women's liberation.

We need to expand that dialogue, because women don't just need to understand the links between what they and trans people suffer in society, they need to realize that the women's and trans liberation movements need each other. Sex and gender oppression of all forms needs to be fought in tandem with the combined strength of these two movements and all our allies in society.

The development of the trans movement has raised a vital question that's being discussed in women's communities all over the country. The discussion revolves around one pivotal question: How is *woman* to be defined? The answer we give may determine the course of women's liberation for decades to come.

The question can't be considered without understanding that women face such constant dangers and harassment, day-in and day-out, that the attempt to define woman is generated by the need for safe space and clear-cut allies. That's a completely valid need. But how can we create safe space for women?

I think that if we define "woman" as a fixed entity, we will draw borders that would need to be policed. No matter what definition is used, many women who should be inside will be excluded.

Let's look first at the question of how woman can or cannot be defined. Some women hold an "essential," or biological definition, that one is born woman. Others, who define themselves as social constructionists, argue that women share a common experience. I don't think we can build women's communities or a liberation movement based on either.

A biological definition of woman is a dangerous direction for the women's movement to take. To accept that biological boundary would mark a definite break with the key principle of the second wave of women's liberation in the United States: that biology is not destiny. Simone de Beauvoir wrote, "One is not born but one becomes a woman."[1] The heart of that wisdom is that one should not be limited in life or oppressed because of birth biology. This is a truth that has meaning to all trans people and all women.

Of course, as a result of the oppression women face growing up in such a violently anti-woman environment, some women draw a line between women as allies and men as enemies. While it's understandable that an individual might do so out of fear, this approach fails as theory. It lumps John Brown and John D. Rockefeller together as enemies and Sojourner Truth and Margaret Thatcher together as allies. This view of who to trust and who to dread will not keep women safe or keep the movement on course.

One of the gifts of the women's liberation movement in the seventies was the understanding that our oppression as women is institutionalized—or built into the economic system. But this same system also tyrannizes entire nationalities, subjugates people because of who they love, denies people their abilities, works people near to death, and leaves many homeless and hungry. And last but not least, this system grinds up those who don't fit a narrow definition of woman and man.

A view that the primary division of society is between women and men leads some women to fear that transsexual women are men in sheep's clothing coming across their border, or that female-to-male transsexuals are going over to the enemy, or that I look like that same enemy. Where is the border for intersexual people—right down the middle of their bodies? Trans people of all sexes and genders are not oppressors; they, like women, rank among the oppressed.

After years of television and Hollywood movies and schooling full of prejudice, all of us have absorbed a biological definition of what is "normal" and what is not. But in a society rife with internal struggle, even a hard science like biology can be misused in an attempt to justify inequality and oppression. While we were dissecting frogs, biological determinism crept into our classrooms.

Biological determinism isn't just a recognition that some people have vaginas and others have penises. It is a theoretical weapon used in a pseudo-scientific way to rationalize racism and sexism, the partitioning of the sexes, and behavior modification to make gender expression fit bodies.

As I argued earlier, historical accounts suggest that although our ancestors knew who was born with a vagina, who was born with a penis, and whose genitals were more multi-faceted, they were not biological determinists. And although women's reproductive abilities contributed to a general division of labor, it was not a hard-and-fast boundary and it was not the only boundary.

It's true that women's ability to bear children and breast-feed in many cases helped to determine an *overall* division of labor. Human babies go through a long period of infancy during which they need to be nursed and nurtured. But by all accounts, childcare in communal cultures was a *collective* task, not the responsibility of each mother, nor of every woman, since not every woman bore children.[2]

I would suggest that we haven't had all the information with which to challenge the cultural construction of the modern view of childcare. For instance, in some preclass societies, both parents went through the ritual pain of bearing a child and both were responsible for infant care.[3]

Any look at the early division of labor in cooperative societies has to take into account the reports by hundreds of social scientists of "women" in early cooperative societies who hunted and were accepted as *men* and "men" who worked among the women and were accepted as *women*. Then why do anthropologists continue to refer to them as *women* hunters and *men* gatherers, particularly when this insistence on their "immutable" biology flies in the face of the way these people were accepted by their own societies?

So although reproduction delineated a rough boundary of human labor, it was not decisive in determining sex/gender. Many communal societies accepted more than two sex/genders and allowed individuals to find their own place within that spectrum.

The people we would call male-to-female transsexuals in these early societies ritually menstruated and wore "the leaves prescribed for women in their courses."[4] That means that *all* the women had a relationship to fertility and birth—including those born with penises. A 1937 account of the North American Mohave by Alfred L. Kroeber describes a male-to-female initiation ritual for youths of ten to eleven years old, which, though provided by a white anthropologist, contrasts with the dominant Western view that sex/gender is fixed at birth.

> In the morning the two women lift the youth and take him outdoors. One of the singers puts on the skirt and dances to the river in four stops, the youth following and imitating. Then all bathe. Thereupon the two women give the youth the front and back pieces of his new dress and paint his face white. After four days he is painted again and then is an *alyha*. Such persons speak, laugh, smile, sit, and act like women.[5]

A further account of the youths after the ceremony shows that they assumed female names. In addition:

> They insisted that their genitals be referred to by female terminology. After finding a husband, they would simulate menstruation by scratching between their legs with a stick until blood was drawn. When they were "pregnant," "menstruations" would cease. Before "delivery" a bean preparation would be ingested that would induce

violent stomach pains dubbed "labor pains." Following this would be a defecation, designated a "stillbirth," which was later ceremoniously buried. There would then ensure a period of mourning by both husband and "wife."[6]

At the other end of the spectrum are accounts that some of the men hunters in communal societies who had been born female were believed not to menstruate.[7] So all the men—even those born with vaginas—were seen as outside the women's reproductive circle.

We need to combat the idea that a simple division of labor between women and men in communal societies has left us with today's narrow sex and gender system. Much evidence exists that many pre-class societies respected many more paths of self-expression. It was the overthrow of communalism and the subsequent division of society into classes that mandated the partitioning of the sexes and outlawed any blurring of those "man-made" boundaries. And we are left with those arbitrary and anti-human restrictions today.

Our histories as trans people and women are inextricably entwined. In the past, wherever women and trans people were honored, you can find cooperative, communal production. And societies that degrade women and trans people are already cleaved into classes, because those patriarchal divisions mandate a rigid categorization of sex and gender.

But how does this understanding help us today? If we reject a fixed biological boundary to define women as a group, what about the view that women share a common oppression? I believe this is also a perilous approach that can particularly lead to glossing over racism and class oppression.

Two broad currents emerged within the second wave of women's liberation in the United States. One was represented by feminists who analyzed women's oppression from a socialist-materialist viewpoint, the other by those who examined the psychological construction of woman. Both branches identified women as a group defined by oppression. Both currents recognized that arguments of biological determinism have been used by the patriarchal ruling classes for centuries as a weapon to justify women's oppression.[8]

However, since the rise of feminism, the definition of "woman" has been increasingly linked to a number of shared bodily experiences, like rape, incest, forced pregnancy, and battering. The underlying assumption is often that this physical oppression, experienced as a result of having a biologically female body, is the defining element of "womanhood." But women are not the only ones who experience the horrors of rape, incest, sexual humiliation, and brutality. And common bodily experiences that the majority of women on this planet share are hauling water and carrying firewood or working on an assembly-line—those are *class* experiences.

Do all women share the same experiences in society? What about the male-to-female transsexual women who have helped build the women's movement over the years? They experience women's oppression on a daily, even hourly basis. So if facing women's oppression defines being a woman, how long do you have to live it before you're "in"? Many lesbians went through a long period of heterosexuality before coming out. Would anyone argue that they should be excluded from lesbian gatherings because they were heterosexual during their formative years?

Do white women share the exact same experience as women of color? Do poor women and rich women share an identical experience? What about the experiences of disabled women, single mothers, lesbians, deaf women? Women endure many different hardships and experiences. The sum total of our experiences and our resulting strengths and insights are just a small part of how many ways there are to be "woman" in this society.

Recently I had coffee with someone I've known since she was a teenager. "I don't think of you as a woman," she explained to me quite cheerily, "but as a very, very sensitive man—the kind that is so sensitive they don't really exist." I asked her how she arrived at this categorization.

"Well," she said, "I grew up without any real power as a girl. So I learned how to use being a woman to get around men's power, and that's not something I see you doing."

What she really meant was she learned to use being "feminine" to get around men's power. But I grew up very masculine, so the complex and powerful set of skills that feminine girls developed to walk safely through the world were useless to me. I had to learn a very different set of skills, many of them martial. While we both grew up as girls, our experiences were dissimilar because our gender expressions were very different. Masculine girls and women face terrible condemnation and brutality—including sexual violence—for crossing the boundary of what is "acceptable" female expression. But masculine women are not assumed to have a very high consciousness about fighting women's oppression, since we are thought to be imitating men.

As the women's movement of the seventies examined the negative values attached to masculinity and femininity in this society, some thought that liberation might lie in creating a genderless form of self-expression and dress. But of course androgyny was itself just another point on the spectrum of gender expression.

And remember the adage that you can't tell a book by its cover? Well, you can't read a person's overall consciousness by their gender expression.

In addition, gender doesn't just come in two brands, like perfume and cologne. Take masculinity, for example, particularly since there's an underlying assumption that the brutal and insensitive behavior of some men is linked to masculinity. Yet not all men dress, move, or behave in the same way. The masculinity of oppressed African-American men is not the masculinity of Ku Klux Klan members. Gender is expressed differently in diverse nationalities, cultures, regions, and classes.

And not all men in any given group express their masculinity in the same way. At a recent speaking event, I couldn't help but notice a man in the audience who was very masculine, but there was something in his gender expression that held my attention. At a later reception, he told me that he learned his masculinity from women—butches had mentored him as a young gay male. He learned one variation of an oppressed masculinity.

Those who are feminine—male and female—don't fare any better when it comes to assumptions about their gender expression. Feminine girls and women endure an extremely high level of sexual harassment and violence simply because of their gender expression. A great deal of woman-hating resides in attitudes toward femininity. And a great many bigoted generalizations are made about femme expression like: "The higher the heels, the lower the IQ, the higher the skirt the lower the morals." So femme women are also not assumed to have a very high consciousness about fighting women's oppression.

And what about males who are considered "effeminate"? Feminists have justifiably pointed out that the label is inherently anti-woman. But it is also anti-trans, gender-phobic, and anti-*feminine*.

The oppression of feminine men is an important one to me, since I consider drag queens to be my sisters. I've heard women criticize drag queens for "mocking women's oppression" by imitating femininity to an extreme, just as I've been told that I am imitating men. Feminists are justifiably angry at women's oppression—so

am I! I believe, however, that those who denounce drag queens aim their criticism at the wrong people.

This misunderstanding doesn't take gender oppression into account. For instance, to criticize male-to-female drag performers, but leave out a discussion of gender oppression, lumps drag queen RuPaul together with men like actor John Wayne! RuPaul is a victim of gender oppression, as well as of racism.

There is a difference between the drag population and masculine men doing cruel female impersonations. The Bohemian Grove, for example, is an elite U.S. club for wealthy, powerful men that features comedy cross-dressing performances. But that's not drag performance. Many times the burlesque comedy of cross-dressed masculine men is as *anti-drag* as it is *anti-woman*.

In fact, it's really only drag performance when it's transgender people who are facing the footlights. Many times drag performance calls for skilled impersonations of a famous individual, like Diana Ross or Judy Garland, but the essence of drag performance is not impersonation of the opposite sex. It is the cultural presentation of an oppressed gender expression.

Our oppression and our identities—as drag queens and kings—are not simply based on our clothing. The term "drag" only means "cross-dressing" to most people. By that definition, we are people who put on garb intended for the opposite sex as a kind of masquerade. It's true that the word *drag* is believed to have originated as a stage term, derived from the drag of the long train of dresses male actors wore. But in fact, it is our gender expression, not our clothes, that shapes who we are.

Hopefully, the trans liberation movement will create a deeper understanding of sex and gender oppression. Everyone has a stake in the struggle to uncover how much cultural baggage is attached to the social categories of man and woman.

In addition, the women's movement has an opportunity to make a tremendous contribution by reaching out to all who suffer from sex and gender oppression. Drag queens and kings, and many women who have not been a part of the women's liberation movement, do not necessarily reflect the same consciousness as those who have been part of a collective movement for change for twenty years. But that doesn't mean that they don't feel their oppression or don't want to fight for their liberation.

The women's liberation movement that shaped my consciousness exposed the institutionalized oppression of women. The movement revealed that inequality begins at a very early age. But simply looking at the differences between what boys and girls are taught only reveals a broad analysis of sexual oppression. Just as girls experience different messages based on whether they are feminine, masculine, or androgynous, boys do too. It's absurd to think that messages of woman-hating and male privilege will produce the same consciousness in a male youth who grows up believing he will be part of the "good-ole boys club" and one who grows up fearing humiliation and violence at the hands of men. If the consciousness of male-to-female transsexuals was shaped early on by "male privilege," then why would they give it up?

What is the consciousness of a child who is assigned one sex at birth, but grows up identifying strongly with another sex? We need to examine how many ways there are to be a woman or a man, and how gender oppression makes sex-role conditioning more complex.

Everyone who is living as a woman in this woman-hating society is dealing with oppression every day and deserves both the refuge of being with other women and the collective power of the women's movement.

All women need to be on the frontlines against *all* forms of sex and gender oppression in society, as well as in fighting all expressions of gender-phobia and trans-phobia. In the simplest of terms, these twin evils are prejudices we have been taught since an early age. Gender-phobia targets women who are not feminine and men who are not masculine. Trans-phobia creates fear of changing sex. Both need to be fought by all women, as well as by all others in society.

As a rape survivor, I understand the need for safe space together—free from sexist harassment and potential violence. But fear of gender variance also can't be allowed to deceptively cloak itself as a women's safety issue. I can't think of a better example than my own, and my butch friends', first-hand experiences in public women's toilets. Of course women need to feel safe in a public restroom; that's a serious issue. So when a man walks in, women immediately examine the situation to see if the man looks flustered and embarrassed, or if he seems threatening; they draw on the skills they learned as young girls in this society to read body language for safety or danger.

Now, what happens when butches walk into the women's bathroom? Women nudge each other with elbows, or roll their eyes, and say mockingly, "Do you know which bathroom you're in?" That's not how women behave when they really believe there is a man in the bathroom. This scenario is not about women's safety—it's an example of gender-phobia.

And ask yourself, if you were in the women's bathroom, and there were two teenage drag queens putting on lipstick in front of the mirror, would you be in danger? If you called security or the cops, or forced those drag queens to use the men's room, would they be safe?

If the segregation of bathrooms is really about more than just genitals, then maybe the signs ought to read "Men" and "Sexually and Gender Oppressed," because we all need a safe place to go to the bathroom. Or even better, let's fight for clean individual bathrooms with signs on the doors that read "Restroom."

And defending the inclusion of transsexual sisters in women's space does not threaten the safety of any woman. The AIDS movement, for example, battled against the right-wing characterization of gay men as a "high-risk group." We won an understanding that there is no high-risk group—there are high-risk behaviors. Therefore, creating safety in women's space means we have to define unsafe behavior—like racist behavior by white women toward women of color, or dangerous insensitivity to disabilities.

Transsexual women are not a Trojan horse trying to infiltrate women's space. There have always been transsexual women helping to build the women's movement—they are part of virtually every large gathering of women. They want to be welcomed into women's space for the same reason every woman does—to feel safe.

And our female-to-male transsexual brothers have a right to feel welcome at women's movement events or lesbian bars. However, that shouldn't feed into the misconception that all female-to-male transsexuals were butches who just couldn't deal with their oppression as lesbians. If that were true, then why does a large percentage of post-transition transsexual men identify as gay and bisexual, which may have placed them in a heterosexual or bisexual status before their transitions? There are transsexual men who did help build the women's and lesbian communities, and still have a large base of friends there. They should enjoy the support of women on their journey. Doesn't everyone want their friends around them at a time of great change? And women could learn a great deal about what it means to be a man or a woman from sharing the lessons of transition.

If the boundaries around "woman" become trenches, what happens to intersexual people? Can we really fix a policy that's so clear about who was born "woman"? And there are many people, like myself, who were born female but get hassled for not being woman enough. We've been accused of exuding "male energy." Now that's a frighteningly subjective border to patrol. Do all women—or *should* all women—have to share the same "energy"?

If we were going to decide who is a "real" woman, who would we empower to decide, and how could the check-points be established? Would we all strip? How could you tell if a vagina was not newly constructed? Would we show our birth certificates? How could you determine that they hadn't been updated after sex-reassignment? DNA tests? The Olympics tried it, but they had so many false results they went back to relying on watching somebody pee in a cup for the drug test as the "sex" test.

I understand that it took the tremendous social upheavals of the sixties and seventies to even begin to draw the borders of women's oppression. When I was growing up, no one even acknowledged that the system was stacked-against women. But the women's liberation movement laid bare the built-in machinery of oppression in this society that's keeping us down. It's not your lipstick that's oppressing me, or your tie, or whether you change your sex, or how you express yourself. An economic system oppresses us in this society, and keeps us fighting each other, instead of looking at the real source of this subjugation.

The modern trans movement is not eroding the boundaries of women's oppression. Throughout history, whenever new lands and new oceans have been discovered, maps have always been re-charted to show their relationship to each other. The modern trans liberation movement is redrawing the boundaries to show the depth and breadth of sex and gender oppression in this society. It is this common enemy that makes the women's and trans communities sister movements for social justice.

What does it mean to be a woman in this society? How many different paths lead to woman? How varied are our experiences, and what do we share in common? Isn't this the discussion we need to have in order to continue to build a dynamic women's movement? And yet, we can't even begin the examination until all those who identify as women are in the movement. It's not a definition that's going to create safe space. Definitions have created some pretty unsafe space for many of us who were born female.

Let's open the door to everyone who is self-identified as woman, and who wants to be in women's space. (Not every woman wants that experience.) Let's keep the door unlocked. Together we can plot tactics and strategy for movement-building. And we can set some good-sense ground rules for what constitutes unsafe behavior.

What should the sign on the door of the women's movement read? I think the key to victory are these three simple words: "All women welcome."

But in addition to fighting women's oppression, we need to recognize and defend other sites of sex and gender oppression and organize an even larger struggle. The women's and trans liberation movements are comprised of overlapping populations and goals. Perhaps the unity of our two huge movements for justice will birth a new movement that incorporates the struggles against all forms of sex and gender oppression.

The combined power of women, trans people, and all of our allies could give rise to a powerful Sex and Gender Liberation movement!

Notes

1. Simone de Beauvoir, as quoted in Monique Wittig, "One Is Not Born A Woman," *The Straight Mind* (Boston: Beacon Press, 1992) 10. See also Simone de Beauvoir, *The Second Sex* (New York: Knopf, 1953).
2. Ann Oakley, "Woman's Work: The Housewife, Past and Present" (New York: Vintage, 1974) 170. For an account of contemporary communal childcare in Vanatinai of Papua New Guinea, based on a matrilineal kinship structure described as taubwaragha ("ancient"/"way of the ancestors") by its people, see Maria Lepowsky, "Gender and Power," *Fruit of the Motherland: Gender in an Egalitarian Society* (New York: Columbia University Press, 1993) 281–306. For a brief account, see John Noble Wilford, "Sexes Equal on South Sea Isle," *New York Times* 29 March 1994:C1, 11.
3. Ann Oakley, *Sex, Gender and Society* (New York: Harper & Row, 1972) 134–135.
4. J. H. Driberg, *The Lango: A Nilotic Tribe of Uganda* (London: T. Fisher Unwin, 1923) 210.
5. Alfred L. Kroeber, "Handbook of the Indians of California," *Bureau of American Ethnology Bulletin* 78 (1925) 748–749.
6. George Devereux, "Institutionalized Homosexuality of the Mohave Indians," *Human Biology* 9 (1937) 498–527, as cited in Richard Green, *Sexual Identity Conflicts in Children and Adults* (New York: Basic Books, 1974) 10.
7. C. Daryll Forde, "Ethnography of the Yuma Indians," *University of California Publications in American Archaeology and Ethnology* 28 (1931) 157; and Edward Winslow Gifford, "The Cocopa," *University of California Publications in American Archaeology and Ethnology* 31 (1933) 294.
8. This is, of course, a very broad categorization of two currents of women's liberation that often intermingled and overlapped. Both were represented by articles and essays on sex and gender in *Sisterhood Is Powerful: An Anthology of Writings from the Women's Liberation Movement*, ed. Robin Morgan (New York: Vintage Books, 1970). Twenty-five years later, these issues are being revisited by contemporary feminists such as Minnie Bruce Pratt, *S/HE* (Ithaca, NY: Firebrand Books, 1995) and Ann Snitow, "A Gender Diary," *Conflicts in Feminism*, eds. Marianne Hirsch and Evelyn Fox Keller (New York: Routledge, 1990).

Key Terms

transgender   A person who has assumed some of the characteristics of the sex to which s/he was *not* assigned at birth, through dress, manner, speech, style of life, choice of sexual partner, and sometimes through limited medical alteration, but who does *not* identify with or as the other sex. Leslie Feinberg describes herself as transgender.

platonic   An often intense but nonsexual relationship.

"Uncle Miltie" Berle   Milton Berle, a former vaudeville comedian, very popular for his variety show on early television. One of Berle's frequent comic acts involved dressing in women's clothing.

butches   Lesbians who assume a pronounced masculine appearance and demeanor. The term "butch" is also used to describe gay men with a hypermasculine appearance or demeanor.

drag queen   Gay men who dress as women.

trans   An inclusive term that includes both transgender and transsexual individuals.

in tandem   In association; together.

Simone de Beauvoir   French feminist philosopher, essayist, memoirist (1908–1986), and companion of philosopher Jean-Paul Sartre.

John Brown   American abolitionist, hanged for treason in Virginia in 1859.

John D. Rockefeller   Founder of Standard Oil; often considered the quintessential American capitalist (1839–1937).

Sojourner Truth   Freed slave and influential speaker for the rights of women and African Americans (ca. 1797–1883).

Margaret Thatcher   Conservative British Prime Minister, 1979–1990.

suffragette   Term applied to women who worked for the extension of the vote (suffrage) to women in the late nineteenth and early twentieth centuries.

Alfred L. Kroeber   One of the founders of American anthropology (1876–1960).

socialist-materialistic   A theoretical perspective (usually called *social materialism*) that considers the primary causes of cultural phenomena to lie in such "material" phenomena as the distribution of valued resources and the power to manipulate them.

sex workers   A relatively recent term applied primarily to prostitutes. The term aims to avoid the stigma that usually accrues to more common words, as well as to make the point that sex workers provide a service for which there is a steady and almost universal demand and which ought not to be condemned.

androgyny   The condition of manifesting both male and female characteristics, whether physically, socially, or psychologically.

transsexual   A person who lives and identifies primarily with and as a member of the sex to which s/he was not assigned at birth. In many industrialized countries, including the United States, transsexuals undergo medical procedures to alter their bodies to conform to the characteristics of their new gender identity. In the United States roughly equal proportions of men and women undergo surgical sexual reassignment.

Trojan horse   According to Greek legend, a huge wooden horse parked at the gates of Troy, a city-state with which the Greeks were at war, and subsequently hauled inside the gates out of curiosity. Under cover of darkness Greek soldiers concealed in the horse crawled out of it and led the Greek army to victory by sacking Troy. The term is now used as a metaphor for any apparently desirable object that conceals disaster.

Discussion Questions

1. Early in this piece Feinberg makes an interesting observation. As she was growing up, she says, she noticed a variety of different kinds of love, but only one that people talked much about: romantic love between a female and a male. Do you think Feinberg is

correct that American culture concentrates on male-female romantic love to the exclusion of other kinds of love? If you disagree, what do you think might be added to romantic love? Why do you think that romantic male-female love is such a focus of Western culture? Do you know anything about other cultures in which it is less emphasized?

2. Americans are clearly uncomfortable with gender ambiguity, and this discomfort usually takes one of two forms. Either we jeer or we laugh. Occasionally we kill. We cannot necessarily tell whether a stranger is American, Samoan, or Paraguayan, and yet this uncertainty does not provoke the anger or humor that uncertainty about gender seems to provoke. Why? What do you think is the reason that the anger derived from (someone else's) gender ambiguity has, in some well-publicized criminal cases, turned murderous? Can you think of any other kind of uncertainty about a person's identity that makes Americans impatient or uncomfortable in a similar way? What is it (or what are they)?

3. Feinberg quotes Simone de Beauvoir as saying "One is not born but one becomes a woman." What do you think she meant by this? It sounds as though de Beauvoir was distinguishing women from men by this kind of experience. Do you think de Beauvoir thought that one is *born* a man, but one must *become* a woman? What would that mean?

4. Because she was a masculine female, Feinberg says she could not use traditional feminine tactics to "get around men's power." What tactics is she referring to here? Do you think these tactics are widely used? Since the traditional "feminine" tactics were useless to Feinberg, she had to develop others to "walk safely through the world." Specifically, what kinds of tactics is she talking about? Do you think that what Feinberg is talking about as feminine strategies are strategies of weakness that will disappear from women's behavioral repertoires as they gain equality with men? Why or why not?

DIFFERENCE, DESIRE, AND THE SELF

THREE STORIES

ARLENE STEIN

This selection is the second chapter of Arlene Stein's book, Sex and Sensibility: Stories of a Lesbian Generation, *in which she presents accounts, drawn from interviews, of the lives of three women who identify themselves as lesbians. As she interviewed lesbians for her book, Stein was struck by how central the accounts of their coming out experiences were to their life stories. The accounts all reflected the importance disclosure had in their narrators' lives, but Stein also noticed the great diversity they represented; there was no single coming out story shared by all. The women discussed in this chapter reflect three different "ways of being lesbian," and their accounts of their coming out, or coming to identify themselves as lesbians, are as different as they are similar.*

Barb is the only one of the three who was always aware of her attraction to females. Even as a child she felt different from other girls, and was unaware of anyone else who had the same desires she did. Though she became sexually involved only with other girls, and then women, she did not formally or publicly identify herself as a lesbian until she was in college, during the heady days of the late sixties and early seventies, when it seemed to many young Americans as though anything was possible. Barb notes that she straddles the "old," prefeminist lesbian world and the "new," feminist lesbian world. And though she credits the feminist revolution of the seventies for helping her to come out, she did not become a lesbian as a result of feminism or any other cause. "It's just the way I am," she says, and she considers only "born" lesbians, like herself, to be "real" lesbians.

Margaret and Ara are not "real" lesbians according to Barb's definition, but they identify themselves as lesbians. Margaret is what Stein sometimes describes as an "elective" lesbian, or a lesbian by choice. Though her early sexual experiences were with men, she came to identify herself as a lesbian primarily through her interpretation of the feminism of the 1970s. Finding sexual relationships with men inherently inegalitarian, and wanting to merge her life more completely with her feminist political convictions, Margaret consciously chose a lesbian identity. Ara, an African American raised in the South, also enjoyed sexual relationships with men, and was briefly married to one. She says that her sexual enjoyment is greater with men, but because she finds it impossible to share a profound emotional bond with them, she identifies primarily as a lesbian. She was in a loving sexual relationship with a woman at the time of the interviews.

In this selection, Stein is at pains to elucidate two primary points: (1) that lesbian identity cannot be separated from the social or cultural context in which it occurs; and (2) that there are many different pathways through which women "come out," or identify themselves as lesbians. For some, lesbian self-identification is based on an early awareness of sexual desire for girls and women; for others it is the result of political conviction; and for still others it is based primarily on emotional attachment.

In reading Stein's chapter, consider the similarities that bind Barb, Margaret, and Ara together, and the issues that separate them. Consider also what these three women (or one or two of them) have in common with the gay men whose experiences are discussed in earlier selections in this reader.

The individual can only be what is possible within some specifically constructed historical world. But individuals, thus constrained, construct and reconstruct such historical worlds by exploiting the distinctive ambiguities of interaction. They bring with them to each of their interactions a unique and inner self.

—Dennis Wrong, "The Oversocialized Conception of Man in Modern Sociology" (1961)

As we have seen, women who reached adolescence and young adulthood during the 1960s and 1970s—at a time when U.S. society was in a period of great social ferment, when gender and sexual norms were being publicly contested—confronted two different accounts of lesbianism. The medical model conceptualized lesbianism in terms of homosexual object choice or desires, which were fixed and immutable. This dominant explanation associated lesbianism with gender nonconformity, exemplified by the mannish woman. To become a lesbian was to reveal something that had before been hidden, to disclose something that occupied the very core of one's "being," and to build an identity on the basis of one's stigma.

In contrast, an emergent account, influenced by social constructionist thought, considered lesbianism to be a product of multiple influences rather than being traceable to a single cause, a lifestyle choice that entailed conscious self-reflection and identification. In the context of the feminist and gay liberation movements, to become a lesbian signified coming to self-knowledge, identifying with the collectivity of other lesbians, and making political commitments.[1]

The discourse of "coming out," as it was used by my interviewees, linked these two conceptions of homosexuality. It imagined the process of homosexual identification as a coming to terms with an "authentic" self, which implied the existence of a "core" sexual orientation, an internal "truth."[2] Yet it situated the development of a lesbian identity as a voluntaristic and reflexive act that challenged the pervasiveness of "compulsory heterosexuality" and was accessible to anyone who possessed the right political convictions. The women I interviewed shared a strong belief in the idea of "coming out," which they generally understood as two linked processes: the consolidation of a personal sense of self as lesbian and the development of a social identity as lesbian, the latter entailing a certain degree of public disclosure. When I began an interview by asking someone how she would describe her sexual identity, most interviewees promptly launched into their "coming out" story.

In one instance, I sat down with a forty-three-year-old woman, a carpenter in San Francisco, and asked her to tell me about her life. No sooner had I turned on the tape recorder than she proceeded to tell me her coming out story, beginning in early childhood and moving through time to the present. It seemed to me that she had told this story many times before. In the course of my research, this scene was repeated time

after time. Immediately after I asked my subjects how they would define their sexual identities, they would embark upon their stories, carefully tracing their biographies in roughly chronological order.

Coming out as a lesbian typically took several years or more.[3] Like a fictional bildungsroman, in which a character achieves self-development by making a challenging journey, the process of coming out moved the individual from one state of being to another.[4] It guided her along a path that ended with the moment of resolution: the "final" achievement of a lesbian/gay identity. The relating of her coming out story was itself an important element of this process, in part because it was an act of disclosure. Though few disclosed their lesbianism to all whom they met, and at all times, the women I spoke with were "out" in many if not most aspects of their lives.

In telling me her story, each woman constructed a personal narrative of sexual identity development that helped to organize her autobiographical experience for herself and for me, the audience. In speaking with individuals, I was often struck both by the pervasiveness of the discourse of "coming out" and by the great variety among the stories themselves.[5] Coming out was a narrative template that was expansive and adaptable enough to accommodate a diverse array of life experiences. Here are three of these stories.

Barb Herman: "Just the Way I Am"

Forty-two-year-old Barb Herman was born to a lower-middle-class Italian family in New York. Barb experienced desires for other girls early in life and acted on these desires in isolation, often thinking that she was "the only one." She thinks of herself as having been a tomboy as a child. "I never played with dolls, and hardly ever played with girls. I wore boys' clothes at age eight or nine."

Barb remembers the 1950s and early 1960s as a time when she was "young and out of control, having all these feelings, and no place to go to talk about them." At fifteen, Barb had a first sexual experience with another girl. It was 1962. At the time, she had no words to describe her feelings, though she was vaguely aware of the existence of other lesbians. It was an experience that she describes as an epiphany, or defining moment. She felt a "mixture of fear and exhilaration. This is home after all these years. I knew that this was what I wanted, but I knew that it was a really bad thing."

Lesbian pulp novels—dimestore fiction sold during the 1950s and 1960s, featuring lurid covers and titles such as *Odd Girl Out* and *Strange Sisters*—told tales of lust, intrigue, and secrecy, of being young and confused, and of being a social misfit. These books remind Barb of her own adolescence, for she "faced the very same kind of struggles" as their characters. Once she had her first homosexual experience, she said, "I felt at peace with myself emotionally. This is home." Quoting the 1952 novel by Claire Morgan (Patricia Highsmith) called *The Price of Salt*, Barb recalled the line: "Nobody had to tell her that this was the way it was supposed to be."

Barb feels that she has always been a lesbian, that it was not at all a matter of choice. To become a lesbian, she simply "discovered" what was "already there." In contrast, she described her first girlfriend, who "turned straight" after a few years: "She flipped out. She became straight after a few years, got married, had kids, and seriously repressed that stuff, her sexual experience with me, her feelings for others. Maybe she had some doubts about really being gay. I couldn't repress it. I never did. I never had any doubts."

Yet it would be several years before Barb could actually name her lesbianism to others. Through her teens and early twenties, Barb had a series of relationships with women but never claimed a lesbian identity in the sense of affiliating with the lesbian

subculture. She was seeing a psychiatrist at the time, who told her that she had "trouble relating to people" and prescribed tranquilizers. Several years after having had her first homosexual experience, Barb befriended Lore, the first "flesh and blood" lesbian she had ever met—the first woman she knew who identified as a lesbian. One day, Lore looked Barb in the eye and said: "You are a lesbian." At the time, Barb said, she scoffed at the allegation, "but it planted some sort of seed." Still, claiming a lesbian identity in a social sense, as a member of a stigmatized group, was not an easy task in the absence of any public lesbian visibility.

> At the time the women's movement was just starting to struggle with lesbianism. I had no patience for it. I had no patience to struggle with them. Even if I said "I am not a lesbian," I think I always knew I was. But it's this funny thing. How you dissociate yourself from things that you're feeling, even if there is a label for what you're feeling in the English language. I always knew I was a lesbian, but I distanced myself from the word. It was too scary to consider. . . . I remember looking at the rise of feminism, and thinking it was hopeful, and that things were moving in the right direction. But I remember thinking or sensing that they're not there yet. It's not all right to be a lesbian—yet.
>
> There were all these strikes going on, and I still didn't quite get all the connections—with the war, with academic freedom, with general alternative education and feminism and black power. There were all these strikes all over campus. Kent State. Riots at Columbia. The world was going to pieces, but I was freaking out about being a lesbian. That was the most important thing to me.

But in 1970, a homophobic incident provided the catalyst for Barb's public coming out. While in college, she was living with a girlfriend and several other people in a communal house. One morning, she awoke to hear her housemates discussing whether the presence of Barb and her girlfriend was "warping the household." That was, she said, "the straw that broke the camel's back." Soon after this, Barb became involved with a radical lesbian political group that had just formed in town. She described attending a first meeting, in 1971: "It was like the messiah had come. There were all these people who were like me. They were all my age. They were lesbians. They were distributing mimeographed copies of 'The Woman Identified Woman.' I quickly realized I was a feminist as well as a lesbian."

Becoming a feminist lesbian meant that Barb could begin to think of her lesbianism in positive terms. It also meant that she could think of her femaleness and her lesbianism as compatible, rather than conflicting. She gained a sense that she could have a social as well as a personal identity as a lesbian.

> The whole period from 1971 was an incredible release. It was great. Because I had gone on marches—civil rights marches and other kinds of demonstrations—before, but none of it seemed to have much to do with my life. It was a thrill to be doing it for me instead of for everybody else. Getting involved in lesbian feminism was a very personal kind of thing. Things were happening very fast; every time you turned around there was more going on, more stuff being written, more things to read and talk about. We were up half the night talking. It was like the racetrack. For a while life was really exciting.

Barb says that she would be a lesbian regardless of these historical changes, but she imagines that she would have been forced to lead a far more secretive, far more unhappy life.

Barb's narrative exhibits many elements of the "dominant" account; she sees her lesbianism as an immutable orientation, fixed at birth or in early childhood. She talked about "knowing" she was a lesbian by age eight, even before she had words to describe her feelings. Adolescent girls vary in the extent to which they know their desires. Some are not at all aware of sexual

feelings, heterosexual or homosexual, while others, like Barb, are deeply conscious of them. Girls with early awareness of their sexual feelings often experience their adolescence as a period in which their embodied sexual desire is simultaneously elicited and denigrated by the dominant culture.[6] One can imagine that girls with early lesbian desires rarely, if ever, receive reinforcement either in the dominant culture or within adolescent peer groups.

Barb identified desires for girls and women at a very early age, experiencing these desires as powerful and unwavering. In the context of the early to mid-1960s, Barb saw herself as virtually alone, having no one to discuss her feelings with. She compared her experiences with those of old dykes, who had come out as lesbians before feminism. "I was sort of an old lesbian. To be an old lesbian meant you were out before feminism. I wasn't out to anyone but myself." Being a lesbian in the mid-1960s was a "long stream of unfinished business." She thinks of herself as straddling the "old gay" and "new gay" worlds because she had same-sex experiences before the late 1960s, before the lesbian/gay movements expanded the social space open to lesbians and gay men. "But I knew when I was eight years old. I probably knew much earlier."

When I asked Barb why she is a lesbian, she replied, "It's just the way I am." Indeed, she found the question itself rather curious. Barb sees her adolescent experiences of difference and her eventual homosexuality as points on a continuum. Her personal identity as lesbian was never really in question. As she grew older and began to affiliate with the lesbian community, those connections gave her a social identity as well, a sense of direction and purpose that went beyond the self, and a way to counter some of the stigma she encountered. She spoke of the important role that the lesbian community played in allowing her to normalize her sexuality.

But the fact that she experienced her lesbian desires early in life has been crucial in shaping her sense of self and the meaning her lesbianism holds for her. Indeed, her identity account resembles the "old gay" account, insofar as secrecy looms large for those who have spent their formative years "managing" their stigma, carefully determining which parts of the self they would reveal to others. She feels that she has lived much of her life in the closet.

Perhaps because of these experiences, Barb tended to accentuate the differences between herself and heterosexual women, viewing lesbians and heterosexuals as two distinct categories, much as did women of an earlier prefeminist cohort. She thinks of lesbianism largely in essentialist terms. She believes that the only "real" lesbians are "born" lesbians—women like her, who have little choice in the matter of their sexuality.

Margaret Berg: "Coming Out through Feminism"

Margaret Berg grew up in New England; she was a red diaper baby, the daughter of Jewish leftist activists of mixed working-class and middle-class backgrounds. To be a woman in the 1950s and 1960s, she said, was to grow up with "the profound sense of oneself as a second-class citizen." Margaret spoke of her need to feign underachievement in school in order to catch a husband. She said that she experienced her heterosexual relationships as largely unsatisfying and her sexual interest in men as often conflicted, motivated more by accommodation to male needs and social expectations than by her own desires. "I had all the feelings about men that we all had; we thought they were like zombies. I felt that I took care of all the men I was involved with. I felt like I was much stronger than they were. I felt like I gave much more than I got." She recalled, "We were growing up in a world that was so invalidating of women.

I straightened my hair, I was ambivalent about being smart, my physics teacher told my parents: she's doing fine for a girl."[7]

The women's movement emerged in the late 1960s to help her make sense of this alienation and situate it in the larger scheme of women's oppression. Margaret compared her exposure to feminism in 1969 to "coming out of a cave." Feminism, she said, was "the most exciting and validating thing that had happened in our lives." It allowed her and others to resolve the dissonance they felt between cultural codes and subjective experience. Within the context of the movement, Margaret developed an analysis and vocabulary for these feelings, seeing her problems in gendered terms for the first time. She began to believe that she had devalued herself as a woman and underestimated the importance of her female relationships.

Because of their growing idealization of other women—a change in attitude made possible by feminism—women like Margaret withdrew from primary relationships with men. This was less a conscious decision than the outcome of the growing separation between men's and women's social and political worlds, at least among the young, predominantly middle-class members of what became loosely called the "movement." At the time, she was romantically involved with a man, but as her women friends became more and more central, he became more peripheral. Eventually, "most of my friends were women, all of my friends were feminists, men were not part of my life. It was all very seamless." Margaret had always thought of lesbianism as something that was involuntary; it was an orientation that one either did or did not "have." But when she was in her early twenties, she became aware of the possibility of constructing her own sexuality and electing lesbianism. As she described it, she was one of those women who "came out through feminism."

When Margaret became involved in her first lesbian relationship, she said, "The only gay women I knew (and *we* wouldn't call ourselves gay) were my friend and myself." Her friend, Jennifer, eventually moved into her apartment. The world they traveled in was that of liberated sexuality and free use of drugs, and there was "a real sense of barriers breaking." She was drawn to Jennifer as a kindred spirit, an equal. "There was a certain reflection of myself I found in her." Margaret recalled that Jennifer had "much more self-consciously identified homoerotic feelings," while hers were more about sexual experimentation and rebellion.

In an effort to make sense of her feelings, and to find support for them, she began to attend a women's consciousness-raising group devoted to discussing questions of sexuality. Practically overnight, through the influence of gay liberation and lesbian feminism, the gathering transformed itself into a coming out group. There Margaret was socialized into the lesbian world. She began to think of herself as a lesbian and call herself one.

> There was a normative sense about discovering women and male domination and how disgusting men could be. Not to be a lesbian was stupid, masochistic . . . something called "lesbian consciousness" developed in our heads. It's hard to reconstruct just how the process occurred. We talked about "coming out" every four or five weeks. That term started having more and more ramifications as our lives changed. Not just making love with a woman for the first time—but every new situation where you experienced and/or revealed yourself as gay.

Within the context of a coming out group, Margaret carved out a place for herself in the lesbian subculture. Earlier, "coming out" had referred almost exclusively to the process of disclosure. But now women who had never experienced themselves as deeply and irrevocably different, but who shared a sense of alienation from gender

sexual norms, could also claim lesbian identities by developing "gay consciousness." The discourse of lesbian feminism conflated feminism and lesbianism. Lesbianism was reenvisioned to signify not simply a sexual preference but a way for women to gain strength and confidence, to bond with other women.

But the political strategy of coming out to others as a means of establishing unity often had the contradictory effect of heightening differences *among* women, and the tension between identity and difference within the coming out group soon became apparent. Margaret describes the "experiential gap" separating the women in the group who were "entering a first gay relationship" and those who were "coming out of the closet":

> One woman was quite involved with a man and left almost immediately—it was never clear exactly why she had joined the group, except that she felt good about women. Another woman pulled out because she felt there was a "bisexual" orientation to the group. . . . Her "coming out" was very different from the rest of ours. She wasn't entering a first gay relationship; rather, she was coming out of "the closet," entering a gay community and acquiring pride in an analysis of who she is. . . . There was a real experiential gap between her and the rest of the group. We had no understanding of the bar scene, of role-playing, of the whole range of experience of an "old gay." I'm sure a lot of this inexperience translated into moralistic arrogance—we were a good deal less than understanding when she called her lovers "girls."

In this clash of cultures we see two different visions of lesbianism: the old dyke world, which valorized gender roles, and the emergent lesbian feminist culture, which rejected gendered coupledom in favor of the communalized sensuality of the group circle dance.

> We all went to our first gay women's dance together. I was very scared by a number of older women dressed sort of

mannishly. Not scared that they'd do anything to me, but wary of being identified with them. I was very relieved when a group of women . . . showed up and we all danced together in a big friendly circle. That was my first exposure to a kind of joyful sensuality that I've come to associate with women's dances. Looking around and seeing a lot of gay women enjoying themselves and each other helped me let go of a lot of my fears and validated the possibilities for growth and pleasure in the relationship with J.

The old gay world conceptualized lesbianism as desire; the new gay world reconceptualized it, more diffusely, as woman identification. Margaret saw differences in the group primarily in generational terms, evidencing the extent to which other distinctions may have been less salient at the time. For younger women, becoming a lesbian was a matter of developing lesbian consciousness, developing a personal sense of self as lesbian. For the second group, the issue was not really *being* a lesbian, a matter of personal identity, but *living* as one, developing a social identity. For Margaret, old dykes, particularly those who were very visibly butch, represented what she might become if she shunned heterosexuality. Gender inversion served as a symbolic marker of lesbianism, warning those who stepped out of their prescribed roles that the taint of lesbianism might soon follow them. But the older women also embodied a kind of protofeminism, a willingness to go against the social grain.

As she tried to figure out her place in the lesbian world, Margaret acknowledged that coming out is "an incredibly hard process." She alluded to the conflict between the dominant essentialist model and an emergent constructionist one. "Many women think there's some magic leap into gayness—that you suddenly lose all fears, doubts, heterosexual feelings. Others are afraid that they weren't 'born gay.' Come-out groups help women deal with all of those feelings. The existence of the Lesbian Mother's Group brought home to us that women are not born lesbians; that women who were both wives and mothers could decide to live with and love other women." After some initial doubts about whether or not she was "really" a lesbian, Margaret assured herself that even seemingly gender-conforming women, women who were once wives and mothers, can be lesbians. These "successful" women who had boyfriends and husbands could also become lesbians—thus, lesbians were not necessarily "failed women."

Her story suggests that some women used the discourse of "coming out" to claim authenticity and gain membership in the lesbian world. Clearly, this was a very different path to lesbianism than the one taken by women whose sense of self as lesbian was less in question, for whom coming out meant "coming out of the closet." While women such as Barb thought of their lesbianism primarily as internally driven, for Margaret and other "elective" lesbians the adoption of lesbianism as a social identity tended to precede the consolidation of lesbianism as a personal identity.

Unlike Barb, Margaret did not trace her lesbianism to early childhood experiences or have the experience of being "not heterosexual" early on—even if she expressed alienation from heterosexual gender norms. Margaret also differs from Barb in her high degree of self-reflexivity, rooted at least in part in her more middle-class background. In general she framed her lesbianism within the development of "lesbian consciousness," viewing her involvement with women rather than men as a political rather than a sexual choice.[8] Because of her history, Margaret held the belief that any woman can choose to be a lesbian. However, she recognized that there were different "types" of lesbians, who exercised greater and lesser degrees of choice over their sexuality.

Ara Jones: "It's a Changeable Thing"

Forty-year-old Ara Jones grew up in the South, the daughter of a manual laborer and a domestic worker. Ara described her life as being shaped equally by her lesbianism and her blackness. She identifies as a lesbian but has long been conscious of the fact that her own desires do not conform neatly with binary sexual categories, homosexual and heterosexual. She says she thinks of her lesbianism as "a changeable thing."

As a teenager, Ara experienced herself as fairly bisexual, though she would not have given it that name at the time. While she was sexually involved with boys, her primary commitments were with other girls.

> I was never boy crazy. I had two boyfriends. It was nice, but it was not like my relationships with girls. It was sexual more than emotional. Sexually it was fine. I think what I did a lot was . . . really separate sex and relationships—it was totally separate. Some people are very vulnerable when they're sexual; for me it was the opposite. I was less vulnerable when I was sexual with someone than when I was talking with them. I think I felt more confident about my body than with who I was.

At twenty-five she entered college and became involved with student organizations, African American and others. By this time, the period of most vocal and visible antiwar and feminist activity had already subsided, leaving behind an institutional infrastructure of lesbian/gay and feminist organizations, publications, and a more accepting climate for minorities of all sorts on her college campus.

Ara became involved with a white woman she met, who was an out lesbian. They fell "madly in love." In the context of this relationship, she began to think of herself as a lesbian. She never particularly identified with the lesbian community, however. This was in large part because it was predominantly white. "I definitely would say that I am a feminist, and a lesbian, but not a lesbian feminist necessarily. Lesbian feminism is too strict for me, and always has been. It's never felt quite right, not quite my experience, not quite comfortable." But once she and her lover broke up, a year later, Ara was forced to reassess her sexual self-definition. "I remember when she left, I felt like, okay: but what am I now? Where do I go? I felt much more connected to her than to a lesbian community. But then I didn't really feel all that connected to the black community by this time either." She continued to date men occasionally, eventually marrying a man whom she met through a friend. After two years, they decided to divorce. She described having "better" sex with men than with women. But with women, she said, she felt a "depth of emotion" that she "couldn't feel with men." She adopted a definition of lesbianism as passionate friendship: "a relationship in which two women's strongest emotions and affections are directed toward each other."[9] Becoming involved with men was "sexually possible but emotionally not." She elaborated, "Sometimes I was more aware of having sexual feelings for men than other times, but I always felt that I was a lesbian as well. In another world, it would be a lot easier. You would just go from relationship to relationship, and male and female sexuality would just sort of be . . . insignificant. But not in this world." The contradictions between these "multiple identities" may have been particularly salient for an African American woman with working-class roots, who was circulating in a largely middle-class world.

After moving to San Francisco in the early 1980s, Ara became a social worker for a county health office. She fell in love with a woman, eight years her senior, whom she met through a mutual friend. When asked whether her lesbianism is a choice, Ara replied, "Yes," adding, "but I'm not straight." Ara feels that her lesbianism is a choice insofar as she could choose to deny what she "really" felt. She could choose to be with men if she wished to fit in, but she has made a choice that fitting in is less important than being "who she is."

> Who I am is changeable. I could have lived my life as a straight person, if Sara hadn't come along. But she did, so here I am. I don't know if I'm a born lesbian, but I sure as hell know this is right for me. I love women. Maybe I'll change. Maybe I won't. So is it a choice? I don't know. Part of it is, part of it isn't.

She is not a lesbian like other women are lesbians, insofar as she was not "born" one, she says. Yet she sees herself as more sexually attracted to women than many of those who call themselves lesbians, particularly many who came out in the context of feminism. Indeed, she was involved with "one of those women" at one point and was sexually dissatisfied. For her girlfriend, she said, lesbianism was about bonding with other women. "It was about making a domestic relationship, making a life together where neither person dominated the other. It was about having a more equal relationship at home where one could be comfortable and not feel squashed by the other person." For Ara as well, lesbianism was about these things, but also about passionate sexuality and intimacy.

As we saw earlier, Barb described her personal identity as lesbian as preceding her affiliation with lesbianism as a social category, while Margaret said the opposite: her affiliation with the group preceded her consolidation of a sense of "deep" identity. For Ara separating out the "personal" and "social" components of lesbian identification and isolating which "came first" is impossible. She talks about her lesbianism in terms of elements that were chosen and elements that were not, and she remains conscious of the disjunction between "dozing" and "being," between engaging in homosexual acts and claiming a homosexual identity: "There are many women like me: women who could've gone either way, depending upon what kind of situation they found themselves in. I probably could've been straight and lived a happy enough life, but women always came first—beginning with my mama. So I became a lesbian. I thought of myself as that even though I didn't usually use the word."

Ara's lesbianism is a choice insofar as acting upon her desires and claiming a lesbian identity are chosen, since originally she experienced her desires as being at least partly fluid and changing. But at the same time, she recognizes that her adoption of a social identity as a lesbian "organized" these desires, diminishing her earlier bisexual inclinations. While embracing a lesbian identity, Ara views it partly as a strategic act, rather than as a direct expression of who she "really is."

Speaking as a Lesbian

The preceding accounts are certainly not an exhaustive sample of different ways of "being" a lesbian. Nor are they intended to be particularly representative in terms of class, age, race, or ethnicity.[10] The stories of Barb, Margaret, and Ara suggest that individuals bring to the process of forming sexual identity a sense of self that has already taken on some shape, and they use the available accounts, or repertoires of meaning, to make sense of that self. These accounts are historical constructions. As women fashion their identities, they study those around them—selecting images to emulate or reject, fitting themselves into the lesbian world(s). This process is historical, situational, and individual.

Coming out takes place in a particular historical context. Women of the baby boom shared a set of broad historical and cultural experiences. The lesbian/gay and women's liberation movements figure prominently in the three life stories, even for those who were not actively political, providing a sense of enlarged possibilities, of expanded cultural resources.[11] Before these movements, traditional conceptions of gender and sexuality had gone virtually unchallenged: men and women were imagined as having separate and distinct roles; sexology and psychoanalysis pathologized sexual "deviants" as biological or psychological aberrations. To claim a lesbian identity was to declare oneself a deviant, an outsider, a queer.

Young women coming to adolescence and early adulthood during the rise of feminism and gay liberation had access to an expanding set of accounts or "scripts" for "doing" gender and sexuality. This cultural context allowed them certain *tools*—meanings, roles, and identities—with which to construct lesbian identities.[12] The discourse of "coming out," which suggested that becoming a lesbian was a positive political act, was also a tool. This elastic narrative template allowed individuals to make sense of their individual experiences and escape the confines of normative heterosexuality and "hegemonic femininity."[13]

Coming out is also a relational process. The family of origin is typically the first audience for trying out one's emerging homosexual identity. For example, some women reported that they had grown up "tomboys," that their families "had always known that they were gay" and had treated them accordingly. This first testing of the waters was typically a negative one, as their homosexual desires were invalidated or made invisible. It was through interaction with other self-defined homosexual men and women later on that an identity was rebuilt and access was gained to accounts that served to legitimate the homosexual experience.[14] Meeting known lesbians made possible more positive, embodied meanings of lesbianism. In the coming out process, individuals assessed those around them, "figuring out" who were the lesbians and whether they might "be one" as well. They evaluated the meanings of lesbianism, questioning whether those meanings helped them to make sense of their own

subjective experiences and whether the stigma attached to such self-constructions was manageable.

And finally, *coming out is an individual process.* Individuals negotiate the meanings, roles, and identities presented to them in different ways. They make sexual choices amid a series of constraints, some arising from individual psychological makeup. The experience and organization of erotic tastes and preferences begin in childhood and continue through puberty, partly forming the sense of self long before an individual's coming out begins. Early experiences of the body and desire seem to play a role in adult sexual identity formation, giving different shape to lesbian identity.[15]

For some girls this process is strongly influenced by "intrinsic" desires and feelings associated with "sexual orientation." Some recall having felt an early sense of "difference," of being "not heterosexual." Barb, who became conscious of her desires for other girls and women when very young, described herself as having been outside of the mainstream, not typically feminine, and not "normal." She struggled to establish a positive sense of herself as lesbian during adolescence, when issues of social identity besides sexuality are also being negotiated.

Those who come out later in life or who experience their sexuality as fluid and malleable may have already dealt with these other issues before they assume a "deviant" sexual identity. They may have established a sense of self as relatively "normal," at least in terms of their sexuality. Margaret and to a lesser extent Ara, because they did not think of themselves as being "not heterosexual" at an early age, felt themselves to be somewhat less different, less deviant.[16] Taking on a lesbian identity at a later stage means coping with somewhat different issues. "It may involve a sense of loss in terms of acceptability and social ease, but losing something one has had is an experience quite different from never having had it."[17]

Experience is mediated by language, so we can never know the "truth" of women's experiences prior to social interaction. "No inner psychology, no desiring subject, no autonomous individual—in short, no *a priori* entity, sexual or otherwise," Roger Lancaster asserts, "precedes social intercourse and awaits its influence." Even if it is often felt as "inner" and "subjective," desire is not part of "nature." Nor is it "opposed to" or "beyond" meaning. It is "a social act carried out through social language."[18] The stories of Barb, Margaret, and Ara suggest women can arrive at a lesbian identity in very different ways; sexual identity is formed by an interplay between factors that are internal and external, personal and cultural.

For Barb, becoming a lesbian meant that she could affiliate with the category lesbian, disclose that affiliation to others, and build a social world around the desires she had for so long kept private. Women like Barb, for whom lesbianism was a matter of deeply felt desires, made up the core group of individuals who would have lived lesbian lives, or at least harbored lesbian desires, even without the lesbian/gay and feminist movements. Their desires for girls and women, felt from an early age, were often accompanied by feelings of gender nonconformity.

Margaret and Ara, on the other hand, might be considered members of the larger grouping of women for whom lesbian identities are more highly dependent upon social context. Neither experienced exclusive homosexual desires from an early age. They did not begin the process of coming out from a position within "a closet," a subjective sense of themselves as highly deviant; their sexual drives toward women were apparently not as strong as Barb's. Margaret became aware of the possibility of defying compulsory heterosexuality when she encountered feminism and gay liberation. For her, coming out as lesbian entailed both developing a "deep" sense of self as lesbian and affiliating with lesbianism as a social

category. Ara combined elements of Barb's and Margaret's stories. Like Barb, she began the process of identity formation with a sense of sexual difference, but for Ara this sense of difference was initially more inchoate and unformed. She recognized her homosexual desires relatively early, but these coexisted with heterosexual desires. Ara saw her embrace of the social category lesbian as somewhat serendipitous rather than as a firm expression of who she "is."

Despite their common use of the "coming out" template, baby boomers told a diverse array of different self stories. To some women, coming out meant "coming home," welcoming the desires they had long affirmed in secret. These individuals experienced a deep, subjective sense of being different early in life, and they saw coming out primarily as a matter of *disclosing* their lesbianism and finding a group of people who would support that disclosure. For others, however, coming out meant "discovering" their lesbianism. For these women, many of whom had "come out through feminism," identification with lesbianism as a sociosexual category often preceded a subjective sense of being different or deviant. Coming out was for them principally a quest to develop a deep sense of self, a matter of *individuating* as a lesbian. Finally, for a third group, whose personal and social sense of lesbianism appeared more fluid and inchoate, coming out entailed both individuation and disclosure in roughly equal measure.

To quote Biddy Martin, "the word *lesbian* is not an identity with predictable content: . . . it is a position from which to speak."[19] Lesbian feminists redefined lesbianism in more expansive, universal terms, making the boundaries between straight and gay worlds less distinct and constructing an oppositional culture founded upon resistance to gender and sexual norms. Though drawing upon common cultural referents, women of the baby boom experienced the process of coming out in very different ways. One might say that they spoke different dialects of the same language of self- discovery and development, a fact that would pose thorny problems as they tried to fashion a collective identity.

NOTES

1. Plummer 1981 calls the dominant account the "orientation" model and the emergent account the "identity construct" model. They have also been referred to as "essentialist" and "constructionist" conceptions.
2. In its most radical form, the discourse of coming out suggested that all women were "naturally" lesbians who had become alienated from their authentic selves through a process of gender/sexual socialization that operated in the service of compulsory heterosexuality. A milder version suggested that many more women were "potential" lesbians, but that the taint of stigma kept the numbers of self-identified lesbians artificially low.
3. Many of my interviewees spoke about their lives in terms that sharply divided the period "before I came out" from that "after I came out," conveying the impression that coming out was a signal event. This event featured an epiphany or "defining moment" that altered the individual and allowed her to see the world differently, changing the fundamental structures of meaning in her life. See Denzin 1989 for a discussion of the role of the "epiphany" in a self story.
4. On the coming out narrative in lesbian fiction, see Zimmerman 1990. For an examination of the notion of the closet, see Sedgwick 1990; for the foundational sociological study of stigma, deviance, and identity "management," see Goffman 1963.
5. I am certainly not the first to note variations among women who self-identity as lesbian. See Ponse 1978; Faderman 1991; B. Vance and Green 1984. Here I have refrained from labeling different "types" to avoid reifying them.
6. Zemsky 1991 cites studies indicating that the mean age at which women recognize and pronounce (at least to themselves) that this sense of difference and disquiet has something to do with lesbianism is approximately fourteen. See also Tolman 1991. Herdt and Boxer 1993 found a disparity between male and female homosexual experiences. For males, first homoerotic sex typically preceded first heteroerotic sex. For girls, however, the average age of same-sex experience is later than the average age of first sex with a male.
7. For a sense of how dominant cultural norms shaped the lives of teenage girls in the 1950s, and how girls resisted these norms, see Breines 1992.
8. A. Rich 1980 and Kitzinger 1987 question whether lesbianism can ever really be a free "choice" or individual sexual "preference" under a system of normative heterosexuality.
9. Faderman 1981, 18.
10. As Weston 1991 suggests in a similar context, "To treat each individual as a representative of his or her race, for example, would be a form of tokenism that glosses over the differences of gender, class, age, national origin, language, religion, and ability which crosscut race and ethnicity" (11).
11. The historical moment shaping the culture when key transitional points occur is what Karl Mannheim [1928] 1952 calls "fresh contact" (148).
12. See Ann Swidler's (1986) conception of culture as a toolbox.
13. This term is R. W. Connell's (1987).
14. Plummer 1975, 148.
15. In this sense, I depart from the tradition of interactionist studies exemplified by Ponse 1978, in which the role of bodily experience is discounted. See Herdt and Boxer 1993 for a fuller explanation of the interplay between cultural and developmental factors in the sexual development of gay youth. During postpuberty, social desires and adjustments match social selves to real-life worlds, a process that is heavily influenced by social norms and cultural symbols and concepts, such as the relative invisibility or accessibility of homosexual persons or cultures.

16. My interviews suggest that stereotypic "butch" or more masculine-identified lesbians were less likely to see their sexual identities as being chosen than were feminine-identified women, though most of the women I interviewed refused such labels as "butch" and "femme." The reasons for this are unclear. Is it because "mannish" lesbians were more "essentially" lesbian in orientation? Or is it because butches were the most identifiable lesbian figures since they stood out, often from an early age, and were more apt to be called lesbian by family members and other authority figures?

17. Burch 1993, 121.

18. Lancaster 1992, 270. This claim is now being contested by a new wave of genetic and other biological explanations for homosexuality, most notably by LeVay 1993.

19. Biddy Martin, quoted in Jay and Glasgow 1990, 6.

References

Breines, Wini. 1992. *Young, White, and Miserable: Growing Up Female in the 1950s*. Boston: Beacon.

Burch, Beverly. 1993. *On Intimate Terms*. Urbana: University of Illinois Press.

Connell, R. W. 1987. *Gender and Power*. Stanford: Stanford University Press.

Denzin, Norma. 1989. *Interpretive Biography*. Newbury Park, CA: Sage.

Faderman, Lillian. 1991. *Odd Girls and Twilight Lovers: A History of Lesbian Life in Twentieth Century America*. New York: Columbia University Press.

Goffman, Ervin. 1963. *Stigma: Notes on the Management of Spoiled Identity*. Englewood Cliffs, NJ: Prentice Hall.

Herdt, Gilbert and Andrew Boxer. 1993. *Children of Horizons: How Lesbian and Gay Youth are, Leading a New Way Out of the Closet*. Boston: Beacon.

Jay, Kayla, and Joanne Glasgow, eds. 1990. *Lesbian Texts and Contexts: Radical Revisions*. New York: New York University Press.

Kitzinger, Celia. 1987. *The Social Construction of Lesbianism*. Newbury Park, CA: Sage.

Lancaster, Roger. 1992. *Life Is Hard: Machismo, Danger, and the Intimacy of Power in Nicaragua*. Berkeley: University of California Press.

Le Vay, Simon. 1993. *The Sexual Brain*. Cambridge: MIT Press.

Mannheim, Karl. [1928] 1952. "The Problem of Generations." In *Essays on the Sociology of Knowledge*, ed. Paul Keeskemeti. New York: Oxford University Press.

Plummer, Ken. 1975. *Sexual Stigma: An Interactionist Approach*. London: Routledge and Kegan Paul.

Ponse, Barbara. 1978. *Identities in the Lesbian World: The Social Construction of a Self*. Westport, CT: Greenwood Press.

Rich, Adrienne. 1980. "Compulsory Heterosexuality and Lesbian Existence." *Signs* 5: 631–661.

Sedgwick, Eve Kosofsky. 1990. *Epistemology of the Closet*. Berkeley: University of California Press.

Swidler, Ann. 1986. "Culture in Action: Symbols and Strategies." *American Sociological Review* 51: 273–286.

Tolman, Deborah L. 1981. "Adolescent Girls, Women and Sexuality: Discerning Dilemmas of Desire." *Women and Therapy* 11 (3–4): 55–69.

Vance, Brenda and Vicki Green. 1984. "Lesbian Identities: An Examination of Sexual Behavior, and Sex Role Attribution as Related to Age of Initial Same-Sex Sexual Encounter." *Psychology of Women Quarterly* 8 (3): 293–307.

Weston, Kath. 1991. *Families We Choose: Lesbians, Gays, Kinship*. New York: Columbia University Press.

Wrong, Dennis. 1961. "The Oversocialized Conception of Man in Modem Sociology." *American Sociological Review* 26: 183–193.

Zemsky, Beth. 1991. "Coming Out Against All Odds: Resistance in the Life of a Young Lesbian." *Women and Therapy* 11 (3–4): 185–200.

Zimmerman, Bonnie. 1990. *The Safe Sea of Women: Lesbian Fiction, 1969–1989*. Boston: Beacon.

KEY TERMS

sensibility   Consciousness of or sensitivity or response to a condition, emotion, or perspective in another individual, or to the general ambience. The title of this piece is a gentle joke, based on the title of Jane Austen's novel, *Sense and Sensibility*.

catalyst   A substance or phenomenon that is essential in producing a reaction or change.

essentialist   A philosophical perspective that considers fundamental identity or qualities (essence) as more significant than function or practice (existence).

invalidating   In this use, a systematic lack of support or refusal to respect, reinforce, or acknowledge the values of an individual or group.

a priori   Latin: from the former; a fundamental assumption on which subsequent conclusions, arguments, or phenomena are based.

DISCUSSION QUESTIONS

1. Early in this article, Stein contrasts what she calls the "medical model" and the "social constructionist model" of lesbianism. What does she mean by these two terms? It seems clear that she prefers one model over the other as a way of explaining why some women identify themselves as lesbians. Which is her preferred explanation, and why? That is, what specifics of the three lives she presents are better accounted for by Stein's preferred explanation? Do you think the other model has any explanatory power in explaining any of the three lives?

2. The Greek philosophers of the fifth century BCE believed that the unexamined life was not worth living, and that to know anything else one must first know himself (they were not very interested in whether a woman could know *her*self or not). Stein follows this line of thought in talking about how lesbian self-identification amounts to a "coming to self-knowledge," or a "coming to terms with an 'authentic' self." Why is self-knowledge so important? In fact, what *is* self-knowledge? And, more obscure, what is an "authentic" self? Isn't this all a lot of sound and fury about something pretty simple: whether an individual has a sexual relationship with her own gender or another? Couldn't we just say, if you want to, go ahead, and if you don't want to, then don't, but why build a whole subculture around the gender of your sexual partner?

3. Barb, like many other children who are not interested in the toys, games, or friends a predominantly heterosexual world considers "appropriate" for their gender, felt as though she was alone. She knew no one else with her interests until she was an adolescent. Yet many Americans believe that informing children about alternative sexual practices and gender roles is harmful, and will confuse or frighten them. What do you think? Why? Do you think more information would have made a difference in the lives of Margaret and Ara? Why or why not?

4. Toward the end of her chapter, Stein expands on a quote from Roger Lancaster, saying "Even if it is often felt as 'inner' and 'subjective,' desire is not part of 'nature.' Nor is it 'opposite to' or 'beyond' meaning. It is 'a social act carried out through social language.'" What are Lancaster and Stein talking about here? What does it mean to say that "desire is not part of nature"? Do you think it is true? Is the quote referring to *all* desire or only specific *varieties* of desire? Restate the quote in everyday language, so that its meaning is clear to the nonspecialist reader. If statements like this one of Stein's have to be analyzed and restated for clarity, why do you suppose they are written in such an obscure way in the first place? (You can't *really* believe Stein is trying to impress us.)

Gender in the Culture of Native Americans and African Americans

Chapter 5

Despite the cultural differences that separate Native Americans and African Americans, and despite significant differences within the two groups, they have an important characteristic in common: Of all U.S. ethnic minorities, they universally had that status imposed on them against their will. No Indian group asked Europeans to invade their territory, and no African asked to be enslaved and transported to what is now the United States. It is not surprising, then, that so many Native Americans and African Americans remain resentful of their original encounters with Euro-Americans and so conscious of the ways in which their present condition and status are derived from events in the past.

Many Americans, particularly comfortable members of the dominant society, are generally intolerant of history, which often seems to them irrelevant to American life in the twenty-first century. They are more specifically intolerant, and sometimes mistrustful, of claims made by Native Americans and African Americans of their ancestors' hardship and oppression, and the resulting disadvantage they themselves suffer today. And many members of the majority population are impatient with accounts of minority cultural variation, which strike them as irrelevant and unrealistic whining. A common feeling of the Euro-American majority is that all Americans ought to pull themselves up by their bootstraps (even when a group may have had no metaphorical shoes). "These minorities need to quit whining and be more like us," is roughly how that argument goes. It is inconceivable to many majority observers that (1) not all minorities *can* achieve middle-class status within their own lifetimes, and (2) that even if they can achieve it, they may not want to accept all the traits of Euro-American culture along with economic comfort.

Among the least recognized and understood cultural differences of Native Americans and African Americans are those related to gender. Euro-Americans may recognize different speech patterns, tastes in food, and styles of celebration. But most people everywhere believe that the gender patterns that exist in their own culture or subculture are natural and universal. To the extent that other patterns differ from one's own, there is a general feeling that they are deviant, wrong, and part of a general problem. As you read through the articles in this chapter, keep in mind the following questions. They will help you organize the information you acquire in your readings, and assist you in recognizing patterns in human interaction and values through time, space, and cultural variation.

1. The issue of gender equality is of great importance to Americans, especially women, as we enter the twenty-first century. This issue is important to others as well, but it has not always been of similar concern throughout time, nor has it been cognized (thought of) in the same way by all peoples. Indeed, what seems to much of the majority population of the United States today as relating to issues of gender equality may be seen somewhat differently by members of other ethnic groups. Consider to what extent and in what ways gender equality and inequality have been manifested among Indian people and among African Americans in the following articles. It is fairly easy to come up with a general impression of an issue like this one, but try to make yourself identify specific incidents and statements in the articles that allow you to come to a specific conclusion. Another issue to consider is what kinds of social, economic, and technological phenomena you might be able to identify as either correlating (going along with) or actually producing relative equality or inequality in the world of gender, and how they change over time.

2. How are gender roles expressed and articulated in African American society now and shortly after the Civil War, and in Navajo and Pueblo cultures now and a hundred years ago—that is, what did men and women do then, and what do they do now? Is there a lot of overlap? Do gender roles change as an individual ages? Does it seem as though there are some "natural" or biological reasons for the gendered division of labor? What are they? Do the activities assigned to one gender account for a difference in prestige accruing to males and to females? Why?

   The account of We'wha, a Zuni gynomimetic (one of several terms used to describe men living as women), is surprising and fascinating to most contemporary readers, and allows us to note the distinction between biologically determined sex and culturally determined gender. Interestingly, Rosen's article on the Memphis riot of 1866 also contains a brief account of a gynomimetic, who was brutally treated when her/his biological identity was discovered. Consider how the two gynomimetics differed with respect to the cultural settings in which they lived, and why. One reflects an elastic notion of gender, and the other a rigid and inhumane notion, at least in the dominant society.

3. How and to what extent do African American and Native American gender roles differ from those that prevail in Euro-American society? Can you make any guesses as to why these differences exist? If you say something like, "It's due to religion," you have gone only part way. *Why* do you think the religious traditions are so different? Similarly, if you say, "Well, they were slaves," you then have to push yourself to try to figure out precisely what it *is* about the condition of slavery that might produce the phenomenon you are considering.

   How has interaction with Euro-Americans shaped African American and Native American gender roles? What have been Euro-American assessments of the differences between their own gendered universe and those of Native Americans and Africans? Do you think these assessments have changed over time? Why? Many members of the American majority think that Indian people are romantic, interesting, or generally "cool," though this is not a common majority perspective on African American culture. As you read the following four articles, try to figure out why these two points of view are so common.

4. As you read through the following four articles, try to formulate a statement about gender that holds true for Native Americans and African Americans despite their very different cultural origins, and that also distinguishes them from Euro-Americans. To what extent does your statement reflect issues of *contrast* and *inequality* with Euro-American society? To what extent may your statement be said to reflect qualities indigenous or native to African American and Native American societies?

WE'WHA, THE CELEBRATED LHAMANA

WILL ROSCOE

This selection is a chapter from Roscoe's book, The Zuni Man-Woman, *which describes not only the Zuni practice of berdache, but the larger cultural context in which it is set. The term* berdache *is derived from a French rendition of a word of Persian origin, and it refers to an institution in which a male assumes the name, manners, clothing, and style of life of a woman, and is considered by his community to be a woman, for all practical purposes. In some communities berdaches may marry men. These are all polygynous societies, in which a man may have more than one wife at a time (if he can afford them, and if he can persuade his wives to agree to the arrangement). Berdache was practiced in many Native American groups in the United States, and those who participated in the practice were called in their own languages by a number of different terms, including "two spirit people." Some Native American populations, especially in the Great Plains, also had an institution through which women might participate in some of the practices of men, including riding to war. These "manly hearted women" were far less common than berdaches.*

One question often asked by modern non-Natives about berdaches and their husbands (if they were married) is "Weren't they really just homosexuals?" This question contains two assumptions based on contemporary Euro-American society: (1) that all humans may be divided into either homosexual or heterosexual; and (2) that persons who manifest gender ambiguity but do not identify themselves as homosexual are trying to "get away" with something. In most Native American societies the dichotomous split between homosexual and heterosexual did not exist. Adults were expected to marry and have children, and even those who were sexually interested in their own gender did not form a self-conscious community of persons with similar sexual interests. A man with a wife who was a berdache was not seen as homosexual. He was, in fact, likely to increase his prestige within the community, since berdaches were often considered unusually spiritually powerful and adept at essential female tasks. Though We'wha was not married, he certainly possessed the spiritual power and practical capabilities often ascribed to berdaches. He was a distinguished and influential member of the community, and in no way a source of embarrassment, comedy, or shame to his family or the larger society.

It is remarkable that Matilda Coxe Stevenson, an intelligent and sophisticated anthropologist, who worked closely with We'wha for many years, apparently was not aware of We'wha's biological sex until late in their acquaintance, or possibly until We'wha's death. This is not because We'wha looked particularly feminine; indeed, photographs show a powerfully built individual with a distinctively male face, though dressed in Zuni women's clothing, and with a Zuni woman's hairstyle. Nor is it because the Zuni kept We'wha's sexual origin a secret. Rather, because the whole Zuni pueblo knew of We'wha's origin and accepted it as a matter of course, there was little occasion to announce it.

In reading the following account of We'wha's life, keep a couple of things in mind. First, consider the general differences between the way the Zuni thought of family organization, obligations, and practices and the way contemporary Euro-American society does. Second,

*consider the assumptions with which Euro-Americans (government bureaucrats and mis-
sionaries) entered the Zuni community. How did these assumptions affect Euro-American
policy and practice, not to mention personal relationships with the Zuni?*

*Native American groups reflect enormous cultural diversity. It would be foolish and
ignorant to believe that this little window into Zuni society gives us a global picture of all
Indian peoples. On the other hand, it does allow us a glimpse of a distinctive, small-scale,
traditional society that shares many traits with other small-scale, traditional Native American groups. Finally, consider this apparent paradox. We'wha was a berdache, and even
though berdaches had an honored place in Zuni society, they were uncommon; they were
not "typical" Zunis. So how is it that we hope to gain insight into Zuni society from an
examination of such an unusual person?*

By any standard, We'wha was a key figure
in Zuni history. Matilda Coxe Stevenson
described him as "the strongest character
and the most intelligent of the Zuni tribe,"
"the most remarkable member of the
tribe," and "the strongest, most active, and
most progressive Indian in the tribe"; while
the popular writer George Wharton James
referred to him as "one of the most noted
and prominent" of the Zunis. Elsie Clews
Parsons called We'wha "the celebrated
lhamana" and "a notable character." And
Robert Bunker, an Indian agent at Zuni in
the 1940s, wrote: "We'wha, that man of
enormous strength who lived a woman's
daily life in woman's dress, but remained
a power in his Pueblo's gravest councils."[1]
Zunis to this day still recall the adventures
and exploits of this famous berdache. And
well they might, for We'wha was at the
center of some of the most dramatic events
at Zuni in the late nineteenth century—
events that shaped the course of Zuni history and left an impression that can be
discerned to this day.

A New Family

We'wha was born in 1849 in a community
that had changed little in the 250 years
since the arrival of the Spaniards.[2] After the
abandonment of the Catholic mission at
Zuni in 1821 following Mexico's independence from Spain, the Zunis were as isolated as they had been at any time in their
history. They were free to practice their
cherished customs and religious ceremonies—and to face their enemies, the
Navajos and Apaches, on their own. "We
were very poor," recalled a Zuni of
We'wha's generation. "There were no white
people, no Mexicans. There was no cloth,
no coffee, no sugar. We slept on skins and
saddle blankets. We had no shoes."[3] But in
the year of We'wha's birth, the Zunis received an official visit from a new invader,
the most powerful yet to enter the Southwest—the Americans. Many of the key
events in We'wha's life unfold against the
background of the Zunis' response to this
development.

Source: Will Roscoe, "We'wha, the Celebrated Lhamana." Chapter 2, pp. 29–52 in Will Roscoe, *The Zuni Man-
Woman*. Albuquerque: University of New Mexico Press, 1991. Reprinted by permission of the University of New
Mexico Press.

When the United States declared war on Mexico in 1846, Gen. Stephen W. Kearny quickly captured Santa Fe, the provincial capital. However, New Mexico's new military government inherited problems not so quickly solved—in particular the warlike Navajos, Apaches, Utes, and Comanches whose bands ringed the territory. In the course of the Spanish colonial era, these Indians had developed a nomadic life-style based on raiding Pueblo and Hispanic villages. In 1846, Kearney dispatched an expedition either to frighten or force the Navajos into peace, but the treaties negotiated that season went unheeded and unratified.[4] In 1849, a second expedition was organized under the command of the territorial governor, Lt. Col. John M. Washington.

Washington's column arrived at Zuni in September. The Zunis, eager to impress the Americans with their willingness to join the war against the Navajos, staged a mock battle as the expedition approached the village. "Guns were fired, dust was thrown in the air," recalled Lt. James H. Simpson, "men on foot and on horseback could be seen running hurry-skurry hither and thither, the war-whoop was yelled, and altogether quite an exciting scene was exhibited." Simpson described the pueblo as it appeared in the year of We'wha's birth:

> The town, like Santo Domingo, is built terrace-shaped—each story, of which there are generally three, being smaller, laterally, so that one story answers in part for the platform of the one above it. It, however, is far more compact than Santo Domingo—its streets being narrow and in places presenting the appearance of tunnels, or covered ways, on account of the houses extending at these places over them. The houses are generally built of stone, plastered with mud. . . .
>
> This is by far the best-built and neatest-looking pueblo I have yet seen, though, as usual, the ragged picketed sheep and goat pens detract not a little from its appearance. . . . These people seem further advanced in the arts of civilization than any

Indians I have seen. They have large herds of sheep and horses, and extensively cultivate the soil. Being far off from any mercantile population, they will sell nothing for money, but dispose of their commodities entirely in barter.[5]

The Americans brought more than military prowess, however. In the nineteenth century, deadly smallpox epidemics repeatedly swept the Zuni village. According to Stevenson, both of We'wha's parents died when he was an infant. This may have occurred in 1853, when smallpox erupted shortly after a party of American emigrants passed through the area. We'wha and his brother were adopted by an aunt, their father's sister. We'wha remained a member of his mother's clan, *donashi:kwe*, or Badger People, with lifelong ceremonial ties to his father's clan, who were *bichi:kwe*, or Dogwood People. His new family included two foster sisters and a brother.[6]

Zuni kinship terms grouped uncles and aunts with parents, and cousins with siblings. Maternal aunts were called "older" or "little" mother, depending on their ages. Paternal aunts performed important rites at key points in the individual's life. Practices like these facilitated We'wha's integration into his new family. According to Stevenson, "the loving gratitude he exhibited for his aunt and her grief at his death afforded a lesson that might well be learned by the more enlightened."[7]

Despite the arrival of the Americans (and sometimes because of it), intertribal conflict increased in the 1840s and 1850s. We'wha grew up with the ever-present threat of Navajo and Apache raids—enemies who would steal crop and livestock, kidnap women and children, and murder men. In 1846, when Navajos attacked thirty miles to the east, at the Zuni farming village of Pescado, and Zuni warriors went out to meet them, an even larger body of Navajos attacked the main pueblo itself. Women and children defended the village for several hours, until the Zuni warriors returned. In 1850, Navajos attacked again, laying siege to the village for sixteen days and carrying off most of the season's crops. On at least two occasions, Navajo warriors breached the main pueblo itself and had to be repelled by residents fighting from the roof tops.[8]

To defend themselves and to launch reprisals, the Zunis bolstered their own military capabilities. They built watchtowers in their corn fields and tended their crops armed while women and children stayed close to the safety of the main village. The great, multistoried pueblo incorporated many defensive features. There were no windows or doors on the ground floors; all access was by ladders that could be quickly raised or dismantled. In the plain surrounding the village, deep pits were dug and lined with stakes—deadly traps for unwary hostiles.[9]

A key element of the Zuni strategy was diplomacy. Throughout the 1850s and 1860s, the Zunis allied themselves with the Americans, hoping to secure desperately needed guns and ammunition. They provided warriors and provisions for military campaigns and outposts; they aided American surveying expeditions that passed through their lands; and they welcomed the development of better roads and communication with trade centers.[10] At the same time, their own military ventures ensured the frequent performance of the scalp dance in the pueblo's plazas. The bow priesthood, or warrior society, grew in size and stature accordingly.

A Zuni Childhood

The events of these years, especially the violent deaths of relatives and loved ones, made a deep impression on We'wha's generation. The military demands of the times, however, did not alter traditional Zuni attitudes regarding a child like We'wha, even though the inclinations of such a youth veered away from the life of the hunter and warrior. Berdache tendencies merely indicated, in Zuni terms, a different "life road" or *'onnane*. Zuni families adapted their child-rearing practices accordingly. Berdaches enjoyed a certain place in the community, the support of their families, appropriate education and training, adult role models, mythological precedents, and the possibility of achieving prestige and respect.

At birth, of course, there was nothing to distinguish We'wha from any other infant. Before the age of five or six his parents called him simply child, or *cha'le'*, without reference to gender. Children of both sexes wore their hair in the same short style.[11] Eventually, however, boys and girls distinguished themselves in a variety of ways. In We'wha's case, a particular configuration of traits, appearing as early as the age of three or four, revealed his berdache inclinations.

The women of a family were usually the first to notice these traits. Among the Hopi Indians, the Zunis' Pueblo neighbors, women discussed their observations of young family members quite candidly. "My little grandson," one Hopi woman explained in a conversation recorded in 1965, "if he comes up here . . . and the children are playing, he'll say, 'I'll be the grandmother, you be the children.' 'She' tries to take the place of the mother, or be the sister or the grandmother. I hear 'her' so many times like that. . . . He talks like a girl. He'll be cleaning the house, and cooking the meal, and that's all he thinks about—the part of the girl." When asked if this worried her, the Hopi grandmother replied, "No. I don't care. We tease him about it, but he doesn't care either."[12]

We'wha, like the young berdache Parsons observed in 1915, may have adopted female kinship terms and other expressions at an early age. Girls, for example, used the same word to address their younger brothers and sisters (*hanni*) while boys used different terms for each (*suwe* and *'ikina*).

Similarly, at three or four, girls began to wear simple cotton slips while boys wore trousers and shirts. But as Parsons and Dissette observed, young berdaches could find ways to distinguish themselves even at this age. We'wha might have worn a much longer shirt than other boys and instead of tucking it into his trousers, left it hanging out like a short skirt, or, like Kwiwishdi, he might have initially donned a single article of women's clothing at first, such as the *bidonne*, which was worn over the shoulders. And instead of playing with other boys, he likely preferred the company and pastimes of girls.[13]

Zuni children enjoyed the run of the great multistoried pueblo. They could chase each other across roof tops, clamber up and down ladders, and scamper through alleys and covered passages. They ran freely in and out of neighbors' houses as well as their own. Boys armed with toy bows and arrows persecuted the village dogs and pigs—their shrieks of delight and howls of pain ringing against the clear sky above—while girls played "bear at the spring," squealing in mock terror when the "bear" chased away the thirsty maidens.[14]

In springtime, hundreds of villagers might file out to the plains west of the pueblo for communal rabbit hunts and game drives. In the summer, children splashed about in the Zuni river and rolled in the sand hills south of the pueblo. Sneaking out to the orchards at the foot of Corn Mountain, they stole peaches left to dry on the rocks above the fields—although their elders threatened dire punishment and the revenge of ogres, cannibals, and Navajos. Boys practiced hunting skills on prairie dogs, rabbits, and birds and learned the strenuous kick-stick races of the men. Girls played with dolls made of baked clay or carved from cottonwood roots. In the fall, there were the endless activities of harvest time—feasts of corn roasted in pits dug in the fields, melons fresh from the vines, and

dances to celebrate the bounty. In the winter, the Zunis trekked to nearby frozen ponds to cavort on the ice. Long nights were passed in the telling of tales and stories to entranced audiences of young and old.[15]

Throughout the year, the never-ending cycle of ceremonial activities incorporated special features for children. In the fall, the Koyemshi clowns arrived with bundles of toys and treats. Cushing relates a typical occasion:

> Toward evening, when all the spectators are gathered in full force, the clowns take up their burdens of toys, and go searching cautiously and grotesquely amid the children as though afraid of the person they sought. When one of them finds the object of his search, he stares, wiggles, cuts capers, and dodges about, approaching nearer and nearer the wondering child and extending the toy he has selected. Finally, the half-frightened little one is induced by its mother to reach for the treasure; as it clutches the proffered gift, the clown suddenly straightens up and becomes grave, and delivers a long, loud-toned harangue. If the toy he has just handed be a bow and arrows, it is given to a boy; if a doll, to either a very little boy, or a girl.[16]

These dolls were carved versions of kachinas and served to introduce children to the elaborate lore of that cult. Kachinas were central in the imaginative and emotional lives of children.[17]

Children shared the interest of their elders in the more dramatic aspects of Zuni religion. According to Bunzel, "They are keen observers of dances, they know songs, and give accurate and lively accounts of ceremonies which they attend; they are interested in sacerdotal gossip; and they orient their activities about great religious festivals."[18] Visits from certain kachinas were anticipated with much excitement. The Kan'a:kwe, for example, appeared only once every four years. In this ceremony, We'wha saw the mysterious berdache kachina, Kolhamana, a role he would one day perform.

As girls got older, they looked after their smaller brothers and sisters, carrying them about on their backs in blankets. They helped their mothers grind corn in work parties of female relatives, enlivened with gossip and song. At the same time, their brothers might be running wildly about the pueblo in gangs, waving long sticks with flaming balls of cotton or wool stuck on the ends. When slightly older, boys organized impromptu dances and were sometimes joined by girls.[19]

Stevenson describes the scene in a Zuni household on a typical evening:

> The young mothers would be seen caring for their infants, or perhaps the fathers would be fondling them, for the Zuñi men are very devoted to their children, especially the babies. The grandmother would have one of the younger children in her lap, with perhaps the head of another resting against her shoulder, while the rest would be sitting near or busying themselves about household matters. When a story was told by the grandfather or some younger member of the group, intense interest would be depicted on the faces of all old enough to appreciate the recital.[20]

Sleeping in a single large room with other family members, Zuni children became aware at an early age of adult sexual behavior. Boys and girls might engage in sex play as early as the age of six or seven. Although adolescent homosexuality has not been recorded at Zuni, there are reports of this behavior among male and female Hopis. No doubt, sexual experimentation took this form at Zuni, too. Parents discussed sexual matters freely with their children, and few young Zunis entered marriage without both knowledge and experience in this area.[21]

The most striking feature of Zuni child-rearing, as most anthropologists have noted, was the relative absence of corporal punishment and the emphasis, instead, on the use of reasoning. Parents, indeed all adults in the household, were sources of unconditional nurturing and support. At the same time, verbal admonishment, exhortation, criticism, and lengthy moral lectures were given freely, along with the threat of shame. The greatest shame was to have a personal shortcoming or error made public. As the anthropologist Li An-Che noted, "All the members of the family besides the parents cooperate to see that the child behaves well. In fact, any member of the community who happens to pass by will say something to correct some misbehavior of a child."[22] Scolded, a child might run away to the house of a relative, but faced with the united front of adults would, sooner or later, submit to their will. At the same time, children benefited from contact with numerous adult role models, male and female, and received training in diverse relationships.[23]

In the case of the occasionally incorrigible child, the Zunis had an extreme recourse in the form of scare kachinas. Given the somewhat fiery temper he became known for as an adult, young We'wha may have once been visited by 'Adoshle or Su:ke. Wearing frightful masks with fangs, bulging eyes, and stringy hair flying in every direction, these terrifying kachinas could appear at any time, at the request of parents or elders. Parsons has described one such visit:

> In a slow, high-pitched voice, loud enough to be heard all over the village, all [kachinas] proceed to berate and lecture the terrified and often wailing children. The children ... are terribly frightened and even the older children may be upset. "You must not mock your parents," all are instructed, "you must mind your mother." "You must not soil the floor after it has been swept up." A boy is told he must learn to look after the horses, a girl that she must look after the baby, she must learn to cook and to grind. And then the "old woman" may catch the little girl's ankles in her crook and drag her over to the grinding stone, pretending to be about to grind her up. Throwing his hair back from over his mask with his

knife, the a'Doshle himself may threaten to cut off the children's ear. . . . If it is cleaning his face a boy has neglected, the ko'yemshi may take him down to the river and, cutting a hole in the ice, wash his face for him or, if so minded, souse him altogether that he may not forget in the future to wash his face early every morning in the river as all well-behaved Zuñi lads are expected to do.[24]

The result of these practices, as Cushing observed, was the development of "admirable self-control" on the part of children. "These dear little brown-eyed, smooth-skinned mites," he wrote, "who tagged me or hung around me by the dozens, though veritable children, dirty and, when at play, noisy to the last degree, were so quaintly old-fashioned in behavior whenever I talked to them or particularly noticed them, and were so gentle to one another and especially to their elders withal, that I came to love them as I have loved no other children on earth."[25] Zuni children learned to conform to ideals of nonaggressive, mild, and cooperative behavior—to be *k'okshi*—and to avoid appearing sulky, greedy, uncooperative, impolite, or lazy, behaviors that were considered "childish." The young boy who delivered the appropriate formal speech upon a visit, the brother and sister who never fought, the youngster who never lost his temper—these were the children who received praise from adults.[26]

A key element of child-rearing, especially for boys, was the religious instruction they received to prepare them for membership in the kachina society. This process started with an initiation held every four years in which all Zuni boys participated. For We'wha, it marked the beginning of his religious career. The ceremony began with the visit of Kaklo in the company of the Koyemshi clowns. A blind bard like Homer, Kaklo was responsible for reciting the epic Zuni origin myth. He was a bustling, officious, and self-important figure, who insisted that the smallest

Koyemshi carry him on his back into the village. When the entourage reached the river, the Koyemshi ignored the bridge and waded into the water, invariable dropping Kaklo in the mud and soiling his beautiful white robes. Through it all, he simply chanted his name, "Kaklo, Kaklo, Kaklo." He repeated his "talk of the first beginning" in each of the six kivas, and each telling took three or more hours. Filled with archaic language and monotonously chanted, few in the audience could follow Kaklo's esoteric version of the origin narrative. Nonetheless, should any of the boys nod or fall asleep, Kaklo struck them roundly on the head with a stuffed duck he carried with him.

Eight days afterward, a score or more kachinas entered the village from the west, led by the great horned serpent Kolo:wisi. These rites culminated in the whipping of the boys in the main plaza. With stiff wands of yucca, the kachinas struck each boy across the back four times. Although covered with several layers of blankets, the blows had their effect. Boys were urged to be brave, but many cried out.[27]

We'wha no doubt was fascinated by these proceedings. He was initiated into the *chuba:kwe kiwitsinne* or south kiva, the kiva of the husband of the midwife who had assisted at his birth.[28] After this, his religious training began in earnest, including memorization of the numerous songs, prayers, myths, and lore of the kachinas, an activity in which We'wha proved especially skilled. Beginning in his teens, he was allowed to join the masked dances. At first, he would have borrowed a mask, but later, by a combination of purchase and initiation, he obtained his own.[29]

We'wha had been adopted into an important and influential household. His foster father, José Palle, was a rain priest. Stevenson described the family as the "richest in Zuñi."[30] They occupied several large rooms in the northwestern corner of the main pueblo block. The apartment was the site not only of Palle's priestly activities, but also the ceremonial chamber of the *lhewe:kwe* or Sword People, an important medicine order.[31] These connections gave We'wha special opportunities to acquire ceremonial knowledge.

Although he received male religious training, once We'wha's berdache orientation was recognized his vocational training came under the direction of female relatives. We'wha learned all the skills necessary for a career in domestic and crafts work. Foremost among them was the endless labor of grinding and preparing corn, the basic ingredient for myriad Zuni dishes: from simple parched kernels and baked ears to gruels, dumplings, mushes, puddings, breads, and the delicate *hewe'* or paper breads, made by pouring thin batters of yellow, blue, red, white, all-color or black corn onto heated stone slabs.[32]

Assisting the women of his household, We'wha daily set out piles of *hewe'* and steaming bowls of mutton stew for an appreciative family. He learned to keep the house neat, according to fastidious Zuni standards, by spraying water on the dirt floor and sweeping it several times a day. In certain chores performed by women— fetching wood, carrying water from the well in jugs balanced on the head, plastering the walls of houses, threshing wheat, winnowing grain and beans, and tending the waffle gardens along the banks of the river—We'wha's strength and endurance was especially advantageous.

We'wha probably received his first instruction in ceramics from a kinswoman with a reputation for skill in the art. Girls were often given lumps of clay to play with. Interest and promise were quickly rewarded. From this followed years of detailed instruction in the procedures involved in pottery-making—from obtaining clay at sites that were often family secrets, to the technique of forming vessels out of coils and painstakingly smoothing

their surfaces, firing them beneath carefully stacked chips of sheep manure, and finally, painting their exteriors in elaborate geometric patterns. To master this art, We'wha had to learn more than technical skills. In decorating their ceramics, Zuni women drew on an extensive knowledge of religious symbols. Indeed, the entire process of pottery-making was surrounded with ritual. The Zunis considered clay to be the "flesh" of Mother Earth. Pots, like humans, were "made beings." Before firing, they were fed wafer bread. Prayers beseeched the success of the endeavor, and sympathetic magic warded off ill fortune. Dreams were an important source of designs for many potters.[33]

We'wha also acquired skills in weaving, learning the complex operation of both the large upright loom for making blankets and the smaller, horizontal loom used for weaving belts and sashes. This was the "classic period" of Pueblo textiles (1848–1880), when distinctive Zuni styles for shoulder blankets, mantas, kilts, breech-cloths, and embroidery flourished. At the same time, Pueblo weavers (and their Navajo counterparts) were also learning to use the new materials brought by American railroads and traders. Wool replaced native cotton (beginning in the Spanish period), and commercial yarns and dyes became common. Photographs of We'wha taken in 1886 show him weaving a traditional stripe design typical of this period.[34]

When We'wha was in his teens, the Americans achieved a military victory against the Navajos that ushered in a new era for the Zunis. In 1864, as a result of Kit Carson's brutal "slash and burn" campaign, the Americans rounded up tens of thousands of Navajos and marched them to a bleak reservation in central New Mexico where they remained for four years. After the Long Walk, as the Navajos referred to the ordeal, intertribal conflict between the Zunis and their neighbors decreased.

The Zunis began to enjoy a new freedom of movement that allowed them to expand their economic and cultural horizons. The old, multistoried pueblo had been designed for defense, not convenience. The Zunis now undertook an ambitious building program. They added doors and windows to ground-floor rooms and moved down from the upper levels of the complex.[35] In 1881, when Lt. John G. Bourke visited Zuni, he found the refurbished pueblo bustling with activity. "The noises in the village are fearful; imagine a congregation of jackasses, quarrelsome dogs, and chickens, bleating lambs & kids, shrill voiced eagles, gobbling turkeys, screaming children and women mourning for two dead relatives. . . . As with the turmoil, so with the effluvia; the place is never policed and I am not going one jot beyond the limits of strict verity when I characterize Zuni as a Babel of noise and a Cologne of stinks."[36]

The Zunis took advantage of the Navajo removal to reoccupy the farming villages at Nutria and Pescado east of the main village. In the last half of the nineteenth century, most cultivation was carried out at these areas and at Ojo Caliente, fifteen miles to the southwest. Zuni families established fields at these sites and constructed summer homes so that they could spend the growing season tending their crops. During these months, the main pueblo was nearly empty.[37] We'wha's family farmed at Doya, or Nutria, fifteen miles northeast at the edge of the Zuni Mountains.[38] Fort Wingate was less than twenty miles to the north, and detachments of troops often passed by or camped in the vicinity. The Zunis constructed an elaborate irrigation system at Nutria, using ditches and hollowed logs to deliver spring water to earth-walled plots of wheat. Ditches and crops required attention throughout the summer, and young people were kept busy with many chores. We'wha may have actually worked in the fields with other boys and men. Cushing's census lists one of We'wha's occupations as "farmer"—a male role at Zuni.

By the late 1870s, as he approached the age of thirty, We'wha enjoyed a secure place within his family and his tribe. Stevenson's report provides occasional glimpses of life in We'wha's adopted family—for example. her description of a typical scene during the period of the winter solstice, when "the elder daughter has her hair dressed by the adopted son, who wears feminine dress."[39] As his foster mother got older, We'wha's domestic responsibilities increased. With his mother's eldest daughter, he helped manage household affairs. While this woman would eventually inherit the house, We'wha enjoyed a sister's right (and obligation) to remain a member of the household for the rest of his life.

A Skirt for We'wha

Although the Zunis had forged a military alliance with the Americans, they remained culturally and socially isolated until the 1870s. Their ceremonial life flourished while they cultivated their fields and crafted goods according to the time-honored technologies of the prehistoric Anasazi. Their farms produced regular surpluses (which they sold to nearby military posts) without metal plows, draft animals, or grinding mills.[40] No Zuni could speak English; only a few knew Spanish. The average Zuni had never met an American face to face. Only one or two had ever traveled as far as the nearest white settlement. Many had not even strayed as far as Ojo Caliente.

But in the 1870s, the geographic, political, and cultural barriers that had guarded the Zunis for centuries came crashing down. The lessening of hostilities with the Navajos opened the way for a new invasion. Anglo and Hispanic herders and ranchers began to encroach on their lands; and traders, Indian agents, missionaries, teachers, and anthropologists began to interfere in their social life. In this onslaught of change, Zuni elders feared for the future of their tribe. "When the trains keep coming and the white people are here, there will be no happiness," Lina Zuni's grandfather told her. "They will build their towns close to you. They will build their houses." As Lina recalled, "We were afraid of the trains and the railroads. We cried."[41]

Formal relations between the Office of Indian Affairs and the Zunis were inaugurated in 1870, when a special agent visited the pueblo. The first American traders licensed to do business at Zuni arrived the following year.[42] In 1877, two more institutions of American culture appeared at Zuni, the school and the church, combined in the form of a Presbyterian mission. These Protestant missionaries were the first Anglos to live at the pueblo. In the next decade, they would be joined by many others. Although these various "agents of assimilation" did not always act in concert, they shared a common philosophy: Indians must be absorbed into American society. They brought the promise of a better life, but they also demanded drastic changes. In the years to come, We'wha would play a prominent role in several key episodes of this confrontation.

The Presbyterian mission to Zuni had its origins in the so-called Peace Policy of the Grant administration. A key element of this policy was the role granted to Christian churches. They were invited to nominate Christians for positions as Indian agents, and they were encouraged to expand missionary efforts. Indian reservations were assigned to various denominations, and Congress appropriated funds to support schools operated by the churches. This policy blurred the separation of church and state, but American churches and church leaders nonetheless dominated Indian affairs until the end of the century.[43]

Although the Presbyterians had accepted responsibility for several Southwest tribes,

they singled out the Zunis because of a threat as alarming to them as paganism itself. In April 1876, two Mormon missionaries had visited Zuni and performed over one hundred baptisms. The following year, a Mormon missionary colony was founded at Ramah, a few miles east of the Zuni village of Pescado. The Pueblo Indian agent, a devout Presbyterian, suspected that the Mormons were as interested in Zuni lands as they were in Zuni souls. He offered the Presbyterian Board of Home Missions six hundred dollars as an annual salary for a missionary-teacher.[44] Praying "that the Holy Spirit may so accompany our mission schools among that people, that they will cut down their sacred groves, and find the blessing of the Gentiles," the Presbyterians accepted the government's offer.[45] Thus began the first Protestant mission to the People of the Middle Place, bringing with it Christianity's double-edged sword of indoctrination to its own beliefs and eradication of the native ones.

Presbyterian minister and medical doctor Taylor F. Ealy, his wife, two daughters, and an assistant teacher arrived on October 12, 1878, to take over the day school founded the previous year. "We arrived here all very well . . .," Ealy reported, "just at the closing exercises of a Devil's Dance. The noise was hideous."[46] Equally disappointing, all of the previous year's students had died in a smallpox epidemic.[47] The next two and a half years at Zuni proved difficult and trying for the Ealy family. In the end, their religious impact was negligible. As the editor of the Ealy journals concluded, the missionaries faced "a frustrating form of passive resistance—the Indians largely ignored the Ealys' well-meaning overtures." Perhaps some of the reverend's technological innovations, like a windmill to grind corn and two steel plows, were more appreciated.[48]

The Ealys rented rooms in the main pueblo and began teaching with only six broken-down desks and few supplies. Attendance fluctuated from two to forty pupils. The Ealys did not speak Zuni, and the Zunis did not speak English. Nonetheless, they tried to teach basic reading and writing skills, and, in the case of female students, housekeeping and sewing.[49] Other aspects of the Ealys' missionizing program targeted basic features of Zuni society, including the traditional division of labor between women and men. Mrs. Ealy wrote that "all the difficult labor, such as grinding the wheat and corn, carrying the water, etc., is done by the women, while the men do the sewing and knitting," and she concluded, "I wish to reverse their labors." When Reverend Ealy installed a windmill for grinding corn, he found the women willing to take advantage of it, but, he observed, "I do think the Indian men of Zuñi are afraid I will take away one of the drudges of the women."[50] Although these early attempts to alter gender roles at Zuni had little impact, they foreshadowed future, more serious efforts by missionaries, teachers, and government agents.

The Ealys' dreary existence at Zuni was greatly enlivened on September 19, 1879, with the arrival of the Bureau of Ethnology expedition. James Stevenson set up headquarters in two borrowed rooms in the mission, and, in Cushing's words, "day after day, assisted by his enthusiastic wife, gathered in treasures, ancient and modern, of Indian art and industry." On October 7, John Hillers took a photograph of the Ealy school. The pupils crouched in front of an adobe building with teacher Jennie Hammaker standing to one side of them and the Reverend Ealy to the other. The most striking figure, however, appears in the middle of the photograph, dressed like a Zuni woman, but taller than any of the other Zunis in the picture, and almost as tall as Reverend Ealy himself. This is the earliest surviving photograph of the celebrated Zuni berdache, We'wha.[51]

We do not know exactly when or how We'wha came to be associated with the Ealys, but it appears that he was already acquainted with them when the 1879 expedition arrived. The surviving portions of Mrs. Ealy's diary include two references to We'wha. In her entry for January 29, 1881, Mrs. Ealy wrote, "We made in all this week five garments; a skirt and two basques for We-Wa, a dress for Grace [a Zuni], a dress and skirt for her sister, besides one for which they found the calico." On January 31 she noted that "Jennie, We-Wa and I washed." Mrs. Ealy's daughter Ruth remembered We'wha as a "Zuni girl" who helped with housework.[52]

No doubt Mrs. Ealy, with two young daughters to look after as well as her teaching responsibilities, needed help with housework and child care. Reverend Ealy noted that when his family had arrived at Zuni, girls and women were among the first to call on them. Perhaps We'wha was among them. In any case, it is likely that We'wha received some kind of payment for his work, probably in the form of goods, like the dresses Mrs. Ealy referred to. He also may have begun to learn some English.[53] According to Zuni tradition, We'wha's role involved even more. Anthropologist John Adair was told that We'wha also served as "matron" at the mission school. Matrons were familiar figures in government Indian schools. They supervised dormitories, kitchens, and laundries; instructed girls in domestic work; and chaperoned small children. Often, they visited homes to teach Indian women Western methods of housekeeping child care, and hygiene. We'wha may have earned this title simply by watching the children and assisting Mrs. Ealy and Jennie Hammaker in the classroom.[54]

We'wha soon discovered that his contacts with outsiders, like the Ealys, could entail drawbacks as well as benefits. In her report, Stevenson includes an account by a Zuni who was attacked by a witch resentful of the narrator's association with the missionary's wife. Anthropologist Dennis Tedlock explains the Zuni concept of witchcraft: "Some people, never one's own kin, are *a:halhikwi*, 'witches,' [sg. *halhikwi*] men and women who get sick at heart when someone has better fortune than they do, or when someone insults or even merely slights them. A witch will wish and plot the death of a person who makes him feel sick, or if that person is too strong, he will hurt him indirectly by attacking someone close to him."[55] Although Stevenson identifies the narrator simply as "a prominent member of the Badger clan," the details of the account fit We'wha:

> I spent some days with the missionary's wife. She gave me a good bed to sleep in and blankets to keep me warm. She was very kind to me, and I was happy in her house, but after a time I grew very ill and had to return to my mother's home. A shaman was sent for and, through the power of the Beast Gods, he was enabled to discover the cause of my illness by placing pinches of sacred meal upon me, which opened to him the windows of my body. He discovered the disease and declared that I had been bewitched, and commanded the material which had been thrust into my body to come forth. He said he saw within me bits of the blankets I had slept between during my stay in the missionary's house, and bits of yarn and calico which the missionary's wife had given me. . . . I do not know, but I think it was the old one-eyed woman who bewitched me. She was jealous of the good times I had at the mission.[56]

As a result of this incident, We'wha made a pledge to join the medicine society of the shaman who had cured him. This was the *beshatsilo:kwe*, or Bedbug People, a division of the Little Fire society. The Bedbug People treated burns, ulcers, cancers, and parasites. In their public rites they performed feats with fire, dowsing themselves with coals and walking barefoot across beds of fire unharmed.[57] Society membership

provided We'wha with additional opportunities to expand his knowledge of Zuni lore and ceremony.

Whatever the full extent of We'wha's contact with the Ealys, it continued until their departure in June 1881. After this, the government and the Presbyterian church maintained "a token form of joint participation" at Zuni, but the school floundered for the rest of the decade. New teachers wondered what, if anything, previous teachers had accomplished. Not until the arrival of Mary Dissette in 1888 did the mission acquire staff whose zeal for the policy of assimilation would prove a match for the Zunis' stubborn resistance to American ways.[58]

In the meantime, as a result of his presence at the mission, We'wha made new friendships that would survive long past the departure of the Ealys, and these would lead him to experiences and places unseen and unimagined by most Zunis of his generation.

Faithful and Devoted Friend

Not long after her arrival at Zuni in 1879, Matilda Stevenson discovered that the "Zuni girl" who helped Mrs. Ealy with housework was "the most intelligent person in the pueblo." Stevenson may have observed We'wha in the role of "matron" at the mission school, for she wrote that his "strong character made his word law among both the men and the women with whom he associated. Though his wrath was dreaded by men as well as women, he was loved by all the children, to whom he was ever kind."[59] Stevenson found We'wha accomplished in Zuni lore and "conspicuous in ceremonials." He was eager to form friendships with outsiders and willing to learn English. This made him an excellent informant. So, while Cushing sought access to information by trying to adapt himself to Zuni ways, Stevenson found a Zuni willing to adapt to her ways, and she cultivated a long-term relationship with him.[60] In fact, the friendship that developed between Stevenson and We'wha grew beyond the roles of anthropologist and informant. Over the course of Stevenson's many return visits to Zuni (in 1881, 1884, 1886, 1891–1892, 1895, and 1896–1897), and during the months that We'wha spent in the Stevenson home in Washington, a genuine friendship emerged between these two remarkable individuals—one of America's first woman anthropologists and Zuni's most famous man-woman.

In one of the few humorous passages in her otherwise sober tome, Stevenson describes the incident that inaugurated her friendship with We'wha. During her stay in 1879, Stevenson decided to introduce soap into the pueblo, and she selected We'wha as her first pupil. Stevenson may not have known that We'wha already had washed clothes with Mrs. Ealy:

> [We'wha] was averse to the work, and at first refused to wash. He looked on in silence for a time while the writer worked. Never having had any experience in that work herself, she soon had most of the water from the tub on the floor and was drenched to the skin. The pupil exclaimed: "You do not understand that which you would teach. You do not understand as much as the missionary's wife; she keeps the water in the tub and does not make a river on the floor. Let me take your place."

After this, We'wha began to wash clothes for members of the expedition. But according to Stevenson, many weeks passed before he would wash and iron without constant urging. "Finally he began to realize that he was accumulating silver dollars from the members of the expedition. Then he declared that he would become a good laundryman and would go to Fort Wingate and wash for the captains' families. This man ultimately became as celebrated as a Chinese laundryman, his own cleanly apparel being his advertising card, and was called upon not only by the officers' families at the garrison, but by the white settlers near and far. Others of the tribe concluded that they, too, would wash their clothes, and consequently a great change for the better took place." Stevenson went on to observe that Zuni men and women each washed their own clothes. "Only a few work for the whites," she concluded, "the men wearing female attire being preferred to the women on account of their strength and endurance."[61] In fact, when Mary Dissette arrived in the pueblo a few years later and requested the tribal council to assign a woman to help her with laundry and housework, they "formally presented" her with the young berdache Kwiwishdi, for there were no women in the village willing to do laundry for pay.[62]

Stevenson's praise for We'wha, in more than one section of her report, contrasts sharply with the style of the detached, objective observer that she affects elsewhere. Of We'wha, Stevenson wrote,

> She was perhaps the tallest person in Zuni; certainly the strongest, both mentally and physically. . . . She had a good memory, not only for the lore of her people, but for all that she heard of the outside world. . . . She possessed an indomitable will and an insatiable thirst for knowledge. Her likes and dislikes were intense. She would risk anything to serve those she loved, but toward those who crossed her path she was vindictive. Though severe she was considered just. . . . Owing to her bright mind and excellent memory, she was called upon by her own clan and also by the clans of her foster mother and father when a long prayer had to be repeated or a grace was to be offered over a feast. In fact she was the chief personage on many occasions. On account of her physical strength all the household work requiring great exertion was left for her, and while she most willingly took the harder work from others of the family, she would not permit idleness; all had to labor or receive an upbraiding from We'wha, and nothing was more dreaded than a scolding from her.[63]

At the same time, We'wha's loyalty to Stevenson was apparent in the extraordinary risks he took to assist her studies. Stevenson describes one of these occasions, during the ceremonies of January 1892:

Although the writer occupied the upper story of the ceremonial house and her door opened upon the roof to which the members resort, on account of the superstitious dread of the powerful medicine of the fraternity, entertained by inmates of the house, great efforts were required to secure photographs on the roof and to enter the ceremonial chamber, in which the writer spent most of the time during the several days' ceremonies. We'wha, a conspicuous character of Zuni, was untiring in her efforts to detain an old father below while the writer secured photographs on the roof, and several times released her when the father had barred the door of her room with heavy stones. The wrath and distress of the old man knew no bounds, and he declared that the writer would bring calamity not only to herself but to all the household.[64]

Remarkably, Stevenson did not discover the "truth" for some years—We'wha was a man. According to Stevenson, his sex was so carefully concealed that she believed him to be a woman "for years."[65] Yet We'wha's maleness hardly seems "concealed" in the several surviving photographs of him. His strong facial features, the musculature in his arms, his hands, his height—how could she have accepted We'wha as a woman? As Triloki Pandey puts it, there was "something opaque" about Matilda Stevenson.[66] This is all the more remarkable when we consider the circumstances of their relationship. Stevenson and her informant worked together closely and for extended periods of time. We'wha even lived with the Stevensons for six months in Washington, D.C., and, according to stories told later, moved about freely in the ladies' dressing rooms. Still, Stevenson continued to believe We'wha was a woman. In her 1904 report,

she stated, "Some declared him to be an hermaphrodite, but the writer gave no credence to the story, and continued to regard We'wha as a woman." Even when Stevenson did discover We'wha's true sex, she wrote, "As the writer could never think of her faithful and devoted friend in any other light, she will continue to use the feminine gender when referring to We'wha." (In fact, as noted earlier, Stevenson used both male and female pronouns when referring to We'wha and other berdaches.)[67]

The exact nature of the relationship between Stevenson and We'wha has been the subject of speculation for many years. John Adair considered the possibility that We'wha and Stevenson were having an affair. Nancy Lurie more realistically concluded that Stevenson's "deep affection and admiration for this remarkable person were entirely that of a close and unquestioning friendship between any two women." Lurie also observed that "Mrs. Stevenson's forthright acceptance of Wé-wha illustrates a degree of scientific and personal sophistication noteworthy for her time and her sex." Indeed, if Stevenson believed We'wha was a woman, she took the berdache to be a woman of her own kind—intelligent, independent, self-confident—an equal worthy of introduction to her own social world in the East.[68]

There is no record of exactly when Stevenson discovered the "truth" about We'wha and under what circumstances. After 1886, Stevenson did not visit Zuni again until 1891 and then again in 1896, the year We'wha died. She probably learned the facts about We'wha on one of these two visits, perhaps not until she observed the preparation of his body for burial.

The irony is that We'wha's true sex was no secret among the Zunis and other white visitors—and this is revealing of Stevenson's relations with the tribe in general. George Wharton James, another visitor at Zuni in the 1890s, wrote that "it was the comments of her own friends, Zunis, that first made me 'wise' to the situation as to her sex."[69] Stevenson, however, was not the only non-Indian to be confused by the role and status of berdaches like We'wha. Despite the obvious signs that suggested otherwise, many Anglos would follow Stevenson in assuming that We'wha was a woman.

Potter and Weaver

Collection of artifacts was a major goal of the expedition, and before leaving to visit the Hopi villages in early October 1879, Mrs. Stevenson commissioned We'wha to make pots that would eventually end up in the National Museum in Washington. Cushing, who had stayed behind in Zuni, wrote to James Stevenson: "The articles which you ordered from We We are not even begun. I have called on her twice relative to them since your departure. . . . I desire you to say to Mrs. Stevenson that I have done every thing I could to get We We at the work. She always says 'Si, Si We-no [*bueno*],'[70] but when we go the next time says she has not begun them, and repeats the same. Today she informed Miss Hamakin [Hammaker] it was too cold to begin."[71]

Judging from Matilda Stevenson's accounts, We'wha was an accomplished potter who shared the deeply religious attitude of Zuni women toward this art. During one of their return visits to Zuni, the Stevensons accompanied We'wha when he collected clay on Corn Mountain. We'wha followed religious protocols all along the way:

> On passing a stone heap she picked up a small stone in her left hand, and spitting upon it, carried the hand around her head and threw the stone over one shoulder upon the stone heap in order that her strength might not go from her when carrying the heavy load down the mesa. She then visited the shrine at the base of the Mother Rock and tearing off a bit of her blanket deposited it in one of the tiny pits in the rock as an offering to the mother rock. When she drew near to the clay bed she indicated to Mr. Stevenson that he must remain behind, as men never approached the spot. Proceeding a short distance the party reached a point where We'wha requested the writer to remain perfectly quiet and not talk, saying. "Should we talk, my pottery would crack in the baking, and unless I pray constantly the clay will not appear to me." She applied the hoe vigorously to the hard soil, all the while murmuring prayers to Mother Earth. Nine-tenths of the clay was rejected, every lump being tested between the fingers as to its texture. After gathering about 150 pounds in a blanket, which she carried on her back, with the ends of the blanket tied around her forehead, We'wha descended the steep mesa, apparently unconscious of the weight.[72]

We know about We'wha's skills in weaving primarily through a series of documentary photographs taken during his visit to Washington and the comments of George Wharton James. James traveled to Zuni in the 1890s and appears to have been a guest in We'wha's house. "On my various visits to Zuni," he wrote, "she always befriended me.[73] In 1920, he published an account and photographs of We'wha in a New Mexico travelogue:

> She was a remarkable woman, a fine blanket and sash maker, an excellent cook, and adept in all the work of her sex, and yet strange to say, she was a man. There never has been, as yet, any satisfactory explanation given, as far as I know, of the peculiar custom followed by the Pueblos of having one or two men in each tribe, who foreswear their manhood and who dress as, act like, and seemingly live the life of, women. We'wha was one of these. . . .
>
> She seldom sang at her grinding, but at a word from her, I have heard as many as a half hundred voices all raised at once in one wonderful unison of melody, from all parts of the pueblo as the women ground their corn and sang simultaneously.[74]

In a manuscript now at the Southwest Museum, he adds:

> Wewa was the attendant at a certain shrine, and was quite a noted character. As will be seen from her picture she was of masculine build and had far more of the man in her character than the woman. Yet she excelled all other of the Zuni women in the exercise of her skill in blanket and pottery making. Her blanketry was noted far and wide, and her pottery fetched twice the price of that of any other maker. . . . Her home in Zuni was full of evidences of her skill. At the time I photographed her she was busy grinding corn meal in one of the rooms of her commodious house, and all around upon the floor were placed baskets and bowls full of vegetables and fruit which she was preparing for winter use.[75]

James was a self-styled expert on American Indian weaving, publishing one of the first books on the subject. Regarding We'wha he wrote, "She was an expert weaver, and her 'pole of soft stuff' was laden with the work of her loom—blankets and dresses exquisitely woven, and with a delicate perception of colour-values that delighted the eye of the connoisseur. Her sashes, too, were the finest I ever saw, and proud indeed is that collector who can boast of one of her weave among his valued treasures."[76]

When Stevenson met We'wha in 1879, the Zuni berdache had just turned thirty. He had survived a turbulent childhood that included tragedy and danger as well as adventure. Raised according to the Zuni understanding of berdaches, he had been trained in domestic skills and the crafts of pottery and weaving. The accounts of Stevenson and James show him to have been especially productive and accomplished in these arts. We'wha was also known for his command of Zuni religious knowledge and practice, having mastered the dual skills of letter-perfect memorization required for learning esoteric material and extemporaneous improvisation employed in relating tales and stories.

We'wha had developed one other prominent characteristic—a combination of self-confidence and innate curiosity that led him to make friends among the Anglos who had begun to visit and live in the village—a trait that would earn him a reputation as a "conspicuous character of Zuni."[77] In 1886, this self-assurance served him well in an adventure that unfolded for him through one of these friends, Matilda Coxe Stevenson.

NOTES

1. Stevenson, "Zuñi Indians," 20, 310, 380; George W. James, "Zuñi and 2 Modern Witchcraft Trails" (typescript, c. 1899), folder 210, carton 8, GWJC; Parsons, *Notes on Zuñi*, 253; Parsons, "Zuñi La'mana," 523; Bunker, *Other Men's Skies*, 99–100. Aside from Bunker's statement, there is no evidence that We'wha formally participated in Zuni political life. Smith and Roberts reported that lhamanas, like women, were not allowed to speak at the public meetings sometimes held in the large plaza (*Zuni Law*, 114). according to Zuni tradition, however, We'wha served as an interpreter for the tribe on official occasions, and this required that he take an oath of office.
2. This date is based on Cushing's estimate of We'wha's age in "Nominal and Numerical Census," ms. 3915, National Anthropological Archives.
3. Bunzel, *Zuni Texts*, 78.
4. Ferguson and Hart, *Zuni Atlas*, 63.
5. McNitt, *Navaho Expedition*, 113, 114.
6. Hart, "Brief History," 23; Stevenson, "Zuñi Indians," 37, 311; Foreman, *Pathfinder in the Southwest*, 141.

7. Stevenson, "Zuñi Indians," 37–38. On kinship terms, see Ladd, "Zuni Social and Political Organization."

8. Ferguson and Hart, *Zuni Atlas*, 60; Abel, *Official Correspondence of James S. Calhoun*, 260, 263, 274; E. Curtis, "Zuñi," 111–112.

9. Bieber, *Marching with the Army of the West*, 206–207; Ferguson and Mills, "Settlement and Growth," 249–250; Ten Broeck, "Manners and Customs," 80.

10. Hart, "Brief History."

11. Ladd, "Zuni Social and Political Organization," 484; Parsons, "Waiyautitsa," 159.

12. Duberman, *About Time*, 219.

13. Parsons, "Zuñi La'mana," 521–522.

14. Cushing, *Zuñi*, 58; Parsons, "Waiyautitsa," 162–163.

15. Stevenson "Zuñi Indians," 354; Leighton and Adair, *People of the Middle Place*, 67; Benedict, *Zuñi Mythology* 1:12.

16. Cushing, *Zuñi Breadstuff*, 605.

17. Young, *Signs from the Ancestors*, 201. See also Sekaquaptewa, "Hopi Indian Ceremonies," 38.

18. Bunzel, "Introduction to Zuñi Ceremonialism," 541–542.

19. Stevenson, "Zuñi Indians," 293–294; Cushing, "Primitive Motherhood," 41.

20. Stevenson, "Zuñi Indians," 293.

21. Leighton and Adair, *People of the Middle Place*, 67; Cushing, "Primitive Motherhood," 41. On sexual experimentation among Hopi children, see Eggan, "General Problem of Hopi Adjustment," 368; Talayesva, *Sun Chief*, 103.

22. Li An-che, "Zuñi," 70.

23. Goldman, "Zuni Indians," 339; Leighton and Adair, *People of the Middle Place*, 71–72; Whiting et al., "Learning of Values," 95; Roberts, "Zuni," 304.

24. Parsons, "Zuñi A'doshle and Suuke," 343–344.

25. Cushing, *Zuñi Breadstuff*, 573; Cushing, "Primitive Motherhood," 37–38.

26. Goldman, "Zuni Indians," 338–340; Whiting et al., "Learning of Values," 108–109.

27. See Bunzel, "Zuñi Katcinas," 975–998; Stevenson, "Zuñi Indians," 102–107.

28. Cushing "Nominal and Numerical Census," ms. 3915, National Anthropological Archives.

29. Stevenson refers to this mask as being among the personal effects buried after We'wha's death ("Zuñi Indians," 313).

30. Ibid., 354.

31. Ibid., 480, 483. In 1917, Kroeber published a map of the village, indicating current and previous locations of various religious groups as well as the clan identification of each household. He places the *lhewe:kwe* chamber in the northwestern corner of the pueblo (see *Zuñi Kin and Clan*, Map 1, "1916 Zuñi House and Clans" and Map 8, "Religious Map of Zuñi"). The same rooms can be located on Mindeleffs 1891 map (in Ferguson and Hart, *Zuni Atlas*, Map 27).

32. See Cushing's analysis of Zuni cuisine in *Zuñi Breadstuff*, 289–343.

33. Hardin, *Gifts of Mother Earth*, 11; Cushing, *Zuñi Breadstuff*, 310–316; Bunzel, *Pueblo Potter*, 54.

34. See Kent, *Pueblo Indian Textiles*, 12–14.

35. Ferguson and Mills, "Settlement and Growth," 247, 252.

36. Bloom, "Bourke on the Southwest," 200.

37. Vogt, "Intercultural Relations," 51–52.

38. Cushing, "Nominal and Numerical Census," ms. 3915, National Anthropological Archives.

39. Stevenson, "Zuñi Indians," 123.

40. Eaton, "Description," 221.

41. Bunzel, *Zuni Texts*, 80.

42. Crampton, *Zunis of Cibola*, 115–16; McNitt, *Indian Traders*, 239.

43. On the Indian policy of this period, see Dale, *Indians of the Southwest*; Fritz, *Movement for Indian Assimilation*; Mardock, *Reformers and the American Indian*.

44. Peterson, *Take Up Your Mission*, 204–207; Vogt, "Intercultural Relations," 55; Bender, *Missionaries, Outlaws, and Indians*, 80.

45. Sheldon Jackson, in Bender, *Missionaries, Outlaws, and Indians*, 83.

46. Ibid., 84. Missionary Andrew Vanderwagen was similarly "appalled" by the Sha'lako dances he witnessed during his first visit to Zuni (Kuipers, *Zuni Also Prays*, 110).

47. Pandey, "Factionalism," 59; Bender, *Missionaries, Outlaws, and Indians*, 81.

48. Bender, *Missionaries, Outlaws and Indians*, 163, 126.

49. Ibid., 90, 96, 198.

50. Ibid., 105, 138.

51. Cushing, *Zuñi*, 59; Bender, *Missionaries, Outlaws and Indians*, 121, 124. I am indebted to Danella Moneta of the Southwest Museum for pointing out We'wha in this photograph (personal communication, 4 April 1985).

52. Bender, *Missionaries, Outlaws, and Indians*, 153,214. Basques were close-fitting bodices.

53. Ibid., 87. According to Dissette, We'wha and Nick Dumaka were the only Zunis who could speak any English when she arrived in 1888 (Dissette to Willard, 3 March 1924, IC, IRAP).

54. John Adair, personal communication, 29 September 1986; U.S. Office of Indian Affairs, *Rules*, 12–13; Dale, *Indians of the Southwest*, 166.

55. D. Tedlock, "American Indian View of Death," 257.

56. Stevenson, "Zuñi Indians," 394. It is interesting to note that We'wha speaks of the missionary's house as if it belonged to his wife, which would be a correct assumption from a Zuni point of view.

57. Triloki Pandey, personal communication, 17 April 1985; Parsons, "Zuñi La'mana," 528; Cushing, *Zuñi*, 96. Cushing does not list a medicine society for We'wha in his census. However, individuals often postponed formal initiation for years, until they could afford the expense of the necessary feasts and gifts.

58. Bender, *Missionaries, Outlaws, and Indians*, 164–165. For the date of Dissette's arrival at Zuni, see Dissette to Willard, 3 March 1924, IC, IRAP (cf. Crampton, *Zunis of Cibola*, 150–151.

59. Stevenson, "Zuñi Indians," 37.

60. Ibid.; Pandey 1972, "Anthropologists at Zuni," 327. Washington Matthews ridiculed James Stevenson's claim that Matilda Stevenson had learned both Zuni and Spanish. "The Indians are just unbosoming themselves to her," he wrote sarcastically to Cushing (Hinsley, *Savages and Scientists*, 199). His doubts about Mrs. Stevenson's language skills were well founded, as evidenced by her confusion of the term *lhamana* and the name of the mythical berdache kachina, Kolhamana—that is, "ko'thlama."

61. Stevenson, "Zuñi Indians," 380.

62. Dissette to Willard, 3 March 1924, IC, IRAP.

63. Stevenson, "Zuñi Indians," 310–311.

64. Ibid., 463.

65. Ibid., 310.

66. Triloki Pandey, personal communication, 17 April 1985.

67. Stevenson, "Zuñi Indians," 310. Stevenson was no doubt referring to Cushing who identified We'wha as an hermaphrodite in his 1881 census. Despite her disclaimer, Stevenson also may have thought, at least for a time, that We'wha was an hermaphrodite. According to Dissette, "Mrs. S. tried to make me believe that Way-weh was an 'Hermaphrodite' but I think she knew better" (Dissette to Willard, 3 March 1924, IC, IRAP).

68. John Adair, personal communication, 29 September 1986, Lurie, "Women in Early American Anthropology," 57. Stevenson's relationship with Clara True was formed on much the same basis (see Chapter 1, note 10).

69. G. James, *New Mexico*, 63–64.

70. This last word is partially illegible, but elsewhere Cushing explained that the Zunis pronounced the Spanish *bueno* as "we-no" (*Zuñi* 59). This suggests that We'wha could speak at least rudimentary Spanish.

71. Cushing to J. Stevenson, 15 October 1879, envelope no. 69, HCC.

72. Stevenson, "Zuñi Indians," 374.

73. G. James, *New Mexico*, 63. See also G. James, *Our American Wonderlands*, 143.

74. G. James, *New Mexico*, 64.

75. G. James, "Zuñi and 2 Modern Witchcraft Trials," *GWJC*.

76. G. James, *New Mexico*, 64.

77. Stevenson, "Zuñi Indians," 463.

References

Abel, Annie H., ed. *The Official Correspondence of James S. Calhoun While Indian Agent at Santa Fe and Superintendent of Indian Affairs in New Mexico.* U.S. Office of Indian Affairs. Washington, D.C.: Government Printing Office, 1915.

Basso, Keith H. "History of Ethnological Research." In *Handbook of North American Indians,* edited by Alfonso Ortiz, 14–21. Vol. 9. Washington, D.C.: Smithsonian Institution, 1979.

Bender, Norman J., ed. *Missionaries, Outlaws, and Indians: Taylor F. Ealy at Lincoln and Zuni, 1878–1881.* Albuquerque: University of New Mexico Press, 1984.

Benedict, Ruth. *Zuñi Mythology.* 2 vols. Columbia University Contributions to Anthropology, vol. 21. New York, 1935.

Bieber, Ralph P., ed. *Marching with the Army of the West, 1846–1848.* Glendale, Calif.: Arthur H. Clark Co., 1936.

Bloom, Lansing Bartlett, ed. "Bourke on the Southwest." *New Mexico Historical Review* 11 (2) (1936): 188–207.

Bunker, Robert. *Other Men's Skies.* Bloomington: Indiana University Press, 1956.

Bunzel, Ruth L. "Introduction to Zuñi Ceremonialism." In *Forty-seventh Annual Report of the Bureau of American Ethnology, 1929–1930,* 467–544. Washington, D.C.: Government Printing Office, 1932.

Bunzel, Ruth L. *Zuni Texts.* Publications of the American Ethnological Society, vol. 15. New York, 1933.

Bunzel, Ruth L. *The Pueblo Potter: A Study of Creative Imagination in Primitive Art.* 1929. Reprint. New York: Dover, 1972.

Bunzel, Ruth L. *Zuñi Katcinas.* 1932. Reprint. Glorieta, N.M.: Rio Grande Press, 1984.

Crampton, C. Gregory. *The Zunis of Cibola.* Salt Lake City: University of Utah Press, 1977.

Curtis, Edward S. "Zuñi." In *The North American Indian,* edited by Frederick W. Hodge, 83–167. Vol. 17. 1926. Reprint. New York: Johnson Reprint Corp., 1970.

Cushing, Frank H. "Primitive Motherhood." In *Work and Words of the National Congress of Mothers, First Annual Session,* 21–47. New York: D. Appleton and Co., 1897.

Cushing, Frank H. *Zuñi Breadstuff.* Indian Notes and Monographs, vol. 8. 1920. Reprint. New York: Museum of the American Indian, Heye Foundation, 1974.

Cushing, Frank H. *Zuñi: Selected Writings of Frank Hamilton Cushing,* edited by Jesse Green. Lincoln: University of Nebraska Press, 1979.

Dale, Edward Everett. *The Indians of the Southwest.* Norman: University of Oklahoma, 1949.

Duberman, Martin B. *About Time: Exploring the Gay Past.* New York: Gay Presses of New York, 1986.

Eaton, J. H. "Description of the True State and Character of the New Mexican Tribes." In *Information Respecting the History, Condition and Prospects of the Indian Tribes of the United States,* edited by Henry R. Schoolcraft, 216–221. Vol. 4. Philadelphia: J. B. Lippincott and Co., 1856.

Eggan, Dorothy. "The General Problem of Hopi Adjustment." *American Anthropologist* 45 (3) (1943): 357–373.

Ferguson, T. J., and E. Richard Hart. *A Zuni Atlas.* Norman: University of Oklahoma Press, 1985.

Ferguson, T. J., and Barbara J. Mills. "Settlement and Growth of Zuni Pueblo: An Architectural History." *The Kiva* 52 (4) (1987): 243–266.

Foreman, Grant, ed. *A Pathfinder in the Southwest: The Itinerary of Lieutenant A. W. Whipple During His Explorations for a Railway Route from Fort Smith to Los Angeles in the Years 1853 and 1854.* Norman: University of Oklahoma Press, 1941.

Fritz, Henry E. *The Movement for Indian Assimilation, 1860–1890.* Philadelphia: University of Pennsylvania Press, 1963.

Goldman, Irving. "The Zuni Indians of New Mexico." In *Cooperation and Competition among Primitive Peoples,* edited by Margaret Mead, 313–353. New York: McGraw-Hill, 1937.

Hardin, Margaret A. *Gifts of Mother Earth: Ceramics in the Zuni Tradition.* Phoenix: Heard Museum, 1983.

Hart, E. Richard. "A Brief History of the Zuni Nation." In *Zuni El Morro: Past and Present*, 19–25. Exploration, Annual Bulletin of the School of American Research. Santa Fe, 1983.

Hinsley, Curtis M., Jr. *Savages and Scientists: The Smithsonian Institution and the Development of American Anthropology 1846–1910*. Washington, D.C.: Smithsonian Institution Press, 1981.

James, George W. "Zuñi and 2 Modem Witchcraft Trials," (typescript, c. 1899), folder 210, carton 8, George Wharton James Collection, Southwest Museum, Los Angeles, California.

James, George W. *Our American Wonderlands*. Chicago: A. C. McClurg and Co., 1916.

James, George W. *New Mexico: The Land of the Delight Makers*. Boston: Page Co., 1920.

Kent, Kate P. *Pueblo Indian Textiles: A Living Tradition*. Santa Fe: School of American Research Press, 1983.

Kuipers, Cornelius. *Zuni Also Prays: Month-by-Month Observations among the People*. Christian Reformed Board of Missions, 1946.

Ladd, Edmund J. "Zuni Social and Political Organization." In *Handbook of North American Indians*, 482–491.

Leighton, Dorothea C., and John Adair. *People of the Middle Place: A Study of the Zuni Indians*. New Haven, Conn.: Human Relations Area Files, 1966.

Li An-Che. "Zuñi: Some Observations and Queries." *American Anthropologist* 39 (1) (1937): 62–76.

Lurie, Nancy O. "Women in Early American Anthropology." In *Pioneers of American Anthropology: The Uses of Biography*, edited by June Helm, 29–81. American Ethnological Society Monograph no. 43. Seattle: University of Washington Press, 1966.

Mardock, Robert W. *The Reformers and the American Indian*. Columbia: University of Missouri Press, 1971.

McNitt, Frank. *The Indian Traders*. Norman: University of Oklahoma Press, 1962.

McNitt, Frank, ed. *Navaho Expedition: Journal of a Military Reconnaissance from Santa Fe, New Mexico to the Navaho Country Made in 1849 by Lieutenant James N. Simpson*. Norman: University of Oklahoma Press, 1964.

National Anthropological Archives, Smithsonian Institution, Washington, D.C. Ms. 3915, Frank H. Cushing, "Nominal and Numerical Census of the Gentes of the Ashiwi or Zuni Indians," n.d. [1881].

Pandey, Triloki N. "Factionalism in a Southwestern Pueblo." Ph. D. diss., University of Chicago, 1967.

Pandey, Triloki N. "Tribal Council Elections in a Southwestern Pueblo." *Ethnology* 7 (1) (1968): 71–85.

Pandey, Triloki N. "Anthropologists at Zuni." *Proceedings of the American Philosophical Society* 116 (4) (1972): 321–337.

Pandey, Triloki N. "'India Man' among American Indians." In *Encounter and Experiences: Personal Accounts of Fieldwork*, edited by André Béteille and T. N. Madan, 194–213. Delhi: Vikas Publishing House, 1975.

Pandey, Triloki N. "Images of Power in a Southwestern Pueblo." In *The Anthropology of Power: Ethnographic Studies from Asia, Oceania, and The New World*, edited by Raymond D. Fogelson and Richard N. Adams, 195–215. New York: Academic Press, 1977.

Parsons, Elsie C. [John Main, pseud.]. "The Zuñi La'mana." *American Anthropologist* 18 (4) (1916): 521–528.

Parsons, Elsie C. [John Main, pseud.]. "The Zuñi A'doshle and Suuke." *American Anthropologist* 18 (3) (1916): 338–347.

Parsons, Elsie C. [John Main, pseud.]. *Notes on Zuñi*. Memoirs of the American Anthropological Association, vol. 4, pts. 3 and 4, 151–327. Lancaster, PA., 1917.

Parsons, Elsie C. [John Main, pseud.]. "Waiyautitsa of Zuñi, New Mexico." In *American Indian Life*, edited by Elsie C. Parsons, 157–173. 1922. Reprint. New York: Greenwich House, 1983.

Peterson, Charles S. *Take Up Your Mission: Mormon Colonizing along the Little Colorado River, 1870–1900*. Tucson: University of Arizona Press, 1973.

Roberts, John M. "The Zuni." In *Variations in Value Orientations*, edited by Florence R. Kluck-hohn and Fred L. Strodtbeck, 285–316. 1961. Reprint. Westport, Conn.: Freedwood Press, 1973.

Sekaquaptewa, Emory. "Hopi Indian Ceremonies." In *Seeing with a Native Eye: Essays on Native American Religion*, edited by Walter H. Capps, 35–43. New York: Harper & Row, 1976.

Smith, Watson, and John M. Roberts. *Zuni Law: A Field of Values*. Papers of the Peabody Museum of American Archaeology and Ethnology, Harvard University, vol. 43, no. 1. Cambridge, Mass., 1954.

Stevenson, Matilda C. "The Zuñi Indians: Their Mythology, Esoteric Fraternities, and Ceremonies." In *Twenty-third Annual Report of the Bureau of American Ethnology, 1901–1902*, 1–608. Washington, D.C.: Government Printing Office, 1904.

Talayesva, Don C. *Sun Chief: The Autobiography of a Hopi Indian*, edited by Leo W. Simmons. New Haven: Yale University Press, 1942.

Tedlock, Dennis. "An American Indian View of Death." In *Teachings from the American Earth: Indian Religion and Philosophy*, edited by Dennis Tedlock and Barbara Tedlock, 248–271. New York: Liveright, 1975.

Ten Broeck, P. G. S. "Manners and Customs of the Moqui and Navajo Tribes of New Mexico." In *Information Respecting the History, Condition and Prospects of the Indian Tribes of the United States*, 72–91. See Eaton.

U.S. Office of Indian Affairs. *Rules for the Indian School Service, 1900*. Washington, D.C.: Government Printing Office, 1900.

Vogt, Evon Z. "Intercultural Relations" and "Ecology and Economy." In *People of Rimrock*, 46–82, 160–190. See Kluckhohn.

Whiting, John W. M., et al. "The Learning of Values." In *People of Rimrock*, 83–125. See Kluckhohn.

Young, M. Jane. *Signs from the Ancestors: Zuni Cultural Symbolism and Perceptions of Rock Art*. Albuquerque: University of New Mexico Press, 1988.

Key Terms

We'wha   The proper name of the subject of this chapter. The apostrophe between the "e" and the second "w" indicates that the "e" is glottalized, or pronounced with a little hiccuping sound, as in between the two syllables of the exclamation "uh oh."

lhamana   The Zuni term for *berdache*, a man who adopts the manners, dress, and activities of a woman.

Elsie Clews Parsons   An early and prominent American anthropologist who worked primarily in the southwestern United States.

berdache   A term deriving from a French version of a Persian word, and referring to an institution by which a male assumes the behaviors and social identity of a female, and is considered by the community to be essentially a woman. The term is also used to refer to individuals who are part of the institution. Berdaches have an honorable place in their societies, and some marry men who also have one or more biologically female wives. The institution of Berdache was found among many Native American groups, especially in the western two-thirds of the United States.

nomadic   Having no permanent residence. Nearly all hunter gatherers are nomadic. They do not live permanently in one place, but move throughout their customary territory according to a seasonal round, according to the availability of food and other resources.

Zuni   The name of a group of Native American farming people who live in a town or pueblo of the same name in northern Arizona.

pueblo   Spanish: town. The term refers to the towns of rock and adobe-built multifamily dwellings in northern Arizona that are home to several Native American groups such as the Zuni and Hopi.

picketed   Tethered.

clan   A group of lineages that consider themselves descended from a common ancestor. Clans have a continuing identity through time and may own property and share responsibility for particular political and religious responsibilities. Members of a given clan must normally marry someone from a *different* clan.

laying siege to   Attacking and surrounding a settlement, cutting off contact with outside support and supplies.

kachinas   Representations of important beings in the supernatural world of Pueblo groups. Senior men impersonate these supernaturals at religious rituals, and small figures or "kachina dolls" are also made, and now sold to tourists.

origin narrative   An account of the creation of the universe. Origin narratives exist in all religious systems.

paper bread   A kind of flaky bread made of ground corn that separates during baking into many very thin layers.

Kit Carson   A frontiersman and "Indian Scout" for the U.S. Army (1809–1868).

shaman   A religious practitioner who interacts directly with supernatural beings and serves as a mouthpiece for them. Shamans are not full-time religious practitioners but also perform the other work expected of members of the community of their age and sex.

hermaphrodite   Someone with sexual characteristics of both males and females.

artifact   An article made by human effort.

"Si, si, we-no [bueno]"   Spanish: "Yes, yes, good." Many Pueblo Indians, especially males, learned some Spanish as a result of interaction with Spanish and subsequently Mexican soldiers, bureaucrats, and missionaries.

DISCUSSION QUESTIONS

1. Anthropologists are very interested in what they refer to as *kinship systems*, that is, the various ways by which different cultures define, describe, and identify the people to whom they are related. The Zuni, like most other Pueblo groups (and even like their traditional enemies, the Navajo and the Apache), are described by anthropologists as having a *matrilineal* kinship system. What this means is that the Zuni calculate their membership in a clan (a group of people tracing their descent from a common ancestor) through the female line only. In a matrilineal system an individual belongs to his or her mother's clan, not his/her father's, and only daughters will pass on this membership to their children. The children of sons will belong to their mothers' clans. Most matrilineal societies are also *matrilocal*. This means that newly married couples go to live with the bride's family. They may not always live in exactly the same place, but they will continue to live near the bride's family and remain associated with them. On the other hand, a man does not lose contact with the family in which he grew up; they usually retain specific important relationships and obligations toward their sons and their sons' children.

    Comb through the account of We'wha's life and community, and provide a description of the distinctive features of Zuni life that reflect the distinctive Zuni matrilineal, matrilocal kinship system. What evidence do you find of the importance of nonmatrilineal kin (that is, an individual's relatives to whom s/he is not matrilineally related)?

2. The dominant, Euro-American culture of the United States has a strong belief in the right of parents to decide how their children are to be raised. Both the federal government and the average American believe that this right should not be interfered with except in the most extraordinary circumstances. Indeed, most Euro-American parents become angry when their children are scolded or corrected by *anyone* other than

themselves, even by a close relative or friend. Some Americans also believe that a little physical punishment is harmless to children, and far less damaging than shaming or public humiliation. Finally, very few Americans would be comfortable, let alone happy, if a son began to refer to himself as a girl, use feminine linguistic expressions, and take up activities reserved specifically for girls. How do these practices and attitudes compare and contrast with those practiced by the Zuni? What do you think might be some of the reasons for the differences in child rearing between the two cultures? What about the idea that every individual has a different "life road"? What are the Zuni and Euro-American limitations to that notion?

3. When they hear terms like *matrilineal* or *matrilocal*, many people believe that they mean the same thing as *matriarchal*. A matriarchal society is one in which women as a group have greater power and authority than the mass of men. And though there are many societies in which certain women have greater power and authority than some, many, or even all men, anthropologists know of no societies that could legitimately be called matriarchies. Popular books, magazines, and television programs continue to write as though such societies have existed in the past, and many people, influenced by these accounts, believe that they have. But no such account has ever stood the test of archaeological scrutiny. On the other hand, the status of women is undeniably higher in some societies than in others, and it is often argued that matrilineal, matrilocal societies, like that of the Zuni, provide women with relative or absolute gender equality. Judging from what you have read in this selection, would you agree? What specific evidence from Roscoe's article would you point to as evidence? Why do you think that matrilineal, matrilocal societies tend to provide women with higher status and greater power and autonomy than is true in patrilineal, patrilocal societies? As always, back up your opinion with evidence from your reading wherever possible.

4. Anglo-American soldiers, bureaucrats, and missionaries were not the first persons of European descent who had passed through Zuni territory. Spaniards and Mexicans of partially Spanish heritage had preceded them, and had left traces of their influence, including remnants of their language. But the Anglo-Americans were a more lasting presence, and their influence was far more pervasive. What are some of the gender-based differences in culture that these early Anglo-American arrivals to Zuni territory noticed, and what was their response to them? How (at least as far as we can tell from this chapter) did the Zuni respond to their new visitors?

The issue of laundry in late-nineteenth and early-twentieth century Zuni territory is interesting. In the first place, in the absence of running water and mechanical washing machines, clothes washing required enormous strength and energy, and yet it was women's work. But laundry was not *ladies'* work. Note that Stevenson speaks of herself as "[n]ever having any experience in that work herself," because, as a member of the educated, upper middle class, she would have had a laundress handle the washing for her and her family. We'wha was at first reluctant to undertake the laundry for Stevenson, though she eventually did so, and with her unusual size and strength became very good at it. Other Zunis also began to do laundry for pay for Euro-Americans in the area. Use the *World of Washing* as a lens through which to explore Zuni-Anglo power and social relations, as well as culture change. Make sure you are specific, and do not trivialize the insights that you can derive from such a mundane activity as doing the laundry.

In My Family, the Women Ran Everything

Emmi Whitehorse

Jane Katz, Editor

Emmi Whitehorse has an MFA (master's degree in fine arts) and is a successful painter with a studio in Santa Fe; she is thus set apart by education and occupation not only from most Americans, but to a far greater extent from Native American women. Yet in her early upbringing and in her outlook on life she is also a respected representative of Navajo women. And her autobiographical sketch gives us a different perspective on a Native American group from the account of We'wha's life in the Zuni Pueblo in the preceding selection.

Like their Pueblo neighbors (and former enemies), the Navajo are both matrilineal and matrilocal. These should not be taken as universal Native American characteristics, however; in fact, most Indian peoples belong to groups that are neither matrilineal nor matrilocal. The Navajo live in close proximity to the Pueblo peoples, mostly on their huge reservation that covers the northeast corner of Arizona with smaller acreage in New Mexico (where Emmi Whitehorse grew up) and Utah. Increasing numbers of Navajo, like Whitehorse herself, now live off the reservation. When the Navajo arrived in the area, they found the Pueblo peoples already ensconced in their high, terraced adobe villages, raising crops in their river-watered gardens in the lowlands. After the U.S. Army forcibly removed the Navajo in the catastrophic Long Walk to the isolated prison reservation in Bosque Redondo (mentioned in the preceding selection), the Navajo were released to occupy a part of their traditional territory, now the modern Navajo reservation (or "Big Rez"). Here they rebuilt their hogans (traditional houses made of timbers plastered with mud and clay) and entered into a life of herding sheep and goats as well as horses and a few cattle. They also planted gardens of corn, beans, squash, and fruit trees. In Navajo society, the land, goats, and sheep usually belong to the women, and are passed to children through the female line. Horses and cattle are more likely to be the property of men.

Traditionally, a Navajo man moved into his new wife's "outfit," or extended family compound, when he married. If he had more than one wife (polygyny was formerly permitted among the Navajo), a man would spend some time at the outfit of one wife and then move to the outfit of the other. The combination of matrilocal residence, where a woman is always surrounded by her own relatives, and the ownership of the major sources of wealth and subsistence (land and flocks) have long made Navajo women well-known for their strength of mind and independence. Though men dominate the realm of religious ritual as priests (singers) and shamans, women shamans also exist.

Clan membership is a vital feature of Navajo identity and group organization. A person retains membership in his or her clan throughout a lifetime, but only women pass on this membership to their children. Since Navajo clans are exogamous (meaning that one must marry outside one's own clan) a father will never belong to the same clan as his own children. A father's clan remains an important part of an individual's life, but most of his or her family obligations and support are articulated through the mother's clan. Thus a mother's brother (and member of one's own class) takes on a very important role in the training of children, particularly of boys. The boy's father will be similarly involved with the training of his sister's son. The outsider status of an in-marrying son-in-law is reaffirmed also by the practice of "mother-in-law avoidance," according to which a man tries never to be alone with his mother-in-law, never to look directly at her, never to speak directly to her or refer to her by name. This practice is known in many cultures in various parts of the world, and it seems to have developed to simplify a relationship that is notoriously difficult to handle—as mother-in-law jokes in our own culture make clear.

The Navajo are well-known for their respect for children's wishes and their general recognition of individual autonomy, even of the very young. Children are expected to contribute to their families' well-being, but they are also taken seriously as thoughtful persons. At one time families arranged the marriages of their children, but this practice has been abandoned. The event that preceded a girl's eligibility for marriage, the puberty ritual, or kinaalda, *continues to be celebrated by many modern Navajo today.*

Indeed, today the Navajo nation forms the largest single Native American group in the United States. Their language and culture are still strong, despite attempts of the Anglo American majority to eradicate both. As the Navajo move into the twenty-first century, they are managing to adapt tradition to the modern world, increasingly on their own terms.

The Santa Fe studio of painter Emmi Whitehorse is a comfortable place. The patio is home to plants, two cats, and a large black rabbit. Inside the converted warehouse, a skylight illuminates Whitehorse's treasures—an abstract "chief's blanket," Navajo[1] fetishes standing like sentinels beside hand-woven baskets, Pueblo pots, and high-tech stereo speakers. The walls are alive with her canvases, which blend European influences with her personal visual language. Figures from her childhood on the Navajo Reservation float in seas of color. Emmi Whitehorse took me on a tour of her work, then we drank tea and she reflected on her passage from shepherdess to "postmodern painter."

My work isn't something mystical that has to be pondered. See this funny little bird? Birds represent different things in different cultures, so when I first showed the painting, everybody thought it was an allusion to some Native American ritual. I said,

"Well, if that's what you want to believe, fine. But I just saw it on a beer label, and I'm painting it." [Laughs.]

I incorporate common, everyday things in my work. I play with images. In these canvases, there are childlike forms. There's a comb, like the one we used to use to beat down the wool and tighten the weaving. I like the shape. There's a little house and an upside-down fork floating in space over denuded trees.

There are female body parts in the works, but they're ambiguous. This big figure started out looking like a bowling pin—you know, elongated head and long body. Then the head disappeared, and the bust came in. In this other painting, there's a woman with a head, but she's armless. [Laughs.] You can see the hips and waist, she has this big strapless ruffly dress on, the kind girls wear to the prom. This upside-down thing here, that's the same female form—I flipped

Source: From *Messengers of the Wind* by Jane Katz, copyright © 1995 by Jane Katz. Used by permission of Ballantine Books, a division of Random House, Inc.

it around—only she doesn't have the ruffly dress on; she's become a chalice.

I don't want to be too literal in the work. I'm ambiguous. I'm interested in the presence of the woman. I'm intrigued by the femininity of the female form.

In my family, the female owned everything, the women ran everything. They owned the land and the sheep. They nurtured and carried the family. The woman was responsible for the survival of the people. So in my work, the female is always very big, she is imposing, she is like this big Goliath in the work. The male image is tiny.

In this other canvas, there's a woman shaped like a vase, like the older Navajo women. Even in old age, I think the women still retain a grace that is unequaled.

My grandmother is like that. She's very giving, and she instilled a lot of traditional values in us without having to preach. She was a weaver. She learned how to weave from her mother. Her work is elegant. She is very finicky, very concerned with what she wears in public. She won't go out on a short trip to the store without putting on her best clothes: a traditional Navajo velveteen top and three-tiered cotton skirt down to her ankles. She used to make her clothes, but now she has trouble seeing, so she has someone make them to her specifications. She's eighty-two, and she's pretty healthy, except for arthritis.

I was born in 1957. I lived with my family in a hogan in a place called Whitehorse Lake on the edge of the Navajo Reservation. It's near Chaco Canyon, New Mexico. Each family lives on a plot of land divided into sections or squares so that each of the relatives can have a section for his or her family. There was my grandmother (I never saw my grandfather), my parents, and five children. Most of the family is still living there.

In olden times, Navajo women would scheme to arrange a marriage for their children to someone from a wealthy family. Wealth meant having cows and horses, or a car. A lot of tribal people were material-oriented, and still are. The mother and grandmother would pick the mate for a girl, but they wouldn't force you. They'd ask you if it was okay first. Our tradition was that the man came to live with his wife's family.

What if a woman was unhappy with her husband? In earlier times, it was easy. she just picked up all his stuff and put it out the door of the hogan, and that was it. He couldn't contest it. He had to go.

The man joined his wife's family basically to ensure the survival of that family. In other words, he sort of became the workhorse. He would haul the wood, and chop the firewood; he'd take care of the sheep too. He'd make sure there was water for the animals. Older men and medicine men were highly regarded. But that was back then.

Our system worked well until the missionaries came and said that we were "living in sin." How can living with nature be a sin? They said that men are supposed to run everything. That threw everything asunder. My generation of young men was greatly affected by the fact that they had to constantly straddle the fence between traditional teachings and western ideals. Unfortunately, many turned to alcohol and destroyed their well-being.

My father worked in California for Amtrak when I was very young, so we children became the caretakers of our animals. We had over two hundred head of sheep. We had to take them out every day to graze. Every spring, Grandmother marked the ears—it was the same as branding. We would help castrate lambs. When little ones were abandoned, we had to bottle-feed them, to be mother to all those motherless lambs. We'd shear the sheep in the spring. We had to use huge shears, and cut each sheep's wool by hand. This would take days. Afterwards, we'd take the wool to market, about fifteen to twenty tremendous burlap sacks. We'd get something like five dollars per pound totaling around five thousand dollars, a substantial amount of money that we would live on for a year. Grandmother also had goats that produced mohair which she used for her weaving.

We'd help Grandmother card the wool after it had been washed. It was a nasty business because wool from the sheep is very dirty and oily. We'd sit and pick all the burrs and twigs out. Using a flat wooden brushlike comb, we'd comb it clean and make little long, flat bundles of wool. While we worked, my grandmother told us creation stories like this one, but only in the wintertime.

Changing Woman was the first woman, born through a sort of immaculate conception. She gave birth to twin boys; the Sun was their father. But because the Sun didn't want children, Changing Woman had to hide their birth, and she raised them in secrecy. When they grew up, they asked who their father was. When Changing Woman could no longer put them off, she told them it was the Sun, and they wanted to go and see him. Changing Woman prepared the boys for the journey. She plucked stars and lightning bolts out of which she fashioned a bow and arrow for each boy. She warned them that their father would try to kill them.

Along their journey, the boys met a gopher who befriended them, and offered to help them outsmart the Sun. When they arrived at the home of the Sun, they announced, "We are the sons of Changing Woman. We know you are our father." The Sun was very angry, and decided to do away with the boys right away. He prepared a sweat for them; he put oversize rocks inside so it would overheat. But the gopher was wise to the Sun; he went inside without being seen, he dug a large tunnel in the middle of the floor that led deep down and to the outside. When the Sun turned up the heat, the boys crawled into this tunnel. Each time the Sun turned up the heat, he would call out to the boys, "How are you doing?" Each time they would answer, "Fine." This went on until the Sun was tired out, and finally the Sun called out to the boys to come out. They emerged unhurt, and the Sun gave in and accepted the boys as his sons.[2]

I asked Emmi Whitehorse if her story affirms her image of woman as a positive force.

Yes. By defying the Sun and having the Twins, Changing Woman liberated her people who had been suppressed by the greedy Sun. She released her people from the underworld where the Sun wanted them to stay; she moved them forward. At one point, I incorporated that story into my painting. See these two figures? They are the Twins.

I was the baby of the family. My siblings had gone off to school, not by their own choice. I wanted to be with them, so I begged my mom to let me go to school. I thought I would play on the swings and merry-go-round all day. She said, "Fine." She enrolled me the very next day! (My mother and my grandmother don't speak English. They never went to school.)

So at a very early age, I went to a Bureau of Indian Affairs boarding school near my home in Whitehorse Lake. I hated it. We were marched around like little cadets: girls were herded around in one area, boys in another. It was very lonely. In the dining room, we were required to sit boy-girl, boy-girl, and that was torture. [Laughs.] All you could do was numb yourself to the whole ordeal.

I wasn't interested in any of the subjects, except art. When we had drawing time, I came alive. That was the only thing I excelled in. That kept me going.

Some of the teachers were very demeaning and made us feel ashamed of our culture. We were forced to wear uncomfortable dresses and hose, with a tight girdle. Boy did we hate it! We couldn't wear our hair loose; it had to be curled, or braided, or piled up on top of our heads to fulfill the school's idea of the "ideal girl."

At Christmas, if we got lucky, we would get gifts, and one year, we all got Barbie dolls. Barbie had a size D bust and a nineteen-inch waist, long legs and blond hair.

We all thought we were supposed to look like her. Well, we found out that no matter how we manipulated our bodies, we could never look like Barbie. We had tanned skin and dark hair. When I got older, I realized we had wasted so much time agonizing over something that could never be, and that didn't need changing! I started drawing the female figure with this pinched-in waist and a big top—I was poking fun at the "ideal figure."

We were only allowed to go home in the summer. At home, mother never pushed us hard; she never made important decisions for us. She never encouraged us to be lawyers or physicians. She let us do what we wanted to do.

During the summer months, I got to participate in some ceremonies. We had a Blessing ceremony when we finished our new home.[3] Once when my mother was sick, she hired a medicine man to come and sing over her, but the medicine man considered us too young to witness it, and sent us away. Did she get well? She must have. [Laughs.]

I didn't have a puberty ceremony because I was away at school, and also I was uncomfortable with the idea of having one. This was the sixties. I thought it was too old-fashioned. Miniskirts were in, puberty rites were not! Now, I think it's such a wonderful ceremony, I should have had it. If I have a daughter I will want her to have one.

In this painting there's a long bundle of sticks used in the girl's puberty ceremony. Your grandmother gives them to you; you use them to stir the blue cornmeal during the ceremony, and you keep them for the rest of your life.

I went to a puberty ceremony when I was around eight years old. The girl who was being initiated into womanhood was about twelve or thirteen. We camped out at the girl's home for a week with all our relatives, men, women and children. Now, I guess you'd drive over every day. With the girl, we spent a whole day grinding the blue corn for the "Navajo cake." When there was enough corn piled up, they would pour it into a big metal container, pour in hot water, add raisins, sweeten it with sprouted wheat (a natural sugar), and it was like a thick pudding. The men would do their part by hauling in water and firewood.

Every morning before sunup, the girl would race out toward the East. We would all line up behind her, grandmothers, mothers and children, as if we were going to run the New York Marathon. Someone would say "Go" and she'd race off. You'd never overtake her, even if you were the fastest runner, because the saying was if you ran past her, you would age quicker than she would. [Laughs.] She would race as far as she could to the East, then she would turn around and run back. It was just a wonderful event.

For the ceremony, the girl was decked out in her best traditional dress and jewelry. Her hair was done up and wrapped with yarn, and a piece of parrot feather with turquoise was tied to her hair.

There were specific songs. I remember the medicine man singing and conducting the ceremony. He was sitting in front of us in the hogan with his legs crossed. My sister and I noticed that he had a hole in the toe of his moccasin. We started giggling hysterically, and my grandmother got angry and chased us out of the hogan. We were put to work gathering firewood and grinding corn. We weren't allowed back in, so we never heard the rest of the ceremony.

Recently, my sister's daughter got married in a traditional ceremony at my mother's home. We all went to help with the wedding preparations. We prepared food for the feast. We butchered a sheep and made mutton stew soup. We cooked various other dishes and of course fried bread.

The bride and groom were dressed in their traditional clothes. He wore a velveteen shirt and blue jeans. The bride wore a purple velveteen blouse and a purple satin skirt with see-through white lace overlaid on the skirt. She had her hair done up Navajo fashion. The couple both wore moccasins.

The bride and groom sat in a corner of the hogan on blankets. The groom's family sat on one side of the hogan, the bride's family on the other side. The groom's mother was a medicine woman, so she conducted the ceremony and said the prayers. It was wonderful to have a woman do that.

The medicine woman poured water over the couple's hands they had to wash before starting the ceremony. A little basket of corn mush was brought in; the couple dipped into the mush with their fingers, marking the four corners as they worked around the lip of the basket, then they ate some.

Next, they opened the floor so that anyone could talk. It all had to do with maintaining a good home and family relationships. Elders counseled the couple on how to be diplomatic. The girl's grandmother told her how to be caring, the boy's father told him how to be giving, financially and emotionally, to his wife. This went on for hours, it seemed, until everybody had run out of things to say and was out of breath.

Finally the food was brought in. The lamb's ribs were given to the groom's family—these are considered a delicacy. The rest of us got to eat mutton stew and fry bread. Everyone ate in a circle around the food.

After the meal, it shifted gears to modern life. Someone from my family had ordered this wonderful three-tiered cake decorated with the plastic image of a couple—a white couple—standing on the very top. [Laughs.] They cut it and passed it out to the guests. There were gifts: a toaster, glasses, a Cuisinart. You didn't get that in the old days. It was bizarre because the first part of the ceremony had been so traditional. But they were young, in fact, they played their favorite music at the end—heavy metal! It was accepted. Everyone went away happy.

After the guests had all left, the bride gathered all the gifts and carried them out to a 1992 Ford Escort, and we watched them drive off.

I thought, well, if I ever decide to get married, I'll have a traditional wedding at night, on my grandmother's land.

In high school, I entered an art contest with a small abstract painting; it won an award, and I got a small scholarship to the University of New Mexico in Albuquerque. The school was male-dominated, and I was very disappointed. When I arrived at my first art history class, I didn't know who Picasso was, I had no idea what modern art was about. I took all the art classes I could, and became a bit more comfortable. I took courses in modern dance, music history and creative writing. I was fascinated. I started showing my work while I was an undergraduate.

I was so happy the day I got my master's degree in fine arts. I sent invitations to all my family and relatives, but my dad was the only one who showed up for the graduation. My sisters were in town, but guess where they went instead. [Laughs.] To a Jimmy Swaggert revival meeting! After the graduation ceremony was over, they came and congratulated me and we all went out for dinner. It was sad that they weren't interested in what I had done, but later I forgave them. The evangelist meeting was more important to them at that time in their lives.

At one point in my life, I suffered from low self-esteem pretty badly. I was trying very hard not to look ethnic. I thought my nose was too big. I guess I was trying to eliminate every trace of who I was. Then a close friend said, "Look at all the things the Navajo are famous for: the weavings, the silversmithing, baskets. These are just as valid as what the Europeans have come up with." It dawned on me that there was this wealth of aesthetic objects my people were creating. Why not be proud of it?

I began looking at the stories my grandmother told me when I was a child, and started incorporating the images into my work. The work became more centered. In some of the paintings you'll see the arc from the bottom of the Navajo wedding basket, or the shape of the cradle board my mother made for me using boards from an orange crate. In another painting, there is a brush made out of dried grass, which Navajo women used to use to brush their hair.

Everything my grandmother stood for I now hold sacred: her love for animals, her limitless compassion for humanity. I would like to be like her when I get older. I will probably trade in my LizWear for a velveteen blouse and a traditional long skirt when I'm sixty years old. [Laughs.]

*—From an interview
with the author, July 15, 1992*

NOTES

1. The alternate spelling is Navaho. In their own language, they call themselves *diné,* which is usually translated as "The People."
2. There are various retellings of the rich origin stories of the Navajos. See *Navajo Creation Stories* told by Teri Keams, Parabola Storytime Series (audio), 1993; Larry Evers, ed., *Between Sacred Mountains: Navajo Stories and Lessons from the Land* (Tucson: Sun Tracks and the University of Arizona Press, 1984).
3. The hogan, or home, occupies a central place in the Navajo sacred world.

KEY TERMS

hogan   The traditional house of the Navajo, made of logs, now usually in an octagonal shaped and plastered with earth, and ideally facing the east, the direction of the rising sun.

Changing Woman   One of the most important and beloved of the Navajo supernaturals. Changing Woman is the personification and guardian of the natural world, including the earth and the rain. As the earth goes through its seasons, Changing Woman moves through her life, becoming an old woman in winter and being reborn as a young girl in spring.

Blessing ceremony   Also known as the Blessing Way, a Navajo ritual that helps to ensure the success of new ventures.

medicine man   The Navajo have a variety of religious practitioners, many of whom are usually referred to by most Navajo as "singers." These are part shaman, part priest, and usually men who have memorized the words to lengthy rituals. If performed properly, these rituals compel the cooperation of the supernatural world in ensuring harmony, prosperity, good health, and the elimination of contamination from illness, death, and enemy forces. Another variety of religious practitioner, including both women and men, are often called "hand tremblers." These practitioners, who are more shaman than priest, diagnose interruption in harmony, such as human and animal illness or polluted wells.

sing   A Navajo religious ceremony conducted by a "singer," a religious practitioner who has memorized the words to lengthy rituals. Sings are intended to restore or maintain the harmony of the universe, and are most commonly employed to heal illness, seen by the Navajo as clear evidence that harmony has been disrupted.

puberty ceremony   A celebration of the physical adulthood of an individual. Male puberty ceremonies are most common in the world and are usually celebrated for a group of boys, since there is no single moment at which a boy may be said to have achieved puberty. In Navajo society the most important puberty ceremony is the *kinaal-da*, or girl's puberty ceremony. Like most girls' puberty ceremonies in the world, *kinaal-da* is celebrated individually, since the onset of menstruation gives an inescapable signal that puberty has arrived.

DISCUSSION QUESTIONS

1. Whitehorse talks about the Barbie dolls that she and the other girls at the BIA boarding school received as Christmas gifts, and the girdles and stockings that the students were required to wear along with their uncomfortable dresses and hairdos. What significance do you see in this story, both in terms of what the school administration was trying to accomplish and in terms of its contrast with Navajo tradition?

2. It is well-known that Indian people have a disproportionate rate of alcoholism. It is likely that part of this may be due to a genetic incapacity for the rapid processing of all forms of sugar, including alcohol. The circumstances of Native American life in the postcontact world, however, are certainly a major component in their frequent tragedy of alcoholism and alienation. Whitehorse mentions alcoholism specifically at one point in her narrative, but she provides many other clues to the difficulties in the Navajo past and present. Comb through Whitehorse's story and describe specifically what events and processes have contributed to an atmosphere to which some Navajo have responded with alcohol. You may wish to draw on a few insights from Roscoe's life of We'wha as well. Why would alcohol seem to help? Despite a high rate of alcoholism among Euro-Americans, many of this group seem to find Native American alcoholism an incomprehensible moral flaw for which there is no explanation. After working on the exercise in this question, do you (still) feel this way? Why might alcoholism be a greater problem for men than for women?

3. Though Whitehorse did not have a puberty ceremony (*kinaalda*) of her own, she re-members one she attended as a child. They remain major ceremonial events in Navajo life, and even a Navajo girl who lives in a Phoenix subdivision may return to her grand-mother's house on the reservation to celebrate her *kinaalda*. In a similar vein, Whitehorse talks about her sister's daughter's traditional (Navajo) wedding. Why are these Navajo traditional observances still so important to young people? Wouldn't it be wiser for them to forget such old-fashioned practices and make a stronger effort to become part of main-stream Euro-American society?

4. Whitehorse's narrative contains a brief excerpt from Navajo mythology, drawn from her grandmother's storytelling. It features Changing Woman and Sun, two major figures in the Navajo supernatural world. Changing Woman both personifies and controls the nat-ural world, including earth and water. As the earth moves through its seasons, Chang-ing Woman changes from a beautiful young girl, to a mature woman, to a gray haired elder—and then is renewed every spring. The Twins, sons of Changing Woman and Sun, were conceived when Sun's warmth and power entered Changing Woman's body. Many of the world's peoples have mythological systems in which the earth is personified as a woman and the sun as a man. Why do you think this is? In many systems (though not the Navajo system), the (changeable) moon is a female deity, while the (unchanging) sun is male. Why do you think changeability is so often associated with women, and constancy with men? The earth is also often associated with women. This is true in rem-nants of European pagan mythology, so many Americans are familiar with the notion of "mother Earth," and the idea seems "natural." But what is so natural about it? That is, why should the idea be so common? One final concept from the fragment of myth that Whitehorse recounts is the enmity between father and sons. Can you think of other myths, legends, or religious stories in which this enmity exists? Does the conflict have a name in Freudian psychology (and in popular American psychology)? Why do you think it is so common? Who is responsible for the conflict—the father or the son(s)? Why?

ROSA LEE

A MOTHER AND HER FAMILY IN URBAN AMERICA

LEON DASH

These excerpts come from a life history of Rosa Lee and her family that is the result of years of work by Leon Dash, an African American reporter for the Washington Post. *The extended life history was initially published as a series in that newspaper, and was then issued as a book. The central character is Rosa Lee, a drug-using ex-prostitute and petty thief, who is, like her daughter, Patty, HIV positive. In order to understand the experiences that shaped Rosa Lee, however, as well as to understand how she shaped others, Dash includes accounts of the lives of her parents, children, and grandchildren. Though Dash is a journalist, not an anthropologist, his perspective is very anthropological. His own middle-class views and values are usually quite clear, but they do not interfere with his ability to interact with his informants in a way that seems both rational and sympathetic.*

The lives of post–Civil War Black sharecroppers were almost unimaginably difficult, and marked by extreme poverty, disease, malnutrition, an almost complete absence of education, as well as political and social isolation. In order to survive, all family members worked on the "share" as soon as they were physically able to do so. The "share" was the portion of the crop brought in by the tenant of a section of large plantation that he was able to retain for his own use and sale. Most plantation owners advanced tenants money against their future harvests, which were often insufficient to pay off the loans. Thus the sharecroppers existed in a morass of perpetual poverty and debt. Since there was no incentive for the white, landowning class to provide easily accessible schools for the children of sharecroppers, and since every hand was needed in the fields, most southern, African American sharecroppers before World War II were completely or nearly illiterate, and unable to do even simple arithmetic. The increased hardships of the Depression, followed by new employment opportunities that resulted from World War II, produced a huge stream of African American and Euro-American sharecroppers moving north in search of a better living. But though the northern migrants had left behind the absolute destitution of the South, life in the North was still extremely difficult. The often segregated schools still offered limited education, and little was done to ensure that poor, Black students attended regularly or came from families that were providing them with backgrounds that would allow them to take advantage of such education as existed. So, few children acquired much education and illiteracy persisted into modern times. Not only was Rosa Lee's mother, who was raised in the South, illiterate, but so were both Rosa Lee, schooled in Washington, D.C., and her daughter Patty, born in Washington, D.C. in 1957.

But other circumstances had changed. No longer did whole families, from eight-year-old children to sixty-year-old grandparents, work the cotton fields. Instead, children went to school (often uselessly), men worked at jobs requiring unskilled labor (when it was available), and women did domestic labor in the households of white people (which, though poorly paid, was nearly always available). The stability of the Black family began to weaken, as the labor of every member of the family was no longer necessary, and as men's employment became less reliable than that of women. With so many men unable to fulfill the ideal of supporting their families, and humiliated by having to rely on their wives' wages, many African American families foundered. These difficulties were exacerbated by the regulations that governed most kinds of public assistance. These regulations required that payments to all but the aged and incapacitated be made to the nonworking, unmarried (divorced, abandoned, or never married) mothers of dependent children. Though public assistance was intended to relieve the kind of dire poverty that had existed before World War II, one of its unintended effects was to erode the fragile bonds of destitute families, already weakened by the increasing unemployment of poorly educated and impoverished men. And then came drugs. Supplanting alcohol as the deadener of choice for impoverished people whose lives were already painful and frustrating, drugs made lives more unendurable and further destroyed the families of the poor.

Reading about Rosa Lee and her family requires a certain exercise of will and humanity. Instead of the kneejerk reaction of "I would never do something so terrible," we need to remember what the actual context of life was for Rosa Lee. These are not simply middle-class people who happen to be poor. They are people whose lives are profoundly different from the lives of the middle class because of the daily realities of the heritage of slavery, the suffocating restrictions of poverty, and the new slavery of drugs. Passing moral judgment on Rosa Lee is pointless and runs counter to the anthropological principles. Our goal is understanding.

Rosa Lee has no trouble remembering when she began hiding her illiteracy.

It was 1953, and she was sixteen years old, separated from her husband of a few months and raising three children in her mother's house near Capitol Hill. It was the last place she wanted to be. Living in Rosetta's house meant living by Rosetta's rules, and those rules were choking Rosa Lee.

Rosetta and her family had come to Washington in the mid-1930s, seeking refuge from their harsh lives as sharecroppers in North Carolina and Maryland. While Earl was alive, and even more so after his death in 1948, Rosetta's domestic work brought in the household's most dependable income.

Just as Rosetta's mother had prepared her to be both a sharecropper and a domestic worker, Rosetta schooled Rosa Lee in domestic work. Long before Rosa Lee turned ten, her mother taught her to scrub laundry on a washboard, to wash a floor so it shined, to make a bed so it looked crisp and neat. Rosa Lee's apartment is a monument to those lessons; no matter how many people are living there, it is always tidy, clean, and well organized.

As the eldest girl, Rosa Lee was expected to do laundry for everyone in the house, by the time she was in the third grade, she was spending hours at the scrub board every week, washing sweaters and shirts. "My mother didn't ask me did I have my homework done," Rosa Lee says. "When she came home from work, she'd say, 'Betcha didn't pull those sheets. Betcha didn't wash those clothes.' School wasn't important to her, and it wasn't important to me."

Source: From *Rosa Lee: A Mother and Her Family in Urban America* by Leon Dash. Copyright © 1996 by Leon Dash. Reprinted by permission of Basic Books, a member of Perseus books, L.L.C.

That was what Rosetta Wright's generation always called "training," says the historian Elizabeth Clark-Lewis. "It was a very bad reflection on the mother, the family, the broader community for a young woman not to be well trained. Training is reflected in what you can do with your hands, be it cleaning the house, washing expertly."

Since the early 1980s, Clark-Lewis has interviewed more than 120 black migrant women from the South. Eighty-three of them were of the same generation and out of the same southern rural traditions as Rosetta Wright. They came to Washington from all over the South in the 1920s and 1930s to work as domestics. About twenty, like Rosetta, were from rural North Carolina. "The reality of domestic work was all pervasive for black women of that generation," Clark-Lewis says.

As I spoke with Clark-Lewis, it became clear why education was such a low priority to Rosetta Wright. She had grown up in a time and place where hard work was the only way rural black sharecroppers could survive. What little education Rosetta managed to get in the segregated schools had not given her the wherewithal to sustain herself and her family. Especially not in Washington. Work did that. And if you were a black woman, work meant domestic work.

Rosetta's parents, Thadeous and Lugenia Lawrence, never had a school to attend, so they did not learn even the rudiments of reading, writing, and arithmetic. Both grew up in the isolation of the forests and swamplands of the Bishop and Powell Plantation near the hamlet of Rich Square, North Carolina, before marrying in 1916. When the white renter of the plantation, Joe Purvis, went broke in 1925, the Lawrences and their children moved to another farm ten miles north, where they sharecropped for its white owner, Charlie Lane, for four years.

Rosa Lee knows little about her grandparents or their experiences. She knows that they picked cotton in North Carolina before coming north a short time before Rosa Lee was born in Washington, but she doesn't know much else. "I don't know if my parents and grandparents came together or not," she says. "No one ever told me about that stuff and I never asked."

Thadeous Lawrence was a big man who almost never smiled. Rosa Lee remembers that, as a child, she though her grandfather's serious demeanor was strange. "He wouldn't laugh or nothing, Mr. Dash," she recalls. "I just remember him sitting in a chair on his porch all day not doing nothing and not saying nothing." She once asked him why he never laughed, and she still remembers his reply. "We've had such a hard time down in them sticks" in North Carolina, he told her, "I don't see much to laugh about."

She didn't understand his response and still doesn't. "What do you think he meant by that, Mr. Dash?" she asks. "That's all I remember him saying."

I respond that her grandparents and parents lived in the South when segregation was rigidly enforced, rural blacks received little or no education, black men were routinely lynched, blacks had no legal rights, and their labor was exploited.

Rosa Lee says she understands what I've said. "I heard them talking sometimes about North Carolina and what they had to put up with, but I never really understood all of it," she continues. "Just bits and pieces."

On the Lane farm, the Lawrences settled into a ramshackle, weather-beaten two-story sharecropper's house on the northern edge of Quarter Swamp. The house is still occupied today, although it has been added on to and covered with dark green aluminum siding. The Lawrences sent their children, Ozetta, Rosetta, Joseph, and Jean, to the two-room schoolhouse at Cumbo, the nearest school available for black children, on the south side of the swamp.

The four Lawrence children were allowed to attend school only when two circumstances converged: when there was no work to be done on Charlie Lane's farm and when the water in Quarter Swamp was low. That did not mean many days at school.

When the water was "up," the children could not use the two-mile-long footpath—a route cut by the longer-legged adult bootleggers—which enabled them to get to school in little more than half an hour. The only alternative was to walk along five and a half miles of dirt road, which took them almost two hours—each way.

The water in Quarter Swamp was often up year-round, even in the cold of winter when there was little farmwork to be done. Rotting swamp vegetation keeps the bogs warmer than the surrounding land, and the running stream agitates the water so it won't freeze. Sometimes, Lugenia Lawrence sent her children along the longer dirt-road route, but most of the time she did not, according to Mamie Barnes, now in her mid-seventies, who attended the Cumbo School with all the Lawrence children. "That swamp didn't freeze over in the winter like you might think it would," remembers Barnes. "The water would be up from melted snow and ice."

Barnes's late husband's first wife was Lugenia Lawrence's sister. She knew all the Lawrences well and is close to Rosa Lee's brother Ben. She's never met Rosa Lee.

Compared to the Lawrences, Mamie Barnes was fortunate. She lived south of the swamp and did not have to contend with crossing the soggy morass at all. She was able to attend classes many more days than they did. She completed the seventh grade when she was fifteen, ending her education to take care of her ailing mother.

"We all went to that school together," says Barnes. "We all was in the same class." The Lawrences "didn't come to school too much 'cause it was too far to walk. And they didn't go to school too much in the

winter. When it snowed, they had to stay home for a long time. If it rained, they stayed home."

Although Barnes was six years younger than Ozetta, and five years younger than Rosetta, the two Lawrence sisters missed so much school "that I went by them in grade. They even stopped school before they moved from Charlie Lane's farm" in 1929.

The white landlords of Rich Square had no interest in encouraging the black sharecroppers to send their children to school. Education was a threat to the sharecropping system that dominated much of the South when Rosetta was growing up in the 1920s; sharecroppers who could read and write might take their labor elsewhere. If they could do math, they might be able to tally up their own debits and earnings, and come to a different reckoning at the end of the harvest, a reckoning that would not leave them in debt to the white landowner.

The Lawrences were in the bottom tier of the three new post–Civil War class formations among African Americans in Northampton County, according to local amateur historian Samuel Glenn Baugham, who knew Thadeous Lawrence. The social hierarchy operated within the rigid confines of racial segregation and discrimination that affected all blacks.

The Lawrences were extremely isolated sharecroppers known as "river" or "swamp" blacks, who lived and worked on the plantations bordering the swamps along the Roanoke River. The river blacks were descendants of the slaves who had worked on the same plantations and, until the Depression, were cut off from even the small flow of humanity that passed through Rich Square. Generally, they had limited or no access to education.

Earl Wright came out of the "piney woods" blacks, the African American sharecroppers from around Rich Square who looked down on and generally ostracized the river blacks. Also the descendants of slaves, they lived in and among the pine tree lots far back from the meandering Roanoke River. They had easier access to education at an all-black school in Rich Square.

The descendants of the African Americans who were "free coloreds" before Emancipation were at the top of this hierarchy. They were better educated and had craftsmen's skills, such as carpentry and masonry, which the two lower groups lacked. Those among them who were not landowners were also the first to migrate North when urban factory employment opportunities first opened up for blacks during World War I.

By the time her son Ben was born in 1932, the fifteen-year-old Rosetta had worked in the cotton fields for a decade. The countless hours spent in the fields changed her body and shaped her soul, and taught her the importance of discipline and stamina. She developed quick, powerful arms and a tough, stern demeanor—a younger version of the grim, brooding woman in the photograph in Rosa Lee's bedroom.

There is no available record of the Lawrence "share" in 1932, no way to know whether the family earned enough to repay the white landowner for the money he had advanced them over the course of the year. According to family lore, Thadeous had a hidden source of income that kept the family from falling into irredeemable debt: a moonshine still. "My grandmother said my grandfather did a lot of bootlegging," says Ben. "He had plenty money! She said sometimes she would not see him for three and four months at a time. By bootlegging, he was able to pay off everything he owed the white landowner.

Many sharecroppers, however, remained perpetually in debt, unable to make their share, yoked to the same landowner year after year. Most could not read or write, add or subtract, so they had no way to challenge the landowner's tally at harvest time. The Lawrences and Wrights were no different.

Ben says his grandparents and father could not read or do arithmetic, but his mother could read a little.

Sharecropping for black farmers was a particularly harsh life, made even harsher by the effect the Depression was having on cotton farmers around Rich Square. In the space of three years, the price of a bale of cotton dropped from $500 to $250. So when Joe Purvis returned to Rich Square after the 1932 fall harvest and offered the Lawrences the opportunity to work with him on a dairy and tobacco farm in St. Mary's County, Maryland, the family decided to leave their friends and relatives and the land they knew so well. Rosetta, her six-month-old son, Ben, and her new husband, Earl Wright, joined the Lawrences on the journey.

Ben and Joe Louis vividly remember the stories that their mother and grandmother told them about their life in southern Maryland. They had almost no money. Meals frequently consisted of whatever they could pick or trap. "They were eating a lot of muskrat and watercress," Joe Louis says. Watercress grew abundantly in the clear springs nearby, and muskrat was then a popular regional dish that the family never got used to. "My mother would say, if she ever got a job and made any money, she was never going to eat another muskrat," Joe Louis remembers. "Had to eat it, because that's all they could trap."

After the 1935 harvest, like thousands of other sharecroppers during the 1930s and 1940s, Rosetta and Earl Wright gave up rural life and headed for the city. The Lawrences stayed behind with three-year-old Ben, afraid that the boy might starve if his parents couldn't find work in Washington. Ben spent his entire childhood with his grandparents. "I was the oldest grandchild and a boy. They favored boys in those days. It was a different time. My mother was a fifteen-year-old teenager when she had me.

She was still living at home. I used to call my grandmother 'Mama.'"

Six months after Rosetta and Earl moved to Washington, the Lawrences followed. The family's sharecropping days were over.

Washington in the 1930s was no land of opportunity for black migrants from the South, especially poor sharecroppers. It was a segregated city, but within the black community was a well-established and educated middle class that traced its roots to the freed slaves who stayed after the Civil War. Over the years, these families had built an extensive network of churches, schools, theaters, and other institutions. It wasn't a closed society, but neither did it reach out to embrace poor migrants from rural areas.

Some of the more fortunate newcomers had friends or family in the city to help them through resettlement. Others, like the Lawrences and Wrights, were on their own. Finding a job, any job, was a challenge.

Most of the jobs then open to blacks—as Post Office clerks and federal agency messengers and cafeteria workers and railroad station porters—went to middle-class blacks who had connections or education, says Portia P. James, the chief researcher at Washington's Anacostia Museum, one of the major repositories of black Washington's history. "You had to have certain resources to get those jobs," James told me. "Those jobs were very competitive. Low-level civil service positions were for the elite of black people. Those weren't considered just regular working-class jobs. Those jobs were considered highly desirable jobs." Middle-class blacks "knew how to take advantage of opportunity," she says. "That's how they got where they were."

For those migrating out of the rural South with farming skills and almost no education, employment opportunities were extremely limited. Thadeous and Earl became general laborers on construction projects, while Lugenia and Rosetta became domestics. This fit a familiar pattern, according to Elizabeth Clark-Lewis. "The middle class was not standing waiting for these people with open arms," she says. "There was a great deal of resistance to them. They had unrefined ways. There were color issues. There were all kinds of class issues. Education issues. Very few men could come in and get a government job, and for most poor, rural women, domestic work was the reality."

As the family grew—Rosetta gave birth to twenty-two children, ten of whom died before reaching adulthood—Rosa Lee became accustomed to bedrooms crammed with too many people and living rooms with no place for private conversation. But one thing that Rosa Lee could never understand was why her brothers could not chop the wood needed to heat the water to wash the endless tubs of sheets and clothes. "Why did I have to do all the work when my brothers could go out and play? I could see them in front of the house. My mother favored my brothers. It was like I was already a day worker and cleaning up behind them. They didn't have to do NOTHING! It used to make me mad! Mr. Dash, I didn't understand it." And she still doesn't understand it all these years later.

"They worshipped boys," agrees Clark-Lewis, explaining the values of Rosetta Wright's generation. "They absolutely adored sons. Sons are their joy." Women like Rosa Lee's mother, she continues, believed that "daughters are to be trained. They are to be worked. They are to be reared! But they are not to be indulged because life is not going to allow them to be indulged. It's part of being African American and female."

Rosa Lee remembers complaining to her mother about the number of chores she had to do and how young she was. "I was still in Giddings [Elementary] School when she gave me the whole house to clean, all the clothes to wash. Mr. Dash, it was just not fair! I told her, too. I stood out of reach of her arm when I did. Like on the other side of the room with something between us. Like a bed or something."

Rosetta Wright would look at her eldest daughter and shake her head, saying, "You're going to find out. This is the only kind of job we can find for black people."

As the first-born girl, Rosa Lee's role was set by the southern traditions that had shaped her mother. "For the older daughter, in particular," says Clark-Lewis, "the mother is so dependent on her carrying the household that the younger ones will have opportunities that the older one just won't have. By the time you are four, there are clear expectations that people have of you. By *eight*, you are considered dull or dim-witted if you cannot carry on almost all the functions of a household. Period!"

While Rosa Lee was still in the early years at Giddings, her smoldering resentment caused her to silently reject her mother's vision of her future. She was determined that domestic work was not going to be the way she survived. "I didn't tell my mother—she would have smacked me in the mouth—but I told myself that I wasn't going to work in white people's houses like she did. I didn't trust white people. I had never heard but that they had done us harm. Why would I want to work in their houses?"

The first-grade classroom at Giddings Elementary School that welcomed six-year-old Rosa Lee in the fall of 1942 was a long way from the Cumbo School that Rosetta Wright had first gone to seventeen years earlier in rural North Carolina. But there was one similarity between the schools that Rosetta and Rosa Lee attended: Both were part of the South's segregated school systems.

Rosa Lee's difficulty with reading and writing began in first grade. She does not remember getting any special help from teachers. "If you didn't learn it, you just didn't learn it," she said.

Then one morning at the beginning of fourth grade in 1946, nine-year-old Rosa Lee saw that school could be something more than a place of idleness and frustration. Although Rosa Lee's classroom was on the second floor, she followed a boy up to his third-floor classroom. "His name was Herman. I went up there and sat in the back. I meddled with the boy, but I saw he wasn't paying me a bit of mind. Then I got my mind off of him and started looking at how Miss Whitehead was teaching." Rosa Lee had heard Miss Whitehead did things differently in her classroom.

Within a few hours, Rosa Lee felt as if she had stumbled into a new school. On the second floor, she and her classmates rotated among four classrooms every day. But Miss Whitehead's students stayed all day in the same classroom and Miss Whitehead handled all the subjects. The students in Miss Whitehead's class had paper and pencils. Downstairs in her classroom, Rosa Lee was not required to write much of anything most of the time.

In Miss Whitehead's classroom, "the students didn't make a lot of noise. They didn't be in the back messing with each other. They were doing their work. I actually sat there and looked around. 'Well, I'll be derned.' This teacher acted like she really cared about her students."

On the second floor, the teachers seemed to spend a lot of time in the hall, talking to each other, while Rosa Lee and her classmates played and "meddled with each other." The teachers would "come back into the classroom if we got too loud. Tell us to be quiet. Then they went back out into the hallway." By contrast, Miss Whitehead's class seemed calm, orderly and exciting.

For three straight days, Rosa Lee climbed the stairs to Miss Whitehead's classroom and sat there, undetected. For the first time in her life, she found school fascinating.

"She was teaching!" she told me. "She made you feel like you were learning something." Rosa Lee planned to stay upstairs forever.

Why weren't the children downstairs taught like that? she asked a girlfriend. The friend told her that the second-floor class was for "slow learners."

No one had told Rosa Lee that she was a slow learner. She remembers angrily cutting her friend off. "I don't want to hear that shit!" Rosa Lee forever felt the sting of the phrase *slow learner*. It was not true that she was slow, but no one ever told Rosa Lee anything different.

It seems difficult to believe, but Rosa Lee went unnoticed in the class for those three days. On the fourth day, she raised her hand to ask a question. Miss Whitehead asked, "Who are you and what are you doing in my class?" She asked Rosa Lee to stay behind during recess.

After the other students left, Miss Whitehead asked Rosa Lee where she was supposed to be, and, Rosa Lee told her the name of her assigned teacher, adding that she preferred to be in Miss Whitehead's class. "But that's not the way we do things," Miss Whitehead told her. "You have to pass to my class."

Rosa Lee told her, "'I can't read, but I can do number work.' I showed her my paper."

Miss Whitehead insisted that she return to her regular classroom.

"But I like the way you teach here," Rosa Lee said. "Why won't you let me come up here?"

"You're not supposed to be up here," she remembers Miss Whitehead saying. "You're supposed to be downstairs."

Rosa Lee retreated to the second floor. "That was the most painful thing. I really wanted to stay up in her room. She was teaching and she made you feel like you were learning something."

Later that school year, Rosa Lee began skipping school frequently. When her teacher would turn her back to the classroom, "I would go right out that side door. Mr. Dash," Rosa Lee tells me one day as we stand inside her second-floor classroom at Giddings, which is now an adult education center. "I would go and get some other kids out of the room. Mr. Dash, I was a bad girl. We would hang on the back steps." On many mornings, she left the house as if she were going to school, but she spent the day roaming the streets of her Capitol Hill neighborhood instead. Rosa Lee says her mother was never notified about her absences. And despite her inability to read, she was promoted to the fifth and sixth grades.

At the end of her sixth-grade year, Rosa Lee's class was called to the assembly hall for its graduation ceremony. She knew she was not graduating so she sat in the last row, trying to hide. "I cried and cried, Mr. Dash," she recalls, sadly. "I didn't know what to do."

It was the spring of 1949 and Rosa Lee had been held back twice during her elementary school years. After the graduation ceremony, a schoolteacher came by her house. The teacher told Rosa Lee and her mother that Rosa Lee would be allowed to attend junior high school in the fall. "She told me I was being passed on account of my age," Rosa Lee said, "not because I had passed any of my classes."

Rosa Lee isn't sure how she made it as far in school as she did, considering her reading problems. Though she would have been allowed to return to seventh grade after Bobby was born, she never did go back to school. She had Ronnie at fifteen, and then, weeks after her sixteenth birthday, she married the father of Alvin, her third child.

Rosetta had insisted that Rosa Lee marry twenty-year-old Albert Cunningham. She told Albert if he didn't marry her daughter, she would report him to the police "on account of I was underage," says Rosa Lee. "I was only fifteen when I got pregnant by him." Rosa Lee didn't love Albert, but she was thrilled anyway. Marriage meant she could leave her mother's house forever. Four months after they married, she was back: her husband beat her after he found out that Rosa Lee had been sleeping with a neighborhood boy who lived in the house next-door to her mother's.

"My face was so swollen my mother didn't recognize me coming in the door," says Rosa Lee. "She told me, 'You don't have to go back to that man.'" Albert came by Rosetta's house that evening looking for Rosa Lee. Rosetta met him at the door and told him Rosa Lee was not ever going back to his house.

Yet those few months of independence made it hard for Rosa Lee to return. She and her mother argued often about Rosa Lee's welfare checks. Rosa Lee wanted the money to come to her, but Rosetta said she was too young. "What are you going to do with it?" Rosa Lee remembers her mother saying, "You don't even know how to pour piss out of a boot."

"I never saw a penny of it!" recalls Rosa Lee. "If I even asked for ten, fifteen dollars so I could have something, I didn't get it."

Rosa Lee craved her mother's love and affection, but she also feared her. She looked at her mother's broad back and powerful hands, and could think only about how to avoid the stinging slaps Rosetta often delivered during their arguments. "My mother classified me as very dumb," Rosa Lee told me one day. "It was almost as if she was making fun of me. I never felt that my mother loved me."

The friction between Rosetta and Rosa Lee, the quick smacks and harsh beatings for any infraction, was not something unique to them; it was a common tradition from the rural black South. "Especially between mothers and daughters," says Portia James. The way Rosetta raised Rosa Lee "seems to be a very typical [southern rural]

upbringing," as opposed to what would be expected in an urban culture.

Rosa Lee saw public housing as her escape. With the help of friends, and without telling her mother, she found her way to the public housing agency one afternoon. She asked a clerk there for help, telling him that she could not fill out the application by herself. The memory of his sneer still causes her mouth to tighten and her voice to thicken. "Back in those days, they didn't give you any sympathy when you said you couldn't read," she says. "It was like, 'So what? It ain't my fault.'" Humiliated, she trudged back to her mother's house. She vowed never again to reveal her illiteracy to someone she didn't know.

"Can you read?" she asked her then-current boyfriend, the boy who lived next-door to her mother. Of course he could read, he told her. Couldn't she?

No, Rosa Lee said defiantly. She sat next to him, brooding silently, while he filled out the applications to switch the welfare payments to her and to get Rosa Lee into public housing.

The showdown with Rosetta came four days later.

Rosa Lee was relaxing on the front porch, feeling good that she had completed her chores for the day, when she felt Rosetta's strong fingers jab her in the shoulder.

"Why didn't you tell me that you went and applied for welfare?" Rosetta demanded.

Rosa Lee had forgotten to check the mailbox. Now it was too late. She decided it was time to stand up to her mother. "I wanted to get me and my kids out of your hair," she remembers saying. "It seems like my kids were getting on your nerves."

Her mother's response was tinged with anger. "They're not the only ones getting on my damn nerves!"

Shaking her head at the memory, Rosa Lee stops narrating the scene for a moment. "My mother was very hard!" says Rosa Lee, before continuing.

Rosetta went on, "I don't know what this is going to prove. I've got to sign that I'm no longer taking care of them."

Rosa Lee had her response ready. "Mama, you're not taking care of them. *I'm* taking care of them. I take care of them all the time. Not only my children. I take care of my brothers and sisters. It's time for me to take my children and leave."

Rosa Lee was praying that this was as far as their conversation would go "because I was scared. She was ready to hit me because I was taking income from her."

Rosetta wanted to know more. Who helped her? How did she know where to send the application?

"I got somebody to help me! You wouldn't help me!" Rosa Lee retorted.

"Who are you talking to like that?" Rosetta said in the tone that Rosa Lee knew well.

"Mama," Rosa Lee pleaded, "you would not help me fill it out."

"How am I going to help you fill it out when I can't even read it myself?" Rosetta shouted.

Rosa Lee was stunned. She had assumed that her mother could read, and did not know that Ben helped Rosetta whenever there were any forms to fill out.

"Why didn't you tell me you couldn't read, Mama?" asked Rosa Lee.

" 'Cause I thought it was none of your damn business!" Rosetta said.

. . .

Patty is sitting up in her mother's bed, dressed in her mother's white nightgown, and surrounded by her mother's belongings. At thirty-four, she is very much Rosa Lee's little girl. Rosa Lee bustles around the bedroom, straightening this and dusting that, although the room is as clean as ever.

Patty's feeling much better today than she did yesterday, when she ran out of money and went into heroin withdrawal.

Yesterday was a day to forget, a day of sweating, abdominal cramps, watery eyes, and a runny nose. When Patty awoke this mild June morning, she was ready to face the world again. Later on, she hopes, her friend Steve Priester will give her money that she can use to buy drugs.

Priester is lounging in a chair, listening as I interview Patty. He is one of Patty's three "boyfriends," as she calls them. They've known each other for about nine months, ever since he moved into an apartment on the ground floor of the building where Rosa Lee and Patty live. When Priester's roommate kicked him out in December, Patty invited him to stay with her for several weeks in Rosa Lee's one-bedroom apartment.

Patty knows little about him, except that he is fifty-seven and comes from West Virginia. He periodically receives a check from relatives there, a small sum of money that he is eager to spend on her. In some ways, their relationship is simple enough: She sleeps with him, he gives her money.

But Priester wants more than sex. He tells Rosa Lee that he loves her daughter and that he intends to break Patty of her drug habit. His declarations seem odd because he knows that his money ends up financing Patty's drug use. Still, his concern for her seems genuine.

More than once, Rosa Lee has complained to Patty about her prostitution. She can't understand why Patty, who is HIV positive, makes no attempt to protect herself or anyone else. Whenever she's been drinking, she's told everyone in their neighborhood that she is carrying the AIDS virus. She's discussed her infection openly around her three boyfriends. They apparently accept that having unprotected sex with Patty exposes them to infection.

When Rosa Lee engaged in prostitution, before anyone ever heard of AIDS, she did it, she says, primarily to feed her children, not her drug habit. There is a difference, she says. Now it kills her to see her daughter travel this road.

"Patty makes me so shamed," Rosa Lee tells me one day. "I tell her, 'When you go outside, Patty, don't you feel those people talking about you? Don't you feel it?'"

And what does Patty say? I ask.

Rosa Lee's lower lip trembles, as it always does when she is upset. "She says, 'Mama, don't get mad at me. Ain't that the way you did it?'"

"You're going to have to take off that damn jacket and tie before we go in there," Rosa Lee said as I parked my car outside the three tan-brick buildings that make up Clifton Terrace.

That was fine with me. It was the last Sunday in May 1988, a hot, humid afternoon, and my shirt was already soaked. We had come to Clifton Terrace to look for Patty. Rosa Lee had offered to introduce her to me.

I had known Rosa Lee for five months at this point and it was only two weeks since her release from the D.C. jail, where we had met and she had agreed to let me spend time with her.

Rosa Lee wasn't sure of Patty's whereabouts. She had heard through the prison grapevine that Patty had turned over her first-floor Clifton Terrace apartment to several New York crack dealers, who were using it as a base of operation. It was a twenty-four-hour-a-day operation, so Patty could not stay in her apartment. She slept wherever she could find a bed.

Rosa Lee hoped that Ducky, who lived on the fifth floor of one of the Clifton Terrace buildings, could tell us where Patty was staying. The last time Rosa Lee had seen Ducky, he had been working for the same New York dealers.

Ducky answered our knock. His slight frame was swimming in a badly wrinkled, pin-striped three-piece suit. The suit was light green. The collar of his tan shirt was open and darkly soiled. The sag in his shoulders, the weary look in his eyes, the way he moved, all made it hard to believe that he was twenty-eight years old.

He listened warily as Rosa Lee explained that I was interested in writing about the family. He said he had just returned from church. "I'm very religious," he said. "I've been born again." As he talked about his renewed commitment to Christ, Rosa Lee shook her head as a warning to me not to believe him.

Finally, I interrupted. "Your mother has told me that you cook powdered cocaine into crack for New York City dealers operating out of your sister Patty's apartment in this building and that you have been addicted to crack for some time now."

Ducky literally jumped in his chair when I began talking. After I finished, he shot his mother a questioning, alarmed look.

"I told him everything, Ducky," Rosa Lee said, "so you can stop all that 'born again' shit."

Ducky's religious cloak fell away. He said that he and the New Yorkers had split. Now he was trying to sell crack on his own.

Rosa Lee asked if he knew where Patty was staying.

"Pussycat's," he said.

Rosa Lee scowled. Pussycat ran an oil joint in an apartment one floor below. Pussycat charged three dollars for entry. She also rented "works"—a hypodermic needle and tourniquet—for three dollars.

I asked Pussycat's real name. "I don't know her real name," Rosa Lee said brusquely. "I wish you'd stop asking me about last names and real names. People don't want you to know that. You might be setting them up to be arrested by the police or something."

Rosa Lee rapped hard on Pussycat's door. Someone opened it a crack. "Hello, Mama Rose," a man's voice said.

The door swung open. When the man saw me, he quickly began to close it. Rosa

Lee stopped the door with the palm of her left hand. "He's with me, Bernard," she said with quiet authority.

Bernard stood aside. Behind him, two women lay on stained sheetless mattresses on the living room floor, their bodies limp. We had found Patty and Pussycat.

It was so hot it was hard to breathe.

"You can go into the back!" Rosa Lee commanded Bernard.

Rosa Lee bent over Patty, who wore black slacks, a red shirt, and no shoes. "Wake up, Patty, wake up," Rosa Lee said, slapping her face. "I want you to meet someone." Each time Rosa Lee slapped her, Patty's eyelids opened for a few seconds.

"This isn't going to work," Rosa Lee said. "You'll have to meet Patty another day."

Two months later, I finally talked with Patty. I met her at the D.C. jail, where she was being held on a drug charge. Narcotics officers had raided her Clifton Terrace apartment seven months earlier. The New York drug dealers who rented her apartment were not there and did not return after the raid, but the policemen found twenty-four packets of crack and $300 in a bureau drawer. A warrant was issued for Patty's arrest on charges of running an illegal establishment. After months of searching, the policemen finally found Patty inside Pussycat's oil joint at the end of June. By this time, a second group of New York drug dealers was working out of Patty's apartment. Patty pleaded guilty to cocaine possession.

Jail meant a forced withdrawal from heroin for Patty, so I didn't know what to expect when we sat down to talk in her cell. She'd been in jail for a month, the longest period she had been without drugs since she was sixteen. But she seemed to be bearing up well. She had gained weight and looked nothing like the emaciated woman I had seen on that mattress.

I know Patty is Rosa Lee's favorite among the eight children, and I mention

to her that Bobby had told me that she is the best at manipulating their mother. Patty agrees and laughs.

"I can manipulate her like she do me," she adds. "I'm just like her. Anything my mother did, I did it. The way she walks, I can walk. The way she talks, I can talk. I just wanted to be like my mother all my life."

Patty has had even less education than her brothers, having gone no farther than the fourth grade. She dropped out at age fourteen when she was pregnant with her son, Junior.

The teenage father of her son had wanted to marry her, but Patty wasn't interested in having a husband. A husband would tie her down, put demands on her. But giving birth to a baby changed her status in her eyes. "Ever since I had a little baby, I was a grown woman," she brags. Two pregnancies with two different men followed Junior's birth. She aborted both because she did not want any more children. One was enough for her to say she was an adult.

As the interview progressed, Patty spoke rapidly looking down at the chewed fingernails of her right hand, just as her mother does when describing some painful or embarrassing incident. I was not prepared for her candor: Within the first hour she told me that a thirteen-year-old male relative had raped her when she was eight. He threatened to hurt her if she told anyone. The assaults continued and the relationship eventually became consensual. It ended when Patty was twenty-two.

I later confirmed her account with the relative, who agreed to discuss it as long as he was not identified. He denied threatening Patty and defended his behavior, saying Patty would often climb into the bed he shared with two other male relatives. When I pointed out the age difference between the two of them, he grudgingly acknowledged, "Yeah, I guess you could say it was rape. I hadn't really looked at it like that."

When Patty was a teenager, Alvin found out about the relative's behavior and beat him up, Alvin later told me.

The first rape happened in January 1966, while Rosa Lee was incarcerated in the Jessup, Maryland, prison. When Rosa Lee was released in July, Patty tried to tell her about it, but she didn't know how. Looking back, Patty says she believes her mother should have known something was wrong, should have wondered why the teenage boy was hanging around her so much. "I feel like she could have done something to stop it."

By the time Patty was born in January 1958, Rosa Lee already had five children, all boys. Rosa Lee named her Donna, but no one has ever called her that. When she was little, she was known as "Papoose," because Rosa Lee thought the shape of her eyes resembled those of a Native American baby. Over time, Papoose became Patty.

When she was young, Patty had long, straight hair that Rosa Lee liked to twist into a single braid down her back. She had her mother's dark skin and her father's round, cherubic face. Otherwise, David Wright didn't have much of a role in her life; when he died in the mid-1970s, Patty didn't even consider attending his funeral.

In the succession of cramped row houses and apartments where Rosa Lee and the children lived during the 1960s, the boys shared mattresses. Patty often slept in her mother's room by herself, since Rosa Lee was working nights at the Ko Ko Club and the 821 Club. When Rosa Lee was shake dancing at the 821 Club, she would practice her routine in front of a mirror in her bedroom. Patty was the only one of her children who was allowed to watch.

Patty was three years old when Rosa Lee began bringing home some of the customers. Rosa Lee thought nothing of having sex with Patty in the room, even in the same bed. As Patty grew older, her mother's nighttime trysts would awaken her. "I would look over and Patty would be sitting up in the bed, wide awake, watching us," remembers Rosa Lee. Patty slept in the bed with Rosa Lee until she was ten years old.

Several months before Rosa Lee was first sent to prison, she caught seven-year-old Patty instructing an older neighborhood boy in sexual intercourse in an upstairs bedroom of the row house Rosa Lee shared with her mother and their seventeen children. Rosa Lee was shocked. She chased the boy out of the house, then sat down to talk to Patty. She wanted to know from whom Patty had learned about sex. Rosa Lee assumed one of her own younger brothers had taught Patty about sex or even initiated her into sexual activity. But that was not the case.

"Patty looked me dead in the face," Rosa Lee recalls, "and said, 'You, Mama.'" Patty recounted in detail lying in bed at night watching Rosa Lee with boyfriends and with tricks. "I had nothing more to say," adds Rosa Lee. "I realized it was my fault. She was just doing what she had seen me do and wanted to imitate me. She's been like that all her life."

Rosa Lee argues she was working as a prostitute so that she and her children could *survive*. "You keep talking about prostitution," she tells me heatedly one day. "I saw it as survival."

In 1969, when Patty was eleven, one of her mother's customers made an unusual request: He asked Rosa Lee if he could have sex with Patty.

There's no way to recapture exactly what went through Rosa Lee's mind as she considered this request. It is not something that she wanted to remember or talk about. After Patty told me about it, I waited almost three years before broaching the subject with Rosa Lee. When I did, she angrily denied that it ever happened and accused Patty of lying. She was sure that if I asked Patty again in her presence, Patty would admit that it was a lie. But I knew Rosa Lee well enough to tell that she was lying and that Patty had told me the truth.

Five months after Rosa Lee's denial, the three of us were spending the day together. We were eating lunch in a downtown restaurant when I gingerly brought up the issue of Rosa Lee prostituting Patty.

Rosa Lee turned to Patty and waited in silence for her daughter to answer.

Patty looked her mother in the eye. "The big fat man," said Patty, and then named him.

Rosa Lee began questioning Patty, as if getting more facts might help jog her memory. "How old was you, Patty?" and "Was I on drugs then?" and "Did he approach me, or did he approach you?"

"He approached you about it," Patty said calmly. "He'd give you the money. Give you about forty and I would get ten dollars of it. That's all I would get. 'Cause I was a little girl. You asked me about it, and I said, 'Yeah, I want to help you.' Remember that? You were feeding everybody and doing it all on your own."

Rosa Lee turned to me. There was pain in her eyes. "Okay," she said. "I just feel so shamed."

Piece by agonizing piece, the story came out. Patty said her mother asked her to have sex with the man, who was then in his mid-forties. Patty agreed. Rosa Lee told the man it would cost forty dollars—twice as much as she had been charging him. The man drove Patty to his home in suburban Maryland. When Patty returned, she put two twenty dollar bills in Rosa Lee's hand.

"Boy, my mind was gone," Rosa Lee says. The man came back to have sex with Patty three or four times. After each time, Rosa Lee asked Patty, "Did he hurt you?" Sometimes Patty would tell her yes, but she continued to have sex with the man on a regular basis.

One morning Patty woke up in severe abdominal pain. She couldn't stand up

straight and couldn't walk, she remembers. An ambulance was called and took her to D.C. General Hospital. She had gonorrhea. She was kept at the hospital for a short period to make sure the infection cleared up.

Rosa Lee decided to use Patty's illness to get more money from the man. She told him that Patty had been taken to the hospital because of complications caused by a pregnancy. Hospital officials were upset because Patty was so young, Rosa Lee told him, and they wanted to know the name and age of the father. The man pleaded with Rosa Lee not to give the officials his name.

Rosa Lee told Patty about her scam and asked Patty to tell the man, when he came to see her in the hospital, that she wanted to abort her pregnancy and needed money to have it done outside the hospital. "When he came, I couldn't stand to look at the *dog!*" remembers Patty. "I hated him!" But she did what Rosa Lee had asked.

"I ain't never seen a man so scared in my life," says Rosa Lee. "He sure didn't want anybody to know that he was having a baby by a baby." He gave Rosa Lee $240 to get Patty an abortion.

There were other men after that, perhaps as many as a dozen. One was a thirty-three-year-old relative. The men offered to pay much more than Rosa Lee's usual rate, $100 or more, amounts that made Patty's head swim. Patty said her mother always asked her if she was willing. Patty never turned her mother down. "I went with the tricks for my mother," she says. "I had a body like I was fourteen. The men was hurting me so bad I could have died. But I seen how hard it was for her to take care of all of us. I love my mother, so I would do it all over again. But I was getting very hurt. . . . At times I wanted to hate her, but I couldn't see myself doing that 'cause my mother's too sweet for that."

The interview has been draining for all three of us. Rosa Lee is hanging her head, unable to look at me or Patty. Patty is relieved, she says, that this part of her story is out and that I am planning to write about it. She wants people to understand why she is the way she is, as she puts it.

"Is this part of the bond between you and Patty?" I ask Rosa Lee, verbally prodding her to lift her head. "Part of the very close relationship that you two share? You don't have that kind of relationship with your other daughter or with any of your sons."

"Yeah," replies Rosa Lee. "We can do things together and I don't hear about it any more from Patty. We all have did things to make money. Trick people out of money."

"I'm curious about why you lied to me when I asked you about it," I say.

Rosa Lee drops her head again, slightly muffling her voice. "I don't know," she says. "I didn't know if I should have went that far."

"Why are you staring at your ring?" I continue. "Look at me!"

Patty laughs. She is enjoying her mother's unease.

Raising her head, Rosa Lee cuts an angry look at Patty. "Me and my daughter," she says in an even voice, "we have been through so much together. And some things I'm very ashamed of, you know. And the things that she had did for us. 'Cause she was attractive and I wasn't. She did things that other girls wouldn't do, like have sex with grown men."

As a fourth grader at Shadd Elementary School in the fall of 1969, Patty stood out for all the wrong reasons. At eleven, she was two years older than most of her classmates.

She had spent three years in the third grade and had never been taught to read. Her attendance was spotty. She was headed for trouble, and her teachers didn't know what to do about it.

The other children teased Patty because she couldn't read. "I hated school," she recalls. "The boys would tease me when I wouldn't do nothing with them. Girls used to do it all the time in front of boys who might like me." They'd say, "She can't even read. Spell cat! Spell I!"

Nancy McAllister—the social worker who had had such an impact on Eric's life—tried to intervene with Patty, making frequent visits to Rosa Lee's apartment in the late mornings, well after school had started. Rosa Lee was always at home and McAllister did not even suspect that she was selling heroin. "But I knew something was going on," she recalls.

McAllister often found Patty at home as well. Rosa Lee would tell her that Patty was sick, but McAllister didn't believe it. She suspected instead that Patty had been staying up late at night. "I'd see her just laying around in bed," she said. "I would get her to go to school."

But what concerned McAllister most was the way Patty dressed on Fridays. "I remember being so amazed at this girl," McAllister said. "She used to come to my office in a wig that reached her waist. She always wore tight, short skirts. At eleven, she was very shapely. Fridays were when most of the men got paid. Those who had jobs."

McAllister asked Patty why she dressed the way she did.

"Oh, this is my evening to do my thing," McAllister remembers Patty saying.

"What thing?" McAllister asked.

"Oh, you know" was all Patty would say.

"Patty never really came out and told me," McAllister continues. "She was really beyond her years. The kinds of things that she would talk to adults about were not kid things." McAllister suspected something was wrong, but she had no conclusive evidence that she could report to authorities. Besides, Patty wasn't the only student whose home life seemed troubled. "The teachers probably had ten or twelve other kids with the same kind of background. It was just overwhelming."

Change the name and go back twenty years, and it's hard to tell the difference between Patty's school record and Rosa Lee's. Both fell behind at an early age. Both began skipping school regularly. Neither one had a parent who believed education was important. Neither one learned to read by the time she dropped out.

There's one more parallel: Rosa Lee was fourteen when she gave birth to Bobby, her first child. Patty was fourteen when Junior was born. And like her mother, that's also when she dropped out of school.

Patty learned about drugs much the same way she learned about sex. By watching.

She was about eleven years old. She had noticed that Ronnie, seventeen, and his girlfriend would lock themselves in his room in the afternoon. Patty wondered what they were doing. She figured she could find out by hiding in their bedroom closet.

"That girl used to hide in my closet," Ronnie remembers. "She used to find out where I'd hide my money and steal it." Patty says she spent the money she stole from Ronnie on doll babies, candy, and ice cream.

After several thefts, Ronnie began checking the closet every time he came into his bedroom. One afternoon, however, Ronnie and his girlfriend didn't bother to check. Anxious to get their fix, they hurried into the bedroom, took out a bag of white powder, cooked it into a liquid, and filled a hypodermic needle. Patty had a clear view through the slightly open closet door. "I watched Ronnie put the needle in his arm," she says.

After Ronnie pushed the liquid into his vein, she watched her brother's worried frown change to a look of pleasure. She stepped from the closet. Neither Ronnie nor his girlfriend showed any reaction until she told Ronnie she wanted to try it. "You better not," he said, "but then again, if you're going to try it, let me hit you first."

Ronnie refused to inject her that day. But, Patty told me, "I knew then, 'Well, I'm gonna try that one day.'"

That day came in late 1973, just a few weeks before Patty's sixteenth birthday. It was the day Patty witnessed her mother and the school crossing guard doing bam and exposed the crossing guard for holding some back. Patty had demanded a hit and Rosa Lee had given in.

As Rosa Lee tells me about this critical moment, she looks pained. She says she did too much "dirty living," that if she hadn't used drugs, her children wouldn't have either. But at the time, she felt as if she had no choice, that she had no way to stop Patty from traveling the same road she had.

A year later, Patty graduated to heroin. A year after that, so did Rosa Lee. By 1976, they were both heavy heroin users. "Our getting high together and even tricking together wasn't like mother and daughter," remembers Rosa Lee. "It was like two sisters."

By the time Patty was sixteen, Junior was two years old. She paid for her heroin with her welfare check, working as a hitter, stealing, pulling any scam she could think of, and "whoring, selling my body," she says. "I didn't like it, but I didn't like me or my mother to suffer." When she went tricking on 14th Street, N.W., Rosa Lee often went along, Patty says, "to watch my back and make sure I didn't get caught up with anything crazy."

Three years later, she had her own apartment in Clifton Terrace, which she shared with a man named Joe Billy, whom she considered her common-law husband. Joe Billy was a 14th Street juggler who kept a little money on him and supplied Patty with all the heroin she needed. She stopped working as a prostitute.

In 1983, the Superior Court's family division took ten-year-old Junior away from Patty because it considered him a "child in need of supervision." Two years later, Joe Billy was arrested on a heroin charge, went into withdrawal in the D.C. jail, suffered a stroke, and died. Patty, without a welfare check or a man in her life, went back into the street. This time she worked as a drug dealer as well as a prostitute.

"I was never as good as my mother dealing," says Patty. "I don't have the patience for it." Soon after she started juggling on the street, she used up $850 worth of heroin belonging to a dealer she was supposed to be working for. "He was looking for me to kill me," she recalls. "He got his girls to jump me. Put a gun in my face. I hid out 'til my mother came home. She paid it off for me. Not all at once. Little by little."

"Patty thinks she's as good as I am at manipulating," says Rosa Lee, laughing. The three of us are sitting around her living room talking about a scheme Patty had tried to pull off to get money out of Rosa Lee a couple of nights before. "She's watched me manipulating and surviving for so long she comes up with scams that she's seen *me* pull! She thinks I've forgotten them."

Patty's latest scam unfolded on a bitterly cold night in mid-February, but cold weather—or any type of bad weather, for that matter—does not stop Patty in her daily quest for drugs. Patty was broke, it was 1:30 in the morning, and the checks that arrive on the first of the month were still two weeks away from delivery. Because of that, Patty could not get credit for heroin or crack from the local dealers. She suspected her mother had some money, probably hidden in her underpants, where Patty couldn't get to it. She enlisted one of her regular tricks to help her in a plan to get money from her mother. Patty entered the apartment with the man, walked quietly past Richard, asleep on the couch, and slipped with the man into her mother's bedroom.

Rosa Lee was sound asleep. Patty punched her several times on the arm to wake her. "Mama," Patty said. "Mama. Wake up! I got to talk to you."

Rosa Lee was tired. She knew Patty had awakened her to talk her out of money for drugs. "Patty, please don't ask me for no money," she whined. "Please don't ask, because I don't have it."

Patty told Rosa Lee that the man with her had let her smoke crack in his apartment, that the man fell asleep and left two billies lying on a coffee table. Patty said she injected both of them. "I knew I could pay for them," Patty told her mother.

"You mean, you knew I could pay for them," shouted an angry Rosa Lee, "but I'm not giving you a goddamn cent!"

Rosa Lee reached over the side of her bed and pulled her large black pocketbook up onto her lap. Patty had not thought of looking in there because her mother *never* left money in her pocketbook when she went to bed. Rosa Lee opened the pocketbook and dramatically pulled out a bill. She was already outacting her daughter. "You see what I got here?" said Rosa Lee. "I got exactly ten dollars."

Patty had seen this dramatic gesture since she was a child. She knew not to believe her mother. She was now convinced that her mother had more money than the ten-dollar bill. Indeed, Rosa Lee had another two hundred dollars in twenty-dollar bills rolled into a tight knot in a stocking and pushed into the top of her underpants. She kept the bed covers up over her stomach so Patty could not see it.

"Get out of my face, Patty!" yelled Rosa Lee.

Her yelling had awakened Richard. He came into the bedroom. He asked what the man was doing in Rosa Lee's bedroom. No one answered Richard, but Rosa Lee said to Patty's friend, "Well, mister, I don't know what happened, but you're not getting any money from me."

Patty began begging Rosa Lee, saying the man would hurt her if Rosa Lee didn't give her forty dollars for the two billies. "I don't give a damn, Patty" was Rosa Lee's only response.

By now, Richard too had figured out Patty's scam and told the man he had to leave. The man, who had seated himself on a chair in Rosa Lee's room, got up and walked out of the apartment without a word of complaint.

Patty looks a little sheepish and Rosa Lee chortles as she concludes the story.

"Ain't no man going to put two billies down in front of a dope addict and fall asleep!" Rosa Lee laughs. "Mr. Dash, even you know better than that!"

Months later, Rosa Lee is telling me in front of Patty how embarrassed she is that Patty is prostituting herself with a lot of the boys and men in their community, and most of them are not using condoms.

"If they think they caught the virus from Patty," says Rosa Lee, "they might come in here and shoot all of us. I can't get her to stop, Mr. Dash, or at least make them wear a condom."

"Is that true?" I ask Patty. "Most of the men don't wear condoms?"

"That's true," Patty stutters, "but it's not my fault. They don't like to wear them. Most of them know I got the virus anyway. If they don't know, they know that I'm a drug addict and a prostitute. Who else is going to have the virus, but *me*! It ain't no secret who gets the virus." All three of her boyfriends, "Howard, Steve, and Anthony, know I have it."

"I'm selling sex for money for drugs," she continues. "I don't care if they use a condom or not. Just pay me my money! It's up to them to use a condom."

"Do they ever express any fear about catching the virus?" I ask.

"No, and I don't bring it up," replies Patty. "What am I going to bring it up for?"

It is a July morning in 1992 and Rosa Lee has Patty on her mind.

We are having breakfast at McDonald's. Rosa Lee is upset: Her latest urine sample at the drug-treatment clinic was "dirty"— the second time she has tested positive for heroin this year. One more strike and she will be required to appear before a team of counselors, who could decide to suspend her from the program.

"Mr. Dash," she says, "I can't go back to the way I used to be."

For more than a year, her urine samples had been clean; she had such a good record that a market developed for her urine among the other methadone patients. In the bathroom, someone would whisper, "Rosa Lee, you clean?" and hand over a dollar or two. The clinic didn't monitor the bathrooms closely, so the risk of getting caught was low. Then, for some reason, she began to slip. Over a six-month period, she used heroin six times. Every time, Patty was involved. Six times is not the same as a daily habit, but it's still not good enough.

Patty is part of the problem, Rosa Lee tells me. If only Patty weren't addicted to heroin, if only Patty didn't bring heroin into her apartment, if only she could get Patty into methadone treatment—if only she could do something about Patty, then she wouldn't be facing the risk of getting thrown out of the program.

She tells me she plans to take Patty to the methadone clinic the next Monday and enroll her. Monday comes and goes without Patty enrolling, and I hear nothing more about it.

In August, Rosa Lee is arrested for shoplifting several expensive scarves from the downtown branch of Hecht's. The day after spending a night in jail, she calls to tell me about the incident. She needed money, she says, to pay off one of Patty's drug debts. The dealer had threatened to hurt Patty.

Rosa Lee is planning to plead guilty. I remind her that the last time she appeared in court, in 1991, the commissioner warned her that another shoplifting charge would land her in jail for a long time. "Why do you have to remind me of that?" an irritated Rosa Lee asks me. "You're like the goddamn voice of doom. 'You know they're going to give you a lot of time, Rose,'" she says, mimicking me. "How do you know so goddamn much, anyway? Did God go on vacation and put you in charge?"

"OK, OK," I plead with her. "I'm sorry I mentioned it."

At her trial in September, she tells Commissioner John W. King that she is guilty. King listens intently as her criminal record is outlined—a total of thirteen convictions for shoplifting and drug-related charges—and then pronounces sentence: two years probation.

Rosa Lee decides to celebrate. On the way back to her apartment, we pick up a pizza. Lucian Perkins, a *Washington Post* photographer who has been working with me since the beginning of the project, arrives.

Patty is happy to hear the good news. As we eat, I notice a flurry of activity. There's a knock at the door. It's Junebug, the drug dealer who lives on the first floor. He and Rosa Lee talk quietly and he leaves. I assume that Patty has persuaded Rosa Lee to buy her a bag of heroin. Sure enough, Patty brings out a metal bottle cap, mixes some powdered heroin with water in the cap, and heats it with a match. She injects herself in her abdomen.

Patty motions to Rosa Lee to lie down. To my surprise, she does. Using the same needle, Patty injects her mother in the leg. Rosa Lee's eyes flutter for a brief second, and our eyes meet.

Patty has allowed Lucian to photograph her before while injecting heroin, but this is the first time that he has seen Rosa Lee do it. Over my left shoulder, I can hear the whir and click of his camera. When we leave, neither Patty nor Rosa Lee says anything about what has happened, and neither do I.

When I return from a few days of vacation, there is an urgent message on my office voice mail from Rosa Lee. I call her. As soon as she hears my voice, she interrupts. "I want to apologize. I know you didn't like what you saw, and I wanted you to know I'm sorry. Very sorry!"

"You don't have to apologize to me," I tell her.

"You can try that on someone else, buddy," she says. "I saw your face when Patty hit me. You were in front of me. I saw your eyes! I'll never let you see me take another hit!"

I hadn't realized that I had shown any reaction, even though it was difficult for me to watch. Nor was I prepared for her apology. After all, she had told me about other slips. Why did it matter so much if I saw it rather than heard about it?

But it did matter. To Rosa Lee, it mattered a great deal.

Over the next several months, the slip-ups stopped. She began badgering Patty once more about having unprotected sex with Priester and other men. She talked about moving again—this time to a senior citizens' housing complex—to get away from the drug traffic in her apartment.

Rosa Lee had tried to cut ties with Patty before, without much success. This time, she told me, would be different: She would make arrangements for Patty to take over her apartment; Patty would pay the sixty-four dollars rent out of her welfare check.

I ask Rosa Lee what she would do if Patty spent the money on drugs and lost the apartment.

"Mr. Dash, that's her business," she said. "I don't care."

KEY TERMS

morass   A swamp; usually used metaphorically to refer to a tangled mess.

Emancipation   The 1863 Emancipation Act, instigated by Abraham Lincoln, which freed American slaves.

DISCUSSION QUESTIONS

1. Rosa Lee, her mother, Rosetta, and her daughter, Patty, all had their first children at fourteen or fifteen. Rosa Lee had eight children, and her mother had twenty-two, of whom twelve lived to adulthood. Can you come to any conclusion about why these women had so many children? Why do you think they began having children so early? (Dash tells us specifically about Patty.) What do you think are some of the results of the early and large families? Consider not only the children's chances for the future, but also their relationships with their parents and the limits these early, large families imposed on their mothers.

2. Rosa Lee's mother, Rosetta, was married, and raised her children with the help of her husband. Though Rosa Lee married, she never developed a long-term, conjugal relationship with any of her sexual partners, and neither did Patty. Why do you think Rosetta's family life was so different from those of her daughter and her granddaughter? Can you make a comparative assessment of these three lives? Is any one of them more rewarding than another? Fewer and fewer American women are waiting to marry or even to establish a long-term conjugal relationship with a man before having a child. Some of these never-married mothers are impoverished women of color, like Rosa Lee and Patty, but others are members of the middle and upper classes. What do you think is going on with the declining rate of marriage, and why?

3. Both Rosa Lee and Patty have had sex with men for money and/or drugs. Patty began, at Rosa Lee's suggestion, when she was eleven. Rosa Lee says she took money for sex in order to feed her children. Though Patty's first ventures into prostitution were intended to help her mother and win her affection, she now says she works as a prostitute for drug money. Drugs and child prostitution aside, what do you think of prostitution? It is extremely widespread and historically persistent; do you think it is possible to eradicate it? Some people argue that a woman's body is her own property, and she ought to be able to earn money from it with any consenting adult in any way she sees fit. How does that argument strike you? Is it possible to discuss prostitution and *not* discuss such issues as drugs and child prostitution?

4. Mark Fleisher, an anthropologist and criminologist who has studied gang members in the Midwest, contends that among the gang members and hangers-on he knows, there are no marriages and no romantic relationships. Male-female relationships, he says (personal communication), are based on exchange: The females provide sex, and the males provide drugs and money. How does Fleisher's assessment fit the lives of Rosa Lee and Patty? It will be possible for you to provide exact evidence from Dash's account to shore up your answer. What has happened to romantic love? Do you think that romantic love is universal? Why? Do you think romantic love requires specific circumstances to flourish? What do you think those circumstances are?

"Not That Sort of Women"

RACE, GENDER, AND SEXUAL VIOLENCE DURING THE MEMPHIS RIOT OF 1866

Hannah Rosen

For reasons that are not entirely clear, many American college students appear to believe that the study of history is a tedious exercise in the memorization of names, dates, and events that are of significance only to sadistic professors. Hannah Rosen's article is a wonderful example of why history is both important and fascinating. The Memphis Riot, though a tragedy to those involved, was not a historical event of the significance of the Sack of Rome or the Fall of Constantinople. Indeed, most Americans who live outside the Southeastern United States have never heard of the Memphis Riot. Why, then, would an article about it be so significant?

First of all, Rosen's account of the riot sets the stage clearly. However much or little we know about the Civil War and its aftermath, we know exactly what events led up to the riot, what went on during the riot, and what its aftermath was. But though helpful, this clarity is not why the article is so valuable.

Like all good historical writers, Rosen goes beyond the events themselves and analyzes them for us. It is not enough to know what happened; we want also to know the significance of historical events. If we cannot understand the significance of historical events, then they are of no more use to us than lists of baseball players' batting averages. If we do understand their significance, then we have some insight into why present events, attitudes, and ideas have evolved as they have. And we are likely to understand more about ourselves, into the bargain.

In reading Rosen's article, try to keep separate four categories of information: (1) events that led up to the riot; (2) the events of the riot itself; (3) the aftermath of the riot; (4) the analysis of events in the riot. Rosen weaves these four elements together so that we can see how they are all related to each other. But part of our job, as readers and students, is to unravel the web so that we can assess the relationships.

The humiliated losers of wars can be a dangerous population. Full of anger and resentment, they seek retribution and vindication wherever they see a likely opportunity. As the Germans looked for a scapegoat after the First World War and found it in the Jews, many southerners after the Civil War found inevitable scapegoats for their defeat in the Black population, nearly all of them former slaves. These newly freed Blacks antagonized many white southerners because of the memories evoked by their very existence. But their removal from plantation slave cabins to formerly forbidden urban areas and their use of urban public spaces were more galling yet to some white southerners, particularly those who felt their own tenuous hold on respectability, legitimacy, and security threatened by competition from emancipated Blacks who were now their neighbors.

Though African American men competed with working-class white men most specifically for labor and income, Rosen suggests that it was African American women who offered working-class white men an opportunity to regain their war-ravaged pride and identity as southern white men. Lower-middle-class white men already felt vulnerable to upper-class white men, and their recent defeat by the Union Army threatened their sense of regional identity and racial superiority. Through the rape of Black women they could assert their superiority not only over Black women, but through them, over the Black men who had failed to protect their wives and sisters. Until accounts of the war in the former Yugoslavia publicized military policies of systematic rape, many modern observers of political strife had managed to forget that rape has been an inevitable companion to war since before the Trojan women watched their husbands, brothers, and sons lose to the Greeks on the plain below the battlements, and knew for certain what fate awaited them.

On June 1, 1866, in the Gayoso House hotel in downtown Memphis, Tennessee, a former slave named Frances Thompson spoke before a congressional committee investigating the riot that had occurred in that city one month earlier. Thompson informed the committee that seven white rioters broke into the house that she shared with another former slave, Lucy Smith. Thompson recounted her efforts to resist the demand for "some woman to sleep with" made by these men. "I said that we were not that sort of women, and they must go." Yet her refusal to have sex proved unacceptable to the intruders. Thompson described to the committee how both she and Lucy Smith were raped.[1]

Frances Thompson was among five freedwomen who recounted being subject to sexual violence during what became known as the Memphis riot.[2] This attack on recently emancipated slaves commenced in the late afternoon of May 1, 1866, and persisted for three days. It took place primarily in the neighborhood of South Memphis, where the freed community of the city was concentrated. The assailants were mostly city police and other lower-middle-class white men, many of whom lived in the same neighborhood with the riot's victims.[3] The riot represented the culmination of increasing

tensions between a growing freed community and white Memphians, above all between African American Union soldiers stationed at the federal army's Fort Pickering in South Memphis and the city's white police force. During the riot at least forty-eight African Americans were killed and between seventy and eighty were wounded.[4] Rioters set fire to ninety-one houses and cabins, four churches, and twelve schools, robbed one hundred freedpeople, and destroyed approximately $127,000 worth of property.[5] Rioters also raped at least five freedwomen.[6] Freedwomen's testimony about these sexual attacks reveals the ways that gender and sexuality became key sites for waging battles over race after emancipation, as rioters struggled to reclaim privileges as white men, and black women struggled to be free.

For African American women to testify in a legal forum about sexual violence was itself a dramatic political act in the battles of Reconstruction. Prior to emancipation, one demonstration of white male dominance of southern society had been the virtual legal impunity with which white men sexually abused African American women. Antebellum laws in the southern states generally excluded female slaves from the legal definition of those who could be

---

Source: Hannah Rosen, "'Not That Sort of Women': Race, Gender, and Sexual Violence during the Memphis Riot of 1866." Pp. 267–293 in *Sex, Love, Race: Crossing Boundaries in North American History.* New York: New York University Press, 1999. Reprinted by permission of New York University Press.

raped, and did not recognize their abuse as a crime.[7] This exclusion was justified in the law by the absence of legal sanction for marriage between slaves and thus the lack of patriarchal rights that could be violated by coerced sexual intercourse outside marriage.[8] This logic dovetailed with widespread imagery representing black women as sexually indiscriminate, consenting to and even pursuing sexual activity with white men, and thus lacking feminine "virtue."[9] It was this quality of "virtue," along with patriarchal rights, that was imagined to be injured in the crime of rape. Thus freedwomen declaring publicly that the violence they had suffered constituted rape, that they were the "sort of women" who could be violated and who deserved legal protection from sexual abuse, represented a radical reversal of both antebellum legal notions and white constructions of black womanhood.

Historians of the Memphis Riot have often pointed to the occurrence of rape to highlight the atrocities and terror that freedpeople suffered over those tumultuous three days.[10] Yet the significance of the specifically sexual form of this violence has not been explored.[11] Sexual violence in the midst of a race riot reveals more than simply extreme brutality. The instances where rioters raped freedwomen reflect the nexus of race, gender, and sexuality within the overall power struggles gripping the post–Civil War South. I will explore this nexus by examining the ways in which post-emancipation struggles over racial relations and identities in Memphis were fought out on the ground of gender and sexuality.[12] Gendered constructions of race emerged in the everyday political conflicts in Memphis in the time leading up to the riot, particularly in contests over the meaning and significance of race transpiring in various arenas of the city's public space. Strikingly similar gendered constructions of race were invoked by rioters when they sexually assaulted black

women. This discursive convergence sheds light on the historical meaning of the sexual violence that occurred during the Memphis Riot. As white southern men struggled to reclaim the power and privilege that white manhood had signified in a slave society, they turned to black women's gender and sexuality as a site for reenacting and reproducing racial inequality and subordination. This politicization of gender and sexuality shaped the perilous terrain upon which freedwomen struggled to render freedom meaningful for themselves and their communities.

Complicating a reading of the sexual violence that occurred during the Memphis Riot is the riot's unexpected postscript. Ten years after testifying before the congressional committee about having been raped, Frances Thompson was arrested for being a man dressed in women's clothing. Thompson's transvestism raises important questions about the form and meaning of the sexual violence that occurred during the Memphis Riot, the full implications of which cannot be explored within the confines of this article.[13] I will, though, discuss the propagandistic use made of Frances Thompson's cross-dressing by conservatives in their efforts to discredit all the women who testified that they had been raped and in general to oppose Reconstruction in Memphis. The newspaper coverage that followed Thompson's exposure as a cross-dresser reveals again the central role that gender and sexuality played in contests over race in the post-emancipation South.

Prior to the Civil War, Memphis's black population had been relatively small: 3,882 people, or 17 percent of the city's inhabitants in 1860. Ninety-five percent of this group were slaves whose public conduct was strictly regulated by city ordinances.[14] Although laws prohibiting slaves' travel through the city without a pass, hiring out their own time, residing away from their owner, or congregating for social or political activities were never fully enforced, city police were empowered to interfere with and constrain the actions of African Americans in the city at all times.[15] Moving about the streets of antebellum Memphis, white and black people observed and experienced racial difference in their everyday lives in part through inequalities in the power to utilize the city's public spaces.

The Civil War permanently altered these racial dynamics in Memphis, where public space was transformed by the resultant change in status and dramatic increase in the number of African Americans. The occupation of the city by the Union army in June 1862 brought thousands of African American migrants to the city. Regiments of black troops were stationed at Fort Pickering, located at the southern edge of the city.[16] Following these troops came their family members and other fugitive slaves seeking the protection of the Union forces. By 1865 these migrants together with African Americans already living in Memphis constituted 40 percent of the city's total population, or just under eleven thousand people, an increase to the antebellum black population on of 275 percent.[17] The significance of this migration for social relations and public activity in Memphis lay not only in its size. In the past, African Americans had been brought to Memphis by force, to be sold in slave markets and to labor in white-owned businesses and homes; after the Union occupation, they entered Memphis as a "city of refuge," a space in which they would be free.[18]

During the Civil War and Reconstruction years, refugees from slavery forcefully entered public spaces in Memphis—the streets, markets, saloons, and other visible spaces of labor and leisure; public sites of legal authority, such as police stations, the Freedmen's Bureau, and courtrooms; civil institutions such as schools, churches, and benevolent societies; and realms of public

discourse such as speaking events, parades, and the Republican press—in anticipation of new rights and freedoms.[19] The political status of these new public actors in Memphis was uncertain. They were no longer slaves, yet they had no formal political rights. Until the Civil Rights Act was passed in April 1866, African Americans were denied even the most nominal legal recognition as citizens.[20] Nonetheless, freedpeople made use of the limited power liable to them to claim many aspects of citizenship. They began their lives in Memphis with expectations for freedom that included the ability to enjoy free movement, social life, and family in an urban community of their own choosing, to be compensated for their labor, and to have these rights protected by law in the form of the Freedmen's Bureau and the police power of the occupying Union army. They expected to be citizens of the city. The reaction of many whites illustrates how powerfully African Americans' public activities in Memphis disrupted whites' previous norms of racial difference rooted in slavery and adumbrated a new nonracialized citizenship. A conflict over public space ensued, as white Memphians sought therein to redraw racial boundaries, delegitimate black people's public presence, and oppose the new power differentials embodied in what they observed around them.

African American women were central actors in the process of laying claim to a new urban citizenship in ways that dramatically transformed public life in Memphis. Women constituted a sizable proportion of those former slaves who made their way to Memphis both during and after the Civil War.[21] White Memphians quickly experienced the reality of emancipation and the changed meaning of race through these women's movement through public space and their use of public authority in the form of the Freedmen's Bureau Court and the police protection of the Union army.[22] Some whites responded by attempting to cast black women's new public presence in a disparaging light.[23] Both white police officers and newspaper editors from the city's conservative press, in their conduct toward and representation of freedwomen in the city's public spaces, enlisted gendered constructions of race, specifically a discourse representing all black women as "unvirtuous" or "bad," and often as prostitutes, to depict black women as unworthy of citizenship.[24] These representations were echoed in the words and actions of rioters who raped black women during the Memphis Riot, suggesting how this violence reflected the confluence of race, gender, and sexuality that structured everyday political conflict in the post-emancipation South.

It was specifically to realize their freedom that African American women migrated to Memphis after the end of the Civil War. Freedwomen fled conditions reminiscent of slavery in the countryside—physical violence, work with no pay, forced separation from family—and came to the city to seek assistance and protection made available by the power of African American Union soldiers and the federal authority of the Bureau.[25] Some came specifically to join, and seek support from, male family members in the Union army.[26] Many women enlisted the aid of soldiers in order to claim possessions, children, and compensation owed them for past labor from abusive employers on the plantations from which they had fled.[27] Thus black women came to Memphis to assert new rights of citizenship—motherhood, property ownership, rights as free laborers—that were guaranteed by state power in the hands of armed black men.

In the city, black women secured other profound, if less tangible, liberties previously reserved for whites. For instance, they fashioned social lives and urban communities that revolved around the grocery-saloons and street corners of South Memphis. In these spaces, freedwomen gathered, danced, and drank with black soldiers, often into the morning hours.[28] Freedwomen also helped build independent black churches in Memphis, such as the Methodist Episcopal Church and various Baptist churches.[29] Former slave women were the backbone of these institutions. They sponsored picnics, fairs, and other public events to raise funds for new church buildings and organized mutual aid societies for the support of church members.[30]

Black women further undermined whites' prior monopoly on public life, and exclusive claims to citizenship, by utilizing the Freedmen's Bureau Court to secure their rights. Freedwomen pressed charges against whites to claim unpaid wages and to protest violent assaults.[31] The impact of legal action at times spilled over from the court into the streets, when whites resisted verdicts and clashed with soldiers making arrests, collecting fines, and confiscating property.[32] Even when cases did not lead to convictions, freedwomen's actions brought charges of white abuse against blacks, and evidence of the new rights and powers of former slaves, prominently into the public eye.[33] Overall, black women's actions after emancipation left indelible marks on Memphis's landscape, changing the city materially and redrawing the racial boundaries around citizenship and freedom symbolized by activities in its public space.

When the presence of freedwomen in Memphis was noted by the conservative press of the city, it was never in reference to victims or opponents of exploitation and abuse. Nor were black women represented as "respectable" church women or "ladies" participating in the civic life of their community. Rather, the rhetoric of newspaper editors and the focus of most reporting suggest efforts to denigrate the public activities of freedwomen in the city by insinuating connections between their presence and an alleged increase in crime and disorder, specifically of "lewd women" or prostitutes, supposedly threatening white Memphians in the city's streets and alleys.[34] Onto the real activities of women in public, in all their variety and unpredictability, was imposed a bifurcated concept of womanhood. As was common in nineteenth-century depictions of urban life in the United States in general, women were represented as inhabiting one of two opposing realities: the delicate, chaste, and virtuous "lady" or the vicious, rude "public woman," or prostitute, the former being the woman whom society must protect, the latter by whom society was threatened.[35] In post-emancipation Memphis, this binary imagery operated along racial lines. Representations of African American women in the conservative press implied their essential relation to the latter category. Depictions were not consistent; the negative characteristics associated with freedwomen were presented at times as menacing and at other times as comical. Together these images appearing throughout commentary on local affairs elaborated the racial power and privilege of whites in Memphis by gendering black women as "bad" women, and often as sexually "dangerous." Newspaper reports labeled black women's presence in the city's public spaces illegitimate and thus challenged their claim to identities as citizens.

For instance, Neely Hunt, a freedwoman, with the assistance of a squad of black Union soldiers, forcibly entered and searched the house of a white family where she believed her child was being held. For this action she was punished not only by the Freedmen's Bureau, which had her arrested, but also by negative characterizations of her in the *Memphis Daily Appeal*. This paper described Hunt as a "negress," who was "enraged," "raving," "threatening," and "us[ing] very abusive and insulting language," in contrast to "the ladies of the house," whose delicate constitutions were allegedly unsettled by this confrontation. The *Appeal* labeled Hunt a liar and

suggested that her deceitful and disreputable character was generalizable to all freedwomen.[36] By identifying assertive black women acting in the public of Memphis with terms such as "negress," the press avoided describing them as "women," distancing them from images of respectable womanhood and associating them with disrepute. Newspaper editors often combined this strategy with other insulting labels, such as when the *Appeal* reported the charge of theft of a pistol made against "an ugly looking negress."[37] Another news item repeatedly used "wench," a term meaning "young female" that also had implications of servitude and sexual wantonness, to describe a black woman charged with drunk and disorderly conduct.[38] Another reported the arrest of five "female roughs of African descent" for disorderly conduct and speculated about the origins of black women's alleged misbehavior: "Freedom seems to have an intoxicating effect on colored females."[39] And the report of a robbery by three black men who supposedly stole a number of hoopskirts editorialized that the skirts were intended as gifts for "some of their dark paramours."[40] Through an assertion of both theft and illicit sexual relations, this report questioned the legitimacy and honor of freedwomen appearing in public in fine clothes.

Images associating black women in Memphis with disrepute and sexual promiscuity circulating in the city's conservative press were reinforced by police action against freedwomen, such as frequent arrests for "lewdness," "vagrancy," and "drunk and disorderly conduct." These arrests, often under false charges and amounting to harassment of black women by police, were then highlighted and exaggerated in newspaper accounts. Some reports implied that a specific incident indicated an epidemic of black prostitution, such as the following: "Six more negro prostitutes were yesterday arrested and brought before the officers of the Freedmen's Bureau, who sent them out to work on different farms in the country."[41] Others used arrests of black women for charges that may or may not have been associated with prostitution simply to assert that those arrested were prostitutes: "Three colored prostitutes were arrested, charged with vagrancy, and were hired out to contractors to go into the country and work," and "Viney Springer, Mary Jane Springer, and Sarah Parker, colored nymphs *du pavé* were arrested for disorderly conduct and incarcerated."[42] These reports make clear the high price freedwomen paid for these arrests, being either imprisoned in the city jail or forced to leave the city and labor on plantations. Although some black women may have been engaged in prostitution or criminal activity, there is evidence that many of these arrests were fraudulent and abusive. A "prominent citizen" reported one such case to the city's Republican newspaper. He had witnessed a white man "kicking a colored woman, who was calling loudly for a 'watch.' Soon a well known officer came running to the rescue, and without asking her for explanations, seized the woman, threw her down, slapped her in the face, dragged her on the ground and finally took her to the station-house and locked her up for disorderly conducted."[43] Other officers, similarly "well known," made a practice of harassing, insulting, and abusing freedwomen. These same officers would be recognized by freedpeople among the Memphis rioters.

One such policeman harassed Amanda Olden, a freedwoman living in South Memphis, with a false charge related to prostitution just days before the riot. Olden was not intimidated by this officer's particular extortion scheme and took her charges to the Freedmen's Bureau. There she recounted that "one Carol or Carrol, a city policeman, came to my house, and compelled me to give him twenty-two dollars at the same time falsely charging me with keeping a house of ill-fame." Carroll told Olden that this money would cover her fine for the charged offense. However, she went to the Recorder of the Police Court the next morning, "ready for an investigation of these false charges . . . this policeman did not appear, nor had he made any report of this action in my case to his proper officer."[44] Through false charges against African American women, city police not only contributed to the representation of freedwomen as "unvirtuous" in Memphis's public, they also attempted to use those representations to exploit individual women in ways that could be hidden from the public under the cloak of that same imagery.

The actions of Officers Welch and Sweatt, the larger of whom was also later identified among the rioters, offer further evidence of police using arrests to denigrate the activities of black women in the public spaces of Memphis rather than to punish real offenders.[45] According to a complaint filed with the Freedmen's Bureau by three black men who had attended a "negro ball," the two police officers intruded into the party and "proceeded to arrest some two or three of the ladies" in attendance. These policemen thus imputed a disreputable character to black women enjoying the privileges of "ladies" in public. Men from the party intervened and forcibly prevented the police from taking the women away. Welch and Sweatt retreated, but soon returned with several armed white firemen, who "cocking their weapons demanded a surrender" and "behaved in a very rough and boisterous manner crying 'shoot the damned niggers.'"[46] That the men and women attending this ball were apparently members of the city's small African American elite seems to have prevented violent incident and allowed the African Americans involved to reassert respectable gender identities as ladies and gentlemen. They received an apology from the firemen, who explained that Welch and Sweatt had "misrepresented the affair," and from the mayor, responding to the provost marshal's complaint that such incidents were "becoming so frequent as to demand attention."[47]

Although most freedwomen did not receive apologies for police misconduct, they did pursue retribution through the courts of the Bureau to defend, and to construct, their rights to enjoy free movement, work, and leisure in the public spaces of Memphis. Certain whites, such as police and newspaper editors, contested those rights as they sought to reassert their control over public space, and over the meanings of race signified by a free black presence in public. The conduct of the Memphis Riot suggests that those three days of violence represented a similar attempt to eviscerate the meaning of African American citizenship and freedom.

It was not surprising that the Memphis Riot began as a clash between black Union soldiers and city police. Since the initial occupation of the city by the federal army, the police force and black troops had been the front lines in an ongoing battle between civilian and military authorities over governance of the city. When their paths crossed in the streets, they often taunted each other, using "very hard language . . . daring each other to fight," concluding at times in serious physical violence.[48] Many observers believed that the police were often the instigators, insulting, shoving, and threatening black men in uniform, and often arresting soldiers under unspecified or fabricated charges and beating soldiers in custody.[49] In the days before the riot, two cases of severe beatings by police led to calls from soldiers for vengeance if such practices were repeated.[50] Given escalating tensions, it would seem not to be a coincidence that several policemen waited until May 1, 1866, the day after most black soldiers had been mustered out of service and forced to turn in their army weapons, to provoke the conflict that began the riot.[51] On this day, the police knew that they now had the upper hand.

Nor was it surprising that the riot began as a clash over freedpeople's activities in public space, in this case a visible and festive gathering of African Americans on a main thoroughfare of South Memphis. On Tuesday afternoon a group of police officers interrupted an impromptu street party on South Street, in which freedwomen, children, and soldiers were "laughing and shouting and making considerable noise."[52] "Some of them [were] hallooing 'Hurrah for Abe Lincoln,' and so on," recalled Tony Cherry, a discharged soldier and participant. "A policeman came along and told them to hush, and not to be hallooing in that way, and another policeman said, 'Your old father, Abe Lincoln, is dead and damned.'"[53] The police sought to silence this defiant tribute to emancipation by arresting some of the soldiers. As the police began to retreat with two soldiers in custody, other soldiers fired pistols in the air or perhaps at the police.[54] On hearing these gunshots and seeing one police officer fall (he apparently slipped and shot himself in the leg with his own gun), the police turned and began shooting indiscriminately into the crowd.[55] Although those few soldiers with weapons fired back, they were overpowered; few white men were injured in the fighting.[56]

Rumors of an uprising of African American soldiers spread through the city, bringing other white men from South Memphis and surrounding areas into the riot. After several hours of what was termed by one observer "an indiscriminate slaughter" of freedpeople by police and white civilians,[57] Union army officers from Fort Pickering arrived to quell the disturbance, forcibly dispersing the crowds and marshalling most black soldiers into the fort. Here soldiers were held over the next few days against their will and despite the efforts of many to leave, rendered powerless to protect their families from the violence that ensued.[58] Around ten o'clock that night, a large crowd of police and white civilians spread throughout South Memphis. Under the pretense of searching for weapons to stop the alleged uprising, rioters intruded into freedpeople's houses and brutalized residents, beginning the looting, assault, murder, arson, and rape that would continue until Thursday evening.

The Memphis Riot was one episode in an ongoing battle over race, citizenship, and rule in the post-emancipation public of Memphis. The riot was a protest among certain lower-middle-class white men against the power freedpeople exercised in public space, and the nonracialized citizenship this power signified. In that sense it was a violent continuation of the efforts of many white Memphians to reclaim privileges for whiteness and to counter new identities and powers for African Americans that challenged white dominance. The freedwoman Hannah Robinson remembered hearing one rioter declare, "It is white man's day now."[59] Throughout the process of reclaiming the "day" for white men, rioters would employ constructions of gender as weapons in efforts to resignify racial difference and inequality.

Rioters acted out meanings of white manhood and insisted on "unworthy" gender identities for African Americans through violence against black women. This can be seen, first, in how certain black women became targets of rioters' violence. Ann Freeman recounted that the party of white men who broke into her home declared that "they were going to kill all the women they caught with soldiers or with soldiers' things."[60] Directing violence against black women because of their relationship to black Union soldiers was made particularly evident in the case of rape. Four of the survivors of rape during the riot were connected to soldiers in ways that figured

prominently in the women's recollections of what they had suffered.

Lucy Tibbs was about twenty-one when she came to Memphis from Arkansas soon after the Civil War broke out. She came to the city with her husband, who by 1866 had found work on a steamboat and was away from home much of the time. She lived in South Memphis with her two small children, and was nearly five months pregnant with her third. On May 1 she was outside when the fighting began. She screamed in outrage as "they broke and run in every direction, boys and men, with pistols, firing at every black man and boy they could see." After observing the shooting death of two soldiers and seeing rioters "going from house to house," she understood that all black soldiers were in danger. She thus encouraged her older brother, Bob Taylor, who had been a member of the Fifty-ninth U.S. Colored Infantry stationed in Memphis, to flee. He ran, but was found dead the next morning near the bayou in back of Tibbs's house. Later that night, a crowd of men broke into her home and stole three hundred dollars. One of these men raped her while "the other men were plundering the house." She later speculated that her home had not been randomly chosen for attack: "I think they were folks who knew all about me, who knew that my brother had not long been out of the army and had money."[61]

Harriet Armour came to Memphis as a slave before the Civil War began. Later she married an African American Union soldier, who was in Fort Pickering during the riots. She lived around the corner from Lucy Tibbs, and she too watched the initial clashes and killings of Tuesday evening. Early Wednesday morning, two men carrying revolvers came to her room.[62] Molly Hayes, a white woman who lived in the adjacent house, overheard these men confronting Armour: "There were two men who came there and asked her where her husband was. She said he was in the fort. They said,

'Is he a soldier?' She said, 'Yes.' . . . The last word I heard him say was, 'Shut the door.'"[63] Armour testified that after they barred her door shut, they both raped her: "[One of the men] had to do with me twice and the other man once, which was the same as three."[64]

Sixteen-year-old Lucy Smith had been raised in slavery in Memphis. Frances Thompson, who was somewhat older, had been a slave in Maryland. At the time of the riot, Smith and Thompson shared a South Memphis home, supporting themselves by taking in sewing, washing, and ironing. Late Tuesday night, seven white men, two of whom were police officers, came to their house and stayed for close to four hours, during which time they robbed Smith and Thompson of many of their possessions and all of their money and food. The rioters threatened to shoot them and set fire to their house. Smith testified that one of these men also choked and then raped her, and that another attempted to rape her. Thompson recounted being beaten by one of the rioters and raped by four. Thompson and Smith also both remembered that the rioters demanded to know why there were red, white, and blue quilts in the house. Thompson later testified, "When we told them we made them for the soldiers they swore at us, and said the soldiers would never have them on their beds, and they took them away with the rest of the things." They also noticed pictures of Union army officers in the room, and as Smith later remembered, "they said they would not have hurt us so bad if it had not been for these pictures."[65]

By raping women associated with black Union soldiers, white men reclaimed their power over representatives of black masculinity, of freedpeople's power and protection in public space, and of federal and military power in Memphis.[66] Rioters demonstrated that black soldiers, now decommissioned, disarmed, and absent, were unable to protect freedwomen from violence. Yet it was not only as women related to soldiers that freedwomen were attacked. Equally important to understanding the sexual form of violence during the Memphis Riot is an analysis of the ways in which rioters enacted particular relations with freedwomen themselves. Through acts of rape, rioters physically overpowered black women. In the process, they also used language and acted in a manner that identified these women as "unvirtuous" or "lewd," in ways reminiscent of the representations of African American womanhood circulating in the conservative press in Memphis prior to the riot. That discourse had offered all white men identities as superior and worthy of power through the denigration of African American women. However, these identities were not necessarily realized in the lives of many white men, whose power was frequently challenged in their everyday interactions with freedpeople. The language rioters used and the scenes they staged around rape reveal how white men attempted to realize that discourse in a tangible way in their own conflicts with freedwomen, and thus attempted to experience for themselves a white manhood that rested on the dishonor of black women.

During the riot, men initiated rape with casual requests for sex and other patterns of behavior that invoked imagery of black women as sexually available to white men. Recall the dialogue described to the congressional investigating committee by Frances Thompson. The seven men who broke into her and Lucy Smith's home in the middle of the night treated their residence as if it were a brothel and demanded that Thompson and Smith act out roles as servants and prostitutes. The men first insisted that they be served supper. Thompson remembered the rioters saying, "they must have some eggs, and ham, and biscuit. I made them some biscuit and strong coffee, and they all sat down and ate."[67] Lucy Smith similarly testified, "They told us to get up and get some supper for them. We got up, and made a fire and got them supper."[68] When finished eating, the intruders announced that "they wanted some woman to sleep with." Thompson recounted that it was when she insisted that she and Smith "were not that sort of women" that the men physically attacked her, asserting that Thompson's claim "didn't make a damned bit of difference."[69] Smith also refused the rioters' demand and the identity they imputed to her. She testified that when "they tried to take advantage of me . . . I told them that I did not do such things, and would not." In response, one of the men "choked me by the neck" and "said he would make me."[70] It was then that these men "drew their pistols and said they would shoot us and fire the house if we did not let them have their way with us."[71]

On the night of May 2, the words and actions of the rioters who assaulted two freedwomen living in adjoining rooms similarly identified these women as "unvirtuous" and sexually available to white men. Elvira Walker described to the congressional committee the following scene: "I was entirely alone; some men came and knocked at my door. They came in, and said they were hunting for weapons. . . . One of them put his hands into my bosom. I tried to stop him, and he knocked down my hands with his pistol, and did it again." This man forcibly touched Walker's body in ways that implied that in his eyes she was not a respectable woman. He then further insulted her. "He . . . said there was $5 forfeit money, and that I must come to the station-house with him." This demand for cash was strikingly similar to Officer Carroll's attempted extortion from Amanda Olden a few days earlier. It suggests that this man was a member of the police force and that he intended to identify Walker with illicit sexual activity.[72]

This theme was continued when the same group of rioters entered the room next door, where Peter and Rebecca Ann Bloom were sleeping. The rioters forcibly removed Peter Bloom from the room, demanding that he obtain the five dollars needed to avoid Walker's arrest.[73] One rioter remained behind. As Rebecca Ann Bloom recounted, "He wanted to know if I had anything to do with white men. I said no. He held a knife in his hand, and said that he would kill me if I did not let him do as he wanted to. I refused. He said, 'By God, you must,' and then he got into bed with me, and violated my person, him still holding the knife."[74] The man who raped Bloom, like those who attacked Thompson and Smith, first solicited her for sex and then employed force when his request was rejected. "Having to do with," a phrase also repeated by Harriet Armour and Frances Thompson in their testimony, referred to sexual intercourse. By asking Bloom whether she had intercourse with white men, this rioter forced her to engage in a dialogue that positioned her as an "unvirtuous" woman. In drawing attention to his whiteness, his words identified her blackness. He simultaneously refused to recognize her identity as a wife, though her husband had just been dragged from the bed in which she still lay. Instead of the respect in theory attributed to married women, the rioter invoked myths of black women seeking sexual relations with white men. When Bloom refused to participate in his fantasy, he forced her under threat of deadly violence.

These sexual assaults, then, were not spontaneous acts of sexual aggression released from "normal" restraints in the pandemonium of a riot. They were, rather, elaborate and, in a sense, "scripted" enactments of fantasies of racial superiority and domination that operated around gendered constructions of racial difference and concluded in rape. In lengthy encounters, assailants employed words and violence to position freedwomen in previously constructed "scripts" that placed them in the role of being "that sort of women who could not or would not refuse the sexual advances of a white man. In these "scripts," white men demanded sex, black women acquiesced, and white men experienced their dominance and superiority through black women's subservience.[75] In this sense, these men attempted to make meaningful to themselves and their audience of other rioters the racist discourses on black women's gender and sexuality circulating in Memphis at the time. Through rape, rioters acted out identities as superior and powerful white men by refusing any recognition of "virtue" and rights to "protection" for African American women. In freedwomen's testimony, there is evidence of their refusal of rioters' "scripts," of their articulation of gendered identity different from the one white men were attempting to impose. When freedwomen rejected the scenes set up by the attackers, the men imposed them with threats or physical force. With their violence, rapists struggled to stage events that "proved"—in a type of causally backward logic—freedwomen's lack of "virtue" by forcing their participation in "dishonorable" acts.

There was a contradiction inherent in these scenes: black women were not in fact consenting, and thus proving their own lack of "virtue"; rather, white men were engaging in extremely "unvirtuous" conduct, forcing women to participate in sexual acts against their will. Rioters contained this contradiction through conduct that erased black women's agency and cloaked white men's force. Through their demands for food followed by sex, or inquiries about freedwomen's sexual partners, rioters invoked antebellum racist imagery of black women as sexually promiscuous and always available for sexual relations with white men, simulating an air of everyday, casual, and consensual sex that belied the terror and violent coercion involved in their actions.[76]

Other aspects of assailants' language further denied that they acted against the will of the women they attacked. Harriet Armour remembered as particularly painful that one of the men who raped her questioned her reason for crying. This man tried to force her to perform fellatio. "Then [he] tried to make me suck him. I cried. He asked what I was crying about, and tried to make me suck it."[77] This rioter's question dismissed the possibility that his actions could cause Armour pain, that she had will or "virtue" that could be violated by such an act. In Lucy Tibbs's case, one of the rioters objected to the conduct of the man who raped her on the grounds of Tibbs's pregnancy. Yet this man's words only further denied the possibility of committing rape against a black woman. Tibbs remembered his saying, "Let that woman alone—that she was not in any situation to be doing that." Although this suggests the perhaps common contradiction between white imagery of black women as sexually "loose" and the reality of white men's interactions with specific black women, his words also implied that had she not been pregnant, she would have been available for sex. As well, his choice of the active voice to describe Tibbs in this moment—"*she* was not in any situation to be *doing* that"—shows a refusal to recognize her lack of consent to sexual intercourse.[78]

That some of the rapes that occurred during the riot took place within a discourse simulating scenes of promiscuous black women willingly engaging in sex with white men did not prevent the attackers from inflicting extreme violence. For instance, Lucy Smith described the violence she suffered:

> One of them . . . choked me by the neck. My neck was swollen up the next day, and for two weeks I could not talk to anyone. After the first man had connexion with me, another got hold of me and tried to violate me, but I was so bad he did not. He gave me a lick with his fist and said I was

so damned near dead he would not have anything to do with me. . . . I bled from what the first man had done to me. I was injured right smart. . . . They were in the house a good while after they hurt me, but I lay down on the bed, for I thought they had killed me. . . . I was in bed two weeks after.[79]

The women surviving rape during the Memphis Riot experienced prolonged physical pain and terror. Each rape was ultimately carried out through violence or threats of death that belied the casual scenes that the perpetrators sought to stage.

Placing this reading of sexual violence in the context of the conflicts over public space leading up to the Memphis Riot reveals another layer to the political meaning of rioters' rape "scripts." By dishonoring black women, white men contested the power these women exercised in the public spaces of Memphis. To identify black women as "loose" women or prostitutes was to imply that they were the "sort of women" who endangered the community if free and unrestrained in public. Through their violence, rioters attacked the citizenship freedwomen had exercised in public by attacking their identities as respectable women. This is not to suggest that this was a consciously designed strategy. The relationship between gendered constructions of racial difference and contests over citizenship was deeply embedded in the discourse circulating among white opponents of Reconstruction in Memphis. The white men who raped freedwomen during the Memphis Riot enacted a fantasy of social subordination that drew on an existing gendered discourse of racial inequality, one that had already politicized gender identities in contests over race, power, and citizenship in post-emancipation Memphis.

The Memphis Riot came to an end on Thursday, May 3, when federal troops spread throughout the city.[80] By that time the murderous events of the past three days had drawn the attention of Republicans in Washington, D.C. On May 14, 1866 Congressman Thaddeus Stevens proposed that a congressional committee travel to Memphis to investigate "the recent bloody riots in that city."[81] Radical Republicans looked to this investigation to provide support for their position that stronger federal intervention into the affairs of southern states was necessary to protect the rights and lives of freedpeople.[82]

Stevens's plan was adopted. A House select committee composed of three congressmen—Ellihu B. Washburne of Illinois and John M. Broomall of Pennsylvania, both Republicans, and George S. Shanklin of Kentucky, a Democrat—arrived in Memphis on May 22. Sixty-six African Americans came before the committee to testify.[83] For the freedwomen who testified about sexual violence, the committee created a forum of unprecedented state power in which they articulated new public identities as citizens and contested racist constructions of black womanhood. For African American women, to testify that they had been raped was a radical act in the context of southern state law and tradition. A legal and cultural refusal to recognize black women's accounts of rape had served a dominant white discourse of racial inequality that bolstered slavery in the antebellum South. Postemancipation imagery of freedwomen as "unvirtuous" drew on this pre-war exclusion of black women from the category of "women" who could be raped. The rioters who raped freedwomen had expressed these same meanings to contest the power that freedwomen were exercising as citizens of Memphis. When black women represented their experience of coerced sexual intercourse with white men as a violation of their will, they asserted a claim to the status of "woman" and "citizen." In the process, they would also counter conventional discourses on womanhood, rape, and "virtue."

Freedwomen employed language of violation and harm in order to identify assailants' actions as rape rather than illicit sex. Rebecca Ann Bloom maintained before the Freedmen's Bureau that the man who got into bed with her had "violated my person, by having connexion with me."[84] Before the congressional committee, Frances Thompson affirmed that she and Lucy Smith were "violated" by the men who intruded into their homes.[85] Lucy Smith chose similar words to describe rioters' actions: they "tried to violate me . . . [and] they hurt me."[86] When asked by Congressman Washburne whether the men who plundered her home had hurt her, Lucy Tibbs responded, "they done a very bad act," and then confirmed Washburne's assumption that by this she meant they had "ravish[ed]" her.[87] Stressing that rioters' actions were imposed against their will, freedwomen refuted the contrary image that rioters had sought to create in the scenes surrounding the actual rapes, namely that the women's experiences were evidence of their own lack of "virtue." Freedwomen further confuted rioters' "scripts" that had denied black women's agency and suffering by recounting the terror they had experienced. Harriet Amour recalled how she cried but was too terrified to call for help.[88] Lucy Smith believed that there were seven men who came into her house on the night she was raped, but "I was so scared I could not be certain."[89] Lucy Tibbs recounted that "I was so scared I could not tell whether they were policemen or not," and described begging her assailants to leave her and her children in peace.[90] This testimony resisted the meanings that assailants had attempted to stage during the riot.

Some of the women who testified had to defend their honor in the face of hostile and insinuating questioning from members of the committee. After answering in the affirmative the chair's question, "Did they ravish you?," Lucy Tibbs still had to contend with the committee's apparent doubt. Washburne continued, "Did they violate your person against your consent?" to which Tibbs again insisted, "Yes Sir. I had just to give up to them. They said they would kill me if I did not." Washburne again suggested the possibility that the attack was somehow a product of Tibbs's own conduct: "Were you dressed or undressed when these men came to you?" She stated that she was dressed. "Did you make any resistance?" the chair then asked. Tibbs responded by sharing with him the information she had used to calculate her safest course of action: "No sir; the house was full of men. I thought they would kill me; they had stabbed a woman near by the night before." Tibbs had heard others report that this same woman had also been raped.[91] Believing that resistance might result in her own death, Tibbs surrendered to the assailant physically. But here, in the committee's hearing room, she resisted both the rioters' and the congressmen's implications that what had happened in some way reflected shame on herself.

Harriet Armour also came under challenging questioning from the committee. She recounted that she had seen no possibility of escape from the men who attacked her, because one of them had barred her door shut. Washburne then asked, "What did he do with the window?" Armour explained that she could not have fled through the window because two slats were nailed across it. "And you made no resistance?" he asked. "No," she answered, repeating that "they had barred the door. I could not get out, and I could not help myself." Yet the suspicions persisted. "Did I understand you that you did not try to prevent them from doing these things to you?" Congressman Broomall asked in disbelief. "Could not the people outside have come to help you?" Armour tried again to explain her strategy to survive the attack:

No, sir; I did not know what to do. I was there alone, was weak and sick, and thought I would rather let them do it than to be hurt or punished. . . . I should have been afraid to call [for help] . . . I thought I had just better give up freely; I did not like to do it, but I thought it would be best for me.[92]

Both Armour and Tibbs had yielded to the rioters' demands in order to prevent further violence, and in the case of Tibbs perhaps to protect her children. Yet their judgment of what to do in such a situation did not conform to the patriarchal framework within which the elite white men on the committee appear to have imagined rape. The congressmen's questioning implied that even under the threat of potentially deadly force, anything but ceaseless resistance to sexual violation raised questions about a woman's "virtue."

Washburne and Broomall may have sincerely doubted Armour's and Tibbs's testimony that they had been raped, because it seemed to these men that the women had not resisted enough. It is also possible that the Republican congressmen's questions were intended to elicit further details so as to shape the testimony in ways that would best represent the women's claims before a national audience.[93] In either case, when faced with the congressmen's apparent uneasiness about their testimony, Armour and Tibbs defended their actions. They made clear that, as much as they had suffered from the rapes they experienced, they did not share the assumption that rape would damage them in ways worth risking death to prevent. Nor did they accept the implications of the rioters, that their submission implied that they were "unvirtuous" women. Armour and Tibbs both firmly maintained that despite physical acquiescence, the sex occurred against their will. To defend their honor and represent the events as violation, the women struggled to make intelligible to the committee a perspective that grew out of

their experiences during the riot, and perhaps out of their experiences as slaves. They had recently lived under a system of slavery in which many women faced the grim choice between submitting to forced sexual intercourse with white men or risking other physical harm to themselves and their loved ones. These women's testimony then implicitly shifted the parameters of patriarchal discourse on rape. By inserting black women's experiences and perspectives into a public discussion of sexual violence, they presented alternative constructions of honorable womanhood. To them, in this context, honor depended more on surviving and protesting injustice than on privileging and protecting a patriarchal notion of women's sexual "virtue."

Perhaps Armour's persistence in demonstrating, under a barrage of hostile insinuation, that her strategy for survival in no way reflected her own dishonor stemmed from the fact that she had already suffered from another's sense that she was less valuable as a woman because of the attack. Cynthia Townsend, a freedwoman and neighbor of Armour, testified that "When [Armour's husband] came out of the fort, and found what had been done, he said he would not have anything to do with her any more." It was clear that Armour suffered enormously from her husband's rejection. "She has sometimes been a little deranged since then," Townsend explained.[94] In her testimony, Armour moved from subject to subject quickly, suggesting that recounting these stories may have been particularly difficult for her, more so than was apparent in other freedwomen's accounts. She segued directly from her description of one man's efforts to force her to perform fellatio to, "I have not got well since my husband went away," thereby connecting the attack with her husband's departure.[95] Armour was the only woman testifying to indicate any ostracism by a member of her community as a result of rape. It is possible that Armour's experience was exacerbated by the fact that she was attacked in daylight and thus suspected that others were aware of what was being done to her ("It was an open shanty, and they could see right in").[96] Any observers were doubtless powerless to stop the attack. Nonetheless, the fact that she understood her ordeal to have been a public spectacle of sorts may have been a factor in her devastation; it may have alienated her from her community, and contributed to her husband's rejection.

What is striking, then, is Armour's courage in coming forward to tell this story again in another public setting, that of the congressional hearing. There was no practical need for Armour or other women to discuss sexual assaults in order to condemn the rioters. When Armour, Lucy Tibbs, Lucy Smith, and Frances Thompson testified before this committee, they all reported other crimes and forms of violence in addition to rape, namely, theft and battery. That they chose to recount having suffered sexual violence, despite the risks involved, suggests that this testimony served ends important to them: the public condemnation of and protest against these acts as violation, and the implicit affirmation of their identities as free women with the will to choose or refuse sexual relations and with the right to be protected by law. Given the conservative pre-riot discourse that imputed dishonorable gendered identities to African American women, and the police harassment of black women in Memphis, both of which were efforts to limit black women's power as citizens, these women's portrayals of themselves as survivors of rape appear as important political acts in African Americans' overall struggle to realize their freedom.[97]

The courage the freedwomen showed in making their suffering public garnered the support of the Republican majority of the congressional investigating committee.

Despite the committee's hostile questioning, freedwomen's narratives served Republican interests in representing southern white men as "unreconstructed" and thus unprepared for self-rule. The committee majority's final report highlighted the rape of African American women to depict the white rioters as uncivilized and dishonorable men. Eleven thousand copies of the report were printed, and it was excerpted in newspapers across the country.[98] Describing the riot as "an organized and bloody massacre of the colored people of Memphis," this report stated,

> The crowning acts of atrocity and diabolism committed during these terrible nights were the ravishing of five different colored women by these fiends in human shape. . . . It is a singular fact, that while this mob was breathing vengeance against the negroes and shooting them down like dogs, yet when they found unprotected colored women they at once "conquered their prejudices," and proceeded to violate them under circumstances of the most licentious brutality.[99]

To bolster this representation of the rape of black women as the ultimate atrocity of the riot, the authors assured readers that Lucy Smith was "a girl of modest demeanor and highly respectable in appearance." They similarly noted that both Harriet Armour and Lucy Tibbs were married—and thus legitimate—women, and that Tibbs had two young children and was pregnant with her third.[100] Through these images of female respectability, the committee's majority sought to preempt accusations of the "dishonorable" character of the women and therefore doubts about their legitimacy as victims of sexual assault.

Images of feminine "virtue" rooted in modesty and submission within marriage had not been part of freedwomen's self-representations when they defended their honor before the congressional committee. In general, freedwomen in Memphis had not shown their definitions of womanhood to depend upon notions of "proper" and submissive femininity. Rather, through their own forceful presence in the city's public spaces, they had claimed identities as women who were active, outspoken, and assertive with regard to their own and their community's rights to live freely as citizens. Yet once freedwomen's narrative concerning rape entered into the arena of national politics, their words were forced into a discourse of womanhood and "virtue" not of their own making.[101] When the congressional committee portrayed freedwomen as victims of rape, they drew on the same opposition between "virtuous" and "unvirtuous" women that conservatives had manipulated prior to the riot in order to reject black women's claims to full citizenship. And, as we will see, this same binary discourse of "virtue" and "vice" would ultimately help conservatives to discredit black women's testimony on sexual violence.

After the congressional investigation, no rioters were arrested or charged with any crimes. Freedwomen's testimony, though, did help to promote several state and national measures that extended greater protection and political power to African Americans during Reconstruction.[102] And the conservative press in Memphis was silenced by the overwhelming evidence to violence enacted by white men presented by the committee's report. The conservative *Appeal*, earlier full of condemnations of black women as deceitful, disreputable, and depraved, offered no immediate critique of the freedwomen who testified that they had been raped.[103]

Ten years later, however, conservatives in Memphis stumbled upon their chance to vindicate white men from charges made in the congressional report and to dismiss the freedwomen's testimony about rape. In 1876 Frances Thompson was arrested for "being a man and wearing women's clothing."[104] Because Thompson's testimony had

occupied a prominent place in the congressional committee's report, her arrest for cross-dressing—an incident that might have received only passing mention in the local press under different circumstances—filled the city columns for days. Her arrest also served the interests of conservatives-turned-Democrats in the 1876 presidential election campaign, which would ultimately mark the end of Reconstruction at the national level and return control over the southern states to white Southerners. In this context, the conservative newspapers contended that Thompson's transvestism proved her testimony about rape to have been a lie.[105]

Thompson herself paid dearly for her supposed crime. After her arrest she was placed on the city's chain gang, where she was forced to wear men's clothing and suffered constant ridicule and harassment from crowds drawn to the scene by mocking press reports.[106] Soon after she completed her prison term of one hundred days, she was discovered alone and seriously ill in a cabin in North Memphis. Members of the freed community moved her to the city hospital, where she died on November 1, 1876.[107] The coroner's report of her death recorded that she was indeed anatomically male.[108]

What can we make of the fact that Thompson—with a woman's identity and a male body—testified that she had been raped during the Memphis Riot? Was she drawing on Lucy Smith's experience of rape to perform for the committee that she too, was a woman?[109] Or had she in fact been raped? Had the rioters been shocked when they discovered the "truth" about her anatomy? Or were they aware in advance that she was anatomically male? Did they attack her because of that fact? Was the materiality of bodies irrelevant, superseded by a "script" of black women's sexual wantonness that mattered most? Unfortunately, there are no sources with which to answer these questions.

There is evidence, though, of a campaign of vilification against Thompson in the conservative press, one designed to refute charges of white southern brutality against African Americans and to oppose Reconstruction policies supported by Republicans. Similar to the disparagement of black women prior to the riot, newspaper editors described Thompson as "lewd," associated her with prostitution, and portrayed her as the epitome of "unvirtuous" gender and sexuality. They attributed to her "vile habits and corruptions," decried her "utter depravity," and accused her of using her "guise" as a woman to facilitate her supposed role as "wholesale debaucher" and "procuress" of numberless young women for prostitution.[110] The papers then used these charges to condemn their Republican opponents, reminding their readers that the Republican Party—now referred to as "the Frances Thompson Radical party"—had relied upon Thompson's "perjurious evidence" to condemn white men in Memphis for violence and brutality.[111]

The conservative press alleged that Thompson's testimony was merely a charade to discredit the words of all the black women who testified that they had been raped during the Memphis Riot. The *Memphis Daily Appeal* criticized Lucy Smith for her corroboration of Thompson's testimony, which was now dismissed as "utterly at variance with the truth." The paper also mocked Smith's claim that she herself had been "violated." The *Appeal* insinuated that Smith did not possess the "virtue" supposedly needed for a woman to protest rape, because—and this they asserted with no evidence—Smith had been "occupying the same bed with Thompson" prior to the riot.[112] The other women who testified were not mentioned by name, but the conservative papers implied that Thompson's transvestism exposed the entire congressional report as "vile slander," manufactured by Republicans solely for political gain. With no new information other than Thomson's cross-dressing, one conservative paper denounced the report: "The evidence of the vilest wretches was received and worded in smooth phrase and published to the world to prove that the Southern people were a set of barbarians and assassins."[113] The *Appeal* went further, enlisting Thompson's image to vindicate all white Southerners from accusations of racist violence during Reconstruction:

> Whenever you hear Radicals talking of the persecutions of the black race in the south, ask them what they think of Frances Thompson and the outrages committed on her by the Irish of this city during the celebrated riots. These pretended outrages in the south are all of a piece with this Frances Thompson affair. It is out of such material as this that all their blood-and-thunder stories are manufactured.[114]

Critics of Reconstruction attempted to supplant recognition of African American women's experiences of sexual violence—now mere "pretended outrages"—with the image of Thompson's allegedly "deviant" and "depraved," cross-dressing male body. Ultimately, Thompson's transvestism was such a powerful tool for conservatives not because Thompson was represented as bizarre or unique, but rather because her image resonated so strongly with the pre-existing conservative discourse attributing dishonorable gender and sexuality to all African American women. It was but a small step from images of women who were "unvirtuous" to images of women who were so "unvirtuous" that they were not women at all.

This postscript to the history of freedwomen's testimony about rape during the Memphis Riot suggests once again how discourses of gender and sexuality played a central role in political struggles over race, following emancipation. Former slaves in Memphis had insisted on their right as citizens to move, live, and work freely in the public spaces of the city. Their actions adumbrated a new social order that challenged the racial hierarchy of the ante-bellum South. White city police and con-servative newspaper editors responded to African Americans' entry into public life in Memphis, among other ways, by con-demning black women in public as prosti-tutes and by depicting them overall as the "sort of women" who were not "virtuous" and therefore not worthy of citizenship. In this way, gender served as a metaphor for racial difference. When emancipation threatened to efface racial inequality, racial difference was reinscribed through the mis-representation and stigmatization of black women's gender and sexuality.

I have tried to show how the rapes that occurred during the Memphis Riot formed part of this same discourse of racialized gender. Rioters who raped freedwomen sought to reassert racial inequality and the privileges of white manhood by enacting antebellum fantasies of black women's sexual subservience and lack of feminine "virtue." During the rapes themselves, and indeed simply by testifying to having been raped, African American women rejected these scripts. Political contests over African American citizenship and freedom following emancipation were partly fought out through battles over gendered constructions of racial difference, battles that included elaborate and contested scenes of horrific sexual domination and violence. Analyzing incidents of rape, par-ticularly in moments of violent political conflict, as part of discourse allows us to begin to understand the multiple histori-cal forces and ideas that have given shape to this form of violence.

NOTES

I thank Cindy Aron, Leora Auslander, Cynthia Blair, Antoinette Burton, George Chauncey, Laura Edwards, Thomas Holt, Pradeep Jeganathan, Linda Kerber, Ann Lane, and participants in the University of Chicago's Gender and Society Workshop for their invaluable comments on versions of this essay, and especially Martha Hodes and Richard Turits for their extensive input. The research was generously funded by the American Historical Association and Carter G. Woodson Institute for Afro-American and African Studies at the University of Virginia.

1. Testimony of Frances Thompson, in *Memphis Riots and Massacres*, 39th Cong., 1st sess., 1865–1866, H. Rept. 101, 196–197 (hereafter *MR&M*).

2. See also testimony of Lucy Smith, 197; Harriet Armour, 176–177; Lucy Tibbs, and affi-davit of Rebecca Ann Bloom, Affidavits Taken before Commission Organized by the Freedmen's Bureau (hereafter FBC) in information on the rapes reported by these women, see testimony of Cynthia Townsend, 162–164; Henry Porter, 167–168; Molly Hayes, 186; Elvira Walker, 193–194; and affidavit of Peter Bloom, FBC, 348, all in *MR&M*.

3. Altina Waller, "Community, Class and Race in the Memphis Riot of 1866," *Jour-nal of Social History* 18 (1984): 235. Police and firemen made up the largest occu-pational grouping of those men identified by Waller as being among the rioters, 34 percent. The next largest category consisted of small business owners, most of whom ran grocery-saloons.

4. Actual casualties may have been much higher. See Report, *MR&M*, 34. See also Richard Banks, "In the Heat of the Night," *Memphis* 15 (1990): 71–72.

5. Report, *MR&M*, 34–36.

6. For the possibility that other women were raped or molested, see testimony of Lucy Tibbs, 161; and Mary Grady, 197, *MR&M*.

7. Hannah Rosen, "Rape as Reality, Rape as Fiction: Rape Law and Ideology in the Ante-bellum South" (unpublished paper, 1989); Jennifer Wriggins, "Rape, Racism, and the

Law," *Harvard Women's Law Journal* 6 (1983): 103–141; Melton A. McLaurin, *Celia, a Slave* (Athens: University of Georgia Press, 1991), esp. Chapter 6; Deborah Gray White, *Ar'n't I a Woman? Female Slaves in the Plantation South* (New York: W. W. Norton, 1985), 152–153, 164–165; and Evelyn Brooks Higginbotham, "African-American Women's History and the Metalanguage of Race," *Signs* 17 (1992): 262–264. See also Diane Miller Sommerville, "The Rape Myth in the Old South Reconsidered," *Journal of Southern History* 61 (1995): 493 n. 34.

8. For instance, lawyers John D. Freeman in *George (a slave) v. State*, 37 Mississippi 317 (October 1859), and B. F. Trimble in *Alfred (a slave) v. State of Mississippi*, 37 Mississippi 307–308 (October 1859).

9. See, for instance, Winthrop D. Jordan, *White over Black: American Attitudes toward the Negro, 1550–1812* (Baltimore: Penguin Books, 1969), 151; and White, *Ar'n't I a Woman?* 27–61.

10. For reference to rape during the riot, see Kevin R. Hardwick, "'Your Old Father Abe Lincoln Is Dead and Damned': Black Soldiers and the Memphis Race Riot of 1866," *Journal of Social History* 27 (1993): 109, 122; Waller, "Community, Class and Race," 234–235; Bobby L. Lovett, "Memphis Riots: White Reaction to Blacks in Memphis, May 1865–July 1866," *Tennessee Historical Quarterly* 37 (1979): 23; James Gilbert Ryan, "The Memphis Riot of 1866: Terror in a Black Community during Reconstruction," *Journal of Negro History* 62 (1977): 243; Jack D. L. Holmes, "Underlying Causes of the Memphis Race Riot of 1866," *Tennessee Historical Quarterly* 17 (1958): 195, 220; Eric Foner, *Reconstruction; America's Unfinished Revolution, 1863–1877* (New York: Harper & Row, 1988), 262; William S. McFeely, *Yankee Stepfather: General O. O. Howard and the Freedmen* (1968; reprint, New York: W. W. Norton, 1994), 277; Herbert G. Gutman, *The Black Family in Slavery and Freedom, 1750–1925* (New York: Vintage Books, 1976), 25–28; and George C. Rable, *But There Was No Peace: The Role of Violence in the Politics of Reconstruction* (Athens: University of Georgia Press, 1984), 39.

11. One exception is Beverly Greene Bond, "'Till Fair Aurora Rise': African-American Women in Memphis, Tennessee, 1840–1915" (Ph.D. diss., University of Memphis, 1996), 96–103.

12. See also Catherine Clinton, "Reconstructing Freedwomen," in *Divided Houses: Gender and the Civil War*, ed. Catherine Clinton and Nina Silber (New York: Oxford University Press, 1992), 306–319; idem, "'Bloody Terrain': Freedwomen, Sexuality, and Violence during Reconstruction," *Georgia Historical Quarterly* 76 (1992): 310–332; Laura F. Edwards, "Sexual Violence, Gender, Reconstruction, and the Extension of Patriarchy in Granville County, North Carolina," *North Carolina Historical Review* 48 (1991): 237–260; idem, "The Disappearance of Susan Daniel and Henderson Cooper: Gender and Narratives of Political Conflict in the Reconstruction-Era U.S. South," in this volume; and idem, *Gendered Strife and Confusion: The Political Culture of Reconstruction* (Urbana: University of Illinois Press, 1997).

13. I am currently working on a separate essay on Frances Thompson. For the purposes of this article, I approach Thompson as a witness to and survivor of sexual assault aimed at African American women. I continue to refer to Thompson as a woman and with feminine pronouns because that is how she identified and chose to live her life.

14. Gerald M. Capers, Jr., *The Biography of a River Town: Memphis: Its Heroic Age* (Chapel Hill: University of North Carolina Press, 1939), 107–108, 110, 164; Kathleen C. Berkeley, "'Like a Plague of Locust': Immigration and Social Change in Memphis, Tennessee, 1850–1880" (Ph.D. diss., University of California, Los Angeles, 1980), 47–48; and Armstead Robinson, "In the Aftermath of Slavery: Blacks and Reconstruction in Memphis, 1865–1870" (thesis presented to the Scholars of the House Faculty of Yale College, May 1969), 26–28. I owe special thanks to the late Professor Robinson for sharing this invaluable study of Reconstruction-era Memphis with me. To compare Memphis's African American population statistics with those of other southern cities for 1860, see Richard Wade, *Slavery in the Cities: The South, 1820–1860* (New York: Oxford University Press, 1969), 326–327.

15. *A Digest of the Ordinances of the City Council of Memphis, from the Year 1826 to 1857; Together with All Acts of the Legislature of Tennessee Which Relate Exclusively to the City of Memphis,* prepared by L. J. DuPree, 1857, 122–126; *Digest of the Charters and Ordinances of the City of Memphis, from 1826 to 1860, Inclusive, Together with the Acts of the Legislature Relating to the City, and Municipal Corporations Generally,* 1860, 85–91, 269, 276, 361–367. Kathleen Berkeley presents evidence of more rigid control of slaves in Memphis than Richard Wade found in his study of slavery in other southern cities. See Wade, *Slavery in the Cities*; and Berkeley, "'Like a Plague of Locust,'" 47–48.

16. Seven black regiments were stationed at Fort Pickering. Arthur L. Webb, "Black Soldiers of Civil War Left Impact on City," *Commercial Appeal,* February (n.d.), 1989. I am indebted to Mr. Webb for a copy of this article.

17. See Robinson, "In the Aftermath of Slavery," 67–68; Berkeley, "'Like a Plague of Locust,'" 168–169; *Census of the City of Memphis, Taken by Joe Bledsoe, under a Resolution of the city Council, Passed April 25, 1865,* Memphis and Shelby County Room, History Department, Memphis Main Public Library; and Ernest Walter Hooper, "Memphis, Tennessee: Federal Occupation and Reconstruction, 1862–1870" (Ph.D. diss., University of North Carolina, Chapel Hill, 1957), 132.

18. Quotation from Louis Hughes, *Thirty Years a Slave: From Bondage to Freedom. The Institution of Slavery as Seen on the Plantation and in the Home of the Planter. Autobiography of Louis Hughes* (1897; reprint, New York: Negro Universities Press, 1969), 187.

19. For feminist conceptualizations of public space and the "public sphere," see, for example, Elsa Barkley Brown, "Negotiating and Transforming the Public Sphere: African American Political Life in the Transition from Slavery to Freedom," *Public Culture* 7 (1994); 107–146; Nancy Fraser, "What's Critical about Critical Theory? The Case of Habermas and Gender," in *Unruly Practices: Power, Discourse and Gender in Contemporary Social Theory* (Minneapolis: University of Minnesota Press, 1989), 113–143; Evelyn Brooks Higginbotham, *Righteous Discontent: The Women's Movement in the Black Baptist Church, 1880–1920* (Cambridge: Harvard University Press, 1993); and Mary Ryan, *Women in Public: Between Banners and Ballots, 1825–1880* (Baltimore: Johns Hopkins University Press, 1990).

    The Republican *Memphis Daily Post* reported the community activities of freedpeople in Memphis. There was no newspaper published by African Americans in Memphis at this time.

20. Foner, *Reconstruction,* 250–251.

21. In 1863 women made up over 40 percent of the 535 adults in a contraband camp in Memphis. John Eaton to Prof. Henry Cowles, March 13, 1863, document H8832, microfilm reel 193, American Missionary Association Archives (hereafter AMA). In 1865 a Freedmen's Bureau census found that women were 59 percent of the 16,509 freedpeople in Memphis and its surrounding areas; see Bond, "'Till Fair Aurora Rise,'" 77.

22. The Freedmen's Bureau established the Freedmen's Court in 1865 to address the exclusion of African Americans from the right to testify in state courts. The Freedmen's Court held legal jurisdiction in all cases involving black people and was presided over by the provost marshal of freedmen. See Board of Mayor and Aldermen, Minutes, book 11, July 21, 1865, 695–697, Memphis and Shelby County Archives, Cossirt Library, Memphis (hereafter MSCA).

23. White Memphians responded with equal hostility to the pretence of African American men in the city, particularly black Union soldiers. For the disparaging portrayals of black men in Memphis by white conservatives, see Hannah Rosen, "The Gender of Reconstruction: Rape, Race, and Citizenship in the Postemancipation South" (Ph.D. diss., University of Chicago, forthcoming), Chapter 1.

24. By "conservative press," I am referring to the partisan newspapers that opposed Reconstruction policies of the Republican Party after the war. For this essay, I use evidence drawn primarily from the *Memphis Daily Appeal.* This paper, despite its somewhat more moderate rhetorical style relative to other conservative papers in Memphis at the time, still frequently misrepresented black women in its local reporting.

25. See, for instance, statements of Lizzie Howard, July 26, 1865; Ellen Clifton, Aug. 3, 1865; Eliza Jane House, Aug. 15, 1865; Mary Rodgers, Aug. 15, 1865; and Jane Coleman, Aug. 26, 1865; entry 3545. Records of the Bureau of Refugees, Freedmen, and Abandoned Lands, RG 105, National Archives and Records Administration, Washington, D.C. (hereafter BRFAL).

26. See statements of Mary Ann, July 31, 1865; Lizzie Howard, July 26, 1865; Elizabeth Jones, July 27, 1865; Hannah Biby, Aug. 2, 1865; Sophia Morton, July 10, 1865; Abraham Taylor, Aug. 1, 1865; Amy Covington, Aug. 10, 1865; Betsy Robinson, Aug. 3, 1865; and Mary Davis, Dec. 13, 1865, entry 3545, BRFAL.

27. See statements of Ellen Clifton, Aug. 3, 1865; Mary Rodgers, Aug. 15, 1865; Elizabeth Jones, July 27, 1865; and Lucy Williams, Aug. 9, 1865, entry 3545, BRFAL.

28. See testimony of A. N. Edmunds, 140; and Tony Cherry, 184, *MR&M*. See also testimony of David T. Egbert, 122; Mary Grady, 187–188; Captain A. W. Allyn, 245; and exhibit no. 2, 358, *MR&M*.

29. See David Tucker, *Black Pastors and Leaders: Memphis, 1819–1972* (Memphis: Memphis State University Press, 1975), 6–8; and Ewing O. Trade to Corresponding Secretary, Aug, 1, 1865, document H8965, microfilm reel 193, AMA.

30. Tucker, *Black Pasters and Leaders*, 8; Kathleen C. Berkeley, "'Colored Ladies Also Contributed': Black Women's Activities from Benevolence to Social Welfare, 1866–1896," in *The Web of Southern Social Relations: Women, Family, and Education*, ed. Walter J. Fraser, Jr., R. Frank Saunders, Jr., and Jon L. Wakelyn (Athens: University of Georgia Press, 1985), 182, 193–194.

31. Statement of Catherine Martin, July 31, 1865, entry 3545, BRFAL; Salena Jones v. Gustavis Fisher, Aug. 1, 1865; and Susan Hill v. H. B. C. Miles, Dec. 1, 1865, Docket Freedmen's Court, entry 3544, BRFAL.

32. Michael Walsh to Ira Moore, June 11, 1866; and Michael Walsh to David Ingram, June 5, 1866, entry 3541, BRFAL. Lieutenant S. S. Garrett to Lieutenant J. S. Turner, Feb. 13, 1866; and statement of Betty Maywell, Dec. 5, 1865, entry 3545, BRFAL. See also "The Negro Again," *Memphis Daily Appeal*, March 3, 1866.

33. See, for example, statement of Elizabeth Burns, Feb. 9, 1866, entry 3545, BRFAL; and from the *Memphis Daily Appeal*, "Cruel Treatment," Feb. 15, 1866, p. 3, col. 1; and "Cruel Treatment," Feb. 23, 1866, p. 3, cols. 1–2.

34. For a discussion of how press accounts of freedpeople in Memphis were interwoven with public conversation about danger in the city, see Rosen, "Gender of Reconstruction" Chapter 1. See also Clinton, "Reconstructing Freedwomen," 313–314.

35. Ryan, *Women in Public*, esp. 73, 76–92.

36. "The Negro Again," 20, *Memphis Daily Appeal*, March 3, 1866; Provost Marshal of Freedmen to George R. Rutter, March 3, 1866, entry 3541, BRFAL.

37. "Freedmen's Court," *Memphis Daily Appeal*, Nov. 26, 1865, p. 3, col. 2.

38. "Sharp Wench," *Memphis Daily Appeal*, March 2, 1866, p. 3, col. 2.

39. "Female Roughs," *Memphis Daily Appeal*, March 2, 1866.

40. "Robbery," *Memphis Daily Appeal*, Nov. 17, 1865.

41. "Freedmen's Bureau," *Memphis Daily Appeal*, Nov. 11, 1865, p. 3, col. 1.

42. From *Memphis Daily Appeal*, "Freedmen's Court," Nov. 29, 1865, p. 3, col. 1; and "Police Arrests Friday Night," April 8, 1866, p. 3, col. 1. *Nymph du pavé* was a euphemism for prostitute; see *The Compact Oxford English Dictionary*, 2d ed. (Oxford: Clarendon Press, 1991), 1191.

43. "Police Protection," *Memphis Morning Post*, June 7, 1866, p. 8, col. 2.

44. Statement of Amanda Olden, April 30, 1866, entry 3545, BRFAL. For the participation of a policeman named Carroll in the Memphis Riot, see testimony of Margaret Gardner, 98; Adam Lock, 115–116; and Dr. Robert McGowan, 126, *MR&M*. For a similar case, see bond for John Egan, April 17, 1866, entry 3545, BRFAL; testimony of Mollie Davis, 200; Ellen Brown, 200; and Mat. Wardlaw, 234, *MR&M*; and "The Riot—Continued," *Memphis Daily Post*, May 4, 1866, p. 8, cols. 2–4.

45. Affidavit of Lemuel (Samuel) Premier, FBC, *MR&M*, 338, identified Sweatt as one of the rioters.

46. Statement of C. C. Swears, Robert Church, and John Gains, Feb. 17, 1866, entry 3545, BRFAL.

47. Ibid.; S. S. Garret to Major William L. Porter, Feb. 17, 1866; and endorsement from Mayor John Park, Feb. 22, 1866, entry 3545, BRFAL.

48. Testimony of Rachel Dilts, *MR&M*, 67. See also testimony of P. G. Marsh, 169; and James H. Swan, T78, *MR&M*.

49. See Benjamin P. Runkle, "Report Concerning the Late Riots at Memphis, Tenn.," in entry 3529, BRFAL; and "Report," 6; testimony of Dr. J. N. Sharp, 154, 156; Dr. D. P. Beecher, 145; James E. Donahue, 199; and William H. Pearce, 218, all in *MR&M*.

50. Testimony of Dr. J. N. Sharp, 167; Margaret Gardner, 98; Ellen Dilts, 64; Rachel Dilts, 67; Andrew Reyyonco, 169; and "Report," 6, all in *MR&M*. See also Runkle, "Report."

51. See report of Captain A. W. Allyn, exhibit 2, p. 358; and testimony of Thomas Durnin, 223, *MR&M*.

52. Benjamin P. Runkle to C. B. Fisk, May 23, 1866, entry 3529, BRFAL. Alex McQuarters noted that there were more women on the street than men. Testimony Taken before Military Commission Organized by General George Stoneman (hereafter MC), *MR&M*, 317. Quotation from affidavit of Albert Butcher, FBC, *MR&M*, 346. See also testimony of Adam Lock, 115–116; J. S. Chapin, 192; and James Finn, MC, 332, *MR&M*.

53. Testimony of Tony Cherry, *MR&M*, 182.

54. Witnesses differed as to where soldiers aimed their initial shots. See testimony of Adam Lock, 116; William Wheedon, 320; Abram Means, 173; C. H. Bowman, 324; Margaret Gardner, 98; and affidavits of Albert Butcher, FBC, 346; and Patzy Tolliver, 351, all in *MR&M*.

55. See Report, 7; testimony of Tony Cherry, 182; Dr. R. W. Creighton, 124–125; Dr. William F. Irwin, 131; and Dr. J. M. Keller, 133–134, all in *MR&M*.

56. See testimony of James Carroll Mitchell, 308–309; and Report, 7–8, *MR&M*.

57. Testimony of Dr. Robert McGowan, *MR&M*, 126.

58. See testimony of George Hogan, 149; Tony Cherry, 185–186; S. S. Garrett, 203–204; Frederick Hastings, 205–208; James Helm, 217; Thomas Durnin, 223–225; and Captain A. W. Allyn, 247, all in *MR&M*.

59. Testimony of Hannah Robinson, *MR&M*, 193.

60. Statement of Ann Freeman, May 22, 1866, entry 3545, BRFAL.

61. Testimony of Lucy Tibbs, *MR&M*, 160–162.

62. Testimony of Harriet Armour, *MR&M*, 177.

63. Testimony of Molly Haves, *MR&M*, 186.

64. Testimony of Harriet Armour, *MR&M* 176–177.

65. Testimony of Frances Thompson and Lucy Smith, *MR&M*, 196–197.

66. See also Hardwick, "'Your Old Father Abe Lincoln Is Dead and Damned.'"

67. Testimony of Frances Thompson, *MR&M*, 196.

68. Testimony of Lucy Smith, *MR&M*, 197.

69. Testimony of Frances Thompson, *MR&M*, 196–197.

70. Testimony of Lucy Smith, *MR&M*, 197.

71. Testimony of Frances Thompson, *MR&M*, 196.

72. Testimony of Elvira Walker, *MR&M*, 194.

73. Ibid.; cf. affidavits of Rebecca Ann Bloom and Peter Bloom, FBC, *MR&M*, 351, 348.

74. Affidavit of Rebecca Ann Bloom, FBC, *MR&M*, 351.

75. "Rape scripts" is Sharon Marcus's term in "Fighting Bodies, Fighting Words: A Theory and Politics of Rape Prevention," in *Feminists Theorize the Political*, ed. Judith Butler and Joan W. Scott (New York: Routledge, 1992), 385–403. The classic reading of the rape of female slaves by white slave owners as an effort to impose a submissive gender on black women is Angela Davis, "Reflections on the Black Woman's Role in the Community of Slaves," *Black Scholar* 3 (1971): 3–15.

76. See also Marybeth Hamilton Arnold, "'The Life of a Citizen in the Hands of a Woman': Sexual Assault in New York City, 1790 to 1820," in *Passion and Power: Sexuality in History*, ed. Kathy Peiss and Christian Simmons (Philadelphia: Temple University Press, 1989), 39.

77. Testimony of Harriet Armour, *MR&M*, 176.

78. Testimony of Lucy Tibbs, *MR&M*, 161.

79. Testimony of Lucy Smith, *MR&M*, 197.

80. See Report, *MR&M*, 3.

81. On the political context of this proposal, see Foner, *Reconstruction*, 243–261. For Steens's motion in the House, see "Journal," *MR&M*, 45.

82. Rable, *But There Was No Peace*, 41.

83. The committee also appended to its report additional testimony collected by the Freedmen's Bureau and a military commission. See *MR&M*, 313–358.

84. Affidavit of Rebecca Ann Bloom, FBC, *MR&M*, 351. Bloom did not testify before the congressional committee; perhaps, like many freedpeople, she and her husband left the city after the riot. See Report, *MR&M*, 2; *Memphis Daily Avalanche*, May 5, 1866, reprinted in MC, *MR&M*, 334; "The Riot—Continued," *Memphis Daily Post*, May 4, 1866, p. 8, cols. 2–4.

85. Testimony of Frances Thompson, *MR&M*, 196.

86. Testimony of Lucy Smith, *MR&M*, 197.

87. Testimony of Lucy Tibbs, *MR&M*, 161.

88. Testimony of Harriet Armour, *MR&M*, 176.

89. Testimony of Lucy Smith, *MR&M*, 197.

90. Testimony of Lucy Tibbs, *MR&M*, 161.

91. Ibid.

92. Testimony of Harriet Armour, *MR&M*, 176.

93. This is suggested by the fact that the hostile questioning came from the two Republican members of the committee, while Shanklin, the committee's minority Democrat, who showed frequent support for white Southerners during his questioning of witnesses, did not ask any questions about rape.

94. Testimony of Cynthia Townsend, *MR&M*, 163.

95. Testimony of Harriet Armour, *MR&M*, 176.

96. Ibid., 177; Cynthia Townsend, 163; Molly Hayes, 186; and Henry Porter, 168, all in *MR&M*.

97. See also Edwards, "Sexual Violence, Gender, Reconstruction"; idem, "The Disappearance of Susan Daniel and Henderson Cooper"; and idem, *Gendered Strife and Confusion*, 198–210.

98. See, for example, "Report of the Committee of Investigation on the Memphis Riots," *New York Times*, July 16, 1866, 1; Rable, *But There Was No Peace*, 41.

99. Report, *MR&M*, 5, 13. Did the authors of this report in fact perceive irony in men acting with "licentious brutality" toward those whom they constructed as inferior others? Or do the quotation marks around the phrase "conquered their prejudices" indicate a recognition that "prejudice" can have a role in, rather than be an obstacle to, fantasies of domination?

100. Report, *MR&M*, 13–15.

101. Laura Edwards argues that this discourse, rather than empowering all women to resist sexual violence, marked only those who remained subservient to patriarchal dictates for women's appropriate behavior as deserving of protection. See Edwards, "Sexual Violence, Gender, Reconstruction." See also idem, *Gendered Strife and Confusion*, 210–213.

102. In addition to expediting the passage of Reconstruction acts in Congress, the congressional committee's report on the Memphis Riot provided the final evidence needed to pass the Metropolitan Police Bill in the Tennessee state legislature. This act, placing control of the city's police force in the hands of a commission appointed by the governor, led to the dismissal of the force that had instigated the riot. See "Metropolitan Police," *Memphis Daily Appeal*, May 1, 1866, p. 2, col. 1. From the *Memphis Daily Argus*, see "The Metropolitan Police Bill," p. 2, col. 1; and "Important Document," p. 3, cols. 3–5, both April 29, 1866; "The Memphis Riots: What Gen. Runkle of the Freedmen's Bureau Thinks about Them," May 12, 1866, p. 1, col. 8; and "The Police 'Head Center,'" May 29, 1866, p. 2, col. 1.

103. Cf. Rable, *But There Was No Peace*, 41.

104. See "A Mask Lifted," *Public Ledger*, July 11, 1876, p. 3, col. 4; "Local Paragraphs," *Memphis Daily Appeal*, July 11, 1876, p. 4, col. 2; and "Local Paragraphs," *Memphis Daily Appeal*, July 14, 1876. See also Elizabeth Meriwether, *Recollections of Ninety-Two Years, 1824–1916* (Nashville: Tennessee Historical Commission, 1958), 180. I thank Gerald Smith for directing me to this source.

105. See, for instance, "Under False Colors," *Memphis Daily Avalanche*, July 12, 1876, p. 4, col. 2; and "Thompson," *Memphis Daily Appeal*, July 13, 1876, p. 4, col. 4.

106. See "Local Paragraphs," *Memphis Daily Appeal*, Nov. 4, 1876, p. 4, col. 2; from the *Memphis Daily Avalanche*, July 18, 1876, p. 4, col. 2; July 19, 1876, p. 4, col. 2; July 20, 1876, p. 4, col. 2; and July 21, 1876, p. 4, col. 1; and from the *Public Ledger*, "Ledger Lines," July 13, 1876, p. 3, col. 3; and July 17, 1876, p. 3, col. 4.

107. "Frances Thompson Dead," *Weekly Public Ledger*, Nov. 7, 1876, p. 3, col. 1.

108. Register of Deaths, Memphis and Shelby County Health Department, 1876–1884, p. 24, MSCA.

109. Thompson appears on a list of freedpeople reporting violence to the Freedmen's Bureau in the days just after the riot. Next to Thompson's name, this list states that Lucy Smith had been raped. See "Report of Casualties and Property Destroyed during the Memphis riots," entry 3529, BRFAL. The entry is ambiguous. It seems to indicate that at this time Thompson did not tell the Bureau that she herself had been sexually assaulted. Even if this were certain, it would not prove that her testimony was fabricated.

110. See in the *Memphis Daily Appeal*, "Thompson," July 13, 1876, p. 4, col. 4; "Frances Thompson," July 14, 1876, p. 4, col. 4; and "Local Paragraphs," July 18, 1876, p. 4, col. 2; in the *Public Ledger*, "A Mask Lifted," July 11, 1876, p. 3, col. 4, and "That Man-Woman," July 12, 1876, p. 3, col. 5; and in the *Weekly Public Ledger*, "Frances Thompson Dead," November 7, 1876, p. 3, col. 5; and in the *Weekly Public Ledger*, "Frances Thompson Dead," November 7, 1876, p. 3, col. 1. Meriwether remembers that Thompson was "discovered" as a result of the accusation by a "respectable negro woman" that her daughter, working as Thompson's house maid, had become pregnant by Thompson (*Ninety-Two Years Recollected*, 180). I found no evidence to confirm this.

111. "Frances Thompson," *Memphis Daily Appeal*, July 14, 1876, p. 4, col. 4; and "Ledger Lines," *Public Ledger*, July 17, 1876, p. 3, col. 3. See also "Ledger Lines," *Public Ledger*, July 14, 1876, p. 3, col. 4.

112. "Thompson," *Memphis Daily Appeal*, July 13, 1876, p. 4, col. 4.

113. "Time Makes All Things Even At Last," *Public Ledger*, July 19, 1876, p. 2, cols. 2–3.

114. *Memphis Daily Appeal*, July 16, 1876, p. 2, col. 1.

KEY TERMS

emancipation Freeing; freedom. In this context the term refers specifically to the freeing of slaves through the Emancipation Act of 1863.

Reconstruction The period after the Civil War during which the victorious Union (northern) forces attempted to "reconstruct" southern culture in the image of the north. The policies of Reconstruction and the northern and African American politicians who administered them were predictably loathed by most white southerners.

antebellum Latin: before the war. The term refers to cultural notions and practices in effect before the Civil War.

tangible Literally: touchable. The word is almost always used metaphorically to mean "concrete."

denigrate Criticize; refer to in negative terms.

nymphs du pavé Hybrid French/English: nymphs of the street, a sarcastic reference to streetwalkers, or prostitutes.

eviscerate Remove the intestines of; gut. The term is often used metaphorically to refer to eliminating the central or most important qualities of an idea or policy.

Discussion Questions

1. What is meant by the notion of "virtue" as it is used in Rosen's article? Are only women "virtuous"? The term is derived from a Latin word that refers specifically to the ideal qualities of *manhood*; what has happened to it over the past two millennia? *Can* the term "virtuous" apply to men as well as women? What constitutes male virtue? Why is it so different from female virtue? Is the notion of virtue in the twenty-first century still as gender specific as it was in the nineteenth? How has it changed? How has it remained the same? Why? Rosen provides some evidence that some of the rioters went to some effort to shape the context of their encounter with their rape victims so that, in their minds, at least, these women could be construed as beyond the pale of "virtue." What kinds of specific activities might be included in this description? Why would these men do this?

2. As members of the congressional investigative committee grilled Black rape victims of the Memphis riot, two perspectives seemed obvious. First, the congressmen felt that the women should have fought hard against their attackers. Second, the women, themselves, felt that death or serious injury was too high a price to pay for avoiding rape. What are the specific historical and cultural circumstances that produced these very different attitudes? Rape is a particular variety of assault. Why should it have such tremendous significance in some cultures? Why is it different from other kinds of assault in U.S. culture and in many others? Why do you suppose that one rape victim's husband left her after he heard about his wife's rape?

3. Rosen tells us, "To [the assaulted freedwomen], in this context, honor depended more on surviving and protesting injustice than on privileging and protecting a patriarchal notion of women's sexual 'virtue.'" This is a very academic style of writing. Restate it in more everyday terms. What is Rosen talking about when she uses the term "patriarchal"? What is so patriarchal about the notion of women's virtue to which Rosen is referring? Do you think this notion of female virtue is the same now as it was 150 years ago? What differences do you notice, and what similarities? What phenomena do you think account for the differences *and* the similarities? This question is clearly related to the previous question, but it takes a slightly different tack in approaching it.

4. Rosen provides a quotation from the conservative Memphis newspaper, the *Appeal*, in which reference is made to "pretended outrages" committed on the transvestite Frances Thompson by "the Irish of the city during the celebrated riots." This is a very interesting quote for at least two reasons. Once it was discovered, ten years after the riots, that Frances Thompson was a male dressed and living as a woman, it was immediately assumed that the rape that Thompson had alleged could not have taken place. What do you make of this? When Thompson's transvestism was discovered, he was sentenced to 90 days on the local chain gang. What is the justification for laws against cross-dressing? Why should it be against the law?

   A completely different issue has to do with the newspaper writer's ascription of the riots to "the Irish." It is difficult for many Americans in the twenty-first century, particularly those who live in western states, to imagine a time when Irish immigrants and Irish Americans suffered severe discrimination at the hands of earlier immigrants and their descendants—but it is a well-documented phenomenon. Indeed, the Ku Klux Klan devoted some of their time in the late nineteenth century to burning crosses on the land of Irish immigrants. The Irish undoubtedly *did* form a disproportionate part of the lower middle class who rioted in Memphis, not because of their naturally vicious dispositions, but because of the frustrations and limitations of the socioeconomic class to which they belonged. What is the motivation for (and the likely result of) the newspaper article's identification of the Irish as responsible for the Memphis riots. What kind of long-term effects does this kind of journalism have? Can you cite specific examples?

Gender in the Culture of Latinas/Latinos and Asian Americans

The cultures of Americans of Latin and of Asian descent contain great internal diversity and are quite different from each other as well. They share one important characteristic, however: With the exception of Spanish-speaking peoples present in what is now the United States at the Treaty of Guadalupe Hidalgo, when Mexico was forced to cede part of its territory to the United States (1848), Latinas/Latinos and Asian Americans chose to emigrate from their native countries. Unlike African Americans, they were not chattel slaves. And unlike Native Americans, they were not living in their original homeland when Europeans invaded the United States.

It seems to be the nature of the human brain to search for patterns. In complex phenomena, like culture, this quest for patterns usually results in simplification, so that satisfying generalizations can be produced. There is nothing wrong with this; it is the behavioral result of a genetically encoded human cognitive trait. The problem arises when people, especially those with power, authority, and wealth, transform generalizations into rigid stereotypes, which then take on a life of their own. Such stereotypes not only blind people to cultural complexity, but are also used to justify inequity and oppression, on the grounds that "they" (whoever "they" are at any given time) aren't like "us." Keep the power of ethnic stereotype in mind as you read the following articles on Latinas/Latinos and Asian Americans. The point is not to polish your sense of guilt, but to recognize how easy it is to slip into the acceptance of unexamined patterns as reality. In order to help guide your thinking, we have come up with four broad issues for you to consider as you work your way through this chapter.

1. In contemplating the issue of gender equality and Latina/o culture, one term probably comes immediately to the mind of most members of the majority American population: *machismo*. What *is* machismo, and how does it operate in Latino/Latina culture? It is common for most contemporary Euro-Americans, especially women, to condemn machismo. Why? How can you account for the development of machismo, and do you see it as having any utility? To what extent does it actually operate in Hispanic society, and to what extent do you see it as a remnant of an earlier cultural ideal? The term *machismo* is Spanish, but

it can certainly be applied to non-Hispanic cultures, as well. Do you see any elements of machismo in the accounts of Asian-American life contained in this chapter? What about Euro-American life?

2. One of the great difficulties shared by immigrants and the children (and grandchildren) of immigrants is the conflicts that inevitably arise between beliefs and practices of the "old country" and those of the new. How do you see these conflicts developing when it comes to issues of gender? The conflicts are not always simple: Parents think X, while children think Y. Sometimes the split may occur between men and women. Often children try to accommodate both their parents' values and those they learn from school and friends, and a hybrid set of values and practices develops. In addition to changing gender attitudes and practices, what other changes do you note?

3. In many cultures the sexuality of women is believed to be a potentially dangerous force that must be strictly controlled. If not, this line of thinking runs, society will crumble, and chaos will reign. The sexuality of men is seen as a natural phenomenon, more akin to gravity, that cannot reasonably be directly limited. To what extent do you see these perspectives as reflected in the articles in this chapter? Explain in detail why you see them or why you do not see them. Why do you think such perspectives are so common? To what extent do you think they exist in majority American culture?

4. As you read all four articles in this chapter, examine your own thinking about gender-based stereotypes of Latinas/Latinos and Asian Americans. If it makes you more comfortable to use the term "generalizations," go ahead. What are they? After completing all the articles, ask yourself again, what was the underlying reality? What seems to have been the distortion factor? What have you learned? Have you altered any of your opinions?

La Conciencia de la Mestiza

TOWARDS A NEW CONSCIOUSNESS

Gloria Anzaldúa

Anzaldúa's article is valuable for at least four different reasons. First, Anzaldúa is a thoughtful observer of the background from which she comes. Sometimes it seems to members of the American ethnic majority that all members of any kind of minority are natural experts on their own backgrounds and are also fascinated by the topic. Of course this is not the case. A Chicana may be no more interested in her ethnic background than a Finnish American or Italian American may be, and may as likely be an expert on detective fiction or social services administration as on Mexican American culture. But someone like Anzaldúa, who is both interested and thoughtful about her cultural heritage brings a special dimension to its study.

Second, as a Chicana lesbian, Anzaldúa combines the perspective of an insider (anthropologists call this an emic *perspective) with that of an outsider (which anthropologists call an* etic *perspective). Both points of view are useful. The insider has cultural understandings that outsiders may never gain, even if they devote their whole lives to the study of a group. But the outsider also brings a useful focus to bear on a culture, since she or he sees aspects of it that insiders simply take for granted and never question. Anthropologists, of course, are always outsiders; it is both the advantage and the limitation they bring to their work. Because her status as a lesbian makes her to some extent an outsider in her own culture, Anzaldúa assesses it more critically than Chicanas/Chicanos who are more fully "at home" in it. And because she is undeniably a part of the culture of which she is also not a part, Anzaldúa understands it thoroughly.*

Third, Anzaldúa is not a social scientist; she is a poet, fiction writer, and essayist. The editors of this collection are both anthropologists, and we are committed to the general perspective of the social sciences. But that is not the only way to acquire information and insight about human values and interactions within the societies people inhabit. Sometimes it is helpful to take a breather, and look at cultures through a different lens. Anzaldúa provides us with just such a lens.

Finally, this selection, which forms Chapter 7 of Anzaldúa's book, Borderlands/La Frontera: The New Mestiza, *contains a lot of Spanish. Many readers who do not speak Spanish may be taken aback by the presence of so much of a language they do not know. But by using it, Anzaldúa makes a brilliant point: She, like the majority of Latinas/Latinos of all origins, has a foot in two very different cultures. Many monolingual English speakers in the United States complain bitterly about the use of languages other than English by immigrants. But Anzaldúa is not an immigrant; she was born in Texas. She uses Spanish and English not because she is unable to express herself well enough to use only one language, but because both languages are part of her birthright and her heritage. In order to maintain her connection to the intimate, Spanish-speaking world and the public, English-speaking world, Gloria Anzaldúa denies neither of those languages. Many American students study Spanish in high school; yet only a very small proportion of them become adept at using the language. Anzaldúa's essay provides a great argument for the increased richness and complexity of expression bilingualism offers, and an equally powerful argument against policies that aim to replace bilingualism, in any group, with monolingualism. For readers who do not speak Spanish, English translations are provided.*

As you read through the following article, consider the cultural elements, both from the larger, Anglo world and the smaller, Latino world that have shaped the gendered universe Gloria Anzaldúa inhabits. Then consider the influences that Anzaldúa, herself, has selected, as guides to shaping a more humane universe.

Por la mujer de mi raza hablará el espíritu.[1]

Jose Vascocelos, Mexican philosopher, envisaged *una raza mestiza, una mezcla de razas afines, una raza de color—la primera raza síntesis del globo*. He called it a cosmic race, *la raza cósmica*, a fifth race embracing the four major races of the world.[2] Opposite to the theory of the pure Aryan, and to the policy of racial purity that white America practices, his theory is one of inclusivity. At the confluence of two or more genetic streams, with chromosomes constantly "crossing over," this mixture of races, rather than resulting in an inferior being, provides hybrid progeny, a mutable, more malleable species with a rich gene pool. From this racial, ideological, cultural and biological cross-pollinization, an "alien" consciousness is presently in the making—a new *mestiza* consciousness, *una conciencia de mujer*.

It is a consciousness of the Borderlands.

Una lucha de fronteras / A Struggle of Borders

Because I, a *mestiza*,
continually walk out of one culture
and into another,
because I am in all cultures at the same time,
alma entre dos mundos, tres, cuatro,
me zumba la cabeza con lo contradictorio.
Estoy norteada por todas las voces que me hablan
simultáneamente.

The ambivalence from the clash of voices results in mental and emotional states of perplexity. Internal strife results in insecurity and indecisiveness. The mestiza's dual or multiple personality is plagued by psychic restlessness.

In a constant state of mental nepantilism, an Aztec word meaning torn between ways, *la mestiza* is a product of the transfer of the cultural and spiritual values of one group to another. Being tricultural, monolingual, bilingual, or multilingual, speaking a patois, and in a state of perpetual transition, the *mestiza* faces the dilemma of the mixed breed: which collectivity does the daughter of a darkskinned mother listen to?

El choque de un alma atrapado entre el mundo del espíritu y el mundo de la técnica a veces la deja entullada. Cradled in one culture, sandwiched between two cultures, straddling all three cultures and their value systems, *la mestiza* undergoes a struggle of flesh, a struggle of borders, an inner war. Like all people, we perceive the version of reality that our culture communicates. Like others having or living in more than one culture, we get multiple, often opposing messages. The coming together of two self-consistent but habitually incompatible frames of reference[3] causes *un choque*, a cultural collision.

Source: From *Borderlands/La Frontera: The New Mestiza* © 1987 by Gloria Anzaldúa. Reprinted by permission of Aunt Lute Books.

Within us and within *la cultura chicana*, commonly held beliefs of the white culture attack commonly held beliefs of the Mexican culture, and both attack commonly held beliefs of the indigenous culture. Subconsciously, we see an attack on ourselves and our beliefs as a threat and we attempt to block with a counterstance.

But it is not enough to stand on the opposite river bank, shouting questions, challenging patriarchal, white conventions. A counterstance locks one into a duel of oppressor and oppressed; locked in mortal combat, like the cop and the criminal, both are reduced to a common denominator of violence. The counterstance refutes the dominant culture's views and beliefs, and, for this, it is proudly defiant. All reaction is limited by, and dependent on, what it is reacting against. Because the counterstance stems from a problem with authority—outer as well as inner—it's a step towards liberation from cultural domination. But it is not a way of life. At some point, on our way to a new consciousness, we will have to leave the opposite bank, the split between the two mortal combatants somehow healed so that we are on both shores at once and, at once, see through serpent and eagle eyes. Or perhaps we will decide to disengage from the dominant culture, write it off altogether as a lost cause, and cross the border into a wholly new and separate territory. Or we might go another route. The possibilities are numerous once we decide to act and not react.

A Tolerance For Ambiguity

These numerous possibilities leave *la mestiza* floundering in uncharted seas. In perceiving conflicting information and points of view, she is subjected to a swamping of her psychological borders. She has discovered that she can't hold concepts or ideas in rigid boundaries. The borders and walls that are supposed to keep the undesirable ideas out are entrenched habits and patterns of behavior; these habits and patterns are the enemy within. Rigidity means death. Only by remaining flexible is she able to stretch the psyche horizontally and vertically. *La mestiza* constantly has to shift out of habitual formations; from convergent thinking, analytical reasoning that tends to use rationality to move toward a single goal (a Western mode), to divergent thinking,[4] characterized by movement away from set patterns and goals and toward a more whole perspective, one that includes rather than excludes.

The new *mestiza* copes by developing a tolerance for contradictions, a tolerance for ambiguity. She learns to be an Indian in Mexican culture, to be Mexican from an Anglo point of view. She learns to juggle cultures. She has a plural personality, she operates in a pluralistic mode—nothing is thrust out, the good the bad and the ugly, nothing rejected, nothing abandoned. Not only does she sustain contradictions, she turns the ambivalence into something else.

She can be jarred out of ambivalence by an intense, and often painful, emotional event which inverts or resolves the ambivalence. I'm not sure exactly how. The work takes place underground—subconsciously. It is work that the soul performs. That focal point or fulcrum, that juncture where the mestiza stands, is where phenomena tend to collide. It is where the possibility of uniting all that is separate occurs. This assembly is not one where severed or separated pieces merely come together. Nor is it a balancing of opposing powers. In attempting to work out a synthesis, the self has added a third element which is greater than the sum of its severed parts. That third element is a new consciousness—a mestiza consciousness—and though it is a source of intense pain, its energy comes from continual creative motion that keeps breaking down the unitary aspect of each new paradigm.

En unas pocas centurias, the future will belong to the mestiza. Because the future depends on the breaking down of paradigms, it depends on the straddling of two or more cultures. By creating a new mythos—that is, a change in the way we perceive reality, the way we see ourselves, and the ways we behave—*la mestiza* creates a new consciousness.

The work of *mestiza* consciousness is to break down the subject-object duality that keeps her a prisoner and to show in the flesh and through the images in her work how duality is transcended. The answer to the problem between the white race and the colored, between males and females, lies in healing the split that originates in the very foundation of our lives, our culture, our languages, our thoughts. A massive uprooting of dualistic thinking in the individual and collective consciousness is the beginning of a long struggle, but one that could, in our best hopes, bring us to the end of rape, of violence, of war.

La encrucijada / The Crossroads

A chicken is being sacrificed
   at a crossroads, a simple mound of earth
a mud shrine for *Eshu*,
   Yoruba god of indeterminacy,
who blesses her choice of path.
   She begins her journey.

Su cuerpo es una bocacalle. La mestiza has gone from being the sacrificial goat to becoming the officiating priestess at the crossroads.

As a *mestiza* I have no country, my homeland cast me out; yet all countries are mine because I am every woman's sister or potential lover. (As a lesbian I have no race, my own people disclaim me; but I am all races because there is the queer of me in all races.) I am cultureless because, as a feminist, I challenge the collective cultural/religious male-derived beliefs of Indo-Hispanics and Anglos; yet I am cultured because I am participating in the creation of yet another culture, a new story to explain the world and our participation in it, a new value system with images and symbols that connect us to each other and to the planet. *Soy un amasamiento*, I am an act of kneading, of uniting and joining that not only has produced both a creature of darkness and a creature of light, but also a creature that questions the definitions of light and dark and gives them new meanings.

We are the people who leap in the dark, we are the people on the knees of the gods. In our very flesh, (r)evolution works out the clash of cultures. It makes us crazy constantly, but if the center holds, we've made some kind of evolutionary step forward. *Nuestra alma el trabajo*, the opus, the great alchemical work; spiritual *mestizaje*, a "morphogenesis,"[5] an inevitable unfolding. We have become the quickening serpent movement.

Indigenous like corn, like corn, the *mestiza* is a product of crossbreeding, designed for preservation under a variety of conditions. Like an ear of corn—a female seed-bearing organ—the *mestiza* is tenacious, tightly wrapped in the husks of her culture. Like kernels she clings to the cob; with thick stalks and strong brace roots, she holds tight to the earth—she will survive the crossroads.

Lavando y remojando el maíz en agua de cal, despojando el pellejo. Moliendo, mixteando, amasando, haciendo tortillas de masa.[6] She steeps the corn in lime, it swells, softens. With stone roller on *metate*, she grinds the corn, then grinds again. She kneads and moulds the dough, pats the round balls into *tortillas*.

We are the porous rock in the stone *metate*
squatting on the ground.
We are the rolling pin, *el maíz y agua,*
la masa harina. Somos el amasijo.
Somos lo molido en el metate.
We are the *comal* sizzling hot,
the hot *tortilla,* the hungry mouth.
We are the coarse rock.
We are the grinding motion,
the mixed potion, *somos el molcajete.*
We are the pestle, the *comino, ajo, pimienta,*
We are the *chile colorado,*
the green shoot that cracks the rock.
We will abide.

El camino de la mestiza / The Mestiza Way

Caught between the sudden contraction, the breath sucked in and the endless space, the brown woman stands still, looks at the sky. She decides to go down, digging her way along the roots of trees. Sifting through the bones, she shakes them to see if there is any marrow in them. Then, touching the dirt to her forehead, to her tongue, she takes a few bones, leaves the rest in their burial place.

She goes through her backpack, keeps her journal and address book, throws away the muni-bart metromaps. The coins are heavy and they go next, then the greenbacks flutter through the air. She keeps her knife, can opener and eyebrow pencil. She puts bones, pieces of bark, *hierbas,* eagle feather, snakeskin, tape recorder, the rattle and drum in her pack and she sets out to become the complete *tolteca.*

Her first step is to take inventory. *Despojando, desgranando, quitando paja.* Just what did she inherit from her ancestors? This weight on her back—which is the baggage from the Indian mother, which the baggage from the Spanish father, which the baggage from the Anglo?

Pero es difícil differentiating between *lo heredado, lo adquirido, lo impuesto.* She puts history through a sieve, winnows out the lies, looks at the forces that we as a race, as

women, have been a part of. *Luego bota lo que no vale, los desmientos, los desencuentros, el embrutecimiento. Aguarda el juicio, hondo y enraízado, del la gente antigua.* This step is a conscious rupture with all oppressive traditions of all cultures and religions. She communicates that rupture, documents the struggle. She reinterprets history and, using new symbols, she shapes new myths. She adopts new perspectives toward the dark-skinned, women and queers. She strengthens her tolerance (and intolerance) for ambiguity. She is willing to share, to make herself vulnerable to foreign ways of seeing and thinking. She surrenders all notions of safety, of the familiar. Deconstruct, construct. She becomes a *nabual,* able to transform herself into a tree, a coyote, into another person. She learns to transform the small "I" into the total Self. *Se hace moldeadora de su alma. Según la concepción que tiene de sí misma, así será.*

Que no se nos olvide los hombres

"Tú no sirves pa' nada—
you're good for nothing.
Eres pura vieja."

"You're nothing but a woman" means you are defective. Its opposite is to be *un macho.* The modern meaning of the word "machismo," as well as the concept, is actually an Anglo invention. For men like my father, being "macho" meant being strong enough to protect and support my mother and us, yet being able to show love. Today's macho has doubts about his ability to feed and protect his family. His "machismo" is an adaptation to oppression and poverty and low self-esteem. It is the result of hierarchical male dominance. The Anglo, feeling inadequate and inferior and powerless, displaces or transfers these feelings to the Chicano by shaming him. In the Gringo world, the Chicano suffers from excessive humility and self-effacement, shame of self and self-deprecation. Around Latinos he suffers from a sense of language inadequacy and its accompanying discomfort; with Native Americans he suffers from a racial amnesia which ignores our common blood, and from guilt because the Spanish part of him took their land and oppressed them. He has an excessive compensatory hubris when around Mexicans from the other side. It overlays a deep sense of racial shame.

The loss of a sense of dignity and respect in the macho breeds a false machismo which leads him to put down women and even to brutalize them. Coexisting with his sexist behavior is a love for the mother which takes precedence over that of all others. Devoted son, macho pig. To wash down the shame of his acts, of his very being, and to handle the brute in the mirror, he takes to the bottle, the snort, the needle, and the fist.

Though we "understand" the root causes of male hatred and fear, and the subsequent wounding of women, we do not excuse, we do not condone, and we will no longer put up with it. From the men of our race, we demand the admission / acknowledgment / disclosure / testimony that they wound us, violate us, are afraid of us and of our power. We need them to say they will begin to eliminate their hurtful put-down ways. But more than the words, we demand acts. We say to them: We will develop equal power with you and those who have shamed us.

It is imperative that mestizas support each other in changing the sexist elements in the Mexican-Indian culture. As long as woman is put down, the Indian and the Black in all of us is put down. The struggle of the mestiza is above all a feminist one. As long as *los hombres* think they have to *chingar mujeres* and each other to be men, as long as men are taught that they are superior and therefore culturally favored over *la mujer*, as long as to be a *vieja* is a thing of derision, there can be no real healing of our

psyches. We're halfway there—we have such love of the Mother, the good mother. The first step is to unlearn the *puta/virgen* dichotomy and to see *Coatlapopeuh-Coatlicue* in the Mother, *Guadalupe*.

Tenderness, a sign of vulnerability, is so feared that it is showered on women with verbal abuse and blows. Men, even more than women, are fettered to gender roles. Women at least have had the guts to break out of bondage. Only gay men have had the courage to expose themselves to the woman inside them and to challenge the current masculinity. I've encountered a few scattered and isolated gentle straight men, the beginnings of a new breed, but they are confused, and entangled with sexist behaviors that they have not been able to eradicate. We need a new masculinity and the new man needs a movement.

Lumping the males who deviate from the general norm with man, the oppressor, is a gross injustice. *Asombra pensar que nos hemos quedado en ese pozo escuro donde el mundo encierra a las lesbianas. Asombra pensar que hemos, como feministas y lesbianas, cerrado nuestros corazónes a los hombres, a nuestros hermanos los jotos, desheredados y marginales como nosotros.* Being the supreme crossers of cultures, homosexuals have strong bonds with the queer white, Black, Asian, Native American Latino, and with the queer in Italy, Australia and the rest of the planet. We come from all colors, all classes, all races, all time periods. Our role is to link people with each other—the Blacks with Jews with Indians with Asians with whites with extraterrestrials. It is to transfer ideas and information from one culture to another. Colored homosexuals have more knowledge of other cultures; have always been at the forefront (although sometimes in the closet) of all liberation struggles in this country; have suffered more injustices and have survived them despite all odds. Chicanos need to acknowledge the political and artistic contributions of their queer. People, listen to what your *jotería* is saying.

The mestizo and the queer exist at this time and point on the evolutionary continuum for a purpose. We are a blending that proves that all blood is intricately woven together, and that we are spawned out of similar souls.

> *Somos una gente*
>
> *Hay tantísimar fronteras*
> *que dividen a la gente,*
> *pero por cada frontera*
> *existe también un puente.*
>
> —Gina Valdés[7]

Divided Loyalties   Many women and men of color do not want to have any dealings with white people. It takes too much time and energy to explain to the downwardly mobile, white middle-class women that it's okay for us to want to own "possessions," never having had any nice furniture on our dirt floors or "luxuries" like washing machines. Many feel that whites should help their own people rid themselves of race hatred and fear first. I, for one, choose to use some of my energy to serve as mediator. I think we need to allow whites to be our allies. Through our literature, art, *corridos*, and folktales we must share our history with them so when they set up committees to help Big Mountain Navajos or the Chicano farmworkers or *los Nicaragüenses* they won't turn people away because of their racial fears and ignorances. They will come to see that they are not helping us but following our lead.

Individually, but also as a racial entity, we need to voice our needs. We need to say to white society: We need you to accept the fact that Chicanos are different, to acknowledge your rejection and negation of us. We need you to own the fact that you looked upon us as less than human, that you stole our lands, our personhood, our

self-respect. We need you to make public restitution: to say that, to compensate for your own sense of defectiveness, you strive for power over us, you erase our history and our experience because it makes you feel guilty—you'd rather forget your brutish acts. To say you've split yourself from minority groups, that you disown us, that your dual consciousness splits off parts of yourself, transferring the "negative" parts onto us. (Where there is persecution of minorities, there is shadow projection. Where there is violence and war, there is repression of shadow.) To say that you are afraid of us, that to put distance between us, you wear the mask of contempt. Admit that Mexico is your double, that she exists in the shadow of this country, that we are irrevocably tied to her. Gringo, accept the doppelganger in your psyche. By taking back your collective shadow the intracultural split will heal. And finally, tell us what you need from us.

By Your True Faces We Will Know You

I am visible—see this Indian face—yet I am invisible. I both blind them with my beak nose and am their blind spot. But I exist, we exist. They'd like to think I have melted in the pot. But I haven't, we haven't.

The dominant white culture is killing us slowly with its ignorance. By taking away our self-determination, it has made us weak and empty. As a people we have resisted and we have taken expedient positions, but we have never been allowed to develop unencumbered—we have never been allowed to be fully ourselves. The whites in power want us people of color to barricade ourselves behind our separate tribal walls so they can pick us off one at a time with their hidden weapons; so they can whitewash and distort history. Ignorance splits people, creates prejudices. A misinformed people is a subjugated people.

Before the Chicano and the undocumented worker and the Mexican from the other side can come together, before the Chicano can have unity with Native Americans and other groups, we need to know the history of their struggle and they need to know ours. Our mothers, our sisters and brothers, the guys who hang out on street corners, the children in the playgrounds, each of us must know our Indian lineage, our afro-*mestisaje*, our history of resistance.

To the immigrant *mexicano* and the recent arrivals we must teach our history. The 80 million *mexicanos* and the Latinos from Central and South America must know of our struggles. Each one of us must know basic facts about Nicaragua, Chile and the rest of Latin America. The Latinoist movement (Chicanos, Puerto Ricans, Cubans and other Spanish-speaking people working together to combat racial discrimination in the market place) is good but it is not enough. Other than a common culture we will have nothing to hold us together. We need to meet on a broader communal ground.

The struggle is inner: Chicano, *indio*, American Indian, *mojado, mexicano*, immigrant Latino, Anglo in power, working class Anglo, Black, Asian—our psyches resemble the bordertowns and are populated by the same people. The struggle has always been inner, and is played out in the outer terrains. Awareness of our situation must come before inner changes, which in turn come before changes in society. Nothing happens in the "real" world unless it first happens in the images in our heads.

El día de la Chicana

I will not be shamed again
Nor will I shame myself.

I am possessed by a vision: that we Chicanas and Chicanos have taken back or uncovered our true faces, our dignity and self-respect. It's a validation vision.

Seeing the Chicana anew in light of her history. I seek an exoneration, a seeing through the fictions of white supremacy, a seeing of ourselves in our true guises and not as the false racial personality that has been given to us and that we have given to ourselves. I seek our woman's face, our true features, the positive and the negative seen clearly, free of the tainted biases of male dominance. I seek new images of identity, new beliefs about ourselves, our humanity and worth no longer in question.

Estamos viviendo en la noche de la Raza, un tiempo cuando el trabajo se hace a lo quieto, en el oscuro. El día cuando aceptmos tal y como somos y para en donde vamos y porque—ese día será el día de la Raza. Yo tengo el conpromiso de expresar mi visión, mi sensibilidad, mi percepción de la revalidació de la gente mexicana, su mérito, estimación, honra, aprecio, y validez.

On December 2nd when my sun goes into my first house, I celebrate *el día de la Chicana y el Chicano*. On that day I clean my altars, light my *Coatlalopeuh* candle, burn sage and copal, take *el baño para espantar basura*, sweep my house. On that day I bare my soul, make myself vulnerable to friends and family by expressing my feelings. On that day I affirm who we are.

On that day I look inside our conflicts and our basic introverted racial temperament. I identify our needs, voice them. I acknowledge that the self and the race have been wounded. I recognize the need to take care of our personhood, of our racial self. On that day I gather the splintered and disowned parts of *la gente mexicana* and hold them in my arms. *Todas las partes de nosotros valen.*

On that day I say, "Yes, all you people wound us when you reject us. Rejection strips us of self-worth; our vulnerability exposes us to shame. It is our innate identity you find wanting. We are ashamed that we need your good opinion, that we need your acceptance. We can no longer camouflage our needs, can no longer let defenses and fences sprout around us. We can no longer withdraw. To rage and look upon you with contempt is to rage and be contemptuous of ourselves. We can no longer blame you, nor disown the white parts, the male parts, the pathological parts, the queer parts, the vulnerable parts. Here we are weaponless with open arms, with only our magic. Let's try it our way, the mestiza way, the Chicana way, the woman way.

On that day, I search for our essential dignity as a people, a people with a sense of purpose—to belong and contribute to something greater than our *pueblo*. On that day I seek to recover and reshape my spiritual identity. *¡Anímate! Raza, a celebrar el día de la Chicana.*

El retorno

All movements are accomplished in six stages, and the seventh brings return.

—I Ching[8]

> *Tanto tiempo sin verte casa mía,*
> *mi cuna, mi hondo nido de la huerta.*
> —*"Soledad"*[9]

I stand at the river, watch the curving, twisting serpent, a serpent nailed to the fence where the mouth of the Rio Grande empties into the Gulf.

I have come back. *Tanto dolor me costó el alejamiento.* I shade my eyes and look up. The bone beak of a hawk slowly circling over me, checking me out as potential carrion. In its wake a little bird flickering its wings, swimming sporadically like a fish. In the distance the expressway and the slough of traffic like an irritated sow. The sudden pull in my gut, *la tierra, los aguaceros.* My land, *el viento soplando la arena, el lagartijo debajo de un nopalito. Me acuerdo como era antes. Una región desértica de vasta llanuras, costeras de baja altura, de escasa lluvia, de chaparrales formados por mesquites y huizaches.* If I look real hard I can almost see the Spanish fathers who were

called "the cavalry of Christ" enter this valley riding their burros, see the clash of cultures commence.

Tierra natal. This is home, the small towns in the Valley, *los pueblitos* with chicken pens and goats picketed to mesquite shrubs. *En las colonias* on the other side of the tracks, junk cars line the front yards of hot pink and lavender-trimmed houses—Chicano architecture we call it, self-consciously. I have missed the TV shows where hosts speak in half and half, and where awards are given in the category of Tex-Mex music. I have missed the Mexican cemeteries blooming with artificial flowers, the fields of aloe vera and red pepper, rows of sugar cane, of corn hanging on the stalks, the cloud of *polvareda* in the dirt roads behind a speeding pickup truck, *el sabor de tamales de rez y venado.* I have missed *la yegua colorada* gnawing the wooden gate of her stall, the smell of horse flesh from Carito's corrals. *He hecho menos las noches calientes sin aire, noches de linternas y lechuzas* making holes in the night.

I still feel the old despair when I look at the unpainted, dilapidated, scrap lumber houses consisting mostly of corrugated aluminum. Some of the poorest people in the United States live in the Lower Rio Grande Valley, an arid and semi-arid land of irrigated farming, intense sunlight and heat, citrus groves next to chaparral and cactus. I walk through the elementary school I attended so long ago, that remained segregated until recently. I remember how the white teachers used to punish us for being Mexican.

How I love this tragic valley of South Texas, as Ricardo Sánchez calls it; this borderland between the Nueces and the Rio Grande. This land has survived possession and ill-use by five countries: Spain, Mexico, the Republic of Texas, the United States, the Confederacy, and the United States again. It has survived Anglo-Mexican blood feuds, lynchings, burnings, rapes, pillage.

Today I see the Valley still struggling to survive. Whether it does or not, it will never be as I remember it. The borderlands depression that was set off by the 1982 peso devaluation in Mexico resulted in the closure of hundreds of Valley businesses. Many people lost their homes, cars, land. Prior to 1982, U.S. store owners thrived on retail sales to Mexicans who came across the border for groceries and clothes and appliances. While goods on the U.S. side have become 10, 100, 1000 times more expensive for Mexican buyers, goods on the Mexican side have become 10, 100, 1000 times cheaper for Americans. Because the Valley is heavily dependent on agriculture and Mexican retail trade, it has the highest unemployment rates along the entire border region; it is the Valley that has been hardest hit.[10]

"It's been a bad year for corn," my brother, Nune, says. As he talks, I remember my father scanning the sky for a rain that would end the drought, looking up into the sky, day after day, while the corn withered on its stalk. My father has been dead for 29 years, having worked himself to death. The life span of a Mexican farm laborer is 56—he lived to be 38. It shocks me that I am older than he. I, too, search the sky for rain. Like the ancients, I worship the rain god and the maize goddess, but unlike my father I have recovered their names. Now for rain (irrigation) one offers not a sacrifice of blood, but of money.

"Farming is in a bad way," my brother says. "Two to three thousand small and big farmers went bankrupt in this country last year. Six years ago the price of corn was $8.00 per hundred pounds," he goes on.

"This year it is $3.90 per hundred pounds." And, I think to myself, after taking inflation into account, not planting anything puts you ahead.

I walk out to the back yard, stare at *los rosales de mamá*. She wants me to help her prune the rose bushes, dig out the carpet grass that is choking them. *Mamagrande Ramona también tenía rosales*. Here every Mexican grows flowers. If they don't have a piece of dirt, they use car tires, jars, cans, shoe boxes. Roses are the Mexican's favorite flower. I think, how symbolic—thorns and all.

Yes, the Chicano and Chicana have always taken care of growing things and the land. Again I see the four of us kids getting off the school bus, changing into our work clothes, walking into the field with Papi and Mami, all six of us bending to the ground. Below our feet, under the earth lie the watermelon seeds. We cover them with paper plates, putting *terremotes* on top of the plates to keep them from being blown away by the wind. The paper plates keep the freeze away. Next day or the next, we remove the plates, bare the tiny green shoots to the elements. They survive and grow, give fruit hundreds of times the size of the seed. We water them and hoe them. We harvest them. The vines dry, rot, are plowed under. Growth, death, decay, birth. The soil prepared again and again, impregnated, worked on. A constant changing of forms, *renacimientos de la tierra madre*.

> This land was Mexican once
> was Indian always
> and is.
> And will be again.

NOTES

1. This is my own "take off" on Jose Vasconcelos' idea. Jose Vasconcelos, *La Raza Cósmica: Misión de la Raza Ibero-Americana* (México: Aguilar S.A. de Ediciones, 1961).
2. Vasconcelos.

3. Arthur Koestler termed this "bisociation." Albert Rothenberg, *The Creative Process in Art, Science, and Other Fields* (Chicago, IL: University of Chicago Press, 1979), 12.

4. In part, I derive my definitions for "convergent" and "divergent" thinking from Rothenberg, 12–13.

5. To borrow chemist Ilya Prigogine's theory of "dissipative structures." Prigogine discovered that substances interact not in predictable ways as it was taught in science, but in different and fluctuating ways to produce new and more complex structures, a kind of birth he called "morphogenesis," which created unpredictable innovations. Harold Gilliam, "Searching for a New World View," *This World* (January, 1981), 23.

6. *Tortillas de masa harina*: corn tortillas are of two types, the smooth uniform ones made in a tortilla press and usually bought at a tortilla factor or supermarket, and *gorditas*, made by mixing *masa* with lard or shortening or butter (my mother sometimes puts in bits of bacon or *chicharrones*).

7. Gina Valdés, *Puentes y Fronteras: Coplas Chicanas* (Los Angeles, CA: Castle Lithograph, 1982), 2.

8. Richard Wilhelm, *The I Ching or Book of Changes*, trans. Cary F. Baynes (Princeton, NJ: Princeton University Press, 1950), 98.

9. *"Soledad"* is sung by the group, Haciendo Punto en Otro Son.

10. Out of the twenty-two border counties in the four border states, Hidalgo County (named for Father Hidalgo who was shot in 1810 after instigating Mexico's revolt against Spanish rule under the banner of *la Virgen de Guadalupe*) is the most poverty-stricken county in the nation as well as the largest home base (along with Imperial in California) for migrant farmworkers. It was here that I was born and raised. I am amazed that both it and I have survived.

KEY TERMS

La conciencia de la mestiza   The consciousness of the mestiza [mixed race woman].

Por la mujer de mi raza hablar el espíritu   The spirit speaks for the woman of my people.

una raza mestiza, una mezcla de razas afinas, una raza de color—la primera raza síntesis del globo   A mixed race, a mixture of refined races, a race of color—the first combined race on the planet.

alma entre dos mundos, tres, cuatro, me zumba la cabeza con lo contradictorio. Estoy norteada por todas las voces que me hablan simultáneamente   soul between two worlds, three, four, my head buzzes with the contradiction. I'm dizzy from all the voices that speak to me simultaneously.

El choque de un alma atrapado entre el mundo del espíritu y el mundo de la tecnica a veces la deja entullada   The collision of a soul trapped between the world of the spirit and the world of technology sometimes leaves it crippled.

un choque   A collision.

la cultura chicana   Chicano culture.

Su cuerpo es una bocacalle   Her body is an intersection.

Soy un amasamiento   I am a kneading together.

Nuestra alma el trabaja   Our soul the work.

opus   A work, as a work of art.

Lavando y remojando el maíz en agua de cal, despojando el pellejo. Moliendo, mixteando, amasamdo, haciendo tortillas de masa   Washing and resoaking the corn in lime water, separating the husks. Grinding, mixing, kneading, making corn tortillas.

metate   Flat stone mortar for grinding, usually grinding corn.

el maíz y agua, la masa harina. Somos el amasijo. Somos lo molido en el metate   the corn and water, the cornmeal. We are the kneaded dough. We are what has been ground in the metate.

comal   Griddle.

Somos el molcajete   We are the mortar.

comino, ajo, pimienta   Cumin, garlic, pepper.

chile colorado   Red chile.

hierbas   Herbs.

tolteca   Toltec. Member of a central Mexican ethnic group whose era of greatest influence predated that of the Aztec.

Despojando, desgranando, quitando paja   Stripping, threshing, removing the chaff.

Pero es difícil   But it is difficult.

lo heredado, lo adquirido, lo impuesto   What is inherited, what is acquired, what is imposed.

Luego bota lo que no vale, los desmientos, los desencuentos, el embrutecimiento. Aguarda el juicio, hondo y enraizado, de la gente antigua   Then she throws away what is worthless, contradictions, mistakes, stupidity. She preserves the judgment of the ancients, deep and rooted.

Se hace moldeadora de su alma. Según la concepción que tiene de si misma, así será. Que no se nos olvide los hombres "Tú no sirves pa' nada Eres pura vieja"   She becomes a shaper of her own soul. According to the notion she has of herself, that's how it will be. Let's not forget the men "You're good for nothing—You're just a woman."

los hombres   The men.

chingar mujeres   Screw women.

las mujeres   The women.

vieja   Woman, broad, old lady.

puta/virgen   Whore/virgin.

dichotomy   Division into two parts.

Coatlapopeuh-Coatlicue   An amalgamation of two Aztec female deities.

Guadalupe   [The Virgin of] Guadalupe. An appearance of the Virgin Mary to the Aztec farmer, Juan Diego, in 1531. The event is said to have resulted in roses blooming in December and the imprint of the Virgin's image on Juan Diego's cloak. The Virgin of Guadalupe is the patroness of Mexico and an important maternal figure in Mexican Catholicism.

Asombra pensar que nos hemos quedado en ese pozo oscuro donde el mundo encierra a las lesbianas. Asombra pensar que hemos, como femenistas y lesbianas, cerrado nuestros corazones a los hombres, a nuestros hermanos los jotos, desheredados y marginales como nosotros   It is amazing to think that we have remained in that dark hole where the world buries lesbians. It is amazing to think that we have, as feminists and lesbians, closed our hearts to men, to our brothers the queers [sic], disinherited and marginalized like us.

jotería   Queer [sic] community.

Hay tantísimas fronteras que dividen a la gente, pero por cada frontera existe también un puente   There are so many borders that divide people, but for every border a bridge exists, too.

corrido   Popular ballad.

los Nicaragüenses   The Nicaraguans.

mexicano   Mexican.

mojado   Wetback.

El día de la Chicana   The day of the Chicana.

Estamos viviendo en la noche de la Raza, un tiempo cuando el trabajo se hace a lo quieto, en el oscuro. El día cuando aceptamos tal y como somos y para en donde vamos y porque—ese día sería el día de la Raza. Yo tengo el conpromiso de expresar mi vision, mi sensibilidad, mi percepción de la revalidación de la gente mexicana, su mérito, estimación, honra, aprecio, y validez   We are living in the night of la Raza [the Chicano people], a time when the job becomes quietude, in the dark. The day we accept what we are, where we are going, and why—that day would be the day of the Raza. I have the obligation to express my vision, my sensibility, my perception of the revalidation of the Mexican people, their merit, esteem, honor, regard, and strength.

el día de la Chicana y el Chicano   The day of the Chicana and Chicano.

Coatlalopeuh   Aztec deity.

sage and copal   Traditional native New World incense. Copal is made from tree resin.

el baño para espantar basura   The bath to scare away rubbish.

la gente mexicana   The Mexican people.

Todas las partes de nosotros valen   All parts of us are worth something.

¡Animate! Raza, a celebrar el día de la Chicana   Wake up, Raza, and celebrate the day of the Chicana!

El retorno   The return.

Tanto tiempo sin verte casa mía, mi cuna, mi hondo nido de la huerta—"Soledad"   So much time without seeing you, my house, my cradle, my deep nest of the orchard—"Solitude"

Tanto dolor me costó el alejamiento   Withdrawal cost me so much pain.

la tierra, los aguacerros   The land, the rain.

el viento soplando la arena, el lagartijo debajo de un nopalito. Me acuerdo como era antes. Una región desertica de vasta llanuras, costeras de baja altura, de escasa lluvia, de chaparrales formados por mesquites y huizaches   The wind blows the sand, the lizard beneath a cactus. I remember how it was before. A deserted region of vast plains, bordered by deep height, of scarce rain, of thickets made of mesquite and huizache.

Tierra natal   Homeland.

los pueblitos   The little towns.

En las colonias   In the rural towns.

polvareda   Cloud of dust.

el sabor de tamales de rez y vanado   The taste of beef and venison tamales.

la yegua colorada   The red mare.

He hecho menos las noches calientes sin aire, noches de linternas y lechuzas   I have missed the hot, airless nights, the nights of lightning bugs and screech owls.

los rosales de mamá   Mama's rose bushes.

Mamagrande Ramona también tenía rosales   Grandma Ramona also had rose bushes.

terramontes   Piles of dirt.

renacimientos de la tierra madre   Rebirths of mother earth.

QUESTIONS FOR DISCUSSION

1. Gloria Anzaldúa describes herself as a Chicana lesbian feminist, a collection of terms that many non-Chicana lesbian feminists may find threatening and alienating. And yet Anzaldúa, without forsaking any of her ethnic, political, or ethical principles is *inclusive* rather than *exclusive*. Exactly what does Anzaldúa mean by the term "new consciousness"? This is something she talks about quite early on in the article. In order to have a *new* consciousness, there has to have been an *old* one. What outlook

(or outlooks) would come under the heading of the "old consciousness"? Why does Anzaldúa consider a new consciousness necessary? What do you think about the issue?

2. Many feminists discuss and analyze what they refer to as "patriarchal conventions," and Anzaldúa is no exception. What, specifically, is meant by this term, not only by Anzaldúa, but by other theorists as well? Does it seem to you that the term is useful? If you compare American society in roughly 1800 with American society in roughly 2000, what changes do you see in the strength and quantity of patriarchal conventions? What patriarchal conventions remain? Do you think they are likely to remain for a long time? Forever? Why? Do you think this is a good thing? Anzaldúa, as a person of color, often uses the term "patriarchal white conventions." How do you think Anzaldúa might argue that patriarchal *white* conventions differ from patriarchal conventions established by persons of color? Do you see a distinction between the two terms, or does it seem to you that all patriarchal conventions are fundamentally the same? Explain.

3. Many philosophers and anthropologists have pointed to the intolerance of Western European-based societies toward contradiction and ambiguity, which they generally trace to Greek philosophy of the fourth and fifth centuries BCE. By "intolerance," they mean that modern people influenced by Greek philosophy (and that means most Americans, whether they are conscious of the influence or not) believe implicitly that a phenomenon (like color or gender or virtue) cannot both *be* and *not be* in the same respect at the same time. You may recognize this as one of the axioms of Euclid, the developer of the geometry so many of us encountered in high school. According to this way of thinking, you cannot be simultaneously black and white. You cannot be simultaneously male and female. You cannot be simultaneously good and bad. And you *must* fall into one of the categories of any pair of opposites.

Anzaldúa says that the new consciousness welcomes contradiction and ambiguity. Why does she say this? What is the advantage to embracing contradiction and ambiguity? How is what Anzaldúa advocates different from being illogical or wishy-washy? What sphere of life is Anzaldúa primarily concerned with? Can you think of other aspects of life in which her advice might be helpful? Dangerous?

4. Though Anzaldúa's article is an examination of cultural phenomena, it does not fall under the rubric of "social science." Why not? If it were the kind of article that most people would label "social science," how would it be different from what it is? What might be added? Deleted? Changed? Charles Dickens's autobiographical novel, *David Copperfield*, is not social science, either, yet it tells us a lot about English Victorian society. Indeed, this is true of all his novels, some of which were specifically cited in parliamentary debates of the time over social policy. In *Bleak House*, another of Dickens's novels, there is a villainous character who spontaneously combusts through his own evil. Though the event is not scientifically possible, it does not detract from the power of the novel. Anzaldúa tells us that "The modern meaning of the word 'machismo,' as well as the concept, is actually an Anglo invention." Most linguists and anthropologists would disagree with Anzaldúa's statement on objective grounds. And yet, like Dickens's spontaneously combusting villain, her point is still "true" in a metaphorical sense. What is the truth contained in Anzaldúa's discussion of the meaning of the word "machismo"?

La Vida

A PUERTO RICAN FAMILY IN THE CULTURE OF POVERTY—SAN JUAN AND NEW YORK

Oscar Lewis

More than thirty years after his death, the anthropologist Oscar Lewis remains both a revered and a controversial figure in academic and social policy circles for his conception and exploration of "the culture of poverty." The following excerpts come from two sources: La Vida (Life), *Lewis's massive narrative based on tape-recorded interviews with an impoverished extended Puerto Rican family, and* A Study of Slum Culture, *which discusses his fieldwork for* La Vida. *Though Lewis was not the first social scientist to employ the technique of tape-recorded interviews, his masterful use of such interviews in creating a multifaceted, complex, and compelling narrative remains unequalled. The seamless streams of consciousness that pour from the mouths of Lewis's informants are the result of skillful interviewing and even more skillful editing.*

From his research in Mexico, Puerto Rico, and the United States, Lewis developed the notion of what he called "the culture of poverty," which is the source of the controversy that still surrounds his work. (See Oscar Lewis, 1966, "The Culture of Poverty," Scientific American *215 (4): 19–25.) According to Lewis, in the industrial (and postindustrial) capitalist world, poverty takes on specific characteristics, which it does not necessarily have in other places and times. These characteristics include unfamiliarity with many institutions of the dominant culture, such as banks, museums, libraries, large department stores, and supermarkets; mistrust of law enforcement and education; an inability to plan for the future and to defer gratification; and high tolerance of violence and psychological and social deviance. These characteristics, Lewis pointed out, were not the willful folly of lazy, selfish people, but a rational, though ultimately self-defeating, response to economic and social conditions over which they had no control, and that condemned them to poverty and oppression. Like all cultures (and subcultures), the culture of poverty, Lewis argued, perpetuated itself through enculturation (the transmission of values). But its root cause, and the condition that ultimately generated and maintained it, is the inequities of developed capitalism.*

Most of the criticism directed at Oscar Lewis comes from those who accuse him of blaming the poor for their own poverty through his statements that the culture of poverty perpetuates itself. This is emphatically not the thrust of Lewis's work. Indeed, though many of Lewis's informants (like people everywhere) are sometimes foolish, cruel, and self-destructive, they are also likely to be intelligent, thoughtful, and comprehensible. In short, they are recognizable human beings struggling to survive and make sense of their very difficult circumstances.

The brief selections from La Vida *presented here provide two views of a common-law marital relationship, that of twenty-one-year-old Simplicio and his somewhat older "wife," Flora. Both Simplicio and Flora are Puerto Rican by birth and upbringing, and though they now live in a Puerto Rican community in New York City, they continue to make trips back to the island and to maintain relationships there. The interviews on which* La Vida *was based were all conducted in Spanish, the native language of Puerto Rico, and English words printed in italics were spoken in English by the informants.*

Reading Simplicio's narrative may prove difficult for many Anglo Americans of the twenty-first century (actually, it would certainly have proven difficult for Flora). Simplicio is in a common-law marriage with one woman, whom he refuses to marry, and whose life he wants to control, while feeling free to establish other sexual relationships at will. But becoming righteously indignant—or furiously angry—at Simplicio is just a waste of time. Instead, try to understand what is going on with these gender roles and gender relations and why. This is the time for analysis, not predictable rage. Our goal should not be to complain self-indulgently that the world is not as we might wish it were, but to try to understand how it is and what some of the reasons might be.

Simplicio's Story

I would rather my wife didn't work outside the house, but Flora is ambitious that way. She leaves for work at seven in the morning and gets home at five-thirty every evening. I don't like that, because if I have a woman, it's so she can take care of my needs. Now my pants are all unpressed. Before, when she stayed home, Flora kept my things nice, and the house was always clean and neat. Her working is no advantage to me in any way; I never see a cent of her wages. In fact, I never have asked how much she earns. When I get paid I give her the money to pay the bills, fifty dollars a week for rent, electricity and food. So Flora's money doesn't do anybody any good. We're going to have a big fight about that someday. I don't spy on her or anything, but I like to keep my woman at home.

With what I earn, I'm sure of a home, food, clothes and everything. I mean, I feel more settled here because I have a home where I rule. That's something I never managed to have in Puerto Rico. There I was like a waif. Nothing in the house was my own. Here, everything, I have is my own, so I think of the future. I have responsibilities, see? I live with Flora, who is a good woman and satisfies me. So I have to make sure I have a decent life and that my woman doesn't ever have to go hungry.

It's true we have our arguments and all that, because when I buy a gift for her she never likes it. I always like the things she gives me, at least I never let her know any different. We quarrel, too, because she doesn't like me to go out with my own relatives. But I do as I please, no matter what she says.

What really drives her wild is my going, out with other women. When she finds out she slaps my face. I control myself so as not to hit back too hard. She's suffered a lot, you see, because her first husband was a drunk. Fontánez gave her money, but he left the house on Thursday afternoon and never showed up until the following Tuesday. I mean, he never gave her love or anything of the kind. I have given her a little love and she has been good to me. With her advice and by controlling me, she has made a man of me. When I met her I was a street

---

urchin. I didn't even wear underclothes. She made me wear them, instructed me, taught me how to dress. And then I'd go out with my girl friends and come back two days later, with lipstick on my clothes and kiss marks all over!

In spite of all that Flora has done for me, I won't marry her. If you marry a woman legally you have to stay with her even if it doesn't work out. You can't remarry. If you fall in love with another woman, you can't have her because you're married to the one before and she's the one who gives the orders. Of course, it's true that if you marry under the law the woman belongs more to you. But there's something forced about it. A man and a woman who marry legally have to put up with each other, no matter what. Suppose I wanted to divorce a woman and she didn't love me either, but refused, out of spite, to let me go. I couldn't do a thing about it. And one couldn't kill her or anything like that. I'd have to stay with her simply because she was my *missus*. And she couldn't leave me because I'd be her husband.

Flora and I stay together for love, because we do love each other. We can both be sure of that because we are under no obligation to stay together. If we weren't in love, each would go his own way. When I get to be thirty-five and, God willing, I have children, then I'll marry. By then I can be perfectly sure of what I want. But not now. I'm only twenty-one and I don't know what life may have in store for me.

Flora's family likes me and is good to me. There's not a two-faced one in the bunch except for that brother of hers. I tell him my secrets and he runs to repeat them to my wife. I spoke to him about it once. "You know how Flora is. Don't play that game of making my wife jealous. I don't go stirring up trouble at your house. I always show you the same face, I'm not changeable or a hypocrite. As I treat you today, I will always treat you." I haven't spoken to him since. I

know myself and I don't want to risk getting mad at him. I'm not what you would call a violent man. I think before I act. But if I'm pushed beyond a certain point, I lose control of myself and don't know what I do.

I don't like to fight. Not me. I like to treat other people with respect and have them respect me too. But sometimes people like to make fools of others and lots of people have tried to make a fool of me. I won't stand for that. There's only one way anybody can make a fool of me—by being nice and getting around me that way. I'll do anything for someone who's good to me but you can't get anything out of me by force. And if anyone tries it, I'll get even. That's why I try not to get into a spot where I'll lose my temper, and I'm trying to break away from my old life. That's another thing I owe to Flora. She has helped me make a decent life for myself. Just think, all my old friends are in jail now, Pipo, Benito, Geño, Johnny, El Indio, the whole bunch except me. I'm the only one who's come up to New York.

Up here in New York the family doesn't mean the same as it does in Puerto Rico. No. Here you go to stay at the house of a relative and they're fond as can be of you, for the first few days. After that they kick you out. You can't do like you do in Puerto Rico, go into a relative's house and say, "Let me have a clean shirt, this one's dirty," and put on the shirt and go your way. Not here. I have gone to my sister and said, "Soledad, lend me one of your husband's coats." And she has answered, "No, I won't. Why should I go around lending things?"

Like when I first came to New York, I went to stay with Felícita. I was only sixteen then and I had left my woman behind in San Juan. Felícita threw her arms around me when I came; she was happy to see me. After a few days I got work and I always gave Fela fifteen dollars on payday. But she got real nasty about it; she thought I ought to turn over my whole pay check to her. She'd curse me and she never gave me anything to eat. If I happened to open the refrigerator she got mad. She's always been that way. When I got home, tired, at five o'clock, she never said, "Here's your dinner." So I went out again and came back about seven after eating a good meal at a restaurant. Sometimes I spent as much as ten dollars a week on food. And I had to pay to send all my clothes to *el laundry* too.

One week I sent Flora some money and Felícita got angry. She refused to take the money I gave her and she told me to get the hell out of her house. Then Edmundo, my brother-in-law, said I had to leave, and Felícita, my own sister, didn't speak up for me.

To show you how Felícita is: one night when I was in her house in La Esmeralda she was saying nasty things about all the Negroes around, especially her own brother-in-law, Crucita's husband, who was there. She went on and on, spoiling for a fight. Finally he couldn't stand it any more and knocked her down. Then I hit him and we started to fight. I really got into *trouble* that time. He picked up a handful of stones and I dared him to throw them. He did. I threw them back and hit his neck. He flung a bottle at me, but I stooped and it didn't hit me. I picked up a piece of the broken glass and drove it into his arm. They had to take him to the hospital.

After that I always went to see Crucita when he was out of the house. Crucita cooked my meals, washed and ironed my clothes, and gave me money. She was so good to me. If I wanted to do anything, she told me to go ahead and do it. She let me eat all I wanted and she never asked for anything in return.

But I have fought with that husband of hers. One time he asked me what was wrong, were we two going to fight? I said, "Fight with you? I should say so! Wait for me here." I went to my house to get a big knife and a baseball bat, but when I came back he was gone. I went looking for him but couldn't find him. Since then I've always been stand-offish with him, polite but distant.

One day he hit Crucita on the mouth. She came to me, bleeding. "Simplicio, my husband hit me."

"He did? But tell me, *chica*, how did that happen?" I asked her about it but I didn't go saying anything disagreeable to him on that account. I know how women are. Never have I interfered in his quarrels but when I was in New York I did send word to Crucita that if I were to go back to Puerto Rico and meet him, and if he were to say something to me, I'd shoot him. The next time we get into a fight, it's him or me. One of us is going to wind up in the graveyard.

Right now Soledad has Benedicto. You can see he's a real man, because he took her out of a bar and set her up in a place of her own. And he loves her children and everything. I say this even though I know he went around saying I was boastful and a queer. But he's good to my sister. Well, one day I was visiting them and they got into a fight. You see, she'd been to Puerto Rico on a visit and Benedicto found out she'd slept with an American there. And her a married woman. But that time Benedicto did something I don't like. He waited until I went home and then he beat her. I don't like that. I never mentioned it to him, though. One shouldn't butt into the affairs of a married couple.

I did talk to Soledad about it later. I told her she'd done wrong and if she didn't change her ways I'd stop going to see her. I said it was wrong to quarrel in front of me. When married people want to quarrel, they should wait until they're alone.

The truth is, I don't think much of my family, except for Crucita and my *mamá*. Because *mamá* is a woman and she has been a good mother, too.

. . .

I went to a bar with Soledad's husband, Benedicto, and I liked it. After that I went every night. I was practically going broke. Then Benedicto sailed off on a ship. I got to thinking, and I said to Soledad, "What shall I do, Soledad? I guess I'd better go get my things in Pennsylvania and find myself a place to live." I looked until I found a place. I paid twenty-two dollars down, plus one dollar for the key. That was two weeks' rent. I paid it in advance, because my money was running out and I was afraid I wouldn't find a job. And if you at least have a place of your own, you're not too badly off.

After finding a place, I went to Pennsylvania to get my things. And you know, it's true that what's done in a year can be undone in an hour. The only things I brought here were the washing machine, the TV set, two lamps, the table and our clothes. I sold all the rest, for twenty-five dollars. And I left the apartment, after painting it and making it so pretty and fixing the bathroom. I left the refrigerator, bed, most of the furniture, new carpets for all the five rooms. I even had something to keep stuff in, a sort of desk, all made of glass. All of that I sold for twenty-five dollars so that I could come here to suffer.

When I finally got my bearings in New York I liked it better than Pennsylvania. It seemed different, see? There's more going on here, many big houses, lots of Puerto Ricans, all sorts of amusements. So I told Flora I was staying here, even though the job I have now is harder than the one in Pennsylvania. But that's not the important thing. Over there, that job was my only chance to work. If they had fired me, what could I have done? Here in New York, if they fire me I'll get another job right around the corner. The factory even gives me life insurance. That way, if something happens to me, my wife will be taken care of. She'll get ten thousand, maybe it's three thousand dollars. That will be some help.

I'm glad I'm a man. That way I don't have to bother with the monthly illness or getting pregnant or anything like that. Not that women are so bad off. They can make themselves pretty, and flirt and all that. And then, a woman doesn't have to go after a man. The man is the one who has to chase after the woman and give up his seat to her and so on. But even so, I'm grateful to have been born a man. Because that way I can work hard to get whatever I want and I can have fun, too, because a man, on account of being a man, can do anything he pleases.

If I fall for a woman, I let her see it. Right now I have one that I courted in our very house, right here in the Bronx. The woman I'm telling you about had moved into the same *building* where we lived. This was during the *Christmas* season and it was snowing. Flora's brother Sotero and I were downstairs. Then this girl came out and began to play in the snow. Her sister came out too. Sotero and I got into the game, Sotero with the other girl and I with mine—Leila she's called. Nothing came of it that day.

After that, both sisters came to call at my house. Then I looked at mine and fell in love with her. I asked Leila where she planned to spend Christmas Eve and said I was going to spend it with my relatives. She asked me if she could go, too. So we dressed up and went over to my cousin's through a heavy snowfall. On the way there I didn't say one word to her. After midnight we returned to my place and there we finally got to talking. Next day, everytime I looked at her, we both had to laugh. On New Year's Eve I kissed the girl on the stroke of midnight, the first kiss I ever gave her. After that we drank and drank until dawn.

Flora realized what was going on and didn't want me to go to Leila's house. But our *toilet* faced the door of her apartment, so I would sneak out through there. When I went to see her we would dance. Flora would call out to me, "Come home now, it's time to sleep."

"Not yet," I'd say. "In a minute." One day Flora came over and punched me. I merely said, "Come on, Flora, be quiet." Then I took her home, put her to bed and went back to Leila.

Sometime later Leila moved to Third Avenue. One night I was there with her when Flora and Soledad appeared. Leila was pregnant and Flora saw she was wearing a maternity dress. The two of them tangled then and there. I simply walked out on both of them, went home to change my shirt, and then out to a bar to drink. But even after that I kept on seeing Leila. Hell, I have a lot of shirts and pants at her house and she washes them for me. I change my clothes over there sometimes. She respects me and does everything I ask her to.

That's why I say that I'm the one who wears the pants at my house. I don't deny that Flora slaps my face and curses me out and all that. I say "yes, yes, yes" to everything. Let her waste her saliva and beat her brain, I do as I please. I go out, have a good time. Then I go home and go to bed without even saying hello to her.

I do my duty as a man of course. I support my family and make people respect my home. I mean, if someone comes around to my place and starts speaking dirty or cursing I say, "Listen, I'm the only one who has a right to speak like that in this house. I'm the one that pays for it." That I do. And to do that, one has to work.

My ambition is to get enough money to go back to Puerto Rico. Then I'd buy a bit of land and make a home of my own to give security to my children, although I have no children yet. And all because Flora won't go to see a doctor and find out if she can be cured and give me a child. Maybe they can't do anything about it now. I have an idea they did something to her at the hospital the last time she miscarried, to keep her from getting pregnant again. She got so sick, you see. I think that's why she's never gotten pregnant again since then, although we

don't do anything to prevent it. I guess I'll have to go make myself some children with some other woman.

I've asked Flora to go to the hospital, because I'm young and would like to have children some day. She says she won't go because she's scared. Well, if she doesn't want to, I won't force her. But she has no right to complain if I try to have children with other women. If I should have a child, ah, I'd take it home with me. If Flora won't accept the child, I'll go to the other woman, the mother of my child.

Seriously, I really have thought that. When Leila got pregnant I felt so good because the child was mine. Leila was seven months gone when she lost the baby. They went to get me at my house about five times that night. But I thought it was a put-up job, see? I didn't believe a word they said. But then I thought it over. By six in the morning I was at her mother's house. And it was the truth. Leila had been taken to that hospital where women go to have babies.

I rushed over but they wouldn't let me in. They said come back that evening at seven. I was so desperately eager to get in that I went ahead of time, at four o'clock, with a big bag of grapes, apples and all sorts of fruit. They wouldn't let me in. I waited there until seven and then they let me in, but they wouldn't let me take the fruit.

Leila stayed in the hospital three days. The baby died. He was a boy. They took him to another hospital to preserve him in alcohol. I felt the baby's death deeply, deeply. And think of it, she miscarried because of me, because I'd scared her half to death. I hardly ever get mad at anybody. But when I do, I go wild. I throw whatever I can get hold of. It's all over in a minute. But in that minute I'm not in this world; I don't know what I'm doing.

This happened on a Thursday when I was over at Leila's. She says to me, "Let's go upstairs. They're having a small dance."

"No," I say, "let's not."

"Oh, come on."

"Well, *O.K.*" When we get there a little old man says to me, "I'm going to put on a record now, especially for your woman. I want to dance with her."

I said no. The old man punched me in the chest. I let it pass. We went back down to Leila's apartment and I locked the door.

About ten minutes later the old man knocks on the door, furious. He yells, "Come on out, you! I'm going to stick you like a codfish."* I opened at once. The old man was standing there with a steel knife in one hand and a small parrot-beaked blade in the other. "I came to get you," he says.

"Oh, forget it," I answered. He pushed on into the apartment. I went crazy. I grabbed a chair and smashed it over his head. I clobbered him. He's been covered with scars ever since. Well, that calmed him down, all right. Then his friends came and took him to the hospital. That was the night Leila lost the baby. She's never gotten pregnant again.

So, if I can't have children of my own, I'd like to keep Gabi, Felícita's son. If they give him to me for good, I'll take good care of him. But they'll have to give me a free hand to bring him up my way, according to my own ideas. I'll give him my name and teach and direct him as I think fit. I'll give him a good education. With me, he can feel he has a father. I'll give him everything he needs and take him places. I wouldn't want him to grow up as I did, with too much freedom. I'll give him freedom, but not absolute freedom. Let him be free, yes, but let him learn to respect me too.

I've had problems with some people here in the Bronx but not gang fights, or anything like that. One time, for instance, I got in between two of my friends who were fighting and one of them socked me over the lip. Another day a boy in a *bar* called me a queer, As far as I'm concerned that's the worst insult! Listen, if they call me *"cabrón"* I don't mind. Because *cabrón* means a man who likes to have a good time, who knows his way around and likes to dance and be gay and have women and more women. So it doesn't bother me in the least to be called *cabrón*. But I won't stand to have anybody call me a queer. Because a queer is a man who likes other men. You can imagine how I felt when that guy called me that. I told him not to call me that and he repeated it. "Oh, so you want to fight?" I said, and he answered, "Sure."

So we went outside. But he brought a friend of his along and they held me and hit me when I was helpless like that. They gave me a black eye and a swollen lip. Then the man who hit me ran away. I turned on the other one, the one who was holding me. "The other one escaped," I said, "but I'll be damned if you do." I socked him hard and broke his head. I'm even with that one now. And the other one is going to get his, too. I haven't seen him since, but I'm watching for him. If I'm sober when we meet, I'll get him. If you let someone make a fool of you, you're sunk. One has to be tough with a character like that.

Those things happen to me when I'm drinking. Truth to tell, I don't even know why I drink. I live my own life, see? I don't have any hard-drinking friends because I don't like that. What I like is going out alone and drinking by myself. I have many friends and I have my cousins, Chango and Tito, who are good guys and side with me. I could go with them if I wanted to. But I don't. I figure that my duty is not to go anywhere from Monday to Friday except to work and back to my home. Friday to Saturday, my entertainment is to drink and go places by myself or, at most, with one

---

*Codfish are flattened out and piled up with a stake driven through them when they are put out to dry.

friend. Saturdays I'm out all night, calling on my sweethearts. There's a little American girl, Sandra, who's mad about me. She works with me. She's eighteen and a virgin. Know what she says to me? "Simplicio," she says, "we can't do anything now because I'm a virgin. But I'm going to marry another man so you can be with me afterward without getting blamed for anything." I say, "Gosh! Go ahead and do it," and I walk off.

. . .

Flora's Story

For me, life in Pennsylvania was simply divine. But Simplicio had problems in his work and we decided to move to New York. Simplicio sold everything we had bought, for only thirty dollars. Crazy! It made me terribly angry and it made me cry too, to think of all the trouble I'd gone through to get my things, all the expense, and then, to have them go for thirty miserable dollars!

So we came here, to New York, and went to Soledad's house. She wanted us to move in with her but I said, "No, I only want to rent a room of our own. A room and a bed, that's all." I didn't want to stay in her house because of all those kids. So we got a tiny little room and we moved into it.

For a while I took care of Soledad's children for her and she paid me twelve dollars, although she used to pay another woman fifteen. But those kids didn't respect me. Sarita is a terrible brat. When I slapped her hands, she'd try to hit me. And so did that Toya. I was going crazy and I told Soledad to get somebody else to look after her girls, but no matter how often I told her, Benedicto would bring them over to me.

I begged and begged Simplicio to let me take a job so we could get a real apartment.

He was only earning forty-six dollars a week, barely enough to pay the food bill. But no, not him. He didn't want me to go out of the house to work because he was afraid I'd fall in love. But he gave in, finally. He himself went with me to the factory where Soledad worked and waited there until they hired me. He even stayed on awhile after I had started working, until the *boss* told him to go because I was busy. Simplicio still gets angry when I work *overtime*. He wants to find me home when he arrives, with the house all neat and his dinner ready.

I have problems with Simplicio. If he has money he spends it right away. That man doesn't care about money. When he shops for food he buys and buys and never thinks of the cost. Listen, he once saw a twenty-two-dollar bedspread and he asked me, "Shall I buy that little bedspread for you?" I said, "No, I have more bedspreads than I need already. Forget it, we can't afford it." So then he got mad. That's why he gives me his money to keep, because he knows he'll squander it, and I save. Aside from little things like that, he's good to me.

Simplicio did play a dirty trick on me once, but he never has since. I had a friend named Leila who used to come to our home with her family. They were starving and I fed them. I treated them like my own sisters. There were three of them, the mother, Leila and her younger sister. I don't like to see anybody suffer, so when they came here I gave them some of everything we had to eat. I even loaned Leila some of my clothes.

Leila hung around the house a lot and I noticed that she often looked at Simplicio. She's one of those women who take one man today and another tomorrow. Mancrazy! I had my suspicions but I said to myself, "Until I catch them at it I won't do anything." And I did catch them!

One day we were at Gina's house. She's a friend of ours. I went out to do some shopping with Gina. "Simplicio, you stay here until I come back," I told him. But when we got back, Catín says to me, "Sotero told Simplicio to go over to Leila's place." Think of that, my own brother serving as go-between! He says that I am his favorite among all his sisters. And yet, look at what he did!

Oh, I got furious! I went to get Soledad, who was at a dance, and together we went to Leila's house. I pushed the apartment door open and there they were, Leila's mother, Sotero and my own Simplicio, talking with Leila in the kitchen. She was wearing a nightgown and one of those flimsy negligees. I went up to Simplicio and said to him, "What the hell are you doing here?" I grabbed him by the shirt and tore it and made a mess of his face, I slapped it so hard so many times. Then I turned on Leila and knocked her down. And the things I said to her: "You dirty bitch, what are you doing, talking to my husband in your night clothes?"

Simplicio broke in, "Look, Flora, I don't give a damn about this woman."

"You dirty bastard! If you don't give a damn about her what are you doing here?" I screamed. "Look here," I said to him, "if you're interested in her, pack up your clothes and go get her an apartment. Forget all about me. She's younger than I am, anyway. Go ahead, get out and leave me." While I raged, Simplicio just stood there weeping. "She's the one that chases after me," he sobbed. "I was just telling her that I would never leave you for her."

Simplicio tells everybody that he loves me too much to leave me, ever. He says, "Flora is the only woman who has been able to make a decent man of me." That is why I give him good advice and tell him, "Simplicio, do this," or "Simplicio, don't do that." Sometimes he grumbles, "Ah, leave me alone. You're always after me." But he always does what I say.

I have lived with Simplicio since he was a mere boy. I almost broke up with him once because he was so young and I so much older. I was ashamed. I still don't believe he loves me. But I love him. I love him truly. He says he loves me but it seems to me he must be lying. Because sometimes he gets drunk and starts insulting me the minute he gets home, "I know you have put the horns on me, so I'm going to kill you." The other day he pushed me in the presence of my brother. I tell him, "But, Simplicio, I haven't done anything wrong." I even cry and I wish I were a little girl again so as not to have to suffer with men the way I do. Then he asks me, "Do you love me?" And I say, "Simplicio, if I didn't love you, would I be living with you? I'm not married to you. If I wanted to leave you I'd do it in a minute."

Now he's set his heart on having a baby. Every time he mentions a baby, it tears my guts out. I keep talking about how hard up we are and how much it costs to bring up children. And I tell him we already have Gabi. But I'm under treatment to see if I can conceive. I want to bear Simplicio a son, a son to love. And besides, sometimes men are more apt to stay quietly at home if they have a child. Simplicio says that if he had a son he would be completely happy and would spend all his time looking after the child and not go out, not even to work.

Simplicio and I have made a solemn promise to each other and we've even shaken hands on it. We said, "When you die, take me with you. If I die first, I will take you." I feel happy now. I do still get into rages sometimes but that is because I love him so much. It's like a madness. I'll carry that cross for Simplicio until I die.

A Study of Slum Culture

Backgrounds for La Vida

Oscar Lewis
WITH THE ASSISTANCE OF
Douglas Butterworth

Marital Conflict

The new-found independence of the working wife was probably the greatest source of domestic conflict among the sample families in New York. Working wives no longer had to rely on their husbands for money for the house or for personal expenses. The women themselves could buy what they and their children needed and could pay to go where they pleased. This freedom had important repercussions for the family, particularly for the husband, who was accustomed to being in control of the family and the purse. Under ordinary circumstances a jealous man, the Puerto Rican husband in New York often became very insecure and distrustful of his wife.

One woman described the problem the men faced in New York:

> In Puerto Rico a woman can't even go for a walk unless it's to the store. If you put on makeup your husband thinks you're in love. But here the women must dress up for work and their husbands can't say anything. They don't know whether their wives really have gone to work or if they've met a lover somewhere.

Women, in turn, resented their husbands' suspicions and insisted upon more equality in the household. The strains on family relationships were often severe and almost every informant commented upon this problem.

> In New York a dog is worth more than a man. Yes, sir, only three things are valued here—dogs, women, and children! As long as you're a minor, you can kill, belong to a gang, steal, or raise hell. No matter what you do, you won't fry, see? Of course, if you're a woman you can get away with anything as long as you live. But if you're a man and over twenty-one and you so much as pick up a stone and aim it at a dog, it means six months in jail. If you hit the dog it's worse. You can't even defend yourself. Women and dogs can attack you any time and you lose the case, no matter what. Know why? It's the law. That's the way it's written, man. And if you've never heard of that law, you're sunk. After you're twenty-one you're an adult and know what you are doing, see?
>
> You need luck in New York, especially to choose a woman and to get married, because here a woman can get away with anything. Suppose you get married. Then one day you come home from work. You've had a hard day. You got out of bed in a hurry, had breakfast in a hurry, went to work in a hurry, and hurried home, tired, worn out. And what do you find? There's your wife in bed with another man. You rush out to get the cops so they can see what's going on. Then, what happens? She wins! Even if you screw your soul working all day long to provide for her needs, she'll win all the same. If you slap her, she'll go and call the cops. Slap a woman! Don't dream of it! You get six

months in jail, see? Not just a fine but jail! If you kill the man, you'll fry for it. That kind of thing isn't allowed here. No, sir!

—Héctor

Marital discord was so intense that it often led to physical violence. In Puerto Rican slums, wife beating was fairly common, but women did not call in the police as often as they did in New York. Our informants, however, were divided in their opinions as to whether or not wife beating had increased since migration to New York; the stimulus to violence on the part of the husbands was greater in New York, but the controls were stronger.

. . .

KEY TERMS

La Esmeralda   A slum in San Juan, Puerto Rico.

cabrón   Literally: male goat, but a common expletive and term of reference that is roughly comparable to the nontechnical significance of the English word, "bastard."

put the horns on   To cuckold; said of a man whose wife is unfaithful to him.

DISCUSSION QUESTIONS

1. Despite Gloria Anzaldúa's disclaimer on the subject of the *real* meaning of machismo, most readers, whatever their backgrounds, would recognize Simplicio's words as a classic reflection of the principles of machismo. Reread Simplicio's narrative, and then boil it down to a "manifesto of machismo." That is, lay out the basic principles that underlie what he says. Simplicio's manifesto contains some internal contradictions, though. What are they? What do you think Simplicio would say if he were asked *why* men can/do/should be allowed to behave in the way he has described? Do you think his answer would be based in his conception of natural history or morality? How do you think Simplicio's manifesto of machismo differs from what an Anglo American man of the early twenty-first century might produce? What might account for the differences?

2. It is clear from comparing Flora's and Simplicio's narratives that there is less than perfect confidence between them. Though what we learn from Flora about herself is pretty similar to what Simplicio tells us about her, Simplicio's self-portrait differs in some important respects from Flora's account of him. Part of this seems to be the result of her ignorance of what Simplicio is actually doing. But another part seems to be the result of Simplicio's unwillingness to present himself as a less than fully macho character. Discuss these two varieties of deviation. Do you think that Flora's description of Simplicio's response to her attacking him for his infidelity is likely to be accurate? Why or why not? If it *is* accurate, then why do you think Simplicio responded as he did? Why do you think Simplicio remains with Flora?

3. Simplicio badly wants children, especially a son. Why do you think this is so important to him? He is, after all, only twenty-one, and he and Flora have very little money. When he talks about the future, and wanting to make a home for his children, he hardly mentions providing for their mother(s). What do you make of this? Simplicio states very clearly that he does not want to marry any woman. Why? An increasing percentage of babies born in the United States recently have been born to unmarried women. Do you think that Simplicio's point of view explains any of the recent and steady increase in unmarried mothers in the United States? What else do you think might help explain it?

4. In *A Study of Slum Culture* Lewis points to the stress working wives are putting on the marriages of Puerto Ricans in the United States. McKee found the same thing to be true of impoverished Mexican-Americans thirty years later on the Texas-Mexico border. What accounts for this stress? Do you see this same stress among middle-class Anglo Americans, also? How have they reacted? Why would there have been a difference in the point at which different ethnic groups in the United States accommodated to the need for women to work outside the household in large numbers? Do you think all ethnic groups will ultimately adjust in roughly the same ways? What will those ways be?

No Name Woman

Maxine Hong Kingston

The following essay is from a book called The Woman Warrior: Memoirs of a Girlhood Spent among Ghosts. *Though the essay reports a story told to the author by her mother in the United States, where Kingston was born, all the action in the story takes place in China. Any reader of this book might then reasonably ask why the essay was included in a book about gender and culture in America. Why, indeed?*

One of the great strengths of the United States is its view of itself as a "melting pot," a place where people from hundreds of different cultures and linguistic backgrounds blend together and become Americans. But as many immigrants and children of immigrants know, and as numerous social scientists have pointed out, the melting pot does not perfectly describe the process of becoming American. There are at least two problems with the notion of the melting pot. First, it takes a while for new immigrants (or their children) to melt, sometimes several generations. And second, some immigrants melt faster than others. Because the earliest immigrants to what is now the United States were nearly all English speakers who came from the British Isles and elsewhere in Western Europe, subsequent immigrants who most closely resembled them had the easiest time fitting into the colonial culture. Those who were not English speakers and/or did not come from Western Europe had a far more difficult time adjusting to the new American culture. To a great extent this was the result of a refusal of the dominant American population to accept newcomers who seemed "foreign," and different from themselves. Indeed, some states and localities prohibited early Asian immigrants from living in certain areas. More shocking, for many years nearly all Chinese women were forbidden to immigrate into the United States, lest a substantial Chinese American population should develop. Little wonder, then, that Asian immigrants often lived near each other, continued to maintain their languages, and protected their culture.

It is important to remember that the development of ethnic enclaves and the maintenance of ancestral cultures and languages, as well as the shunning and discrimination experienced by many Asian immigrants, had been part of the experience of earlier generations of European immigrants, some of whose descendants then forgot their ancestors' experiences. In the cities of the Northeast, mid- and late-nineteenth-century Irish immigrants saw signs posted by employers that read "No Irish Need Apply." In parts of the upper Midwest, Scandinavian immigrants settled together in communities in which they could maintain their ancestral cultures. And in New York (and many other places) German immigrants continued for several generations to send their children to "German school" after the public school day was over, so that children would continue to be fluent in their parents' and grandparents' language. But with the passage of time, as these children ceased to be thought of as "hyphenated" Americans, they looked at new immigrants, many of them from Asia, with a jaundiced eye—just as their own ancestors had been viewed fifty or a hundred years earlier.

Kingston explains the setting of her story without seeming to deliver ethnographic information. But it might be wise to restate a couple of things. First: China is a patrilineal, patrilocal society. That is, membership in a family is passed down only through the male line. Females may technically be part of their fathers' families but to a great extent they function as part of their husbands' families, to which their children all belong. When a girl marries she goes to live in her husband's household and only rarely makes visits to her natal family after that. Her closest associations after her marriage will be with the other women of her husband's family, and with her children. Because they do not carry on their family line but go to live elsewhere, and because their labor, though essential, is considered insignificant, women have traditionally had very low status in Chinese families. Eventually, a senior woman, the grandmother of a family, for example, may achieve importance among her relatives. But girls are not desired as children, and their wishes are seldom considered. Traditionally, marriages have been arranged in China, primarily with an eye toward increasing family wealth and solidarity. The notion of romantic love is simply not an issue for either of the prospective spouses. The first duty of the newly married couple is to produce sons to carry on the husband's family line, and a husband's first obligation continues to be to his parents, specifically, and to his family in general.

It is hard for many Americans to accept these cultural notions, so different from contemporary Western ideas. But remember that our job in reading about them is not to pass moral judgment, but to understand. On the other hand, for Americans like Maxine Hong Kingston, caught between the China of her parents and the United States of her classmates, it is difficult to decide how to balance with a foot in each world.

"You must not tell anyone," my mother said, "what I am about to tell you. In China your father had a sister who killed herself. She jumped into the family well. We say that your father has all brothers because it is as if she had never been born.

"In 1924 just a few days after our village celebrated seventeen hurry-up weddings—to make sure that every young man who went 'out on the road' would responsibly come home—your father and his brothers and your grandfather and his brothers and your aunt's new husband sailed for America, the Gold Mountain. It was your grandfather's last trip. Those lucky enough to get contracts waved goodbye from the decks. They fed and guarded the stowaways and helped them off in Cuba, New York, Bali,

Hawaii. 'We'll meet in California next year,' they said. All of them sent money home.

"I remember looking at your aunt one day when she and I were dressing; I had not noticed before that she had such a protruding melon of a stomach. But I did not think, 'She's pregnant,' until she began to look like other pregnant women, her shirt pulling and the white tops of her black pants showing. She could not have been pregnant, you see, because her husband had been gone for years. No one said anything. We did not discuss it. In early summer she was ready to have the child, long after the time when it could have been possible.

"The village had also been counting. On the night the baby was to be born the villagers raided our house. Some were crying. Like a great saw, teeth strung with lights, files of people walked zigzag across our land, tearing the rice. Their lanterns doubled in the disturbed black water, which drained away through the broken bunds. As the villagers closed in, we could see that some of them, probably men and women we knew well, wore white masks. The people with long hair hung it over their faces. Women with short hair made it stand up on end. Some had tied white bands around their foreheads, arms, and legs.

"At first they threw mud and rocks at the house. Then they threw eggs and began slaughtering our stock. We could hear the animals scream their deaths—the roosters, the pigs, a last great roar from the ox. Familiar wild heads flared in our night windows; the villagers encircled us. Some of the faces stopped to peer at us, their eyes rushing like searchlights. The hands flattened against the panes, framed heads, and left red prints.

"The villagers broke in the front and the back doors at the same time, even though we had not locked the doors against them. Their knives dripped with the blood of our animals. They smeared blood on the doors and walls. One woman swung a chicken, whose throat she had slit, splattering blood in red arcs about her. We stood together in the middle of our house, in the family hall with the pictures and tables of the ancestors around us, and looked straight ahead.

"At that time the house had only two wings. When the men came back, we would build two more to enclose our courtyard and a third one to begin a second courtyard. The villagers pushed through both wings, even your grandparents' rooms, to find your aunt's, which was also mine until the men returned. From this room a new wing for one of the younger families would grow. They ripped up her clothes and shoes and broke her combs, grinding them underfoot. They tore her work from the loom. They scattered the cooking fire and rolled the new weaving in it. We could hear them in the kitchen breaking our bowls and banging the pots. They overturned the great waist-high earthenware jugs; duck eggs, pickled fruits, vegetables burst out and mixed in acrid torrents. The old woman from the next field swept a broom through the air and loosed the spirits-of-the-broom over our heads. 'Pig.' 'Ghost.' 'Pig,' they sobbed and scolded while they ruined our house.

"When they left, they took sugar and oranges to bless themselves. They cut pieces from the dead animals. Some of them took bowls that were not broken and clothes that were not torn. Afterward we swept up the rice and sewed it back up into sacks. But the smells from the spilled preserves lasted. Your aunt gave birth in the pigsty that night. The next morning when I went for the water, I found her and the baby plugging up the family well.

"Don't let your father know that I told you. He denies her. Now that you have started to menstruate, what happened to her could happen to you. Don't humiliate us. You wouldn't like to be forgotten as if you had never been born. The villagers are watchful."

Whenever she had to warn us about life, my mother told stories that ran like this one, a story to grow up on. She tested our strength to establish realities. Those in the emigrant generations who could not reassert brute survival died young and far from home. Those of us in the first American generations have had to figure out how the invisible world the emigrants built around our childhoods fits in solid America.

The emigrants confused the gods by diverting their curses, misleading them with crooked streets and false names. They must try to confuse their offspring as well, who, I suppose, threaten them in similar ways—always trying to get things straight, always trying to name the unspeakable. The Chinese I know hide their names; sojourners take new names when their lives change and guard their real names with silence.

Chinese-Americans, when you try to understand what things in you are Chinese, how do you separate what is peculiar to childhood, to poverty, insanities, one family, your mother who marked your growing with stories, from what is Chinese? What is Chinese tradition and what is the movies?

If I want to learn what clothes my aunt wore, whether flashy or ordinary, I would have to begin, "Remember Father's drowned-in-the-well sister?" I cannot ask that. My mother has told me once and for all the useful parts. She will add nothing unless powered by Necessity, a riverbank that guides her life. She plants vegetable gardens rather than lawns; she carries the odd-shaped tomatoes home from the fields and eats food left for the gods.

Whenever we did frivolous things, we used up energy; we flew high kites. We children came up off the ground over the melting cones our parents brought home from work and the American movie on New Year's Day—*Oh, You Beautiful Doll* with Betty Grable one year, and *She Wore a Yellow Ribbon* with John Wayne another year. After the one carnival ride each, we paid in guilt; our tired father counted his change on the dark walk home.

Adultery is extravagance. Could people who hatch their own chicks and eat the embryos and the heads for delicacies and boil the feet in vinegar for party food, leaving only the gravel, eating even the gizzard lining—could such people engender a prodigal aunt? To be a woman, to have a daughter in starvation time was a waste enough. My aunt could not have been the lone romantic who gave up everything for sex. Women in the old China did not choose. Some man had commanded her to lie with him and be his secret evil. I wonder whether he masked himself when he joined the raid on her family.

Perhaps she had encountered him in the fields or on the mountain where the daughters-in-law collected fuel. Or perhaps he first noticed her in the marketplace. He was not a stranger because the village housed no strangers. She had to have dealings with him other than sex. Perhaps he worked an adjoining field, or he sold her the cloth for the dress she sewed and wore. His demand must have surprised, then terrified her. She obeyed him; she always did as she was told.

When the family found a young man in the next village to be her husband, she had stood tractably beside the best rooster, his proxy, and promised before they met that she would be his forever. She was lucky that he was her age and she would be the first wife, an advantage secure now. The night she first saw him, he had sex with her. Then he left for America. She had almost forgotten what he looked like. When she tried to envision him, she only saw the black and white face in the group photograph the men had taken before leaving.

The other man was not, after all, much different from her husband. They both gave orders: she followed. "If you tell your family, I'll beat you. I'll kill you. Be here again next week." No one talked sex, ever. And she might have separated the rapes from the rest of living if only she did not have to buy her oil from him or gather wood in the same forest. I want her fear to have lasted just as long as rape lasted so that the fear could have been contained. No drawn-out fear. But women at sex hazarded birth and hence lifetimes. The fear did not stop but permeated everywhere. She told the man, "I think I'm pregnant." He organized the raid against her.

On nights when my mother and father talked about their life back home, sometimes they mentioned an "outcast table" whose business they still seemed to be settling, their voices tight. In a commensal tradition, where food is precious, the powerful older people made wrongdoers eat alone. Instead of letting them start separate new lives like the Japanese, who could become samurais and geishas, the Chinese family, faces averted but eyes glowering sideways, hung on to the offenders and fed them leftovers. My aunt must have lived in the same house as my parents and eaten at an outcast table. My mother spoke about the raid as if she had seen it, when she and my aunt, a daughter-in-law to a different household, should not have been living together at all. Daughters-in-law lived with their husbands' parents, not their own; a synonym for marriage in Chinese is "taking a daughter-in-law." Her husband's parents could have sold her, mortgaged her, stoned her. But they had sent her back to her own mother and father, a mysterious act hinting at disgraces not told me. Perhaps they had thrown her out to deflect the avengers.

She was the only daughter; her four brothers went with her father, husband, and uncles "out on the road" and for some years became western men. When the goods were divided among the family, three of the brothers took land, and the youngest, my father, chose an education. After my grandparents gave their daughter away to her husband's family, they had dispensed all the adventure and all the property. They expected her alone to keep the traditional ways, which her brothers, now among the barbarians, could fumble without detection. The heavy, deep-rooted women were to maintain the past against the flood, safe for returning. But the rare urge west had fixed upon our family, and so my aunt crossed boundaries not delineated in space.

The work of preservation demands that the feelings playing about in one's guts not be turned into action. Just watch their passing like cherry blossoms. But perhaps my aunt, my forerunner, caught in a slow life, let dreams grow and fade and after some months or years went toward what persisted. Fear at the enormities of the forbidden kept her desires delicate, wire and bone. She looked at a man because she liked the way the hair was tucked behind his ears, or she liked the question-mark line of a long torso curving at the shoulder and straight at the hip. For warm eyes or a soft voice or a slow walk—that's all—few hairs, a line, a brightness, a sound, a pace, she gave up family. She offered us up for a charm that vanished with tiredness, a pigtail that didn't toss when the wind died. Why, the wrong lighting could erase the dearest thing about him.

It could very well have been, however, that my aunt did not take subtle enjoyment of her friend, but, a wild woman, kept rollicking company. Imagining her free with sex doesn't fit, though. I don't know any women like that, or men either. Unless I see her life branching into mine, she gives me no ancestral help.

To sustain her being in love, she often worked at herself in the mirror, guessing at the colors and shapes that would interest him, changing them frequently in order to hit on the right combination. She wanted him to look back.

On a farm near the sea, a woman who tended her appearance reaped a reputation for eccentricity. All the married women blunt-cut their hair in flaps about their ears or pulled it back in tight buns. No nonsense. Neither style blew easily into heart-catching tangles. And at their weddings they displayed themselves in their long hair for the last time. "It brushed the backs of my knees," my mother tells me. "It was braided, and even so, it brushed the backs of my knees."

At the mirror my aunt combed individuality into her bob. A bun could have been contrived to escape into black streamers blowing in the wind or in quiet wisps about her face, but only the older women in our picture album wear buns. She brushed her hair back from her forehead, tucking the flaps behind her ears. She looped a piece of thread, knotted into a circle between her index fingers and thumbs, and ran the double strand across her forehead. When she closed her fingers as if she were making a pair of shadow geese bite, the string twisted together catching the little hairs. Then she pulled the thread away from her skin, ripping the hairs out neatly, her eyes watering from the needles of pain. Opening her fingers, she cleaned the thread, then rolled it along her hairline and the tops of her eyebrows. My mother did the same to me and my sisters and herself. I used to believe that the expression "caught by the short hairs" meant a captive held with a depilatory string. It especially hurt at the temples, but my mother said we were lucky we didn't have to have our feet bound when we were seven. Sisters used to sit on their beds and cry together, she said, as their mothers or their slaves removed the bandages for a few minutes each night and let the blood gush back into their veins. I hope that the man my aunt loved appreciated a smooth brow, that he wasn't just a tits-and-ass man.

Once my aunt found a freckle on her chin, at a spot that the almanac said predestined her for unhappiness. She dug it out with a hot needle and washed the wound with peroxide.

More attention to her looks than these pullings of hairs and pickings at spots would have caused gossip among the villagers. They owned work clothes and good clothes, and they wore good clothes for feasting the new seasons. But since a woman combing her hair hexes beginnings, my aunt rarely found an occasion to look her best. Women looked like great sea snails—the corded wood, babies, and laundry they carried were the whorls on their backs. The Chinese did not admire a bent back; goddesses and warriors stood straight. Still there must have been a marvelous freeing of beauty when a worker laid down her burden and stretched and arched.

Such commonplace loveliness, however, was not enough for my aunt. She dreamed of a lover for the fifteen days of New Year's, the time for families to exchange visits, money, and food. She plied her secret comb. And sure enough she cursed the year, the family, the village, and herself.

Even as her hair lured her imminent lover, many other men looked at her. Uncles, cousins, nephews, brothers would have looked, too, had they been home between journeys. Perhaps they had already been restraining their curiosity, and they left, fearful that their glances, like a field of nesting birds, might be startled and caught. Poverty hurt, and that was their first reason for leaving. But another, final reason for leaving the crowded house was the never-said.

She may have been unusually beloved, the precious only daughter, spoiled and mirror gazing because of the affection the family lavished on her. When her husband left, they welcomed the chance to take her back from the in-laws; she could live like the little daughter for just a while longer. There are stories that my grandfather was different from other people, "crazy ever since the little Jap bayoneted him in the head." He used to put his naked penis on the dinner table, laughing. And one day he brought home a baby girl, wrapped up inside his brown western-style greatcoat. He had traded one of his sons, probably my father, the youngest, for her. My grandmother made him trade back. When he finally got a daughter of his own, he doted on her. They must have all loved her, except perhaps my father, the only brother who never went back to China, having once been traded for a girl.

Brothers and sisters, newly men and women, had to efface their sexual color and present plain miens. Disturbing hair and eyes, a smile like no other, threatened the ideal of five generations living under one roof. To focus blurs, people shouted face to face and yelled from room to room. The immigrants I know have loud voices, unmodulated to American tones even after years away from the village where they called their friendships out across the fields. I have not been able to stop my mother's screams in public libraries or over telephones. Walking erect (knees straight, toes pointed forward, not pigeon-toed, which is Chinese-feminine) and speaking in an inaudible voice, I have tried to turn myself American-feminine. Chinese communication was loud, public. Only sick people had to whisper. But at the dinner table, where the family members came nearest one another, no one could talk, not the outcasts nor any eaters. Every word that falls from the mouth is a coin lost. Silently they gave and accepted food with both hands. A preoccupied child who took his bowl with one hand got a sideways glare. A complete moment of total attention is due everyone alike. Children and lovers have no singularity here, but my aunt used a secret voice, a separate attentiveness.

She kept the man's name to herself throughout her labor and dying; she did not accuse him that he be punished with her. To save her inseminator's name she gave silent birth.

He may have been somebody in her own household, but intercourse with a man outside the family would have been no less abhorrent. All the village were kinsmen, and the titles shouted in loud country voices never let kinship be forgotten. Any man within visiting distance would have been neutralized as a lover—"brother," "younger brother," "older brother"—one hundred and fifteen relationship titles. Parents researched birth charts probably not so much to assure good fortune as to circumvent incest in a population that has but one hundred surnames. Everybody has eight million relatives. How useless then sexual mannerisms, how dangerous.

As if it came from an atavism deeper than fear, I used to add "brother" silently to boys' names. It hexed the boys, who would or would not ask me to dance, and made them less scary and as familiar and deserving of benevolence as girls.

But, of course, I hexed myself also—no dates. I should have stood up, both arms waving, and shouted out across libraries, "Hey, you! Love me back." I had no idea, though, how to make attraction selective, how to control its direction and magnitude. If I made myself American-pretty so that the five or six Chinese boys in the class fell in love with me, everyone else—the Caucasian, Negro, and Japanese boys—would too. Sisterliness, dignified and honorable, made much more sense.

Attraction eludes control so stubbornly that whole societies designed to organize relationships among people cannot keep order, not even when they bind people to one another from childhood and raise them together. Among the very poor and the wealthy, brothers married their adopted sisters, like doves. Our family allowed some romance, paying adult brides' prices and providing dowries so that their sons and daughters could marry strangers. Marriage promises to turn strangers into friendly relatives—a nation of siblings.

In the village structure, spirits shimmered among the live creatures, balanced and held in equilibrium by time and land. But one human being flaring up into violence could open up a black hole, a maelstrom that pulled in the sky. The frightened villagers, who depended on one another to maintain the real, went to my aunt to show her a personal, physical representation of the break she had made in the "roundness." Misallying couples snapped off the future, which was to be embodied in true offspring. The villagers punished her for acting as if she could have a private life, secret and apart from them.

If my aunt had betrayed the family at a time of large grain yields and peace, when many boys were born, and wings were being built on many houses, perhaps she might have escaped such severe punishment. But the men—hungry, greedy, tired of planting in dry soil—had been forced to leave the village in order to send food-money home. There were ghost plagues, bandit plagues, wars with the Japanese, floods. My Chinese brother and sister had died of an unknown sickness. Adultery, perhaps only a mistake during good times, became a crime when the village needed food.

The round moon cakes and round doorways, the round tables of graduated sizes that fit one roundness inside another, round windows and rice bowls—these talismans had lost their power to warn this family of the law: a family must be whole, faithfully keeping the descent line by having sons to feed the old and the dead, who in turn look after the family. The villagers came to show my aunt and her lover-in-hiding a broken house. The villagers were speeding up the circling of events because she was too short-sighted to see that her infidelity had already harmed the village, that waves of consequences would return unpredictably, sometimes in disguise, as now, to hurt her. This roundness had to be made coin-sized so that she would see its circumference: punish her

at the birth of her baby. Awaken her to the inexorable. People who refused fatalism because they could invent small resources insisted on culpability. Deny accidents and wrest fault from the stars.

After the villagers left, their lanterns now scattering in various directions toward home, the family broke their silence and cursed her. "Aiaa, we're going to die. Death is coming. Death is coming. Look what you've done. You've killed us. Ghost! Dead ghost! Ghost! You've never been born." She ran out into the fields, far enough from the house so that she could no longer hear their voices, and pressed herself against the earth, her own land no more. When she felt the birth coming, she thought that she had been hurt. Her body seized together. "They've hurt me too much, she thought. "This is gall, and it will kill me." With forehead and knees against the earth, her body convulsed and then relaxed. She turned on her back, lay on the ground. The black well of sky and stars went out and out and out forever; her body and her complexity seemed to disappear. She was one of the stars, a bright dot in blackness, without home, without a companion, in eternal cold and silence. An agoraphobia rose in her, speeding higher and higher, bigger and bigger; she would not be able to contain it; there would no end to fear.

Flayed, unprotected against space, she felt pain return, focusing her body. This pain chilled her—a cold, steady kind of surface pain. Inside, spasmodically, the other pain, the pain of the child, heated her. For hours she lay on the ground, alternately body and space. Sometimes a vision of normal comfort obliterated reality: she saw the family in the evening gambling at the dinner table, the young people massaging their elders' backs. She saw them congratulating one another, high joy on the mornings the rice shoots came up. When these pictures burst, the stars drew yet further apart. Black space opened.

She got to her feet to fight better and remembered that old-fashioned women gave birth in their pigsties to fool the jealous, pain-dealing gods, who do not snatch piglets. Before the next spasms could stop her, she ran to the pigsty, each step a rushing out into emptiness. She climbed over the fence and knelt in the dirt. It was good to have a fence enclosing her, a tribal person alone.

Laboring, this woman who had carried her child as a foreign growth that sickened her every day, expelled it at last. She reached down to touch the hot, wet, moving mass, surely smaller than anything human, and could feel that it was human after all—fingers, toes, nails, nose. She pulled it up on to her belly, and it lay curled there, butt in the air, feet precisely tucked one under the other. She opened her loose shirt and buttoned the child inside. After resting, it squirmed and thrashed and she pushed it up to her breast. It turned its head this way and that until it found her nipple. There, it made little snuffling noises. She clenched her teeth at its preciousness, lovely as a young calf, a piglet, a little dog.

She may have gone to the pigsty as a last act of responsibility: she would protect this child as she had protected its father. It would look after her soul, leaving supplies on her grave. But how would this tiny child without family find her grave when there would be no marker for her anywhere, neither in the earth nor the family hall? No one would give her a family hall name. She had taken the child with her into the wastes. At its birth the two of them had felt the same raw pain of separation, a wound that only the family pressing tight could close. A child with no descent line would not soften her life but only trail after her, ghost-like, begging her to give it purpose. At dawn the villagers on their way to the fields would stand around the fence and look.

Full of milk, the little ghost slept. When it awoke, she hardened her breasts against the milk that crying loosens. Toward morning she picked up the baby and walked to the well.

Carrying the baby to the well shows loving. Otherwise abandon it. Turn its face into the mud. Mothers who love their children take them along. It was probably a girl; there is some hope of forgiveness for boys.

"Don't tell anyone you had an aunt. Your father does not want to hear her name. She has never been born." I have believed that sex was unspeakable and words so strong and fathers so frail that "aunt" would do my father mysterious harm. I have thought that my family, having settled among immigrants who had also been their neighbors in the ancestral land, needed to clean their name, and a wrong word would incite the kinspeople even here. But there is more to this silence: they want me to participate in her punishment. And I have.

In the twenty years since I heard this story I have not asked for details nor said my aunt's name; I do not know it. People who can comfort the dead can also chase after them to hurt them further—a reverse ancestor worship. The real punishment was not the raid swiftly inflicted by the villagers, but the family's deliberately forgetting her. Her betrayal so maddened them, they saw to it that she would suffer forever, even after death. Always hungry, always needing, she would have to beg food from other ghosts, snatch and steal it from those whose living descendants give them gifts. She would have to fight the ghosts massed at crossroads for the buns a few thoughtful citizens leave to decoy her away from village and home so that the ancestral spirits could feast unharassed. At peace, they could act like gods, not ghosts, their descent lines providing them with paper suits and dresses, spirit money, paper houses, paper automobiles, chicken, meat, and rice into eternity—essences delivered up in smoke and flames, steam and incense rising from each rice bowl. In an attempt to make the Chinese care for people outside the family, Chairman Mao encourages us now to give our paper replicas to the spirits of outstanding soldiers and workers, no matter whose ancestors they may be. My aunt remains forever hungry. Goods are not distributed evenly among the dead.

My aunt haunts me—her ghost drawn to me because now, after fifty years of neglect, I alone devote pages of paper to her, though not origamied into houses and clothes. I do not think she always means me well. I am telling on her, and she was a spite suicide, drowning herself in the drinking water. The Chinese are always very frightened of the drowned one, whose weeping ghost, wet hair hanging and skin bloated, waits silently by the water to pull down a substitute.

KEY TERMS

Gold Mountain   A colloquial term used in China to refer to the United States, because of its potential for permitting immigrants to gain wealth.

Ghost   A term of contempt and reproach, indicating complete rejection by the family that ordinarily reveres and nourishes the spirits of dead family members.

almanac   Here, a book of supernatural information, including instructions on how to predict the future.

miens   Aspects; countenances; appearances.

atavism   Throwback to an ancient or ancestral trait or phenomenon.

agoraphobia   Fear of going into public places.

not origamied into houses and clothes   Not folded into representations of houses and clothes that were often made for the dead and then burnt, so that they would ensure the happiness and prosperity of their spirits. Origami is the Japanese, not Chinese, art of paper folding, but the term is used here metaphorically.

DISCUSSION QUESTIONS

1. One of the questions that might first occur to an American reader, especially an American reader not of Chinese descent, is this: Why did the villagers attack? In trying to construct an answer to this question, consider what kind of a threat the illicit pregnancy posed to the village in the eyes of those who lived there. Perhaps even more important than the pregnancy itself, what about the young woman's family's tolerance of it? What message did the villagers receive from the family's tolerance? In the United States today tolerance for formerly "illicit" pregnancy is increasing at a very rapid rate. But there are still some behaviors that seem to provoke widespread rage and righteous indignation on the part of American communities. What kinds of behaviors can you think of that fit this description? Do they seem in any way similar in effect or conception to the illegitimate pregnancy of No Name Woman?

2. Why did the villagers rage against the pregnant woman and her family, and not against the man who was the father of her baby? There are several strains to this answer; make sure you don't give in to the easiest one only. In most societies in which illicit pregnancy is strongly condemned (and this is certainly not a universal practice), it is usually the mother who suffers greater condemnation than the father, if, indeed, he suffers any. Why do you think this is so? In the United States today increasing numbers of births involve unmarried women, and the rate will probably continue to go up. What

social, cultural, and economic forces do you think are contributing to this phenomenon? How do you think American society now reacts to unmarried mothers?

3. Why did Maxine Hong Kingston's mother tell her the story of No Name Woman? On the surface, perhaps, the answer to this question seems obvious. But there are plenty of other ways the author's mother might have chosen to pass on the same basic information. Why did she choose to do it this way? How does the tale of No Name Woman differ from the kind of stories with a moral most modern American mothers would be likely to tell their children?

4. What lessons did the author take away from her aunt's tragic story? There is the obvious one, of course: Do not allow yourself to be seduced. But there are several others. What are some of them? Do you think that this story will lose its warning power for succeeding generations of the author's family? How do you think a boy—say, the author's brother, if she had one—would have reacted to this story? Do you think his mother or father would have told him the story?

THEN CAME THE WAR

YURI KOCHIYAMA

JOANN FAUNG JEAN LEE, EDITOR

These two short oral narratives recount two very different lives: one of a Philippine-born man who grew up in the United States in the 1950s and 1960s, and the other of a Nisei (first-generation Japanese-American) woman who came of age in an internment camp during the Second World War. Neither narrative takes gender as its specific subject, but we can derive some interesting insights into gender from both of them.

Both Merina and Kochiyama describe their gradually growing awareness of their separation from the majority, Euro-American population of the United States. Kochiyama spent her school days unaware of racism, and was, as she says, "red, white, and blue . . . very American." Though her mother kept reminding her that she was Japanese, she insisted that she was really American. Her father was a small businessman; her mother a housewife, and her two brothers went to the University of California at Berkeley. Yuri Kochiyama, herself, went to a junior college and then looked for employment. Despite the Japanese birthplace of her parents, this was in many ways a classic American family. Even the pattern of sending the two sons to a university and the daughter to a junior college was not specifically Japanese; it was common in Euro-American families, too, before the war, when many daughters had no postsecondary education at all. It was not considered necessary, since daughters would work only until they married, after which their husbands would support them. What would be the point of higher education for them? Certainly Kochiyama did not seem to resent her lack of education, and greatly enjoyed her job in a small department store.

Victor Merina, on the other hand, seemed to experience less internal conflict over his mixed heritage, the Filipino traditions his parents worked to maintain at home, and the American culture he absorbed from the larger world around him, at school and among friends. Only when he became involved in fistfights with neighborhood boys who accused him of being Japanese did Merina begin to realize that he was perceived as different from the Euro-American majority. The identification as Japanese was particularly hard on members of a Filipino family who had themselves fought the Japanese. But to the majority of the U.S. population, all Asians were the same. Merina's pronunciation of English was marked by the speech patterns of his parents' Tagalog (which he, himself, did not speak), and this also reinforced his sense of "differentness" from other Americans.

As you read through the two following narratives, consider the following range of variables and the differing ways in which they intersect:

1. *Time: Merina grew up in the 1950s and 1960s, while Kochiyama was almost twenty years older.*
2. *Place: Merina lived in several places in the United States, including the Southeast, while Kochiyama grew up in the tightly knit northern California community of San Pedro.*
3. *Family integration into American culture: Though both authors' parents were foreign born, Merina's father was a member of the U.S. military, and the family often lived on military bases.*
4. *Authors' identification with U.S. majority culture, as well as with parental culture.*
5. *Gender: To what extent were the two authors' experiences shaped by the facts of their differing identities as male and female?*

Yuri Kochiyama is sixty-seven, Japanese American, and was born and raised in San Pedro, California. She got married and moved to New York after World War II. She now teaches English to foreign students.

"I was red, white and blue when I was growing up. I taught Sunday school, and was very, very American. But I was also very provincial. We were just kids rooting for our high school.

"My father owned a fish market. Terminal Island was nearby, and that was where many Japanese families lived. It was a fishing town. My family lived in the city proper. San Pedro

was very mixed, predominately white, but there were blacks also.

"I was nineteen at the time of the evacuation. I had just finished junior college. I was looking for a job, and didn't realize how different the school world was from the work world. In the school world, I never felt racism. But when you got into the work world, it was very difficult. This was 1941, just before the war. I finally did get a job at a department store. But for us back then, it was a big thing, because I don't think they had ever hired an Asian in a department store before. I tried, because I saw a Mexican friend who got a job there. Even then they didn't hire me on a regular basis, just on Saturdays, summer vacation, Easter vacation, and Christmas vacation. Other than that, I was working like the others—at a vegetable stand, or doing part-time domestic work. Back then, I only knew of two Japanese American girl friends who got jobs as secretaries—but these were in Japanese companies. But generally you almost never saw a Japanese American working in a white place. It was hard for Asians. Even for Japanese, the best jobs they felt they could get were in Chinatowns, such as in Los Angeles. Most Japanese were either in some aspect of fishing, such as in the canneries, or went right from school to work on the farms. That was what it was like in the town of San Pedro. I loved working in the department store, because it was a small town, and you got to know and see everyone. The town itself was wonderful. People were very friendly. I didn't see my job as work—it was like a community job.

"Everything changed for me on the day Pearl Harbor was bombed. On that very day—December 7, the FBI came and they took my father. He had just come home from the hospital the day before. For several days we didn't know where they had taken him. Then we found out that he was taken to the federal prison at Terminal Island. Overnight, things changed for us. They took all men who lived near the Pacific waters, and had anything to do with fishing. A month later, they took every fisherman from Terminal Island, sixteen and over, to places—not the regular concentration camps—but to detention centers in places like South Dakota, Montana, and New Mexico. They said that all Japanese who had given money to any kind of Japanese organization would have to be taken away. At that time, many people were giving to the Japanese Red Cross. The first group was thirteen hundred Isseis—my parents' generation. They took those who were leaders of the community, or Japanese school

teachers, or were teaching martial arts, or who were Buddhist priests. Those categories which would make them very 'Japanesey,' were picked up. This really made a tremendous impact on our lives. My twin brother was going to the University at Berkeley. He came rushing back. All of our classmates were joining up, so he volunteered to go into the service. And it seemed strange that here they had my father in prison, and there the draft board okayed my brother. He went right into the army. My other brother, who was two years older, was trying to run my father's fish market. But business was already going down, so he had to close it. He had finished college at the University of California a couple of years before.

"They took my father on December 7th. The day before, he had just come home from the hospital. He had surgery for an ulcer. We only saw him December 13. On December 20th they said he could come home. By the time they brought him back, he couldn't talk. He made gutteral sounds and we didn't know if he could hear. He was home for twelve hours. He was dying. The next morning, when we got up, they told us that he was gone. He was very sick. And I think the interrogation was very rough. My mother kept begging the authorities to let him go to the hospital until he was well, then put him back in the prison. They did finally put him there, a week or so later. But they put him in a hospital where they were bringing back all these American Merchant Marines who were hit on Wake Island. So he was the only Japanese in that hospital, so they hung a sheet around him that said, Prisoner of War. The feeling where he was was very bad.

"You could see the hysteria of war. There was a sense that war could actually come to American shores. Everybody was yelling to get the 'Japs' out of California. In Congress, people were speaking out. Organizations such as the Sons and Daughters of the Golden West were screaming 'Get the "Japs" out.' So were the real estate people, who wanted to get the land from the Japanese farmers. The war had whipped up such a hysteria that if there was anyone for the Japanese, you didn't hear about it. I'm sure they were afraid to speak out, because they would be considered not only just 'Jap' lovers, but unpatriotic.

"Just the fact that my father was taken made us suspect to people. But on the whole, the neighbors were quite nice, especially the ones adjacent to us. There was already a six AM to six PM curfew and a five mile limit on where we could go from our homes. So they offered to do our shopping for us, if we needed.

"Most Japanese Americans had to give up their jobs, whatever they did, and were told they had to leave. The edict for 9066—President Roosevelt's edict[1] for evacuation—was in February 1942. We were moved to a detention center that April. By then the Japanese on Terminal Island were just helter skelter, looking for anywhere they could go. They opened up the Japanese school and Buddhist churches, and families just crowded in. Even farmers brought along their chickens and chicken coops. They just opened up the places for people to stay until they could figure out what to do. Some people left for Colorado and Utah. Those who had relatives could do so. The idea was to evacuate all the Japanese from the coast. But all the money was frozen, so even if you knew where you wanted to go, it wasn't that simple. By then, people knew they would be going into camps, so they were selling what they could, even though they got next to nothing for it.

"We were fortunate, in that our neighbors, who were white, were kind enough to look after our house, and they said they would find people to rent it, and look after it till we got back. But these neighbors were very, very unusual.

"We were sent to an assembly center in Arcadia, California, in April. It was the largest assembly center on the West Coast having nearly twenty thousand people. There were some smaller centers with about six hundred people. All along the West Coast—Washington, Oregon, California—there were many, many assembly centers, but ours was the largest. Most of the assembly centers were either fairgrounds, or race tracks. So many of us lived in stables and they said you could take what you could carry. We were there until October.

"Even though we stayed in a horse stable, everything was well organized. Every unit would hold four to six people. So in some cases, families had to split up, or join others. We slept on army cots, and for mattresses they gave us muslin bags, and told us to fill them with straw. And for chairs, everybody scrounged around for carton boxes, because they could serve as chairs. You could put two together and it could be a little table. So it was just makeshift. But I was amazed how, in a few months, some of those units really looked nice. Japanese women fixed them up. Some people had the foresight to bring material and needles and thread. But they didn't let us bring anything that could be used as weapons. They let us have spoons, but no knives. For those who had small children or babies, it was rough. They said you could take what you could carry. Well, they could only take their babies in their arms, and maybe the little children could carry something, but it was pretty limited.

"I was so red, white and blue, I couldn't believe this was happening to us. America would never do a thing like this to us. This is the greatest country in the world. So I thought this is only going to be for a short while, maybe a few weeks or something, and they will let us go back. At the beginning no one realized how long this would go on. I didn't feel the anger that much because I thought maybe this was the way we could show our love for our country, and we should not make too much fuss or noise, we should abide by what they asked of us. I'm a totally different person now than I was back then. I was naïve about so many things. The more I think about, the more I realize how little you learn about American history. It's just what they want you to know.

"At the beginning, we didn't have any idea how temporary or permanent the situation was. We thought we would be able to leave shortly. But after several months they told us this was just temporary quarters, and they were building more permanent quarters elsewhere in the United States. All this was so unbelievable. A year before we would never have thought anything like this could have happened to us—not in this country. As time went by, the sense of frustration grew. Many families were already divided. The fathers, the heads of the households, were taken to other camps. In the beginning, there was no way for the sons to get in touch with their families. Before our group left for the detention camp, we were saying goodbye almost every day to other groups who were going to places like Arizona and Utah. Here we finally had made so many new friends—people who we met, lived with, shared the time, and gotten to know. So it was even sad on that note and the goodbyes were difficult. Here we had gotten close to these people, and now we had to separate again. I don't think we even thought about where they were going to take us, or how long we would have to stay there. When we got on the trains to leave for the camps, we didn't know where we were going. None of the groups knew. It was later on that we learned so and so ended up in Arizona, or Colorado, or some other place. We were all at these assembly centers for about seven months. Once they started pushing people out, it was done very quickly. By October, our group headed out for Jerome, Arkansas, which is on the Tex-Arkana corner.

"We were on the train for five days. The blinds were down, so we couldn't look out, and other people couldn't look in to see who was in the train. We stopped in Nebraska, and everybody pulled the blinds to see what Nebraska looked like. The interesting thing was, there was a troop train stopped at the station too. These American soldiers looked out, and saw all these Asians, and they wondered what we were doing on the train. So the Japanese raised the windows, and so did the soldiers. It wasn't a bad feeling at all. There was none of that you 'Japs' kind of thing. The women were about the same age as the soldiers—eighteen to twenty-five, and we had the same thing on our minds. In camps, there wasn't much to do, so the fun thing was to receive letters, so on our train, all the girls who were my age, were yelling to the guys, 'Hey, give us your address where you're going, we'll write you.' And they said, 'Are you sure you're going to write?' We exchanged addresses and for a long time I wrote to some of those soldiers. On the other side of the train, I'll never forget there was this old guy, about sixty, who came to our window and said, 'We have some Japanese living here. This is Omaha, Nebraska.' This guy was very nice, and didn't seem to have any ill feelings for Japanese. He had calling cards, and he said 'Will any of you people write to me?' We said, 'Sure,' so he threw in a bunch of calling cards, and I got one, and I wrote to him for years. I wrote to him about what camp was like, because he said, 'Let me know what it's like wherever you end up.' And he wrote back, and told me what was happening in Omaha, Nebraska. There were many, many interesting experiences too. Our mail were generally not censored, but all the mail from the soldiers was. Letters meant everything.

"When we got to Jerome, Arkansas, we were shocked because we had never seen an area like it. There was forest all around us. And they told us to wait till the rains hit. This would not only turn into mud, but

Arkansas swamp lands. That's where they put us—in swamp lands, surrounded by forests. It was nothing like California.

"I'm speaking as a person of twenty who had good health. Up until then, I had lived a fairly comfortable life. But there were many others who didn't see the whole experience the same way. Especially those who were older and in poor health and had experienced racism. One more thing like this could break them. I was at an age where transitions were not hard; the point where anything new could even be considered exciting. But for people in poor health, it was hell.

"There were army-type barracks, with two hundred to two hundred and five people to each block and every block had its own mess hall, facility for washing clothes, showering. It was all surrounded by barbed wire, and armed soldiers. I think they said only seven people were killed in total, though thirty were shot, because they went too close to the fence. Where we were, nobody thought of escaping because you'd be more scared of the swamps—the poisonous snakes, the bayous. Climatic conditions were very harsh. Although Arkansas is in the South, the winters were very, very cold. We had a pot bellied stove in every room and we burned wood. Everything was very organized. We got there in October, and were warned to prepare ourselves. So on our block, for instance, males eighteen and over could go out in the forest to chop down trees for wood for the winter. The men would bring back the trees, and the women sawed the trees. Everybody worked. The children would pile up the wood for each unit.

"They told us when it rained, it would be very wet, so we would have to build our own drainage system. One of the barracks was to hold meetings, so block heads would call meetings. There was a block council to represent the people from different areas.

"When we first arrived, there were some things that weren't completely fixed. For instance, the roofers would come by, and everyone would hunger for information from the outside world. We wanted to know what was happening with the war. We weren't allowed to bring radios; that was contraband. And there were no televisions then. So we would ask the workers to bring us back some papers, and they would give us papers from Texas or Arkansas, so for the first time we would find out about news from the outside.

"Just before we went in to the camps, we saw that being a Japanese wasn't such a good thing, because everybody was turning against the Japanese, thinking we were saboteurs, or linking us with Pearl Harbor. But when I saw the kind of work they did at camp, I felt so proud of the Japanese, and proud to be Japanese, and wondered why I was so white, white when I was outside, because I was always with white folks. Many people had brothers or sons who were in the military and Japanese American servicemen would come into the camp to visit the families, and we felt so proud of them when they came in their uniforms. We knew that it would only be a matter of time before they would be shipped overseas. Also what made us feel proud was the forming of the 442 unit.[2]

"I was one of these real American patriots then. I've changed now. But back then, I was all American. Growing up, my mother would say we're Japanese. But I'd say 'No, I'm American.' I think a lot of Japanese grew up that way. People would say to them, 'You're Japanese,' and they would say, 'No, we're Americans.' I don't even think they used the hyphenated term 'Japanese-American' back then. At the time, I was ashamed of being Japanese. I think many Japanese Americans felt the same way. Pearl Harbor was a shameful act, and being Japanese Americans, even though we had nothing to do with it, we still somehow felt we were blamed for it. I hated Japan at that point. So I saw myself at that part of my history as an American, and not as a Japanese, or Japanese American. That sort of changed while I was in the camp.

"I hated the war, because it wasn't just between the governments. It went down to the people, and it nurtured hate. What was happening during the war were many things I didn't like. I hoped that one day when the war was over there could be a way that people could come together in their relationships.

"Now I can relate to Japan in a more mature way, where I see its faults and its very, very negative history. But I also see its potential. Scientifically and technologically it has really gone far. But I'm disappointed that when it comes to human rights she hasn't grown. The Japan of today—I feel there are still things lacking. For instance, I don't think the students have the opportunity to have more leeway in developing their lives.

"We always called the camps 'relocation centers' while we were there. Now we feel it is apropos to call them concentration camps. It is not the same as the concentration camps of Europe; those we feel were death camps. Concentration camps were a concentration of people placed in an area, and disempowered and disenfranchised. So it is apropos to call what I was in a concentration camp. After two years in the camp, I was released."

After the War

"Going home wasn't much of a problem for us because our neighbors had looked after our place. But for most of our Japanese friends, starting over again was very difficult after the war.

"I returned in October of 1945. It was very hard to find work, at least for me. I wasn't expecting to find anything good, just something to tide me over until my boyfriend came back from New York. The only thing I was looking for was to work in a restaurant as a waitress. But I couldn't find anything. I would walk from one end of the town to the other, and down every main avenue. But as soon as they found out I was Japanese, they would say no. Or they would ask me if I was in the union, and of course I couldn't be in the union because I had just gotten there. Anyway, no Japanese could be in the union, so if the answer was no I'm not in the union, they would say no. So finally what I did was go into the rough area of San Pedro—there's a strip near the wharf—and I went down there. I was determined to keep the jobs as long as I could. But for a while, I could last maybe two hours, and somebody would say 'Is that a "Jap?"' And as soon as someone would ask that, the boss would say, 'Sorry, you gotta go. We don't want trouble here.' The strip wasn't that big, so after I'd go the whole length of it, I'd have to keep coming back to the same restaurants, and say, 'Gee, will you give me another chance.' I figure, all these service men were coming back and the restaurants didn't have enough waitresses to come in and take these jobs. And so they'd say 'Okay. But soon as somebody asks who you are, or if you're a "Jap," or any problem about being a "Jap," you go.' So I said, 'Okay, sure. How about keeping me until that happens?' So sometimes I'd last a night, sometimes a couple of nights that no one would say anything. Sometimes people threw cups at me or hot coffee. At first they didn't know what I was. They thought I was Chinese. Then someone would say 'I bet she's a Jap.' And I wasn't going to say I wasn't. So as soon as I said 'Yeah,' then it was like an uproar. Rather than have them say, 'Get out,' I just walked out. I mean, there was no point in fighting it. If you just walked out, there was less chance of getting hurt. But one place I lasted two weeks. These owners didn't want to have to let me go. But they didn't want to have problems with the people.

"And so I did this until I left for New York which was about three months later. I would work the dinner shift, from six at night to three in the morning. When you are young you tend not to take things as strongly. Everything is like an adventure. Looking back, I felt the people who were the kindest to me were those who went out and fought, those who just got back from Japan or the Far East. I think the worst ones were the ones who stayed here and worked in defense plants, who felt they had to be so patriotic. On the West Coast, there wasn't hysteria anymore, but there were hostile feelings toward the Japanese, because they were coming back. It took a while, but my mother said that things were getting back to normal, and that the Japanese were slowly being accepted again. At the time, I didn't go through the bitterness that many others went through, cause it's not just what they went through, but it is also what they experienced before that. I mean, I happened to have a much more comfortable life before, so you sort of see things in a different light. You see that there are all kinds of Americans, and that they're not all people who hate Japs. You know too that it was hysteria that had a lot to do with it.

"All Japanese, before they left camp, were told not to congregate among Japanese, and not to speak Japanese. They were told by the authorities. There was even a piece of paper that gave you instructions. But then people who went on to places like Chicago where there were churches, so they did congregate in churches. But they did ask people not to. I think psychologically the Japanese, having gone through a period where they were so hated by everyone, didn't even want to admit they were Japanese, or accept the fact that they were Japanese. Of course, they would say they were Japanese Americans. But I think the psychological

damage of the war time period, and of racism itself, has left its mark. There is a stigma being Japanese. I think that is why such a large number of Japanese, in particular, Japanese American women, have married out of the race. On the West Coast I've heard people say that sixty to seventy percent of the Japanese women have married, I guess, mostly whites. Japanese men are doing it too, but not to that degree. I guess Japanese Americans just didn't want to have that Japanese identity, or that Japanese part. There is definitely some self hate, and part of that has to do with the racism that's so deeply a part of this society.

"Historically, Americans have always been putting people behind walls. First there were the American Indians who were put on reservations, Africans in slavery, their lives on the plantations, Chicanos doing migratory work, and the kinds of camps they lived in, and even too, the Chinese when they worked on the railroad camps, where they were almost isolated, dispossessed people—disempowered. And I feel those are the things we should fight against so they won't happen again. It wasn't so long ago—in 1979—that the feeling against the Iranians was so strong because of the takeover of the U.S. embassy in Iran, where they wanted to deport Iranian students. And that is when a group called Concerned Japanese Americans organized, and that was the first issue we took up, and then we connected it with what the Japanese had gone through. This whole period of what the Japanese went through is important. If we can see the connections of how often this happens in history, we can stem the tide of these things happening again by speaking out against them.

"Most Japanese Americans who worked years and years for redress never thought it would happen the way it did. The papers have been signed, we will be given reparation, and there was an apology from the government. I think the redress movement itself was very good because it was a learning experience for the Japanese people; we could get out into our communities and speak about what happened to us and link it with experiences of other people. In that sense, though, it wasn't done as much as it should have been. Some Japanese Americans didn't even learn that part.

They just started the movement as a reaction to the bad experience they had. They don't even see other ethnic groups who have gone through it. It showed us, too, how vulnerable everybody is. It showed us that even though there is a constitution, that constitutional rights could be taken away very easily."

NOTES

1. Executive Order No. 9066 does not mention detention of Japanese specifically, but was used exclusively against the Japanese. Over 120,000 Japanese were evacuated from the West Coast.
2. American soldiers of Japanese ancestry were assembled in two units: the 442 Regimental Combat Team and the 100th Infantry Battalion. The two groups were sent to battle in Europe. The 100th Battalion had over 900 casualties and was known as the Purple Heart Battalion. Combined, the units received 9,486 purple hearts and 18,143 individual decorations.

VISITING THE HOMELAND

VICTOR MERINA

JOANN FAUNG JEAN LEE, EDITOR

Victor is a Filipino American who lives in California and works as a reporter for the L.A. Times. He is forty years old and is married to a German Irish American. He has two sons.

"I remember the stories my parents told us when we were growing up, and I try to convey them to my children. The very little Tagalog I know happens to be a song which I sing to my children. I think that it is important to have these little things which we and our children can remember.

"I was born in a hospital on a military base in Manila. So my sister and I grew up as army brats because we moved around a lot. In the Philippines my father was a guerrilla and fought in the mountains during the war. The U.S. Army made those guerrillas Philippine scouts—sort of an auxiliary force—during the war. So after

World War II, he joined the U.S. Army as an enlisted man.

"I grew up partly in California, went to elementary school in Kansas, came back to California and went to high school in Kentucky. In Kansas, in a neighborhood where we lived off the base, the Kansan students there thought I was Japanese, so I had some run-ins with students in the elementary schools. This was in the 1950s. My father was really upset about this because he fought against the Japanese in World War II. This was still a sensitive thing to him. We lived on Kiowa Street, and everyone called me the Kamikaze of Kiowa Street. We fought a lot about that.

"Another thing that reminded me of how different I was was going to speech impediment class. Several of us would be taken to the attic of the school. The other people were there for stuttering and other impediments. I went because of my accent. Today, I still recall this vividly. I couldn't pronounce the r's. I grew up in an environment where my parents have strong Filipino accents. For instance, my father would call cockroaches, 'COKE-ROCHES.' I mean, that's the way it was pronounced. I grew up in the house like that.

"One time I had an oral report where I used the word, 'COKE-ROCHES,' and everyone burst out laughing. I had absolutely no clue what they were laughing at. I always thought that's the way it was pronounced. I was having trouble saying r words, and so I would have to go to this attic a few times a week and I would have to crow like a rooster, to make the 'er' sound. So I would say, 'er-er-er-er-er, er-er-er-er-er.' I remember sitting there and the teacher would come to me and say, 'Well, how is the rooster coming?' I would say, 'er-er-er-er-er.' Once the kids learned that that was why I was up there, people would greet me with rooster crows.

"I remember going home to my father and telling him how people laughed at me when I said 'COKE-ROCH.' And he just roared with laughter. He said, 'I always thought that's the way people said it.' He took it fairly well.

"But as a child, you are being corrected at school, and you go home and correct your parents. Then you start to wonder if there are other things they aren't saying right. There was so much pressure to be accepted. I think what it did was made me reticent about speaking out in public. I was afraid to volunteer answers in class. I guess what struck me so about that oral report was that I stood up there and was proud of what I was saying, and the laughter just took the floor out from under me. Everyone just zeroed in on that.

"Looking back, my resentment went beyond having a physical impediment. They were telling me the way I pronounced things which was exactly the way my parents pronounced words, was wrong. So on one hand we were corrected, and then turned around and wanted to correct our parents.

"In the South, when I was there (we were on the Kentucky-Tennessee border), it was okay for me to date and go out with Anglo women in the small town nearby. And that was fine. I was sixteen and going to high school. My father was stationed at the military base, and I had a girlfriend in town. But then one time I was walking in the town with a black friend of mine from the army base, and all of a sudden, the girlfriend of this girl I was dating was telling me I would have trouble going out with her again. So I said, 'Why is that?' She said 'Because you were seen with a black guy, and her family is really upset.' I was shocked. At the time, I didn't feel I was objectionable, but all of a sudden I have a black friend, and suddenly I became objectionable. So in that sense, there is a feeling that there are whites, and blacks, and Asians. Filipinos are somewhere in the middle.

"There was much more pressure for blacks to pair off with their own kind. I remember there was a black football player and a black cheerleader in high school. People were trying to get the two of them together. But the football player didn't feel attracted to her. I could understand how he felt. It would be like people saying to me, 'Hey, Vic Merina, go out with a Filipino girl.' There were only two other Filipino families in town at the time, and one of them had all boys, so it would have been like saying, 'You can only date this one Filipino girl.' The thing that was discriminatory and affected me much more than the racial issues was class rank. My father was an enlisted man, and the girl I was seeing was a colonel's daughter. That was much worse than any racial issue.

"My parents encouraged the Filipino culture at home. The one thing we all regret now—and it stemmed from language problems like the 'COKE-ROCH' incident—they didn't want us to learn Tagalog (the main language of the Philippines), or a dialect from their islands, which is called Ivatan. At first they spoke both dialects at home with my sister and I. But after the incidents of language in school, they made a conscious decision not to mix the languages. So they didn't speak any Tagalog to my sister or I when we were growing up. In retrospect, we all regret that now.

"One of the things in the Filipino culture is 'Utang na loob.' In the crassest form, it is like quid pro quo. But it really means that you owe a debt to someone who helps you. And it is a very strong cultural and traditional trait there. If someone helps you in schooling or to get your education, you owe that individual. It's not that if you help someone, you expect them to pay you back. But in the culture, that's what happens. You feel the need to reciprocate.

"Even when it comes to eating a meal, there are certain things we still practice at home. What we saw readily, as we were growing up, and it still happens today in my parents' home, is that we would have friends come over, and if you have a meal, everyone takes some food home afterwards. I don't do that in my family now. But we like for our children to visit my parents' house because the vestiges of the culture are present there. I feel saddened that this sort of tradition will be lost after my parents' generation."

Going Home

"When I was in the Philippines to cover the Revolution in 1986, I visited my parents' old home in Batanes (a group of islands located in the northern part of the Philippines). When we were in the airport in Manila trying to get to Batanes, the seats were all booked, and we couldn't get on the plane. So the photographer and I were going around, talking to people, trying to get them to sell their tickets to us. We were willing to buy the seat for however much they wanted, just to get on the plane. So a group of people found out that I was a Merina, and they asked me if I was related to Eloy (my uncle), so I said, 'Yes, I'm Victor Merina from the United States.' So when they found out that I was related to my uncle, they began giving us their seats to get to Batanes. They said, 'No money, no money. Just go see your family.' And they wanted to share food they had brought with them. Getting off the plane in Batanes, it was nothing but a dirt runway. But all these people were lined up, and I thought somehow the word had gotten out and they were there to see us. But no, these people were there just to greet anybody who came from the plane. My uncle was there, but he wasn't there to see me. They were just waving to people when they arrived. And when the plane left, the same thing happened. My uncle said, 'When ever the plane comes, we just come to greet people and to say goodbye.' Even strangers. It was just the friendly thing to do. That was our first experience in Batanes. And that was the way it was throughout.

"When the word spread that I had come, people would come, and just deposit things at our door. Food, little gifts, the outpouring of warmth was incredible. The people had this big feast for us. They went out in the fishing boats to get fish, they cooked all day, slaughtered a pig and got vegetables from the fields. There were groups of people doing this. It was a real communal thing. At the end, these women in their eighties were wrapping up all these little things of food and giving it out.

"There was no entertainment there, no movie houses. So each of these houses would have kids riding on bicycles holding blackboards saying which movie was showing at which movie house. As it turns out, the movie house was just the family home, with a Betamax, and they would be showing cassettes. And they would come out and give you popcorn and stuff like that.

"When I was there someone had just bought a chain saw. Its price was equivalent to a year's wages. So there was a crowd of people at his home watching him cut logs because it was a big thing. And people had brought wood for him to cut for them.

"There are at most a few thousand people living in the Batanes Islands. In our village, there are maybe a few hundred. My uncle was the village elder, and he settled disputes between neighbors. He also chose people to do public works projects. One time when we were there, a young wife came over and needed my Uncle Eloy because there was a dispute over a chicken. Someone had accused a neighbor of stealing her chicken. He had to go out and mediate this dispute, and then came home to dinner.

"Several of my aunts and my uncle could barely speak English, so my cousins had to translate for us. Then they would try to teach me phrases in Ivatan. Some of them didn't even speak Tagalog.

"I want my children to be exposed to what I saw when I went back to the Philippines. I want them to see, like in Batanes, where people have very little money, where the material goods that we have come to accept and rely on in this country mean much less. They have this feeling of family camaraderie and they've retained the culture. They can see that one of the greatest things about the Filipino culture is the helping of one another; and this blend of old folk ways with a Catholic religion would be tremendous for my kids to see. It made the culture real for me, when I saw it."

Food

"Food is important because it provides a time when the family gathers. For instance, when you make lumpia—it's like a wonton wrapped dish—it is a family thing. I like to have my children go over and help my parents make lumpia. You have to wrap and while you wrap, you sit around and talk. Just chatting and talking and all this, making this meal together. As I've grown up, that's always been a part of the culture. You sit there, and make these dishes, and the family talks, and it extends all the way to the end, when you wrap things up, and send the extra food home with the guests. So food is very important.

"When my wife came to California to meet my parents for the first time, they made this huge, very important meal. When she left to go back to New York where she lived, they packed this huge thing for her, and she was stunned. She asked, 'How much food do you people make?' My folks don't have a lot of money—just the military salary. But no matter where you go it seems this is typical of Filipino families I know. Even the poorest families have all this food. What helps them, like my parents for instance, is they've always had a garden. They grow a lot of their food. They also grow fruit trees. So a lot came from what they grew. It wasn't like buying everything. There was always an abundance. I have never through all the years, felt a time when there wasn't enough: not just enough to eat, but to give away.

"When my college classmates first visited us, my parents were concerned they wouldn't like Filipino food. So they made an entire dinner of Filipino food and an entire dinner of American food. The first couple of times I wondered why they made so much food. And finally my mother told me, it was in case they didn't like the Filipino food. Because my parents were concerned my friends wouldn't enjoy the food, they made extra stuff.

"I think being a Filipino male today helps me professionally, rather than hurts. That is in part because there is a renewed emphasis in my profession, and in the world, on Asian matters—the Pacific rim. And now there is this worldwide interest in what's going on in Asia. Because of the changeover from Marcos to Aquino, and the elections coming up in 1992 in the Philippines—I think all that, and the realization that the Philippines has some bearing on defense, and the growing number of Filipino immigrants in this country—all that speaks to the point that it is going to be more and more important to have people who are sensitive to the culture. I think we're at a point now, where we're starting to have our literature, and a lot of information on the experience of that."

Key Terms

Isseis   Japanese-born residents of the United States. This group is distinguished from the Nisei, or first generation of American-born Japanese-Americans, like Yuri Kochiyama, herself.

Tagalog   Pronounced TaGAlog. The most widely spoken language of the Philippines. Numerous other languages are also spoken in the islands.

Discussion Questions

1. Victor Merina points out that in the southern town in which he went to high school, it was acceptable for him to date Euro-American girls. It would not, however, have been acceptable for an African American high school boy to date a Euro-American girl. What is the underlying justification for this difference? Do you think the status of Asians as being something like "honorary whites" still prevails in the United States?

2. Kochiyama talks about how American she felt as a girl and young woman, and how stunned and betrayed she felt to be considered a potentially traitorous Japanese by the U.S. government. She points to the large number of Japanese-American women of her generation who have married Euro-American men, partly in an effort to eradicate the stigma of being "less" than American. Do a little checking in the data compiled by the Bureau of the Census, and see what kinds of statistics you can come up with for Japanese-American women born from 1920 to 1945, and the ethnicity of their husbands. Try comparing these Japanese-American women to other Asian-American women of the same age. What do you find? Do you think Kochiyama's interpretation is correct?

3. At the end of his narrative, Merina says he thinks it is an advantage to be a Filipino male because of the increasing American interest in Asia and the Pacific Rim countries. Does this seem true to you? Does it seem to you that members of other ethnic minorities have certain advantages in contemporary American culture? Which? Why? Merina says specifically that he thinks Filipino *males* have an advantage. Do you think this advantage (either for Filipinos or for other ethnic groups) is gender specific?

4. Kochiyama's narrative is interesting simply as an account of the effects of racist American policy on a young Japanese-American woman. But it is even more interesting to consider the insights she has derived from her own experience as it applies to other ethnic groups. How would you characterize her position? How does this position fit in with Kochuyama's view of Euro-Americans, found in the body of her narrative?

THE COLLEGE EXPERIENCE CHAPTER 7

The articles in this chapter offer three ways of examining the experience of higher education as it reflects and is shaped by the complexities of gender in American culture:

1. Dorothy Holland's article suggests that the American female preoccupation with romance frequently shapes and limits women's educational experience and their expectations for life after college.

2. The study of women in the University of Michigan class of 1967 investigates the effect of a major cultural upheaval, the women's movement of the 1960s and 1970s, on women's lives. The study explores the expectations, plans, and actual activities of women who embraced the women's movement, as well as those who rejected it, and points out that few women could ignore it.

3. The report of the American Association of University Women charts the ways in which events and circumstances of life shape educational and occupational pathways, and examines how these pathways vary by gender.

The approaches of the three studies are quite different, but they are united by a common theme: the interaction and articulation of gender and education. Each study explores the role of gender in shaping how and when—or *if*—higher education will play a role in an individual's life. In addition the studies all investigate the role of higher education in shaping individuals' options for the future.

Though the AAUW report discusses the educational and career choices of men as well as women, the focus in all the articles in this chapter is on women. As you read through the chapter, consider the largely undiscussed roles of male students. To what extent are men affected by the notion of romance? Do they approach it differently? Why? The original historical model of romance in the Western world was developed and articulated during the middle ages by men. Why should it now seem to be such a female preoccupation? What about the upheavals of the 1960s and 1970s? Were there any cultural events in that era that had as great an effect on men as the women's movement did on women? What about the women's movement itself? Its impact on women is easy to see, but as Mao Tse-tung pointed out, women hold up half the sky. So when their grip changes, men will certainly feel the results. What kinds of results *have* men experienced from the women's movement? How do men deal differently with education from the ways in which women do?

At the beginning of the twenty-first century most women, whether they describe themselves as feminists or not, would agree that they have benefited from the gains of the women's movement. To a great extent these gains begin in higher education and are then played out in the world of work. In reading this chapter, consider exactly what educational and social changes have made these benefits possible. Consider also whether there have been any costs to the benefits, and who has paid them. Though it is possible that we are dealing with a "win-win situation," in which there are no losers, most benefits come with unexpected cultural costs, at least in the short run, that must be "paid" by some segment of society. Sometimes the costs are the result of benefits to one group that can be produced only by withdrawing benefits from a previously privileged group (a "zero sum game"). In other situations the benefits newly accruing to one portion of the population may indirectly cause some disadvantage to another portion because it ceases to be able to compete effectively once the "ante is upped."

The benefits to women of increased education seem clear, but it is worth asking what the costs are, and who pays them. Do all women benefit equally? Who is most likely to benefit, and who is least likely? Can the costs be neutralized over time, and through what kinds of cultural change? Women do not form a monolithic group, despite the possession of two x chromosomes! They vary at least by age, wealth, ethnicity, and social class, and these dimensions of contrast certainly affect the ways in which they participate in education, and in the consequences that education has for their futures.

As you read through this chapter, try to construct for yourself a cohesive and integrated account of American gender and higher education in the last half of the twentieth century. Try to extrapolate from the events of the past into predictions for the future. What do you see as continuing gender-based problems for the twenty-first century? What kinds of solutions would you recommend to address them? What gains do you expect will be made in this century?

How Cultural Systems Become Desire

A CASE STUDY OF AMERICAN ROMANCE

DOROTHY C. HOLLAND

The title of Holland's article may seem academic, but it is actually quite dramatic. What it states so blandly is that what Americans consider to be one of the most fundamental human emotions—romantic love—is actually to a great extent the result of socialization, the process of coming to accept cultural norms and values. And in her article Holland provides an example of this process of socialization.

The contention implicit in the title is that the "commonsense" notion that romance is natural and universal is incorrect. Instead, Holland demonstrates that a powerful interest and an emotional commitment to romance are produced in women students at two southern universities by exposure to the "culture of romance" endemic in these institutions. Further, this focus is promoted and perpetuated by the half of the female student population who are already convinced practitioners of the culture of romance.

Holland's original intention in exploring the influence of peer groups among women students was to assess their influence in shaping students' career aspirations. What she found, however, was that vastly more time, energy, and interest were devoted to the planning and discussion of romance than of careers, and she consequently shifted the focus of her study. Her interest in the role of the peer group, however, remained. Over time, Holland contends, the majority of students she studied came to share the romantic perspectives and practices of the fifty percent of their peers who were already confirmed practitioners of romance. As they gained experience, and as the salience of romance and their identification with it increased, even students who had originally resisted became Educated in Romance *(the title of a book of which Holland is co-author). Thus a cultural system (the overwhelming importance and pursuit of romance) became desire (the powerfully felt need for heterosexual romantic attachment).*

One of the most interesting portions of Holland's article concerns the underlying assumptions on which the culture of romance is based. When the editors of this collection have discussed this issue with their own students, it has proven very controversial and provoked lively debate. The central issue of the controversy seems to be the feeling on the part of many students that despite the accuracy of Holland's general contention that a culture of romance exists among women students in American universities, their own personal romantic relationships should not be included in the general culture of romance. Further, many students feel that their own romantic relationships are unique, and that they are not bound by what they consider the calculated (or even cynical) assumptions that Holland contends govern such romantic relationships. Other students, apparently those who are not involved in romantic relationships at the time of the discussion, consider Holland's account more accurate. As you read Holland's article, keep this student-based disagreement in mind. Does the controversy stem from a disagreement between the emic perspective (that of the insiders of a particular culture or subculture) and the etic perspective (that of the outsiders to a culture or subculture)? Usually anthropologists employ these terms when they are discussing an "exotic" culture, one very different from their own. But it is also useful to consider these two perspectives when examining disagreements within a population or group of one's own culture.

. . . she took him to the prom . . . he was about 26 . . . he was with a whole lot of girls, it wasn't like he was just talking to her . . . she really didn't know what she was getting into . . .

Americans speak of romance as though it were a "natural" activity which most find intrinsically motivating and which most, by the time they reach a certain age, engage in at a reasonable level of competence. In the quote, Cylene, a woman in the study to be described, alludes to a much less frequently encountered conception, namely that "affairs of the heart" are an area of expertise. This chapter addresses the infrequent recognition that expertise in romantic pursuits is learned and that the motivating force of romance—as culturally constructed in the United States—may not come about automatically, but rather is formed in the learning process. The larger issue concerns the ways in which cultural models come to have "directive force."[1]

In the study, we followed Cylene—the woman quoted above—and twenty-two other women for a year and a half, through three semesters of college. The study was designed to investigate how women's peer groups affected their choice of career. As it turned out, much of the women's time and energy, much of what they said in their interviews, and much of what we observed in participating in their peer activities had to do with romantic relationships. Because the women were interviewed again and again over the time period, it was possible to follow their developing ideas and skills with the conduct of romantic affairs. Because we were participating in some of their peer activities, it also was possible to describe the social interactional context in which these ideas were developing. This paper describes the women's process of learning about romance as that process is discernible from the interviews and participant observation. It relates their developing expertise and involvement with romance to Spiro's (1982) levels of cognitive salience of cultural systems and to Dreyfus's (1984) stages of the development of expert knowledge. The cultural model of romance acquired motivating force as the women developed mastery of it and their mastery, in turn, depended upon their development of a concept of themselves as actors in the world of romance. Although American culture tells us that the urge to romance is "natural"—that the directive force is supplied by nature—the study suggests that the desire for romance is formed during the learning process and that this process occurs in the context of social interaction.

Source: Dorothy C. Holland, "How Cultural Systems Become Desire: A Case Study of American Romance." Pp. 61–86 in *Human Motives and Cultural Models,* ed. Roy G. D'Andrade and Claudia Strauss. Copyright © 1992 Cambridge University Press. Reprinted with the permission of Cambridge University Press.

Processes of Internalization and the Directive Force of Cultural Meaning Systems

The larger issue of the chapter is a perennial one for the social sciences: is it that meaning systems "become a desire" or, more mundanely put, that a cultural system directs or motivates people to action? This question is central because it lies at the interface between the collective and the individual and is implicated in any theory which purports to explain important processes such as social reproduction. Parsons alludes to the importance of the issue in an essay he published in 1961. In his opinion, the question of the relations of "social structure" and "personality" had been solved by a convergence between Freud's account of ego, superego, and id and Durkheim, Cooley, and G.H. Mead's accounts of society. His excitement was evident: "This convergence is one of the few truly momentous developments of modern social science . . ."

Parsons's enthusiastic assessment notwithstanding, there was, and continues to be, serious contention within the social sciences and within anthropology in particular as to the proper conceptualization of the relationship between society, behavior and the "presocial" nature of humans. In anthropological accounts the issue is phrased in terms of culture. To what extent does culture determine behavior? Is culture—defined as collective interpretations of social and material experience—but an after-the-fact labeling of deep-seated human needs and concerns stemming, say, from psychodynamic forces or perhaps from inbuilt materialist orientations? Or, taking the opposing view, are cultural meaning systems influential to the point that they profoundly shape and define human needs (Henriques *et al.* 1984:11–125, Spiro 1982:47–51)? As Spiro points out, these assumptions determine one's interpretation of the problem of the directive force of cultural systems.

If culture is assumed to define and determine individual human needs, then the challenge is to explicate the form and nature of the cultural model and so its power to dictate action. The directive force is supplied by the cultural model itself. Most cognitive anthropologists take culture to be profoundly important in determining human motivation and thus adopt this first approach.

If, on the other hand, culture is conceived as a surface labeling of deep-seated human needs, then questions about the directive force of cultural systems become questions about how the cultural system—the surface form—is harnessed to and so derives its power from underlying psychodynamic forces. This second approach can be found in the cognitive anthropology literature as well. The cognitivist position does not exclude the possibility that cross-culturally variable meaning systems are but gilt upon a more fundamental psychodynamic, materialist, or even structuralist substrate (see Quinn 1987 and Hutchins 1987 for examples of connections between cognitivist approaches and psychodynamic analyses). A third approach—one that emphasizes the formation of motivation during development—is less familiar in the cognitive anthropology literature. This third position is the one that is taken here (see also Harkness *et al.*, Quinn, and Strauss).

In the neo-Vygotskian developmental approach that informs the present paper, thought and feelings, will and motivation, are *formed* as the individual develops. In the context of social interaction, the individual comes to internalize cultural resources, such as cultural models, language, and symbols, as means to organize and control her thoughts and emotions. To use Vygotsky's terms, these internalized cultural devices enable and become part and parcel of the person's "higher mental functions." Becker's

(1963) analysis of the use of marijuana provides an example of the kind of study and conclusions implied by Vygotskian theory.[2] Although Becker does not refer to Vygotsky's concepts, his study of how people become inveterate pot smokers indicates that the motivation to smoke pot is developed in the learning process. Becker's findings challenged the then prevalent ideas that either personality traits or the physiological effects of the drug itself motivated use. He found that the full measure of the motivation to smoke was not brought by the individual to the activity of pot smoking, nor was the individual fully compelled to continue smoking by the nature of the drug. Rather the compelling nature of activity developed and was maintained in the context of interaction with others. The neophyte not only learned how to use the drug from others, he also learned how to attend to and value the experience from others. Similarly, although one may not wish to draw any sort of parallels between using drugs and being involved in romance, the present research suggests that the compelling nature of romantic pursuits comes about, or is constructed, *in the process* of learning the cultural system.

The Study

The study was originally designed to investigate college women's decisions about their future careers and the relationship of those decisions to their peer activities. A three-semester period, from near the beginning of the informants' freshman year to the middle of their sophomore year, was chosen for intensive study. Over the course of the study, researchers conducted monthly interviews with the women and participated with them in various of their campus activities. The interviews—"talking diary" interviews—were open-ended and designed to encourage respondents to discuss their experiences and concerns in their own

terms. A second type of interview, the "life history" interview, was conducted near the end of the study, in the middle of the women's sophomore year. Details of the ethnographic study and of the survey study that followed it are presented in Holland and Eisenhart (1981, 1990).[3]

The following is a close analysis of approximately half of the cases. The 200 or so pages transcribed from each woman's "talking diary" and life history interviews were combed for passages about male/female relationships, as were the notes from the peer activities that we observed. The remaining cases have been reviewed, but not as systematically. Although "American" is sometimes used to designate the group that supplied the material analyzed here, it should be kept in mind that the sample is both small and from the southeast. There were subcultural differences between the black and white women's interpretations of romantic relationships, but those differences are not relevant to the argument here. Descriptions and analyses of these differences can be found in Holland and Eisenhart (1988a, 1989, 1990).

The next section briefly describes the context in which the women were learning about and carrying out romantic relationships. The discussion then turns to an analysis of the ways in which the individual women differed in their engagement with and knowledge of the world of romance. The findings of the research, summarized in a phrase, are that romantic expertise, identification of self as a romantic type, and the compelling force of the cultural system co-develop as part of a socially assisted, interrelated process.

The Social and Cultural Importance of Romance at the Two Schools

At both Bradford and SU social activities usually involved or related to the conduct of romantic encounters and relationships.

Going out with, or seeing, friends of the opposite sex ranked high on the list of valued activities, and places where one might meet new men and women, such as parties, mixers, or the local bars, were favored locations. The women and their friends also spent a lot of time talking about potential romantic partners and their own and others' cross-gender relationships. Attractiveness—as validated by attention from a man or men—contributed in a major way to a woman's status in the peer system (Holland and Eisenhart 1988b, 1990: Chapter 7).

The romantic sphere of life was especially important to the women of SU. Those who experienced less success at coursework than they had expected began to emphasize romantic relationships even more than they had. Relationships with women were subordinated to relationships with men. At both Bradford and SU, although in different ways, romantic relationships often interfered with relationships with other women (Holland and Eisenhart 1989).

The themes of male/female relationships also dominated a vocabulary that the students used to talk about one another. Women knew literally hundreds of words for types of men: "jerks," "jocks," "cowboys," "frattybaggers," "brains," "pricks," etc. and vice versa (Holland and Skinner 1983, 1987). And romance figured in the semiotics of clothes and personal adornment.

The Cultural Model of Romance

An earlier study at SU of the meaning of the gender-marked terms and of the descriptions of male/female encounters and relationships had suggested that student discourse about romantic and close cross-gender friendships presupposed a "cultural model" of how such relationships develop. To understand the students' talk one had to know what the students considered unremarkable or took for granted about these relationships (Holland and Skinner 1987).

Since their ideas about the world of romance are important background information for the analysis to follow, the results of the earlier project are briefly summarized here.

As with other cultural models, the cultural models of romance that we inferred posited a simplified world populated by a set of agents (e.g., attractive women, boyfriends, lovers, fiances) who engage in a limited range of important acts or state changes (e.g., flirting with, falling in love with, dumping, having sex with) as moved by a specific set of forces (e.g., attractiveness, love).[4]

Holland and Skinner (1987) concluded that when the young adults talked about their acquaintances, friends, and (potential) romantic partners in terms of gender-marked types such as "hunks," "jerks," "Susie sororities," or "dumb broads," they were assuming that the talk would be understood in relation to a simplified world of cross-gender relationships. In the simplified world posited by the cultural model, cross-gender relationships progress in a typical way:

> An attractive man ("guy") and an attractive woman ("girl") are drawn to one another.
>
> The man learns and appreciates the woman's qualities and uniqueness as a person.
>
> Sensitive to her desires, he shows his affection by treating her well, e.g., he buys things for her, takes her places she likes, and shows that he appreciates her and appreciates her uniqueness as a person.
>
> She in turn shows her affection and interest and allows the relationship to become more intimate.

The model also describes the motives or purposes of such relationships:

> The relationship provides intimacy for both the man and the woman.
>
> The relationship validates the attractiveness of both the man and the woman.

And the model accounts for some exceptions:

> In some cases, the attractiveness or prestige of the man is less than that of the woman. He compensates for his lower prestige by treating her especially well.
>
> If the woman's attractiveness is the lower of the two, she compensates by being satisfied with less good treatment from the man.

The hundreds of gender-marked names that the young adults in our study used, as it turned out, designated, for the most part, "problematic" types of males and females—problematic in relation to the taken-for-granted progress of male/female relations posited by the cultural model. They cause such relations to go awry. "Jerk" provides an example: "jerks" are lowly, negatively evaluated types. In the definitions given by our informants, "jerks" were described as "insensitive" and "stupid." But the definitions did not fully spell out why a "jerk" was considered to be such a negative type or why women found them disgusting and irritating. The reason became clear when a "jerk" was considered as a relevant character in the world posited by the cultural model. A "jerk" is a type who is neither attractive *nor* sensitive to women. He cannot compensate for his low prestige by treating the women especially well. He's too stupid or too "out-of-it" to discern her special qualities and anticipate her desires. He cannot figure out the things that he could do to make her feel well treated. He may be so insensitive, in fact, that he cannot even tell that she dislikes him. Because he cannot "take the hint," he will not leave her alone and thus he becomes more and more irritating as time goes by.[5]

Not only were the women in our study expected to know the cultural model of romantic relationships and these many types who populated the world of romance, they also were constantly exposed to model-based interpretations of their own behavior.

In short, life among women students at both universities was dominated in large part—both socially and culturally—by romance. Social activities and relationships—including relationships between women—often revolved around romantic encounters or around talk about romantic relationships. Status was interpreted, especially for women, in relation to attractiveness. The students shared ways of communicating about and conventions for interpreting romantic relationships. And one's goals, intentions, and qualities were likely to be interpreted according to these ideas about romance.

Differences in Romantic Expertise and Involvement

In the peer situation just described, with its emphasis on romance, with its constant enactments of, and talk about, romantic relationships, individual differences in expertise and involvement were obscured or masked. Knowledgeability about the types of men and the ways romantic relationships work was more-or-less assumed. Further, in as much as romance was assumed to be a natural activity, a basic level of competence in the conduct of relationships was presumed.[6]

American culture does not generally treat romantic relationships as an area of expertise. The women did not usually talk about romance and romantic relationships as something at which one is good or bad, expert or inexpert. Love and romance were more often talked about fatalistically, as something which happened to one, not something that one affected. Unsuccessful relationships were more often attributed to character flaws, to the luck of the people involved, or mismatches in interests rather than to a lack of skill or expertise.

Nonetheless, despite all the alternative ways of talking about romance, there was some talk that turned upon questions of expertise and competence. The women did sometimes see themselves or others as having made mistakes. They had a sense of romantic situations that were "challenges" or situations that they were too inexperienced or "too young" to handle. They sometimes assessed themselves and others as more or less proficient at romantic activities and the world of romance.

Judging from the women in the study, this latter, infrequently articulated idea, of differing levels of expertise, seemed to be the more accurate view. The more common taken-for-granted notions of similar levels of competence and involvement with romance did not hold up. A close look at the women as individuals revealed that some were quite ambivalent about romance American style and had less than compelling images of themselves in romantic relationships. Further the women differed in their facility with romantic situations. The next section describes those differences in their "involvement" with the world of romance; the section following, their different levels of expertise in conceiving and responding to romantic situations.

Involvement in the World of Romance

For some of the women, romance was much more "salient" or present in their thoughts. Apart from, but related to, the "salience" of romance, there was another aspect of involvement: identification of self in the world of romance. These two aspects of involvement are discussed in turn.

The Salience or Directive Force of the American Cultural System of Romance

Spiro (1982:48) describes five levels of "cognitive salience" of cultural systems. At the next to highest level of salience, a cultural system *guides* action. At the very highest level, it *instigates* action. For some of the women, everyday life was translated into, or seen through the lens of, the cultural

model of romance. Judging from the observations of the women's peer activities, and from their interviews, romantic involvements—actual or hoped for—occupied a lot of their time and thoughts. They spent much of their time being with boyfriends, talking about boyfriends, looking for boyfriends, adjusting their plans and activities to boyfriends than did others. For others romance was less salient; they spent time instead on other things such as classes, clubs or committees, friends or family relationships.

For several of the women, the salience of romance changed over the course of the study. In some cases, romantic activities became more important; in others, less. As will be developed in more detail in later sections of the paper, these cases helped to tease out not only the concomitant aspects of increasing and decreasing salience, but also the various factors that affected the rise and fall of salience.

Experiences in non-romantic pursuits sometimes occasioned changes in a woman's emphasis on romance. Holland and Eisenhart (1988b) describe several of the women who came to college proud of having done well in high school and then grew upset when their university grades were not as good. As time went by, they gradually became less involved with their school work and instead switched their attention and time to romantic pursuits. Romance became an even more salient system for them.

Friends were another impetus to romance. Peers generally encouraged the pursuit of romance as in the case of Susan which is described in a later section of the paper. Sometimes, however, they stimulated opposition to the cultural system and for one woman, Sandy, may have figured in her eventual loss of interest. For her, the decrease in salience was dramatic.

At the beginning of the study, Sandy seemed interested, along with her dormmates, in finding a male romantic partner

("You can have the blondes, I get the dark-haired . . . cute ones"). But, as time went by, she had trouble establishing the kind of relationships that she wanted with men at college. During this period, she also learned that a potential boyfriend back home did not feel similarly attracted to her and, later, she learned that he was involved with another woman. Her friends all seemed to be having similarly unhappy romantic experiences as well. At the same time, Sandy began to feel that she did not fit in with the other students at SU. "In my hometown, I was pretty much respected in the community and accepted for what I am, or was, in that community. [I was] basically your non-conformist, and I dressed to suit me. But when I came down here . . . got the impression that here I was a sloppy little girl and I didn't have any class or I didn't have any style . . ." She came to stress friendships even more than she had before and to concern herself about helping her friends. "Friendships were and probably still are one of the most important things to me. They were important to me not so very much socially. They were important to me as a person . . . I pride myself in my friendships." As the study progressed, she came to develop a very special friendship with one woman, Leslie. Despite the jealousy of her other friends and the admonitions of her parents who felt that she was not availing herself of all her options at college, Sandy felt it important to pursue her friendship with Leslie. "Our friendship is terrific . . . I just would like to spend more time . . . [so far] it's all been crammed into one semester there's probably not gonna be another time in my life when I can just sit down and just be friends."

Eventually Sandy came to spend all her time with Leslie. She had begun her freshman year with an emphasis upon romantic relationships with men, but for the various reasons discussed dropped those interests altogether. For her, such romantic attachments became markedly less salient and her identity as an attractive woman in the world of romance, as culturally construed, became unimportant to her.

Identification with the World of Romance

Aside from the importance or quantity of time devoted to romance, the nature of the woman's relationship to romance varied. Some of the women seemed to have an idea of themselves as participants in the world of male/female relationships—as beings in the romantic world—and to accept their romantic selves as real parts of themselves. Others either had an unclear image or sensed a discrepancy between themselves and the role(s) they were acting out. Of the cases reviewed in depth (roughly half of the twenty-three), at least one woman, Susan, explicitly contested the way romance was conceived and enacted in the student culture. Another—Natalie—had more or less explicitly devalued some aspects of the taken-for-granted ideas of romance and marriage as important to her.

The women's process of identifying with the romantic world took place in the context of constant social input. Their peers, and sometimes their professors, cast them as romantic actors. Although she was not pleased by her professor's typing of her as a romantic/sexual character, Delia's account provides a graphic example of such casting. One day she had gone to class dressed in a skirt and blouse.

> And I sit in front . . . of the class, and my teacher says, "What's this? What's this? Della, where's she at?" And I just sat there looking at him 'cause he looked dumb looking around me. . . . and he said, "Oh, there's Della." He looked my legs up and down, up and down, and the whole class [was] looking at him. He said, "Oh, oh, I see. I see, Della, I see. Oh, oh." . . . I was so embarrassed; the whole class was looking at me.[7]

In another case, Karla told about a seduction attempt by a former teacher. The events took place during the study and were described over several interviews. Karla's story consisted of the following episodes. She ran into a former teacher of hers from high school. He was a teacher she had liked and respected and she continued to value his opinions highly. He gave her a book to read—a book by Freud—and they made plans to discuss it later. She read the book and went to meet him ready to have an intellectual discussion. Instead she found out that he wanted to be her lover. She deflected his advances. Because he had a family, she had not thought of having a romantic relationship with him and she disapproved of his invitation. He persisted. When she finally made her reluctance clear he became angry and told her that "intellectuals" were not concerned about whether their lovers were married or not.

These attempts to interpret or identify the women in certain sorts of romantic or sexually related male/female relationships were fairly explicit and direct. In addition to many such cases we also observed an abundance of cases in which the attributions were more indirect. Even comments such as "Oh, you're wearing your add-a-beads," could be an abbreviated reference to a romantic type. At the time of the study, "add-a-beads" were popular among sorority women. Such a comment on clothing, or even a look, was sufficient to communicate an interpretation—in the "add-a-bead" case, that one was acting out a certain femininity and style of carrying out romantic relationships.

Sometimes the women accepted these frequent interpretations of self as a romantic type, sometimes explicitly rejected them, and sometimes ignored them. It was clear in the interview, for example, that Della—quoted above—rejected her professor's casting of her in a sexual role. In Karla's discussion of her experience with

the high-school teacher, she ignored the teacher's claim that intellectuals really did have different moral codes when it came to extramarital affairs and that if she wanted to be an intellectual she had better change her ideas about romantic relationships. In another case, however, Cylene seemed to be entertaining the possibility that a characterization of her as a romantic type was true. Her father had told her that she wanted so many things—a house, a car, a boat—that she was going to "kill" her man. The gist of her father's comment was that she expected her boyfriend to treat her too well—to supply her with too many material possessions. She did not dispute his characterization and, in fact, went on to consider his statement as a possibly valid interpretation.

The women seemed to winnow the possible interpretations and accept some parts while rejecting others. Natalie, for example, talked explicitly about a vision of herself that she had formed as a young child and had since given up at least in part. "'Marrying rich' is just a term for marrying the whole ideal guy . . . that's just a thing that most everybody thinks about . . . a good-looking rich man who loves me very much and won't let me cook . . . and lives in a big house." By the time she participated in the study Natalie said she had discarded a piece of this vision of herself as a married woman. For various reasons, including her sister's experiences with a husband who could not hold a job, Natalie had decided to prepare herself to earn money so that she would not have to depend upon her future husband for economic support. She said that she no longer envisioned being financially supported.

Despite the fact that the women were frequently supplied with images of themselves in the world of romance, and despite the fact that many of their peers seemed to have sorted through various interpretations and arrived at a fairly stable view of themselves as participants in the romantic world, some had failed to form such an identity. They had no clear idea of a possible "romantic" self that engaged them—either as a self to avoid or a self to realize.[8] Susan, for example, had an extremely unsettled and ambivalent identification with romance.

Susan's ambivalence surfaced in many ways. At one point, for example, she spoke of her trip out West and what a beautiful place it was for a romance, but said that she had not got involved with anyone because it was "too much trouble." Her boyfriend, as will be described later, seemed more of an accommodation to peer demands than a reality. Further, she was openly critical of one of the motives, summarized earlier, for romantic relationships: the idea that boyfriends should be a source of prestige. She took the researcher to her dorm precisely to show her the way in which the girls brought their boyfriends to the lounge to "show them off." In Susan's opinion boyfriends were not for showing off.

During most of the study, Susan spent a lot of time thinking about the sort of lifestyle she wanted to have. Her dilemma seemed to be a choice between becoming what she considered a "socialite" or becoming a "hippie." By the time of the study she was inclined to reject the upwardly mobile, upper-middle-class lifestyle that she felt pressured—perhaps by her family—to embrace. This struggle, which occupied a lot of her time and efforts, related both to her ambivalence about her studies and, of direct relevance to this paper, to her ambivalence about romantic relationships. Reliance upon boyfriends as a source of prestige as emphasized in the student culture seemed to remind her of socialite women in her hometown. These women, in Susan's mind, were typified by their frequent attendance at the country club where they talked on and on about their rich husbands. Her feelings about socialites—and

her distaste when she thought about herself as one—made it difficult for her to identify with the world of romance at SU.

In addition to the case of Susan's explicit reluctance and overt criticisms of the idea of romance as construed on campus, there also were cases in which the women—including Susan—participated in relationships without their hearts being totally in them, so to speak. These women had or were participating in romantic relationships according to the accepted cultural notions but they told us of a distance between their true feelings and the ways they were acting. Cylene, for example, talked about how she had had a steady boyfriend in high school, but that, looking back, she probably had had him as a steady not because she was particularly attached to him and did not want to date other men, but because she was worried about people "talking."[9]

The person who was most straightforward about the felt distance between her actions and her true feelings was again Susan. Although some of the others also had absentee boyfriends who primarily seemed to be useful excuses for not going out with other men, Susan's way of talking about Howard, her boyfriend, clearly revealed her limited involvement in the relationship. She talked explicitly in the interviews about their awkwardness with one another when they did get together. She also made statements about Howard that were in a stereotyped tone of voice that indicated she was not serious. For example, in describing her feelings about Howard's decision to attend a university more than half way across the country from her university, she said: "I don't know exactly when he's going but, um, I'm sure I'll see him sometime. So . . . heartbreak, sob and everything like that!" In another instance when an "older" man from a nearby city tried to persuade her to go out with him, she told the interviewer: "But 30 years old, that's old. I mean I'm 18 years old. I don't want to go out with someone who's 30. It's not that bad but—shucks, I don't want to go out with anybody but Howard. He's worth the wait."

Although she was not as ambivalent as Susan, Natalie also seemed to participate only half-heartedly in activities where one might meet potential romantic partners. Natalie did attend many parties and mixers but seemingly only for appearance's sake. As she presented herself in the interviews, Natalie was actually much less involved in romantic endeavors than most other women in the study, and had much more of herself invested in her schoolwork. She constantly talked in the interviews not about boyfriends but about her schoolwork and her interactions with her family. She appeared to be not much identified with the world of romance. As she described it, her earlier childhood vision of herself as a romantic partner (described earlier) had largely disintegrated as she watched her sister's marital troubles. She spoke in positive terms of becoming romantically involved with a man in the future, but, at least as she spoke of her vision of this future relationship in the interview, the vision was vague and without detail.

What these cases and the previous ones suggest is that although they were constantly cast as romantic actors in the world and treated as though they were seriously involved with (potential) romantic relationships, the women's involvement with romantic pursuits varied. Some resisted being identified as romantic participants, some opposed pieces or parts of the views of romance that they associated with their peers, some had strategies for avoiding or circumscribing their romantic experiences, and many indicated a recognition that the way they felt was at odds with the way they were acting out a relationship.

The women's involvement varied along two interrelated dimensions: salience and

identification. About half of the women defined themselves in large part as (potential) romantic partners and devoted a great deal of time and energy to romantic pursuits. Others like Susan had an unclear or contested identification and some like Natalie and Cylene (as she described herself in high school) had a sense of distance between their actions and their identifications. They devoted less time and energy to romantic activities and their identifications were of a different quality from those of persons who defined themselves in large part as romantic types. For Sandy, her identification with the world of romance—one in which she perhaps saw herself as a hurt or rejected admirer—was not sufficiently compelling or salient to keep her involved in the pursuit of a boyfriend. Over the period of the study she lost what interest she had had.

To reiterate, the general point is that the women in the study were not all equally involved with the world of romance and that the components of involvement—salience and identification—proved to be interrelated. Talk about men, focus on men, orientation toward romantic relationships with men—as noted in the observations and as came through in the interviews—seemed to be positively correlated with the degree to which the women talked about and acted toward themselves as actors in the world of romance. Those such as Cylene, Natalie, and Susan, all in their different ways, seemed less personally involved in their romantic relationships and activities than many of the other women. Although they participated in these relationships and activities, their comments conveyed a sense of distance, a lack of emotional involvement. Correspondingly, their degree of talk and concern about romance in the interviews was less than for the women such as Karla who did identify with the world of romance and for whom such relationships and activities were salient.[10]

Expertise in Formulating and Responding to Romantic Situations

In addition to degrees of involvement with the world of romance, the women in the study also seemed more or less expert at the conduct of romantic relationships. They differed in the extent that they relied upon the directions and motivations of others and in ways that they formulated and responded to problematic situations. The women who gave the impression of being less knowledgeable or less expert were those who closely copied and took directions from others, who attended to relatively circumscribed parts or aspects of relationships, and who had trouble generating possible responses to romantic situations.

Adopting the Words and Directives of Others

The women's ways of talking about men and relationships with men conveyed different degrees of facility with the cultural ideas. One woman, for example, had sufficient knowledge of campus types to be able to extract the essences of the types and put them together in a skit. She and some of the other women also were facile in talking about their own strategies for handling relationships. Karen, for example, talked about "keeping the upper hand," in a relationship and Rosalind about "putting one man up front." While Karen and Rosalind may not have invented these strategies—described later—they seemed to be fully at ease with describing and putting them into action. Susan, on the other hand, as will be described later, seemed to be constrained to repeating and attempting to carry out the directives of others.

In the case of "getting the upper hand," Karen was describing her behavior toward Hal, a man that she had just met. She was trying to convince him that she was attractive—possibly more attractive than he was. A woman who is less attractive than a man she goes out with—according to the cultural model—compensates for her relative lack of attractiveness by settling for less good treatment and by allowing the relationship to become intimate faster than she might wish. On the other hand, if she is more attractive than the man, he compensates for his relative lack of attractiveness by being especially sensitive to and attentive to her. Karen tried to get the upper hand by giving Hal the idea that other men were interested in her. She did this by giving him the impression that she was going out with other men, that she had a boyfriend back home and that she had a fuller social calendar than he did.

In the case of "putting one man up front" Rosalind a woman at Bradford—intended to play up her involvement with only one man. At Bradford, romantic relationships were complicated by one's having to maintain integrity and self control. A way to lose control was by having information about one's emotional investments become known to those who might use it to try to manipulate one or to interfere in one's relationships (Holland and Eisenhart 1989). Rosalind's idea was to emphasize one man as the person that she was primarily interested in, thereby deflecting attention from the others.

Both the idea of "getting the upper hand" and "keeping one man up front" were strategies for achieving the valued outcomes of romantic involvements while avoiding bad outcomes. These strategies seemed to be ones that the women themselves had decided to use and could describe without too much trouble. Susan, on the other hand, gave the impression of repeating and trying to act upon what others had said.

During the first year and a half of her college career, Susan talked about gender relations in a variety of ways—ways that for the most part could be traced to her friends. During this period she was searching for a group of friends. She cast about and struck up friendships with a variety of women having different lifestyles and orientations and different ways of talking about men and gender relations. In the interviews she sometimes talked about her friends' relationships in terms that we knew from the observations were terms her friends used. Lee, a friend of Susan's, was having to fend off sexual advances from the owners of the restaurant where she worked. In describing Lee's troubles with her employers, Susan said that a guy at the café had "pinched Lee on the buns and told her to loosen up." In another description of the same incident, Susan said that a "Greek was messing with her [Lee]." Words such as "buns" and "messing with her" were not the types of words that Susan used in other interviews to describe somewhat similar situations.

Susan described another friend's, Patricia's, relationships as being "open" or "not open," "serious" or "not serious." Speaking of one of Patricia's relationships she says: "It seems really good, the relationship they have, because they talk a whole lot, and its a lot more open [than the] relationship that she had with George, as far as saying what she wants and feels." The "openness" of Lee's (the other friend's) relationships was not something Susan talked about, presumably because Lee did not talk about them in those terms.

Susan used euphemisms to talk about a topic—the sexual aspects of gender relations—that she seemed not to discuss with her friends. For example, she told the interviewer that she had learned that a potential boyfriend was "homosexual" and that she was relieved: "[I'm] glad not to have to worry about that [sex] with him anymore." Knowing Patricia and some of Susan's other friends, one doubts that any of them would have referred to sex as "that."

Susan also seemed willing to adopt the arguments of others regarding herself. In one interview, for example, Susan described a situation (referred to above) in which an "older" man was trying to get her to go out with him. The man originally had called Susan's dorm in search of a woman who had previously lived there. Susan answered the phone. They began to talk and he asked her out. She put him off by saying that she had homework and eventually told him she had a boyfriend back home—Howard. The man was not so easily put off. She admitted to going out with someone else besides Howard. The man argued that if she went out with other people in the area then she should go out with him. He almost had her persuaded. In the next interview, although she eventually returned to her boyfriend-back-home position, Susan debated about going out with the man. She said, "But I guess I should meet him, you know, he seems like a pretty interesting person to meet."

By the end of the study Susan had settled more or less upon one group as her primary set of friends and her talk about men and gender relations had begun to conform to the way her group talked about such relationships.

It could be suggested that, in Susan's case, the motivation to participate in romance, as well as the words, were initially supplied by her friends. She did not find the culturally defined motives for romantic relationships—prestige and intimacy—sufficiently attractive to overcome her discomfort with romantic encounters. And, as pointed out, she even disputed one of the motives—prestige—as a proper motive for relationships.[11]

Nonetheless, in her sophomore year, Susan began to look for a boyfriend in earnest. It appeared that her efforts were spurred by her desire to participate in the same activities and talk that her friends did. She needed to find a boyfriend in order to be like her group of friends. Indications of the difficulty she had in making these attempts and of the support supplied by her friends in the activity are clear in the following passage. She had just told the interviewer that she would like to find a boyfriend and the interviewer had asked her how one goes about finding one. "You just scope out the crowd first . . . see I found this guy that I'm interested in . . . But I never see this guy so that makes it difficult . . . I get all nervous and paranoid so I can't ever talk to him. Its pretty funny, all my friends are like: Go talk to the guy, Susan. Let's go talk to him. *I just can't.*" In the follow-up interviews, especially the one conducted in 1987, Susan evidenced more positive associations with romantic experiences, but in 1980 her motivation seemed to be supplied by her friends.

Scope or Overview of Romantic Situations

Besides their facility with ways of talking—and presumably thinking—about relationships, the women seemed to vary in the scope or overview that they had of romantic relationships. Susan, for example, answered the interviewer's question about finding a boyfriend in terms of small-scale, step-by-step procedures that one could follow at a mixer or a party. In contrast, Karen and Rosalind with their strategies of getting the upper hand and keeping one man up front seem to be paying attention to a larger chunk or bigger-scale view of the relationship.

Another comparison of the women's different levels of analysis or overview is presented by the following. Paula, a woman at SU, became annoyed at starting relationships with men she was meeting at parties only to find that they were also going out with her friends. Following several similar experiences, she decided that meeting men at parties did not work. In contrast, a woman at Bradford similarly was having trouble with the men she was meeting. She, however, thought that the men behaved as they did because the women outnumbered the men at Bradford. Because they were in

demand, the men, she thought, were unjustifiably arrogant and expected more from the women than they were entitled to.

> At this school, it's about six girls to one guy . . . so the ugly [guys] . . . think they look like heaven and will try to [talk to you] all the time. It's really sick . . . Some of these guys have the cutest girlfriends, and I don't know how they got them . . . He must have the money. That's the reason why an ugly guy could get a fairly decent-looking girl. He has one of two things: a car or he's got money . . . And most of the guys here that look good, they're real dumb and . . . as far as holding a conversation, just forget it; I'd rather talk to a wall . . . But with so many girls to one guy, he gonna get somebody regardless of how he act.

This latter woman seemed to have a fairly broad overview of the relationship between men and women at Bradford while the former woman at SU seemed to have learned from trial and error that the relationships started at parties did not work out the way she wanted them to.

Generating Responses to Romantic Situations

Besides the differences in the overview or scope of analysis of romantic situations and problems, the women also seemed to vary in how rapidly they came up with responses. In the case of Della and the teacher who embarrassed her in class, according to her interview, she was stymied and could not think of any sort of response. The only way she could think of to stop him from making further such remarks was to avoid him.

Susan's processes of responding to the romantic situations described earlier seem different from the ones that Karla described in her interviews. Recall Susan's process of thinking about her move regarding the man who called her dorm and asked her out. At least in terms of how she talked about the situation in the interview, Susan did not seem to have any overview of the situation or hypothesis about what he was doing. She consciously thought through the calls, the man's arguments and her various reactions, such as her feeling that he was old. She eventually fell back upon the absentee boyfriend to make up her mind and it was not clear at all how she might put off the man should he call her back. He already had argued against her "Howard" excuse. Karla's story about the former teacher's attempt to seduce her—at least in the way she told it—revealed a different sort of process. Karla seemed to form a hypothesis about the situation and the man and then to have devised—more or less at once—a response. She had to change her hypothesis several times when things did not go as expected. Each time, however, she seemed to form a new hypothesis and a new response without having to work through the situation piecemeal as Susan did. As an aside, she was finally successful when she had a friend of hers—a very large football player—call up the high-school teacher and tell him that he better leave her alone or else. After the telephone call, the teacher left Karla alone.

Discussion

Although the women in the study all participated in student society at the two universities and so were exposed constantly to social activities organized around romantic relationships and to shared interpretations of romance, they varied in their identifications with the culturally constructed world of romance. Not all of them found it compelling or salient. Further they also varied in their apparent expertise with the conduct of romantic relationships. The less expert women seemed to repeat the words and follow the directions of others. They also seemed to have less of an overview of romantic relationships and to have to work harder to come up with responses to romantic situations. Perhaps it comes as no surprise that those who were less identified with the world of romance and for whom it was less salient also were the ones who were less expert with the relationships. Those who were resisting, avoiding, lacking in interest, and enacting romance without having their hearts in it were the ones who were less expert.

The research suggests, in other words, that involvement—the salience of and identification with the cultural system of romance—co-developed along with expertise. If the woman had not developed a clear identification of herself in the world of romance—an image of herself that mattered to her—then romance was not likely to be very salient for her and she was not likely to be very expert in conducting romantic relationships. Similarly, if for some reason she had not been able to develop expertise than she was unlikely to have formed much of a romantic identification. Salience, identification, and expertise appear to develop together as an interrelated process—a process that was continually supported and shaped in the context of social interaction.

The research findings on the interrelations of expertise, identification, and salience are corroborated and informed by theoreticians such as Spiro (1982) and Dreyfus (1983, 1984). As shall be discussed, each is concerned explicitly with only one dimension—Spiro with cognitive salience, Dreyfus with expert knowledge. Nonetheless, references to the other dimensions—including, I will argue, identification—are present in both analyses.

Spiro (1982) describes the varying intensities of the directive force of cultural symbols and explains why these symbols are more or less motivating for different individuals. His scheme (p. 48) depicts five levels of the "cognitive salience" of cultural systems that can be summarized as follows: (1) the actors *learn about* the doctrines; (2) the actors come to *understand* the meanings of the doctrines as they are interpreted by specialists; (3) the actors, in addition, *believe* that the doctrines are true, correct, or right; (4) the doctrines come to structure the actors' perceptual worlds and *guide* their actions; and (5) the doctrines further come to *instigate* their actions.

Spiro is especially concerned to point out that cultural systems may or may not reach a very high level of cognitive salience and so may or may not have anything to do with instigating or even guiding an individual's behavior. Although he was primarily interested in discussing religious systems in his article, his differentiation of different levels of cognitive salience certainly applies to the present findings regarding the culturally constructed activity of romance. There were women in the study for whom romance—American style—was more or less cognitively salient. Also of relevance to the research reported here is that Spiro found it necessary to refer to knowledgeability. His first two stages are devoted to the individual's developing knowledge of the system. The individual, his scheme implies, must develop at least a certain mastery of or expertise with the cultural system, before he or she will find it motivating. In the present study, salience appeared to co-develop with expertise.

Dreyfus (1983, 1984), in contrast to Spiro, is interested in the development of expert knowledge. He too proposes five stages: (1) novice stage; (2) advanced beginner stage; (3) competency stage; (4) proficiency stage; and (5) expertise stage. Since he opposes the more traditional conception of expert knowledge, it is necessary briefly to describe his stages. Dreyfus denies the usual idea that expertise develops through the formulation of more and more sophisticated rules or propositions from which inferences are more and more rapidly drawn. Dreyfus argues that it is primarily novices and advanced beginners—not experts—who rely upon rules. Those who are more advanced have a more comprehensive, "three-dimensional" understanding of the system, be it a game such as chess, a sensorimotor skill such as driving, or a contentionalized or culturally interpreted system of relationships such as romance.

In the novice and advanced beginner stages, the individual's knowledge is organized into rules and maxims. These rules, which the learner has probably heard from others, address single elements or aspects of the situation. They are like steps in step-by-step recipes for winning the game, driving the car, or finding a boyfriend. Susan's rules about scoping out the crowd come to mind.

With competency, the various elements of the situation become organized into a gestalt. The individual learns to think in terms of broader elements or chunks of the overall situation. Karen's concept of getting "the upper hand" in her relationship with Hal is an example of such a chunk.

At the competency stage, one must work consciously to arrive at possible responses and assessments of those responses. At the more advanced stages of proficiency and expertise, the experience of arriving at a response changes. The generation and assessment of responses becomes less conscious. Susan's process of thinking about her response to the man who called her dorm and asked her out exemplifies a less proficient stage than that represented in Karla's account of her response to her former teacher's attempt to seduce her.

Dreyfus's stages seem plausibly represented in the present research, but it also seems telling that just as Spiro did not restrict his levels of salience to salience alone, Dreyfus does not restrict his scheme to expertise alone. In order to describe the changes from advanced beginner and competency to more advanced stages, Dreyfus finds it necessary to speak of emotional involvement and sense of responsibility in the system.

The shift between the advanced beginner stage and the later stages of competency, proficiency, and expertise is marked, wrote Dreyfus, by a qualitative change in the relationship between the individual and the system. The individual comes to experience herself not as following rules or maxims taught by others but as devising her own moves. Dreyfus (1984:30) described this change as obtaining a sense of responsibility in the system. Perhaps a better phrasing would be to say that the individual gains a sense of being in the system—as understanding him or herself in terms of the activity. She identifies herself in the world as described by the cultural system:

> The novice and the advanced beginner applying rules and maxims feel little or no responsibility for the outcome of their acts. If they have made no mistakes, an unfortunate outcome is viewed as the result of inadequately specified elements or rules. The competent performer, on the other hand, after wrestling with the question of a choice of perspective or goal, feels responsible for, and thus emotionally involved in, the result of his choice.

In play, as described by Vygotsky (1978), the child suspends other possible interpretations of things in the environment and becomes caught up in a pretend world. Her desires become related to "a fictitious 'I,' to her role in the game and its rules" (p. 100). Her motives become defined by the motives of the game. Here, as described by Dreyfus, the individual gets caught up in a particular game or cultural system and sees himself or herself as an agent in it. As with play, the overall activity is emotionally engaging. Dreyfus also argues this sort of participation is necessary for further mastery:

> An outcome that is clearly successful is deeply satisfying and leaves a vivid memory of the situation encountered as seen from the goal or perspective finally chosen. Disasters, likewise, are not easily forgotten.

With competency the situation becomes "three dimensional" and the individual is "gripped" by it:

> The competent performer, gripped by the situation that his decision has produced, experiences and therefore remembers the situation not only as foreground and background elements but also as senses of opportunity, risk, expectation, threat, etc. These gripping holistic memories cannot guide the competent performer since he fails to include them when he reflects on problematic situations as a detached observer. As we shall see, however, these memories become the basis of the competent performer's next advance in skill (1984:30).

Notice that the emotional involvement or identification comes only after a certain degree of competence is reached and that this degree of emotional involvement is necessary for further mastery. Phrasing this same point in a different way, Dreyfus (1983), in a talk about the acquisition of expert knowledge in the game of chess, says:

> It seems you can't acquire these skills [of having a complex view of the situation] unless you're taking the game very seriously; it won't help to just be reading book games. There's the story that Bobby Fisher, whenever he plays even a book game, says: "Pow, got him, killed him that time!" even though there's nobody [no live opponent] there.

If Dreyfus's notions of the development of expertise are accurate, then identifying oneself as an agent in the system—an actor in the world as system—an actor in the world as defined by the game, is a necessary precursor to mastering the system beyond a certain level. One has to develop a concept of oneself in the activity and want either to realize that self or avoid it.

Interweaving the Two Schemes

Although explicitly focused on their separate concerns, Spiro's and Dreyfus's schemes interrelate. Dreyfus is describing expert knowledge; however, he writes that emotional involvement is necessary for the achievement of his fourth stage of proficiency and fifth stage of expertise. Emotional involvement is also important in Spiro's account of the motivating force or cognitive salience of a cultural system. And, in turn, Spiro's scheme implicates knowledgeability. His first two levels explicitly refer to the knowledge that the individual has of the system. Put together, the two schemes begin to describe an integrated process of the development of expertise and cognitive salience. I would also argue that both schemes predicate what I have interpreted as "identification" with the cultural system.

Dreyfus vaguely describes a sense of responsibility as necessary for the development of expertise. He argues that one cannot go to the more advanced stages of proficiency and expertise without conceiving of oneself as devising one's own moves rather than relying upon the rules and maxims learned from others. Spiro (p. 48) describes the corresponding stage as the stage of believing—one comes to think of the system as being "true, correct, or right." His article is devoted to explaining why a patently impossible—to a western scientific mind—world of the supernatural could seem true.

I would argue that the key development that occurs around the third stage in both schemes is best phrased as "identification"—the formation of a concept of self as an actor in the culturally devised system. Spiro suggests that belief is crucial for advancement to higher levels of salience. Belief probably is relevant, but it may not be sufficient. An assessment that a world—a culturally interpreted world—lacks validity, truth, correctness, or rightness may indeed affect whether an individual can conceptualize or personalize the system as relevant to him or herself. Even in the case of romantic relationships which may not strain scientific credulity as do the religious systems Spiro considers, Susan, for example, had trouble seeing herself in the world of romance as interpreted by her peers. She had trouble because she disagreed with the association between boyfriends and prestige. The world did not seem right to her. However, there may be other reasons besides credulity that one does not form a valued identity in a cultural system. Sandy apparently continued to "believe" that the world of romantic male/female relationships existed. She did not come to doubt the world, rather her concept of herself in such a relationship was uninspiring and became even less so in comparison to her valued conceptions of herself in her other close relationships.

Identification—as the more inclusive process—seems to describe better the point or phase in internalization where the system that one has been socially interacting, according to the instructions and directions of others, becomes a system that one uses to understand and organize aspects of oneself and at least some of one's own feelings and thoughts (see also Quinn and Holland 1987:12–113).

Summary and Conclusions

This paper has presented a case study of young college women's internalization of the cultural system of romance. The interviews and observations of twenty-three women followed over a year-and-a-half period revealed processes through which romance—as culturally constructed in the southeastern United States—becomes (or fails to become) compelling. The larger issue at hand is the directive force of cultural systems and what the process of learning a cultural system reveals about its motivating force.

The women in the study belied Americans' commonsense notions that romance is naturally compelling, naturally salient, and an area of competence that automatically appears when one reaches a certain age. The commonsense notions imply a homogeneity of interest and competence that was not found in the present research. The women were more or less expert with romantic relationships and more or less compelled to pursue romantic activities. Further, the commonsense notions underplay the pivotal significance of social intercourse in the formation of romantic interests and skills.

A close look at the women's developing involvement and expertise suggests that expertise, salience, and identification with romance co-develops as part of an interrelated process and that this process is integrally connected to social context. In accord with D'Andrade's (1986a) point that cultural models generate rather than provide a means to satisfy pre-existing goals, the present study suggests that relative beginners may neither know nor find the rumored motives for romantic activity—prestige and intimacy—especially enticing. Further, their knowledge of the conduct of romantic relationships may be rather piecemeal, their overviews of romantic situations rather vague, their responses to romantic situations rather labored, and they may not have developed any engaging visions of themselves as a participant in the world described by the cultural system.

For the women in the study, the cultural interpretation of romance became salient and compelling as their expertise with romantic relationships increased and as they came to form an engaging interpretation of themselves in the world of romance. Women who were vague and unclear or resistant to seeing themselves in the world of romance were the who were less expert and who found romance relatively unimportant in their lives. Women who were

more expert were those who clearly identified with the world and for whom romance was highly salient.

The research was not originally conducted to study the internalization of cultural models of romance and so must be regarded as tentative and incomplete. However, Spiro's (1982) scheme depicting the five levels of cognitive salience of a cultural system and Dreyfus's (1984) five stages of the development of expertise both corroborate and inform the research findings. A beginning attempt was made to interweave schemes of cognitive salience and expertise by showing their interrelationships and by suggesting, in the case of the Spiro and Dreyfus schemes, certain reformulations. Specifically, it was suggested that "identification" with the culturally theorized world be substituted for Spiro's concern with belief and Dreyfus's emphasis on a feeling of responsibility for generating one's own moves.

Ethnographic case studies of internalization, such as this one and that of Becker (1963), for example, make it very clear that the social interactional context of learning must be taken into account. The relationship of the social interactional context of learning romance to the development of expertise, salience, and identification was not the focus of the present paper; nonetheless, the ubiquitous presence of peers as participants in romantic relationships and talk about romantic relationships, as coaches and "motivators" and as targets of opposition, was alluded to at many points. Although the women were not all expert enough or self-engaged enough in the system of romance to find it compelling in and of itself, they all were certainly propelled into the activities by the urgings of others. Further, those that resisted, rebelled and failed to form identifications with the romantic world did so in part in reaction to their peers.

If expertise, salience, and identification do co-develop in an interrelated process, as argued in this paper, then our descriptions of cultural content—by implication—become even more complicated than we had thought. The manner of formulating the content—as rules and maxims or gestalts (in the way of an expert)—implies a level of expertise, a level of salience, and a level of identification that may in fact be appropriate for describing only a small subset of the people studied. The description may falsely imply a homogeneity of expertise, salience, and identification, as well as homogeneity of content.

Randall (1976) and others argued that ethnoscience's formulation of cultural knowledge in terms of referential function and taxonomic organization falsely presupposed that cultural knowledge is organized for "scientific analytic" purposes as opposed to, say, more practical tasks. If the conclusions drawn here are correct, then the way an anthropologist describes a cultural system also may (falsely) presuppose that the system is known by most at a particular level of expertise, with a particular level of identification, and a particular level of salience.

What may already have been perceived now becomes more clear. There is the strong possibility that we have been describing cultural systems whose content has been mastered by, and whose directive force is compelling for, only a subset of the population.

And what are the characteristics of that subset and the relationship of that subset to the remainder of the population? Unexamined assumptions of homogeneity are a problem not so much because they may be unjustified according to the canons of scientific sampling and generalization, but because they permit inattention to the social distribution of cultural knowledge and its role in the reproduction of power relations. Assumptions of homogeneity deflect attention from the important processes of social conflict, the social symbolism of knowledge, and the processes and consequences of individual resistance that are important, even in the present research on an everyday and common activity. Expertise with romance, the salience of romantic activities, and the formation of one's view of oneself in the world of romance co-develop as part of an interrelated process that occurs within, and is sensitive to, the social-interactional context. Thus, the directive force of romance—the compelling nature of romance—integrally depends upon social as well as cultural forces.

NOTES

1. The research reported here was done with Margaret Eisenhart. She and several others, including William Lachicotte, Laurie Price, Melford Spiro, Claudia Strauss, and two anonymous reviewers, made helpful suggestions and comments on earlier drafts of the paper. Roy D'Andrade first alerted me to Spiro's stages of cognitive salience. D'Andrade's ideas and the papers and comments of the other panel members at the time of the A.A.A. symposium have affected the paper as well. I also would like to thank the women who participated in the study.
2. For a general discussion of Vygotsky and references to his work see Wertsch 1986. Elaboration of Vygotskian concepts pertinent to this paper can be found in Holland and Valsiner 1988. For one of the few translated papers of Vygotsky's directly addressed to motivation, see Vygotsky 1987.
3. The study participants were drawn from two universities—twelve of the women were attending Bradford University (Bradford), a historically black school, and eleven were attending Southern University (SU), a historically white school. Both universities are

located in the southern United States. Bradford, the smaller and less well funded of the two universities, draws students of predominantly black, lower-middle-class backgrounds while SU draws students of predominantly white, middle-class backgrounds. In some other respects the two schools are similar. Both are state universities. At both schools the ratio of women to men is about the same (60:40). The original study was carried out in 1979–1981.

The names of the universities and all personal names are pseudonyms. Inconsequential but potentially identifying details in the quotes have been changed.

4. Cultural models are shared, conventional ideas about how the world works that individuals learn by talking and acting with their fellows. Defined cognitively, cultural models consist of "schemas" that guide attention to, drawing inferences about, and evaluation of, experience. These schemas also provide a framework for organizing and reconstructing memories of experience (Quinn and Holland 1987).

5. The research that produced the cultural model was conducted at SU in the late 1970s and included an analysis of some of the interviews that are the basis of the study described here. Because only a few men were interviewed in the latter study we describe the model as one held by women. Women at Bradford used similar sorts of terms and, in their descriptions of romantic relationships, seemed to rely upon similar ideas about attractiveness and the respective roles of the male and the female. For them, however, there was an emphasis on self-determination and self-protection that entered into their interpretation of male/female relationships. Further details are given by Holland and Eisenhart (1989, 1990) along with a discussion of the possible historical roots of the differences between the black and white women's interpretations of male/female relationships.

6. Kessler and McKenna (1978) discuss a similar process in the case of gender attributions and interpretations. Even inexperienced transsexuals in the United States find that it is not difficult to be convincing as a member of the opposite sex. Once an attribution of gender is made, most make efforts to interpret a person's deportment as gender-appropriate. Although the corresponding studies have not been conducted, it is probably the case that a basic level of romantic expertise is assumed to be a natural correlate of attaining a certain age.

7. Both Della and Karla, in the cases that follow, were embarrassed and offended by being cast into the world of gender relations in what they considered to be inappropriate situations by men they considered inappropriate partners. While most of the interpretations of themselves as potential romantic/sexual partners were not taken amiss, these were. The women in the study were learning of their vulnerability to romantic/sexual typing regardless of their wishes to be so typed (see Holland and Eisenhart 1990, Chapters 7 through 10).

8. Markus and Nurius's (1987) article "Possible Selves: The Interface between Motivation and the Self-Concept" is relevant to the research here. From their review of the social psychological research, they argue, among other points, that individuals form personalized images of themselves in various situations—e.g., visions of oneself receiving a Nobel Prize. These visions motivate actions to realize these possible selves. There also is evidence that some images of possible selves are negatively evaluated so that one works to avoid the realization of such an image.

9. As previously mentioned and as described more fully elsewhere (Holland and Eisenhard 1989, 1990), the black women at Bradford were concerned about maintaining self-direction and self-control. Since knowledge about one's behavior and feelings can be used by others to manipulate one, having a steady boyfriend—as opposed to going out with a number of boyfriends—becomes a way to control information.

10. As the study progressed, Cylene and especially Susan became more involved with romantic relationships. Examples of women who were greatly involved with romance and identified themselves as such are given later. More extensive examples and discussion can be found in Holland and Eisenhart (1990, Chapters 9 and 10).

11. Susan's process of learning is a good example of the internalization of social discourse (Vygotsky 1987, Wertsch 1986).

REFERENCES

Becker, Howard S. 1963. *Outsiders: Studies in the Sociology of Deviance*. New York: The Free Press.

D'Andrade, Roy. 1986a. Cognitive Anthropology. Paper presented at the 1986 American Anthropological Association meetings in the symposium, Psychological Anthropology: Appraisal and Prospectus, Philadelphia, PA.

D'Andrade, Roy. 1986b. Cultural Schemas as Motives. Paper presented at the 1986 American Anthropological Association meetings in the symposium, The Directive Force of Cultural Models, Philadelphia, PA.

Dreyfus, Hubert L. 1983. Telling What We Know: The Making of Expert Systems. Talk presented to the conference, The Brain and the Mind. Available from National Public Radio, N1—831207.01/02-c. Washington, D.C.

Dreyfus, Hubert L. 1984. What Expert Systems Can't Do. *Raritan* 3(4):22–36.

Henriques, Julian, Wendy Holloway, Cathy Urwin, Couze Venn, and Valerie Walkerdine. 1984. *Changing the Subject: Psychology, Social Regulation and Subjectivity*. London: Methuen.

Holland, Dorothy and Margaret Eisenhart. 1981. *Women's Peer Groups and Choice of Career*. Final Report. Washington, D.C.: National Institute of Education.

Holland, Dorothy and Margaret Eisenhart. 1988a. Moments of Discontent: University Women and the Gender Status Quo. *Anthropology and Education Quarterly* 19(2):115–138.

Holland, Dorothy and Margaret Eisenhart. 1988b. Women's Ways of Going to School: Cultural Reproduction of Women's Identities as Workers. In *Class, Race and Gender in U.S. Education*, Lois Weis, ed. Buffalo: SUNY Press. Pp. 266–301.

Holland, Dorothy and Margaret Eisenhart. 1989. On the Absence of Women's Gangs in Two Southern Universities. In *Women in the South*, Holly Mathews, ed. Athens: University of Georgia Press. Pp. 27–46.

Holland, Dorothy and Margaret Eisenhart. 1990. *Educated in Romance: Women, Achievement and College Culture*. Chicago: University of Chicago Press.

Holland, Dorothy and Debra Skinner. 1983. Themes in American Folk Models of Gender. *Social Science Newsletter* 68(3):49–60.

Holland, Dorothy and Debra Skinner. 1987. Prestige and Intimacy: The Cultural Models Behind Americans' Talk about Gender Types. In *Cultural Models in Language and Thought*, Dorothy Holland and Naomi Quinn, eds. Cambridge: Cambridge University Press. Pp. 78–111.

Holland, Dorothy and Jaan Valsiner. 1988. Symbols, Cognition and Vygotsky's Developmental Psychology. *Ethos* 16(3):247–272.

Hutchins, Edwin. 1987. Myth and Experience in the Trobriand Islands. In *Cultural Models in Language and Thought*, Dorothy Holland and Naomi Quinn, eds. Cambridge: Cambridge University Press. Pp. 269–289.

Kessler, Suzanne J. and Wendy McKenna. 1978. *Gender: An Ethnomethodological Approach*. New York: John Wiley.

Markus, Hazel and Paul Nurius. 1987. Possible Selves: The Interface between Motivation and the Self-Concept. In *Self and Identity: Psychosocial Perspectives*, Krysia Yardley and Terry Honess, eds. Chichester: John Wiley. Pp. 157–172.

Parsons, Talcot. 1961. *Social Structure and the Development of Personality. Studying Personality Cross-Culturally*, B. Kaplan, ed. Evanston, IL: Row, Peterson. Pp. 165–200.

Quinn, Naomi. 1987. Love and the Experiential Basis of American Marriage. University of Virginia Center for Advanced Studies Working Paper Series.

Quinn, Naomi and Dorothy Holland. 1987. Culture and Cognition. In *Cultural Models in Language and Thought*, Dorothy Holland and Naomi Quinn, eds. Cambridge: Cambridge University Press. Pp. 3–40.

Randall, Robert. 1976. How Tall is a Taxonomic Tree? Some Evidence for Dwarfism. *American Ethnologist* 3(3):543–553.

Spiro, Melford E. 1982. Collective Representations and Mental Representations in Religious Symbol Systems. In *On Symbols in Anthropology: Essays in Honor of Harry Hoijer*, J. Maquet, ed. Malibu: Udena Publications. Pp. 45–72.

Vygotsky, Lev S. 1978. The Role of Play in Development. In *Mind in Society: The Development of Higher Psychological Processes*, M. Cole, V. John-Steiner, S. Scribner, and E. Souberman, eds. Cambridge, MA: Harvard University Press. Pp. 92–104.

Vygotsky, Lev S. 1987. The Problem of Will and Its Development in Childhood. In *The Collected Works of L.S. Vygotsky*, Vol. I: *Problems of General Psychology*, Norris Minick, trans. New York: Plenum Press. Pp. 351–358.

Wertsch, James V. 1986. *Vygotsky and the Social Formation of Mind.* Cambridge, MA: Harvard University Press.

KEY TERMS

ego   In Freudian terminology, the conscious, individual self. (Latin: I.)

superego   In Freudian terminology, the ethical, moral aspect of an individual's psyche. (Latin: superior I.)

id   In Freudian terminology, the basic (biologically) primitive element of the individual's psyche, from which the ego and superego are derived. (Latin: it.) Freud, himself, though schooled in the classics, used not Latin but his vernacular German for what English speakers know as the ego, the superego, and the id.

neo-Vygotskian, Vygotsky   Lev Semenovich Vygotsky (1896–1934) was a brilliant Russian psychologist whose work was little known to the Western world until thirty or forty years after his death. Vygotsky's work, pursued largely in isolation from Western thought because of the political climate of his time, represents cognition as articulated with the social world. Today students recognize similarities to the work of major Western thinkers, such as Sapir and Whorf, though Vygotsky was unaware of most of the intellectual work of the West. The term "neo-Vygotskian" refers to contemporary thought that strongly reflects Vygotsky's perspective.

neophyte   Novice; beginner.

Bradford, SU   Pseudonyms given by Holland to colleges at which she collected data.

salient   Prominent; striking; noticeable.

gestalt   German: form; shape. A coherent entity that is perceived in its entirety rather than as an assemblage of individual components.

maxims   Pithy, significant statements.

ethnoscience   A school of anthropological linguistic thought that focuses on the analysis of various systems of classification and their constituent words.

referential function   Objective meaning, significance, or purpose.

taxonomic organization   Organization into a system of classification.

DISCUSSION QUESTIONS

1. Holland never defines "romance" or "romantic love." Nor does she describe the history of romance, as a specific style of behavior that originated in Western Europe in the middle ages. Yet most readers will have little difficulty in understanding what Holland means when she talks about the "culture of romance." But just to keep ourselves honest, what is romance? Is it the same thing as romantic love? How is romantic love different from other kinds of love? What other kinds of love are there? Romantic love, in Holland's discussion (and in Madison Avenue's) seems to be based to a great extent on physical appearance. Do you think this is true? Are other kinds of love based on appearance? Can romantic love exist *without* the spur of a desirable physical appearance?

2. Holland provides a model that lays out the way in which romance works. Does her model seem accurate to you? Why or why not? What changes would you make in the

model to render it more accurate? Holland discusses exceptions to her model that seem particularly interesting. Social scientists sometimes refer to the notion of "positive assortative mating," which for our purposes here means primarily that people tend to become romantically involved with partners who are generally considered to be similar on a scale of attractiveness. Does your experience confirm Holland's exceptions—that is, that when the woman is substantially less attractive than her male partner, she accepts less good treatment, and when a man is less attractive than his female partner, he has to be especially nice to her? Why are the obligations of the less attractive partner different depending on gender?

3. All cultures in the world have rules that organize and interpret love and sexual expression. Are you aware of any that organize these phenomena differently from the way they are organized in majority American culture? What are they, and what are the differences? You may come from such a culture yourself, or have friends or relatives who do. Or you may have read about such cultures. What would U.S. culture be like without the cultivation of romance? How would the arts be different (painting, movies, television, literature)? What about clothing? Marriage? Life in school?

4. Holland's research involved only women. Most similar investigations have involved primarily or exclusively women. Why? Though it is women who are usually thought of as "sex objects," men seem to be most frequently cast as "romance objects." Why? Do you think this characterization is accurate? Where (or how) do you think men fit into the culture of romance?

THE UNIVERSITY OF MICHIGAN CLASS OF 1967

THE WOMEN'S LIFE PATHS STUDY

SANDRA S. TANGRI AND SHARON RAE JENKINS

This article is valuable and interesting on a number of different grounds. First, its organization and writing are unusually clear and straightforward. Second, it provides an account of the effects of the Women's Movement on the first generation of women college students to be affected by it. Third, it follows the women in its study through fifteen years, from their senior year in college through interviews fourteen years after graduation. For one of the editors of this collection (McKee), the study is even more interesting, since she graduated from college in 1966, and so is very nearly part of the same age cohort as the students involved in the Michigan study.

The authors' characterization of the University of Michigan is very important in understanding who its students are. Though a large public institution, the academic prestige of the University of Michigan is great: The University is very selective; its expectations for performance are high; and its students are conscious of their participation in an elite educational experience. Not surprisingly, the educational attainments of the parents of many University of Michigan students are relatively high, as are their family incomes.

In 1967 a group of 200 graduating seniors were selected for interviews that were expected to continue periodically for a number of years into the future. Eventually this group dwindled to 117 in 1981, as interviewers and participants lost track of each other. Still, a longitudinal study of this many participants is in itself valuable. The participants of the study on which this article is based were made up of equal numbers of Role Innovators, Moderates, and Traditionals, based on their choice of future occupation. This division into thirds did not reflect the proportion of these groups among women students at the University, where Moderates and Innovators comprised only 10 percent each of all students. But for the purposes of the longitudinal study, it was essential to have roughly equal numbers of each group.

As a group, the Innovators were initially distinguished from the Traditionals and Moderates by their family backgrounds: more education and more money at home. They were, however, not distinguished by their romantic success, as researchers in the 1960s (and possibly the twenty-first century) might have thought. Innovators were as likely as anyone else to have romantic relationships, and more likely to have male friends who were not romantic partners. In other ways, of course, they were different from the Moderates and Traditionals. They planned less traditional careers; they planned to marry later; and they expected to have fewer children.

But what is interesting about graduates in all three groups is that as time passed, their expectations for the future were so often unrealized fourteen years later. The table on page 382 presents this information in graphic form; it contrasts the expectations of participants as graduating seniors with what the women had actually done by the time they were interviewed in 1981. Overall, fewer were married; most had given birth to fewer children than they had expected to; many had acquired more education than they had intended to; more were employed than had expected to be; and the ranks of the Moderates had thinned out, as former Moderates became either Innovators or Traditionals. As you read the article, consider why you think these changes occurred and whether you think they are still occurring among women college students today.

The article contains four brief sketches of participants who represent different configurations of life paths: Innovators, Traditionals, those who became more Traditional, and those who became Innovators. These little portraits are enjoyable because they put faces or personalities to the general descriptions of participants. They also allow us to understand them as thoughtful, intelligent (and remarkably insightful and articulate) participants in a rapidly changing world. Though the women are quite different in some respects, they share several traits. The most common regrets seem to be that they did not acquire additional education earlier, and that they did not insist on more participation in household tasks from their husbands or partners early on in the relationships. This is another issue to consider as you progress through the article: To what extent do you think the current generation of college women has learned from the experiences of their mothers' generation?

Participants in the Michigan study generally agreed that the Women's Movement had had a definite impact on their lives, both for better and for worse. Improvements included the greater opportunities open to women after the gains of the Movement. But some women, particularly Traditionals, also felt resentment in the aftermath of the Women's Movement. Though they had elected to stay at home with their children, according to the traditional American pattern, they felt that they were being judged negatively by many people, particularly by feminists, for not fulfilling their "potential" as educated women by having careers. This is a point of view that continues to be discussed by women at the beginning of the twenty-first century, and the issue has clearly not yet been resolved.

The women discussed in this chapter entered the University of Michigan in 1963 and graduated in 1967; that is, they are quintessential members of that turbulent cohort called the 1960s generation. Like many other colleges and universities, the University of Michigan used social science research methods to try to understand the needs and behavior of its student body in those years. This effort resulted in the Michigan Student Study (Gurin, 1971), which formed the basis for the Role Innovators Study (Tangri, 1969, 1972, 1974), which in turn grew into the Women's Life Paths Study (Tangri and Jenkins, 1986; Ruggiero and Weston, 1988).

The Michigan Student Study gathered extensive interview and questionnaire data on subjects' relationships with family, friends, faculty, and classmates, on their college activities, experiences, and attitudes, and on their future plans, including plans for careers and families. Pursuing her interest in women choosing role-innovative occupations, Sandra Tangri collected additional personality and questionnaire data on a stratified random sample of women from the Michigan Student Study. The first wave of these data (the Role Innovators Study) was collected during the spring of

1967 from 200 graduating seniors. Three years later, 152 of the women were interviewed by telephone or returned a mailed questionnaire. The most recent data were gathered by questionnaire from 117 women in 1981, when they were in their middle thirties. For this follow-up, Tangri was joined by a research team consisting of Jan Hitchcock, Sharon Rae Jenkins, and Jo Ruggiero and assisted by Karen Chandler.

The initial focus (the Role Innovators Study) was on finding predictors of nontraditional occupational choice by looking at family background, personality, and experiences in college that could explain why some women chose to go into fields that were then predominantly occupied by men. The next focus was on the question of whether and how these occupational choices were pursued. The researchers looked broadly at the full range of circumstances of the women's lives, as well as at specific work and educational experiences. We report here on the complex ways in which these women have organized their lives, on their satisfactions and dissatisfactions, and on how they view their experiences and the contexts shaping those experiences.

In this chapter, we review the. history and context of the study, summarize and

Source: Sandra S. Tangri and Sharon Rae Jenkins, "The University of Michigan Class of 1967: The Women's Life Paths Study." Pp. 259–281 in *Women's Lives through Time*, ed. Kathlees Day Hulbert and Diane Ticktor-Schuster. Copyright © 1993 Jossey-Bass, Inc. Reprinted by permission of Jossey-Bass, Inc., a subsidiary of John Wiley & Sons, Inc.

integrate our quantitative findings, and present narrative portraits of four women who represent four different life paths delineated in the study: continuous Role Innovation, continuous Traditionality, movement toward Role Innovation, and movement toward Traditionality. Finally, we discuss two emergent issues raised by a number of our women: women's exodus from teaching careers, and new complications in relationships among women.

The Historical Context

The years 1967 to 1981 saw dramatic shifts in demographic trends affecting women's life patterns. These trends include reduced and delayed childbearing, a rising divorce rate, increased single parenting by women, and increased women's labor-force participation (Gerson, Alpert, and Richardson, 1984). The "sex map of the occupational world" (Bird, 1968) started shifting, to a significant degree, toward gender desegregation in politics and in the professions.

In 1967, there was one woman in the U.S. Senate and there were eleven in the House of Representatives. By 1981, the numbers had risen to two and twenty, respectively. In 1967, only one of the mayors of major metropolises was a woman; in 1981, 8.4 percent of these mayors were women. The first women elected state governors in their own right (rather than as governors' widows) began to take office during the 1970s and the first woman was appointed to the U.S. Supreme Court in 1981. Thus, more women not only were working—and working more of their lives—but also were entering a greater variety of fields (specifically, fields that had long been the nearly exclusive provinces of men). National data show dramatic increases in the proportions of women going into the physical sciences, life sciences, and social sciences at the baccalaureate level (National Science Foundation, 1984) and into

dentistry, medicine, and law (National Center for Educational Statistics, 1980, 1987). These trends were not temporary: the percentage of women in these fields has continued to grow.

The University Context

The University of Michigan is a land-grant college conforming to the "multi-versity" concept of public higher education in the United States. Even in the early 1960s it was large (25,000 to 30,000 enrollment), recruiting students both nationally and internationally and boasting many renowned graduate programs and professional schools (still very sex-segregated), as well as a strongly research-oriented faculty. It was often referred to as the "Harvard of the Midwest."

While there, the class of 1967 witnessed teach-ins on the Vietnam war and the resurgence of political consciousness that swept American campuses during that time. Issues of population growth, environmental degradation, free speech, and self-determination for students were discussed in the student paper the *Michigan Daily*, the coffeehouses and the "quad." But there was not much evidence of change in the traditional expectations associated with sex roles. Fraternities and sororities were strong on campus. It was still men's prerogative to initiate dating. No women were visible in campus politics. In fact, Matina Horner's research (1972) on women's motives for avoiding success was conducted on this campus in the mid 1960s. There was a contradiction between the pressure for achievement in the sciences (for both sexes, a pressure induced by the Sputnik I launching in 1957) and the pressure for women to be "feminine" (that is, not competent in "male"—scientific—fields). Yet the campus activism of this time was one of the roots of the modern women's movement: after the Democratic convention of 1968, held a little over a year after this cohort graduated, activist women who had worked for civil rights and against the Vietnam war took up their own cause as their male counterparts continued to relegate them to coffee-making duty.

The Women's Life Paths Study

It was in this context that Theodore Newcomb and Gerald Gurin began the Michigan Student Study (Gurin, 1971), a broad study of young-adult development at the college, with a strong focus on the sources of student protest. It followed two cohorts of entering students through their four years at the university. The study provided a wealth of information about these students, including their responses in their senior year to a questionnaire item asking what occupations they intended to enter. This information provided the basis for stratification of our sample.

Students' responses to this question were coded for sex ratios in those occupations at the time. Of the 350 women from the class of 1967 who participated in the Michigan Student Study, 80 percent wanted to go into Traditional female occupations (those in which half or more of the workers were women), 10 percent wanted to go into Moderate occupations (in which 30 to 50 percent of the workers were women), and 10 percent wanted Role-Innovative occupations (in which fewer than 30 percent of the workers were women). For her doctoral dissertation on the determinants of Role-Innovative occupational choices, Tangri (1969, 1972) selected a stratified random sample of 200 women to begin the Role Innovators Study. Of these 200 women, one-third were classified as *Role Innovators*, one-third were *Moderates*, and one-third were *Traditionals*. (These included all of the Role Innovators, all of the Moderates, and a random sample of the Traditionals.)

Shortly before graduation, these women were asked in a group testing session to provide some additional information. Most important, they wrote brief stories in response to five written Thematic Apperception Test (TAT) cues (the same ones that Horner used), such as "Carol is looking into her microscope." The resulting stories were scored, by established methods, for fear of success (Horner, 1972) and need for achievement (Jenkins, 1987b). The request for a description of "the kind of person you want to marry" received open-ended descriptions which were scored for content-analytical measures of a woman's expectation that her husband's life or her own would involve effortful responses to challenges or would be more concerned with security. These measures were used to determine whether the women were interested in achievement for themselves or were displacing their achievement concerns onto their hypothetical future husbands. This study of women's occupational aspirations became the Women's Life Paths Study. Information about the women's backgrounds (parents' education; employment; attitudes; family relationships), occupational decision making, college experience (friends, faculty, classes, extracurricular activities), and plans for families, careers, and further education had been gathered in 1967 by the Michigan Student Study. Information about graduate education, jobs, and family formation was gathered in 1970, through a mailed questionnaire and interviews, from 152 of the original sample (Tangri, 1974). In 1981, through a mailed questionnaire returned by 117 of the same women (Tangri and Jenkins, 1986), we brought all the information about education, work, and family up-to-date. Some issues were revisited. Perceptions of parents were asked about in 1967 and 1970 (to explore issues of identification with parents). Strength of commitment to the labor force was asked about in 1967, 1970, and 1981. Story protocols scored for motivation were collected in 1967 and 1981. Anticipation and then experience of conflict between marriage or children and having a career was asked about in all three years (with the question "Do you feel any conflict between marriage and career?"), as were hopes and aspirations for the future. Career commitment in 1967 and 1970 was measured by combining responses to three questions about whether the respondent planned to work after getting married, whether she planned to work after having children, and when she would return to work after having children. Career outcomes in 1981 have been evaluated in a variety of ways—as role innovation (Tangri and Jenkins, 1986), as work involvement (Ruggiero and Weston, 1988), as labor-force participation (Jenkins, 1987a), as motive-congenial, motive-arousing, or not motive-relevant (Jenkins, 1987b), and in terms of specific careers (Jenkins, 1989). In this way, longitudinal research allows us to follow the development of women in different careers.

Family Background and Personality

The women in this sample were born around the end of World War II and represent the leading edge of the baby boom. Almost half were eldest or only children, and most of their parents probably experienced the Depression as teenagers and young adults; even parents from economically privileged families would have been aware of the stress on their communities and on the nation. The war years had brought the parents new stresses; many of them (and many of the sample's other relatives) probably served in the armed forces and supporting services. The sample's mothers and aunts had been swept into the labor force in the resulting economic and patriotic boom and provided new models of women employed in nontraditional roles. Even when they wished to continue working, many of

the same women then found themselves pushed out of the labor force by public pressure and propaganda when the servicemen returned. It was among them that Betty Friedan first diagnosed "the problem that has no name" (Friedan, 1963); it was about them that Marilyn French (1977) wrote *The Women's Room*.

Although the University of Michigan is a public institution, the sample was economically privileged. Most of the women's fathers and one-quarter of their mothers had completed college; another one-quarter of the mothers had at least some college education. One-third of the fathers and 10 percent of the mothers had advanced or professional degrees. About 40 percent of the mothers had been employed for more than five years since marriage. In 1967, 86 percent of the families had total annual incomes of more than $10,000, and about 40 percent made more than $20,000 per year (the median family income at the time was $7,933).

The Women as College Seniors

Compared to the Traditionals, the Role Innovators were reared with higher family incomes, better-educated parents, and mothers who were employed longer and in more role-innovative jobs (Tangri, 1969). The women whose mothers were employed longer rated their own future careers as more important when they were college seniors, and they planned more often to return to work after having had their own children, aspired to higher degrees, and were more willing to assert their career intentions with prospective husbands. Their taking these positions predicted greater labor-force participation on their part in the years 1967–1981 (Jenkins, 1987a).

Although cross-sex parental identification had been hypothesized to predict role innovation, the findings suggested a more complex picture. Role-innovative daughters did see themselves as more like their fathers than their mothers or like neither parent, but they described closer relationships with their mothers than with their fathers, despite their feeling that their mothers did not understand them and disagreed with them on their college goals. These findings suggest substantial independence from both parents, with the Role Innovator feeling warmly toward her mother, with whom she disagrees, and seeing herself as similar to her father (perhaps only because of a shared work orientation). Among the Role Innovators, however, those whose mothers had more education saw themselves as more like their mothers than their fathers, even though they still disagreed with their mothers on college goals and felt that their mothers did not understand them well. Role-innovative daughters of less educated parents showed more psychological distance from both parents but were not necessarily more conflicted. For most of these women, role-innovative aspirations would have represented upward socioeconomic mobility.

The characteristics that most strongly differentiated Role Innovators from Traditionals had to do with personality and motivation. The Role Innovators were more autonomous and individualistic and were motivated by the desire to do their very best in their future careers. They also expressed more doubts about their ability to succeed and about identity, findings that reflect the fact that the academic choices they made were more difficult and more socially ambiguous. Traditionals were more likely to displace their achievement concerns onto their hypothetical future husbands and were more likely to choose their occupations because they wanted to work with people, felt confident of their ability to do the work, and thought that these careers would not interfere with running a household but would promise a secure future.

Despite the relatively privileged nature of the sample, almost half the women worked for pay during college, often more than ten hours per week. The more hours they worked, the greater their labor-force participation in the fourteen years after graduation (Jenkins, 1987a).

Occupational choice was not easy for this cohort, which had grown up with the restless mothers described in Friedan's *The Feminine Mystique* (1963) and did not yet have the role models that emerged during the late 1970s and early 1980s. Two-thirds changed their prospective occupational choices during college, and half of these women reported having experienced a problem or crisis over occupational decisions. Many of these women (40 percent) were still very concerned as seniors with vocational decisions.

Concurrently at this university, Horner (1972) was developing her measure of the motive to avoid success, and this measure was included in the Role Innovators study. The amount of "fear of success" imagery seen in this study was comparable to that seen in Horner's own, but Role Innovators and Traditionals did not differ in their levels of "fear of success." Neither was there any behavioral evidence that Role Innovators were rejected by men: Role Innovators and Traditionals did not differ in the number of romantic relationships with men that they listed among their ten closest friendships, and the Role Innovators listed more nonromantic friendships with men, which may reflect their larger number of male classmates.

Because the Michigan Student Study included most members of the class of 1967 of both sexes, it was often possible to obtain the actual responses of our subjects' closest friends. For 114 of the women in our sample, at least one of the top three close friends listed had also provided data for the Michigan Student Study. Traditionals had more men friends who said they would disapprove of their wives' having careers, or who saw a wife's career either as meeting her obligation to use her education or as allowing her to avoid boredom or other negative consequences of not working. Role Innovators' men friends, by contrast, supported a wife's career because of the attractions or benefits it would have for her. A Role Innovator was also more likely to have a steady, serious relationship with a teaching fellow or a laboratory assistant in her own field.

The women friends of Role Innovators were not necessarily Role Innovators themselves, but they did give greater importance to having a career themselves after college than the women friends of Traditionals did. Role Innovators also gave greater importance than Traditionals did to the part played by college friends in choice of occupation. Overall, Tangri (1969) found surprisingly little support for the idea that college peers provided social support for the women's role innovation. The Role Innovators themselves felt that only their parents had influenced their occupational choices and had done so significantly more than university faculty members, advisers, counselors, or friends. Faculty members were important, however, in the selection of the first academic major and may have had an indirect effect on choice of occupation.

There is also substantial integrity within each group in how work and family priorities have been organized. Women who had role-innovative aspirations in 1967 also tended to want to marry later and have fewer and later children than the other women, and they usually did so. They also had stronger commitments to work and career advancement, and they reported more conflict over wanting both marriage and a career. The combination of stronger work commitment, greater anticipated conflict, and longer postponement of family formation constitutes a reasonably functional constellation of values.

Women who were Traditionals as seniors chose their careers sooner in their lives, for altruistic and affiliative reasons and for security, but they also found staying home once children were born more attractive. They expected to live both for and through others and to rely heavily on the stimulation provided by husbands' life challenges. Role Innovators, by contrast, planned to rely on their own efforts for their own satisfaction (Tangri, 1969).

The Women in their Middle Twenties

Between 1967 and 1970, most of these women shifted away from work, particularly from role-innovative work, as they started their families, pursued graduate training, or worked in traditional fields that they would later abandon. Nevertheless, their aspirations in 1970 predicted that there would be a shift back into the labor force. There was also a smaller number of women (about one-fifth of the sample) who moved in the opposite direction, doing more role-innovative work than they had aspired to as seniors.

The women's specific occupational choices were still changing three years after graduation. About one-third said that their aspirations had been vague in college, and a few more (40 percent) said that they had changed fields since graduating or planned to change fields soon. Half of the women said that they were doing what they had aspired to do as seniors. Some would change their minds in the next ten years, but most would not.

In 1970, half of the women in the sample were employed full-time. Slightly over one-fifth were full-time homemakers, one-sixth were full-time students, and fewer than one-tenth were employed part-time. Many were part-time students, either in degree programs or in advanced courses. Only one-quarter reported no further schooling by 1970; about one-third had at least some graduate school experience, and another third had taken at least some professional or business school courses. The full-time students, especially the doctoral students, were mostly Role Innovators. The Traditionals were mostly working full-time, but nearly one-third of the Traditionals had already earned master's degrees.

By 1970, 61 percent of the women in the sample were married, and 15 percent had children. Women who were Role Innovators in 1967 were less likely to have married by 1970, and married women tended to become more Traditional. In general, the two-thirds of the sample who had married seemed to have chosen husbands whose attitudes matched their own aspirations, with Role Innovators more likely to have supportive than unsupportive husbands and more willing to assert their career intentions with them in either case. The Role Innovators, who had agreed with the statement "I want and intend to have a career; my husband will have to take that for granted and adjust accordingly," subsequently experienced greater labor-force participation through 1981 (Jenkins, 1987a). Women with supportive husbands reported less conflict between marriage and a career. Women whose husbands disapproved of their having careers were more likely to reject career goals entirely, in favor of homemaking.

Women who became more Traditional between 1967 and 1970 were more likely to be married and especially to have children and were more likely to have had lower career commitment in 1967. They had been less interested in 1967 in "being famous" someday, had planned a later rather than a rapid return to work after having children, and had displaced their achievement interests onto their hypothetical future husbands, describing the men they wanted to marry as leading exciting, challenging lives. Their descriptions, in 1970, of their future plans indicated that many of these women

expected to return to role-innovative or moderate careers; others, traditionally employed, were considering more innovative career changes.

The Women in Their Middle Thirties

By 1981, the reversal anticipated in 1970 was nearly complete. Three-fourths of the women were employed (most of them full-time), and only one-fifth were neither employed nor looking for jobs. The number of Role Innovators had increased by 25 percent over 1967 (from 37 to 46), the number of Moderates had decreased 42 percent (from 38 to 22), and the number of Traditionals had increased by 17 percent (from 41 to 49). [See table on page 382.] Over half the sample's most recent jobs (whether or not the women were currently employed) were in role-innovative occupations.

Nevertheless, within these general trends there are significant continuities at the individual level. The majority of the sample (61 percent) was as role-innovative in 1981 as in 1967. Despite rather dramatic detours between 1967 and 1970, or between 1970 and 1981, the longer span shows greater continuity, particularly on the occupational dimension.

In education, these women far exceeded the goals they had stated as seniors in college, even though a few (10 percent) did not earn the degrees they had planned to earn. Only one-quarter of the women stopped with the bachelors degree, as they had planned to do, and three-fifths of the higher degrees were earned by women who had originally wanted less.

The women's marital experiences also departed from the expectations they had expressed as seniors, but less so than their educational, work, and childbearing experiences. All but one of these women had intended to get married, but only four-fifths had done so by 1981 (including eleven divorced women and two widowed women

OUTCOMES, 1970–1981

THE EXPECTATIONS AS SENIORS		WHAT THEY HAD DONE BY 1981	
Did not want to marry	<1%	Had not married	14%
Wanted to marry within 2 years	69%	Married within 2 years	67%
Wanted to marry in 3–10 years	30%	Married in 3–10 years	20%
		Got married when wanted	43%
Did not want children	12%	Had no children yet	28%
Wanted 2 children	24%	Had 2 children (including husband's)	38%
Wanted more than 2 children	62%	Had more than 2 children	17%
Number of children wanted	3.5	Number of children had	1.4
		Had as many children as wanted	14%
Wanted children within 4 years	44%	Had children within 4 years	33%
Wanted children after ≥ 4 years	43%	Had children after ≥ 4 years	38%
		Had children when wanted	33%
Planned to stop at B.A.	59%	Stopped at B.A.	33%
Planned to get master's degree	27%	Got master's degree	38%
Planned to get Ph.D. or professional degree	14%	Got Ph.D. or professional degree	28%
Wanted to have a career	46%	Spent no more than one year out of labor force	44%
Felt family-career conflict	25%	Felt family-career conflict	50%
Role Innovators	32%	*Role Innovators*	39%
Moderates	32%	*Moderates*	19%
Traditionals	36%	*Traditionals (including full-time homemakers)*	42%

who remarried). In 1981, at about age thirty-five, sixteen (14 percent) had never married, and seven were divorced without having remarried. At least two women (including one mother) were in lesbian relationships; since we did not ask directly about sexual orientation, this figure is probably an underestimate. Among those who were married, most (69 percent) had wanted in 1967 to marry within two years of graduation. About the same number did marry within two years of graduation (not necessarily the same women). In fact, fewer than half the sample (43 percent) had married within two years of when they had wanted to in 1967; about an equal number (one-fifth each) married either earlier or later.

The spouses and partners of the women in our sample were described in 1981 as strongly supportive of the women's careers. Three-quarters of the women reported that the spouse or partner would (or did) like the idea of their working; one-fifth said that it would be all right with him (or her). One-quarter of the women reported that their spouse or partner would approve of their working primarily because the work was attractive to them, and this was the most frequent response (28 percent). One-fifth said that the spouse or partner was most persuaded by financial considerations. At this time, according to what the women said, more spouses or partners would have seen it as the women's duty to hold a job (10 percent) than would have cited the women's duty to stay home (6 percent).

Asked to describe their husbands' or partners' feelings about their working, the women mentioned financial benefits most often (36 percent). Unqualified support was reported by 23 percent, and another 24 percent said that their husbands or partners would be proud of their achievements. Although only 8 percent reported that their husbands or partners were resistant to their working, 23 percent cited the importance of women's not failing in their traditional responsibilities for household management and child care. Overall, 45 percent of the women reported that their partners supported their working or helped them get what they wanted out of working; 20 percent said their partners resisted or indirectly hindered their working.

The disparity between desires (1967) and fulfillment (1981) in the number and timing of children was quite dramatic. In 1967, the women wanted an average of 3.5 children; in 1970, they wanted 2.5 children; in 1981, they had an average of 1.4 children. Four women's families included their partners' children from previous marriages. Obviously, few women (14 percent) had as many children as they originally had wished to have, and the vast majority (72 percent) had fewer. Only one-third had actually started families when they originally had wanted to; about one-fourth had not had any children by 1981.

Related to the decrease from desired to actual family size and to the increase in labor-force attachment was the increase in the number of women who felt that combining marriage and a career, or children and a career, created conflicts for them. The number reporting conflict rose, from one-fifth of the sample in 1967 to one-third in 1970 to one-half in 1981. Conflict increased the most for married women and for women with children. Women who became more Role-Innovative from 1967 to 1981 reported the least conflict (Tangri and Jenkins, 1987).

Asked to explain their feelings about marriage-career conflict, 18 percent reported that they already had both and were either managing or not feeling conflict. Another 18 percent said that they had chosen a family over a career, and 13 percent said that they had chosen a career over a family. Each of the following kinds of conflicts was described by 10 to 15 percent: conflicting time demands, conflicts between a couple's dual careers, and conflicts related to the demands of the husband's career on his wife, the husband's or partners support, and the husband's or partner's resistance.

Several women cited their own perfectionism, either at home or at work, as a source of conflict. Underlying a number of the women's responses to questions about conflict between a career and a family was a sense of the difficulty of reconciling high performance standards in both areas with the real limitations imposed by finite time and energy.

For some women, this difficulty was felt as an unresolvable conflict, in which the choice of work was seen as selfish and the choice to meet children's needs was expressed with great moral conviction: "When one creates a child, that child deserves love and attention. A career robs the child of much of that love and attention due to lack of time. . . . I feel my first responsibility is to my child, not work or study. Any work or study I do must be the least destructive to mothering."

Others were able to reconcile this opposition by seeing connections between these roles and their own well-being (including their capacity to perform in several roles concurrently) and benefits for the well-being of family members, including children.

A high school administrator married to a teacher for eleven years said that she experienced no marriage-career conflict: "It makes me a whole person and a good role model for my child." Being a mother, she said, was "even more work and more rewarding than I thought," and it changed her feelings about working: "I've got to compromise. Work is no longer my priority. I have to leave school at a decent time."

A college professor with two children, married to a lawyer for ten years, wrote, "A working mother is always in a dilemma: Are you doing enough as a mother and professional? . . . I am a perfectionist and very demanding and therefore experience a lot of guilt. However, the guilt has greatly reduced this year!" Asked how being a mother had changed her feelings about work, she said, "I appreciate my job even more—when there are pressures of mothering, the job is a release, and vice versa! It is also a juggling act, and my husband is a great help."

A part-time newspaper reporter with two children, married for thirteen years to a business executive, said, "The contrasts of raising and dealing with children and handling job challenges are mentally healthy for me. Each side gives me perspectives on the other."

Portraits of Continuity and Change

We would like now to flesh out this picture, already presented in numerical terms, with the self-descriptions offered by the women as they answered questions about various aspects of their lives. We offer four self-portraits, which we feel capture the dominant characteristics of the four groups of women in this study: those who were Role Innovators throughout, those who were Traditionals throughout, those who became more Role-Innovative over the course of the study, and those who became more Traditional. The names have been changed.

Ann, a Role Innovator Throughout

Ann worked without interruption over the course of the study, was married, and has one child. She changed careers three times, but all of them were Role Innovative. In her senior year, she wanted to be a college professor. In 1970, she was working full-time as a computer programmer, and then she advanced into systems design. In the early 1970s she changed again and became a lawyer. By 1981, she had advanced to senior attorney for a computer corporation. Looking back, she says that she changed careers because her skills are better suited to the corporate environment and because she wanted to reduce stress and her working hours. She feels that this has been a bit of a compromise, which she made "in order to fulfill my job as a mother and to enjoy my daughter." Her major satisfaction is that "people are appreciative of my performance, [and] the job makes good use of my training and abilities." Nevertheless, she would like more "challenge and responsibility" and expects soon to have "a somewhat more responsible job, which may involve longer hours and more stress." She has been helped in getting what she wants out of working by her "intelligence [and] willingness to work hard" and hindered by her "inability to be 'assertive' enough."

Her first marriage, of eleven years, ended in 1979, two years before the last follow-up. She has been involved with a computer scientist for the past three years, and they have a daughter. He is "a good father," but he and Ann are not getting along very well right now. The relationship is important to her because he's the "father of my daughter, he's caring, and he needs my help." His major activities are "computer science, sailing, cars, and life crises." She feels conflict between her relationship and her career: "Both require a great deal of energy and mine is often limited; my partner sometimes resents my career achievements." She says he is ambivalent about her working because he "likes the income and my independence; but sometimes he feels threatened or envious of my success. He likes me to handle the household and day care." She is not very satisfied with his participation in household chores.

Children and career do conflict, she says, because there is "only so much energy and time to devote to either, but, overall, having a career is necessary for me in many ways, even though I love my daughter more than anything." Mothering has changed her feelings about work: "I cannot become involved in a job with a great deal of travel, stress, or more than forty hours per week, and I do not want to." Looking back at her life so far, she says that she wishes she had "demanded more from those around me."

Barbara, a Traditional Throughout

Barbara has concentrated on her family but has also worked part-time fairly steadily. As a senior, she wanted to be a physical therapist, and she has continued taking courses in this and related areas since 1967. She says that having a career was important to her, but this career was a bit of a compromise. She would have preferred to study medicine or fine arts, but these fields conflicted with her family responsibilities, required too much additional schooling, or met with objections or discouragement from others.

Three years after graduating, she was working full-time in her field. In 1967, she had wanted and intended to have a career and expected her future husband to adjust. Looking back, in 1981, she said that her goals back then were "to gain a supervisory position as a physical therapist in a large hospital rehabilitation facility," but by 1981 she preferred "to work independently and perhaps to teach" because of "my own maturity, an increase in my own

self-confidence." She interrupted her career in 1972, when her first child was born, and returned to work part-time two years later.

In 1981, she found satisfaction in the chance to "observe patients' improvement with treatment" but was dissatisfied with her lack of control over her own patient load. She said that her most recent job had involved some compromise because of "my children's activities." She was hindered in getting what she wants out of working by "other involvements—children, and my current desire to work in various volunteer activities."

Barbara has been married for fourteen years to a businessman and has two children. Regarding marriage-career conflict, she said, "My husband generally supports my work. I feel a need to devote time to my children and husband at this time." Her husband likes the idea of her working because "he feels I am happier/more stimulated when I am working. We have enjoyed the extra money." She is fairly satisfied with others' participation in household chores; the division of labor in the home is fairly sex-stereotypical (she does most of the child care, and her husband takes care of most of the repairs).

Mothering has changed her feelings about working: "I feel it is difficult to divide time between the two. My work or my children suffer depending on which I emphasize most—when [I was] working 45 hours a week, children had less attention. Now work is not as good because children are my priority." Children and career conflict: "I feel to be really good in a career, one must devote full time to it."

In retrospect, she "would prefer to have attained an advanced degree immediately following my B.S.—perhaps to have gone to medical school." Looking ahead, she says: "I would like my husband to attain the degree of success to which he aspires. I plan to devote much of the next several years to raising my children—and being active in my community. Once the children are older, I wish to pursue my career."

Carol, Who Became More Traditional

Carol has focused on her family to the exclusion of work. As a senior and a Moderate in 1967, she wanted to be a high school history teacher. She expected to stop with the B.A. degree but said that a career was important to her and stated both career and family goals as part of her future life. In 1970, she was teaching full-time. She wanted to have a career and expected her husband to adjust. Nevertheless, she left the labor force in that year to have the first of her three children. In 1981, she said that she would not return to teaching but said, "I haven't the slightest idea what I want to do yet."

She has been married for thirteen years to a doctor who has a major administrative position in his hospital and who "feels that anything that would make me happy is OK with him as long as it doesn't interfere with my managing the house." Their relationship is important: "He's very independent in his work and very successful, he's very gifted, but I realize that he counts on me as his best friend." She is not very satisfied with his participation in household chores; she does most or all of everything: "My husband never offers any assistance with anything."

Regarding child-career conflict, she says, "I have very strong feelings that a person should do what she feels is most acceptable. I could not personally work and raise young people successfully; I'd have too many guilt feelings." Mothering changed her feelings about a career: "Children need a lot more discipline, love, and care than I realized before I had them," she says. "Financially, I don't have to work. Because my husband depends on me to run the household and care for the children, which

I find to be very time consuming, I'm in no hurry to find a job."

In retrospect, she says, "I would have demanded more participation by my husband very early in our marriage. We have been married too many years for him to change and he won't—if I had realized this early enough, our marriage might be very different."

Dorothy, Who Became More Role-Innovative

Dorothy has focused on work to the exclusion of marriage and children. In 1967, she planned to be a psychologist (a Moderate occupation then), although she planned to get only a B.A. She saw her career as important and described both a family and a career as part of her future life. In 1970, she was working full-time as an interviewer and computer programmer and "still looking for a good teaching position" while taking courses in premedical sciences. She then went to dental school full-time. This was very much a compromise: she would have preferred to become a physician but was not accepted into medical school because she was "not a 'traditional' student." She gave several reasons for going to dental school: "1. A few positive contacts with professional women. 2. Coming to view myself as responsible for my own life. 3. The view that my ability to influence community changes will increase with my increasing credentials and expertise." In 1981, she was starting a private dental practice after a five-year stint in a clinic. She said that she had changed her occupational goals for the following reason: "I grew up and realized that traditional female vocations weren't especially satisfying, rewarding, or offering potential for my future satisfaction." What helped her get what she wanted from working was, in her words, "my own perseverance in developing the job and the working relationships necessary to function."

Shortly after finishing dental school, Dorothy married a government administrator. "I love my husband and he is very supportive and tolerant of me, my moods and needs," she says. The relationship is important because of "the intimacy, trust, sexuality, and closeness." She says he likes the idea of her working: "He feels that everyone should have meaningful work. I am more interesting to him as a 'worker.'" Nevertheless, she reports feeling conflict between marriage and a career. "There are times when time demands of my career interfere with my relationship with my husband. Sheer fatigue is often a problem." She rates herself as not very satisfied with their sex-stereotypical division of household labor: "Although my husband will help with domestic tasks if I ask him, he will rarely initiate an activity or offer to assist me when I'm cleaning, cooking, or doing laundry." She is undecided about having children: "The responsibilities of childrearing would be nearly totally mine, and would take time and energy from my career."

In retrospect, she says, "I would have pursued a graduate degree right after my B.A. I would have had children before getting so involved in my career. I would have pursued a more general degree, not the highly technologically oriented one I have received." Regarding her future life, she says, "I would like to become more involved in community affairs and in politics; to raise children, either natural or adopted, and to have an economically self-sufficient practice."

Creating and Responding to Social Change

We asked the women in our sample to respond to a variety of open-ended questions, and their sometimes long and impassioned answers brought to light several issues that represent points of friction between larger cultural trends and women's individual lives. Most notable among these issues are the women's exodus from elementary and secondary school teaching and evidence of both support and strain in relations among women at both the ideological and the personal level.

Exodus from Teaching

Elementary and secondary school teaching were the most frequently chosen occupations among these women in 1967, preferred by 28 percent of the sample. (College teaching was also a common choice, at 19 percent.) As seniors, these women struggled less than their classmates did with vocational decisions, having made an early decision to teach. They were more likely to give "working with people" and/or "helping others" or "helping society" as reasons for their career choices. They did not differ from women who chose other careers in the priority that they gave to having a family relative to having a career (Jenkins, 1989). In retrospect, however, several women cited parental pressure to go into teaching. A former elementary school teacher, now at home rearing three children, said that in 1967 teaching "was a good job for a woman—good pay, good hours." Looking back, teaching seems to her to have been a compromise, made because of "pressure from parents—what a good job for a woman was—a secure job" and her own "need for a job that allowed for marriage and a family." In 1981, she preferred business, marketing, law, or banking.

By 1981, large numbers of these women had migrated to more role-innovative occupations: into college-level teaching or teaching in less traditional contexts, or out of teaching altogether and into business and the traditionally male-dominated professions. This migration was inspired both by the desire for broader, better-rewarded, and more challenging opportunities and by specific dissatisfaction with teaching.

One group of former teachers seemed motivated by specific intrinsic achievement concerns. A lesbian former high school teacher began graduate school for a master's degree: "Once I was there, I liked it and realized that I could do better than be a high school teacher. . . . I realized that I had set my sights too low, and there were more interesting and challenging jobs that I could get with an advanced degree. I had formerly thought I could only ever be a teacher or a nurse." Another woman got her M.B.A. and became a cost analyst and investment tracker after eleven years as an elementary school teacher: "Mental boredom and lack of career opportunities (salary, challenge, responsibilities, and promotion) were crucial elements which started my exploration of other careers—plus the school system has a terrible track record of promoting women." In retrospect, she wishes that she had "quit teaching sooner—at age twenty-five." This group exemplifies the women who entered noncollege teaching with a high need for achievement, experienced further achievement-motivation arousal by the task characteristics of the teaching situation, and then changed to careers with social structures that provided opportunities for achievement and thus offered more frequent and intense achievement rewards (Jenkins, 1987b, 1989).

College teaching also seems to have served an important transitional role for many women. One-fifth of the sample expected to teach in college in 1967; in 1981, 14 percent were college faculty members, but only three of these were the same women. College teaching may serve as a stepping-stone occupation that combines a sex-stereotypical task role with higher status and greater financial and intellectual rewards than are available in noncollege teaching. The training, visibility, and professional contacts available in college teaching may enable women to pursue better-paying jobs in the private sector (Jenkins, 1989).

Strains among Women

Although the women in our sample were generally appreciative of the positive effects of the women's movement, some also expressed feelings of strain regarding their place in our changing social world. In their spontaneous comments at the end of the questionnaire, many cited the importance of feminism as a positive force in their personal and/or career lives. Ann, the physical therapist, said, "I feel that the women's movement was significant in raising my own self-esteem and in improving/raising my own feeling about women."

Some full-time homemakers seemed to feel compelled to defend the legitimacy of their choices and the importance to the world of rearing their children well. They cited pressure to have a career and devaluation of the social contribution of mothering, pressure that they attributed to other women. A Moderate with two children, now working as a part-time newspaper reporter and doing volunteer work and community service, expressed annoyance:

> I have felt susceptible to current pressures, from women's groups especially, about working women. I have felt the pressure as "unless I have a paying job, I'm not very valuable to society, or not too exciting." Now that I have a respectable part-time job, I can more clearly see how futile it is to make personal decisions based on cultural trends. I feel angry at messages that I pick up, such as "Women who are worth anything have a career plan." I would joyfully welcome messages promoting thoughtful mothering. For me, though, my job has truly added excitement and satisfaction to my life. I also care about my mothering role.

A former high school teacher, who in 1981 was rearing her three children while working part-time as a bookkeeper for her dentist husband and as a property manager, commented as follows:

> So many girls are postponing marriage and children for a career. Those who choose a

career over a family are missing out on what life is all about—sharing yourself intimately with others—putting their needs over your own. I am not a martyr, and often reach my limit—but I really feel so fortunate to be a wife and mother. Sounds corny? Of course, the ideal would be to have so much energy, you could do both simultaneously—and my hat goes off to those women!

In the remarks of a former teacher, now a homemaker of nine years for her two children, we hear a muted dysphoria: "For women of my age, it is so important to come in contact with women who have broken away—who are not sitting in their suburban homes all day, arranging junior League meetings!" Other women expressed feelings of inadequacy and self-doubt, as well as tentative hope for a "legitimizing" career in the future. Carol, the former high school teacher who became more of a Traditional and had been home rearing her three children since before 1970, noted that the questionnaire "made me reflect on the past ten years of my life, which were totally committed to raising our family. It made me feel inadequate. I really haven't done much for myself—I mostly live for others—however, I'm happy. Maybe when you question me again in ten years, I'll be able to feel as though I've done more for myself." A full-time mother of two, who had taught as a substitute until 1974, offered the following comment:

I feel like a throwback to the "housewife" of the 1950s. In my day-to-day life, however, I really don't think I am. I do still use my brain, my creativity, and my independence, but most of my "duties" are traditional. I strongly support the [proposed] ERA [Equal Rights Amendment] and feel women should have freedom of choice. I have deliberately chosen my present role and am sometimes uncomfortable with myself for half-believing outside influences who demean my role.

Both overtly and covertly, these responses give the impression that Traditional women felt attacked and devalued for their choices, even when they felt sure of their adequacy and legitimacy.

At the same time, Role Innovators also expressed dissatisfaction with how they are treated, especially by other women. A medical research scientist with three children described her problem:

One of the hardest things for me is to find and keep female friends. We have moved quite often, due to my husband's internship, residency, and being drafted. But in addition to this, there are rarely any wives in my neighborhood or place of work who are married with children and who have a "serious" professional career. I have always joined neighborhood book clubs and craft groups whenever we move anywhere new. I am always well accepted until they find out I have a Ph.D. Then they treat me differently and have trouble relating to me. Some act as if they couldn't possibly carry on a conversation with me when they ask me what I do at work. They can't seem to understand that I am human, too, and that I am raising children like them, that I cook dinner, pay bills, shovel snow like them! Sometimes I don't tell anyone I have an advanced degree because I can't stand the isolation. Sometimes I am very lonely.

We should note that painful perceptions of other women are shaped by both temporal and societal contexts. Temporally, almost all the women in each group (that is, employed women and women working at home) will at some time experience the circumstance of the other. Those working at home generally have been and will again be in the labor force. Those now employed outside the home often have been and may again be spending time at home with small children, or for other reasons. Perspectives on each life-style are shaped by current but temporary circumstances. These are not two permanent camps of different individuals.

Societal failure to provide care for children whose parents work outside the home sets up a situation in which parents who are at home can get sucked into the resulting vacuum (Silverstein, 1991). This contributes to feelings of inequity in those who offer to help out.

Several women made insightful comments such as this one, on historical and intergenerational change:

> We have been the generation, I believe, that was most influenced by the early women's movement. All intelligent women, whether they work inside or outside the home, have in some way been touched. I have a strong sense of being a straddler of two eras in women's roles—of wanting both home and family, but being nagged somewhat by a sense of not fulfilling my talents because I'm not working. A woman once described my feelings/dilemma: our generation feels the need to be the mother of five, maintain a perfect house, and play first string with the Boston Symphony. My hope for my daughters is that whatever choice they make in life, they will not have any doubts about the wisdom of their choice for them. And for me—that I will someday come to peaceful terms with the choices I have made.

Despite these tensions, there was also optimism:

> I seem to realize now—at the age of 36!—how very strong *women* can be. I feel as if I am in the "spring" of my life with many new paths and opportunities ahead of me. As if I have reached the mountain meadows after a long and difficult hike. I want to develop a career and also keep my family unit intact. I feel a great deal of responsibility in this. I love my husband and children dearly—but with insight also! I very much need a mentor in my task of developing a career—and I hope that I find one. Every generation of women seems to have a different task or challenge. My paths are different from those of my mother—but my daughter's will definitely be different from mine. I think

research needs to be done in the area of parental expectations, and college mentors. I feel that U Mich lacked in this area and I'm going to think long and hard about campus selection for my daughter. Right now I can definitely see the advantage to a women's campus.

Conclusions: The Paths They Walked

In a poetry reading by Ray Gwyn Smith, which one of the authors attended during initial analyses of these data, the following lines stood out: "It didn't matter which path she walked./What mattered was the sense she made of it." Among our findings from the first wave of data in the Women's Life Paths Study were several items that laid to rest myths about career-oriented women, misconceptions that may sound quaint today but were common at the time (Helson, 1972). In college, the career-oriented Role Innovators did not identify with their fathers in preference to their mothers; rather, they took their more educated working mothers as role models. Although they saw themselves as less extremely feminine and conventional and more intellectual, self-reliant, and depended on by others, they did not reject the core female roles of wife and mother. They were not wallflowers; they had as many romantic and casual relationships with men as their Traditional peers did. Their commitment to their future careers even while they were in college, and especially the importance they gave to advancement opportunities, were greater than among women going into female-dominated professions, so that their decisions to continue working cannot be viewed as having been made by default when other alternatives failed. In fact, choosing supportive boyfriends (and eventually husbands) seemed to play some role in helping them pursue their career goals, despite feelings of conflict.

Our longitudinal approach enabled us to compare these women's plans in college to their adult life paths and to ask questions about continuity and change. In 1981, the majority of the women in the sample (61 percent) were classified as Role Innovators or Traditionals, as they had been in 1967. Despite rather dramatic detours in the intervening years, due mostly to early family formation, the longer time span shows great continuity, particularly on the occupational dimension.

The original Role Innovators, true to the values they expressed as seniors in college, were more likely to be working full-time, had taken less time out from the labor force, and were overwhelmingly (81 percent) working in role-innovative occupations. Early graduate training helped them consolidate their career plans and persist in setting and pursuing their goals. For some women, it involved a new appreciation of their abilities and an increase in educational aspirations. These women most often resolved marriage-career conflicts by remaining single, postponing childbearing, having fewer children than the other women, and choosing spouses who supported their career aspirations. The 1981 Role Innovators who had not begun with role-innovative aspirations in 1967 came to share most of these characteristics (except for having remained single).

Many Traditional seniors were employed full-time in their chosen fields after college, delaying their family formation somewhat and reducing their expected family size. Although some of them returned to work in these fields after having children, others, especially among noncollege teachers, moved into role-innovative careers that sometimes required their returning to school as reentry students. This phase often intensified feelings of marriage-career conflict; for those with nonsupportive husbands, divorce sometimes resulted.

Early full-time homemaking was most common for women who as seniors had wanted to marry and have children early.

These women resolved their marriage-career conflicts by forgoing careers. They were more likely to choose husbands who preferred homemaking wives and to take vicarious pleasure in their husbands' achievements in lieu of pursuing careers of their own. Even so, many of them returned to the labor force and/or to higher education earlier than they had expected to as college seniors, and some of these moves were in role-innovative career directions. Such moves were often accompanied by increased feelings of marriage-career conflict.

In this study, the general trends over time regarding occupational attainment, marriage and childbearing patterns, and conflicts experienced over combining marriage and a family reflect and contribute to the larger social changes of which this cohort is a part. More women in our study were employed in 1981 than expected to be in 1967; fewer were married, and they had fewer children. They attended graduate school, attained advanced degrees, and worked in role-innovative occupations beyond their 1967 aspirations as a group. They are also experiencing more conflict between marriage (or childrearing) and a career than they thought they would.

A far cry from the women whom Freud saw as having finished their lives and development by middle age, these women in their middle thirties—Traditionals, Moderates, and Role Innovators—are clearly engaged in an active, conscious struggle to define themselves and design their own choices, mindful of the social changes they are creating. From a woman who had to begin again after her first marriage ended comes an eloquent testimony to the pain and joy of living in "interesting times":

> My coevals have had the best and worst of the decade. In 1967 we reasonably expected marriage, motherhood, and successful husbands by whom we could be defined; albeit with plans to go back to

school ourselves or to work "someday." Losing that expectation is awfully harsh when mixed up with the liberation of and changing career/life goals of women just a few years younger, who always expected to have careers as well as what we expected. I'm a survivor, proud of it, and no doubt not the only woman my age who's had to shift gears. We're the ones, I think, who really do have it all!

ACKNOWLEDGMENTS

We want to thank Jo Ruggiero and Jan Hitchcock for their collaborative work on the 1981 data collection and Karen Chandler and Kathy MacDonald for extensive coding of open-ended data. This research has been supported by National Institute of Mental Health (NIMH) grant no. 5-F1-MH-30,493-03, U.S. Department of Labor grant no. 91-34-71-02, funds from the Urban Institute to Sandra S. Tangri, grants from the Henry A. Murray Research Center of Radcliffe College to Jo Ruggiero and Sharon Rae Jenkins, funds from Providence College to Jo Ruggiero, funds from the University of California at Santa Cruz to Sharon Rae Jenkins, funds from Harvard University to Jan Hitchcock, and by funds from the Mobil Foundation granted to Radcliffe College and awarded to Sharon Rae Jenkins. The 1967 and 1970 data sets are archived at the Henry A. Murray Research Center, Radcliffe College, and are available for secondary analysis by qualified researchers.

REFERENCES

Bird, C. *Born Female*. New York: McKay, 1968.

French, M. *The Women's Room*. New York: Summit Books, 1977.

Friedan, B. (1963). *The Feminine Mystique*. New York: Norton, 1963.

Gerson, M., Alpert, J. L., and Richardson, M. "Mothering: The View from Psychological Research." *Signs*, 1984, *4*(3), 434–453.

Gurin, G. *A Study of Students in a Multiversity*. Final report, contract no. OE-6-10-034. Ann Arbor: Office of Education, University of Michigan, 1971.

Helson, R. "The Changing Image of the Career Woman." *Journal of Social Issues*, 1972, *28*(2), 33–46.

Horner, M. "Toward an Understanding of Achievement-Related Conflicts in Women." *Journal of Social Issues*, 1972, *28*(2), 157–175.

Jenkins, S. R. "A Life Course Approach to Woman's Career Involvement." Paper presented at the 95th annual convention of the American Psychological Association, New York, 1987a.

Jenkins, S. R. "Need for Achievement and Women's Careers over 14 Years: Evidence for Occupational Structure Effects." *Journal of Personality and Social Psychology*, 1987b, *53*, 922–932.

Jenkins, S. R. "Longitudinal Prediction of Women's Careers: Psychological, Behavioral, and Social-Structural Influences." *Journal of Vocational Behavior*, 1989, *34*, 204–235.

National Center for Educational Statistics. *Fall Enrollment in Colleges and Universities*. Washington, D.C.: Government Printing Office, 1980, 1987.

National Science Foundation. *Women and Minorities in Science and Engineering*. Washington, D.C. Government Printing Office, 1984.

Ruggiero, J. A., and Weston, L. C. "Work Involvement Among College-Educated Women: A Methodological Extension." *Sex Roles*, 1988, *19*, 491–507.

Silverstein, L. B. "Transforming the Debate About Child Care and Maternal Employment." *American Psychologist*, 1991, *46*(10), 1025–1031.

Tangri, S. S. "Role-Innovation in Occupational Choice Among College Women." Unpublished doctoral dissertation, University of Michigan, 1969.

Tangri, S. S. "Determinants of Occupational Role-Innovation Among College Women." *Journal of Social Issues*, 1972, *28*(2), 177–200.

Tangri, S. S. *Effects of Background, Personality, College, and Post-college Experiences on Women's Post-graduate Employment*. Final report, contract no. 91-34-71-02. Ann Arbor: University of Michigan, 1974.

Tangri, S. S., and Jenkins, S. R. "Stability and Change in Role Innovation and Life Plans." *Sex Roles*, 1986, *13*(11/12), 647–662.

Tangri, S. S., and Jenkins, S. R. "Marriage-Career Conflict: Expecting It, Using It, Minimizing It." Paper presented at the 95th annual convention of the American Psychological Association, New York, 1987.

OTHER STUDY REFERENCES

Hitchcock, J. L. "Emotional Adaptation to Life Changes in a Post-World War II Cohort of College-Educated Women." Unpublished doctoral dissertation, Harvard University, 1984.

Jenkins, S. R. "Person-Situation Interaction and Woman's Achievement-Related Motives." Unpublished doctoral dissertation, Boston University, 1982.

KEY TERMS

dysphoria   A general negative feeling (in contrast to euphoria).

coevals   Persons of the same age; agemates. (The word has nothing to do with "evil.")

DISCUSSION QUESTIONS

1. One of the most common issues discussed in Tangri and Jenkins's article is the conflict between family and career. By 1981 half the women interviewed felt such a conflict, though only half that many had expected to feel it when they were interviewed as college seniors. What, specifically, are the components of a family-career conflict? Why do you think that only half the women interviewed experienced such conflicts? Do you think that as time goes on more or fewer women will experience such conflicts? Why? Few studies like this one include both men and women, and few researchers are likely to ask men if they expect to experience conflicts between family and their careers. Why?

2. One of the most interesting phenomena noted by Tangri and Jenkins is the movement of women out of the Moderate category into the Innovator category (which increased from 32 percent to 39 percent) and the Traditional category (which increased from 36 percent to 42 percent). Why did this happen? The answer to this question requires two separate lines of analysis, since the two moves were caused by quite different phenomena. Do you think that the same kinds of moves continue to go on today, roughly twenty years after the last interviews reported in this article? Why or why not?

3. The terms *feminism, feminist,* and *feminine* all occur in this article. How do the authors use the terms? Do you think these three terms are generally used in the same way in which the authors use them? What definitions would you provide for these three terms? How do you think most Americans of your generation (whatever that is) react to the three terms? What is your reaction to them? Do you think a man can be a feminist? Why or why not? Can a feminine woman be a feminist? Why or why not? Are you a feminist? Why or why not?

4. The women interviewed for the Michigan Study were very conscious of the effect of the Women's Movement on their lives. The editors of this collection have generally found

that their students are much less aware of changes in American life as a result of this Movement. This is not surprising, since the earliest changes were probably the most dramatic, and they occurred quite a while ago. Still, it is important to consider specifically how life in the United States has changed since the late sixties. What cultural changes can you point to in the realm of gender roles, relations, activities, and values that are specifically the result of the Women's Movement? How might your life be different if the Movement had not occurred? Do you see aspects of American life having to do with gender in the twenty-first century that you think still need to be changed? What are they? Do you see any gender changes that have had a negative effect on the quality of life in this country?

GAINING A FOOTHOLD
WOMEN'S TRANSITIONS THROUGH WORK AND COLLEGE

AMERICAN ASSOCIATION OF UNIVERSITY WOMEN

This excerpt from a report commissioned by the American Association of University Women presents information on three pathways followed by both men and women after high school. The questions addressed by the report fall into two sets of contrasts:

1. *How do the circumstances, goals, and views of individuals vary according to whether they have gone straight from high school to college, from high school to full-time work, or from work to college?*
2. *How do the circumstances, goals, and views of individuals in these three lifepaths vary by ethnicity and gender?*

These contrasts impose organization on questions such as the following: Why do individuals make the choices they do as to whether to pursue higher education directly after high school or at a later time—or not to pursue it at all? Do men and women make these decisions for the same reasons or different ones, and how do they vary across ethnic lines? To what extent does a man's or woman's marital status or the presence of children condition educational or occupational choice?

For most Americans, the image of a college or university is of a huge collection of buildings surrounded by lawns and playing fields, while the image of a college student is of a young person between eighteen and twenty-two. As the introduction to this report points out, however, a university is increasingly a systematically organized collection of information and interactions transmitted electronically, and a student is increasingly likely to be nontraditional. These nontraditional students are usually well over twenty-two; they often work full time; and they may have families to support. And these older students are frequently nontraditional in other ways as well. Their educational progress may follow a more circuitous route than that of younger students, a trait particularly characteristic of women students. Also, contrary to the expectations of educational policymakers, their approach to education may be less instrumental (or "practical") than that of traditional students, something that is also more pronounced among women than among men. Finally, there is the issue of family demands, which fall disproportionately to women and thus have a greater impact upon their life paths, whether academic or not, than they do upon those of men.

This excerpt presents an account of the data collected for the AAUW through "focus groups" (directed small group discussions) and telephone interviews. The information is organized in a readable narrative that packs a lot of information into a clear and well-organized summary. Despite the excellent organization, however, the piece contains so much information that the reader must work hard to keep track of all the findings discussed, and to keep in mind the profile of each group described. Along with keeping track of which group does what, consider why the various groups might make the choices they do.

The Research Context

If experts are correct, higher education institutions—and their students—may look radically different in the 21st century. Consider the following:

- At his inauguration as The Johns Hopkins University president, William Brody predicted that "we will witness the transformation of the university from a physical campus, or specific geographic location, to a dispersed, virtual campus." He urged that "we must view the educational process not as a finite encounter lasting a few semesters, but as a lifelong continuum." A U.S. Department of Education report concurs with some of Brody's vision. It speculates that postsecondary education will increasingly be delivered in "module" form—distributed throughout a person's life—rather than in the discrete package of a four-year bachelor's degree.

- Chancellor Donald Langenberg of the University of Maryland also imagines

"virtual universities," where learning will occur "wherever students can connect to the World Wide Web. Students will be able to move easily among educational institutions," he speculates, "perhaps enrolling at several real and/or virtual universities, or perhaps studying one subject at the high school level and other subjects with college professors." A universal "college-credit banking system" will have to evolve." Students will "demonstrate their mastery of certain skills at different points in their lives and will receive certificates of achievement" that will contribute to a performance portfolio.

- A former University of Michigan president imagines 21st-century higher education as a "knowledge industry" characterized by a "shift in focus from faculty members and their specialties to the needs of all kinds of students at various points in their lives."

- Finally, even high school graduates sense shifts on the higher education landscape. Research based on a series of national forums with honors students

Source: From pp. 3–18 in "Gaining a Foothold: Women's Transitions through Work and College." Washington, D.C.: AAUW, 1999. Reprinted by permission of the American Association of University Women (AAUW).

reveals a broad belief that higher education "does not necessarily mean a four-year college or university education." Students agree that they can "profit from many kinds of higher education institutions," including technical colleges, and that college education, in any case, should be "for a lifetime."[1]

These visions of higher education in the next century share a conviction that both education and the definition of the "student" are becoming more fluid and flexible. People are making educational decisions throughout their lives, rather than limiting their choice to whether or not to go to a four-year college immediately after high school.

Second, they recognize that higher education's infrastructure is changing and may need to change further to accommodate more diverse students, not only by race and ethnicity, but by age and learning needs. Students over age 40 represent the fastest-growing age group in postsecondary education, yet only 27 percent of students in this group receive financial aid for returning to school. Older students are more likely to work full-time, study part-time, and have family commitments. Higher education institutions often do not match the needs of this growing population of students, who are eager to go back to school and to combine work with formal education. Even among young students, there has been "a substantial increase" in the numbers who combine work and education, according to The National Center for Postsecondary Improvement. Between 1984 and 1994, the proportion of students engaging simultaneously in college and work increased by nearly eight percent.[2] Additionally, more students who move directly from high school to college are taking longer than the traditional four years to complete their bachelor's degrees.

Visions of the 21st-century university also recognize that economic and technological changes invite, and perhaps demand, more interaction among education, school, and work. The popular idea of "lifelong learning," with people developing their knowledge, skills, and interests throughout their lives, is in part driven by economic and technological changes that require the frequent updating of skills. Additionally, the workplace has changed from offering cradle-to-grave job security to a more fluid (or volatile) economy characterized by downsizing, outsourcing, "task employment," temporary work, self-employment, and rapid technological change. This new context of work will probably stimulate more interaction between educational and occupational worlds in the future. "School to Work" programs in the 1990s, for example, which combine high school coursework with internships and apprenticeships, have already intermeshed the classroom and work settings as dual sites for teaming. In this new economy, women can realistically expect to make more transitions—by choice or necessity—between their career or job and their education.

Women, specifically, may also find that their need for education changes as their lives take different turns—from a welfare mother struggling to get off public assistance to a mid-level manager attempting to break through the glass ceiling; from a woman graduating from college and beginning her career to one returning to school in order to reenter the job market after raising children. If women are to be equipped to face these changes, we need to know more about how, when, and why education affects these transitions, the barriers women face, and the effects of education on their careers and lives.

Goals of the Report

In light of these changes in higher education and the economy, this research explores how and why women make educational transitions. It focuses on the factors that influence women as they move from high school to work, from high school to college, and from the workforce back to school.

The AAUW Educational Foundation's overall goals in this research are to:

- Explore the institutional factors that affect women's decisions at different transition points
- Compare men's and women's experiences of transitions
- Understand the complex interaction of personal, social, cultural, economic, and institutional variables that influence how, when, and why educational transitions occur
- Understand how women make decisions about schooling and education
- Clarify how institutions create obstacles or opportunities for women making educational transitions

Study Methodology

Qualitative Phase

Lake Snell Perry and Associates conducted focus groups in September and October 1998. Areas of inquiry included challenges, opportunities, motivations, expectations, and goals for the future; decision-making processes; institutional obstacles, barriers, or incentives to pursue postsecondary education; sources of information; views on two-year versus four-year schools; and a retrospective examination of participants' own educational and career choices.

This research phase consisted of 10 focus groups: in Atlanta, one group of white boys ages 16–19 and one racially mixed group of women, ages 20–30, both groups transitioning from school to work; in Los Angeles, one group of young Latinas, ages 16–19, and one group of minority women, both groups with experience at a two-year institution or community college; in Altoona (PA), one group of white women with educational experiences similar to their counterparts in Los

Angeles, and one group of lower-income white women who went to work before continuing their education; in Baltimore, one group of white girls, ages 16–19, and one group of African American girls in the same age group; and, finally, in Chicago, one group of African American women who worked before returning to school, and one group of upper-income white women who followed a similar pattern.

Because of the limited number of respondents and the restrictions of recruiting, this research phase must be considered in a qualitative frame of reference. This phase of the study cannot be considered reliable or valid in the statistical sense. It is intended to provide insight, knowledge, and opinions about issues and concerns to help enrich and shape the quantitative phase of the research, which does provide statistically valid information.

Quantitative Phase

In December 1998 and January 1999, DYG, Inc., conducted a national telephone survey of 1,070 respondents undergoing one of the following three transitions: high school to college, high school to full-time work, and work back to postsecondary education.[3] Each transition was defined as follows:

- Transition Group #1: High School to College. These respondents, identified as "School to College" in this report, met the following criteria:
- Graduated from high school in the past three years
- Went directly to an accredited higher education program (a two-year or four-year college, full- or part-time)
- Did not work full-time before college (summer jobs the exception); do not work full-time while in college

DYG, Inc., conducted 317 interviews with this group (212 women, 105 men).

- Transition Group #2: Work to College. These respondents, identified as "Work to College," met the following criteria:
- Worked Full-time for at least a year after high school and before attending college or graduate school
- Currently enrolled full-time in a post-secondary degree program (a two-year, four-year, or a graduate/professional program)
- Can still be working part-time or full-time while in school

DYG, Inc., conducted 453 interviews with this group (345 women, 108 men).

- Transition Group #3: High School to Work. These respondents, identified as "School to Work," met the following criteria:
- Graduated from high school in the past several years
- Did not go on to college
- Work at least 20 hours per week

DYG, Inc., conducted 300 interviews with this group (200 women, 100 men).[4]

All statistically significant differences cited in the report are reliable with a 5 percent margin of error.

· · ·

Executive Summary: Key Findings and Conclusions

AAUW Educational Foundation commissioned *Gaining a Foothold: Women's Transitions Through Work and College* to learn more about the differences and similarities among distinct groups of students making education-related transitions. As a Foundation that produces research on the themes of gender, equity, and education, we had a particular interest in understanding how men and women navigate educational transitions.

One crucial, overall finding of *Gaining a Foothold* is that "students" are a far more

heterogeneous population than that of 18-year-olds who pack their bags and leave for college immediately after high school graduation. While others have spoken of the "track" or pipeline from high school to college, this report uses the metaphor of a "spiral" to denote, among other things, the continuing role of education over a woman's lifetime as she moves in and out of postsecondary education. Many students—by choice or necessity—follow a circuitous path through postsecondary education rather than a straight line from high school, to college, to graduate or professional school, to career. The diversity of the student population by age, race, ethnicity, socioeconomic status, academic preparedness, and educational interests and needs will become only more pronounced as the next century progresses.

In light of these changes, institutions, educators, researchers, policymakers, counselors, K-12 teachers, and individuals can benefit from rethinking crucial educational concepts such as access, social equity, and institutional services and design.

This research describes three groups of students and prospective students—those moving from high school to full-time work ("School to Work"), those moving from high school to college ("School to College"), and those moving from full-time work back to college[5] ("Work to College"). It explores how and why women and men make educational decisions; the institutional obstacles and opportunities they face; the interaction of education and other life changes such as marriage, divorce, and parenthood; and their views of how colleges might be more responsive and accessible to a broader range of students. The report is designed to help reconceptualize the identity and needs of the "student," and to help K-16 institutions meet the needs of these specific populations, by contributing a new dimension to the body of research on educational transitions.

Choices and Chances:
The Decision-Making Process

Significantly more women than men who moved from high school to the full-time work force report that not attending college was a decision based on circumstances or "forces beyond [their] control." Fewer women than men respond that the decision was "basically their own choice."

- Male high school graduates who moved into the work force were significantly more likely than their female counterparts to:
  - cite a lack of interest in college and a belief that they could "get a decent job" without college as "very important" factors in their decision
  - describe their employment as a "career" rather than "just a job"
  - have never seriously considered going to college in the first place.
- Conversely, a significantly higher percentage of School to College men report that they "feel like [they] got pushed into college by other people" and "never really made the decision [themselves]" (17 percent of men to 8 percent of women).

Goals and Aspirations

Women have a dual agenda for attending college. Whether going to college straight from high school or after working for some time, they attend college for both economic (career, income) and self-fulfillment (personal enrichment) reasons. Women in all college-bound groups place more emphasis on self-fulfillment than do men.

- There is a misperception that nontraditional students return to school to learn specific skills to further their careers. This overlooks the desire for personal enrichment and general intellectual development that is an especially pronounced goal for women across the transition groups.
  - Nine out of 10 School to College and Work to College women judge pursuing "a career that is interesting and

personally fulfilling" to be a "very important" reason for attending college. Almost eight out of 10 women in both groups—and significantly more women than men in the School to College groups—choose "personal enrichment" as a very important goal. Obtaining a better-paying or a well-paying job is judged a very important goal by seven out of 10 and almost eight out of 10 Work to College and School to College women, respectively.

- Women returning to school, especially, emphasize quality-of-career issues in focus group conversations. They seek jobs that have inherent value and meaning and for which they receive not only financial compensation—which is important—but work flexibility, autonomy, and satisfaction.
- Younger students going straight to college from high school are more likely to see a college diploma as a necessary credential than older, returning students.
  - Sixty percent of School to College women and men say getting "the piece of paper" or a necessary credential is a very important goal, in contrast to 38 percent of Work to College students.
- There are more significant differences in goals for college by sex among School to College students than among Work to College students.

Obstacles and Barriers
Money Matters

Money is cited as the most significant obstacle for both men and women contemplating higher education. Over one-half of the School to College group and about two-thirds of each of the other two groups say that "a lack of money and/or financial aid" was an obstacle to going to college. In some cases, however, money affects men and women differently:

- Women moving from high school to work are significantly more likely than men in that group to say that a lack of money is a barrier to education (69 percent to 55 percent) and that college is too expensive for them (71 percent to 58 percent).

- School to Work women are also significantly more likely than men to feel that better information about financial aid would have made them "much more likely" to go to college (51 percent to 33 percent).
- Women are significantly more likely than men (32 percent to 19 percent in the Work to College population) to say that credit card debt was a barrier to going to college.
  - People of color, in comparison to whites, are more likely to say that credit card debt poses an educational barrier (41 percent to 26 percent in the Work to College group).
  - The problem of credit card debt begins as early as high school and is more pronounced for women than men. Fully one in five School to Work respondents cite credit card debt as a obstacle to college.

*Academic and Test Performance Anxieties:
The Story of Self-Fulfilling Prophecies?*

Anxiety impedes some from attending college. The source of anxiety most often cited as an obstacle to attending college is "nervousness about the academic requirements," mentioned by almost half of the School to College group and by 36 percent of the School to Work group.

- Approximately one-quarter to one-third of women in each of the three groups say that anxiety about SAT scores is an obstacle to college.
- Among the School to College students, women are significantly more likely than men to cite SAT scores as an obstacle (34 percent to 22 percent).
- More people of color than whites who did not attend college immediately after high school feel that doing away with standardized tests would have made them "much more likely" to go to college (37 percent to 20 percent).

It is important to note that these students were impeded from applying to college by anxieties about low scores, not by low scores themselves.

- Significantly more School to Work men than women (20 percent to 9 percent) cite their feeling that "it was too difficult to get accepted" as a "very important" obstacle to college.
  - People of color and students from families with incomes under $40,000 are also significantly more likely to be deterred from college by a feeling that it would be too difficult to get accepted.

Skepticism about SAT Fairness and Accuracy

- College-bound students do not perceive the SAT to be an accurate predictor of academic performance. Only 15 percent of School to College women and 25 percent of School to College men judge them to be accurate gauges of future college performance.
- Roughly half of the women in the two college-bound groups feel that students who can afford SAT preparation classes have an unfair advantage, and between one-third and half of the women in these groups feel that the SAT is a fair and unbiased measure of ability. Only slightly more college-bound men—roughly one in four—feel that the SAT is a fair and unbiased measure of ability.

Treatment of Women and Minorities in College

- On the whole, women in all three transition groups perceive college to be an inviting place for them. Only about one-fifth of women in the two college-bound groups agree that the "treatment of women in higher education" or "society's attitude toward women" creates an obstacle to college.
- School to Work women who did not go to college do not feel that college is a "tougher place for women" (only 16 percent say college is tougher for women). Men's and women's opinions are similar on the issue, with 18 percent of men agreeing that college is tougher for women than men.

- College appears somewhat less inviting for people of color, roughly one-third of whom in the college-bound groups agree that the "treatment of racial and ethnic minorities in higher education" poses an obstacle for them.

Guidance Counselors: A Missed Opportunity?

Over half of all three groups (57 percent of the School to Work group, 59 percent of the School to College group, and 62 percent of the Work to College group) report being somewhat satisfied or not satisfied at all with their guidance counselor experience.

- Students who report having average or below average grades are especially likely to feel that their "guidance counselors did not give [them] enough time or attention."
- In focus group conversations, participants felt that counselors sometimes determined whether or not a student was "college material," and focused on what they could not do immediately following graduation instead of providing more concrete, long-term guidance about how the student might eventually achieve a stated goal.

The Information Gap: What They Don't Know Hurts Them

There is a strong consensus that students would benefit from more information about the college application and selection process. Fully 72 percent of the School to Work group, for example, speculate that better information about colleges, degrees, and programs would have made them more likely to attend college.

- Across all three transition points, women are significantly more likely than men to agree that better information would have influenced their decision. One in three School to Work men feels that more information would have had "no effect at all" on their decision, in contrast to only one in five women.

- When it comes to getting information, nothing succeeds like success: Students across all three transition points who report having received above average SAT scores and above average grades are significantly more likely to report that they "knew a lot" about the college selection process.
- Income affects students' perceptions of how much information they received. Almost all of the School to College respondents (94 percent) who report family incomes under $50,000 feel that they needed "much more information," in contrast to 80 percent of those with family incomes over $50,000.
- Information about careers is even harder to come by than information about college. About one-third of both the School to Work and School to College group agree that it was difficult to get information about careers. Twenty percent of the School to College set, in contrast, feel it was difficult to get information about college.
- Women are more eclectic in their decisionmaking than men, reporting that a wider variety of sources of information, ranging from campus visits to books, were "very influential" in their thinking.
- Students who report knowing a lot about college are more likely to attend a four-year school, while those who do not are more likely to attend a two-year school.

Life Stages/Educational Transitions

Age Is More Often Cited as an Obstacle by Returning Women than Men

- Although adult students now account for nearly half of college enrollments overall, significantly more women than men feel that their age posed a barrier to college. Of those Work to College women who said they were older than their fellow students, 18 percent cite age as an obstacle, compared with only three percent of their male counterparts.

*Spouses Appear as Obstacles
or as Irrelevant to the Educational Transition*

- Twenty-one percent of the married Work to College students report that "lack of spouse support" was a "significant obstacle." In another question, 32 percent respond that being married had "no effect" on their decision to go back to school.

The Paradox of Children

- Seventy-five percent of the School to Work group (men and women) who were pregnant or caring for children at the time they graduated from high school report that "having to care for children" was a very important reason they did not go to college. A vast majority—82 percent—name it as the "single most important" reason for not seeking postsecondary education.
- Although parents seeking further education may often face institutional barriers and obstacles, children also emerged in focus group research as powerful motivators and incentives for women to return to or continue school.
- Students with children need more time and flexibility. The highest percentage of the School to Work group (28 percent) choose "more financial aid for anyone who needs it" as the single most important thing that would have influenced their transition. However, among those with children, the highest percentage—26 percent—choose "more flexible scheduling of classes to accommodate outside demands," and the second-highest percentage (19 percent) choose colleges offering day care services. Another 19 percent choose "more financial aid" as the single most important factor.
- Work to College students with children face a broader range of obstacles than their counterparts without children. Obstacles they deemed to be "significant" included credit card debt, nervousness about academic requirements, lack of motivation or desire, low grades in high school, anxiety about SAT scores, society's attitude toward women in general, treatment of women in higher education, and a spouse's or partner's lack of support.

- Work to College parents also differ in their judgment that the "treatment of women in higher education" constitutes a significant obstacle (13 percent of respondents with children in comparison to 5 percent of respondents without children).
- School to Work parents are significantly more likely than their childless peers to receive little or no encouragement for education from their friends and spouses, and are more likely to report that parents and teachers were "not an influence at all" in their transition.

Perceptions of Education, Economy, and Careers

The Future Job Market

- Roughly two-thirds of the Work to College and School to College groups say that they did consider economic projections and the future job market when they made their educational decision. The ratio is reversed, however, in the School to Work group, where 63 percent report that the economy did not influence their decision or transition.

Although high school students bound for college feel that they have considered economic realities in their decision, other research shows that college-bound students—both men and women—dramatically overestimate their chances of getting professional jobs, for example, and express little interest in the career areas likely to grow in the next century.

Computers "Take Over"

- All respondents—from both sexes, all ages, races, and ethnicities, and across all transition points—firmly believe that computers are, in a high school woman's words, "taking over the world."
- Fully 85 percent of the Work to College and 78 percent of the School to College groups agree that "it is almost impossible to get a decent job today without a firm knowledge of computers." Seventy percent of the School to Work group feel that computer skills are "very important" to getting a good job today.

The High Educational Bar

Almost unanimously, respondents undergoing any transition, and from all social backgrounds, feel that a high school degree is essential for getting a good job. Substantial numbers now report that a college degree is the minimum prerequisite for career success.

- Roughly one-third of the two college-bound groups believe a college degree is "essential" for a good job. Between 94 percent and 96 percent agree that "in the future, it will be even harder to get a decent job without a college degree."
- Views of the college decree and formal education are somewhat ambivalent, however. Although respondents place great value on high school diplomas and, to a lesser extent, college degrees, larger percentages of respondents in all three transition groups rate "having people skills," "real world work experience," "interviewing well," and "critical thinking skills" as essential for a good job. Forty percent of the School to Work group believe that "you don't really need to go to college today to get a decent job."
- People of color agree that a postgraduate degree is an "important" factor significantly more often than whites. They cite the degree as "essential" almost twice as often as white respondents across all three transition groups.

Solutions: Making College More Accessible and Equitable

Community Colleges Rate Highly as Role Models of Institutional Flexibility, Affordability, and Parent-Friendly Campuses

- Most students, including those in four-year colleges and universities, judge community colleges quite positively. Not unexpectedly, the most favorable ratings of community colleges come from the Work to College group and students with children.

- Seventy-five percent of the Work to College group agree that community colleges offer a better deal financially than four-year colleges.
- Eighty-three percent of Work to College students enrolled in two-year schools agree that community colleges are better for students with children. A majority—65 percent—of the Work to College students in four-year schools also agree with the statement.
- Parents in the Work to College group are significantly more likely than those without children to agree that community colleges are better for:
  - Students who work
  - Getting personal attention from faculty
  - First-generation college students
  - Convenience
  - Flexibility in scheduling

Money Matters

- "More financial aid for anyone who needs it" was the item most often favored by women to make college more accessible, significantly more than men in two groups. Each of the transition groups also cite tax incentives to make it easier for people to continue their education as one of their top three recommendations. Across all three groups, two-thirds to over three-quarters of women favor more financial aid and tax incentives.

Better Sources of Information Needed about Financial Aid

- Significantly more women than men across all three transition points strongly favor better sources of information about financial aid as an improvement that would make going to college easier. Fully 80 percent of School to Work women, compared with 66 percent of School to Work men, favor better sources of information, which would include more user-friendly, accessible, and streamlined financial aid information.

*More Information about College
and Careers—and More Tangible Information*

- Women students, especially, prefer tangible—human, face-to-face—sources of information, and all students feel that they would have benefited from more career and college information as they considered their decision.

Employer Incentives: Rare but Highly Effective

- Employers and co-workers lent encouragement to very few employees in either the Work to College or the School to Work groups. Only about two in 10 say they were strongly encouraged by someone at their workplace to return to school. Nor do employers typically offer financial incentives for employees to pursue college. Yet those Work to College group who did receive financial incentives overwhelmingly reported (75 percent) that it was an important factor in their return to school.

Day Care Services

- Seventy-four percent of the Work to College parents say more "day care and schedules to accommodate students with children" is a "large help" in returning to school, and almost all assess it as at least somewhat of a help.
- Seventy-four percent of School to Work parents say that day care services would make them "much more likely" to attend college.

*Returning Students Favor
Institutional Flexibility*

- Women returning to school are significantly more likely than men to value more flexible scheduling of classes (69 percent to 53 percent) and more flexibility regarding the length of time needed to complete different programs (55 percent to 40 percent). Evidently, women returning to school feel especially stretched for time and imagine that they would benefit more from flexible schedules and timetables.

NOTES

1. William Brody, "A University Campus in which Bits and Bytes Replace Bricks and Mortar," *Baltimore Sun*, February 26, 1997, p. 11A; U.S. Department of Education, "Building on What We've Learned: Developing Priorities for Education Research," May 24, 1996, p. 71; Donald Langenberg, "Diplomas and Degrees are Obsolescent," *Chronicle of Higher Education*, "Point of View," September 12, 1997; Julianne Basinger, "Former Michigan President Seeks to Turn Higher Education into a 'Knowledge Industry,'" Chronicle of Higher Education, Web site (www.chronicle.com), January 22, 1999; The National Collegiate Honors Council Forums, *Preparing for a Good Future: What Kind of Education Do We Need After High School?* (Englewood Cliffs, NJ: John Doble Research Associates, Inc., 1997), p. 2. See also Terry O'Banion, "A Learning College for the 21st Century," *Community College Journal*, 66, 1995–1996 (December/January), pp. 18–23, which envisions a learning college that allows the learner to select options among prescribed modules, opportunities for collaboration with other learners, tutor-led groups, and other options.
2. Ernest Freeman and the Institute for Higher Education Policy, *Life After Forty: A New Portrait of Today's and Tomorrow's Postsecondary Students* (Washington, D.C.: Institute for Higher Education Policy, 1997); National Center for Postsecondary Improvement, *The Transition from Initial Education to Working Life in the United States of America* (Stanford, CA: NCPI, 1998), p. 6.
3. Some of the respondents may have recently completed a transition.
4. Additional Methodological Notes: Interviews lasted, on average, 24 minutes. At least four callbacks were made, staggered by day of week and time of day, to ensure that even the busiest respondents were reached. Follow-up appointments were scheduled with respondents who could not complete the interview when first contacted. Professional interviewers wee utilized, with at least one supervisor always on hand. The sample

was a mix of random digit dial (RDD) and, for students, the listed sample was obtained from American Student List. The listed sample was drawn to be as representative as possible, including students from all regions of the nation, public and private schools, and most competitive and least competitive schools.

5. We use the term "college" for continuity; however, students returning from work to college, or students combining full-time work and at least 20 hours a week of college, may be pursuing completion of a bachelor's degree, a two-year associate's degree, a certificate, or a postgraduate degree. "College" encompasses each of these elements of post-secondary education.

KEY TERMS

concur   To agree.

infrastructure   Internal organization. The term is often used to refer to the organization of structures and institutions for the delivery of government services.

qualitative   Having to do with the nature of phenomena. *Qualitative* assessments or descriptions are often contrasted with *quantitative* assessments or descriptions, which aim not to explore the phenomena so much as to provide a numerical or statistical account of them.

quantitative   Having to do with a numerical or statistical analysis of phenomena. *Quantitative* assessments are often contrasted with *qualitative* assessments or descriptions, which aim at providing an exploration of the phenomena.

heterogeneous   Composed of elements of a variety of different kinds or origins.

DISCUSSION QUESTIONS

1. What would you say is the principle or topic according to which the findings of this study are organized? Why do you think the authors chose to organize their data in this way? What other organizing principles might have been chosen? What would have been the advantages to those principles? What disadvantages might they have had?

2. One of the more interesting and discouraging findings of the AAUW study is the lack of self-confidence that women report more frequently than men. There is no category in the report labeled "self-confidence," yet it appears throughout the excerpt presented here. Where do you find evidence of women's lack of self-confidence? Where do you find evidence of men's lack of self-confidence? Why do you think men's level of self-confidence seems to be so much higher than women's? Do you think that over time this disparity will decline?

3. An interesting project would be to use the data contained in the AAUW report to construct narrative profiles of men and women in each of the three categories the study designated: high school to college, high school to work, and work to college. In constructing your profiles, try to use as much qualitative data as you can find, though most of your data will be quantitative. In the process of constructing this narrative profile, you may as well also construct purely quantitative profiles. When you have finished, what have you found? Do the gender profiles present a different picture from the one presented in the report itself? How? Why? Do the narrative profiles seem in any way different from the purely quantitative profiles? How? Why? If you were writing up a report of the findings of the AAUW research, what style of presentation would you have chosen? Why?

4. More men than women report that they were simply not interested in higher education when they finished high school, and more women than men return to college after

work. Why do you think this is true? In constructing your answer, consider a variety of possible contributing causes: the socialization of boys versus the socialization of girls; the grades received by boys versus those received by girls in high school (girls' grades are higher overall); the kinds of jobs available to male versus female high school graduates; the differing ways in which family responsibilities weigh on men and women at different times throughout their lives; and finally, the effects of divorce on men and women (this may actually be seen as part of the previous category).

CONCLUSION

The concluding chapter of this reader focuses on two important themes we have encountered throughout this book—diversity and work. Johnnetta B. Cole in "Commonalities and Differences" takes a thorough and reasoned look at gender in the United States in terms of diversity among women. She addresses many dimensions of diversity—among them, class, ethnicity, and sexual preference. She shows what difference these and other variations make in women's lives in areas such as sexuality, reproduction, work, religion, and politics. Yet along with differences among women she also finds some significant similarities. This article is an excellent review of the issues and the literature on gender and sociocultural diversity in the United States. Cole's position as a prominent anthropologist, a black woman, and a leader in the struggle for social equality gives her a particularly illuminating vantage point.

One of the spheres of life that Cole analyzes is work, and one of the commonalities she finds among U.S. women is that "when women live in households with men or with men and children, women are 'in charge' of the housework. Thus if women also work outside the household, they do a 'double shift,'" to cover the housework and childcare. This whole issue of balancing careers and families is taken up in the next piece by Elizabeth Perle McKenna, but with a new twist—a focus on men. McKenna sees that the dichotomy between the male world of work and the female world of domestic activities (discussed at the very beginning of this reader) is breaking down. She then looks at the consequences and meanings of this change for men.

COMMONALITIES AND DIFFERENCES

JOHNNETTA B. COLE

Cole's article draws attention to a grave error made by the 1960s women's movement: It ignored differences among women in terms of, for example, class and race. As a result, the '60s movement stayed a white, middle-class concern that was rejected by many other women. Cole herself, a black woman and an anthropologist, was one of many women, both inside and outside the middle-class "women's movement" to redress this situation and to ensure that other women's voices were heard. In so doing, these women ushered the women's movement into a new phase that sought to come to terms with diversity. "Commonalities and Differences" was a significant contribution to that effort.

This article is also significant for its tone and purpose. Class chauvinism, ethnocentrism, and in some cases outright racism, lay behind the failure of the 1960s movement to attract women outside the white middle class. But Cole does not get trapped in or bemoan the past. Rather she moves on and asks in a straightforward and refreshingly objective way: Are there commonalities among U.S. women? "Is difference a part of what we share or is it, in fact, all that we share?" Do women, as women, share aspects of oppression, and, if so, what are they? Note throughout this article Cole's stylistic use of "US women" and "U.S. women."

Cole raises her questions about U.S. women's commonalties and differences in terms of five spheres of women's lives: work, families, sexuality and reproduction, religion, and politics. For each sphere she first examines what she sees that all U.S. women share. She then discusses the differences among women in terms, where relevant, of class, race, ethnicity, religion, age, sexual preference, geographical location, and physical ability. The result is a comprehensive and rich review of the experiences of U.S. women in all their diversity.

This article was published in 1986; thus many of the statistics on women's work or participation in politics are somewhat outdated. Significantly, however, most of the overall gender patterns that Cole discusses have not changed in the intervening fifteen years. What has changed since her article was published, however, is that gender in the United States is no longer considered apart from issues of socioeconomic and cultural diversity.

Cole finds that along with their diversity, there is a great deal that U.S. women share. For example, in the sphere of "work" she finds that women tend to work in sex-segregated jobs and earn less than men for comparable work. In the sphere of "sexuality and reproduction" she notes that women are subjected to cultural attitudes and values that "categorize all women as sexual objects who either live up to or fall short of the ideal female sexual being." Women are also victims of sexual crimes across the board. Yet in all the five spheres of women's lives, the differences among women in terms of race, class, sexual orientation and so on are very real. Cole concludes that all U.S. women share oppression, but the content and in some cases the magnitude of that oppression are significantly shaped by the differences among women. Women in the United States are, then, both bound by similarities and divided by differences.

If you see one woman, have you seen them all? Does the heavy weight of patriarchy level all differences among US women? Is it the case, as one woman put it, that "there isn't much difference between having to say 'Yes suh Mr. Charlie' and 'Yes dear'?" Does "grandmother" convey the same meaning as "abuela," as "buba," as "gran'-ma"? Is difference a part of what we share, or is it, in fact, *all* that we share? As early as 1970, Toni Cade Bambara asked: "How relevant are the truths, the experiences, the findings of white women to black women? Are women after all simply women?" (Bambara 1970: 9)

Are US women bound by our similarities or divided by our differences? The only viable response is *both*. To address our commonalities without dealing with our differences is to misunderstand and distort that which separates as well as that which binds us as women. Patriarchal oppression is not limited to women of one race or of one particular group, women in one class, women of one age group or sexual preference, women who live in one part of the country, women of any one religion, or women with certain physical abilities or disabilities. Yet, while oppression of women knows no such limitations, we cannot, therefore, conclude that the oppression of all women is identical.

Among the things which bind women together are the assumptions about the way that women think and behave, the myths—indeed the stereotypes—about what is common to all women. For example, women will be asked nicely in job interviews if they type, while men will not be asked such a question. In response to certain actions, the expression is used: "Ain't that just like a woman?" Or during a heated argument between a man and a woman, as the voice of each rises and emotions run high, the woman makes a particularly good point. In a voice at the pitch of the ongoing argument, the man screams at her: "You don't have to get hysterical!"

In an interesting form of "what goes around comes around," as Malcolm X put it, there is the possibility that US women are bound together by our assumptions, attitudes toward, even stereotypes of the other gender. Folklorist Rayna Green, referring to women of the Southern setting in which she grew up, says this:

> Southern or not, women everywhere talk about sex. . . . In general men are more often the victims of women's jokes than not. Tit for tat, we say. Usually the subject for laughter is men's boasts, failures, or inadequacies ("comeuppance for lack of up-commance," as one of my aunts would say). Poking fun at a man's sexual ego, for example, might never be possible in real social situations with the men who have power over their lives, but it is possible in a joke. (Green 1984: 23–24)

That which US women have in common must always be viewed in relation to the particularities of a group, for even when we narrow our focus to one particular group of women it is possible for differences within that group to challenge the primacy of what is shared in common. For example, what have we said and what have we failed to say when we speak of "Asian American women"? As Shirley Hune notes (1982), Asian American women as a group share a number of characteristics. Their participation in the work force is higher than that of women in any other ethnic group. Many Asian American women live life supporting others, often allowing their lives to be subsumed by the needs of the extended family. And they are subjected to stereotypes by the dominant society: the sexy but "evil dragon lady," the "neuter gender," the "passive/demure" type, and the "exotic/erotic" type.

However, there are many circumstances when these shared experiences are not sufficient to accurately describe the condition of particular Asian American women. Among Asian American women there are those who were born in the United States, fourth and fifth generation Asian American women with firsthand experience of no other land, and there are those who recently arrived in the United States. Asian American women are diverse in their heritage or country of origin: China, Japan, the Philippines, Korea, India, Vietnam, Cambodia, Thailand, or another country in Asia. If we restrict ourselves to Asian American women of Chinese descent, are we referring to those women who are from the People's Republic of China or those from Taiwan, those from Hong Kong or those from Vietnam, those from San Francisco's Chinatown or those from Mississippi? Are we subsuming under "Asian American" those Pacific Island women from Hawaii, Samoa, Guam, and other islands under U.S. control? Although the majority of Asian American women are working-class—contrary to the stereotype of the "ever successful" Asians—there are poor, "middle-class," and even affluent Asian American women (Hune 1982: 1–2, 13–14).

It has become very common in the United States today to speak of "Hispanics," putting Puerto Ricans, Chicanos, Dominicans, Cubans, and those from every Spanish-speaking country in the Americas into one category of people, with the women referred to as Latinas or Hispanic women. Certainly there is a language, or the heritage of a language, a general historical experience, and certain cultural traditions and practices which are shared by these women. But a great deal of harm can be done by sweeping away differences in the interest of an imposed homogeneity.

Within one group of Latinas there is, in fact, considerable variation in terms of self-defined ethnic identity, such that some women refer to themselves as Mexican Americans, others as *Chicanas*, others as Hispanics, and still others as Americans. Among this group of women are those who express a commitment to the traditional roles of women and others who identify with feminist ideals. Some Chicanas are monolingual—in Spanish or English—and others are bilingual. And there are a host of variations among Chicanas in terms of educational achievements, economic differences, rural or urban living conditions, and whether they trace their ancestry from women who lived in this land well before the United States forcibly took the northern half of Mexico, or more recently arrived across the border that now divides the nations called Mexico and the United States.

Women of the Midwest clearly share a number of experiences which flow from living in the U.S. heartland, but they have come from different places, and they were and are today part of various cultures.

> Midwestern women are the Native American women whose ancestors were brought to the plains in the mid-nineteenth century to be settled on reservations, the black women whose fore-bears emigrated by the thousands from the South after Reconstruction. They are the descendants of the waves of Spanish, French, Norwegian, Danish, Swedish, Bohemian, Scottish, Welsh, British, Irish, German, and Russian immigrants who settled the plains, and the few Dutch, Italians, Poles, and Yugoslavs who came with them. (Boucher 1982: 3)

There is another complexity: when we have identified a commonality among women, cutting across class, racial, ethnic, and other major lines of difference, the particular ways that commonality is acted out and its consequences in the larger society may be quite diverse. Ostrander makes this point in terms of class:

> When women stroke and soothe men, listen to them and accommodate their needs, men of every class return to the workplace with renewed energies. When women arrange men's social lives and relationships, men of every class are spared investing the time and energy required to meet their social needs. When women run the households and keep family concerns in check, men of every class are freer than women to pursue other activities, including work, outside the home. But upper-class women perform these tasks for men at the very top of the class structure. . . . Supporting their husbands as individuals, they support and uphold the very top of the class structure. In this way they distinguish themselves from women of other social classes. (Ostrander 1984: 146)

Suppose that we can accurately and exclusively identify the characteristics shared by one particular group of women. For each of the women within that group, into how many other groups does she want to, or is she forced to, fit? Or can we speak of similarities *only* with respect to a group such as Puerto Rican women who are forty-three years old, were born in San Juan, Puerto Rico, migrated to New York City when they were five years old, work as eighth-grade school teachers, attend a Catholic church, are heterosexual, married, with two male and two female children, and have no physical disabilities?

Then there is that unpredictable but often present quality of individuality, the idiosyncrasies of a particular person. Shirley Abbott, describing experiences of growing up in the South, contrasts her mother's attitude and behavior toward the black woman who was her maid with what was the usual stance of "Southern white ladies."

> I don't claim that my mother's way of managing her black maid was typical. Most white women did not help their laundresses hang the washing on the line. . . . Compulsive housewifery had some part in it. So did her upbringing. . . . There was another motive too. . . . Had she used Emma in just the right way, Mother could have become a lady. But Mother didn't want to be a lady. Something in her was against it, and she couldn't explain what frightened her, which was why she cried when my father ridiculed her. (Abbott 1983: 78–79)

Once we have narrowed our focus to one specific group of women (Armenian American women, or women over sixty-five, or Arab American women, or black women from the Caribbean, or Ashkenazi Jewish women), the oppression that group of women experiences may take different forms at different times. Today, there is no black woman in the United States who is the legal slave of a white master: "chosen" for that slave status because of her race, forced to give her labor power without compensation because of the class arrangements of the society, and subjected to the sexual whims of her male master because of her gender. But that does not mean that black women today are no longer oppressed on the basis of race, class, and gender.

There are also groups of women who experience intense gender discrimination today, but in the past had a radically different status in their society. Contrary to the popular image of female oppression as being both universal and as old as human societies, there is incontestable evidence of egalitarian societies in which men and women related in ways that did not involve male dominance and female subjugation. Eleanor Leacock is the best known of the anthropologists who have carried out the kind of detailed historical analysis which provides evidence on gender relations in precolonial North American societies. In discussing the debate on the origins and spread of women's oppression, Leacock points out that women's oppression is a reality today in virtually every society, and while socialist societies have reduced it, they have not eliminated gender inequality. However, it does not follow that women's oppression has always existed and will always exist. What such arguments about universal female subordination do is to project onto the totality of human history the conditions of today's world. Such an argument also "affords an important ideological buttress for those in power" (Leacock 1979: 10–11).

Studies of precolonial societies indicate considerable variety in terms of gender relations.

> Women retained great autonomy in much of the pre-colonial world, and related to each other and to men through public as well as private procedures as they carried out their economic and social responsibilities and protected their rights. Female and male modalities of various kinds operated reciprocally within larger kin and community contexts before the principle of male dominance within individual families was taught by missionaries, defined by legal status, and solidified by the economic relations of colonialism. (Leacock 1979: 10–11)

Even when there is evidence of female oppression among women of diverse backgrounds, it is important to listen to the individual assessment which each woman makes of her own condition, rather than assume that a synonymous experience of female oppression exists among all women. As a case in point, Sharon Burmeister Lord, in describing what it was like to grow up "Appalachian style," speaks of the influence of female role models in shaping the conditions of her development. In Williamson, West Virginia, she grew up knowing women whose occupations were Methodist preacher, elementary school principal, county sheriff, and university professor. Within her own family, her mother works as a secretary, writes poetry and songs, and "swims faster than any

boy"; her aunt started her own seed and hardware store; one grandmother is a farmer and the other runs her own boarding house. Summarizing the effect of growing up among such women, Lord says:

> When a little girl has had a chance to learn strength, survival tactics, a firm grasp of reality, and an understanding of class oppression from the women around her, it doesn't remove oppression from her life, but it does give her a fighting chance. And that's an advantage! (Lord 1979: 25)

Finally, if it is agreed that today, to some extent, all women are oppressed, to what extent can a woman, or a group of women, also act as oppressor? Small as the numbers may be, there are some affluent black women. (In 1979, less than 500 black women had an income of over $75,000 a year. Four thousand black men had such an income, as compared to 548,000 white men who were in that income bracket. [Marable 1983: 101–102].) Is it not possible that among this very small group of black women there are those who, while they experience oppression because of their race, act in oppressive ways toward other women because of their class? Does the experience of this society's heterosexism make a Euro-American lesbian incapable of engaging in racist acts toward women of color? The point is very simply that privilege can and does coexist with oppression (Bulkin et al. 1984: 99) and being a victim of one form of discrimination does not make one immune to victimizing someone else on a different basis.

We turn now to an overview of each sphere of women's lives on which succeeding sections will focus: work, families, sexuality and reproduction, religion, and politics. These spheres are examined first in terms of commonalities and shared experiences among US women. Then the coin is turned, exposing differences among US women due to our respective class, race, ethnicity, religion, age, sexual preference, geographical location, and physical ability.

Work

Women work. All over the world women work. A comprehensive view of women's work in the United States must include slave labor, wage labor, unpaid household labor, and voluntary work. In that sense, all women in the United States work whether in prisons (a form of slave labor), out in the "marketplace," in their own households, or for a charitable cause.

The organization of women's labor in the United States has changed over time and in response to the particular economic system in effect. Native American women labored under precapitalistic conditions in their nations and societies prior to European conquest. With colonialism and the advent of capitalism, especially after the rise of industrialization, labor became a commodity and a new sexual division of labor began for most women and men in the United States. Men worked outside of their homes for wages and women continued to work within their homes, without wages. But it is important to note that this new sexual division in the location and valuing of labor did not fundamentally change the type of work women did in precapitalist society: nurturing and socializing of children, care and maintenance of the home, and domestic manufacturing.

Within the sphere of work, major commonalities among women can be stated in terms of two propositions. First, when women work outside of their households, they tend to work in sex-segregated jobs and receive less pay, for comparable work, than men. Second, when women live in households with men or with men and children, the women are "in charge" of the housework. Thus, if women also work outside of the household, they do a "double shift."

Doing "women's work" and getting "women's pay" are phrases which capture the plight of the largest segment of female workers. About 60 percent of the women in the U.S. labor force today (38 million women) work in sex-segregated jobs. Over 99.5 percent of secretaries, 96 percent of registered nurses, and 94 percent of telephone operators are female. Of all jobs, an estimated 96 percent are segregated by sex, with paychecks reflecting the difference between women's pay and men's.

Now two decades after the 1963 Equal Pay Act and Title VII of the Civil Rights Act, women as an aggregate group in the labor force earn 60 percent of what men earn (Shalala 1983: 3). A study by the National Academy of Sciences sums up the situation in these terms: Not only do women do different work than men, but they are also paid less for what they do. The more an occupation is dominated by women, the less it pays. Yet here too, one cannot avoid reference to differences: the discrepancy between what white women and men earn is less than that between what women of color earn and what is earned by men (Shalala 1983).

Housework is not included in calculations of the U.S. Gross National Product, but it is certainly very much a part of the day-to-day lives of the overwhelming majority of US women. Women doing housework carry out all those tasks which, if done at the dry cleaners, in restaurants or by maids, would require men's wages to shoot up. Thus, women in traditional marriages who do housework and care for children not only work for free, but work for free for their husband's employer. Although "full-time housewifery" is a declining occupation for women as two wages becomes a necessity for increasing numbers of U.S. families, housework continues to be, primarily, women's responsibility. To the extent that increasing numbers of US women work outside of our households, increasing numbers do a double or second shift. Following eight hours of work for less pay than a man would receive, most women in the labor force return home to husband, or children, or both, and begin their "second shift." Women who work outside of their households put in almost as many hours sweeping, cleaning, dishwashing, laundering, and shopping as women who are "housewives." A wife who does not work for wages spends a minimum of forty hours a week maintaining house and husband, and a minimum of thirty hours per week if she does work for wages. Thus, while "outside" employment may mean a degree of economic independence, it does not mean emancipation.

Time-budget studies have found that women still do most of the housework, an average of 70 percent, while husband and children each do about 15 percent. Many women note that even when they manage to get their husbands or grown children involved, the cleaning and cooking and shopping remain "their tasks." Before picking up the broom or turning on the vacuum cleaner, most men will likely ask: "What do you want me to do?" or "How can I help you?"

Perhaps the most telling case of the intimate association of women with housework is what happens in the homes of affluent women who are relieved of the drudgery of doing housework themselves. They become, instead, the managers of the drudgery of domestic work done by other women.

It was not until World War II that large numbers of women in the United States began to work outside of their homes. Until then, Euro-American women who lived with their husbands worked outside their home only if they were professional women or extremely poor. Afro-American women, on the other hand, have a long history of working outside of their own households. This particular experience was grounded in the peculiar and barbaric institution of slavery; and after "emancipation," there was often domestic work available for them but not for black men.

In 1963 Betty Friedan described the "problem without a name" as the feeling of boredom and unfulfillment of white suburban middle-class housewives. Yet even in 1963 when she wrote *The Feminine Mystique*, more than one-third of all US women were in the work force; and recent economic circumstances have led unprecedented numbers of women of all racial and ethnic groups and of middle- as well as working-class origin into the paid labor force.

Among women in the paid U.S. work force, a major difference revolves around the kinds of jobs we hold. When viewed as "aggregate groups"—women of color versus Euro-American women—women of color are far more likely to work in less skilled and lower-paying jobs. About 25 percent of Chinese American women still work under harsh conditions in garment shops. In California's "Silicon Valley" women make up 75 percent of the assembly line work force, as they do along Route 128 outside of Boston and in the antiunion, "right to work" state of North Carolina. Forty percent of the workers in these electronics factories are immigrant women. On the West Coast, the majority of the women are Filipinas, Thais, Samoans, Mexicans, and Vietnamese (Fuentes and Ehrenreich 1983).

The situation among Native American women is, in a quantitative sense, the worst of any group of women in the United States. They have the lowest income of any group in the country: while the median yearly income for all Native American women was $1,697 in the 1970s, for those in rural areas it was even less—$1,356. More than a third of all Native American women are employed in service occupations, nearly twice the national average. The plight of American Indian women is reflected in the startling reality that their average life expectancy is in the mid-forties.

Another difference among women in the sphere of work has to do with the amount and intensity of discrimination they face on the job. Women are paid less than men; that is the general rule. And the reason is quite simply that employers find it profitable to do so. "Not only [can] women be forced to absorb unemployment and seasonal work, and to perform the most tedious jobs, but their availability to do so [is] used as a threat against men to keep men's wages and resistance down" (Baxandall et al. 1976: xv). But within this general context of wage discrimination, different women experience other forms of discrimination. For example, in a study of discrimination against lesbians in work places (the first such study of its kind), the researchers conclude that many lesbians both anticipate and experience discrimination in the labor force (Levine and Leonard 1984: 710).

Women's ability to find work also varies. This is well documented in the difference between unemployment for white women and women of color. Bureau of Labor Statistics' figures for July 1985 show the jobless rate as 13.2 percent for black women and 5.7 percent for white women. For comparative purposes, it is interesting to note that for the same period, the jobless rate was 5.6 percent for white men and 12.6 percent for black men, reflecting the decades-long trend of black unemployment at least twice the rate for whites. Unemployment figures of stark proportions which receive very little attention are those of women with disabilities. Estimates are that between 65 percent and 76 percent of disabled women are unemployed. More stark and not so well known is the situation of disabled women of racial and ethnic minorities (Fine and Asch 1981: 233).

And finally, there is diversity among women in terms of whether or not they even need to work. One of the characteristics of upper-class women is their involvement in voluntary or charitable work. The

sharp contradictions between the experiences of poor and working-class women, and those of upper-class women, are evident in the response of one of the latter when asked to talk about her voluntary work: "Every summer I get about eighty kids from the [city's black ghetto] and bring them out for a day at my place in the country" (Ostrander, 1984: 126).

What can we conclude about the world of work experienced by women in the United States? Very importantly, work has a centrality in our lives. What kind of work we do, whether or not we work outside of our households, for whom we work, the pay we receive, and the conditions under which we work are key questions not only in shaping the material conditions of our lives, but also in helping to define who we are, as we view ourselves and as we are viewed by others.

Among US women there are radical differences in the answers to these questions. Some women own or are among the owners of the very plants where others work for exploitive wages and under oppressive conditions. Some women clip stock coupons from investments in companies whose profits come, at least in part, from the labor power of other women. Some poor women are the recipients of the charity work of upper-class women. These class divisions cannot be swept away by rhetorical references to a united sisterhood among all US women.

There are also, in the world of work, sharp divisions along racial and ethnic lines. What the overwhelming majority of women of color experience in the work world—whether that is a world of unskilled labor or corporate management—involves "adding insult to injury." In addition to being victims of sex discrimination in employment, Afro-American, Latino, Asian American, and Native American women also experience racial discrimination. And it is this double jeopardy which places women of color at the very bottom of all those comparative statistics between "white" and "nonwhite" women in the labor force.

Not in spite of but in addition to these class and racial differences among US women, there are common, although not identical, experiences among US. As a rule, housework is "women's work." As a rule, the kind of work women do in the labor force is different from that which men do, and as a rule it is labor for which there is less pay.

Families

Among women of different backgrounds, there is no sphere of life, no institution which stirs controversy as does *the family*. It is not only a question of debating similarities and differences among families; it is a matter of widely divergent positions as to what ought to be the very future of *the family*. At stake is a normative issue—what should happen to *the family*—and a political agenda—what is in the best interest of women.

In U.S. society, the term *family* is often used to include and sometimes to stand for "household"; sometimes it means the "nuclear family," i.e., husband, wife, and children; and sometimes the term refers to all of those to whom one has a kinship relationship. Often the term "relatives" is used to distinguish extended family from immediate or nuclear family. "Household," which is actually a spatial term referring to residence, is often a more appropriate term than *family* because it describes a domestic economy which may or may not be limited to biological kin.

Despite the considerable variation in the people *families* are composed of today, the dominant ideology in the United States still presents a family consisting of one man who goes off to earn the bacon, one woman who waits at home to fry it, and roughly 2.5 children poised to eat it. The reality is

that no more than 7 percent of all families in the United States are of this type.

While women are the sole bearers of babies and the primary nurturers of children, not all women have children. What sets up a commonality among women is the widespread presumption that those without children are unfortunate individuals who indeed wanted children, but were unable to have them.

While responsibility for young children is shared by most women, how they discharge that responsibility can and indeed does differ. For example, in the homes of the upper class, women can and often do delegate child care responsibilities to other *women*, "nannies" paid to serve as surrogate mothers. Women at the other end of the class continuum also "have help" with the tasks of mothering, but the circumstances involve networks of kin, neighbors, and friends who are not paid monetary sums but are bound together by mutual support and reciprocity. Thus, the children of the rich and the children of the poor are often cared for by individuals other than their biological mothers—but the details of those two situations are in fact quite different. In both cases, the biological mother is "freed" from the day-to-day constraints of child care. In one case, it permits her to engage in voluntary work, to visit with friends, to shop, or to engage in other activities which are not those of necessity. In the other case, the poor woman who is "relieved" of child care responsibilities spends her day working for wages which are not sufficient to monetarily compensate the relative or friend caring for her offspring.

Carol Stack describes the intricate web of relationships in which young black children grow up in the poor urban ghetto where she carried out her research.

> The individual can draw upon a broad domestic web of kin and friends—some who reside together, others who do not.

Residents in The Flats characterize household composition according to where people sleep, eat, and spend their time. Those who eat together may be considered part of a domestic unit. But an individual may eat in one household, sleep in another, contribute resources and service to yet another, and consider herself or himself a member of all three households. (Stack 1981: 352)

Among working-class white families, there is often a sizeable discrepancy between the ideal of an autonomous nuclear family and the necessity of pooling, borrowing, and sharing resources.

It is women who bridge the gap between what a household's resources really are, and what a family's position is supposed to be. Women exchange babysitting, share meals, lend small amounts of money. . . . The working class family literature is filled with examples of such pooling. (Rapp 1978: 288)

Thus in the variety and importance of friendship and kinship networks for coping with the demands of daily living, working-class white families share a great deal with poor black, as well as poor white, families. What distinguishes the conditions of these families, however, is not only that more material resources are available to the white, working-class family. Families of the black poor are constantly battling against racist ideology and institutions. Middle-class status and the even less common status of the black upper class can offer some protection against racist attitudes and practices; however, no black family can be totally shielded from white racism. This reality was starkly captured by Malcolm X when he asked an audience at Harvard: "What do you call a black person, man or woman, with a Ph.D.? The answer," Malcolm said, "is 'nigger'."

What of the white middle-class family, the suburban family described by Betty Friedan in *The Feminine Mystique*? Until recently women in these families tended to have full-time responsibility for child care and housework because necessity did not drive them to work outside of their homes. Bell Hooks, recalling those days of *The Feminine Mystique*, writes:

During the early stages of the contemporary women's liberation movement, feminist analyses of motherhood reflected the race and class biases of the participants. Some white middle class, college-educated women argued that motherhood was a serious obstacle to women's liberation, a trap confining women to the home, keeping them tied to cleaning, cooking and child care. Others simply identified motherhood and childrearing as the locus of women's oppression. Had black women voiced their views on motherhood, it would not have been named a serious obstacle to our freedom as women. Racism, availability of jobs, lack of skills or education and a number of other issues would have been at the top of the list—but not motherhood. Black women would not have said motherhood prevented us from entering the world of paid work because we have always worked. (Hooks 1984: 133)

What is clear from this discussion so far is that the opinions of various women about their families address different realities.

The extent to which women are defined in terms of their familial roles and responsibilities is captured in these words of an Asian woman:

But Asian women are not only oppressed by this American government and society which is based only on what is profitable, Asian women are also oppressed inside our communities by the force of Asian feudal tradition. This tradition continues to define us as so-and-so's daughter, mother, or wife. Such feudal ideas serve to keep us quiet and think "family first." Endless layers and rituals of obligation try to smother us, make us lose ourselves, or we must be "bad" mothers, "bad" daughters and "bad" wives. Is there a balance? (Hohri 1983: 44)

A similar point is made by Ann Wolfe in her discussion of role models for Jewish women, and the extent to which these models come into conflict with feminist perspectives.

> Has tradition enabled these women (fairly affluent and well educated) to feel secure both as women and as Jews? Who are the Jewish heroes that we hope will instill our children with pride in their Jewishness? If we are to believe the texts used in Jewish schools, women, I regret to say, are not much in evidence. One series of widely used Sunday school books about heroes in Jewish history describes thirty-two heroes. Only *one* of these is a woman who is seen as a hero in her own right: Henrietta Szold. Yet her biographical sketch ends with this curious statement: "God made her childless so that she might be mother of thousands." Need I say more? Seven other women are mentioned in these texts—but only in relation to their men: a selfless mother, a devoted daughter, a loyal wife. (Wolfe 1976: 47)

Implicit in the critique of the family voiced by many in the women's movement is that women do all of the work in their households and families but are not given commensurate decision-making powers. Yet, while black women do in fact participate in family decision making more frequently than whites, they are charged with being "black matriarchs"! It seems clear that there is a relationship between decision making in a family/household and contributing monies received from outside the unit. Ostrander makes this point concerning upper-class women:

> One source of subordinance among upper-class women—as a general mode of accommodation and in family decision-making—is the class tradition of women turning over their inheritances to their husbands to manage. When the women give up the control of their money, they give up the freedom to order their own lives and the ability to speak with an equal voice in family decisions. This is not surprising. Low economic power has long been shown to be related to low decision-making power in families in other social classes. (Ostrander 1984: 65)

Here then, in a very striking way, we see a commonality among women in families: the denial of decision making based on economic dependence on men; and conversely, decision-making powers which come with economic independence.

What can we conclude from hearing these various voices on *the family*? It's clear that for women, *families* (in the sense of the kin and fictive kin with whom they live and share a domestic economy) are a source of support in some cases and an obstacle to a woman's development and growth in others. Thus when we talk about women and their *families*, we need to be clear about whom we speak: is it the elderly woman living alone, spending her days wishing that her *family* would spend time with her or ask her to do things for them? Is it the super rich widow who also lives alone and makes a great effort to keep all of the money-hungry *family* from coming around? Is it the poor "bag lady" on the city streets, moving in the winter from one nowhere to another—a woman "freed" of the responsibilities of caring for children and housework, who finds her only *family* are those who drop something in her outstretched palm? Or when we speak of *family* do we mean all of the individuals who provide the support which poor and working women must have if they are simply to make it from day to day? Or is *family* those who live with an upper middle-class woman, helping to create, as Betty Friedan put it, "the problem that has no name"? Is *family* that group of similarly disabled women who stick very close to each other, forming a ring of protection from the gaping stares or disregard of the abled? Or is family those who live within a particular household made up of two lesbian women and the boys and girls whom they brought there from previous relationships? *Family* for US women is "all of the above" and more.

Deep emotional and ideological meanings are wrapped up in the concepts and realities of women in families. Nowhere is this emotion more evident than in certain debates between middle-class white women and women of color.

Rayna Rapp, an anthropologist who has written on families in contemporary U.S. society, describes the emotional nature of the issue when she notes that within the women's movement

> many of us have been to an archetypical meeting in which someone stands up and asserts that the nuclear family ought to be abolished because it is degrading and constraining to women. Usually, someone else (often representing a Third World position) follows on her heels, pointing out that the attack on the family represents a white, middle-class position, and that other women need their families for support and survival. Evidently both speakers are, in some senses, right. And just as evidently they aren't talking about the same families. We need to explore those differing notions of family if we are to heal an important split in our movement. To do so, we must take seriously the things women say about their experiences in their families, especially as they vary by class. (Rapp 1978: 278–279)

We need also to listen to what women say about experiences in families as they vary by race, ethnicity, and by all other characteristics of family members. If we listen to what different women say about their experiences in their diverse family arrangements, we will acknowledge and come to understand that for women as a group, as well as for individual women, life in families is contradictory—involving restrictions, constraints, and oppressive acts on the one hand and support, protection, comfort, and indeed joy on the other.

Sexuality and Reproduction

Sexuality and reproduction, while closely tied by much of the ideology which surrounds women, are not the same. In order to focus more clearly on the diverse and similar ways in which they are viewed, practiced, and denied, each is discussed here in relative isolation. Actions which violate women's sexuality and personhood (rape, battering, pornography, and so forth) are discussed in the section on politics, for fundamentally they are abusive acts of power.

Sexuality

What is it about sexuality which all US women can be said to share? Certainly the biological characteristics of the female body are a "common denominator" among women. However, the possession of those characteristics is not as important as how they are viewed within a culture and how that cultural view is affected by individual sexual orientation, race, ethnicity, class, age, and other considerations.

One thing shared by US women is the fact that we are the subjects of attitudes, values, practices, a folklore, and "humor" which categorize *all* women as sexual objects who either live up to or fall short of the ideal female sexual being.

US women are being measured against an objectified notion of female sexuality which is eternally young, never fat but "well developed," heterosexual, submissive to "her man," *and* capable of satisfying him sexually. It is striking how this ideal image cuts across racial, ethnic, and class lines. Yet the responses of women to this objectified notion of femaleness are different, as are notions of how close certain groups of women come to the ideal. Indeed, issues of race, ethnicity, and class are very evident in stereotypes of black women as "loose and sexually hyperactive," Asian American women as "exotic/erotic," and affluent women as more prudish than working-class women.

Ideal images of men are also in effect. Indeed, objectification of one gender requires objectification of the other. The difference is that in the case of women, the ideal physical being, carriage, and general personhood are grounded in notions of submissiveness and powerlessness as opposed to strength and power.

The white middle-class women at the forefront of the early women's liberation movement leveled sharp criticisms against this view of women's sexuality and what they considered the oppressive aspects of women's sex lives. Some of these women advocated the destruction of the "double standard" and others called for female sexual permissiveness (a possibility made all the easier because of more ready access to birth control). Lesbian separatists claimed that women should reject all heterosexual relations in favor of nonrepressive homosexual bonds.

Many women, Afro-American women, for example, reacted strongly to these views. In some, perhaps many cases, heterosexist attitudes or "prudishness" were at the base of the reaction. Other Afro-American women, however, were reacting to white middle-class women's indulging themselves in discussing and experimenting with sexuality while black and poor women were struggling to make it through another day in a white racist, capitalist society. The response of many working-class white women was also less than positive as they drew on traditional working-class attitudes about sex and sexuality (Rubin 1976). For many women in Native American, Asian American, and Latino communities, these public discussions of sex and sexuality raised difficulties particular to varying cultural norms. For some Christian fundamentalist women, such open discussion of sexual questions was blasphemous.

There was no all-embracing sisterhood on these questions or on other issues related to women and sexuality. As the women's liberation movement developed through the 1970s, so, too, did a far-ranging discussion of lesbianism as a sexual preference *and* as an empowering choice. However, the discussion was most often centered among middle-class, white women. Yet then, and even more so today, strong voices of lesbian women of various racial and ethnic groups argued for recognition of the particularities of their experiences.

While affirming what is shared with other lesbians, Anita Valerio speaks of her Blackfoot heritage and some of the feelings she experienced in returning to her people:

> Perhaps in the old days, in some way or other I could have fit in there. But today, my lesbianism has become a barrier between myself and my people. What to say when my grandmother or aunt asks if I've met a boyfriend? The perennial lesbian problem—how to tell the folks and what to tell them. . . . Five years ago I dreamt myself walking out of my home in Littleton and out to a flat, long desert. There, beneath a shelter of poles and sticks, an old Kainah woman sat. . . . The old lady looked at me a long time, then she said, "You will return to the Indian way." (Valerio 1981: 44–45)

Audre Lorde, in an open letter to Mary Daly, puts succinctly the important difference color can make for two women who otherwise share a great deal:

> Within the community of women, racism is a real force in my life as it is not in yours. The white women with hoods on in Ohio handing out KKK literature on the street may not like what you have to say, but they will shoot me on sight. (If you and I were to walk into a classroom of women in Dismal Gulch, Alabama, where the only thing they knew about each of us was that we were both Lesbian/Radical/Feminists, you would see exactly what I mean.) (Lorde 1984: 70)

Lesbians of poor and working-class backgrounds have spoken of their alienation from "a brand of lesbianism" associated with the women's movement of the late sixties and seventies:

> The history of my brand of lesbianism is the story of women who ran from towns like the one I fled, who joined the army, navy, or air force or who were busted when discovered with another girl and thrown into juvie hall. Or it is a quieter story of women who form a culture different from the feminist one—a life led in gay bars on Friday and Saturday nights, if you have a lover; every night, if you don't. It is about drinking too much and playing pool with style. It is an underground that runs through the phone company, the Teamsters Union, the Bank of America, and the grocery counters of this country. (Hollibaugh 1984: 2)

An issue which has most clearly divided many women of color from those white women advocating separatist politics is that of relating to men. For many Afro-American, Asian American, Hispanic, and Native American women, who share a range of oppressions with men of their group, a radical feminist position of total separation from all men, who are perceived as the enemy, does not match their day-to-day experiences or aspirations. Lesbian women of color witness the oppression they share with men of color, and they often see their own ultimate liberation as no less a racial than a gender/sexual question. Some of these dynamics are exposed in this passage from a letter written by a Chinese American woman to her mother.

> I understand all too clearly how dehumanized Dad was in this country. To be a Chinese man in America is to be a victim of both racism and sexism. He was made to feel he was without strength, identity, and purpose. He was made to feel soft and weak, whose only job was to serve whites. Yes, ma, at one time I was ashamed of him because I thought he was "womanly."

> When those two white cops said, "Hey, fat boy, where's our meat?" he left me standing there on Grant Avenue while he hurried over to his store to get it; they kept complaining, never satisfied. . . . I didn't know that he spent a year and a half on Angel Island; that we could never have our right names; that he lived in constant fear of being deported; that, like you, he worked two full-time jobs most of his life; that he was mocked and ridiculed because he speaks "broken English." And Ma, I was so ashamed after that experience when I was only six years old that I never held his hand again. (Woo 1981: 145)

Reproductive Rights

There is a definitive association of women with a childbearing function—and that association cuts across racial lines, ethnic and religious lines, class lines, and most others as well. Yet, not all women can have children and not all women wish to.

There are also differences in the ways that women respond to reproduction and to what they assume are their reproductive rights. These issues are explored in greater detail in Part III. A few summary comments are offered here on three aspects of reproduction: controlling reproduction (birth control), halting reproduction (abortion), and the loss of an ability to reproduce (sterilization).

Women's views are quite divergent on these issues. There are differences along racial, class, and religious lines. And there are intensely emotional battles and even violence as some women and men on the political right attack and even bomb abortion clinics.

Certainly birth control is not an issue on which all US women are united. In addition to the official anti-birth control position mandated for women by the Catholic church, the Nation of Islam, and other religious groups, a widespread argument in several communities of color (Afro-American, Native American, and Puerto Rican especially) is that those who use or advocate birth control participate in a racist effort to limit or eliminate those populations. Regardless of the politics of today's advocates, birth control has been closely aligned with the eugenics movement and with other explicitly racist positions. As Angela Davis notes, the racism and class bias of the early birth control movement argued that it was a right for the privileged and a duty for the poor (Davis 1983).

Women are also divided over the question of abortion. Antiabortionists are quite capable of refusing abortions for themselves. What is at stake is their insistence on making a similar choice for all other women. And although the antichoice forces (men and women alike) push a single-issue line, in reality their position is about an all-encompassing, fundamentalist moral order with right wing politics and a definite place for women—as subservient as possible. Women who participate in this antifeminist, antiabortion backlash present a serious problem for those who argue that all women are sisters.

Legislative and judicial reversals in a woman's right to decide about her reproductive powers and the means to carry out her decision cause disproportionate suffering among women of color and poor women. In the years before abortion was legalized in New York State, for example, 80 percent of deaths from illegal abortions were among black and Puerto Rican women.

The most criminal assault on women's reproductive rights is forced sterilization. Once again, it is women of color, poor women, and most of all poor women of color who experience this unwanted loss of reproductive powers. In the 1970s an estimated 24 percent of all Native American women of childbearing age, and an estimated 35 percent of all Puerto Rican women of childbearing age had been sterilized. Of the women sterilized through federally subsidized programs, 43 percent were black. Although figures are not available on

what percentage of these sterilizations were voluntary, those working in the antisterilization movement argue that the majority are clearly forced on women. Those who have organized and fought hardest against "la operación" are Puerto Rican women, Afro-American, Native American, and other women of color. That there has not been more active effort in this area from white women's groups is a source of bitterness among many women of color.

In the ongoing women's movement, questions of sexuality and reproduction remain at the heart of heated discussions, radical responses, divisions, and creative possibilities for change. Although when stripped to the most fundamental levels these issues are biological, the moment they are put into action, or even discussed, culture comes into play, and they become social issues. How, by whom, against whom they are put into action or denied expression becomes a matter of power, that is to say, politics.

Perhaps sexuality and reproduction are so controversial because of the pervasiveness with which ideology in mainstream U.S. culture has reduced women to sexual and reproducing objects. Large numbers of women, armed with a political movement, have fought against that reductionism and sometimes used the very issues of sexuality and reproductive rights as metaphors for an all-encompassing liberation of women.

This discussion illustrates the extent to which issues of sexuality and issues of reproduction are subject to the duality of shared yet divergent experiences that characterize other spheres of women's lives. In that sense, it may be better to speak of female sexualities and modes of reproduction.

Religion

If asked to hold forth on the topic of "religion in the United States" a response of many would be: "Which one?" Which one indeed? A listing of what are called the world's "great religions" practiced in the United States would bring the count to six: Buddhism, Christianity, Confucianism, Hinduism, Islam, and Judaism. Such a listing does not include the traditional spiritual ways of Native Americans, nor the many syncretized religions, combining, for example, traditional African religions with Christianity (Santeria among Cubans, Spiritualismo among Puerto Ricans). And listing the so-called great religions practiced in the United States does not begin to indicate the multitude of denominations, sects, and cults that exist within them.

The point is simply that on the question of religion in the United States, most would begin with an assumption of diversity, rather than an ecumenical approach which seeks to identify and build on points of commonality among denominations and religions. Adding women to the phrase—"women and religion in the United States"—conjures up further images of diversity. Then what are the commonalities among US women in the sphere of religion? There are two obvious ones. First, in each of the "world religions" practiced in the United States the proper place for women is defined, and it is on the whole a subservient one. And second, women are the backbone of organized religions but rarely serve as the leaders of the churches, synagogues, mosques, and temples in which they are practiced.

Woman's Place

Through affirmations or challenges, religions reflect the dominant values in a society and in large measure mirror the social order. It is not surprising then that in the major religions practiced in the United States, the role of women in religious practice and in society is defined in the holy religious writings as a subservient one.

Christians certainly disagree about the extent to which biblical passages defining women's second-class status should be taken literally. Yet, regardless of interpretation, such passages do not assign women an equal position with men. And as many feminists point out, when women are "praised" or given special attention, the Bible most often casts them in the role of mother.

In Judaism, there is an ongoing debate on women's roles in the synagogue and their responsibilities and rights as women of the Jewish community. In terms of synagogue services, one of the earliest issues raised in the mid-1970s was that of the mehitzah, the barrier which separates women and men during prayers. Another issue was that of counting women in the minyan (the prayer quorum). Many but not all Conservative synagogues voted to do so. Women as rabbis was yet another major issue, and in 1972 Sally Preisand became the first woman to be ordained a rabbi. Today both Reform and Reconstructionist movements have ordained well over seventy women rabbis, and the Conservative movement ordained its first twelve women in 1985.

But these changes have not come without conflict, and the debates continue. The Orthodox movement remains firmly opposed to allowing women to participate equally in religious life. Instead, women's special responsibilities in creating a Jewish home and raising the next generation of Jews are emphasized. According to an Orthodox rabbi, woman's role as mother is designed by God:

> It is not easy to form children in the Jewish mold and prepare them to become Jewish adults, and such a task would not have been primarily assigned to women had they not been especially prepared for it, physically, psychologically, intellectually, and spiritually, by Almighty God Himself. (Heschel 1983: xviii)

Women as the Backbone of Organized Religions

> Women are expected to sing in the choir, serve on the usher and stewardess boards, participate in the missionary society, cook

in the kitchen, teach children in the Sunday School, and serve in all those positions that men regard as "women's work." But unlike men, women are not encouraged to enter the ministry. (Cone 1984: 132–133)

James Cone thus describes the specific situation in most black churches. But with a few variations here and there, it is a description applicable to religious bodies throughout the United States.

Casual observations and scholarly studies indicate the predominance of women in many religious activities. Black women represent more than 70 percent of the black church. Many hypotheses are offered to explain this phenomenon: it is women who are "in charge" of the morality of a community, and thus, they are in greater attendance in services; for many women religious services serve as something of a psychologically and sexually fulfilling experience; it is the one "public" activity which all groups encourage women to participate in, and on and on. It seems that the same explanation offered for the widespread involvement of black people in organized Christian churches can be applied to the question of why women are also there in great numbers. Despite the Bible's purported message to black people that as Ham's children they shall be the hewers of wood and the drawers of water, there is also the message that Jesus is the savior, and he shall set you free. Such a mixed message is also given to women: the Bible assigns a second-class status to women but also offers solace, comfort, and inspiration to them as an oppressed group.

While women are the "backbones" of churches, synagogues, and mosques, they are rarely the "heads." Throughout black history, some black women have served as preachers, but it was always an uphill battle as they often had to prove their call to the ministry to an extent not required of men. Women are still excluded from the ordained in some black churches.

Although fear of female leadership in organized religion is not often voiced in clear and unequivocal terms, it is possible to find such statements. For example, historian Lucy Dawidowicz remarks in reference to female leadership in synagogues:

> Women are efficient; they can organize, raise funds, bring order out of chaos. They can turn the shul into a Hadassah chapter. Not that I disapprove of Hadassah, its activates, of its ladies. But I do not like the idea of their taking over the synagogue. To my mind, the assumption by a woman of rabbinic or priestly function in the synagogue undermines the very essence of Jewish tradition. (Heschel 1983: xx)

Within the range of women's experiences in the sphere of religion, there is also a debate which echoes divisions we noted in the discussion on "the family." The women's movement has criticized organized religion for the role it plays in suppressing women. And, there is a call for radical changes by scholars who challenge the male-centered references to the deity, and the use of theological references to "keep women in their place" (Christ and Plaskow 1979; Daly 1973; Goldenberg 1979). In some cases, the call is for women to leave male-dominated organized religions and affiliate themselves with feminist spiritual groups.

The response of many women of color, as well as poor white women, is that the church for them is a shelter from economic and racial discrimination. Until those forms of discrimination end, or other institutions take over functions now carried out by these religious bodies, women will, it is argued, remain faithful to these traditional male-dominated religions.

Today, there are two movements which bring into sharp contrast how different women can be in their views of the spiritual world. On the one hand are the "born again" Christians, who adhere to a world view that calls for a return to "the old ways," to the most fundamentalist traditions in Christianity. On the other hand, there are women who, as a part of their feminist world view, call for a radical overhaul in the language, beliefs, and rituals of organized religions in order to remove the male bias at the very center of it all. This chasm between these two sets of women once again challenges us to recognize similarities without ignoring distinctions; to see differences without blurring commonalities.

Politics

In turning to politics, the final sphere of women's lives explored in this book, there is a sense in which we have come full circle. For "the woman question," whether discussed in the specifics of work, family, sexuality and reproductive rights, or religion, is at the base a question of power, and power is politics. In the broadest terms, we can say that women in the United States, in comparison with men, are defined as "other." From language to the highest political offices, men are the standard and women the other. Women have fewer choices about what they will do in the world of work. Women receive less pay for comparable work. Women are more often assigned secondary roles in public and religious activities. Women are challenged more in terms of their reproductive rights and sexual powers. And women are clearly more subject to sexual violence. The shorthand terms we use are that women are oppressed, or we speak of the need for women's liberation in connecting the status of women with a movement to change that status.

With all of the provisos noted earlier in terms of variations based on class, race, and other factors, the most striking commonality among US women is that as a group we do not wield political power

comparable to that of men, especially white men of an affluent class. The areas of difference include perceptions of the specifics of our political status, actual differences in our respective political power, and our various views on how the status of women can be changed.

One way of looking at women's oppression in the political sphere is to note that nowhere in the United States are women represented in large numbers in sustained positions of leadership. The U.S. social order systematically excludes people of color, poor folks, and women from any significant degree of leadership and power.

But women are not totally powerless, for where there is oppression there is also resistance, and resistance is by its very nature the exertion of a degree of power. However, as far as organized political power is concerned, women are still a very long way from being proportionally represented. Geraldine Ferraro's vice presidential candidacy notwithstanding, there is still deep-seated discrimination against women in U.S. politics. Only about 10 percent of elected officials in the United States are women, and they are heavily concentrated in local government. Though women may be seen campaigning for political office, both Democratic and Republican parties are hesitant to nominate them for winnable Congressional seats. Nine out of ten female Congressional candidates run against incumbents, and they are frequently served up as sacrificial lambs with very little financial or other support from their party.

Although sixty-five women ran for the U.S. House of Representatives in the 1984 election, the number in the House remained 22, the *only* black woman Representative being Cardiss Collins of Illinois. And the defeat of the Equal Rights Amendment, although a complex issue, is a symbol of women's lack of sufficient organized political power.

US women are bound by a common second-class status, yet, from an idea here and there to fully developed philosophies and ideologies, there is tremendous variation concerning *how* women's liberation is to be achieved. The many ideologies will be discussed more completely in the introduction to Part V. Here it is important to indicate the range of approaches.

The many different ways women seek to achieve gender equality are somewhat captured in this litany: feminism, radical feminism, cultural feminism, nationalist feminism, socialist feminism, feminist socialism, lesbian feminism, Third World lesbian feminism, feminist coalition politics, women in electoral politics, socialism, utopianism, indigenous traditionalism, indigenous socialism, and the list goes on and on.

How is the daily struggle viewed? A reading of the literature from the center of the women's movement indicates a range of responses, though, in general, the theoretical works speak of the struggle against patriarchy. The source of patriarchy is of course under dispute. Some argue a causal relationship with capitalism, others argue that patriarchy predates and antedates capitalism. A more straightforward rendition of this notion holds that the struggle of women is against all of the vestiges of male control and oppression of women—as expressed in attitudes and behavior which range from sexist language to male monopoly of political and economic power. From an activist perspective, the heart of the women's movement today is for greater participation and power in electoral politics; for equal pay for comparable work; for reproductive rights; and against pornography and all forms of sexual exploitation and violence.

It would be difficult to find a group of women of color who would argue against the need for each of these changes. However, while they would not deny the importance of these arenas of struggle, they would necessarily place them within the context of their daily lives. And within their lives, women of color are twice as likely to be unemployed as are white women; their life expectancy is years less than that of white women; they are fifteen to twenty-nine times more likely to live in substandard housing and receive no or inadequate health care; and their children are far more likely to receive a substandard education. Racism is the only explanation for why these conditions of women of color are so dramatically different. Thus, their struggle against sexism cannot be divorced from their struggle against racism. The history of the National Black Women's Club movement illustrates this point. As with the nineteenth-century women's movement, the club movement among Afro-American women was fundamentally organized by "middle-class" women. And at the same time that these black women in the 1900s addressed some of the same issues that were on the agenda of the women's movement of that era, there were other issues—racism being the most pronounced—which white women did not address in a consistent and frontal way. The continuation of black women's clubs and organizations today, and similar formations among other women of color, rests on the primacy which these women give to the continuing struggle against racial inequality. (For a discussion of the National Black Women's Club movement, see Giddings 1984: 95–117.)

At the center of the women's movement, there is the tendency to "level oppressions," that is, to suggest that all women are equally oppressed. Note this point in an historical context:

As a prison house for the women themselves, the notion of Southern ladyhood was almost as effective as slavery. No one knew this better than Mary Chestnut. "All married women, all children, and girls who live on in their father's houses are slaves," she wrote with brutal finality. (Abbott 1983: 91–92)

There is no such "finality" in the view of many Afro-American women who know that the experience of their foremothers as slaves was brutally worse than that of the white Southern ladies who were their mistresses. In a modern day setting, "Poor women and women of color know there is a difference between the daily manifestations of marital slavery and prostitution because it is our daughters who line 42nd Street" (Lorde 1984: 112).

There is then a real danger in arguing that the oppression of every woman is equal to the oppression of every other woman. Yet there is also a danger in forcing every oppressive experience into a hierarchy such that it must be judged as more or less important than every other one and, therefore, more or less deserving of political action. Clearly, we need to find ways of acknowledging the various forms of women's oppression without losing sight of what are in fact differing degrees of exploitation. As Barbara Smith puts it:

> In a white dominated, capitalist economy, white skin, and if you have it, class privilege, definitely count for something, even if you belong at the very same time to a group or to groups that the society despises. Black women cannot help but resent it when people who have these privileges try to tell us that "everything is everything" and that their oppression is every bit as pervasive and dangerous as our own. From our frame of reference, given how brutally racism has functioned politically and historically against people of color in the United States, such assertions are neither experientially accurate nor emotionally felt. (Bulkin et al. 1984: 76)

Of all the ways in which women's oppression—that is to say, women's powerlessness—is expressed, none is more blatant than the reality that, far beyond what is the case for men, women are potential victims of sexual harassment, sexual exploitation, and sexual violence. Battering, rape, and incest are the most physically violent forms. Sexual harassment involves sexual advances by men in a position to intimidate or unjustly exert their power in a job or classroom situation. Such advances are offensive, possibly psychologically damaging, and professionally disastrous to women. Sexual exploitation includes that form of prostitution in which a woman "agrees" to participate in sexual acts but does so because she has concluded that she has no alternative source of money, and pornography, which reduces women to their "sexual utility."

These various assaults against women are best characterized not as sexual acts but as acts of violence which dramatically signal women's powerlessness. These acts of psychological and physical violence cut across age lines. As recent exposés indicate, child molesting is not some isolated horror, but a widespread crime—which disproportionately affects little girls. And rape is among the special fears of older women in our cities. The increasing use of female children in pornographic movies and pictures is also an indication of the extremes of misogyny.

The severity of the physical and psychological pain which women suffer as a result of these various forms of sexual violence cannot be overstated. The conditions are such that most, if not all women, are in fear of such violence at some point in their lives. Susan Jacoby interviewed a group of women, all in their forties, most of whom grew up in first- and second-generation Jewish or Italian immigrant families. In their East Flatbush women's group, the following exchange took place:

> "I confess I don't feel much of a sense of sisterhood when I see pictures of Gloria Steinem with her streaked hair and slinky figure. I feel somehow that these people don't know how it is to be getting older

with very little money and education. They have it a lot better than we do—it's not true that we're all in the same boat." Another woman disagreed: "Well, there's one thing that we all have in common— we're all afraid of muggers and rapists when we walk down a dark street at night. And that's something we have in common with the colored women who live right here in East Flatbush, even though most of us are better off financially than they are." (Baxandall et al. 1976: 388–389)

However, because *all* women in the United States live with the possibility that they will be sexually abused, harassed, raped, or battered does not mean that the actual experience with such violence is the same for all women.

It is tempting to say that all women are bound by the recurring suggestion, innuendo, or outright assertion that whatever sexual abuse they suffer, it is basically the woman's fault: "She shouldn't have been walking down that dark street"; or "If you wear a blouse like that you're asking for it." Yet throughout U.S. history, there has been a glaring exception to this "rule": it is the prevailing assumption that rape is most often committed by black men and that the victims are white women. In this case, blame is laid on the "oversexed" black male.

This use of the myth of black men's "super sexuality" as a coverup for other issues and problems is not new. Ida B. Wells, the great Afro-American antilynching warrior, found that of 504 black citizens lynched between 1896 and 1900, only 96 had ever been accused of rape. Thus, although rape was often the rationale for lynching black men, the charge brought against the accused was seldom rape. Rather, at the heart of the lynchings of black men was their "threat" to the labor market privilege of white men.

The myth is that white women are the victims of rape and black men are the rapists. The reality is that black women, other women of color, and particularly poor women of color are disproportionately the victims of this sexual violence. A study undertaken in Chicago indicated that black women are eighteen times more likely to be raped than white women (Joseph 1978: 3). And the reasons are clear.

> There are particular conditions that account for high incidents of rape—systematically sanctioned conditions—which are the results of institutional racism. Blacks are disproportionately over-represented in the lower socio-economic groups and the material conditions of their lives include poorly lighted and poorly policed living areas, exposures to the insecurities of public transportation, brutal family relations, and communities filled with the army of the walking wounded (the drug addicts, winos, superflies, and crazies). Since street crimes are by and large neighborhood crimes, these existing conditions account for the high incidence in intra-racial rape and other crimes. (Joseph 1978: 3)

Thus, women in the United States share a status of oppression, and perhaps the most traumatic expression of that status is in our potential victimization in sexual crimes. Yet once again, we note the tempering influence of race and class on women's experiences.

This exploration of five spheres of women's lives has made the point that on a certain level of generality, there are definite commonalities among US women; and on particular levels of specificity, there are differences among us of considerable importance. The oppression of women cuts across lines of class, race, ethnicity, age, religion, sexual orientation, region, and physical abilities. Yet, these same realities create the specific content of the oppression. The significance of this point is captured by Audre Lorde:

> Certainly there are very real differences between us of race, age, and sex. But it is not those differences between us that are separating us. It is rather our refusal to recognize those differences and to examine the distortions which result from our

misnaming them and their effects upon human behavior and expectations. . . .

Too often we pour the energy needed for recognizing and exploring differences into pretending those differences are insurmountable barriers, or that they do not exist at all. This results in a voluntary isolation or false and treacherous connections. Either way, we do not develop tools for using human differences as a spring board for creative change within our lives. (Lorde 1984: 115–116)

REFERENCES

Abbott, S. 1983. *Womenfolks: Growing Up Down South.* New York: Ticknor and Fields.

Bambara, T. C., ed. 1970. *The Black Woman: An Anthology.* New York: Signet.

Baxandall, R., L. Gordon, and S. Reverby. 1976. *America's Working Women: A Documentary History—1600 to the Present.* New York: Vintage.

Boucher, S. 1982. *Heartwomen: An Urban Feminist Odyssey Home.* New York: Harper & Row.

Bulkin, E., M. E. Pratt, and B. Smith, eds. 1984. *Yours in Struggle.* Brooklyn, N.Y.: Long Haul Press.

Christ, C. P., and J. Plaskow, eds. 1979. *Womanspirit Rising: A Feminist Reader in Religion.* San Francisco: Harper & Row.

Cone, J. H. 1984. *For My People: Black Theology and the Black Church.* Maryknoll, N.Y.: Orbis.

Daly, M. 1973. *Beyond God the Father: Toward a Philosophy of Women's Liberation.* Boston: Beacon Press.

Davis, A. Y. 1983. *Women, Race and Class.* New York: Vintage.

Fine, M., and A. Asch. 1981. "Disabled Women: Sexism Without the Pedestal." *Journal of Sociology and Social Welfare,* VIII(2): 233–248.

Fuentes, A., and B. Ehrenreich. 1983. *Women in the Global Factory.* Boston: South End Press.

Giddings, P. 1984. *When and Where I Enter.* New York: William Morrow.

Goldenberg, N. R. 1979. *Changing of the Gods: Feminism and the End of Traditional Religion.* Boston: Beacon Press.

Green, R. 1984. "Magnolias Grow in Dirt: The Bawdy Lore of Southern Women." In *Speaking for Ourselves,* M. Alexander, ed., pp. 20–28. New York: Pantheon.

Heschel, S., ed. 1983. *On Being a Jewish Feminist.* New York: Schocken.

Hohri, S. 1983. "Are You a Liberated Woman?" *East Wind: Politics and Culture of Asians in the U.S.* 2(1): 42–45. California: Getting Together Publications.

Hollibaugh, A. 1984. "The Sympathy of the Blood." *Village Voice,* June 25, 1984, pp. 22–25.

Hooks, B. 1984. *Feminist Theory: From Margin to Center.* Boston: South End Press.

Hune, S. 1982. Asian American Women: Past and Present, Myth and Reality. Unpublished manuscript prepared for conference on Black Women's Agenda for the Feminist Movement in the 80s, Williams College, Williamstown, Mass., November 12–14, 1982.

Joseph, G. I. 1978. Rape—Race—Rapism. Unpublished manuscript.

Leacock, E. 1979. "Women, Development and Anthropological Facts and Fictions" In *Women in Latin America: An Anthology from Latin American Perspectives,* pp. 7–16. Riverside, Calif.: Latin American Perspectives.

Levine, M. P., and R. Leonard. 1984. "Discrimination against Lesbians in the Work Force." *Signs* 9(4): 701–710.

Lord, S. B. 1979. "Growin' Up—Appalachian, Female, and Feminist." In *Appalachian Women: A Learning/Teaching Guide,* S. B. Lord and C. Patton-Crowder, eds., pp. 22–25. Knoxville, Tenn.: University of Tennessee.

Lorde, A. 1984. *Sister Outsider.* Trumansburg, N.Y.: Crossing Press.

Marable, M. 1983. *How Capitalism Underdeveloped Black America.* Boston: South End Press.

Ostrander, S. A. 1984. *Women of the Upper Class.* Philadelphia: Temple University Press.

Rapp, R. 1978. "Family and Class in Contemporary America: Notes Toward an Understanding of Ideology." *Science and Society* 42 (3, Fall): 278–300.

Rubin, L. 1976. *Worlds of Pain.* New York: Basic Books.

Shalala, D. E. 1983. Big Sister Is Watching You: A Feminist View of 1984. Unpublished speech prepared for delivery at the opening session of the 32nd Biennial Convention of the American Association of University Women, San Francisco Hilton and Tower Hotel, Saturday, June 25,1983.

Stack, C. 1981. "Sex Roles and Survival Strategies in an Urban Black Community." In *The Black Woman Cross-Culturally*, F. S. Steady, ed., pp. 349–367. Cambridge, Mass.: Schenkman.

Valerio, A. 1981. "It's in My Blood, My Face—My Mother's Voice, the Way I Sweat." In *This Bridge Called My Back*, C. Moraga and G. Anzaldúa, eds., pp. 41–45. Watertown, Mass.: Persephone Press.

Wolfe, A. 1976. "The Jewish Woman." In *Dialogue on Diversity*, B. Peters, and V. Samuels, eds., pp. 42–49. New York: Institute on Pluralism and Group Identity.

Woo, M. 1981. "Letter to Ma." In *This Bridge Called My Back*, C. Moraga and G. Anzaldúa, eds., pp. 140–147. Watertown, Mass.: Persephone Press.

DISCUSSION QUESTIONS

1. Cole points to differences among U.S. women and how these differences affect their experience of gender inequality. But what about men? Discuss how differences in, for example, class, ethnicity, and age affect men's experiences *as men* in U.S. society.

2. Given Cole's description of diversity among U.S. women, to what extent do you think a united "women's movement" is realistic in the opening decade of the twenty-first century? Would you predict that the commonalities will outweigh the differences, or will the differences override the commonalities? On what factors might the outcome depend?

3. Most feminists in the twenty-first century take it for granted that the "women's movement" will be an enduring part of the American cultural landscape, whatever hopes they may have for its future changes. What about the possibility that the women's movement may cease to exist at some time in the future because it is no longer necessary? Does that seem possible or likely to you? What would the United States have to be like for the women's movement to be unnecessary?

MEN, WORK, AND IDENTITY

ELIZABETH PERLE MCKENNA

A lot has been written about women and work in the United States. The literature covers conflicts between women working outside the home and "family values," gender inequalities and sexual harassment in the workplace, and women's problems with balancing home and career. But what about men? How do they fit into this picture and these controversies?

This reader opened with discussion of the important dichotomy between male-public/female-domestic spheres of life that has so profoundly shaped gender in American society. But for the most part this dichotomy has been discussed in relation to its constrictions on women, or the problems it generates for women today as they participate in ever greater numbers in the workforce. How do all of these issues look when we shift our focus to men?

These questions are taken up by Elizabeth McKenna's article on men, work, and identity. This piece is from her book, When Work Doesn't Work Anymore: Women, Work and Identity. *A great deal of the book covers her own experience as a high-powered and high-earning professional woman who quit her job to "get a life," including time for her marriage and children. Rather than seeing this as a "step back" for women, McKenna questions the whole link between work and identity for both women and men in contemporary U.S. society. She moves the problem of "balancing" work and home onto a new level with some provocative implications for everyone, men and women.*

McKenna shows how deeply the idea of "provider" has been tied to masculinity in American culture, and how strongly male identity has been tied to work. She interviews a number of men who, as husbands and fathers, are struggling with different options in response to the considerable increase in working women. Those she interviews range from fathers who have chosen to be stay-at-home dads while their wives support their families to fathers who adamantly insist on their roles as sole providers for their wives and children. With these interviews she provides a deeper understanding of the link between work and masculinity and the changes that some men are themselves making in relation to their own identity as men.

Michelle Rosaldo, who analyzed the male-public/female-domestic dichotomy and whose classic article opened this book, said that in the end, gender equality could only come about if men entered the domestic sphere. McKenna makes a similar point. But she also discusses how "success" itself needs to be redefined; how it needs to move away from money and professional advancement and toward inclusion of personal and family relationships. For gender equality, it is not just the activities of men and women but our "success culture" that needs to change.

My husband makes a good living. It's a great statement. It simultaneously locates his exact worth in the world and represents the complete appeasement of my father's concerns for his daughter. Some burdens still pass from man to man. While I was learning that I could do the same job as any guy for the same pay, I also inhaled the fragrance of security (and potential luxury) promised by marrying a man with a good job. These two understandings bestowed on me a sense of freedom, of choice. Not that I wanted to depend on a man. I spent two decades fending for myself, enjoying the profound benefits of being a woman of independence. But I'd be less than honest if I didn't say that somewhere deep in the back of my brain, nestled in the darkest folds, lay the comforting notion that somehow, some way, I would be taken care of one day.

Until my husband became the sole source of consistent income in our family, though, I had never really considered what that equation "good provider equals security" meant from anyone else's point of view, notably my husband's. Because I had been making a good salary, he hadn't had to face his unaired assumptions about it either. But the day I woke up jobless and depressed with no vision of what I planned to do in the future, he—who so actively supported my leaving—went to work in a bit of a blue funk. Which, over time, blackened to an inky cloud.

History, cultural expectations, and experience accounted for the change in his weather: my husband had been here before. Like some other men at the front of the baby-boom curve, he had lived under two different sets of rules in two different incarnations, all before he'd even officially hit midlife. In his first marriage he played the role of the traditional male provider. His wife stayed home and raised their children. He never thought twice about being the one who went off to the office every day. His life was not so different from his father's and neither were his expectations, obligations, or responsibilities. He lived surrounded by a company of men who rode the same trains, coached the same soccer games, turned in the same expense reports. They were doing what they were raised to do. They were doing what was right and worthy.

"What are you so worried about?" he'd ask me in frustration when I protested that he just didn't understand, I *had* to work for my own self-esteem, for my sense of independence. "I make enough money for you to stay home if you want." At the time he was not thinking about the psychological importance work held for me. But, to be fair, I underappreciated how extremely hard he had worked over many years to be able to say that sentence with all the confidence he could. My husband loves me and when I was miserable, he wanted to give me the gift of the freedom to work out the confusion in my life without having to ride the subway every day.

But when I took him up on his offer, that small, dark cloud collected on his emotional horizon. Now it really *was* up to him. Now he couldn't entertain fantasies of joining the senior pro golf tour or becoming a therapist or a stockbroker or Mr. Mom. Although he had gladly taken the complete financial weight of our lives onto his shoulders, something deep within him simultaneously bridled at the extinction of even the possibility of freedom. A grimness set in, his mood heavy with the knowledge his options had just shrunk to almost zero.

Reading this, I think my husband will protest that he had no reservations whatsoever about his offer—which will be the truth. But that doesn't mean that underneath everything there wasn't also a quiet, slow deflation as the second income slowed to a trickle and then dried up completely. An income that had represented a potential safety valve and cushion. Even though he was doing what was expected—more, he was doing what he wanted—it just wasn't fair, on some level, that I got to quit and he didn't.

Some days I would joke around and say that when I was rich, he could stop work and play golf every day. "I can't wait!" he'd respond, and go off to work. But even though most men will say something like that, it would be very hard for them to actually do it. So much of who they are depends on what they do—or don't do. Most of my husband's human contact takes place in his office—it's his main community. He's worked with the men and women there for more than twenty years—they are a big part of his life. Besides that, my husband's position confers on him an identity and a sense of worth. He's proud of the fact that he can afford to support the people he loves; it makes him feel that his days have meaning and purpose. When his work is going well, it gives him great personal satisfaction. It confirms to him that he has a place in this world, a job to do. He's busier than he wants to be, travels much more than he likes, but in spite of the hassles his work fires him up in a place that very few other things in life can reach. For him—and for many of his friends—to assume any role other than that of the main provider means an enormous rearrangement of values and pride and identity has to take place. For these men, work gives more than self-definition and fulfillment; it brings (as women well know) independence and a measure of control over life. It's a right women fought hard to get. And I've yet to meet a man who wanted to part with any control whatsoever as far as his life and career were concerned.

My husband is an extremely smart man. He is quite aware that there are many alternatives to the way he works. He knows that there are ways to cut his income that would result in more time at home, more time with me, with our child. He appreciates that I could be the one to go to work every day and that he could raise our son. He understands that there is still very little societal support for any of those alternatives. For a man like my husband, the first one in his family to go to college, the first one to break into the executive ranks, those choices represent a diminishment of the possible. More than that, they represent a step off the path of the American Dream. Becoming a success, making the most of the hard-won opportunities in his life, is more than a badge of honor, it's something that gives esteem, meaning, shape, and purpose to his life. In the face of that kind of power it's pretty easy to let these alternatives remain simply ideas.

Little boys still get the message by our example that their career paths and their lifelines lie locked together. Even though women now comprise half the workforce, rather than broaden the message to include other values, or rearrange the top priority we assign to the gathering of money, power, and success, we have simply extended the same set of values to little girls. If we, the adults, haven't broadened our definition of a successful life to include with equal worth the values of caring for community, connection, and service; if we continue to value the ten hours we work to buy a car with a CD stereo less than the equipment they purchase; what choice do we really give anyone who moves away from the success we worship as a society?

When my father came home to this country after fighting in World War II, he went to law school on the GI Bill. He knew opportunities his parents never had known. He had known poverty and promise. He delighted in giving me an easier life than he'd had. My father believed that social and economic mobility knew only one true direction—up. It was his duty to make sure his family benefited—not for power's naked sake but for the sustenance and pleasure and growth of those he loved. But long after I have been self-supporting, my father still works as though my life depended on it. For the men of my father's generation, being a man and being a provider were almost synonymous. For him, who he is and what he does are fused so completely that I have often thought that the moment he stops working he will stop breathing. It wouldn't surprise me. I've seen it before.

A Business Built for Providers and Heroes

Author Warren Farrell cited a study that demonstrated that the image and equation of masculinity as breadwinner in this country was so powerful that it would actually be easier for a man to have his sex changed than to undo the social and cultural conditioning about what it meant to be a man in our society.[1] Even though what we call a traditional family—with the homemaker mom and sole-provider dad—accounts for less than three percent of American families today,[2] this tenacious image is the one centrally installed in most baby boomers' mental wiring. According to this picture, men get their identities and their worth mostly from the work they do. Society rewards men with its approval according to how much influence a man wields, how important a man's work is to the community, or how much money he produces.

In May of 1996, when Admiral Jeremy Boorda committed suicide, I couldn't help but think that he represented a tragic, if extreme, example of how dangerous the work-equals-life equation had become. A proud man, an accomplished man, Boorda was a true American success story. He rose through the ranks to the top of the Navy by the sweat of his own efforts, the first enlisted man in its history to do so. When it was charged that he might not have been entitled to wear certain of the medals he sported, rather than blacken the office to which he had devoted forty years of his life, he killed himself. When something threatened to go hideously wrong with his job, there was no other side of him that he could rely on to sustain him as a human being. "He so identified with the uniform he wore . . . that in the end, he was apparently unable to separate his real self from his naval persona," *Newsweek* magazine concluded.[3] For Boorda the stain of dishonor at work was enough to render his whole life a tragic failure.

Boorda is of the generation that still presides over most of business. His values—while exaggerated—aren't so different from the values of the men who exclusively inhabit the top seats at *all* of the *Fortune 500* companies and a huge majority of the positions in the upper echelons. While we justly focus on the implications of that skewed amount of power on women's lives, for the first time in history research is showing that younger men (beginning with the baby boomers) are also being negatively affected by outdated work and family values. For that generation, what a man

did for a living wasn't merely about putting food on the table. What and how much he provided determined the importance, value, and meaning of his life and of his children's.

This is the way that work—and by extension, manliness—became endowed with a kind of sacredness and power way beyond its actual activities. The moment that survival was no longer the exclusive reason men left home every day, work and masculinity became synonymous. If work failed, the man failed. That is what makes Boorda's death such a modern morality tale. The tragedy lies not in his dishonor but in the fact that he didn't *have* to die for what he did or didn't do (some contend he had actually earned the right to wear the medals). He didn't die for his country, he didn't die for his family, he died for his office. Although Boorda died by his own hand, is he so very different from the legions of men who kill their days or the quality of their lives in return for more money, more power or prestige? What about the thousands of men who sit grim faced in traffic jams, commuter trains, or the subways every day on their way to the offices to fulfill their role as the male provider? Or the men who travel for work and spend many weeks, if not months, away from their families and friends?

Warren Farrell says, "Men are taught to be human doings; women are taught to be human beings." He feels the paradox of masculinity is that "a man becomes 'someone' by forfeiting himself to a corporation, the armed services, or other organizations." He points out that the word *hero* derives from the Greek *ser-ow*, servant or slave. In Farrell's view, "Work has never worked for men as human beings. The very purpose of work, historically, has been survival; men sacrificed themselves and their time to feed their families. In exchange, they received respect, approval, love, and immortality in the memories of others." Farrell feels men's problem is that they have learned to define power as "feeling obligated to earn money." Thus, in his view, the more a man gives up his life to work, the more "heroic" he becomes and the more society esteems him. Today's work environment continues to create and perpetuate that kind of "heroism," and a working man is still judged—and loved—for what he produces for others. This stereotype hasn't changed much since the 1950s. But for today's baby-boom generation, it no longer is a comfortable fit.

"The corporate world, stuck in the mentality of the 1950s, too often still operates on the notion that the American worker is a male with a wife at home to tend to all the family issues,"[4] observes psychologist Rosalind C. Barnett, author of a major NIH-backed study of men, women, and work. Studies like hers and others show that neither men nor women believe anymore in that model of work where work is most holy. Yet, as Barnett observes, it's "hard to rip out of our heads the images that we believe to be eternal truth—which are, in fact, merely the residue of an atypical time."[5]

Authors Barnett and Rivers report their research categorically showed that "it is simply not true that a job is more important to a man than his family."[6] But they emphasize how unaware business today seems to be of this fact. While seminars are offered on ways to reduce stress, stop smoking, or meditate, there is virtual silence on the topic of balancing work and family—the domain, these companies feel, of women. "Until men realize that family issues are not the sole domain of women, nothing is going to change," state the authors. They go on to say that until corporations rearrange their priorities and men realize that the unwritten rules are killing their chances at any semblance of balance, "the emotional health of American men will remain in jeopardy."[7]

Moreover, the landmark study found that the "traditional" division between men and women—that men work and do and women care and feel—simply no longer exists. Quite emphatically, the research showed that a man's home life, a man's marriage, and a man's children are as important to his sense of happiness and his identity as they are to a woman's.[8] The study echoed what other current research shows, that "more men are willing to trade raises and promotions to spend time with their families."[9] These are the private and true beliefs of men today. But they run headlong into the definition of being a good man (a good provider) that these men received growing up. That definition just might have made sense forty years ago when in exchange for hard work a man could expect to be taken care of by his company for life. But in the light of the new economic realities of downsizing and the extinction of corporate loyalty, cleaving to this definition is punitive. The clash of the way men really identify themselves today and the old messages that run around in their heads is leaving them with the feeling they are caught in pincers, squeezed between who they are supposed to be and who they want to be, how they are supposed to work and how they want to live. Today, it is just plain dangerous for a man's sense of well-being to give his work the kind of power to determine his self-worth and identity.

My husband found this out the hard way. In the middle of my writing this book, he discovered that his position was being rearranged off the organization chart. With a tap of the delete key much of who he was and much of what he cared for was wiped away. Since he knew about the change before most others in his company, he had to pretend to be who he had been for quite a while. Standing by him at a corporate function one night, I could see the way people treated him with respect and deference. He had earned both. A man came up to me and told me how much people thought of my husband. I wondered if he would say such nice things if my husband were no longer the number-two man in his company. I wondered if my husband wondered the same thing. I knew in that moment that it was going to take a while for him to sort out the man and the work. It had been a long time since he'd had to.

Separating the Role and the Man

Because the messages about work and masculinity are so knotted up and tangled together, any examination of the subject makes most men touchy at best. They may want to leave work, but they don't feel they can without giving up a good deal of what they were taught it means to be a man. When author Wendy Kaminer left the practice of law to become a writer, she found herself the object of male envy. "I can't tell you the number of male lawyers who used to come up to me," she recalls. "They'd say, 'I'm so jealous; I've always wanted to do that!' and I'd say, 'It's easy. Just quit your job and go live in a garret.' They had all these fantasies about it. Really, they were as free to do it as I was. Except they weren't." The images about what it meant to be a successful man depended too heavily for these men on having a successful work life. And a successful work life was not defined by an insecure income. Consequently, men are boxed in, left with a Hobson's choice—work hard and be seen as a success or be less than a real man.

Unlike men, women have a socially (if not personally) acceptable alternative—go home and be a wife and mother. When I left my job, I had an immediate identity—inaccurate and incomplete as it was—as a mother. The fact that I became a writer and continued to work full-time got lost under the more socially obvious other role. Had my husband been the one to quit, he would have had a very different experience—he would be an unemployed ex-something. He would still be defined by what he once did.

This link between identity and work is beginning to break down, however, as the baby-boom generation experiences an insecurity in work that their fathers never did. A January 1997 *New York Times* poll reported that 80 percent of men and women interviewed said they knew someone who had—or they had themselves—lost a job in the past two years. The sacrifice involved in a hero's life makes increasingly less sense when it goes unrecognized or discounted. If a man works hard (or sees his friends doing so) and loses his job anyway, the incentive for propping up the model that worked a generation ago drops to nearly nothing. Still, getting past the silent and lethal corollary to the provider equation—the one that says that failure to succeed proves that the man himself is the failure—means enormous rewiring for men. For many it's still better to die trying. And if the insurance industry's figures are correct, that is precisely what men are doing—an average of four years earlier than women.

But men do know something is wrong. Ask a man with a young daughter if he wants her to be able to do what he does for a living. "Of course," he will say. Then ask him if he wants her to work the *way* he works. It won't take him very long to say, "No way." For an increasing number of men work is beginning to be something that is simply not worth dying for.

One of the amazing statistics affecting men today is that 48 percent of women in married couples provide half or more of the family income. And if a woman is separated, divorced, widowed, or heads a single-parent household, the percentage is even higher—64 percent.[10] More and more, women are the benefit providers. This profound change causes some necessary confusion as the roles come loose from their economic anchors. When economic factors are no longer driving the roles each person plays in a relationship, we begin to see how stubborn the old messages are. We have internalized them and we find them echoed to us from the structures and attitudes in our employment and our communities. In actual practice, however, the exclusivity of the breadwinner-as-man model is finished forever.

Indeed, when a man no longer *has* to be the provider, who is he and why does he work? Michael Lancaster, a fifty-year-old corporate strategist for an international technology company, has spent a good deal of time, recently, asking himself those questions. After almost thirty years in his company he was tired of all the travel and the pressure in his office, but he had two years left before the generous stock benefits offered to him were fully vested. Mike had enough money to be comfortable, though, and his wife, Linda, made a very good living as a very successful software designer. They had been talking about leaving the New York area for a different life and had just decided on a two-year plan to do so when they found out that Mike's position was being eliminated because of a reengineering. He wasn't being asked to leave—in fact the president of the company went out of his way to tell Mike how valuable he was to them—but he was being offered positions of much less responsibility and importance.

Rather than see this event as an opportunity to cut down on what had been bothering him about his job, Mike was devastated. "I feel a horrible loss of domain," he said. "And I hate the fact that people are talking behind my back." Because some of Mike's peers were benefiting from the change, they had known that his job was being eliminated well before Mike did. "I feel betrayed and deceived. I had been a partner with these guys for years. It's kind of humiliating."

Mike's wife, Linda, shakes her head as she muses, "You know, it's not just Mike who is affected by this. Our whole family is shaken up. It's not the money either. I make enough for us to live on and besides, the company I work for is about to be bought and I have lots of stock because I was here in the beginning. It's more about Mike's ego and sense of importance. Our eleven-year-old son said to me the other day, 'I hope Dad doesn't do something stupid.' Even he relied on Mike's position—he bragged about him to his friends. But Mike is so hurt, we can all feel it. I don't need him to have this big job to love him. But I do need him to like himself. And I think he's going to be absolutely lost without a big job. It made him feel important. Respected. He took so much pride in building the company and helping people. I don't know what he's going to do to replace that; so much of what he thinks is best about him comes from his work. It's breaking my heart to see it."

Mike admits that on top of the betrayal, he has fears about his future. "I always said I wanted to go back to school and teach history. But now I don't know if that will satisfy me. I was proud of the job I did. People respected me. I am going to miss that so much. I know I'm not 'Mike Lancaster, corporate executive,' but without my position I'm not sure who I am."

Mike's situation draws into bold relief how work becomes woven into men's egos and self-esteem. There is no equally valuable alternative in Mike's mind to what he has been doing for a quarter of a century. Even in the face of a new kind of freedom, Mike feels he needs and wants the work to complete him. He is like the Gilded Age characters in Edith's Wharton's *The House of Mirth*. "The doors stood open," she observed. "But the captives had forgotten how to get out."[11]

I Am Not My Father (or Am I?):
Questioning the Roles

Forty-year-old Andy Rosenthal, an editor at *The New York Times*, is all too aware of the conundrum in which Mike has found himself. Andy, like many of his baby-boom contemporaries, is trying to figure out how to live his life in the face of the twin pressures of old messages and a work environment that hasn't changed since his father's time. Not only that, Andy wants to have a good career *and* a good life. He doesn't want to define himself by what he does or have his work and his ego (in the best sense of the word) inextricably wedded together.

Andy typifies his generation. Research has shown that the children of the "Organization Man" of the 1950s have very different values about their work than those of their fathers. Less competitive, more cooperative, and concerned with their families and communities, they want a different relationship with their work.[12] It's not that they don't want to work hard, but like Andy, they don't want to be slaves to their jobs. They, like Andy, know all too well the messages they received as boys about what made a man worthy or not.

Growing up, Andy understood clearly that as a man, he had a definite role to play in this culture. "You had to work and you had to succeed and you had to be, if not rich, then famous," he recalled. "In my family I had a father who had a very high-powered career and a mother who was totally devoted to two jobs: raising three boys, and promoting my father's career." When, after thirty-eight years of marriage, Andy's parents divorced, he watched his mother go through a profound loss. "She is seventy-one and has done a lot of really great things in her life, but she feels like it's all been wasted." Andy was determined to live his life differently. After his first marriage didn't work out, he feels his values shifted from "thinking I was going to be happy ninety percent

from my job and ten percent from my personal life to thinking I had to have a life outside of work I found fulfilling and rewarding and that wasn't related to whether or not I became executive editor or the emperor of Siam." Andy married again, to an attorney, and a year or so later they had a son. And with the birth of his child Andy found that he was suddenly in the midst of a pitched battle with all the old roles and instructions.

Part of not living his life based on his work meant, for Andy, being a good father and taking on a great deal of the responsibility for the care of their son. After his wife went back to work, they alternated days in which one of them would have to leave work earlyish to get home. "On the days when it's my turn, I just have to stand up and walk out the door, even if I'm in mid-sentence. I feel very complicated about that. I feel good in a sense—that I'm fulfilling the responsibilities that I think are important and that I'm meeting my commitment to my child and to my wife and that I am taking seriously what I said I was going to do. But at the same time it makes me very nervous, as it has been trained into me that work is a higher calling than fatherhood and that I am abandoning my higher calling for my lower calling. I am walking out the door in the middle of a bunch of responsibilities, and I can't get it out of my head that if the work exists, then I have to do it. Because that's what I've been taught. I'm trying not to value myself that way. I'm trying to change my mind, but it's very hard. Because part of the work ethic I was given was—you just do it."

Andy admits that his great fear about having a child was always that he would not have the strength to push work away and focus on him—that he would end up being a father like his own father. When Andy's son was born, he discovered firsthand how much subtle pressure there was for him to be just that. He found that "apart from my friends, there's not a lot in society that tells you that it's okay to be a father first." At work Andy found people, although outwardly supportive, commented on the length of time (two weeks) that he had spent away from the office when his son was born. "Nobody called me up and said, 'You have to come back to work.' But the message was fairly clear when I came back that this was a bad thing. People couldn't just come out and say, 'What are you? Some kind of lazy fool? What kind of man are you, anyway?' One man said to me, 'What were you doing during those two weeks? Standing by the crib and gazing adoringly at your son?' The message there was 'Spending time at home is not valuable. Spending time at work is valuable. And you're a wimp.'"

Still, Andy decided to place his principles on the line. A month or so later he took another three weeks off, even though his company does not give paternity leave. "I wanted to establish that it is possible to take time off. That it is possible to be a male person with a big career and take time off to stay home with your kids. Because a lot of my colleagues are having babies here, I wanted to be clear to them that if they wanted to take time off, they could do it. That it is ridiculous to set things up so that men feel like they can't take time off. Not even productive. Why would you want to have a group of guys sitting around moping because they haven't had time to bond with their babies? They aren't even doing their work right."

These principles, however, had a flip side for Andy. They came at a cost to him. He found that if he was going to take time off, leave at a reasonable hour, he probably wasn't going to become the big success he had been raised to be. "Why do I have to make the choice between being a successful person at work and being a successful father?" he asked with full understanding that working mothers ask

this question almost every day. "Maybe it's not possible to be king of the hill and a good father. So maybe you wind up making a choice. You make it two thirds the way up the hill and wind up being perfectly happy there." Easier said than done when a man judges himself by how much of his potential he has realized in his career.

As much as Andy was able to make some peace with his ambitions, he was unprepared for his ambivalence about being the provider. After all, he had married a woman who worked and made a good income. After a few months back on the job his wife began to think about staying home with the baby; Andy found he had very mixed feelings. While he understood her desires, he found himself deeply divided on the issue. "I always said I didn't want to marry my mother—that I wanted to marry a career woman with her own identity—which I defined as a job. Yet, now that we have this baby, I think it would be fine if she wanted to stay home. I actually don't know how I feel about this. To some degree it worries me. I'm afraid that it will feed all the parts of me that will easily accept the idea that I am just a working individual and not a whole person and I'll just settle into that role—that my wife and kids would become a unit apart from me, one that I will come home and visit. The male-provider role is worrisome for me too. There's anger and frustration associated with it. I tried so hard to be a liberated man and now I feel that I have to be my father. It's infuriating. I spent so much time learning to view women as equals and now it's like 'You're turning into a girl again.' I know these are irrational thoughts and I don't really mean them, but they are real." Andy feels that if his wife does decide not to continue her career for a while, they will have to work very hard not to settle into roles they don't really like. Andy doesn't want to be reduced to breadwinner at the cost of being an outsider to his own family.

And it's not just the roles that concern Andy—there's the question of money. "We had a lifestyle based on being as unconcerned as possible with our finances. We bought cars and motorcycles and went on expensive vacations. We live in a nice house. If my wife stops working, either our lives will change or I will have to pursue an even bigger job," he says, and he doesn't like either option particularly. One represents less security and comfort and the other less time and life outside of work. Andy resents that those are the available choices. After years of trying to value himself more broadly than by the job he performs, fatherhood has thrust all the old values back in his path. He is having a hard time thinking that to be a good father means that he probably won't end up where he would have without a family. But he knows, too, that there is a critical difference between him and the older generation. Unlike his father, who lived through poverty, the Depression, and World War II, he is part of a generation that feels it has the birthright to ask questions. Andy may not be able to completely avoid the old roles, but, like his contemporaries, he can begin to ask challenging questions without social censure. He knows he is part of a society where he can ask of himself, "At seventy, looking back over my life, am I going to be happier with my wife and kids? Or because I had a job with a big title?"

By valuing his family and his work equally, Andy is taking the first steps in a revaluing process that will ultimately break work's determining dominance over his life and self-worth. He and his friends, who are also questioning their roles, are beginning to inch away from their fathers' lives and value system. On a fundamental level they have to shake the foundation of their lives in order to broaden their options in life. As these men introduce (on an equally valuable basis) more traditionally "female" concerns and values into the discussion, they start a process that results in changing not only their predetermined roles but also the way the business itself works.

Cultural Resistance

This kind of revolutionary thinking breeds strong reactions. Moving away from the equation "good provider equals good man" means going against most of the cultural instruction men get about being a man. Men still work in a world where a majority of their male peers think that work is, on balance, fine the way it is. It is very important to emphasize that not every man wants things to change. For many men (and increasingly many women) work still represents a retreat. "Work is men's world. And once the boundaries are blurred, they lose their hegemony. Work for many men is still about closing the door on that messy, nasty undisciplined world at home," comments Letty Cottin Pogrebin. Of course almost no man will admit to this as it appears to cast him in an unflattering light. But many men say it in other ways. They say that their wives are better at taking care of the kids, more patient, more forbearing. For other men like Ron, a sales director of a magazine company, work is fulfilling and exciting enough to compensate for seeing his kids only a few hours a day. He explains that he and his wife are more comfortable with the traditional roles—not because of tradition, but because of who they are as individuals. They both love their work, but Ron doesn't think he's cut out to be a full-time father. He loves what he does and feels that his more than twenty-year career has borne fruit. When he married and had children, work started to mean something different. But unlike Andy, having kids simplified and clarified things for Ron. "It all changed when I became a father. Until then Jessica worked. We had no responsibilities, we had lots of money. Not much was on the line. But after our first kid was born, we agreed that we wanted one of us to be home and raise him. It just happened that Jesse wanted to do it and I didn't. It could have been the other way around. But I get a lot of satisfaction out of making money now. My ambition has increased and I've never enjoyed work more. I'm proud of the fact I can give my family a good life. Besides," he says, "there are real benefits to coming home at the end of the day and not having to be the authority all day long. I get to amuse my kids."

But even men like Ron feel they are working more from choice than from obligation. While he acknowledges they need money, he also realizes that the income could have come just as easily from wife as from him. They chose a traditional arrangement. Had both wanted to work, they might have been forced into making some difficult concessions. The exclusivity of the male-breadwinner role may have broken down, but men still relish it for the sense of purpose and contribution it provides. There's not much incentive to change things if seventy-five percent of it is working well. And as long as women continue to do most of the work of the home, most of work will still work for men. Besides, for those men who have moved their lives away from a work-centered life, they are all too aware of the difficulties.

No one knows this better than Peter Martin, a former Boston-based newspaper editor. Peter and his wife, Cathy, decided to move to a university town in the midwest so that Cathy could take a tenure-track position teaching in an excellent department. "We moved out here with the understanding that she was going to be the primary breadwinner and I was going to be the primary caretaker," Peter recounts. "Philosophically, I had no problem with that. I approved of it. I embraced it. I was proud of it. In practice, though, it has created problems." Peter and Cathy are very

honest with their concerns and are particularly afraid that honestly addressing the problems of defying gender stereotypes will play into the hands of the backlash. They both are extremely careful to state that their arrangement is a work in process, not an example of why it can't be done. But their experiences amply demonstrate the nature of society's and even their own resistance to such revolutionary cultural change.

"I scare people," Peter says. "I go in and do PTA work at my daughter's school one day a week and I get strange looks from parents. I can see that they are thinking, *What is that man doing here?* I think some people think I'm a child molester. Others give me more credit than I deserve—like I'm a saint or hero. Obviously, I'm neither of those things. But they can't figure out what I'm doing and why I'm not in an office somewhere."

It's not just his community that looks at Peter askance. "Both my parents and my in-laws are horrified by my life, each in their own ways," he says with resigned good humor. "Cathy's parents certainly expected her to marry a good provider. Don't get me wrong; she was expected to work too. She was raised in as feminist a household as one was likely to find in that era. But her parents certainly expected that Cathy's work would be secondary and that she would not have to worry about being the primary breadwinner." Not only that, Peter thinks Cathy herself is surprised to find this so.

"Though we never said so out loud," Cathy says in a separate interview, we both came into this marriage with a rather traditional idea that he would probably make more money than I would, be more successful in conventional terms. I even think I picked a career where I thought I could do something interesting and support myself to a certain degree but also have flexibility. My mother worked part-time and my father had the full-time role. That was part of my inheritance." For Cathy and for Peter the fact that she makes more money than he does in his new freelance writing career bothers neither of them per se. It's just that they don't have enough money, period. Her academic salary can't comfortably support the family, and because of where the college is located, there aren't many jobs for Peter.

Cathy's biggest worry is that somewhere down the line, Peter will say, "What have I done with my life?" and regret the decisions they made. She ventures, too, that she is somewhat divided in her feelings about her life. On the one hand she is pleased that their principles have driven their counter-cultural arrangement—she is happy that her daughter will grow up with strong, nongendered examples of her parents' roles; on the other hand she admits that she feels she has a set of expectations that weren't met. That she doesn't feel taken care of and she doesn't even want to be the one who provides health benefits. "Very simply, why don't I have a nicer lifestyle? In retrospect," she observes, "I expected it was going to happen through my husband. Unless I'm kidding myself, I don't feel let down by him—I think, actually, he's been very bold. It's just that I want my daughter to have new clothes and be able to go to private schools. And I really worry that at some point in the future, Peter will regret having traded his career for my professional happiness. That he will say, 'I threw it all away for this?'"

Peter says he has no real concerns about having left the career path; ironically, it's Cathy who is most worried. She admits that she is still influenced by the cultural dictates about what satisfies men even if she doesn't believe in them intellectually. She doesn't want Peter to miss experiencing conventional success in his life. She also doesn't really want to be the primary financial support all her life. She worries that her daughter will be the one who pays the price for their living out of the sphere of conventional success. In the face of those fears it becomes difficult to appreciate the unvalued side of the equation—that their daughter will have grown up without the example of fixed gender roles and that she will have spent an equal amount of time with both her mother and her father.

For Peter and Cathy, operating outside of convention has allowed them both to clearly see the cultural baggage they not only confront in others but carry within themselves. They know that the pull of the expected roles' values is fierce. It still precludes most men from participating in any life other than the traditionally masculine. "There is too much of a price for men to pay if a man elects a nontraditional choice," Pogrebin observes. "He gets called a wimp, he loses his place in line. The men don't sacrifice money for time, because they will get zapped."

Thinking Outside the Box

For all their extremely sincere questioning and experiments Andy, Ron, and Peter are still thinking about their lives within the confines of a box whose walls, floor, and ceiling are made up of the culture's prevailing beliefs about work and masculinity. Their assumptions about what constitutes success and mediocrity and failure are still much like those of their parents. Even Peter, who is quite intentionally flaunting convention, says he has given up trying to be a success. What he hasn't done is to redefine success on new terms that suit his life. But without a group of like- and open-minded adventurers, doing otherwise is almost impossible. Peter says that there are other male "trailing spouses" where he lives, but any attempt to discuss the psychological or even logistical problems of having a career from their isolated location quickly dwindles into surface chitchat. None of the men is accustomed to trying to solve his problems within a supportive community. They still operate like lone wolves. Not having a successful career carries enough of a shameful tinge that these men remain apart from each other, reluctant to discuss what makes them unhappy in their lives.

If men want to begin to develop a broader definition of success, if they want to move away from the box, they need only look as far as the nearest women in their lives to help them with an alternative model. For women truly know the limits of the success culture. As perpetual outsiders they see much more clearly how much of the way they work is unnecessary. Women have this clarity precisely because they go to work every day in a world designed to meet men's needs, not women's. "Very few women buy into the system completely in the way the guys do," says Anna Quindlen. "I think many more women put on the camouflage to get by, but at a certain point in their lives they say to themselves, *Work is what I do, but it's not who I am*. Whereas men are still really invested in a work-is-everything kind of thing." And it's hard to get the desire, no less the ability, to creatively imagine a different work world when most of it still works.

But a few things are propelling men toward a new way of looking at who they are and what they are worth. As the jobs on which they have depended become less and less secure, the question of choice in work is introduced into the discussion. They see former peers building their own businesses (more out of necessity than virtue, initially, but they are proceeding nonetheless). They see the women in their lives forging new relationships with their work either in terms of hours or location, and earning incomes as good as or better than theirs. As men like Andy strive to be more a part of their families, they are understanding the painful trade-offs required. And as men start to experience some freedom from the economic burden of masculinity, it's beginning to force them to think about work and success in different terms.

Added together, all these changes work to create meaningful choices for men—not just between career success or a personal life but in what constitutes success itself. The door to redefining and revaluing men's lives opens a crack. As long as men and women have thought about their lives within the narrow confines of the conventional success box, men have resented women for their putative ability to choose, while women have resented they've been made to do so. Letty Cottin Pogrebin remembers that when she was writing *Growing Up Free*, she interviewed a little boy who said, "Girls are lucky; they get to wear skirts *or* pants." "There was this perception by this little boy that girls had more privileges because they had choices. But no man wants to wear a skirt; it's not something men desperately want. I don't know too many men who want to stay home full-time, they want someone they trust to stay home full-time. They may want the income of the wife but if they don't need it, they are just as happy to have their wives stay home. Men are still quite comfortable about that. But women aren't comfortable with the choice, they are apologetic in the same way that women in the fifties and sixties were apologetic when they worked outside the home." Once we step out of the box, the choices start to look entirely different. The "nonwork" values immediately become part of the discussion. Our definition of what is successful and valuable begins to expand to include more of the things in life that go on outside of the glass towers and factories while the sun is up. All of the things that we have, for years, allowed to remain separate and unequal.

As long as we stick to the old roles and definitions of success, we are necessarily left with only two choices—either we work or we go home. But in accepting those alternatives we miss the real issue, which is that the choices themselves reflect an outdated and artificial division of human life. The either/or nature of our options is nothing but a hangover from another era, and it suits neither men nor women anymore. "I think the transformation that has to happen is not 'either/or' but 'and,'" comments Gloria Steinem. "It isn't that we are either inside corporations or outside with our own businesses transforming values and patterns. We have to do both. And, indeed, we would anyway because women need work." As men lose their work or see their peers break down the all-or-nothing forms of work, it gives them permission to imagine (with dignity) a whole, more balanced life. It allows men to transform their sets of values about themselves to include all of life that the workday excludes.

The Gifts of Transformation

External events may be forcing men to seek alternatives, but there are powerful internal incentives at work as well. As Warren Farrell says, "What's in it for a man is that when he discovers his children, he discovers what life is about. He is directly connected to love, whereas before he was indirectly connected to love. The problem with the male system was that the more money he produced for the people he loved, the further away he had to be from the people he loved. That's what I call the male tragedy. The incentive for the men's revaluing of their lives and roles is that now they will be directly connected to love. A man will be appreciated for the meal he cooks, not depreciated for

being away from home while the meal was being cooked."

Gloria Steinem concurs. "What's killing men is the masculine role. If you take out of the death statistics those men whose death could reasonably be attributed to the stress of work and the masculine role, women and men would have close to the same life expectancy. So this is not a bad deal," she concludes. "You get to be a full human being instead of hating your 'feminine' qualities, and distancing yourself from women because they awake these qualities within you. And you even live longer."

Although this perspective seems to come from a certain deep maturity, many young men in their twenties clearly see the wisdom in valuing more equally all the options in their lives. They are building futures for themselves that hint at a deep difference in their value systems. They clearly see that building a life on the assumption that work will always be there is a risky, almost insane, proposition. These young men and women grew up, too, seeing their mothers work. They came of age believing that the sexes were equally capable. For this group there has been a drawing together of the personal and professional worlds. The wall that separated work and home, which was built along gender lines, appears to be coming down.

Consultant Janet Andre reports that she is seeing many "Gen X" men who are saying that their personal life is as valuable to them as professional achievement. She feels that "the women are influencing the men. I have a twenty-eight-year-old friend who went to one of the military academies. He has a military career. He recently married a high-achieving woman who is now getting her CPA. He now has a challenging assignment, after which, he says, he is considering getting out because his wife can't have a career if he stays in and she wants a career. That's the deal they made before they got married." Besides, Andre says, her friend acknowledges that his wife is much more ambitious than he is. He is more interested in teaching or politics and government. He would rather that she be the high-powered business type. "This is a kid who went to a tough, elite school," she emphasizes. "He's very smart, a high achiever, but she has had a big influence on his life because of her own self-confidence. And it has freed him to be who he wants to be." Andre feels that by the time her friend and his wife get to their mid-thirties, they are not going to have to face the either/or choices that men and women have to face with their lives and their careers. "In order to get talented people companies are going to have to drop their sexism," she says, "and recognize that the work can be done differently. The absolute system based on a male who spends very little time with his children and has a complete support system at home is a dinosaur. It's like school closing in the summer. We have a whole school system built around having the summer off to tend the crops and kids can't even work because of child labor laws. A lot of these senior guys want to be there for their kids now. A lot of the twenty-year-olds want to arrange their lives differently. All this is going to force huge change."

The workplace is not going to change, however, until a critical mass of men demands that it change. And for that to happen, what a man considers valuable about himself and his life has to undergo a revaluation. The women's movement could happen quickly because it didn't change the values of the success culture; it strove to make them equally available. But what now we define as valuable must be broadened. No real change is going to happen until it is as estimable for men to do the traditional work of women as it is for women to do the work previously reserved for men. And we are probably a generation or two away from that moment. "Until men are raising babies and children as much as women are, until men cook what they eat, clean what gets dirty, work won't change," comments Gloria Steinem. "I still get young women in audiences standing up asking, 'How can I combine career and family?' I always tell them, 'You can't until men are asking that question too. You can't do it all by yourself. You can't be superwoman, it's impossible. You have a right to have a partner and a society that behaves as if families matter.'"

There is a shift happening in the balance of power in the workplace. Not just between the sexes but also between the generations. It can wipe away the old, punitive ways we work. It can begin to create management practices that work for the people of today, not forty years ago. It's in men's best interest to stop working by the unwritten rules. If it's true that men today value their lives outside of work as much as women do—and research proves it is—then they have to join women's fight to reconstruct the way we work and create a new, broader definition of success. But as long as family and personal-life issues appear to be the province of women, nothing will change. These concerns will stay on the margins of work's agenda. Men are beginning to see that there are enormous psychological, emotional, and physical rewards in store for them if work changes. They will get to live their lives, know their children, contribute to their communities. They can have a deeper, broader sense of identity and self-worth founded on more than what they do. Men and women both have the need of and the right to stimulating work and rewarding personal lives. Together, we can create the necessary changes.

NOTES

1. Warren Farrell, "The Human Lib Movement: I," *The New York Times*, June 17, 1971, p. 41 citing the California Gender Identity Center's research.
2. Rosalind C. Barnett and Caryl Rivers, *She Works/He Works: How Two-Income Families Are Happier, Healthier, and Better Off* (San Francisco: HarperCollins, 1996), p. 5.
3. "A Matter of Honor," *Newsweek*, May 27, 1996, p. 24.
4. Barnett and Rivers, op. cit., p. 6.
5. Ibid., p. 49.
6. Ibid., p. 56.
7. Ibid., p. 57.
8. Ibid., p. 6.
9. Ibid.
10. *Women: The New Providers*, op. cit., p. 33.
11. Kennedy's Fraser's essay "Warmed Through and Through," in her *Ornament and Silence: Essays on Women's Lives* (New York: Alfred A. Knopf, 1996), p. 74.
12. Barnett and Rivers, op. cit., p. 144.

DISCUSSION QUESTIONS

1. Most surveys suggest that working women living with working men continue to perform about two-thirds of the housework and childcare. What do you see as the primary obstacles to men's greater participation in the domestic sphere?
2. What have been your own observations (of yourself, if you are male, or of fathers, brothers, husbands, if you are female) of men participating in the domestic sphere? Based on these observations, would you agree with McKenna that the boundary between male-public/female-domestic spheres is genuinely breaking down? What evidence supports your opinion?
3. What impact, if any, do you think that more gender-equal activity in the domestic sphere would have on other gender issues, such as violence against women, sexual harassment at the workplace, and discrimination against women in pay levels, raises, and promotions?